This wax impression, bearing the abbreviated name of Jesus
encircled by the inscription
"The seal of the Superior of the Society of Jesus"
(SIGILLVM PREPOSITI SOCIETATIS IESV),
was made from the seal used
by St. Ignatius when he was the first general
of the order, 1541-1556.
The medieval spelling of *prepositi* is noteworthy.
This same seal was also used by St. Ignatius' earlier successors
and by General Congregations II-XI (1565-1661),
XIII (1687), and XV-XIX (1706-1758).
St. Ignatius' secretary, Juan de Polanco, used it
upon the official text of the *General Examen* on October 9, 1558,
and Lorenzo Maggio, Secretary of the Society, put it
upon the ameliorated text
of the *Constituciones de la Compañía de Jesús*
which was approved by General Congregation V (1593-1594).
In the series of volumes,
Monumenta Historica Societatis Iesu,
there are interesting facsimiles
in *Constitutiones Societatis Jesu,* Volume II, pages 123 and 727,
and *Fontes Narrativi,* Volume I, on the title page.
The photograph was taken
by the Reverend Algimantas Kezys, S.J.
The seal itself is now preserved in the Jesuit curia in Rome.

A HISTORY
OF THE
SOCIETY OF JESUS

WILLIAM V. BANGERT, S.J.

A HISTORY
OF THE
SOCIETY OF JESUS

THE INSTITUTE OF JESUIT SOURCES

St. Louis, 1972

IMPRIMI POTEST: Very Reverend Gerald R. Sheahan, S.J.
Provincial of the Missouri Province
May 18, 1971

IMPRIMATUR: John J. Cardinal Carberry
Archbishop of St. Louis
March 10, 1972

©1972 The Institute of Jesuit Sources
Fusz Memorial, St. Louis University
3700 West Pine Blvd.
St. Louis, Missouri 63108

Printed in the United States of America
Library of Congress Catalog Card Number: 78-188687
ISBN 0-912422-05-x

TO THE MEMBERS OF THAT SOCIETY

which Saint Ignatius wished to be known by the name of Jesus

Published through the aid of funds

donated by Mrs. Rose Monaghan

of Milwaukee, Wisconsin,

in memory of her beloved husband,

James L. Monaghan, Junior,

August 5, 1898 — March 5, 1965

CONTENTS

MAPS

IN HISTORIES OF EUROPE and the world since the age of Emperor Charles V the Jesuits appear with notable frequency. Struck by this recurrence, students and readers of history occasionally look for a relatively brief but comprehensive account of the Society of Jesus. Surprisingly, there is in English no work of this kind which incorporates the important scholarly findings in the strong rush of research on the Jesuits which has been in progress the past fifty years or so. This inadequacy I have tried to remedy.

This work, essentially introductory in character, is designed to be kept within the limits of a single volume. Despite the inevitable compactness I have made an effort to keep to the fore the fluid and dynamic qualities of the Society's history. Each moment in the Society's experience was a stepping stone which was at once a creation by the past and a point of departure for entering the future. During this perennial onward movement the Society constantly retained a readily identifiable character as a fellowship with unique qualities. This unbroken movement and this essential character I have tried to register in the conviction that a priceless clue to what the Society is and what it can do at any one moment of history is to be found in what it has been and what it has done in the past. To trace the Society's course through the skies of history is to record the continuous movement of a particular planet. This is the kind of tracing I have hoped to make.

A work of this nature is never completely in focus. The Society of Jesus as a religious order has worked, as it is doing today, alongside secular priests, other religious, and laymen, so that its enterprise should be seen for what it is, a single thread in the broad fabric of the Church's history. There were hundreds of other threads. A Capuchin, François Le Clerc du Tremblay, was the famous Éminence Grise and close confidant of Cardinal Richelieu; a Carmelite, Domingo Jesús-María, by his fervent eloquence galvanized the council behind Johann Tzerclaes, graf von

Tilly, and Maximilian of Bavaria just before the critical battle of the White Hill in the early stage of the Thirty Years War; an Oratorian, Richard Simon, made the first modern breakthrough in scriptural studies and is rightly hailed as "The Father of Biblical Criticism;" a Franciscan, Cristóbal de Rojas y Spinola, was the most energetic Catholic ecumenist of the seventeenth century; an Augustinian, Hans Ulrich Mergerle, was the most effective preacher among the Catholics in the German-speaking lands of the eighteenth century. Here the spotlight is naturally on the Jesuits, but the poised historical judgment must be ever attentive to the significant persons, incidents, and trends in the Church's history outside the circumference of this particular beam.

Nearly three centuries ago the French Church historian, Louis Sébastien Le Nain de Tillemont, rightly insisted on a knowledge of secular history as essential for an understanding in depth of church history. The direction taken by the Jesuits was often altered by wars, failure of wheat crops, international diplomacy, mass hysteria, industrialization, and innumerable other events and circumstances. The encomienda system in colonial Spanish America, the imperial contests of the seventeenth and eighteenth centuries, the Italian *risorgimento,* the principles of democratic government as realized in the United States were often the real helmsmen who marked the channel the Society would take. While I must in general suppose a knowledge of this secular background, I have, here and there, explicitly given it some attention in order to illumine how its threads were often closely entwined with the threads of the Jesuit record.

Various ways of dividing this work suggested themselves, but no one was completely without difficulty. As can be seen from the chapter headings, I decided on a basically chronological presentation. In each chapter, except the first and last, I made further divisions according to the main areas in which the Society labored. This method has the special value of warding off the oversimplified general judgment and of illustrating at any one moment the complexity of the Jesuit experience. At times, however, events refused to be boxed into neat compartments. For example, the attempt of some Jesuits during the rule of Claudio Aquaviva to change radically the Society's Constitutions had repercussions in Rome and Spain. I have dealt with this episode in the section on the generals in Rome as well as in the section devoted to Spain. I have followed the same pattern in my presentation of the debates about the Chinese and Malabar rites. The first two chapters are relatively short and rather sparsely documented. Others have written learnedly and extensively on St.

Ignatius and the early years of the Society. The restricted length of these initial chapters has meant the sacrifice, reluctantly made, of an extended and detailed study of the significance of the Jesuit appearance amid the religious, cultural, and social ferment of the sixteenth century. This has been done admirably elsewhere, most recently by the late H. Outram Evennett in *The Spirit of the Counter-Reformation* (Cambridge, England, 1968).

The limitations of space forced me to omit several important Jesuits as well as some significant Jesuit achievements and failures. To do otherwise would result in a thick logjam of names and events. Certain omissions will displease some readers, but unanimity about who and what should appear in a volume of this nature is an impossible ambition. I have, for example, of set purpose omitted Jîří David, the Czech authority on Russia, who almost certainly composed the first textbook in western Europe for the study of the Russian alphabet and language; Rafael Landívar, the superb Latin poet from Guatemala; Giuseppe Brasanelli, the artist of the Paraguayan Reductions; Girolamo Saccheri, the Italian mathematician, notable for his adumbrations of non-Euclidian geometry; George Tyrrell, the Irish writer and prominent figure in the Modernist movement; Daniel Seghers, the Flemish brother and renowned painter of flowers; the two brothers, Étienne Martellange and Lorenzo Tristano, who ranked among the better architects of their age; the two scholastics, Domenico Zipoli, who created impressive Baroque music and died on the foreign missions, and Jean Gresset, whose delightfully barbed critique of French manners in the eighteenth century incurred the anger of the government, which demanded his dismissal from the Society.

I have also deliberately passed over some important episodes of Jesuit participation in public and diplomatic life, such as the presence of Odon Pigenat at the sessions of the *Conseil Ses Seize* in Paris before the conversion of Henry IV; the appointment of Manuel Fernandes to Portugal's Council of State; the mission of Francesco de Malines and Paolo Casati to Queen Christina of Sweden before her conversion to the Catholic faith. In treating of a religious order so large and diversified I had to be content with soundings here and there.

Three works that lie before me are *La Nouvelle Mission de la Compagnie de Jésus au Liban et en Syrie 1831* by G. Levenq, S.J. (Beirut, 1925), *53 Jahre Österreichischer Jesuiten-Mission in Australien* by Peter Sinthern, S.J. (Vienna, 1924), and *Quelques Aperçus sur la Mission de Java* by H.J.M. Koch, S.J. (Djokja, 1925). These, and several others too, reproach me for the scant attention I have given to certain areas of the world. Indeed, some countries I have not even mentioned. It was impossible, for example, to pass in review the dozens of new nations into which Latin America was fragmented during the nineteenth century. Limited space dictated this austerity.

A glance at the bibliography, in which I have listed only those authors to whom I have made explicit reference, will indicate but some of the many scholars to whom I am indebted. It is a special pleasure to mention that two are former students of mine, Nicholas P. Cushner, S.J., and John J. Godfrey. There are eight Jesuits to whom I am especially grateful: George E. Ganss, the general editor of the Institute of Jesuit Sources, whose editorial proficiency and wisdom are matched only by the warmth of his fraternal charity; William A. Carroll, who showed me the correspondence between John Adams and Thomas Jefferson on the Society; Theodore J. Cunnion, James J. Hennesey, Robert E. McNally, Clement J. McNaspy, and the late Edward A. Ryan, who read, in whole or part, the typescript and made many excellent suggestions. I am also indebted to Hugo J. Gerleman and Mrs. Seymour Rosen for the patient and meticulous care with which they helped in preparing the text for the press. In proofreading the galleys, three Jesuit scholastics, Arthur C. Bender, who also composed the Index, Francix X. Clooney, and Arthur R. Madigan, gave me invaluable help. I wish to thank them publicly.

William V. Bangert, S.J.

Fordham University, Bronx, New York
March 12, 1972

A HISTORY
OF THE
SOCIETY OF JESUS

Chapter 1

THE FOUNDER AND HIS LEGACY
1491–1556

IN THE CATHOLIC CHURCH there is today a body of men known *The Early Life* as the Society of Jesus, each of whose thirty-three thousand *of Ignatius* members looks back into the past for his way of life to a man *of Loyola* who lived through the first half of the sixteenth century. This man, courtier and gentleman, soldier and campaigner, student and teacher, ascetic and mystic, was Ignatius of Loyola.

Ignatius was born, most probably in 1491, in the austere and stolid castle of the Loyolas in the Basque province of Guipúzcoa, the last of eleven children — or possibly thirteen, certainty being impossible because of the destruction of the records — of Beltrán Yañez de Oñaz y Loyola and Marina Sáenz de Licona. At his baptism at the church in Azpeitia he received the name Iñigo de Oñaz y Loyola, probably in honor of the Benedictine saint, Iñigo de Oña. In a letter of 1537 he first used Ignacio, possibly out of devotion to St. Ignatius of Antioch, known for his veneration for the name of Jesus. Amid the striking beauty of the Basque countryside with its massive mountains, rich pasture, and plentiful streams, Ignatius spent his early years and formed his first attitudes within a family whose roots went deep into the Middle Ages, whose home of rough-hewn stone blocks evoked memories of feudal strife, and with whom the highest values were an intense loyalty to the Catholic faith and deep fidelity to the code of medieval chivalry.

Seemingly marked by his father for a career in the Church, Ignatius learned at an early age the rudiments of reading and writing. Death took his mother when he was very young. His father died when he was about sixteen, but not before he had made an important decision about the education of his youngest son. Ignatius, manifesting no inclination for ecclesiastical studies, felt a strong attraction to the dash and glory of a military career. Don Beltrán therefore sent him, probably in 1506, to Arévalo to Juan Velázquez de Cuéllar, chief treasurer of the royal court, under whose guidance he was to receive the basic formation of a Spanish gentleman and courtier.

3

During these years, while Velázquez continued to be an important person in the official family of the queen, Ignatius was intimately associated with the royal retinue and there developed habits of exquisite courtesy, graciousness of manner, and delicate refinement, habits which he never lost. At Arévalo, Ignatius also widened his reading as he became acquainted with the literature of the day. He filled his young mind with the extravagantly false idealization of woman and subtly sensuous expression of human love which he found in *Amadís de Gaula* and other works of the same genre. Dressed in clothes of bright colors, sporting a scarlet cap on his blond curls which reached to his shoulders, with sword and dagger at his waist, Ignatius found his pleasure in military exercises, the company of women, and sins of the flesh. It was a life marked, as Ignatius himself confessed, "with a great and vain desire to win honor." [1]

In 1516, in the wake of the complex changes after the death of King Ferdinand, Juan Velázquez fell into disfavor at the court. Ignatius stayed with his patron during his days of humiliation until the ex-treasurer died a year later at Madrid. His next decision brought him close to a potential field of battle and the opportunity to realize his fond dreams of soldierly exploits. At Pamplona, in command of royal troops, was the duque de Nájera, a powerful figure on the Spanish frontier and a relative of the Loyolas. Ignatius went to Navarre in 1517 and became part of the duke's command. For almost four years Ignatius filled his days with jousts, the chase, business of the duke, and continued reading of romances.

Among the several theatres of war in which the Hapsburgs and the Valois tried to settle their differences were the mountainous passes of Navarre. The Navarrese, seething with anger at the memory of how Ferdinand the Catholic had appropriated their lands south of the Pyrenees, welcomed the French when they marched on Pamplona in the spring of 1521. The situation looked hopeless to Francisco de Beaumont, designated by the duque de Nájera to command the Spanish defensive at Pamplona, and he marched away. To Ignatius this withdrawal was

For a list of the ABBREVIATIONS used here, such as *AHSJ*, see page 514 below. BIBLIOGRAPHICAL DATA, usually abridged in these footnotes, can be found at the back of the book in the alphabetized Bibliography or by means of the Index.

1 P. de Leturia, S.J., *Iñigo de Loyola* (Syracuse, 1949), pp. 44-46, 52-53.

disgraceful flight in which his sense of honor would not allow him to take part. He rallied around him the men who were willing to defend Pamplona's citadel and prepared for the assault by the French. Then the governor of the fortress and his captain wanted to surrender. Ignatius refused to concur and argued so persuasively that he inspired them with his own gallantry and turned their weak-heartedness into martial valor.

On May 20, 1521, the best artillerymen of Europe had set up their cannons before the walls. The French offered terms of surrender. Ignatius persuaded the governor not to accept them. Because no priest was present Ignatius, following a custom of the Middle Ages, confessed his sins to a comrade. Then he took his post on the breastworks. For six hours the French pounded the citadel, and finally part of the wall crumbled and the infantry prepared to pour in. In the breach stood Ignatius, sword drawn to meet the attack. And there he fell, his right leg shattered by a shell. Surrender of the garrison followed immediately. So closed the military career of Ignatius of Loyola in the full realization of his dreams of gallantry and courage in the service of his monarch.

The French treated their wounded prisoner with that delicate courtesy which prompted them to carry him in a litter to Loyola, but which could never be a substitute for surgical competence, so distressingly wanting when they tried to set his broken leg. At Loyola the doctors of Azpeitia tried to remedy the mistakes of the French. It was an agonizing experience, and years later Ignatius spoke of it as "butchery." He failed to rally after the operation, became more and more weak, received the last sacraments, and almost died. Then came a turn for the better and his strength gradually returned. However the doctors had left his leg in a condition intolerable to a man who still would be the gallant courtier and soldier. The sections of the broken bone did not mesh smoothly and evenly, one piece actually resting astride another. This caused a noticeable protrusion and made the leg shorter than the other. Ignatius could not abide this deformity and insisted on another operation even though it entailed agony of the worst kind. No pain was too great a price to preserve the ideal appearance of the knight in arms. The operation was almost a complete success. Ignatius had but the slightest limp and he could once more wear tight-fitting hose. But the protracted period of convalescence did more than restore damaged health. It transformed his mind and heart.

As the days dragged on, Ignatius requested some books on chivalry to while away the time. There were none to be had in the Loyola castle, but the ladies who were caring for him brought him the *Life of Christ* by the Carthusian Ludolph of Saxony and the popular medieval lives of the saints, the *Golden Legend,* by the Dominican Jacopo da Varazze (Voragine). As he turned the pages of the latter he read about the prowess of men who were described as "Knights of God," dedicated to the "eternal Prince Jesus Christ." In the *Life of Christ* he read about the magnanimous leader Christ, whose wish it was that his followers walk as "holy knights" and gaze into "the mirror of his Passion" and find there the courage to suffer the hardships of battle. A new procession of thoughts began to cross his mind. He discovered a wondrous nobility in the lives of the saints and he felt attracted to the completeness of their dedication to Christ. Then these thoughts yielded to the old, familiar ones about military glory and feats of chivalry. Then once more reflection on the valor of the saints prevailed. Ignatius became curious about these inner experiences and he closely analyzed the ebb and flow of his thoughts. Worldly ones left his heart empty and restless; spiritual ones brought profound peace and gladness. He sought the causes for this striking diversity, and concluded that it was the devil who stirred up the vain thoughts with all their unrest and that it was God who inspired his spiritual reflections with their calm joy. By an exceptional power of inner concentration and reflection, which became one of the characteristic marks of his growth in sanctity, Ignatius arrived at a fundamental and central idea: Christ is King, the saints are his knights, the human soul is a battleground of a momentous conflict between God and Satan.[2] Ignatius' admiration for the saints, expecially in their heroic penance and hard labor for Christ, grew into a firm resolve to do just as they had done. A close friend of Ignatius in later years, Juan de Polanco, remarked that Ignatius was ever the magnanimous man who ambitioned great things.[3] Certainly magnanimity and ambition for high sanctity were the marks of his start on a new way of life. One specific form which his resolution took was a decision to make a pilgrimage to the Holy Land.

Ignatius' generosity received an extraordinary reward. One night as he lay awake, he beheld very clearly the Blessed Virgin Mary holding the Child Jesus. With the great spiritual joy which he experienced went a deep disgust for his past sins, especially those of impurity. Three years before his death, when

2 Ibid., pp. 95-98.
3 *FN*, II, 518-519.

he was dictating his *Autobiography*, Ignatius said that from the time he saw Our Lady he had never given the slightest consent to a suggestion against chastity.

By early March, 1522, ten months after he fell in battle at Pamplona, Ignatius judged that he was well enough to start out on his pilgrimage to Jerusalem. Mounted on a mule, dressed in the colorful apparel of a courtier, he started southward toward Aránzazu. There he stopped at the shrine of Our Lady, and stood watch during the night. Then he turned eastward. After about fifteen days of travel he approached the famous shrine and Benedictine abbey of Montserrat, purchased a pilgrim's tunic of rough cloth, a staff, gourd, and sandals. He reached the monastery in the morning of March 21. There he conferred with Juan Chanones, a wise and saintly director, and after careful preparation made a general confession to him on the 24th. He donated his mule to the monastery, turned over his sword and dagger to Chanones to be hung on the grill in front of Our Lady's chapel, gave his gentleman's clothes to a beggar, and then, garbed in his pilgrim's robe and with staff in hand, prayed through the night before the Blessed Virgin's altar.

Before dawn of the 25th, Feast of the Annunciation, Ignatius attended Mass and quickly left Montserrat. He had decided to delay his journey toward the Holy Land for a few days in order to note in a copy book some ideas that had particularly impressed him, a practice he had started during his months of recuperation at Loyola, but fearful that possibly someone might recognize him at the shrine, he went to a little town, about twelve miles away, called Manresa. It was a decision fecund with the most penetrating and transforming of spiritual experiences. The short stay of a few days which he had planned lengthened into almost an entire year.

At Manresa Ignatius gave free rein to his resolve to rival the saints in his rejection of the worldliness of his past life. The once fastidious knight, now with unkempt hair and untrimmed fingernails, went from door to door begging his daily bread as children taunted him as "old man sack." During most of his stay at Manresa the Dominicans kindly provided him with a small cell in their priory. He helped the sick at the hospital, attended daily Mass and Vespers at the cathedral, and spent seven hours each day on his knees in prayer. Sometimes he sought the solitude of a cave in the rough and rocky hillside. His corporal austerities were severe and terrible.

Great and intense interior joy carried Ignatius along at the inauguration of this new manner of life, but very soon proved to be but the threshold to an agonizing period of excruciating misery and distress. Scruples assailed him; doubts about the completeness of past confessions tortured him. Taste for prayer disappeared. For several months the agony continued. With the full power of his voice he called to God for help and cried that he would willingly go even to a puppy-dog if it would lead him to a remedy for his suffering. One day he felt a strong temptation to destroy himself. To win the grace of interior peace he decided to undergo a long fast, and for a week, with no mitigation of his long prayers and his harsh penances, he took neither food nor drink. His confessor, learning what he was doing, told him to discontinue the fast. The scruples disappeared only to return in two days as his past sins passed through his mind like links in a chain.

Then came a day of vigorous decision. In his growth in understanding the movements of his soul, Ignatius began to discern the roots of his scruples and determined never more to confess his past sins. Serenity of soul returned, and with it came an abiding assurance that his deliverance from this fearful trial was an act of God's mercy. What followed was even more wonderful. Into Ignatius' soul poured wave after wave of extraordinary graces which raised him to the heights of mystical experience and brought him visions of the Holy Trinity, Christ Our Lord, and the Blessed Virgin. One day, near the river Cardoner, enlightenment of supreme brilliance filled his mind. Years later, when recalling this decisive experience, Ignatius tried to explain the depth and breadth of his insight into the supernatural by a comparison: Never in his whole life had he received at one moment an interior enrichment comparable to that which he enjoyed at the Cardoner. So true was this that, even if all the graces he later received and all his self-acquired wisdom should be gathered into a single comprehensive insight, it still could not equal in profundity and illumination the experience at Manresa. From then on he was, in his own words, "another man." He had entered into the company of the greatest mystics in the history of the Church.[4]

During this crucial period of his life Ignatius began to compose a little book which became a landmark in the history of Christian spirituality. Although he augmented, altered, and refined the text until its publication in 1548, the key ideas or core of the

4 *DeGuiJes*, pp. 30-32, 40, 44-46; Hugo Rahner, S.J., *The Spirituality of St. Ignatius Loyola* (Westminster, Md., 1953), pp. 48-58.

booklet were clearly in his notes when he left Manresa. Called the *Spiritual Exercises,* this small volume is not a spiritual treatise such as the *Introduction to the Devout Life* of St. Francis de Sales, but is rather a series of practical instructions on methods of prayer and examination of conscience, on ways to arrive at an unbiased decision, on plans for a variety of meditations and contemplations, all aimed to help an exercitant discover God's will for him and to carry it out with vigor. Systematically organized into a coherent body, these directives demand a most intense response from a man's faculties and powers. The *Spiritual Exercises* is not a book for reading; it is a manual to be translated into personal activity. Stamped with a sense of practical purposefulness which reaches its full development in a significant decision about the choice of a way of life, or if one's way of life is already determined, about its greater sanctification, the Exercises point the way to a magnanimous and loving embrace of God's will in the service of his Divine Majesty.

Ignatius divided the *Spiritual Exercises* into what he called "weeks," four of them in all. These weeks are flexible in their length and do not necessarily correspond to a group of seven days, although in their totality they usually equal about thirty days. The first week, with its great purifying meditations on the malice of sin and the sufferings of hell, preceded by a solemn consideration of man's basic purpose in the world, highlights the service, unvitiated by unruly passions, which man owes the Divine Majesty. The second, third, and fourth weeks are dominated by the person of Christ, presented in all his compelling nobility and attractiveness as he summons all men to follow him. In the second week, St. Ignatius presents Christ as he moves through the successive stages of his earthly life, completely rejecting the principles and attitudes of the worldly-wise, deliberately embracing a life of poverty and humility, lovingly enduring the contempt of men, in a supreme dedication of self to the unalloyed fulfillment of his Father's will. The insistently repeated prayer is for the grace to know Christ more intimately, to love and follow him more closely. As the meditations and contemplations advance, there is a mounting absorption with Christ as he unfolds the nature of his conflict with Satan and the character of his own way of life. At the moment of formulating the important decision which should affect the entire future of one's life, Ignatius pointedly recalls the basic spiritual principle: progress in the spiritual life is made in proportion to the surrender of self-love, self-will, and self-concern. The ultimate norm is ever the greater praise and glory of God. To carry out such a brave

9

resolve, which is really a scalpel making a deep and painful incision into the body of man's selfishness, a rare courage is needed. Ignatius points to Christ as the source of this mettle. In the third week of the *Exercises* he directs the exercitant to contemplate Christ as he moves with sublime fortitude through his Passion to his terrible death, and as in the fourth week he radiates the glowing joy and serenity of the Resurrection.

This compact organism of directives, if responded to with generosity of soul, should stamp a man for life and leave him with a firm and resolute determination to achieve what is for God's greater service as it appears at the moment of decision. The logic of the First Principle and Foundation, at the threshold of the first week, and the élan of the contemplation on the Kingdom of Christ, immediately before the second week, join and in their fusion create the noble and beautiful ideal of companionship with Christ in the service of the Divine Majesty.[5] In the formation of the Jesuit the *Spiritual Exercises* have ever been and still remain an indispensable means to set the novice on the highroad to heroism and sanctity.

It can never cease to be a source of marvel that this little volume came from the pen of a man who but a year before had, in his enchantment by the romances like *Amadís de Gaula,* been spinning a web of images of himself as the chivalrous knight before a lady fair or as the spirited soldier in the thick of battle. Only the action of the Divine Artisan in his creation of this Christian mystic can account for what Ignatius brought forth. In a style that is taut, plain, difficult in its solicitude for exactness, sharp, like the jagged face of a rocky precipice, the *Spiritual Exercises* are a trophy of the bitter contest waged in Ignatius' soul between Christ the King and the Prince of Darkness. This revelation of his personal experience under God's grace is one of the most precious legacies Ignatius has left to his Society.

The *Spiritual Exercises,* however, have had an influence not at all restricted to the Society, for they are one of the basic documents in the modern era of the Church's history. Their

---

5 *DeGuiJes,* pp. 593-601. John Bossy has edited the 1951 Birbeck Lectures of the late H. Outram Evennett in *The Spirit of the Counter-Reformation* (Cambridge, England, 1968). On pp. 43-66, 126-130, Evennett in one of the lectures, and Bossy in a postscript, discuss the cultural and literary influences, aside from personal mystical graces, on Ignatius in his composition of the *Spiritual Exercises.*

words and phrases have entered into millions of minds and hearts through retreats, missions, sermons, and spiritual counseling, and have created a body of the faithful alert to the call of Christ the King inviting them to do battle under the standard of the Cross against the power of Satan. Large pieces of the cloth of modern spirituality bear the stamp of Manresa.

Toward the end of February, 1523, Ignatius left Manresa on the first leg of his journey to Venice, point of embarkation to the Holy Land. At Barcelona, at Rome where he had gone to obtain the pope's blessing and permission for his pilgrimage, and at Venice where he waited passage from mid-May to mid-July, Ignatius followed a program of great austerity, begging his food and often sleeping without roof. On July 24 he sailed from the city of the lagoons, and after a little more than a month, at sea, with the usual experiences of contrary winds, calms, and storms, he landed at Joppa on August 31. Three days later, with his twenty fellow-pilgrims in silent and reverent procession, guided by the Franciscan custodians of the holy places, he entered Jerusalem. The days which followed were an inspiration for Ignatius, filled as they were by visits to places blessed by their associations with Christ: the Holy Sepulchre, the river Jordan, Bethlehem, and the Mount of Olives. He determined that here was to be his abode for the rest of his life. The Franciscan superior, with his practical knowledge of the serious danger such a plan could entail because of the uncertain and uneasy relations between the Christians and the Turks, very decisively vetoed the pilgrim's resolve. On September 23, after nineteen memorable days, Ignatius and his companions started back to Joppa. Three and a half months later, after a perilous voyage compounded by heavy seas, stinging winds, and driving snow, he was once more in Venice, in January, 1524.

With the collapse of his high hopes to remain in the Holy Land, Ignatius had to find another orientation for his future. Since his days at Manresa he had felt an insistent desire to help other souls to achieve their divine purpose, and this now took specific form in a resolve to study for the priesthood. The days of the long-planned pilgrimage to Jerusalem were over, and yet he remained a pilgrim for a long time to come, as for thirteen years he held faithfully to the hard and stony road to holy orders.

Ignatius returned to Spain and there began the first period of a long program of study, three and a half years at Barcelona, Alcalá, and Salamanca. At Barcelona, in his thirty-third year, he sat in a grammar class with youngsters and under the direction of Jerónimo Ardévol doggedly applied his untrained mind for

11

two laborious years to the mastery of Latin declensions and conjugations.

Through these years Ignatius was the welcome guest of a devout and generous family, the Pascuals, who reverenced the poor, penitential, and prayerful student. Ignatius begged his food, cared for the sick in the hospitals, taught catechism to children, walked about even in the winter in shoes without soles. His influence was widespread. Some women of aristocratic families became his warm admirers and three young men elected to share his way of life. His profound mystical experiences, elevating the charm of his natural gentility, broke through his indigent appearance and touched the souls of others. One of the characteristics of Ignatius' spirituality was his disposition to seek God in all things, which was reflected, as the Polish Jesuit, Mikolaj Lenczycky (Lancicius), recorded, in the warm smile with which he would seem to draw others into his very self, because in them he beheld the image of Christ.[6]

On the completion of his study of grammar Ignatius went in March, 1526, to Alcalá, seat of Ximenes' famous university, fresh and buoyant in the vigor of its youth. Here Ignatius, during a little more than a year of study, made a serious mistake. Ignorant of the need for order and gradation in the conquest of learning, he directed his attacks against several different fronts at once, the logic of De Soto, the physics of St. Albert the Great, the theology of Peter the Lombard. He ended up with nothing but a head full of confused and undigested ideas to show for his many months of labor. This mistake however had a resonance far beyond Alcalá and Ignatius' personal intellectual advancement, for when the time came for him to direct the Jesuit educational venture, he insisted on a graded hierarchy of aims and methods.

At Alcalá his mélange of courses did not deflect Ignatius from his habitual charity, and it was precisely this penchant for helping others which brought to an abrupt close his career at the University. He and the companions who joined him at Barcelona, all dressed alike, soon became popular in the city for their ability to discourse movingly and effectively on spiritual topics. The Inquisitors, sensitive to the current of illuminism in Spain's history, investigated the situation which became suddenly aggravated by the disappearance of two women, a mother and her daughter. These women, contrary to Ignatius' advice, went on a pilgrimage to Jaén. What was an inconsequential incident

6 *FN*, III, 658-659.

grew into a mighty issue, fed by the irresponsible gossip which placed the blame on Ignatius. The Inquisitor had him placed in prison while he looked into the rather ridiculous tempest. After about a month and a half of confinement, Ignatius heard the sentence: he must put aside his pilgrim's robe for clothes then in style, and he must desist from teaching, either publicly or privately, under pain of excommunication. The latter judgment was a grievous blow to his strong desire to help others, and to avoid this enforced silence he and his companions left for Salamanca around June 21, 1527.

The venerable old university town was far more curt in its reception to Ignatius than Alcalá. Ignatius arrived in early July, 1527, and left in mid-September. He was in the city less than two weeks when he was chained with one of his friends in a dirty cell. The Dominicans of the Convent of San Esteban had cordially invited him to dinner. Then they questioned him about his manner of life and his teaching. Ignatius remained as a guest at San Esteban for three days when the vicar general of the diocese entered the case and ordered that the suspect be imprisoned. Ignatius submitted his text of the Spiritual Exercises for official scrutiny. The cross-examination on theology continued. At Manresa, Ignatius saw with great clarity the nobility of following Christ even in humiliation, and the indignity of his confinement only nourished his fervent commitment to that ideal. The future archbishop of Burgos, in a gesture of sincere sympathy, visited him and inquired about his condition. His reply was the natural outpouring of the man of Manresa. "I assure you that there are not so many fetters and chains in Salamanca as I wish to bear for the love of God; indeed, even more." After twenty-two days in jail Ignatius heard sentence: he and his companions were orthodox in doctrine and unblemished in morals, and so they were free to continue their usual way of life except for explaining, until they had had four more years of study, the distinction between mortal and venial sin. Piqued by what he felt was an unfair restriction, especially in view of the acknowledged soundness of his teaching, Ignatius made another of those momentous decisions which opened the door to a unique and fertile phase in his life. He resolved to quit Spain and pursue his studies at the University of Paris.

About two weeks after his release from prison and after settling with his companions to remain at Salamanca until he had made arrangements for them at Paris, Ignatius started out, with a small donkey loaded with his books, on the wearying journey eastward through Spain to Barcelona, where he received alms from his

friends, and then northward through France to Paris. He arrived
at Paris on February 2, 1528.

*In Paris
and Rome*
Ignatius spent seven years at Paris, years of great achievement as he more fully qualified himself for the priesthood. His
first move at Paris actually was in a sense a step backwards.
With an innate aversion for any lack of thoroughness, he enrolled
at the spartan-like College of Montaigu in order to repeat grammar and humanities. So, at thirty-seven years of age he again
took up the study of Latin. He stayed at this institution for a
year and a half.

Very early he felt the severe pinch of poverty, which in turn
seriously hampered his studies. Assured free shelter at the Hospital of St. James, he begged his daily bread, but soon realized
that asking charity consumed precious time. A Spanish friar advised him to go to Flanders during the summer months of
vacation and there ask the Spanish merchants at Bruges and
Antwerp for the financial help necessary to carry him through
the academic term. Ignatius did this for three years, including
a trip to London in the third year. Then the generosity of the
merchants made it no longer necessary to leave Paris since they
forwarded their alms directly to him.

In October, 1529, he began his philosophy courses at the College of Sainte Barbe. In March, 1533, he received his Licentiate,
and the year following his Master's degree. In 1533 he also
began his course in theology under the Dominicans at their convent on Rue Saint-Jacques.[7] His education, hitherto shaped in
large measure by the medieval tradition of courtly refinement
and knightly chivalry experienced at Loyola and Arévalo, was
now broadened by another legacy from the Middle Ages, the
philosophy of the Schoolmen and the theology of St. Thomas
Aquinas. Among the intellectual dispositions he took with him
from Paris two were pronounced: an admiration for the system
and organization of studies at the University and a predilection
for the teaching of the Angelic Doctor.

Meanwhile Ignatius gave the Spiritual Exercises to a number
of his fellow students, communicating to them the intense fire
of love for God within his own soul. The companions whom he
had won in Spain, for a variety of reasons, dropped by the way-
side. The early chronicler of the Society of Jesus, Juan de
Polanco, likened this little band to a premature birth, not long-

7 P. Dudon, S.J., *St. Ignatius of Loyola* (Milwaukee, 1949), pp. 142-143.

lived. But at Paris six who committed themselves to his ideal of apostolic action remained faithful to the end. The first was a blond, comely Savoyard of most friendly and sweet disposition, Pierre Favre.

Pierre, a student at the College of Sainte Barbe and roommate of a student from Navarre only six days older than himself, Francis Xavier, welcomed Ignatius into his quarters in the Fall of 1529 when Ignatius quit the College of Montaigu for Sainte Barbe. Pierre and Francis were then twenty-three years old. Favre as a shepherd boy in his Alpine home at Villaret early felt drawn to a life of holiness and when twelve years old, while out in the fields with his sheep, made a vow of chastity. He overcame his father's reluctance to send him to school by his tears of disappointment. After nine years of study at Thônes and La Roche, he began his university studies at Paris in 1525.

When Pierre met Ignatius he was in the throes of deep interior anguish caused by scruples and temptation, further aggravated by his indecision about his vocation in life. So distressed was he that he would willingly have retreated to a desert to live on nothing but herbs if only he could find freedom from his suffering. He had been helping Ignatius in his study of philosophy, and one day revealed to him the affliction of his soul. It was a day of great blessing for Pierre, for by that act he had placed himself in the hands of one of the more eminent spiritual directors in the history of the Church.[8]

Ignatius instructed Pierre in the recognition of the causes of scruples and outlined for him a program of prayer, eradication of defects, weekly confession, and Holy Communion. Peace descended on Pierre's soul, and with tranquillity came the resolve to follow Ignatius in a life of service to Christ Our Lord. After a month given to making the Spiritual Exercises under Ignatius' direction, Pierre was ordained to the priesthood in May, 1534.

Francis Xavier (Francisco Javier), handsome, buoyant native of Navarre, had a benefice ready for him at Pamplona, and at first held himself somewhat aloof from the Basque student, fifteen years older than himself. Ignatius, however, by his kindness and help in finding financial assistance for Francis, broke through the initial reserve, and Francis, once touched by the noble ideals of Ignatius, did as Favre had done, and thus forged the link, never to be broken, between the names of Loyola and Xavier.

8 W. V. Bangert, S.J., *To the Other Towns: A Life of Blessed Peter Favre* (Westminster, Md., 1959), pp. 28-29.

Sometime about October, 1532, Ignatius became especially friendly with the twenty-two-year-old, urbane, and gracious Portuguese, Simão Rodrigues. The next year he met the twenty-one-year-old, intelligent, and fearless Castilian, Diego Laynez, and the eighteen-year-old, versatile, and articulate Toledan, Alonso Salmerón, and a year still later another Castilian, the twenty-four-year-old, blunt and candid Nicolás Bobadilla. All of them felt the pull of Ignatius' magnetic spirit and elected to ally themselves with him in the service of Christ.

The first major problem the little group had to face was to determine what specific shape and form their ambitions would take once they had finished their studies. After long and serious discussion they decided that their field of labor would be among the Moslems in the Holy Land. To make more secure the bond of unity among themselves and to strengthen their determination, they resolved to pronounce three vows: poverty, chastity, and a journey to Jerusalem. If the last vow should be impossible to carry out, they would go to Rome and place themselves at the disposal of the pope.

On the feast of Our Lady's Assumption, 1534, the seven students left the Latin Quarter in the morning and walked to the small chapel in honor of St. Denis on the slope of Montmartre. In the crypt Pierre Favre, the only priest among them, offered the Holy Sacrifice of the Mass. At the Communion he turned, faced his kneeling friends and held the Sacred Host before them as each in turn pronounced the three vows. He gave them Holy Communion, then turned to the altar, made the vows himself, and consumed the sacred species. That day they spent on the side of the hill, simply enjoying the gladness they felt in their hearts. They had formed a tightly knit little company — not indeed a religious order — and this scene has ever remained one of the most precious treasures in the traditions of the Society of Jesus. Forty-three years later Simão Rodrigues remarked that the recollection of that day was ever for him a source of fervor and "unspeakable wonder." [9]

A few months later Ignatius became seriously sick and the doctors advised that he should seek relief by a return to his native air. In the spring of 1535, having arranged that his companions should meet him in Venice on the completion of their studies, he designated Pierre Favre as their leader and set out for Spain. Actually he did not remain in Azpeitia very long, only about three months, but he made an unforgettable impression

9 *MonBroet*, pp. 457-458.

on his countrymen by his sermons, catechism lectures, and insistence on lodging in the Magdalena hospital rather than at the Loyola castle. Toward the end of July he left Azpeitia, and by way of Javier, Almazán, and Toledo, where he met the families of Francis Xavier, Diego Laynez, and Alonso Salmerón, and transacted some business for his friends, he traveled through Valencia and Genoa to Venice where he arrived in December, 1535. The year 1536 he spent in the Serene Republic, devoting his attention largely to the continuation of his studies in theology.

At Paris, meanwhile, three more students at the University joined the group left behind by Ignatius. Favre, with that skill which won from Ignatius the handsome tribute that Pierre was unequalled among the early Jesuits in the art of conducting the Spiritual Exercises, guided through a month's retreat his friend and former classmate in Savoy, the priest Claude Jay, another priest, the handsome and stately Paschase Broët from Picardy, and the joyful and innocent Jean Codure from Seyne in the shadow of Mont Blanc. All three elected to make their own the ideals expounded to them by Favre.

The renewal of the shameful and selfish conflict between the two great Catholic princes of Europe, Charles V and Francis I, made it necessary for Favre and his charges to advance the date of their departure for Venice. They all won their Master's degree and in November, 1536, left Paris. After an exhausting journey on foot through a terrain muddied by winter rain, swept by piercing winds, and patrolled by detachments of soldiers, they ascended into the passes of the Alps, trudged through snow often over their knees, and finally, "joyful in spirit and safe in body," as Favre recalled, arrived at Venice on January 8, 1537. There they found Ignatius awaiting them.

From that January, 1537, when they were but a little brotherhood ambitious for the service of God in the Holy Land, until September, 1540, when they would receive papal approbation as a religious order with the name of Society of Jesus, only three and a half years were to pass. But for these men, still ignorant of the high destiny prepared for them, they were years of groping along uncertain paths and of carefully searching for God's will in the rapidly shifting circumstances of their life. Their paramount desire was to obtain passage to the Holy Land, but this met frustration at every turn. Since the winter months were off-season for ships to Palestine, Ignatius and his friends spread out among the hospitals of the city and, to the amazement of the Venetians, tended the sick, scrubbed the floors, buried the

17

dead. During Lent, Ignatius sent his companions to Rome to request the pope's blessing on their journey to Jerusalem and his permission for the non-priests to receive the sacrament of holy orders. Ignatius himself did not go because at Rome were two influential men who, he had good reason to believe, might be prejudiced against his project. They were Gian Pietro Carafa, co-founder of the Theatines, and Doctor Pedro Ortiz, special envoy of the Emperor Charles V at the papal court. But it proved to be the latter who, in a dramatic change of front, gave the group a cordial welcome and arranged that they be received by Pope Paul III. The audience was a rather singular one, since Ignatius' friends, at the pope's request, carried on a discussion in theology during Paul's meal, but it proved to be to their best advantage. The breadth of their learning made a deep impression on the pontiff, who with manifest gladness granted their request. This meeting was an important moment in the advance of the Catholic Reform, the significance of which those who looked on could scarcely surmise, as Alessandro Farnese, pope of the new papal orientation, stood with arms outstretched in benediction over the kneeling figures of Favre, Laynez, Salmerón, and the others, men to be among the most penetrating lights in the reillumination of the faith in Europe.

Back in Venice, all those not yet priests, save Salmerón who was too young, were ordained on June 24, 1537. So intimately did they appreciate their new spiritual gift that they deferred the offering of their first Masses until after forty days of prayer and penance. In groups of two or three they scattered to different parts of the Venetian Republic. The austerity of Ignatius, Favre, and Laynez in an abandoned, ramshackle convent at Vicenza, living on the bread they begged and sleeping on the ground, was a gauge of the determination of these men to have no part in the spirit of worldliness. In September all assembled at Vicenza, and, on a day or days unknown to us, the newly ordained, save Ignatius and Rodrigues who waited even longer, celebrated their first Masses.

Once more, during the summer of 1537, their hopes to go to the Holy Land were crushed since war clouds were gathering over the Mediterranean as tensions increased between Venice and the Ottoman Empire. In October, therefore, they decided once more to disperse, this time to preach in different towns of northern Italy while Ignatius, Favre, and Laynez went to Rome. Before they separated they made an important decision. By now people could not fail to observe their unity and would naturally inquire about the nature of their group. Since Jesus Christ was their model and since he it was to whom they dedicated their entire life, they decided to identify themselves as the *Compañía de Jesús,* Society of Jesus.[10] So, in the inspiration of this name, Jay and Rodrigues journeyed to Ferrara, Xavier and Bobadilla to Bologna, Broët and Salmerón to Siena, Diego Hozes, a new member whom Ignatius had received at Venice, and Codure to Padua.

Toward the end of November, Ignatius, Favre, and Laynez briefly interrupted their journey to Rome and stopped at a chapel in a little place, nine miles from the city, called La Storta. Here Ignatius received one of his mystic graces as he beheld God the Father, and close to the Father Christ with his cross, both looking on him with love. He heard the Son say, "My desire is that you be my servant," and the Father, "I shall be propitious to you at Rome." This vision left Ignatius with an increased desire that his little band be known as the Society of Jesus and with a deeper confidence in God's protection regardless of what Rome might have in store for them.[11]

The welcome they received in the Eternal City was heartening. While Ignatius gave the Spiritual Exercises, Favre and Laynez, by appointment of the pope, lectured on scripture and theology at the Sapienza. By Easter of the following year, 1538, all the others had come to Rome and were reunited with Ignatius in a small house near the Trinità dei Monti. Despite a violently irrational outbreak of slander against them, which was inspired by the followers of an Augustinian friar whom they had admonished because of the Lutheran overtones in his sermons, these men made a deep impression at Rome. Ignatius, with dogged tenacity of purpose, not only broke the back of the campaign of lies but, by going directly to Pope Paul, obtained an official statement from the governor of the city that he and his companions were blameless in their life and teaching. In several of the churches of the city they preached, much to the gratified amazement of the faithful, who had learned to expect sermons only during Lent and Advent. During the bitter and terrible winter that fell upon Rome at Christmas, 1538, when famine drove hundreds into the city from the countryside only to drop in the streets exhausted, frozen, and starved, they moved into this melancholy scene, picked up the frozen unfortunates, carried them to their house, now near Ara Coeli, fed them, and

10 *FN,* I, 204; II, 595-596. On this name, see *ConsSJComm,* pp. 345-349.
11 *FN,* I, 313, fn. 37; Bangert, *To the Other Towns,* p. 299, n. 17.

warmed them with the food and firewood of their own begging. Thousands felt the mercy of these men during five terrible months.

Late in November, 1538, in the realization that the little flame of hope which they had of going to Jerusalem had been extinguished, they went to Pope Paul and placed themselves entirely at his disposal, even if he should desire that they go to the Indies or any other part of the world. The pope gladly accepted this magnanimous offer. Pierre Favre interpreted this event as the quasi-foundation of the Society of Jesus.[12]

Within two years this quasi-foundation developed into the full and complete groundwork of papal approbation of the Society as a religious order. One of the factors which set this development in motion was the seriously imminent danger that their unity of five years and more would be broken and destroyed. In March, 1539, Broët received orders from Pope Paul through Cardinal Gian Pietro Carafa to go to Siena, accompanied by one of his friends, and there inaugurate a reform in the monasteries of Sant' Agnese and San Prospero. This was the opening wedge. Other prelates importuned Ignatius for his friends. Therefore, toward the end of Lent, 1539, they began a series of discussions which lasted for several months on what they would have the precise nature of their Society of Jesus to be. Every page of the proceedings at these conferences is redolent with the prayerfulness, sincerity, and thoroughness which each of these men brought to this problem. It was clear from the beginning that they were unanimous in their desire to preserve some sort of unity; but the capital point which remained dark and hidden during nearly a month of searching debate, fortified by prayer and penance, was that of adding to their vows of poverty and chastity, the vow of obedience to one of their number. They recognized that the inclusion of the vow of obedience would mean their assumption of the obligations of the religious life. In mid-April they finally concluded that they should take this momentous step. How keenly they felt the gravity of their decision they showed in a special ceremony reminiscent of the day of vows at Montmartre. On April 15, Pierre Favre celebrated Mass, and at the Communion asked each if it was his will, dependent on the approbation of the pope, to form a religious order and if it was his intent to join it. Each answered affirmatively and then

12 *FN*, I, 541.

received Holy Communion from Pierre.[13] Through May and into June they continued their discussions on several aspects of the structure and work of the Society they envisaged.

The next step was to petition the pope for his approval. Ignatius, therefore, drew up in a few pages a compendium of their decisions, which, despite its brevity, forecast the spirit of the future Jesuit *Constitutions*. The opening words of this militant document form a strong link with the *Spiritual Exercises:* "Whoever desires to serve as a soldier of God beneath the banner of the cross in our Society. . . ." Some of the fundamental points about the Society as expressed in this "Formula of the Institute" were: its apostolic spirit, looking primarily to the advancement of souls in Catholic doctrine and life; its loyalty to the Holy See, expressed in a special vow to go anywhere in the world at the pope's behest; its devotion to poverty by the sacrifice of the individual's right to the possession of property; its prompt and persevering obedience to the general; its sacrifice of the traditional and beautiful chant in common of the Divine Office in the interest of gaining time for apostolic action.

The time could hardly have been less propitious for the creation of a new order in the Church because of the disrepute of many religious communities and the conviction of some prelates that their number should be curtailed. The formal presentation to the pope of Ignatius' Formula was followed by a year and three weeks of suspense and uncertainty. The cardinals who, at one time or another, were commissioned to examine the document were of two minds. Cardinal Gásparo Contarini favored prompt approbation. Cardinal Giralomo Ghinucci hesitated, in his fear of Lutheran influence, about the omission of choir. The hard core of opposition came from Cardinal Bartolomeo Guidiccioni, who had strong feelings against religious and who seemed to lean toward the drastic reduction of all orders of men to merely one, matching the general category of secular priests. Ignatius had a strong redoubt to be taken in this fixed judgment of Cardinal Guidiccioni, and he brought to his energetic assault both supernatural and natural weapons. He promised almighty God that he and his handful of priests would offer three thousand Masses; they sought letters of commendation from persons of influence who had seen their work. From Ferrara, Parma, Lisbon, Bologna, Siena, messages conveying the warmest praise poured into Rome. Guidiccioni finally weakened to the extent that he was willing to lift his objection if the number of the com-

13 *Cons*MHSJ, I, 1-8.

munity were limited to sixty. On September 27, 1540, Pope Paul, adopting Guidiccioni's restriction, gave formal approbation by the bull *Regimini militantis ecclesiae*. The Society of Jesus, as a fully canonical religious order, had become a reality.

A matter of paramount importance which called for early attention was the election of the general. During Lent, 1541, six who were able to be present convened at Rome with Ignatius. The ballots of these six, as well as the ballots of Favre, Xavier, and Rodrigues, which had been sent from Germany and Portugal, showed that Ignatius was their unanimous choice. With the greatest reluctance and only on the strong counsel of his confessor, Ignatius accepted the office. On April 22, 1541, he and his companions in Rome went to St. Paul Outside-the-Walls and pronounced their solemn vows as members of the Society of Jesus. In 1544 Pope Paul III removed the earlier restriction to sixty men and in 1550 Pope Julius III solemnly confirmed the Society in the bull *Exposcit debitum*. Very soon the members of the order became known as Jesuits — those peculiarly associated with the name of Jesus — at first in a pejorative sense, then more generally as an expression of esteem.

Early Expansion   Ignatius had inlaid into the character of this little group the idea of mobility and action, an idea which they all eloquently expressed in the oblation they had made of themselves to the pope to go to any part of the world he should desire. Even before he gave his formal approbation of the Society, Paul began to use these men in areas outside Rome. In 1539 he sent Paschase Broët to Siena whence came reports of the startling renovation of the town which he was achieving by retreats to university students and by his popular sermons. The same year Paul dispatched Pierre Favre and Diego Laynez to the Duchy of Parma where by the Spiritual Exercises they created a fervor, before unknown, for the sacraments of penance and the Holy Eucharist. Claude Jay's first orders took him to the strife-ridden town of Bagnorea where by his gentle charity he won the hearts of all, reconciled old enemies, and started a general return to the sacraments. Speaking of the daily number of confessions, he wrote: "At present I cannot get away from the church until midnight. On some mornings I find that they have scaled the walls and are actually settled inside my house waiting to go to confession." [14] Pope Paul, the same year, used Nicolás Bobadilla on the delicate mis-

14 *MonBroet*, pp. 265-267.

sion of reconciling Juana of Aragon with her husband Ascanio Sforza at Ischia, which was but the first in a rapid series of moves which took him for priestly work to Gaeta, Naples, Bisignano.

Very soon the talents and zeal of these men were being channeled into other important works of the most diverse kind: diplomatic and quasi-diplomatic missions for the Holy See, professorships at universities, theological counseling at the Council of Trent, the administration of schools, the foreign missions. In the fall of 1541 Alonso Salmerón and Paschase Broët, as papal nuncios, undertook the short-lived and frustrating mission to sorry, distressed Ireland, almost completely under the tight control of Henry VIII, in order to bolster the waning fidelity of the chieftains to the Church. In October, 1540, Pierre Favre was directed to accompany Doctor Pedro Ortiz of the emperor's diplomatic corps into Germany for the religious debates between Catholics and Protestants scheduled at Worms and Regensburg. Protocol did not permit Pierre to speak with Melanchthon and his associates, but by his superb facility in conducting the Spiritual Exercises, his attractive manner, and his charism for conversing on spiritual subjects, Favre brought new resolution to German prelates and priests. The first Jesuit to enter Germany, he reached the conclusion that the people of that country were not turning to Lutheranism because of any logic of doctrine but because of the widespread breakdown in Catholic life, even among the clergy.[15] At Worms, Speyer, and Regensburg he initiated, especially by his influence on ecclesiastical leaders, the great contribution of the Society of Jesus to many areas of Germany, the restoration of their ancient religious heritage.

The university lecture hall was an early post for the men of the Society. As early as 1537, Favre and Laynez taught scripture and theology at the Sapienza in Rome. In 1543 Claude Jay was at Ingolstadt when the veteran champion of the faith, Johann Eck, died, leaving vacant a key chair in the theological faculty at the university. Duke William of Bavaria invited Jay to take the post. Claude declined, in part because he feared that a professorship, demanding by its very nature a degree of stability, would be a check to what he felt was one of the hallmarks of the Society, its mobility. Only on the insistence of Bishop Robert Wauchope, internuncio in Germany, did he yield and undertake a series of lectures at the university on the epistles of St. John. This was an important experience for Claude since it deepened his knowledge of the religious situation in Germany and jarred

15 *MonFabri*, pp. 48-49.

him into an awareness of the deplorable quality of the education of the priests. In a sharp reversal of judgment he became an energetic advocate of Jesuits entering the field of formal education.[16] Six years later, after an absence from Ingolstadt on other apostolic business, Jay returned to the lecture hall, this time joined by Alonso Salmerón and a young Dutch priest, Peter Canisius.

The paramount event in the movement of reform within the Church was the Council of Trent. Three days after the Council was opened in December, 1545, Jay arrived as the representative of Cardinal Otto Truchsess von Waldburg of Augsburg. Pope Paul asked Ignatius for more of his men for this great enterprise, and Ignatius assigned Favre, Laynez, and Salmerón. Only the last two arrived at the tiny Tyrolese town since Pierre, taken by a virulent fever in the summer of 1546, died at Rome, just a little over forty years of age. With their wide erudition and careful scholarship Laynez and Salmerón gave invaluable assistance behind the scenes to the bishops. And on the floor, with facile eloquence, they elucidated several points of dogma to the general assembly. So began the truly distinguished Jesuit contribution to the success of this milestone in the history of the Church.

Highly specialized as was such work at Trent and in the universities, it did not keep the first Jesuits from a wholehearted dedication to popular preaching and the introduction of the Spiritual Exercises through the length and breadth of Central and Western Europe. Each of them, apart from Ignatius who remained at headquarters in Rome, had soon piled up hundreds and even thousands of miles of travel through a bewildering list of towns and cities. Claude Jay, for example, worked at Bagnorea, Faenza, Brescia, Regensburg, Ingolstadt, Dillingen, Worms, Augsburg, Ferrara, Vienna. Salmerón gained a reputation as one of the great pulpit orators of the day by his preaching at Rome, Naples, Modena, Bologna, Verona, Belluno, Venice, Ferrara. Using as his tool primarily the Spiritual Exercises, Favre won by his gentle and attractive manner the affections of many, nct only for himself but also for the Society he represented, in Parma, Worms, Speyer, Regensburg, Mainz, Cologne, Louvain, Lisbon, Valladolid. While on his many travels, especially in Germany, Pierre occasionally found time to note in a diary, known as his *Memoirs* (*Memoriale*), the changing experiences of his in-

16 *MonBroet*, pp. 289-290.

terior life. With its passages of moving simplicity the *Memoirs,* revealing an innocent, affectionate, prayerful soul, ever docile to the inspirations of the Holy Spirit, has remained one of the most precious spiritual treasures of the Society.[17] Thus, in almost a haphazard way, this infant among religious orders became more and more well known in Europe as its priests, generally at the disposal of bishops as well as the pope, moved about with startling alacrity.

One of the most striking responses to the message of the Jesuits was the large number of men who sought admission into the order. In 1540 the Society numbered ten; by 1556, the year Ignatius died, about a thousand. At Parma, several, including Antonio Criminali, the Society's proto-martyr, and Benedetto Palmio, destined to be one of the great popular preachers of Italy, found their vocation in meeting Favre and Laynez. At Louvain there was among the students of the University a remarkable outburst of enthusiasm for the Society's ideals, engendered by the eloquence of the scholastic, Francisco Strada, and the spiritual counseling of Pierre Favre. Favre sent eight of these students to Coimbra and one to Cologne for their training. In Portugal, due chiefly to the influence of Simão Rodrigues and the encouragement of King John III, the early Society developed as nowhere else, and by 1544 there was a community of forty-five in the university town of Coimbra.

If news from Portugal brought joy to Ignatius it also brought sorrow. The trouble arose from the waywardness of no other than one of his first companions, Simão Rodrigues. This cultivated Portuguese gentleman, entrusted with the responsibility of guiding the Society in his native land, evidenced an instability and recalcitrance which pushed Ignatius almost to the point of dismissing him. With fatherly tact and love, however, the general brought his unruly subject to the path of sorrow, penitence, and rededication to his earlier ideals. Rodrigues made up for his failings by the composition of one of the most precious and informative documents on early Jesuit history, *The Origin and Progress of the Society of Jesus,* which was published only in 1869.

Of all the new Jesuits the two most eminent were the Dutchman, Peter Canisius (Pieter De Hondt), and the Spaniard, Francis Borgia (Francisco Borja). In 1543 Canisius went through the Spiritual Exercises under the direction of Favre at Mainz and

---

17 Bienheureux Pierre Favre: *Mémorial, traduit et commenté* par M. de Certeau, S.J., "Collection Christus," no. 4 (Paris, 1959), pp. 7-11; Bangert, *To the Other Towns,* pp. 172-175.

on his twenty-second birthday vowed to become a member of the Society of Jesus. With this retreat in a Rhineland city began the fifty-four years of incredible labor of the man to be known as Germany's second Boniface. Francis Borgia, urbane and refined grandee of Spain, viceroy of Catalonia and duke of Gandía, chanced to meet Favre and Antonio Araoz and became captivated by the spiritual horizon which they opened to him. On the death of his wife in 1546, Francis resigned his high position in the Spanish aristocracy and became a Jesuit, bringing to his new way of life all the spiritual intensity that had stamped his career as a servant of the crown.

The early increase in numbers was a happy development since, amid the great variety of works in which the Jesuits became engaged, Ignatius was able to accept and develop two which have become identified with the Society in a special way: education and the foreign missions.

Schools   Education as a form of the apostolate, in the broad sense that it included preaching and teaching catechism, was part of the origins of the Society. But very soon Ignatius, faced with the problem of training the men whom he had admitted into the order, had to give thought to the matter of education in the formal sense. Adopting the suggestion of Laynez, he set up residences in university towns where the scholastics would follow the courses in the schools. By the end of 1544 there were seven of these residences in Europe. Gandía was the decisive place where the Society turned down the road to the apostolate of education for secular students. In 1545 Francis Borgia founded at Gandía a college for the training of Jesuit scholastics. The rector arranged some public demonstrations of the disputations in philosophy which so impressed some of the families of the city that they requested that their children be allowed to attend the classes. Borgia seconded the request, and in 1546 Ignatius gave his consent. Two years later the faculty offered courses in the humanities to the Gandian youth.

This development in Spain was not the only one that constrained Ignatius to reflect on the apostolate of the school. In 1543 the Portuguese at Goa asked Francis Xavier, who had arrived there the year before, for some Jesuit teachers in the local college of Diogo da Bourba. Xavier's report on this type of work was enthusiastic. From Germany, Claude Jay wrote that the Society could engage in no more essential work in that distressed country than teaching. In Sicily the Viceroy, Don Juan de Vega, a personal friend of Ignatius, in his hope of raising the religious and cultural tone of the island, urged the municipality of Messina to ask Ignatius to open a school for the youth of the town. Ignatius responded in most magnanimous fashion with the dispatch of ten carefully chosen Jesuits, including Jerónimo Nadal, Peter Canisius, and André des Freux. With the formal inauguration of the school in Messina in October, 1548, the Society started its first school in Europe primarily for secular students. Messina was the heavy body of the opening wedge whose fine, thin edge was Gandía.

Ignatius moved with care in his appraisal of this new apostolate, especially because of the problems it raised in relation to the mobility and poverty which he desired in the Society. But once it became clear in his mind what excellent service to the Church could be rendered in the field of education, he applied to this new enterprise all his talents for organization, and on December 1, 1551, he recommended to the Society in a circular letter the inauguration of colleges throughout Europe. Guided in great measure by reflection on his own personal experience, he advanced the cultivation of the intellectual life through the study of literature in the form of the ancient classics, of philosophy as developed primarily by Aristotle, and of theology in which St. Thomas was the master. With independence of judgment he envisaged an educational structure for which he took the stones from the ancient world of the classical authors, the medieval world of the great universities, and his contemporary world of Renaissance passion for humanism. Because of local circumstances not every Jesuit school could offer the full curriculum, some being limited to literature and philosophy, and others just to literature. Theology in fact rarely got beyond the seminary. But Ignatius' ideal was clear. From its inception the Jesuit school became one of the more influential exponents of the spirit of the Catholic reform. Bringing renewal to all classes of society, it gave validity to the vaunt of many early Jesuits: *Puerilis institutio renovatio mundi*. The people of Billom spoke of the Jesuit enterprise in their town as "a rebirth of the infant Church." [18]

A pressing need in this new work was the formulation of norms and instructions to guide administrators and teachers in the schools. Soon several plans or tracts appeared, one by Annibal du Coudret at Messina in 1551 which Polanco entitled *The Plan of*

---

18 *IdeaJesUn*, pp. 153-167; F. de Dainville, S.J., *La naissance de l'humanisme moderne* (Paris, 1940), pp. 359-360.

Studies at Messina (*De ratione studiorum Messanae*), and three by Nadal. Nadal's first was dated 1548 and called *The Constitutions of the College at Messina* (*Constitutiones Collegii Messanensis*); the second, 1552, and known as *The Arrangement and Order of a University* (*De studii generalis dispositione et ordine*); the third, 1553, and entitled *Rules for the Classes in the Colleges* (*Reglas para los studios de los collegios*).[19] These documents were the first drafts of the continual probing, sifting, and adjusting that went on for a half-century before the final charter was formulated in the *Plan of Studies* (*Ratio studiorum*) of 1599. On this gradual development of an educational charter the stamp of Ignatius was clear. The University of Paris was the school of his predilection, and by his insistence that the methods of Paris be adopted, he guaranteed that Jesuit schools would have certain basic characteristics: a distinctly graduated order of studies; a respect for the varying capacity of the students; an insistence on class attendance; an abundance of exercises. The order in a school so tightly organized was worlds apart from the confusion Ignatius experienced, to his own loss, at Alcalá, and from the chaos he saw in the contemporary Italian schools where classes were infrequent and the students were free to elect their courses. The College of Sainte Barbe was the cradle of Jesuit pedagogy, and Ignatius by his genius gave classical studies a stability and an expansion and a popularity which Erasmus, great humanist that he was, was not able to achieve.

The most illustrious of all the centers of learning established by Ignatius was the Roman College, opened in 1551. On this institution, where experimentation in methodology and textbooks was extensive and which he desired to be the model of all Jesuit schools, Ignatius lavished his constant and tender attention. He summoned to its faculty some of the best scholars of the Society, men like André des Freux, Martín de Olave, and Manuel de Sá, and so started a tradition of professional excellence that has been a challenge to generations of Jesuits.

In the eight years between 1548, when the college at Messina was opened, until 1556, the year of his death, Ignatius started in Europe thirty-three schools for secular students and gave approval for the opening of six others. Gandía had been a crossroads in Jesuit history where the Society of Jesus started down the long and seemingly unending highway of the apostolate of the classroom.

19 *MonPaed* (1965), I, 17-28, 93-106, 133-163, 185-210.

The second principal work with which the Society of Jesus became identified very early was that of the foreign missions.
Conspicuous as was the Jesuit expansion in Europe, it was
matched by a diffusion overseas even more remarkable because
of the difficulties, met and overcome, arising from staggering distances, unfamiliar cultures, strange languages, and even Christian perfidy. When Ignatius died he had his sons established in
the East Indies, Japan, Brazil, the Congo, and on their way to
Ethiopia. All of these ventures he started with the generous
encouragement of Portugal's high-minded monarch, John III,
and it was from Lisbon and under the flag of St. Vincent that the
first Jesuit missionaries sailed away from Europe on to the open
seas. The prime exemplar in the glorious missionary tradition of
the Society, still vibrant in the 7,000 Jesuits who today labor in
the field afar, was Francis Xavier.

Xavier's assignment to the Far East was ultimately a consequence of the anxiety of King John III of Portugal to bring the
faith to the teeming millions in his vast colonial empire. Doctor
Diogo de Gouvea, Portuguese head of the College of Sainte
Barbe at Paris, recalled the zealous group of men around Ignatius of Loyola and recommended them to his monarch as possible missionaries. Through his ambassador at Rome, King John
asked Ignatius for help. Although there were only six of the
group in Rome at the time, Ignatius picked two, Simão Rodrigues
and Nicolás Bobadilla. A serious illness prostrated Bobadilla, and
Ignatius on March 14, 1540, informed Francis Xavier that he was
to go instead. Xavier's reply was simple, "Fine. I'm your man."
Two days later he was on the road to Lisbon. So impressed was
King John by the two Jesuits that he decided to keep at least one
in Portugal for the wide opportunities for priestly work there.
Rodrigues he retained, and on April 7, 1541, his thirty-fifth birthday, Xavier with Micer Paul, a secular priest who lately had
entered the Society, and Francisco Mansilhas, a Portuguese vol-
unteer and aspirant to the priesthood, sailed down the Tagus on
the seven-hundred-ton *Santiago* for the Indies.

The journey was a fatiguing one of more than a year. During
the long months on the open seas when monotony was aggravated by the cramped quarters, the crudeness of unpalatable
food, and frequent spells of nausea among the passengers, the
qualities of Xavier's beautiful character, his tender charity for
others, his gaiety of spirit, his intense prayerfulness, glowed all
the more brilliantly. On May 6, 1542, the lumbering *Santiago*
reached Goa, the capital of Portuguese India.

Xavier was in the Far East ten years and his labor there falls

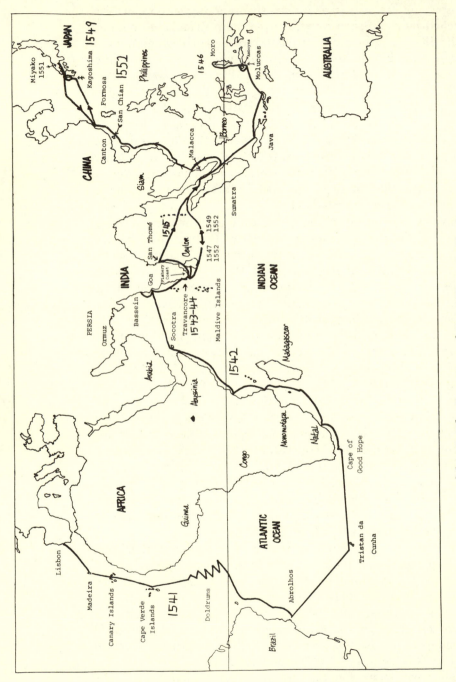

Map 1. The Journeys of Saint Francis Xavier
Drawn by Robert F. O'Connor, S.J.

into four general phases: teaching among the people of the Fishery Coast; a reconnoitering journey across about four thousand miles of ocean to the Moluccas; the establishment of the faith in Japan; vain efforts to enter China.

Francis stayed about four months at Goa, which became headquarters for the Jesuit contribution to the great missionary drive in the Orient, already under way some forty years and manned chiefly by the Franciscans and Dominicans. In September, 1542, leaving Mansilhas and Micer Paul to work in the capital, Xavier started on his first expedition, to the poor pearl fishers who lived along the fifty miles of desolate seashore on the eastern side of Cape Comorin, the southern extremity of India. He faced an unusual problem along the Fishery Coast, for of the thirty thousand inhabitants living on a barren, sandy, and hot coastline, about twenty thousand had, eight years before, received baptism without any preparation because the priests were ignorant of the language. Not only had he to be concerned with converting the pagans but he had to instruct these new Christians. With the help of some of the natives who had a smattering of Portuguese he translated into Tamil the Sign of the Cross, the Creed, the Our Father, the Hail Mary, the Confiteor. Painfully he memorized these prayers, and then began the more painful process of teaching them to the people. From village to village, under a broiling sun and on a diet of rice and an occasional fish, Francis traveled in the endless process of instructing and trying to detach the poor people from their ancient heathen practices. Adding to the mountains of difficulties was a dynastic war which had broken out for the throne of the monarch of Cape Comorin.

For almost two years, with the exception of a few months after October, 1543, when he returned to Goa to obtain the help of Mansilhas and some catechists, Francis remained on the arid Fishery Coast. Toward the end of 1544 his perseverance received its reward. In Travancore, on the southwestern coast of India, among the fishing folk of Macua who knew of the conversion of their neighbors and who realized that the adoption of Christianity would bring Portuguese protection against Mohammedan marauders, there was a general movement toward the Church. Francis advanced through the fourteen villages as the untiring teacher, and in one month baptized more than ten thousand.

The limits of his responsibility were the outer bounds of the Portuguese possessions in the Far East, the fabulous Moluccas four thousand miles beyond India. For almost four years, after a short visit at the shrine of St. Thomas, from August, 1544, to

March, 1548, when he arrived back at Goa, Francis was on the move, assessing opportunities for missionary work, translating prayers and instructions into the Malayan tongue, teaching the natives, counseling European merchants, sailors, and colonists. In ships where discomfort was a constant companion he crossed the Bay of Bengal to Malacca, wealthy and dissolute entrepôt between India and the Far East, then past the dense vegetation of the Malayan peninsula, the long island of Java to the fabled Moluccas, source of Portuguese wealth in spice, especially nutmeg. In jostling rowboats under a fierce sun he visited Amboyna, Ternate, and Moro. His travels widened his initial experience at Goa of the presence within the Portuguese empire of two contending moral forces, the nobility and high mindedness of certain Europeans in whom he found strength and encouragement, and the avarice, meanness, and lust of others who were his constant heartache. The four years of stress and exhaustion were outbalanced by the invaluable personal appraisal he was able to make of the places where priests could be stationed to best advantage.

Francis' task was a serious one, but grimness and stiffness never replaced his brightsome charm, and he carried on, as one observer mentioned, with laughter in his mouth. His letters to his fellow Jesuits in Europe revealed that he renewed his energies at the font of the Spiritual Exercises. "If one takes on these hardships for the sake of Him for whom we should bear them, then they will turn into sources of great refreshment. . . . It is my belief that the man who knows how to carry the cross of Christ will find rest in these labors." [20] This spirit, with the rare exception, permeated the other Jesuits. Of Antonio Criminali, then at Cape Comorin with six others, Xavier wrote to Ignatius on January 14, 1549, "Take my word for it. He is a holy man, born for the missions out here. Please send more like him. We need them. The people of Cape Comorin are his cherished comrades. To Christians, natives, and Saracens he is extraordinarily dear." In June of the same year some tribesmen pierced him with their lances and gave the Society the first of its martyrs, numbered in 1905 at 907.[21]

Malacca became for Francis a kind of peak from which he broadened the rim of his apostolic horizon, for it was there he

20 *EppXav*, I, 127.
21 Ibid, II, 29–30; I. H. Dugout, S.J., *Nos martyrs: Catalogue des Pères et Frères . . . qui . . . ont sacrifié leur vie* (Paris, 1905), p. 62.

encountered two strangers who aroused his interest in China and Japan. On his way to the Moluccas he met a Portuguese who discoursed about the mysterious Chinese empire, closed to the outside world but with whose people Portuguese merchants carried on a surreptitious trade. Xavier asked newly made friends at Malacca to discover all they could about this secretive land. On the return trip from the Moluccas he was introduced to a man named Yajiro from a country which the Portuguese discovered only five years earlier, Japan. Yajiro depicted for Francis a people of advanced civilization and richly developed culture. Francis, therefore, decided that Japan must enter into his planning for the future. Yajiro, who was anxious to become a Christian, he sent ahead to Goa for instruction in the faith.

It was also at Malacca that Francis first met some of the great flow of Jesuit reinforcements from Europe into Asia, three of them as well as a fourth who had entered the Society in India. For six weeks he briefed these newcomers and then dispatched them to the Moluccas. His letters to his Jesuit brethren in Europe electrified them. King John of Portugal, stirred deeply by the report of the ten thousand Francis had baptized at Travancore, directed that this news be announced in the churches, and arranged for the sustenance of a hundred Jesuits at Coimbra and the dispatch of twelve to India in early 1546. Father Araoz advised Ignatius that Xavier was doing by letter as much in Spain and Portugal as he was accomplishing in the Indies by his preaching.[22]

Francis was back at Goa in March, 1548. For a year he concentrated on the organization of the mission, arranging for the disposition of the other Jesuits and posting them at Goa, San Thomé, Quilon, Bassein, Ormuz and other distant places. He decided that he himself would go to Japan.

On Palm Sunday, 1549, accompanied by Father Cosme de Torres, Brother Juan Fernández, and Yajiro, the Japanese recently baptized and named Paul of the Holy Faith, and carrying impressive letters of recommendation from both the viceroy and the bishop of Goa, Francis set sail from Goa. By the end of May they were at Malacca. Late in June, on a Chinese junk, they started on the nine weeks' journey which concluded on August 15th, the fifteenth anniversary of the vows at Montmartre, as Francis stepped ashore at Kagoshima, capital of

---

22 *EppMixt*, I, 225; Bangert, *To the Other Towns*, pp. 245-258.

Japan's most southern kingdom. Then began two and a half years of loving labor among the people he was to call "the delight of my heart."

The home of Paul of the Holy Faith in Kagoshima, soon filled with inquisitive visitors, was the first sounding board for the missionaries. As with Tamil on the Fishery Coast and Malayan at Malacca, in the Japanese language Francis met a wall that had to be breached before he could advance. Through several months, while studying with Torres and Fernández under Paul's guidance, he wrote into a notebook in the native tongue a lengthy exposition of the Catholic faith. This he read, both at Paul's house and from a temple terrace. Conversions were not many, perhaps about two hundred, but the shift was pronounced enough to arouse the anger of the Buddhist monks, who induced the daimyo to prohibit sternly further conversions.

This abrupt halt to his preaching at Kagoshima gave Francis the occasion to put into operation the core of his carefully developed plan for the conversion of the country. He determined to contact both the University of Hiei-zan and the emperor at Miyako, the present Kyoto, far to the north. From the emperor Francis hoped to obtain imperial permission to tell the Japanese people about Christ; at the university he ambitioned the creation of liaison with the great universities of Europe, especially his own Paris, which would then send a stream of Catholic scholars into Japan. Leaving Paul of the Holy Faith in charge of the converts at Kagoshima, he started on his journey with Torres and Fernández in September, 1550.

At the island of Hirado, a hundred and fifty miles northwest of Kagoshima, Francis left Torres, and with Fernández continued, as winter set in, for roughly another one hundred and fifty miles over wretched roads and on windswept ships to Yamaguchi, city of a powerful daimyo. There they read their exposition of the faith from their notebook, only to meet general scorn and contempt. For still another two hundred and fifty miles Francis, with feet uncovered, swollen and bleeding, trudged through snow, freezing streams, a source of wonder to the good Brother companion.

Miyako, the city of his high hopes, rewarded him for his suffering with rebuff. The university forbade strangers to enter its precincts. An audience with the emperor was out of the question without the presentation of gifts. Francis and Fernández stayed only eleven days in the royal city, but long enough to discern that the emperor was an impoverished and impotent ruler, a mere phantom of former splendor. Francis' grand design

34

was ill-advised, based on sadly erroneous information about the social and political structure of the country. With quick adaptation to the real condition of things, he formed a fresh plan: Since the daimyo of Yamaguchi was a prince of genuine power who would be impressed by only a display of grandeur, Francis decided to appear before him garbed in fine robes, carrying his artistically inscribed letter of credence (he had been constituted an ambassador of Portugal) and bearing an elaborate assortment of presents. Back to Hirado he and Fernández journeyed and then with Portuguese help equipped himself for the novel adventure.

Ouchi Yoshitaka of Yamaguchi, properly impressed, received Francis and Fernández most cordially. Enthralled by the clock, spectacles, music box, wine, and other presents brought by his visitors, he not only gave Francis permission to preach but also placed an unused Buddhist temple at his disposal for living quarters. Visitors stormed the residence to find out the doctrines of the strangers. In two months converts numbered five hundred. Xavier was delighted with them, so intelligent, so anxious to learn, so complete were they in their devotion to their new belief.

While Francis was teaching he was also learning. He found that in the estimation of the people of Japan the most eminently erudite men of the world were the Chinese, and that it was to the great empire across the sea they looked for their inspiration and guidance in art, philosophy, and religion. Knowledge of this cultural dependence intensified Xavier's earlier preoccupation with China and caused him to veer to the opinion that the conversion of China might be the most effective key to the conversion of Japan. An invitation by the daimyo of Bungo to visit his domain became the first in a series of incidents that led Francis to leave Japan and make the decision to attempt entry into China.

In the fall of 1551 Francis traveled to Bungo where he was delighted not only by the warm welcome from the ruler but also by meeting an old friend, Duarte da Gama, captain of a Portuguese ship in harbor. Da Gama delivered to Francis his first letters since his arrival in Japan. These gave him a mixture of good news and bad, opening up a panorama of an inspiring apostolate by his fellow Jesuits on the Fishery Coast, Malacca, Cochin, Ormuz, and at the same time disclosing the arrogant and autocratic conduct of the superior at Goa, Antonio Gómez. Xavier decided to return to India in order to reassess conditions there and procure help for Japan. Leaving Torres and Fernández in charge of the Catholics, he sailed from Bungo with Da Gama in mid-November, 1551.

Near the islands off Canton, Da Gama made contact with another Portuguese ship, captained by another friend of Francis, Diogo Pereira. Pereira had heard stories of the misery of Portuguese merchants who, caught as smugglers, were locked in the jails of Canton. From these prisoners with their pleas for help came the suggestion that Portugal send an embassy to Canton to establish peaceful relations between the two countries. Francis seized upon this idea. If he could persuade the viceroy at Goa to appoint Pereira as Portuguese ambassador to China, he could join the official party and so make a beachhead for the faith in the Celestial Empire. Pereira agreed. In mid-February, 1552, Francis was back at Goa.

His stay at the capital was but a short two months before he sailed on Easter Sunday, with the viceroy's approval of his plan, for the great Chinese venture. As at Miyako he saw the abrupt frustration of his great plan for the conversion of Japan, so too at Malacca he had to witness the rude shattering of his optimistic design for entry into China. Don Alvaro da Gama, son of the renowned explorer and captain of the Malaccan sea, bluntly refused, for reasons not clear, to allow Pereira to proceed as Portuguese ambassador. Standing amid the wreckage of his highest hopes, Francis, in his dream of opening vast empires to Christ, refused to be stopped. Stripped of the support of an official ambassador, he managed, by the end of August, 1552, to join the Portuguese merchants at San Chian (Changchuen), an island only two miles from the mountains of China and thirty miles from Canton.

Francis spoke with Chinese merchants in an effort to find one who would dare to transport him to Canton. The Portuguese pleaded that he not risk certain imprisonment. Francis' mind was clear: Far better to be taken captive for love of God than to be free and running away from the cross. He finally discovered a Chinese who, for three hundred and fifty-three cruzados worth of pepper, agreed to give him transport. The sailing date was set for November 19.

Francis eagerly waited for the ship that never came. Half starved, frozen by biting November winds, in a miserable little hut, he fell ill. A little after midnight, December 3, a faithful Chinese friend put a candle in the dying man's hand and watched as he breathed his last. For the Society of Jesus China became a mission of special predilection and the atelier of some of its most gifted sons, who have always found unfailing inspiration in the refined Basque gentleman who died desolate on dreary San Chian in the China Sea.

At his death Xavier left fellow Jesuits stationed, in a neatly organized pattern, along the great seaways of the Indies as well as in schools in the Portuguese colonies at Bassein, Ternate, Malacca, Cochin, Thana, and Quilon. To assist Torres and Fernández in Japan he had sent Baltasar Gago and two Brothers. Slowly the number of converts grew, including men of distinction, so that by 1554 there were about six hundred at Bungo, fifteen hundred at Yamaguchi, and two hundred at Hirado. Promise of further success came with the arrival of two dedicated men, Luís de Almeida, merchant and surgeon, who entered the Society in Japan, and Gaspar Vilela. But there was also promise of future distress, for the outbreak of a local conflict at Yamaguchi in 1554 forced many Catholics into exile and cut the Catholic population to three hundred. Brilliant light and somber shadows were ahead for the mission in Japan.

Like a great weight on one arm of a balance counterpoising a weight on the other arm, the vast Portuguese colony of Brazil in the West matched the wide area of the Indies in the East. The first Jesuits assigned to Brazil sailed into the broad and beautiful Bahía de todos os Santos on March 29, 1549, a party of six, unusually apt to grapple with the thorny problems indigenous to the colony. The superior was the thirty-two-year-old cultivated nobleman of broad vision and quick initiative, Manuel da Nóbrega. With him were Fathers Juan de Azpilcueta, a facile linguist, Leonardo Nunes, a dynamo of energy, Antonio Pires, an architect and jack-of-all-trades, Brothers Diogo Jácome, a carpenter, and Vicente Rodrigues, a schoolmaster.

Very soon the colony felt the impact of this concentrated variety of talent. Two weeks after their arrival, the Jesuits had organized children of the Portuguese colonists and nearby natives into classes of writing, singing, religious instruction. Within five months they baptized a hundred natives and were preparing five to six hundred catechumens. From their rude mud hut at São Salvador, later known as Bahía, grew the Collegio Maximo, the cradle of Brazilian culture. Between 1549 and 1553, while Francis Xavier was establishing the church in Japan and preparing to enter China, Nóbrega and Nunes edged their way along the coast north and south of Bahía, stopping at places like Pernambuco, Ilhéus, Pôrto Seguro, São Vicente, and assessing the apostolic possibilities. Nóbrega described his travels as running up and down the coast to feel the pulse of the land. And of the Basque, Juan de Azpilcueta, he wrote to friends in Europe,

"With such fervor does he run from place to place that he seems to set the mountains ablaze with the fire of his charity." [23]

Behind the long string of Portuguese settlements on the ocean loomed the deep and mysterious forests, peopled by the roaming, fickle tribes of Tupi Indians. The Jesuits recognized that it was part of their task to carve out of these primeval materials order and stability, which are the bases of civilization, if the faith was to enjoy any permanence. In 1553 Nóbrega made a bold decision. He climbed into the mountains behind São Vincente, to the vast and splendid plains with which he fell in love, and there marked a site, which with a school and seminary he envisaged as the nerve center for the apostolate of settling the natives in community. Such were the origins of São Paulo.[24]

In 1550 four more Jesuits arrived, followed three years later by the most illustrious of all who went to Brazil in that era, the nineteen-year-old sickly and badly crippled scholastic, José de Anchieta. Through forty-four years this native of Tenerife in the Canaries — he was called *O Canarino* because of his melodiously sweet voice — dedicated his high intelligence, prodigious memory, and intense industry to the Brazilian mission. Nóbrega and Anchieta met on December 24, 1553, at São Vicente, and in that meeting began one of the great fellowships in mission history. Within six months after his arrival Anchieta had composed a rough draft of his grammar of the Tupi-Guaraní language in which he transferred its softly spoken sounds into Latin characters. With his skill in rhyme and verse he wove Christian concepts into native songs, and soon the forests were ringing with the voices of native youngsters praising the Holy Trinity, Christ Our Lord, and his Blessed Mother. The same burning spirit, derived from the Spiritual Exercises, which radiated through the letters of Xavier from the East, inspired the reports of Anchieta from the West.

Fifteen hundred and fifty-four was a year of tragedy. Nunes, one of the pioneers known because of his rapid movement from place to place as "the flying Father," was lost at sea on his return to Europe to report on the mission. Two lay Brothers, Pero Correia and João de Sousa, sent by Nóbrega into the forests to try to make peace between two warring tribes, the Tupis and the Carijos, were killed by Carijos, the first of the Society to shed their blood in Brazil. With these losses and with men spread thin in modest schools at Ilhéus, Pôrto Seguro, Espírito Santo,

23 *MonBras*, I, 141.
24 Ibid., I, 36.

São Vicente and among the Indians, the pleas for help to the Jesuits in Europe became a chorus: "The natives are starving for spiritual food. Why do not the fathers and brothers come to allay this holy hunger?" "The heathens here await the outpouring of your blood as foundation stones for the new church. Come." "The harvest is immense. We need workers." But the plea, reaching beyond a call for other missionaries, was also for drums, flutes, fishhooks, tools. To achieve the transformation of the Brazilian forests the Jesuits welded into a close union the two powerful influences of religion and civilization.

In contrast to the rich promise of the missions in the Indies, Japan, and Brazil, the first Jesuit ventures into Africa, all sponsored by the Portuguese Province, either moved slowly or met with complete frustration. In 1548 two Jesuits entered Morocco, and two others the Congo. In 1555 those in the Congo were expelled because they split with the ruler, who initially was hospitable, on the question of polygamy. The same year two penetrated Ethiopia, possibly the most auspicious of all the African areas. Almost from the beginning, however, chicanery dogged the Jesuit efforts there. As the head of this country with its large population of Monophysite Christians ruled the wily Negus named Claudius. In the face of imminent subjection by Moslem invaders, Claudius promised Portugal, in a bid for assistance, that he would unite his people to the Roman Church. The Portuguese, in stirring campaigns, repelled the Moslems. Claudius' fair promises promptly evaporated. The Moslems once more took the offensive, and once more Claudius appealed for help, requesting of King John III, as a sign of his good will, a patriarch and a band of missionaries. King John chose Pierre Favre for the patriarch's office, but Pierre had died even before the monarch had dispatched his request to Ignatius. The man chosen in Pierre's place was one of Favre's own recruits for the Society, João Nunes Barreto. Although it was Ignatius' firm principle that members of the Society should reject all ecclesiastical honors, unless ordered to accept by the pope, he did not object in Barreto's case since the patriarchate of Ethiopia was actually a door that opened to extreme hardship and dire poverty rather than to glory and honor. As two coadjutor bishops Barreto received two other Jesuits, Andrés de Oviedo and Melchior Carneiro. Four months before Ignatius died, on March 30, 1556, the recently consecrated patriarch sailed from Lisbon for his rendezvous with frustration and thwarted hopes.

A year before Barreto left Europe the Jesuits at Goa had become involved in the Ethiopian mission. The viceroy, who desired to prepare the way for the patriarch, sent two Jesuits, Father Gonçalo Rodrigues and Brother Fulgencio Freire to the court of Claudius. They assessed the situation realistically. Not only did the Negus' interest in Rome merely rise and fall according to the proximity of Moslem marauders, but his vassals would hardly tolerate such a drastic change in the religious orientation of the country. It was a rueful Rodrigues who returned to Goa with the gloomiest of prospects for the patriarch.

Although this early experience in Ethiopia foreshadowed what would be in that distressful country, despite occasional shafts of light, a story darkened by the heaviest of clouds, it did not sound the characteristic note of the general Jesuit mission experience during Ignatius' last year. Nor should it distract from the vast significance of one of the great cultural developments of history to which Ignatius contributed. The first half of the sixteenth century was part of the stirring age of overseas discovery; it was also part of the brilliant era of humanism. The amalgamation of discovery and humanism Ignatius, by his two chief apostolates, the schools and the missions, helped to achieve. He sent his men across the Atlantic and to the Far East; there they started schools. The great European men of letters dreamed of reuniting Christendom on a basis of a common humanism. Ignatius went further. Looking overseas, in the Jesuit school on a far distant shore he saw a superb instrument to bring countless pagans into the Church. This important union of discovery and humanism he did not create, but he and his Society fostered it on an uncommon scale.[25]

Last Years of Ignatius

From 1540, the year Paul III confirmed the Society, until 1556, the year of his death — sixteen years in all — Ignatius left Rome on but a few occasions, to Montefiascone, Tivoli, and Alvito, either to conduct business or reconcile enemies. He hoped to open personally a mission in Africa and to make a pilgrimage to Loreto, but in each case circumstances made it impossible.[26] He remained at headquarters, guiding with a father's tender love and wide wisdom the work of his sons on four continents. Either personally or through his devoted secretary, Juan de Polanco, he sent them some six thousand letters. But the greatest legacy he

25 F. de Dainville, S.J., "S. Ignace et l'Humanisme," *Cahiers Universitaires Catholiques* (1956), 458-479.

26 P. de Leturia, S.J., "Conspectus Chronologicus Vitae Sancti Ignatii," *Estudios Ignacianos. Revisados por el P. Ignacio Iparraguirre, S.J.* (Rome 1957), I, 29, 33, 35, 40, 43, 47.

left for their instruction and inspiration, aside from the *Spiritual Exercises,* was the *Constitutions of the Society.*[27]

To build on the bull of approbation and the forty-nine points decided on in the spring of 1541 naturally fell to Ignatius. For six years, interrupted by business and spells of sickness, he made but slow progress. In 1547 he appointed as secretary Juan de Polanco. This competent and affable Spanish gentleman filled the part to perfection, relieved Ignatius of many of his burdens, and allowed him to concentrate on drawing up the *Constitutions.* At the beginning of this document Ignatius placed what he called the *General Examen,* a summary expression of the nature and scope of the Society of Jesus designed for the instruction of those who aspire to become Jesuits. Herein, he stressed a two-fold preoccupation of his: the need for high selectivity in the choice of aspirants to the Society, and the total abnegation of self-love which is required of the individual Jesuit. Emphasizing the apostolic character of his Company, he formally stated that its end is not only the salvation and perfection of the individual Jesuit but also the salvation and perfection of other men.

Ignatius divided the *Constitutions* into ten parts. In these he explained both the external structure and interior spirit of the Society. Authority and jurisdiction he placed primarily and fully in the general congregation, an assembly of delegates from the whole Society; and secondarily and by participation, in the various superiors. The general congregation, composed basically of the provincial and two professed fathers from each province, elects the general, who holds office for life. Departing from the traditional manner whereby provincial and local superiors were chosen in chapters of each province, Ignatius decided that the general should be invested with the power to appoint the other superiors. Into the structure of the Society he built several classes, or what are commonly called "grades." There are those who are priests or who are studying for the priesthood, and those who are not destined for holy orders. In the former category there are novice scholastics who, on the completion of the novitiate, pronounce the simple and perpetual vows of religion and become approved scholastics. After their intellectual training, ordination,

---

27 For English translations, see L. J. Puhl, S.J., *The Spiritual Exercises of St. Ignatius* (Chicago: Loyola University Press reprints, 1968), and St. Ignatius of Loyola, *The Constitutions of the Society of Jesus: Translated, with an Introduction and a Commentary,* by G. E. Ganss, S.J. (St. Louis: The Institute of Jesuit Sources, 1970), abbreviated in these notes as *ConsSJComm.*

and a concluding year of spiritual formation known as tertianship, they pronounce their final vows, either solemn or simple.
Those who are outstanding in virtue and learning pronounce
solemn vows, to which they add a fourth, to go anywhere in the
world the pope might assign them. These are known as the
professed. The others pronounce simple vows and are known as
spiritual coadjutors. Among those who are not destined for holy
orders and whose business it is to care for the temporal needs
of the Society in offices such as cook, mechanic, bookkeeper,
there are three grades: the novices, the approved coadjutors
who pronounce at the end of the novitiate simple vows, and the
formed temporal coadjutors who, after ten years, pronounce
simple final vows.[28] Other details, usual in any religious order,
about such matters as the admission of candidates and the dismissal of subjects, Ignatius treated with impersonal canonical
language.

But the *Constitutions* are at once impersonal and full of character. Through them throbs the same living spirit which Ignatius
had projected into the Spiritual Exercises. The individual Jesuit,
as envisaged by Ignatius, abhors utterly the predilections of the
world, and desires with all his strength what Christ loved and
embraced; ambitions to imitate and resemble Christ even if this
should entail suffering repudiation by others; esteems the pursuit of holiness of far greater moment than learning or other
human gifts; seeks God in all things. In the sixth part, where
he treated the vows of religion, Ignatius manifests the same
sensitivity to the primacy of the spiritual. In expressive language he called on each Jesuit to love poverty as a mother in his
surrender of his possessions and in his declination of recompense
for his services. This gratuitousness of service had a significance
far beyond the holiness of the individual Jesuit because it meant
that in the vast network of the Society's schools, save in the last
two centuries when social conditions dictated a change, education was given without return. St. Ignatius further called on
the Jesuit to resemble in his chastity the purity of the angels.
But nowhere more than in obedience did he urge his sons to the
complete surrender of self-love. He exhorted them, in their selfless desire to find God's will and imitate Christ, who because
of love for his Father was obedient unto death, that they "be
ready to receive the superior's command just as if it were coming from Christ our Savior." Ignatius, convinced that the union
of wills among Jesuits was their chief means to serve God, re-

28 On these grades, see *ConsSJComm*, pp. 65, 71, 81, 232, 349–356.

garded obedience in the spirit of Christian faith and love as the hallmark of the members of the Society of Jesus. He crowned the *Constitutions* by a succinct restatement, given in the tenth and last part, of the essential place of the spiritual in the life of the Jesuit, calling on him to endeavor to make himself "an instrument in the hands of God."

With all the preoccupation of this kind Ignatius nevertheless never slurred over in a careless way his choice of human means in the apostolate. For two problems, among others, he showed wide concern: the training of the scholastics and the education of secular students in the Society's schools. To these he devoted the fourth part of the *Constitutions*. The educational goal he envisioned was the formation of the cultured man, Catholic in outlook, and capable of participating intelligently and zealously in contemporary civil, cultural, and religious life. Always conscious of choosing the apt means, he traced for the Jesuit scholastic an educational path that took him through the humanities, philosophy, Scripture, positive and scholastic theology, and terminated in the cultivated, articulate, and clear-thinking master of the Church's doctrine. Ignatius' concepts showed comprehensiveness in their embrace of the humanities, philosophy, and theology; flexibility in their adaptation to the needs of time and place; practicality in their concern for the abilities of the students; completeness in their attention not only to the mental but also the moral faculties of the person; contemporaneousness in their susceptibility to the best in the current world.[29]

In this wide concern for education Ignatius drew upon an idea which resounds with frequency through the *Constitutions* — 130 times according to Joseph de Guibert — and stamps the Jesuit's purpose both in his personal holiness and the sanctification of his fellow men: the glory of God, and especially the greater glory of God, as the basis of decisions. The Society is preoccupied with "the more," what is *more* to God's honor and glory.

By November, 1551, Ignatius had finished the great task. He sought the impressions of several of the professed fathers. Save for a few suggestions of change in details they gave their approval. Ignatius then sent Nadal on the important mission of explaining the body of legislation to the Jesuit communities in Italy, Spain, Portugal, Germany, and Austria.

The *Constitutions*, immensely influential on newer religious congregations, especially of women, is one of the basic docu-

29 F. Rodrigues, S.J., *A Formação intellectual do Jesuita* (Porto, 1917), pp. 7-37.

ments in the history of religious life in the modern era. With their apostolic bent, their departure from monastic form, their engagement with the world, their alertness to current needs of the Church, their harmonization of intense activity and habitual prayerfulness, they have given vision to many holy souls inspired to raise up other religious families.

Viewed as part of the long tradition of religious life in the Church, the *Constitutions* hold a unique place. At least two reasons make this so. First, the *Constitutions* and the body of men who embraced them saved the religious order as an institution for the Church militant. In the sixteenth century, with the hammering of the humanists, the growth of associations of priests and collegiate establishments, and the policy of pruning advocated by some Roman officials, the religious order had, in the opinion of some, reached its sunset in the Church. This Ignatius by his creativity forestalled. He set aside four ancient and key forms of the monastic structure: lifelong residence in one community; decision-making on major issues by individual communities in chapter assembled; the choosing of its superior by each individual community; the chanting of the divine office in Choir. Ignatius with his freshness elected that detachment, mobility, disposability be the Jesuit marks. And second, the *Constitutions* despite their evident modernity, reached into the earliest centuries of the Church and rescued from dissolution one of the key concepts of the religious life, that of the superior being in every way the spiritual father of the individual subject. Through the centuries after Pachomius, in the development of feudal government, the practice of *in commendam* whereby, for financial or other reasons, the office of abbot was "commended" to one who was not a member of the community (in post-Reformation France Protestants occasionally held this position) had disastrous results. By removing from the community the one person on whom devolved by rule the responsibility of teacher and guide in things spiritual and temporal, it corroded an essential hinge on which hung the vitality of religious life. Ignatius, cutting through the layers of ruin accumulated through the centuries, unearthed the precious pearl at the heart of the intimate, Christlike relationship between superior and individual religious.[30] In this respect Pachomius' Egyptian desert came to life again in Renaissance Rome.

30 D. Knowles, *From Pachomius to Ignatius* (Oxford, 1966), pp. 59-62, 94.

Serious sickness had frequently delayed Ignatius during this enormous undertaking. But in bringing it to completion he had created a precious heritage for his sons. The one thousand or so Jesuits who immediately survived him, as well as those of subsequent centuries, could turn to the *Constitutions* and discern in them, clearly and beautifully delineated, the heart of Ignatius and the directions by which they could make their hearts like to his. The final prostrating sickness came in the summer of 1556. On July 31, Ignatius breathed his last.

In the sixty-five years between the birth of St. Ignatius and his death great changes in his personal life occurred. They have had a momentous impact on the history of the Church and the world. The courtier and soldier became the pilgrim and student; the pilgrim and student became the priest and apostle; the priest and apostle became the creator of a renowned religious family.

Conclusion

The spirit that sprang from the fountains of Loyola and Manresa flowed through the channels of the *Spiritual Exercises* and the *Constitutions* of the Society of Jesus into the hearts of thousands and became incarnate in the lives of the Jesuits who at Ignatius' death labored not only in Europe but also in India, Japan, Africa, and Brazil. It was a spirit of companionship with Christ in the service of the Divine Majesty.

Within the sixteen years from the papal approval of the Society to the death of Ignatius, Jesuits became engaged in numerous facets of the Church's life: education, foreign missions, retreats, diplomatic missions, the reform of religious communities. Ancient cities of Europe and newly discovered lands overseas received the stamp of Manresa. The flow of extraordinary graces which Ignatius personally received from God has been called *une invasion mystique*.[31] From him, at his headquarters in Rome, to the four corners of the world flowed another wave, which might be styled *une invasion apostolique*.

The Society's *invasion apostolique* was not an isolated incident in the life of the Church. As part of the sixteenth century, it has a wider and deeper significance in its relation to the other many and varied fonts of holiness of that era, St. Philip Neri, St. Cajetan, St. Thomas of Villanova, St. Theresa, St. John of the Cross, all of whom gave force and freshness — apart from the challenge of the Protestants — to the massive wave of the Catholic reform.

31 *DeGuiJes*, p. 72.

Chapter 2

EVER WIDENING HORIZONS
1556–1580

The Generals DURING THE TWENTY-FIVE YEARS after the death of Ignatius three generals ruled the Society, Diego Laynez (1558-1565), Francis Borgia (1565-1572), and Everard Mercurian (1573-1580). It was a period of extraordinary growth, both in manpower and the expansion of activities. By the end of Mercurian's life five thousand Jesuits — five times the number under Ignatius — were operating one hundred and forty-four colleges — one hundred and thirteen more than under Ignatius — besides residences, professed houses, and novitiates, and they had widened their missions overseas to include Florida, Mexico, and Peru.

Laynez, Two years passed after Ignatius died before Diego Laynez
1556–1565 was elected general on July 2, 1558, the long delay being due in large measure to the impossibility of assembling a congregation because of the strained relations, even to the point of war, between Pope Paul IV and King Philip II of Spain. The uncertainty of these years was aggravated by two complex and embarrassing difficulties, both relative to the interregnum government of the Society. The first concerned the identity of the vicar-general. Two years before his death, during a period of sickness, Ignatius named Jerónimo Nadal as vicar, but with the return of his strength he again took the Society's business into his own hands. Then, shortly before he died, he turned over the administration of the order to Juan de Polanco and Cristóbal de Madrid. When the end came, with Nadal a thousand miles away in Spain, Polanco summoned the few professed fathers who were about Rome to choose the vicar-general. They unanimously elected Diego Laynez. Laynez had some misgivings about the legality of his position, since some Jesuits felt that Nadal had been deprived of authority justly his by reason of Ignatius' ear-

46

lier appointment. But Nadal settled this problem by his support of the choice of Laynez.[1]

The second difficulty was the creation of the fractious and mercurial Nicolás Bobadilla. This unpredictable man came forward with the principle that, since the Constitutions had not yet been ratified by the Society, the government of the Society should devolve upon Ignatius' earliest companions, those he referred to as the "founding fathers," as a sort of cabinet of equals. To the dismay of his fellow Jesuits he sent to Pope Paul IV, a pontiff with many reservations about the Society, a memorial in which he criticized Ignatius as an autocrat and the Constitutions as a maze of confusing and unintelligible directions. Nadal spoke up with vigor and scathingly devastated Bobadilla's pretensions. The highminded Dominican Cardinal, Michele Ghislieri, appointed by the pope to adjudicate the case, persuaded Bobadilla to drop his irresponsible plan. With the return of internal peace and the assembly of twenty professed fathers in Rome in June, 1558, the Congregation was able to convene, and Diego Laynez was elected general with thirteen of twenty votes.

Among the important pieces of business in the Congregation was the consideration of the Constitutions of the Society. With the exception of a few minor changes, the fathers ratified the document as it had come from the pen of Ignatius. Before they had disbanded, however, two basic points in the Society's organization, the life-term of the general and the omission of choir, were strongly challenged by Pope Paul IV. In a stormy audience which the vehement pontiff gave Laynez, he told the general that the Jesuits must chant the Divine Office in common and that the general's term should be for but three years. Dutifully the communities of the Society took up the practice of choir and continued for a year until Paul died in August, 1559. After the pontiff's death, Laynez heard the universal agreement of five distinguished canon lawyers that Paul's orders, verbally given, yielded at his death to the legally promulgated bulls of earlier popes and ceased to carry any further obligation. Hence the general instructed his subjects to discontinue the chant of the Divine Office in choir.[2]

Toward the end of his seven years as general, Laynez was able to give but limited time to his great responsibility, since for

1 M. Scaduto, S.J., *Storia della Compagnia di Gesù in Italia,* vol. III, *L'epoca di Giacomo Laínez. Il governo* (1556-1565) (Rome, 1964), pp. 15-18.
2 Ibid., 116-120.

two and a half years, from July, 1561, until January, 1564, he was absent from Rome on missions for the new pontiff, Pius IV, first at the Colloquy of Poissy in France, and then at the closing sessions of the Council of Trent. He had a most dependable aid in that indefatigable traveler, Jerónimo Nadal, who continued the essential work, initially committed to him by Ignatius, of visiting Jesuit community after community and explaining with his alert intelligence and wisdom to men of diverse nationalities the purpose, structure, and internal spirit of the *Constitutions*. No one in those early days did more to create a unity of mind and heart among the Jesuits than this man with the ability to make the printed pages of the *Constitutions* vibrant with the life of Ignatius himself.

Saint   On January 19, 1565, Laynez died. On July 2 of the same year,
Francis Borgia, by twenty-three votes of thirty-one in the Second General Con-
1565–1572 gregation, Francis Borgia became general. By a series of far-
reaching decrees this congregation showed that it was alert to a number of problems created by the rapid expansion of the Society. Growth, gratifying as it was, carried with it the danger of weakening the appreciation for the interior life of prayer and of impairing by sheer numbers the sense of unity among the Society's members. Judging that the Society had taken on works beyond its resources, the congregation warned against the indiscriminate acceptance of schools. Borgia then set out to close some of those already started. In its concern for the formation of the scholastics and orderly administration, the congregation called for the establishment of a novitiate and a house of studies in each province. To safeguard the close unity which Ignatius had stressed, it decided, in what has proved to be a step of immense wisdom, that every three years delegates, one from each province, should meet at Rome to determine whether there be cogent reasons for summoning a general congregation. This body is known as the congregation of procurators. (The Thirty-first General Congregation of 1965-1966, while maintaining the substance of this valuable institution, modified its composition. In the future, every other congregation of procurators is to be composed of the provincials rather than elected delegates.) Feeling that, for the preservation of Ignatius' legacy of deep esteem for a life of union with God, it might be wise to lengthen the time of prescribed prayer, the congregation of 1565 gave the general power to decide according to what he judged best. Borgia then directed that, besides the two quarter-hour examinations of conscience, one at noon and one at night, an hour

should be devoted daily to prayer. This gradually developed into what became known as the "morning meditation." In 1581 the Fourth General Congregation decreed that "the pious and salutary custom, as it was introduced by Reverend Father Borgia, should be retained."

This legislation, hardly noted, if at all, by historians concerned more with the external experience of the Jesuits, was of great importance, for it marked a pull, justified in the eyes of many dedicated Jesuits because of the inroads of tepidity, away from the mind of St. Ignatius on the basic issue of prayer in the Society. This it did in two ways: first, by its nature it could tend to obscure what should be cut into each Jesuit's soul with diamond sharpness, Ignatius' insight that the Jesuit, professedly dedicated to laborious apostolic toil, should, by "seeking God in all things," find in his work undertaken in a spirit of charity and obedience no less a strong link of union with God than in formal prayer; and second, it could lead to a practical departure from Ignatius' profound respect for individual souls with their wide differences of needs in mind, heart, and body, and in the gifts they receive from the Holy Spirit.[3]

St. Ignatius expressed one of the basic intuitions of his brilliant creative spirit in his desire that the Jesuit "seek God in all things." Modern scholarship has uncovered a multitude of texts which bear the same message as the letter which Ignatius sent to one of the most indefatigable Jesuit pioneers in the Far East, Gaspar Berze. To Berze he wrote: "If the country where you are proves to be less conducive to meditation than this part of the world, so much the less is there reason for extending meditation there. . . . Where there is a complete ordering of all to the divine service, everything is prayer. This idea must penetrate every member of the Society, for whom exercises of charity take a very considerable amount of time from prayer. Still more, it must not be thought that in these works of charity less pleasure is given God than in prayer."[4] For Ignatius, work undertaken in obedience and in the service of the Lord had a sacramental character in which his sons were to find God as readily as in formal prayer. From this position he refused to be budged by requests from some Spaniards for an hour and a half of pre-

---

3 R. E. McNally, S.J., "St. Ignatius, Prayer, and the Early Society," *WL*, XCIV (1965), 113-115; 118-120; see also *DeGuiJes*, pp. 86-90, 169, 192-196, 205, 222, 227-229, 237, 552-554, and M. A. Fiorito, S.J., "Ignatius' Own Legislation on Prayer," *WL*, XCVII (1968), 149-224.
4 *EppIgn*, VI, 91.

scribed prayer. Nadal he reprimanded for his sympathy with this petition from Spain. To Francis Borgia, strongly inclined toward long periods of prayer, he wrote in 1549: "It is worth realizing that man gives service to God not only when he prays. . . . In fact, there are times when more service is given to God in ways other than prayer." [5]

St. Ignatius also had deep respect for the workings of the Holy Spirit in individual souls. He stood against the creation of a universal norm applicable to a large group of men with widely different gifts, natural and supernatural. Each Jesuit's prayer was unique and personal, corresponding to "the degree of grace imparted to him by God." In the *Constitutions,* [342, 582], he made a distinction between the Jesuit in training and the Jesuit completely formed. For those in training and growing in the spiritual life he traced out a daily program of great simplicity: besides Mass, each was to make two examinations of conscience, recite the Office of the Blessed Virgin Mary (or other prayers) until an hour had been spent in prayer throughout the day; and they were to get personalized direction from their superior or spiritual director. He was most concerned that they grow in the mastery of "finding God in all things." For those whose training was finished Ignatius insisted that, beyond the examinations of conscience, "it does not seem wise in those things pertaining to prayer, meditation, and study, nor in the bodily exercise of fasting, vigils, and other practices, which concern the austere chastisement of the body, that any rule be set down save that which discreet charity will compose for each, provided that the confessor shall be consulted and, where there is doubt as to what is best, the matter be referred to the Superior." [6] It was for the formed Jesuit, intent on a life of union with God, to work out with his superior or confessor a program of prayer and penance consonant with his personal needs and the demands of his apostolic work. The norm of "discreet charity" allowed for flexibility under the workings of the Holy Spirit.

At the base of this kind of prayer St. Ignatius presupposed in the individual Jesuit a deep and pervasive spirit of self-denial. His teaching rings clearly in these words from the *Spiritual Exercises,* [189] "For everyone must keep in mind that in all that concerns the spiritual life his progress will be in proportion to his surrender of self-love and of his own will and interests." This conviction, brought to an apostolic task assigned by obedience

5 Ibid., XII, 652.
6 *ConsSJComm,* [582] on pp. 259-260.

and undertaken in faith and charity, gives the Jesuit the capacity to pray as Ignatius taught. Only the mortified man can enter fully into Ignatian prayer. But by the time of Borgia, in the judgment of some historians which others however reject, the intensity of this conviction began to lessen. The members of the congregation, unanimous in their desire to insure the preservation of a prayerful spirit within the Society, split on the way to achieve this. In the debates the French and the Germans advocated adherence to Ignatius' teaching. The more numerous Spaniards, Portuguese, and Italians supported the new approach. The latter prevailed and the congregation passed its important legislation on prayer. This the Fourth General Congregation confirmed in 1581. After that the hour's meditation was a major feature in the making of the spiritual cachet of a Jesuit's life.

In 1966, however, the Thirty-first General Congregation made a momentous change. Inspired by the desire of the Second Vatican Council that religious communities find spiritual renewal in fidelity to the inspiration of their founders, the congregation confirmed St. Ignatius' teaching on prayer in the Society. It decreed that formed members, guided by "discreet charity" and their superiors, may develop a plan of prayer most suited for their particular needs. This return *ad fontes ignatianas* brings to the modern Society a deepened awareness of what its founder envisaged and hoped for.

With Borgia's failure to insist on fidelity to Ignatius' basic intuition in regard to prayer went an ingrained predilection for some older practices of religious life.[7] He preferred a monastic garb, in contrast to Ignatius' rejection of distinctive dress, and wore his rosary, as indeed did other Jesuits, on his cincture, even on journeys. Once, shortly before his death, Catherine de Médicis asked him for his rosary as a relic. In 1566, when the advance of the Turks became ominous, he introduced the recitation of litanies by the Jesuit communities. But when the Moslem menace faded, he ordered that the litanies be retained, a kind of custom specifically rejected by Ignatius.

Francis however was not alone in altering the course originally mapped out for the Society. Three years after Borgia was elected general, Pope Pius V, a Dominican, questioned the private

---

7 O. Karrer, S.J., "Borgia's Influence on the Development of Prayer-Life in the Society of Jesus," *WL*, XCVI (1967), 349-357. This is a section, translated by G. W. Traub, S.J. and W. J. Bado, S.J., from Karrer's *Der Heilige Franz von Borja, General der Gesellschaft Jesu, 1510-1572* (Freiburg-im-Breisgau, 1921).

recitation of the Divine Office in the Society. Fearful, as he said, that the Jesuits, so much in contact with the world, would by their failure to chant the Divine Office become "black as chimney-sweeps," he ordered them to take up this ancient and venerable practice, at least in modified form. He also ordered that all Jesuit scholastics pronounce solemn vows before ordination, thus removing the distinction between the grade of the solemnly professed and that of the spiritual coadjutors in the Society's structure. These papal changes, however, were in force only five years when Gregory XIII, within a year of his election, abrogated them.

One of Borgia's main preoccupations was the foreign mission field. The dispatches which he sent to the Jesuits overseas, embodying most sensible norms of action on such matters as the more careful instruction of converts and the danger of dissipating one's energies, testify to the breadth of his apostolic vision. It was he who suggested to Pius V that the missions of the Church be placed under a central commission of cardinals, an idea which in 1622 blossomed into the important Congregation for the Propagation of the Faith.

Mercurian,   Francis Borgia died on October 1, 1572. The Third General
1573–1580   Congregation opened on April 12, 1573, under a dark cloud caused by two separate and discordant factors: first, a regional feeling of resentment against the Spaniards then current among some Jesuits; and second, an antipathy, forcefully expressed by the Portuguese monarchy, toward the New Christians, those converts, real or pretending, from the Jewish faith who resided in the Iberian peninsula.

In some areas Jesuits resented Spanish prominence in the Society. The first three generals had been Spaniards; so also were several other higher officials. Spanish superiors in Italy, ignorant of Italian ways, governed in a style which Pedro Ribadeneyra called *a la española*. In some Roman circles, therefore, there was the desire that the next general be from another nation. Pope Gregory XIII shared this view. Through Cardinal Alessandro Farnese he informed Polanco of his feeling. Polanco sensed that the anti-Spanish sentiment was directed largely against his own person since he, so well versed in the Society's government as secretary under Ignatius, Laynez, and Borgia, was a likely choice as general. He therefore, with his accustomed magnanimity, asked the pope that his own name be suppressed but not that an entire nation be excluded in the election.

Three days after the opening of the congregation, with Salmerón and a few others, he went to Gregory to ask his blessing. Gregory inquired about the nationality of previous generals. He remarked that he would like to see a non-Spaniard elected. Polanco respectfully protested, pointing out that each delegate was obliged to vote for the man he thought most qualified, and that the debarring of an entire nation might make the fulfillment of that obligation an impossibility. Gregory insisted that his preference was for a non-Spaniard, and mentioned Everard Mercurian, a Belgian, as a possibility. Again Polanco protested. Gregory stopped him, gave his blessing, and dismissed his visitors with the words: "Go in peace and run a good election." [8]

The second discordant factor that affected the congregation was the antipathy of the Portuguese monarchy to the New Christians. This came to the fore with the arrival of the Portuguese delegates headed by Leão Henriques. Henriques acted as the intermediary through whom King Sebastian and Cardinal Henry most insistently asked the pope that he not permit the election of a New Christian as general of the Society. At the same time a story was abroad in Rome that Polanco was either a Jew or looked with sympathy toward the New Christians. April 22 was the date set for the election. A few days before, Henriques received another letter from King Sebastian to be delivered to the pope. On the 21st he rode to Frascati where Gregory was then staying. Sebastian's missive, another regal intervention to forestall a man with Jewish blood becoming the Jesuit general, merged with Gregory's personal desire that a Spaniard not be elected. Since Spain was the principal country with a New Christian population, an efficacious way to satisfy the Portuguese monarch, and at the same time achieve his own desire, was to give a clear-cut order that a non-Spaniard be elected general. Gregory's personal preference hardened into a command. [9]

On the 22nd Tolomeo Gallio, the Cardinal of Como, entered the aula of the congregation and announced that the pope clearly forbade the election of a Spaniard. Distress swept through the assembly at the removal of their freedom of choice. All eyes turned on the Portuguese as the villians of the piece. Henriques, appalled at the extreme results to which his action had led, with genuine sorrow, expressed his regret and offered to speak to the pope. With four other delegates he went to Frascati and earnestly

8 A. Astráin, S.J., *Historia de la Compañía de Jesús en la Asistencia de España* (Madrid, 1902-1925), III, 9-10.
9 F. Rodrigues, S.J., *História da Companhia de Jesus na Assistência de Portugal* (Porto, 1931-1950), II, i, 345-349.

asked Gregory to restore to the congregation its complete liberty. Reluctantly Gregory withdrew his command, but insisted that his personal preference for a non-Spaniard remained. The next day, on the first ballot, the congregation chose Everard Mercurian.

This fifty-nine-year-old native of Marcour in Belgian Luxembourg, known for his prudence and sense of proportion, brought to his new task a wealth of administrative experience gained as provincial, assistant, and visitor in Germany and France. In two ways especially, during his seven years in office, he employed his great executive gifts: first, in the composition of rules, which he issued in 1577, for a number of important positions in the Society where uniform norms of action were essential, such as provincial, rector, minister, treasurer, master of novices; and second, in the sifting, evaluating, and synthesizing of the growing amount of directives and suggestions for the schools. The Third General Congregation, reflecting the need felt by Jesuits, both in administration and in the classroom, of a clearly defined code on education, commissioned Mercurian to examine and estimate the mass of material already at hand. Building on the experimentation of Nadal, the man who had contributed most to the evolution of a plan of studies was Diego Ledesma, who had been associated with the Roman College most of his Jesuit life. Gifted with a happy combination of wide breadth of view and diligent concern for minute details, he devoted much time between 1562 and 1575, the year of his death, to the organization of the studies at the Roman College. Among the papers he left at his death were seven preliminary drafts of a *Plan of Studies,* an incomplete work called *The Plan and Order of Studies at the Roman College,* (*De ratione et ordine studiorum Collegii Romani*), and many jottings. In his manuscripts Ledesma achieved a neat balance between his clear general statement of educational goals and his precise disposition of classes, time-order, exercises, and methods. Other professors also contributed suggestions about curricula and procedure. A great mass of material had gathered, and it was to the study and evaluation of this as a step toward a comprehensive code on studies that Mercurian had directed his energies when death took him on August 1, 1580.

Grown to a little over five thousand men in twenty-one provinces, one hundred and forty-four colleges, ten professed houses, twelve novitiates, and thirty-three residences, the Society had need for coordination of procedures and methods among its widely spread members. Mercurian, by promulgating rules for various positions and by the impetus he gave to the systemization of the schools, answered that need. Consolidation was the mark of his term.

The Jesuits stood before the Italian people primarily as teach-
ers. The expansion of schools was phenomenal, a one hundred per cent increase over the twenty established in the Italian peninsula at the time of Ignatius' death. Town after town clamored for a Jesuit school, but in the very flush of the exhilaration of growth such embarrassing factors as inadequate foundations and shortage of manpower caused superiors to brake their enthusiasm and to proceed with caution. Salmerón, as provincial of Naples, knew what it meant to be torn between the exigency of the admiring Italian people and his inability to give them what they wanted. Around 1565 he had to turn down requests for schools from Atri, Benevento, Salerno, Capua, Pozzuoli, and Cosenza. Juan de Polanco had to remind him, as he begged for more men, that Naples was not the only province of the Society clamoring for reserves.[10] In the north of Italy several schools, in close proximity to each other and accepted under the urging of St. Charles Borromeo, had to be closed eventually.

In this busy hive of schools the Roman College reigned as the glorious queen. To its classrooms the generals summoned from other countries some of the Society's most gifted professors. Germany was present in Christoph Klau (Clavius) whose mathematical genius found unique expression in the Gregorian Calendar; Spain contributed the two penetrating speculative theologians, Francisco de Toledo, and Francisco Suárez; Portugal, the Scripture scholar, Manuel de Sá; France, the distinguished humanist, Pierre Perpinien. Most eminent of all was the native of Montepulciano whom Gregory XIII assigned in 1576 to the recently created chair of Controversial Theology, Robert Bellarmine. For twelve years this superior scholar, with a wide experience gained as preacher and teacher in Florence, Padua, and Louvain, delivered his lively, penetrating lectures on Catholic theology and its relevance to the current problems raised by the Protestants. These lectures, printed in three volumes (1586, 1588, 1593), were the substance of his *Inquiries into Controverted Points of the Christian Faith,* a masterpiece of intellectual integrity in its single-minded search for truth and a model of charitable argumentation in its freedom from rancor and vituperative expression so prevalent in that age. Doctor Matthew Sutcliffe, chaplain of Queen Elizabeth, spoke for many of Bellar-

10 *MonSalm,* I, 367.

mine's opponents when he called the *Inquiries* new "stables of Augaeus containing an infinite heap of dung," and Bellarmine himself "a braggart dunghill of a soldier."

Despite the fulminations of Sutcliffe, the *Inquiries* reached a high peak in the long mountain range of theology. Their appearance had a threefold historical significance: first, they portrayed the Church as it was generally conceived by Catholics in the sixteenth century after its long medieval development and Renaissance experience with the strong stress on its juridical and hierarchical structure, although Bellarmine, as well as others, also wrote of it as the mystical body of Christ; second, they placed in clear relief the positions of the Protestants as seen by the Catholics of the sixteenth century, crystallizing the encounters on such central issues as the primacy of the papacy and the visible character of the Church; and third, they did much to set the tone for Catholic thinking on the Church for the next three centuries. In the late eighteenth century, Johann Adam Möhler unearthed once more the rich patristic ideas about the Church as the mystical body and started a new current of thought. But even as that current deepened through the nineteenth century, Bellarmine's influence remained strong and helped mold the powerful ultramontane sentiments which culminated in the definition of papal infallibility by Vatican Council I. The *Inquiries* were therefore contemporary and of long range authority, epitomizing the Catholic ecclesial ideas of the cardinal's day, and at the same time being a wellspring of theological thought for the three centuries that followed.

Staffed by scholars of such competence and of diverse provenance, such as Bellarmine, Suárez, Clavius, and Sá, the Roman College kept lively contact with the intellectual movements of the day and understandably became what Montaigne called it, "a nursery of great men." Through the initiative of Pope Gregory XIII the radius of the Society's influence in the training of priests at Rome was lengthened. In addition to his generous support of the Roman College and the German College, Gregory entrusted the Hungarian College, the Greek College, and the English College to the Jesuits.

After their schools, the Jesuits had probably no more effective medium for direct contact with large groups of people than through confraternities and associations formed for the cultivation of a deeper spiritual life among the laity.[11] From the earliest

---

11 E. Villaret, S.J., "Les premières origines des Congrégations Mariales dans la Compagnie de Jésus," *AHSJ*, VI (1937), 25-57.

days of the Society these organizations sprang up in town after town. It was not long before Trapani, Padua, and Messina each had its confraternity set up by Jerónimo Nadal. Faenza and Brescia could point to like achievements by Claude Jay. And there were many more. A striking characteristic of these congregations was the emphasis on a deeply interior and intense Christian life. Vary though they did in details, the rules stressed frequent Holy Communion, meditation, and examination of conscience. In 1540 Pierre Favre capped his instructions to his many friends in Parma with the exhortation: "Even aim at not missing confession and Holy Communion at least once a week." A second trait was the strong apostolic orientation pointing to works of charity among the poor, the sick, the uneducated, the social castaways. A third mark was the broad spectrum of people these congregations embraced: lawyers, artisans, youth, aristocrats, magistrates, and other specialized groups. But of that great number, one especially had a magnetic appeal for the youth in Jesuit schools, the Sodality of the Blessed Virgin Mary. At the Roman College in 1563 was a young Belgian Jesuit, Jean Leunis. Having first gathered with regularity some of his students in a classroom for a brief period of prayer and spiritual reading, Leunis then organized an association in which the young men, under the protection of the Blessed Mother, promised to follow a program of prayer, sacramental life, and practical charity. The idealism of Leunis' enterprise was contagious, and thirteen years later, throughout the Jesuit schools, there were thirty thousand youths dedicated to a life of more than ordinary holiness in the Sodality of the Blessed Virgin Mary.

It is not often that a novitiate is blessed by the presence of a saint among its first novices. In 1567, on the Quirinal, Borgia opened the Roman Novitiate of Sant' Andrea, and on August 15, one year later, an eighteen-year-old novice died. He was the manly and delightful Stanislaus Kostka. Son of a Polish nobleman and student at the Jesuit College in Vienna, he gave the measure of his determination to respond to God's call to the Society, against the set opposition of his angered father and brutal brother, by the fatiguing journeys he made on foot from Vienna to Augsburg, and then to Rome where Borgia received him into the novitiate. Of singular innocence and devotedness to Our Lady joined to undeviating singleness of purpose, he was carried off by a fever, leaving to recently opened Sant' Andrea the happy memories of a joyous son who had been among the first to enter its walls.

The cardinal event of the Catholic Reform continued to be the

Council of Trent. Protracted as no previous general council had been, it survived ominous threats of disaster and gave the Church a deeply needed corpus of doctrinal and pastoral teaching. In the exacting task of formulating with clarity and precision the conciliar decrees, the Jesuits played an important part. Peter Canisius, Claude Jay, and especially Diego Laynez and Alonso Salmerón, were absorbed at long intervals in the exhausting round of research, reports, conferences, general assemblies, and by their competence brought new courage to hearts grown faint about the efficacy of the Council. During the second period (1551-1552), for example, Laynez and Salmerón arrived at Trent on July 27, 1551, only to find the Council almost completely bogged down and few delegates in attendance. Their advent raised the spirits of the leaders who exclaimed in relief: "Now we believe that there will really be a council." During the third and final period (1562-1563), Peter Canisius wrote from Trent to Francis Borgia on June 18, 1562: "It is the general opinion here that Father Alonso [Salmerón] is the Number One man among the theologians of the Council. He has brought great honor to the Society." [12] Peter added that he was sure that Laynez, expected soon, would enhance even more the spirit of good will toward the Society. On the involved question of episcopal jurisdiction which almost wrecked the Council, Laynez spoke with such brilliance and erudition in defense of papal prerogatives that even the sour and biased Paolo Sarpi called the speech a masterpiece. With the same solid learning he and Salmerón discoursed on the sacrifice of the Mass and the sacraments. It was only fitting that these two Spaniards, dear friends from their youth, should be present at the moving session when Cardinal Giovanni Morone on December 4, 1563, closed the work of eighteen painful years and one of the most fruitful episodes in the Church's history. In plotting the course through very troubled waters they had been close to the men at the helm.

Having become through its spiritual purpose, so vividly made manifest at the Council, a formative part of the Catholic Reform, and through its commitment to humanistic studies a dynamic influence in the Renaissance, the Society quite naturally made wide use of that relatively new instrument, so effective in the hands of theologians and humanists, the printing press. The pattern of the characteristically catholic interests of the Jesuits as writers was discernible in their early publications in Italy: the sixteen volumes, solid and erudite, of Salmerón's commentaries

12 *B. Petri Canisii epistulae et acta*, ed. O. Braunsberger, S.J., III, 461-462.

on Holy Scripture; the edition by André des Freux and Émond Auger of *The Epigrams* of Martial; the short treatises on frequent Holy Communion and meditation on the life and death of Christ by Fulvio Androzzi; and the several spiritual tracts, particularly the *Practice of the Christian Life* (*Essercitio della vita cristiana*), by the fluent Gaspar Loarte. Sacred Scripture, theology, asceticism, history, the classics, all claimed a share in the earliest Jesuit essay in publishing and gave evidence of the fresh headwaters from which would flow fecund streams into the cultural fields of Europe.

More spectacular perhaps than their entry into various fields of literature was the close association of the Jesuits with a new vogue in architecture. On June 26, 1568, a day of colorful ceremony in Rome, Cardinal Alessandro Farnese laid the foundation stone of the church of the Gesù which he was erecting for the Jesuits. Farnese's church became a kind of prototype of baroque religious architecture. During the second half of the sixteenth century, Renaissance architectural forms ran through the various expressions of the mannerist style associated with Michelangelo and gradually developed into what became known as baroque. It caught on. A few years after the Gesù had been started, the Oratorians built their Chiesa Nuova and the Theatines their Sant' Andrea della Valle. These three churches were massive hall-like and spacious structures which were among the more impressive baroque achievements in Rome. They exemplified the baroque preoccupation with the expression of a dominant sense of unity. Integrated into the architectural scheme were elaborate paintings, rich embellishments, and gilded forms. Light played against shadow. Strong curves abounded. And over all ruled the ideal of a grand and impressive unity. Architecture, painting, sculpture, all ran together in a dynamic and grand effort to achieve a perfect harmony.[13]

This integration of structure and color the Jesuits did not achieve until the middle of the seventeenth century, and in this sense their church did not enter immediately into the fullness of the baroque era. The delay at the Gesù underlined a key problem which the Jesuits faced: the patron. In the conception and

Architecture

---

13 *Oxford Companion to Art,* 10th ed., s.v. "Baroque," pp. 108-109. An important work which appeared too late for me to use is *Baroque Art: The Jesuit Contribution,* edited by R. Wittkower and Irma Jaffe (Bronx: Fordham University Press, 1972), 144 pp. with 64 plates.

decoration of the church the Jesuits were dependent on the ideas and plans of the patron, Cardinal Farnese. The Jesuits, concerned with the acoustics, wanted a flat roof. Farnese and his architect, Giacomo Barocchio de Vignola, insisted on a dome. Farnese died in 1589. The interior decorating, hardly begun, stopped. The Farnese family did not have the same interest as the Cardinal and declined to finance any further embellishment. The Society tried to raise funds but with limited success, and the work moved along sporadically. Giovanni Baglione, who did one painting, complained that the Jesuits were in arrears in paying him and kept putting him off. For more than a century, the Gesù, only partially decorated, was rather bleak.[14]

Some modern historians of liturgy censure the baroque church and style. Despite the criticisms of these scholars, who write from their own particular angle of interest, the baroque church made an immense spiritual impact. For the people it radiated a profound spirituality rooted in the rapture and exaltation of the Risen and Living Christ.[15] It spoke of the triumph of Christian hope. And unlike so many earlier churches, the baroque edifices gave the people an open range of vision so that they could clearly see the altar and the dramatic action of the Mass. Within the spacious area the people were also able to assemble to hear the sermons, those most important tools of instruction constantly used by the Jesuits in their apostolate.

Despite these assets some Jesuits of the time felt out of sympathy with the splendor of the baroque style. In 1611 Louis Richeome published his *Spiritual Painting. The Art of Admiring, Loving, and Praising God in All His Works,* in part a criticism of what he judged to be architectural extravagance. He called for austerity and simplicity of style. Critically he wrote of such ornaments as "Ionic columns crowned with scroll-like adornments, pilasters, pedestals, paintings, and reliefs."[16] Yet, despite Richeome's dissent, Jesuits generally as time went on embraced the baroque style and built in Europe and overseas impressive churches of that kind. In Austria, Bavaria, Franconia, Spain, and the colonies, the Jesuit presence was often identified with a baroque church.

14 F. Haskell, *Patrons and Painters* (New York, 1963), pp. 65-67; A. G. Dickens, *The Counter Reformation* (New York, 1969), pp. 165-170.
15 J. Jungmann, S.J., *The Mass of the Roman Rite: Its Origins and Development* (New York, 1951), I, 142; L. Bouyer, *Liturgical Piety* (Notre Dame, 1954), pp. 5-9, 43-44; E. I. Watkin, "The Splendour of Baroque," *The Tablet* (London), CCXXII (1968), 387-388.
16 F. Haskell, *Patrons and Painters,* p. 68.

The outstanding leaders of the Society in Spain during this period of uncommon growth were Francis Borgia and Jerónimo Nadal. Their achievement gained in impressiveness because of the opposition they encountered from two of the most potent forces of the day: the crippling bureaucratic machinery of Philip II and the extravagant nationalism at the Spanish court.

His Catholic Majesty was the sun around which revolved every aspect of Spanish life. Unfortunately for Borgia and Nadal, they were not always in the path of the rays from the royal orb. Philip restricted Nadal's freedom of movement; forbade Spanish Jesuits to leave the country for other parts of Europe lest they suffer the taint of heresy; and prohibited the export of Spanish currency for the support of such institutions as the Roman College. Philip's chariness about the Jesuits impelled Pius IV to write the king a spirited defense of the Society.

Spaniards looked upon themselves as the Catholics without equal in the world, in whom was realized the fullness of the Christian faith. Antonio Araoz funneled this spirit into segments of the Spanish Society. Resentful because he was dropped to the position of provincial of Castile while Borgia was made superior in all Spain, this onetime responsible Jesuit turned into a narrow and blind nationalist of the worst kind. Openly hostile to other Jesuits like Nadal, Polanco, and Borgia because of their willingness to admit men of Jewish extraction into the Society, angrily determined against the use of Spanish funds for the Roman College, and irritated that the general made his residence in Rome rather than Spain, this disappointed and disgruntled man became the darling of the Spanish court and a personal friend of the influential Ruy Gómez de Silva, the príncipe de Éboli. He augmented his nationalistic ideas with others which struck at the internal structure of the Society, especially in his pleas that superiors be chosen not by the general but by chapters in each province. Other Jesuits imbibed Araoz' attitudes. Mercurian delegated Pedro Ribadeneyra to try to check the rising momentum of criticism. In 1577 this facile and ready writer published a ringing defense of the Society's institute, but it failed to stop the fury of the terrible storm that was building up to lash the Spanish provinces during the next generalate.

Borgia and Nadal braved the opposition with fortitude. On Borgia fell the disfavor of the Inquisition because of his unconcealed sympathy for the imprisoned archbishop of Toledo, Bartolomé de Carranza; the inquisitor general placed on the Index a spiritual work which Borgia had published years before and which in no way offended orthodoxy; a stream of slander, tagging him as a fugitive from justice, followed him on a routine visit to Portugal. In those dark hours the patient, gracious spiritual gallantry of this nobleman shone with a brilliance which gave inspiration to his fellow Jesuits.

Jerónimo Nadal's spirit lost none of its magnanimity because of the spiteful tactics of Araoz, the pitfalls of Spanish bureaucracy and the irritating surveillance of the crown. By his exposition of the *Constitutions* to his fellow Jesuits, who received him with enthusiasm and delight, he contributed mightily to the formation of their interior spirit. Even while Araoz was creating a pull in Spain away from the rest of the Society, Nadal was binding hundreds of Jesuit hearts to other Jesuits throughout the world.

Two more serious tendencies appeared in the Spanish Society at this time: an extreme rigorism among some superiors and a desertion of the Society's apostolic purposes for the purely contemplative life. Deviating from the kind and considerate attitude asked of them by their rule, some superiors wanted to introduce the use of jail and flogging to maintain discipline. During the three-year period, 1565-1568, Francis Borgia, as general, had to admonish all four Spanish provincials because of their rigidity and sternness.[17]

Through Spain at this time was running a strong current toward the contemplative manner of living, and to this many Jesuits were yielding. Ignatius had been adamant in withstanding it, but after his death it made deep inroads. Many Jesuits became Carthusians. In 1574 the rector at Valencia lamented that in a short time he lost five of his community to the local charterhouse. The rector of the novitiate at Montilla combined the traits of the rigorist and the contemplative by exhausting his novices with arduous toil while he himself spent the entire day in his room.[18] To aggravate the situation, a wave of false mysticism was then moving across Spain in the heterodox teaching of the Alumbrados or the Enlightened Ones. Mercurian had genuine cause for alarm, and to meet this very real peril he sent a visitor to Spain.

Unfortunate enough to be caught between the hammer of the visitor and the anvil of the contemplative drift within the Society was one of the more distinguished spiritual directors of the day, Baltasar Álvarez. The question at issue reduced itself, in one precise form, to the kind of prayer that might be used in

17 Astráin, *Historia*, II, 267-270, 446-447, 454-459.
18 Ibid., III, 76-77, 81-82.

the Society. Álvarez had held several important posts in the Society and for a while was the esteemed spiritual director of St. Theresa of Ávila. He himself had received the gift of infused contemplation and he taught those he judged were properly disposed the great worth of infused prayer. He did not neglect teaching the methods of prayer set forth in the *Spiritual Exercises;* nor did he fail to stress that total self-abnegation insisted on by St. Ignatius. He clearly taught that no opposition existed between the methods in the *Spiritual Exercises* and contemplative prayer; nor between the apostolic vocation of the Society and higher prayer. The visitor, brusque and unfeeling Diego de Avellaneda, backed up by Mercurian, told Álvarez to desist. Alvarez obeyed promptly. His doctrine, as well as that of others like Antonio Cordeses, was irreproachable and in later years was incorporated into the teaching of Diego Álvarez de Paz and Luis de la Puente, but Mercurian faced at that precise moment the prospect of a whole segment of the Society losing sight of its apostolic objective. To avoid this calamity he acted rather rudely and without sensitivity for the positive and orthodox values in some of the more distinguished spiritual writers in Spain's history. The general and pervasive trend in Spain toward contemplative prayer he could not alter, and its dangers and aberrations continued to trouble the Society into the next generation.[19]

Meanwhile, in Portugal, the successive reigns of King Sebastian, Cardinal Henry, and Philip II of Spain, all affected the Society. Coimbra continued to be the great seedbed of missionaries. As King John had made this college the apple of his eye, Cardinal Henry, an active promoter of letters, ambitioned making Évora a thriving intellectual center. He followed up his foundation of a Jesuit college at Lisbon in 1565 with the placing of three colleges at Évora under the care of the Society.

Both Coimbra and Évora were graced by a theologian and philosopher who possibly was the greatest metaphysician in the history of the Society.[20] Pedro da Fonseca, known as "The Portuguese Aristotle," gave impetus, form, and direction to the revival of scholastic philosophy in the sixteenth century. This he did chiefly by his *Dialectics* (Cologne, 1567) and his four-volume *Commentary on the Metaphysics of Aristotle* (Lisbon, 1577-1589). In the former he integrated with immense clarity the

19 *DeGuiJes,* pp. 225-229.
20 J. F. Gomes, "Pedro da Fonseca: Sixteenth Century Portuguese Philosopher," *International Philosophical Quarterly,* VI, 632-644.

Organon and later doctrines of logic. In the latter, his most important work, he not only manifested originality and independence of mind but he also shaped an initial effort to establish the autonomy of metaphysics, which Suárez carried to completion. Alive to the humanistic preoccupations of his age, he brought to his work a fine philological vigor in his examination of Aristotelian texts and the ideal of presenting his doctrine in precise and clear language. Aged seventy-one, he died in 1599. Portugal, as a colonial power, was an exporter of men. Made an intellectual power by Fonseca and others, she became an exporter of ideas.

Two Jesuits gave generous service as tutors to the young, unrealistic King Sebastian, in whose veins flowed the blood of the mentally troubled Queen Juana of Spain. Both Luis Gonçalves da Câmara, who was a hero to his royal student, and Gaspar Mauricio Serpe tried to dissuade the unstrung king from his foolish dreams of crusading against the Moors in Africa. In the fateful campaign of 1578, when Sebastian charged to his death in a wild cavalry attack, Serpe was captured by the enemy and beheaded.

The year 1580 was a difficult one for the Portuguese as they beheld the troops of Philip II sweeping into their country to begin the sixty years of Spanish occupation. Luis Alvares provided an inspiring moment during this sorry episode. In the cathedral of Évora he preached a stirring sermon, calling for Portuguese unity against the invader. But all his eloquence and his theme of blood, sweat, and tears could not stop the best infantry in Europe. So began the ordeal of Jesuit superiors, trying to keep their Portuguese subjects from voicing their thoughts about the invaders from the east.

France Like every institution in France at this time, the Society of Jesus felt the harsh impact of the sanguinary and violent struggle between the Catholics and the Huguenots. During that merciless conflict made memorable by the regency of Catherine de Médicis, the massacre of Vassy and the massacre of St. Bartholomew's Day, the Jesuits, despite reverses and impediments, continued to expand. By 1575 there were three hundred and sixteen men in two provinces. By 1580 they were conducting fifteen colleges.

The distribution of the colleges is an index to the peculiar pattern of the Society's growth. With the exception of three, of which two, Verdun and Pont-à-Mousson, were in the east, all the schools were in the south and central area of France. The only one in the north was the College of Clermont in Paris. In the provinces, Auvergne, Lorraine, Nevers, and others, the Jesuits

planted their roots at the cordial invitation of important churchmen like the cardinals of Tournon, Lorraine, and Armagnac, or
noblemen like the duc de Savoie and the duc de Nevers, or city
governments like that of Lyons. In Paris, however, many in the
Parlement and the University let them know that they were not
welcome.

The bishop of Pamiers, Robert de Pellevé, hearing the glowing reports about the Jesuit school at Billom, persuaded the
Society to open a college in 1559 at Pamiers in the heart of a
Calvinistic enclave. Cardinal François de Tournon, distressed
that the University at Tournon had become a foyer of Calvinism,
managed to transfer that institution of several hundred students
to the Society in June, 1561. Bishop Guillaume du Prat received
his wish that there be a school in the upper part of Auvergne to
match Billom in the south when in 1563 the Jesuits inaugurated
classes at Mauriac. The initiative and influence of Cardinal
Georges d'Armagnac brought Jesuit education to Rodez and
Toulouse; that of Cardinal Alessandro Farnese to Avignon; that
of Cardinal Charles de Lorraine to Pont-à-Mousson; that of the
duc de Savoie to Chambéry and the duc de Nevers to Nevers.
Other schools were opened at Lyons, Bordeaux, Verdun, Bourges.
The trend was evident. Through the encouragement of men in
high places the Society had entered into the religious and cultural
life of France.[21]

This experience was nevertheless neither facile nor without
anguish. Difficulties abounded in plenty, the two most severe
being the pinch of poverty and the havoc of the religious wars.
If the cardinal of Tournon and Bishop Guillaume du Prat showed
their solicitude about the material welfare of their schools,
others failed in an appalling way to provide adequate foundations. Pamiers was an extreme example. The bishop did not
translate into practical financial support his interest in checking
Calvinism, and as a consequence the founding fathers had to
live in a disgraceful hovel without doors or windows. At other
places the faculty had to subsist on starvation diet, as meager
sometimes as just dry bread, plums, and water. At Avignon one
day in 1578 the brother in charge of purchasing found not a sou
in the treasury to pay for provisions. During his visitation of the
French colleges in 1568, Nadal counseled superiors that they

21 H. Fouqueray, S.J., *Histoire de la Compagnie de Jésus en France*
(Paris, 1910-1925), I, 363-387, 434-451, 452-475, 500-513, 514-531,
594-615.

realize their responsibility to see that better endowments for the schools were guaranteed.

War was the other major impediment. Constantly the alarms of battle between Catholic and Calvinist rang through the land. Forced recesses were common as the columns of Huguenots maneuvered and pillaged. In the spring, 1562, the Baron des Andrets moved on Tournon and demanded the expulsion of the Jesuits. Realizing that the whole population would suffer if they remained, twenty-four Jesuits, disguised and in the dark of night, quietly quit the town. A year passed before they could return. In 1561 the staff at Pamiers, retreating before the Huguenot onslaught, closed the doors of their school, not to be opened again until after seventy years.

Many of these pioneer teachers were also effective preachers. Émond Auger, a man of wide-ranging gifts, whose piercing sermons have marked him as among the first four or five great Jesuit preachers of all time, initiated the rich and glorious tradition of Jesuit pulpit oratory in France. Far more convincing than the military sallies of The League, the ardent and colorful words of this Champagnois brought back Calvinists to the Church by the thousands. In scenes reminiscent of apostolic days depicted in the Acts of the Apostles, whole colonies of Huguenots throughout central and southern France, such as the nearly two thousand in Lyons alone, returned to the faith of Clovis and St. Louis.

Auger was not alone in this work. The Jesuit colleges became natural centers from which priests radiated on preaching excursions into the neighboring towns and villages. Foreign Jesuits gave powerful aid to their French brethren. They included the Italian, Antonio Possevino, who found only a faint flicker of the faith in Dieppe in 1570 and within a few days led two thousand back to the Church; and the Belgian Olivier Mannaerts, who, building on Possevino's foundations, converted four thousand more of the Dieppois; and the Spaniard, Juan de Maldonado, whose name was writ large in the reformation of Poitou.[22]

The Huguenot challenge uncovered among Catholics a frightening ignorance of their faith and clearly demonstrated the need of basic doctrinal instruction. Auger, known because of his eloquence as the "Chrysostom of France," earned by the publication of a catechism still another title, "The French Canisius." Not quite of the excellence of Peter Canisius' in Germany, Auger's work nevertheless filled a gap which could wait no longer to be stopped.

22 Ibid., 535-536, 545-547.

This same period saw the origins of another Jesuit tradition in France as glorious as that of sacred oratory. Preaching by deed was the hallmark of the men who through the centuries sacrificed their lives for the poor people struck down by the epidemics which periodically swept through the land. At the head of this distinguished roll was the first provincial of France, the gentle and self-effacing Paschase Broët, who made the supreme sacrifice on September 14, 1562. At Avignon seven followed his example. Then in 1580, three at Paris; in 1582, two at Bourges; in 1583, four at Nevers; in 1585, five at Bordeaux, ten at Pont-à-Mousson, and two at Tournon. These statistics indicated the pattern of the normal Jesuit response to the terrible epidemics that frequently plagued Europe before the discoveries of modern medicine. By 1907 at least 2,094 had died in this role throughout the world. Later research has shown that there were more.[23]

In contrast to the welcome they received throughout the provinces, the Jesuits in Paris met an unceasing barrage of bitter criticism from Gallican and Calvinistic interests strongly entrenched in Parlement and the University. Their first problem, inherited from the earlier period, was to obtain legal recognition of their corporate existence in the country. For five years after Ignatius' death Paschase Broët and the indefatigable Ponce Cordogan, by memoranda and interviews, did not let the monarch forget the Jesuits' case, but they were caught in the cross-fire of the centuries old struggle between the crown and the aristocracy. In February, 1560, Francis II confirmed the letters patent which had been issued by Henry II, recognizing the Society of Jesus in France, but which for nine years had lain disregarded in Parlement's record office. Parlement, its self-confidence increased by the weakness of the regency, refused to register the document. On April 25 the king issued new letters patent. Parlement skillfully used tactics of delay. On October 9, Francis ordered Parlement to comply with his royal wishes, but death took the young monarch soon after and the struggle was inherited by the ten-year-old Charles IX. On December 23, Catherine de Médicis, acting for her son, delivered letters patent confirming those of Henry II and Francis II. Again Parlement slyly procrastinated, and finally commended the question to either the Estates General, or a general council, or the religious colloquy scheduled to be assembled at Poissy in 1561.

23 Ibid., 316; II, 68-77; A. Poncelet, S.J. *Histoire de la Compagnie de Jésus dans les anciens Pays-Bas* (Bruxelles, 1927), II, 468-469; I. H. Dugout, *Nos martyrs*, p. 71.

It was at Poissy that a breach was made in the wall of delay and the Jesuits finally received their legal recognition, albeit in a severely narrow form. Contrary to the wishes of the pope, who was then thoroughly preoccupied with the Council of Trent, Catherine de Médicis, in an effort to bring peace to sorely rent France, called for religious discussion at the town of Poissy, and invited the well-known Protestant apologists, Theodore Beza and Peter Martyr. Forty-six Catholic bishops attended. Pope Pius IV, dreading the outcome of these discussions on dogma, and fearful that France might be deflected into heresy, sent to the colloquy Cardinal Ippolito d'Este, and Fathers Laynez and Polanco. Two things were made luminously clear at the queen mother's abortive council: first, the serious prospect of further Huguenot gains, intimated by the belligerent speech of Beza on the Holy Eucharist, and the bold, aggressive words of Peter Martyr; and second, the presence in France of a redoubtable champion of the Church in the new religious order whose general, Diego Laynez, not only expounded with brilliance, clarity, and precision the disputed points of dogma but also, with startling and audacious courage, publicly advised Catherine de Médicis that it was no business of hers to try to resolve questions of faith.

Eventually the question of the legal status of the Jesuits in France came up. Led by such emphatic admirers of the Society as the cardinals of Tournon, Bourbon, Lorraine, and Armagnac, the hierarchy generally favored the act of registration. But the situation was extremely delicate. The hard Gallican bishop of Paris, Eustache du Bellay, who resented the Society, could not be ignored, especially since the immediate effect of approval would be the legal recognition of the College of Clermont in his diocese. Hoping that the aggressiveness of the Calvinists would temper Du Bellay's antipathy to the Society, the bishops designated him to draw up the formula of legal recognition.

The bishop's firm document, however, revealed no change of heart. The main point, extremely restrictive in nature, was that the Society was recognized not as a religious order but as a corporation and a college, and this only on certain conditions: that its members adopt a title other than Society of Jesus; that they be completely under the jurisdiction of the bishop; that they be subject to the common law without any private rights; that they renounce any privileges founded on papal bulls which were contrary to the jurisdiction of the Paris Parlement. De Tournon and other friendly bishops, displeased with the constricted nature of Du Bellay's work, felt nevertheless that another opportunity to champion the Society in common might not soon arise, and therefore on September 15, 1561, signed the document. Five months later Parlement enacted its act of registration. The Society, aggrieved by the humiliating conditions, but aware of the acute need for instruction in the faith among the youth of France, submitted and assumed the title, "Society of the College of Clermont." [24] It was a compromise, but Laynez was determined to use it to full advantage. He planned to station at the College professors of superior qualities and to make it the most celebrated school of the Society. And so ended one distinct phase of the Jesuit struggle in Paris.

The second, like the first, was embedded in a mire of legalism. It revolved about the question of the right of the Society of the College of Clermont to conduct public classes. The center of opposition was in the University of Paris, intellectual custodian of a strong animosity toward the papacy, now fortified among some members by a pronounced sympathy for the doctrines of Calvin. The Society had two objectives: to obtain official approval as teachers and to receive incorporation within the organizational framework of the University. In the first they succeeded; in the second, they failed.

Having purchased with money left them by Bishop Guillaume du Prat the large and commodious Hôtel La Cour in the heart of the university area, the Jesuits filed their formal petition for approval as teachers — technically known as *Lettres de scholarité*. They timed their request perfectly, since Jubin de Saint Germain, the rector at the time — the rector was changed every three months — was a Catholic and of open mind about the presence of the Jesuits in Paris. He granted the request.

On February 22, 1564, classes opened at the College of Clermont under the direction of two especially competent scholars, both Spaniards, Miguel Venegas, who taught humanities, and Juan de Maldonado, who lectured on philosophy and starting the next year, on theology. They created a sensation in the Latin Quarter. By their luminous exposition and broad erudition, traditional courses in humane letters and philosophy became fresh and new-minted. Crowds of excited students, attracted especially by Maldonado, filled the classrooms. By 1570 the numbers had risen to over a thousand, and some arrived two or three hours before the lecture in order to be sure of a seat.[25]

24 Fouqueray, *Histoire*, I, 253-257.
25 J. M. Prat, S.J., *Maldonat et L'Université de Paris* (Paris, 1856), pp. 161-188.

Juan de Maldonado, native of Estremadura, formed intellectually at the University of Salamanca during the years of its vibrant literary and theological renaissance, in face of the pressing problems raised by the Protestants, broke with the older methods of commentary on the *Sentences* of Peter the Lombard and of syllogistic argumentation refined to sharpness of a needle point. With his intense and broad culture, he showed how theology, studied in the documents of Scripture and patristic writings, was the unique way to satisfy the intellectual curiosity of the age. Laynez had hoped that the professors at the College of Clermont, by the compelling brilliance of their teaching, would turn the Society's enemies into admirers and friends. However, a directly opposite reaction set in. Embarrassed by the dwindling numbers of their students, who were deserting them for Maldonado and his brethren, the lecturers of the University became more intransigent and irreconcilable in their position, pursuing through the years after 1564, on one front and then another, their relentless campaign to dislodge the distasteful College of Clermont.

The complex issue eventually went through the court and ended in the chambers of Parlement. On April 5, 1565, Parlement rendered its decision. Maintaining a delicate balance between the two parties, it declared the Jesuits free to teach, but denied them the right of incorporation within the University. But this did not satisfy the Society's enemies. They then concentrated their fire on Maldonado. Finally, in 1577, they obtained their objective. Pope Gregory XIII, concerned about the ceaseless turmoil at Paris, expressed his desire that Maldonado leave the College of Clermont. Bourges became the new home of the brilliant teacher. The maledictions of the men of the University snapped the Spaniard's ties to Paris, but in doing so they set him free to compose his masterpiece, *Commentary on the Four Gospels* (1596-1597), for at Bourges he found the leisure to write. Breaking with the common and traditional form of exegesis and directing his attention primarily to the literal meaning of the text, Maldonado composed several volumes of scriptural commentary (not published until after his death) which still merit respect for the lucidity and perceptiveness of their exposition.

At the end of this period the Jesuits were still teaching at Paris. No resolution, satisfactory to both sides, of the problem of aggregating the College of Clermont to the University had been achieved. This legal impasse was symbolic of the wider, graver, and more basic tension which prevailed between the Church and its enemies. The uncertainty that hung over the Jesuit enterprise in France was of a piece with the problematical resolution of the contest for supremacy in the kingdom between Catholic and Huguenot.

Germany reached a milestone in its history in 1555 with the religious Peace of Augsburg. Lutherans and Catholics had fought to a standstill, and the emperor was constrained to recognize officially the Lutheran presence in the empire. Consolidation of the Catholic position demanded a profound spiritual renovation. To this restoration of a vigorous Catholic life the Society, yearly increasing at a steady pace, made a worthy contribution. In 1579 the Rhineland Province, from which the Belgian had been separated fifteen years before, numbered 234 men. In the same year the Upper German Province, from which Austria had been divided sixteen years earlier, numbered 170 men. The Austrian Province in 1585 had 210 men on its roster.[26]

The major symbol of the Jesuit role in this renaissance of Catholic strength, resilience, and enterprise was the college. Peter Canisius, at the time Claude Jay opened the College at Vienna in 1552, requested Ignatius to pray that King Ferdinand and the Duke of Bavaria would sponsor another at Ingolstadt. "Then," said he, "other princes in Germany, as the need for colleges is borne in on them, will gradually fall into line in imitation of them." Peter was correct. Requests for Jesuit colleges multiplied, and by 1580 from Paderborn and Heiligenstadt in the North to Luzern, Innsbruck, and Hall in the South, from Trier in the West to Vienna and Graz in the East the three German-speaking provinces were either operating or just at the point of opening nineteen schools. Not all of these colleges developed to the same dimensions or with the same rapidity. Among the larger were the one at Trier which grew from a student body of 550 in 1564 to 1,030 fourteen years later, that at Würzburg from 160 students in 1568 to 700 in twenty-two years, that at Mainz from 30 in 1561 to 500 in five years. The smaller schools included that at Graz which had 200 students in 1578 and 363 six years later, and that at Molsheim which expanded from 84 students in 1580 to 125 in two years. These institutions, notably on the university level, had more than a religious import. In the rough chaos brought to the intellectual life of Germany by the Reformation, many students left their own country for the universities of Paris, Louvain, Douai, and Pavia. To stem this debilitating

26 B. Duhr, S.J., *Geschichte der Jesuiten in den Ländern Deutscher Zunge* (Munich, 1907-1928), I, 95.

emigration new universities were needed, and reform in the older ones was imperative. The bishops called on the Jesuits. By the early seventeenth century no Catholic university within the Empire, save Salzburg, which was in the hands of the Benedictines, was founded or maintained without Jesuit help. The Society had saved university life within the Catholic regions of the Empire.[27]

In Hungary, where the part not under the domination of the Turks had become extensively Protestant, the Jesuit origins were very modest. At the invitation of Archbishop Miklós Oláh of Esztergom they arrived in 1561 and shortly after opened a college at Nagyszombat. These German and Hungarian institutions became colonies of Catholic learning and devotion in a besieged area into which, like an aqueduct, the Society carried the strong stream of spiritual renovation and intellectual ferment from the rest of the Catholic world.

Jesuit At times this awakening found colorful expression. In 1574 the
Drama students at the Jesuit school in Munich produced a play by one of their teachers, Georg Agricola. The play was entitled *Constantine*. The town itself, beautifully decorated, was the stage. One thousand actors took part, and it lasted two days. The climactic point was the splendid entry of Constantine into Rome after the battle of the Milvian Bridge with the emperor driving four span of horses and surrounded by four hundred horsemen in glittering armor. This event, a cultural landmark in Munich's history, evidenced the rich resources of creativity and imagination the Jesuits were tapping in Germany.[28]

It also vividly portrayed one of the major achievements of the Jesuit schools throughout Europe: the cultivation of drama. In 1551, three years after the opening of the Collegio Mamertino in Messina, the Society's first school in Europe primarily for externs, the Jesuit students there produced a tragedy. In 1558, also at Messina, the students put on a comedy written by the Spanish Jesuit, Francisco Stefano, entitled *Philoplutus. The Sorry Outcome of Avarice*. At Vienna, in 1555, the students began a long Jesuit dramatic tradition in that city with the production of *Euripus. The Emptiness of All Things*. At Córdoba, in 1556, the

---

27 Ibid., 92-166; S. d'Irsay, *Histoire des Universités Françaises et Étrangères*. (Paris, 1933), I, 345, 356.

28 J. Janssen, *History of the German People* (St. Louis, 1905-1910), XIII, 200.

young men produced *Metanea,* a work by one of their masters, Pedro de Acevedo.[29]

The Jesuits had a twofold didactic purpose in the encouragement of drama: to give the students the opportunity to demonstrate in a lively and entertaining way their skills in grammar and rhetoric, and to impart in an engaging way the doctrinal and moral teaching of the Church. In the beginning the plays were in Latin, the core of the school curriculum. The subjects and themes were usually biblical or historical and had titles like *Goliath, Hercules, Samson, Nabuchodonosor, Constantine.* The plays often exploited the tensions that characterized the various expressions of baroque art, that between virtue and vice, God and man, eternity and time. Within a very short time the simple origins developed sparklingly as the Jesuits introduced the vernacular languages, music, dancing, orchestras, and large groups of actors. Probably no phase of Jesuit education evolved so extensively and into so many varied and lively forms as the drama.

Among the leaders in the introduction of the vernacular and music into the school plays were the Spanish Jesuits. They employed the vernacular very early. Sometimes they had the prologue presented in Spanish. Sometimes they used a dialogue in Latin and Spanish as a means to distinguish between the noble and plebeian characters, the former speaking Latin, the latter Spanish. Sometimes they inserted Spanish verse forms. The most famous Spanish Jesuit dramatist of the early years, Pedro de Acevedo, experimented widely. In 1556 in his *Metanea* he mixed Latin prose and Spanish verse; in 1562 he composed the prologue in Spanish verse of eleven syllables; in 1566 he presented *Athanasia,* the Latin prose of which was broken by three entr'- actes in Spanish verse. Jesuits in other countries were not far behind. In 1580 at Pont-à-Mousson the students put on *The Maid of Orléans* in French. Two years later the Jesuits at Lucerne received permission to present plays in German. And in 1588 the schools of the Austrian province were allowed to produce interludes in German.[30]

In the use of music and dancing the Spaniards were again leaders. In 1558 the students at Ocaña produced a tragic-comedy, *Joseph,* which included music and dancing. Ten years later in Munich, an elaborate ballet was part of the play, *Samson,* and a

29 Edna Purdie, in *The Oxford Companion to the Theatre,* 3rd ed., s.v. "Jesuit Drama," p. 508.
30 Ibid., 508-510.

grand chorus sang the music prepared by Orlando di Lasso. In 1582 at Innsbruck the play, *Tobias,* was really an Italian *Singspiel* or operetta, an early indication of the enormous influence that the Italian opera was to exert on the Jesuit drama, especially in Austria and southern Germany.[31]

In the use of decor and stage settings, the Italian, Spanish, and German Jesuits broke early from the original simple forms. In 1573 in Rome the students presented a play on the Last Judgment against a background of vast vistas that gave a fearful picture of the lot of the damned. In 1580 at Seville the students produced *San Hermenegildo,* in which a large frontispiece represented the city and on one side stood a tower, the prison of the saint, and on the other side a second tower filled with fireworks. In Munich, in 1573, the young men produced *Constantine,* mentioned above. In Germany these Jesuit plays, possibly more than anything else, revealed in a highly visible way the spontaneity and vitality of the Catholic Reform.[32]

Scholarship and schools were not the only Jesuit preoccupation. Gathered together in the Society's archives in Rome are the reports of both superiors and subjects from all corners of central Europe on their labors outside the classroom. The businesslike paragraphs and the cold columns of statistics echo but feebly the voices of Jesuits once heard preaching, catechizing, administering the sacraments in town and village and countryside. In 1573, for example, Johann Rethius reported on the Lenten preaching of Peter Brillmacher at Speyer three times a week, of Gregor Wolfschedl at Augsburg three times a week, of Martin Leubenstein at St. Mauritz twice a week. In 1564 Martin Stervordian described his six months' preaching tour with Jean Couvillon and Georg Schorich in lower Bavaria. In 1569 Schorich informed Borgia of the thousands at Landshut who heard him and received the sacraments.[33]

Nothing, however, reveals so impressively the growing strength of the faith as the reports on the administration of the sacraments. At Easter of 1560 the priests at the Jesuit church in Vienna heard 700 confessions; in 1569, 3000; then, after a falling off, 3,540 in 1584. At Graz, when the college was opened in 1573, only twenty received Holy Communion at Easter at the Jesuit chapel. Two years later there were 500, eight years later more than a thousand, and double that in 1590. In Freiburg in Switzerland hardly five or

---

31 Ibid., 511, 513; Janssen, *History of the German People,* XIII, 199-200.
32 Purdie, *The Oxford Companion to the Theatre,* pp. 511-512.
33 Duhr, *Geschichte,* I, 471-473.

six people received Holy Communion at Christmas. The Jesuits opened a school there in 1582 and could report that 600 had received that year. In Passion Week of the next year over 2,000 made their confession. In Cologne, in 1576, 15,000 received Holy Communion at the Jesuit chapel. Five years later the number reached 45,000. In the same period at Trier the increase was from 13,000 to 22,000.[34] Pierre Favre, the first Jesuit to work in Germany, had judged from his experience that the danger of heresy would recede if the people were led to a love of the sacramental life. "If the heretics," he observed, "should see in the churches the practice of frequent Communion, with the faithful receiving their Strength and their Life, some weekly, others every two weeks, not one of them would dare to preach the Zwinglian doctrine of the Holy Eucharist."[35] The statistics in the Jesuit records bear testimony to the accuracy of Favre's diagnosis.

During this remarkable burst of expansion with its inherent danger of deviation from St. Ignatius' spirit, the one priest who could best assure that each Jesuit community was a coin from the mint of the Society's *Constitutions* was the tireless apostle of the highway, Jerónimo Nadal. Nadal loved Germany. He had traveled throughout western Europe as visitor and had given his heart to every Jesuit school he visited, but his summary observation was: "With me Germany is at the top of the list since its needs are so acute." To his fellow religious, often working in severe poverty, often surrounded by hostile elements, Nadal by his joyful, amiable, buoyant spirit communicated a will to carry on.[36]

Continuing to be, in the words of another Jesuit, "The pride and ornament of all Germany" was Peter Canisius. During this quarter-century he traveled approximately 20,000 miles through Germany, Italy, Austria, Bohemia, Switzerland, preaching, founding colleges, counseling bishops and princes, encouraging his fellow Jesuits, ever gentle, kind, warmhearted. His responsibilities were often heavy, as when in 1556 he was made provincial of the newly created Province of Upper Germany, which embraced Austria, Bohemia, Bavaria, and the Tyrol. Others marveled at the frequency with which he turned out his books, all directed to some immediate need. Catechetics continued to be a constant concern, and in 1558 he published his *Shorter Catechism,* a de-

34 Ibid., 439-441.
35 *MonFabri,* p. 196.
36 *MonNad,* II, 488-510; J. Brodrick, S.J., *The Progress of the Jesuits (1556-1579)* (London, 1947), p. 175.

lightful and instructive medley of doctrine, woodcuts, and verse. Later editions revealed his untiring concern for improvement and greater effectiveness. The composition which tried Peter most and with which he never felt at ease was the beginning of what was designed to be the Catholic answer, in two massive volumes, to the giant Protestant venture into Church history, the *Centuries of Magdeburg*.

During the twenty-five years since the death of St. Ignatius, the Catholic Church in Central Europe grew in beauty, vitality, and spiritual splendor. The nineteen Jesuit colleges had done a great deal in the restoration. And Peter Canisius, turning sixty years of age in 1581, had been a leading designer.

Poland   Contained between Germany and Russia, the Kingdom of Poland in the late sixteenth century embraced a medley of different states, Poland proper, the grand principality of Lithuania and its Ruthenian territories, the duchy of Mazovia, Livonia, royal Prussia, ducal Prussia, and the duchy of Courland. The vast area of Lithuania became an organic part of the Polish Kingdom in 1569 when by the Union of Lublin the parliament of the grand principality amalgamated with the Polish *sejm*. King Sigismund II Augustus called his kingdom a *Rzeczpospolita* – a commonwealth of nations. Over this commonwealth fell the shadow of a serious spiritual crisis in the sixteenth century. Peoples, traditionally faithful to the Catholic Church, were abandoning their old loyalty for the Protestant cause. Two men especially halted this defection, Cardinal Stanislaus Hosius, prince-bishop of Ermeland, and King Stephen Bathory. Both leaders relied greatly on the Society and opened the way for Jesuit participation in one of the greatest trials of Poland's religious life.

Early Protestant success and resourcefulness appalled the ubiquitous Peter Canisius, who in 1558 attended the Diet of Piotrkow as theological advisor to the papal legate. What he observed in his travels to Kraków, Lowicz, and Piotrkow caused him to advise Laynez that the fate of the Catholic Church depended on the stability and fortitude of the bishops and the monarch. But the hierarchy was weak, and in the face of Protestantism King Sigismund II Augustus was both indecisive and theologically befuddled. By 1569 the Protestants held close to half of the seats in the Senate, and if episcopal senators were not included, actually out-numbered the Catholic peers. Before 1600, 2,000 Catholic churches had fallen into Protestant hands.

But quietly and undramatically the Protestant advance was halted, and a reanimated Catholic body took up the offensive.

Stanislaus Hosius became bishop of Ermeland in 1551. In 1565 he invited the Jesuits to conduct a college in East Prussia at Braunsberg. Stephen Bathory, elected king in 1575, brought the Society to Kraków in Little Poland, Riga in Livonia, and Polotsk in Lithuania. The college at Vilna, also in Lithuania, he elevated to the dignity of a university.

The Poles took to the Society, and the Society in turn, with its interior power of adaptation to widely variant national traits and characters, took to the Poles. In 1575, only ten years after the founding of the college at Braunsberg, Mercurian created the province of Poland. The Poles, attracted by the carefully organized program of instruction and impressed by the climate of civilization and intelligence about the Jesuit schools, filled the classrooms. The alumni moved into the nation's social and political life, and the Catholic cause began to receive intelligent and devout leadership. From the schools catechists and preachers radiated into the country, and men of the eloquence of Fathers Karnkowiski and Stanislaw Sokolowski made great inroads into the Protestant holdings. At this time of crisis appeared the greatest of them all, a writer and pulpit orator, who for nearly a half-century helped lead the way in the Catholic restoration. Piotr Skarga entered the Society in 1568, four years after his ordination. Catholic Poland knew that it had a gifted champion in its midst when it heard his powerful sermons and read his cogently written *The Unity of the Church of God* (1577).[37]

In the Netherlands, among the alert, enterprising people at this strategic crossroads of German and French culture, the Society, once established, expanded most rapidly. But this was the period when the fever of independence was spreading against Spanish rule and when Alessandro Farnese was pursuing his adroit policy of driving a wedge between the Catholic provinces of the south and the Calvinist controlled provinces of the north. The four colleges and other residences of the Society could not avoid being among the casualties of the discord and turbulence.

The legal recognition of the Society in the Netherlands, which St. Ignatius had not been able to obtain, Pedro Ribadeneyra finally secured through his patient diplomacy at the court of Philip II. The first college, opened at Tournai in 1562, was soon followed by others among the French-speaking population at Dinant, Saint-Omer, Cambrai, Douai, and Liège. In 1575 the

The Low Countries, England, and Other Areas

37 L. von Pastor, *The History of the Popes*, XX, 401-405; XXIV, 125-127.

Flemings received three schools, at the great banking center of Antwerp, at Bruges, and at Maastricht. Mainly Spaniards first staffed these colleges.[38]

The provinces united against Spain in the Pacification of Ghent of 1576, and the Jesuits, protected by the Spanish crown and with the patriotic movement therefore closed to them, had to abandon their institutions and leave the Netherlands. This exile lasted nine years, until 1585.

Roots of Jansenism Most memorable of the Society's engagements in the intellectual and spiritual life of the Netherlands was its challenge to the theological speculation of a group of scholars at Louvain, headed by Michel de Bay (Baius). Baius, in his teaching on St. Augustine, developed a theology which exaggerated both the natural goodness of man before the fall of Adam and the evil suffered by human nature after the fall. With alternatingly misplaced optimism and pessimism he cut across the great realities of grace, human freedom, Christ's redemptive work, with an interpretation that was alien to the faith. His obliteration of the distinction between the natural and supernatural orders revealed the strong impress of Calvinism in his system. This was the origin of the powerful and influential movement which soon developed into the tradition of Jansenism. From the start Jesuit theologians took a decided stand against the doctrine of Baius, thus committing themselves and their successors to one of the most protracted and complex struggles in the history of theology. The Jesuit engagement could not have begun more auspiciously. In 1570, the twenty-eight-year-old, recently ordained Robert Bellarmine, with beautiful lucidity, clear logic, and broad erudition, began his six years of counterattack at Louvain against the aberrations of Baius. It was Bellarmine's introduction, on a broad scale, to the intellectual contests of his intensely controversial age.[39]

In this period of religious crisis, when it was generally the rulers who set the religious pattern of their countries and guided the religious allegiance of their people, the Holy See placed considerable importance on keeping contact with the various European courts. At times the popes employed Jesuits on these delicate missions. Those so engaged were never very many, but the importance of their work was far out of proportion to their

---

38 Poncelet, *Histoire*, I, 158, 163-180.
39 J. Brodrick, S.J., *Robert Bellarmine. Saint and Scholar* (Westminister, 1961), pp. 27-30.

numbers, since it carried the possibility of saving the faith of an entire realm.

Scotland was one such kingdom. In 1561 Queen Mary had returned from France, young nineteen-year-old widow of the late Francis II, to find the tide of Presbyterianism running strong against the Church. On her strategy depended the fate of the Catholics. Pope Pius IV dispatched the Dutch Jesuit, Nikolaas Floris (Goudanus) of Gouda, to urge the queen to take a militant stand in the mold of Mary Tudor of England. Covertly Floris entered Edinburgh in 1562. His arrival somehow discovered, he went into hiding for two months as the pulpits resounded with exhortations to the Scots to capture "the ambassador of anti-Christ" and wash their hands in his blood. Finally, on July 24, 1562, Floris spoke secretly to Mary at Holyrood. He found it a fruitless meeting since her reply to papal exhortation was evasive and noncommittal. Disappointed as he was, he left Holyrood with a deep sympathy for the lonely young lady in the center of a storm of hate, meanness, and deceit.

Four years later another Jesuit acted as representative for another pope to the same Queen of Scots. Pope Pius V, of like mind as his predecessor about the need for a strong and vigorous stand in Scotland, chose an Italian bishop, Vincenzo Laureo, to urge Mary to cut down the men who were faithless to her and give to the realm an example of her set purpose. To prepare the way for Laureo, a Scots Jesuit, Edmund Hay, was sent ahead. On January 14, 1567, Hay gave Mary a preview of the drastic tenor of the bishop's message. The queen brushed the proposal aside, asserting that she would not bear responsibility for spilling even disloyal blood of her subjects.[40]

Sweden was another kingdom with which the Holy See had temporary and tenuous contact. For ten years, 1574-1584, it seemed that victory might be snatched from the Protestants in that northern nation. This hope rested largely on a small group of Jesuits. The Swedish Mission developed in three stages, each guided by a man of skill: the first by Stanislaw Warszewicki, the second by Laurentius Norvegus, the third by Antonio Possevino.

The focal point on which the three Jesuits converged was the Lutheran King John III, who leaned toward the Catholic faith and who was married to the Catholic Princess Catherine of Poland. In 1574 Warszewicki was sent to Stockholm to attend the queen. John was impressed by the Jesuit and evidenced interest in becoming a Catholic. But he made it clear that his conversion

40 Brodrick, *The Progress*, pp. 193-205.

would be dependent on three dispensations: for a married clergy, for Holy Communion under the species of both bread and wine, for the vernacular at Mass, all three in one way or another identified in that age with Protestantism. He also insisted that the conversion of his people would have to be a gradual process.[41]

Warszewicki appealed to his superiors for a Jesuit who knew the Swedish language. This opened the way for the intelligent and original Norwegian, Laurits Nielssen, usually known as Laurentius Norvegus. A native of Tönsberg in Norway, at the age of twenty he went to Copenhagen to continue his education. There he met some Jesuits working secretly. At their urging he went to Louvain, where he became a Catholic and a Jesuit. In the spring of 1576 he arrived at Stockholm. King John was delighted with his vast learning and dialectical skill and promptly made him president and lecturer in theology at the recently founded Royal College of Stockholm. Not revealing his identity and confining his lectures to noncontroversial subjects, Laurentius Norvegus built up an impressive school. By the spring of 1579 he had seventy students registered, including thirty Lutheran ministers. Meanwhile he drew King John closer to the faith.[42]

Officials at Rome, apprised of these developments, wanted more information. The pope therefore dispatched the gracious and knowledgeable Antonio Possevino. Garbed as the ambassador of the Holy Roman Empire officially carrying the news of the recent demise of the Emperor Maximilian, Possevino arrived in Sweden in December, 1577. By his clear and logical reasoning he convinced the king that he should become a Catholic, and assured him that the authorities at Rome were trying to work out a solution to his peculiar problems. Somehow or other — perhaps by an overoptimistic interpretation of Possevino's remarks — John concluded that Gregory XIII would grant Sweden a married clergy, the chalice for the laity, and the vernacular in the Mass. In mid-May he took the definite step. On the 16th and 17th he renounced Lutheranism and received Holy Communion. Soon after, Possevino left Stockholm for Rome where he presented the king's plan for the gradual conversion of Sweden behind the facade of the triple dispensation. He also outlined his own grand scheme for the conversion of the northern nations, one major item of which called for the foundation

---

41 O. Garstein, *Rome and the Counter-Reformation in Scandinavia, 1539–1583* (Oslo, 1964), p. 77.
42 Ibid., pp. 94-97.

of seminaries for Scandinavians at Braunsberg, Olmütz, and Vilna. The Roman Curia however refused to grant the requested dispensations. Then the pope, designating Possevino as vicar apostolic to Scandinavia, Russia, and the Baltic regions, directed him to return to Sweden.[43]

Possevino reached Stockholm in July, 1579, and found an angry king. John had already heard of the curia's decision on his requests, and in disgust had withdrawn from the Church. Diplomatic issues, which touched practically every religious question of that age, came prominently to the fore. John faced the problem whether to join Sweden to the Catholic bloc or the Protestant bloc in the alignment of nations. With diplomatic acumen he chose a policy of neutrality. In this delicate situation Possevino made a hazardous decision. Placing all his hope in the one card of forcing the king to choose one side or other, he ordered the Jesuits in Sweden, about eight of them at this time, to throw off the veil of secrecy and reveal to the people that they were Catholic priests.[44]

This move failed. John refused to budge from his neutral position, although, because of the public clamor, he ordered Laurentius Norvegus, the best known of the foreigners, to leave the country. With Laurentius gone Possevino saw no purpose in his remaining longer, and in August, 1580, leaving five of the Society to carry on, he left Sweden. One bright ray shines through the shadows of this impasse. During his latter visit Possevino had sent at least thirty-two young Scandinavians to continental seminaries. When he left he took sixteen others with him. The five Jesuits who stayed behind faced a highly dubious future. Four years later, as will be seen in the next chapter, with their status undermined by Possevino's negotiations in another papal diplomatic mission, this time between Poland and Russia, they too quit Sweden.

Laurentius Norvegus and Possevino had failed in Scandinavia. To embitter their defeat, differences had broken out between them. Some haunting questions hang over the history of the Swedish mission: Was Possevino wise in trying to force King John's hand in early 1580? Might not John's gradualism have worked in a country where the Catholic faith was still very much alive if Rome had granted the dispensations he requested? Sweden might have become a great Catholic outpost of the North, and there might not have been a Protestant Gustavus

43 Ibid., pp. 159-162, 169.
44 Ibid., p. 201.

Adolphus to sweep through the Empire with the force of a whirlwind during the Thirty Years' War.

Ireland was another country which Rome feared would be lost to the Church. But Ireland's link to the Holy See remained firm, and in the securing of that tie the Society contributed in a significant way. Limited in number, the Jesuits had to make a choice of the area of their apostolate, whether the walled towns and cities with their old Anglo-Norman population or the country peopled by the ancient Gaels. They chose the former. The English government, having suppressed the Anglo-Norman monasteries and thereby erased the source of Catholic education, built up an Anglican school system, reaching from the parish to Dublin College, which was opened in 1542, and having for its avowed purpose "the Reformation of the Realme, and to breed in the rudest of our people resolute English hearts." To contest this Protestant ambition the Jesuits, through the succeeding centuries, concentrated on Catholic education.[45]

The priest who spearheaded the Society's Irish mission was David Wolf, a Limerick man. On January 21, 1561, with the authority of apostolic nuncio, he reached Cork. For seven years he moved with superb endurance among the people, filling vacant episcopal sees, instructing, administering the sacraments. Captured by Protestants, he spent five years in the squalor of a dungeon in Dublin Castle until his escape in 1572. He then gave his great energies to helping, in Portugal, Spain, and Italy, his friend James Fitzmaurice launch an expedition against the English forces in Ireland. Under circumstances not clarified by known documents, his connections with the Society were severed in 1576-1577.[46]

About 1565 the educational beginnings were made, at Limerick. But English pressure made the school take to the road and settle temporarily at Kilmallock, Clonmel, and Youghal during the next fifteen years, developing in the process that "itinerant," "straggling" school system about which Anglican prelates complained. The blood of a martyr marked it in its infancy when on October 25, 1572, the Irish scholastic, Edmund Daniel, died for the faith. In 1564, Daniel and William Good, Englishman and future companion of Antonio Possevino in Sweden, entered Ireland, instructed by the Holy See in its ignorance of

45 T. Corcoran, S.J., *Clongowes Record* (Dublin, 1932), pp. 6-8.

46 M. da Costa, S.J., "The Last Years of a Confessor of the Faith: Father David Wolf," *AHSJ*, XV (1946), 127-143.

the Irish situation, to set up a university modeled on Paris and Louvain. Daniel, known as Edmund the Irishman, taught in the school in Limerick. But the mayor of the town turned informer, Daniel was captured and, when he refused to take the Oath of Royal Supremacy, was hanged, drawn, and quartered at Cork, the first Jesuit to shed his blood for the faith on European soil.[47]

The main hope of the faith in the England of anti-Catholic penal laws lay in the secular priests trained at William Allen's seminary at Douai. Two of these excellently formed men, Thomas Woodhouse and John Nelson, were captured and, while awaiting execution in London Tower, requested that they be admitted into the Society of Jesus. They were the first Jesuit martyrs to die in England, Woodhouse in 1573 and Nelson in 1578. After much urging by Allen, Mercurian decided to create an English Jesuit mission. Just a month and a half before the general died, three Jesuits, Fathers Edmund Campion and Robert Persons and Brother Ralph Emerson, landed in disguise on the coast of Kent. All three were to know the efficiency of the English government's spy system.

Another people for whom Pope Gregory XIII felt deep con- *The Near East* cern were the Maronites, those Christians of Lebanon who were united to Rome since the reign of Innocent III in the high Middle Ages. A war-torn Middle East had made communications between the Maronites and Rome a practical impossibility for centuries, but in 1578 the patriarch notified the pope of his desire to reconfirm the old ties of unity. For this delicate mission Gregory chose two Jesuits, Tommaso Raggio and Giambattista Eliano, both Hebrew and Arabic scholars. The two priests made a survey of religious conditions among the Maronites and discovered that a number of dogmatic errors and erroneous customs had infiltrated their church during these centuries of isolation among Moslem and schismatic peoples. They made their report to Rome, and in 1580 Eliano, this time accompanied by Giovanni Bruno, returned to Syria, conducted a synod in the monastery at Quannobin where, with splendid Maronite cooperation, they corrected the aberrations. Pope Gregory, delighted by the success of the mission, founded in Rome the Maronite College and placed it under the supervision of the Society.[48]

47 Brodrick, *The Progress of the Jesuits,* pp. 234-235.
48 Pastor, *History,* XX, 491-494.

The Far East   Luis Gonçalves da Câmara, in a letter of May, 1561, expressed to Nadal his wonder at the missionary challenge which
faced the Province of Portugal. With the Tordesillas line of
Pope Alexander VI in mind, he saw in the Indies, the Moluccas,
Japan, China, and along the coast line of Brazil and Africa,
millions who depended on the zeal of the Portuguese to receive
the light of faith. To this challenge the Jesuits of Portugal,
aided by other nationalities, responded with distinction, and
place names like Goa, Malacca, Yamaguchi, Macao, Belém, Rio
de Janeiro, Luanda became as familiar in the records of the
Society as Naples, Augsburg, Cologne, Valladolid, and Coimbra.

Of all the fields within the Portuguese sphere of influence the
Orient attracted the greatest number of missionaries. St. Francis
Xavier, whose letters raised the eyes of many a Jesuit beyond
the confines of Europe, turned out to have been the bellwether
in a vast migration of priests, scholastics, and brothers to the
lands of the Far East. At first the groups were small, three, four,
or five men. In 1574, however, forty-two, of whom thirty were
Spaniards and six Italians, assembled at Lisbon for the sailing.
In 1578 fourteen sailed; in 1579, twelve, in 1581, fourteen.[49]

This mounting number of men, scattered over vast areas,
made careful coordination of efforts imperative. On September
6, 1574, Alessandro Valignano arrived at Goa as visitor and
began to apply to the complex problems of the missions his
powerful organizational ability and breadth of understanding.
This thirty-five-year-old native of Chieti, tall and handsome, intelligent and resourceful, labored for thirty-two years in the
Orient and left his stamp on the Church in India, Japan and
China. The name of Xavier evokes memories of the origins and
early expansion of the Jesuit missions in the Far East. That of
Valignano recalls the succeeding era of consolidation.

An impetuous and choleric temperament somewhat marred
this great Italian's government. With a tendency for facile gen-
eralizations he expressed little regard for the Portuguese. The
Indians, in contrast with the Japanese and Chinese, had so little
merit in his eyes that he ruled against accepting them into the
Society. About 450 of his documents have survived. They provide an interesting study of a human mind. Events in the Far
East were in a state of constant flux, and these writings reveal
the evolution and modification of Valignano's judgments as his
knowledge grew through thirty-three years in the Orient.[50]

49 Rodrigues, *História,* II, ii, 453-461.
50 *DocInd,* IX, 19*-20*.

The Society's Indian experience of the previous thirty-two years Valignano studied carefully. Virtue and defect blended in this experience. The years 1571-1572 brought a dreadful epidemic to Goa. Students at the Jesuit College of St. Paul cared for the sick. Many died, joining in a bond of Christian charity several of their teachers who also made the supreme sacrifice. About forty Jesuits of the Indian province died in the four-year period, 1569-1573, some at sea, others during the plague.[51] On the Fishery Coast Father Henrique Henriques was finishing half of his more than fifty years among the Paravas. His letters reflect the beautiful unobtrusive spirit of this tireless missionary, who supplemented his labors with one of the first Konkani grammars to be published. In such unselfishness Valignano could not help but find encouragement. But he also recognized deficiencies. A number of Jesuits came to India unprepared for the work there. Some, Valignano felt, volunteered and were sent just to get a change. He therefore insisted on a careful evaluation of the qualifications of the men before their assignment to the missions.[52]

After Valignano had left for Macao and Japan a great new vista opened for the Jesuits of India in 1579. From Akbar, great mogul of an empire touching the Himalayas in the north and reaching from Bengal to Kabul and beyond, came an embassy with a request for some Jesuits to explain Christianity. This intelligent and religiously inclined potentate had brought to his capital at Fatehpur Persian, Moslem, and Brahmin theologians to argue in his presence the truth of their creeds. He now wanted to hear the Christian side. The vision of the great mogul, baptized and starting a massive turning to the Church of India's interior, was overwhelming. Three fathers were chosen for this exciting mission, Rodolfo Aquaviva, thirty-year-old, gentle and prayerful nephew of Claudio Aquaviva, Francisco Henriquez, Persian convert from Islam, and Antonio de Monserrate, a Catalonian. They left Goa on November 17, 1579, and three and a half months later arrived at enchanting Fatehpur.

The debates were ceremoniously conducted in a magnificent assembly hall, in the center of which stood a richly decorated pillar which was the focal point for four graceful bridges that led to four galleries. In these galleries sat the spokesmen for four religions, Mohammedan Mullahs, Persian Sufis, Hindu Brah-

51 Ibid., VIII, 11°-12°.
52 J. Humbert, S.J., in a review (*AHSJ*, XXXVI [1967], 176-179) of *DocInd*, VIII and IX.

mins, and the Jesuits, all looking down to the throne on which sat the powerful ruler whose intelligence they aimed to win. Aquaviva, for all his mildness, was a vehement debater, and Akbar had to caution him against offending the sensitivities of his adversaries. The debates dragged on, and after seven months Aquaviva wrote to Goa that the Mohammedans had not budged a fraction from their positions. Akbar, who openly displayed his kind feelings for Aquaviva by publicly walking with him with his arm about his neck, confided to the priest that the mysteries of the Trinity and the Incarnation were the stumbling blocks to his acceptance of Christianity. Then the debates were abruptly suspended. Toward the end of 1580 a rebellion broke out in Kabul. Akbar prepared for war, Henriquez returned to Goa and Monserrate accompanied the army. Aquaviva remained at Fatehpur, devoting his time to the study of Persian, to prayer, and penance.

A year and a half earlier, on July 25, 1579, Alessandro Valignano landed in Japan to start his visitation of the Jesuit mission there. Momentous changes in the national life of the country had taken place since Francis Xavier left Father Torres and Brother Fernández there twenty-eight years before, and these changes had extensive influence on the work of the Society there. The Japan Xavier left was literally *Sengoku*, the "Country at War." The feudal chaos, caused by the constant shifting of the sixty-six provinces in a bewildering series of alliances, worked both for and against the Jesuits, balancing, on the one hand, a friendly reception in one province against a hostile one in another, but on the other hand, seriously obstructing by the constant imminence of war the stability of the mission. Ten years before Valignano arrived, it had been clear that Japan was leaving behind the era of sectional conflict and, under the aegis of a strong ruler, Oda Nobunaga, was on the road to national cohesion and unity. The fortunes of Christianity, like so many other strands in Japan's life, were falling into the hands of this central figure.

The Jesuit reinforcements, who had brought the total to fifty-nine men, of whom twenty-eight were priests, when Valignano arrived, included such resourceful and able men as Baltasar Gago, Gaspar Vilela, Luís Frois, and Brother Luís de Almeida. These men learned by personal experience the heartache of trying to teach Christianity in a turbulent, restless society. At Yamaguchi, for example, some 1,500 had received baptism, but a revolution in 1556 brought in a hostile daimyo, and twenty years passed before a priest could again reside there. On the island of Hirado, Gago baptized within a month about 1,400 persons. In 1560 the daimyo, hitherto friendly, changed colors and launched a persecution against the Catholics. At Miyako Vilela's initial successes, supported by an official carte-blanche to preach, were checkmated by political and military unrest in 1561, in 1563, and from 1565 to 1569.[53]

The demands on the fortitude and courage of the Jesuits were great. Loneliness amid a strange and often hostile people was perhaps the greatest hardship. For six years Vilela did not see a fellow European, and for three years, because he could not obtain the necessary articles, he was not able to say Mass. Gago received but one letter from Goa in six years. He had to flee Hakata when 2,000 ruffians in an outbreak of violence stormed the city, only to fall into the hands of bandits, who for three months held him captive and threatened him with death. His nerves shattered by these experiences, the broken man had to return to India in 1561.[54]

By 1569 the formidable figure of Oda Nobunaga was rising above the country and putting together its fragments. In April of that year this masterful and feared leader gave an interview to Luís Frois at Miyako. For two hours Nobunaga, seated on a drawbridge as he superintended the work of construction of a castle, spoke familiarly with Frois. The prince clearly liked the Jesuit, and with this rather informal meeting began a remarkable friendship between a declared agnostic and a Christian missionary which promised well for the future of the Church in Japan.[55]

A year later Francisco Cabral replaced Xavier's first companion, Cosme de Torres, as superior of the mission. Cabral had the strong conviction that the advance of the Church's work could best be attained by the conversion of the princes, since for their subjects the will of the prince was law. A new phase in the Jesuit work opened when between 1570 and 1578, as more and more princes received baptism, a mass movement toward the Church developed. In 1571 Gaspar Vilela, worn-out veteran of seventeen years on the mission, left for Goa, estimating that there were 30,000 Catholics in Japan. Eight years later the number was 150,000.

---

53 J. Laures, S.J., *The Catholic Church in Japan* (Tokyo, 1954), pp. 43-47; 54-57.
54 Ibid., pp. 38-40, 46.
55 C. R. Boxer, *The Christian Century in Japan, 1549–1650* (Berkeley, 1951), pp. 59-60.

These figures are, however, equivocal and evasive. In such large proportions they certainly do not represent a bloc of Catholics unselfishly committed to the faith and free of all unworthy motivation. The profession of Christianity became for several princes who wanted to participate in the Portuguese trade a convenient cord to bind an understanding with the western merchants. Velvet caps, Cordovan leather, fine glassware, and especially coveted Chinese silk, supplanted principles of religious profession. Many of the general population accepted Christianity because it was imposed from above by their princes. Striking examples of mass conversions were at Omura, Amakusa, and Bungo. At Omura the daimyo Sumitada, baptized in 1563, decided in 1574 to crush paganism. With exile decreed for pagans, twenty thousand received baptism in 1575. In 1577 Sumitada had not a single pagan under him in a community of fifty to sixty thousand. At Amakusa, where in 1571 there were only forty Catholics, there were by 1579, following the baptism of the prince and princess, ten thousand, the entire population of the fief. In Bungo progress had been slow. But upon the conversion of the lord, Sorin, in 1578, the number of Catholics rose from 2,500 to 6,000 in a year.[56]

Many of these conversions were deeply sincere, but no one could look into the seeds of time and say which grain would grow and which not. Valignano readily recognized that it was the Portuguese carrack, loaded with wares, which was emerging as a cardinal problem in the work of the Jesuits in Japan.[57]

The world of learning owes a great debt to these pioneer Jesuits, for it is largely through their voluminous writings, both in formal history and in correspondence, that the important developments in Japan's political life in this era were recorded. The only Europeans who viewed the process at close range, they have given a picture that is far more reliable than that drawn by the national records. Frois wrote a lengthy history. His letters, and those of Gago, Vilela, and Organtino Gnecchi-Soldi, gave vivid descriptions of the staggering beauty of the palaces, distinguished by their superb cedarwood, gold-leaf decorations, and gleaming mirrors. They portrayed at length Buddhist festivals, temples, the national character. So complete were these descriptions that the Roman editors of the reports, objecting to what they termed the "prolix and detailed" nature of the letters and in reproof of such "unedifying" pictures of Buddhist sects

---

56 Laures, *Catholic Church in Japan*, pp. 86-87, 92-93.
57 Boxer, *The Christian Century*, pp. 92-99.

and temples, quite ruthlessly wielded the censor's pencil. But scholars of recent times, in the editing of hitherto unpublished reports, have repaired somewhat the mutilations of an earlier day, and, with the danger of disedification now quite remote, have shown the Jesuits in Japan to have been most intelligent and acute reporters.[58]

The missions to Africa were in four different areas: Ethiopia, Egypt, about the Zambesi river, and Angola. The first three, in- spired one way or another by misinformation and even decep- tion, started the Jesuits on the vain search for the pot of spiritual gold at the end of the rainbow.

In Ethiopia, by his protestations of desire to lead his Monoph- ysite people into the Catholic Church, the Emperor Claudius had set in motion the wheels of the Jesuit mission to his coun- try. But, as seen in the previous chapter, the Jesuit delegation of 1555 to the emperor unveiled the emptiness of his high- sounding assurances. Nevertheless Andrés de Oviedo, auxiliary bishop to João Nunes Barreto, the patriarch, in a gallant effort to rescue the mission from utter collapse, set out to find some possible strand of sincere purpose in the emperor's thinking by which he might tie the Ethiopian Church to Rome. In 1557 he led a party of five Jesuits to the royal court. It was the start of an effort of forty years, fertile only in the superb personal hero- ism of these six men. Oviedo debated with the Monophysite theologians, wrote a work entitled *The Primacy of the Roman Church*, but all he gained from Claudius was angry opposition. Claudius' successor banished him to the desert for his success in making some converts. To Pope Pius V, who thought of termi- nating the enterprise, Oviedo sent a beautiful protest in terms of Christ's love for a single soul. In 1577, after twenty years of searing hardship, the heroic bishop died. Two of his companions had preceded him, both murdered, one by robbers, the other by Turks. The three others stayed to the end in the desolate wasteland, the last, the loveable and childlike Francisco Lopez, dying in 1597, twenty years after Oviedo and forty years since they all had first gone to the court of Claudius.[59]

Concurrently with Oviedo's mission, Jesuits were trying, on another and more civilized front, to undo the work of the Mo- nophysites. In 1561 Cristóbal Rodríguez and Giambattista Eliano, a convert from Judaism, arrived in Alexandria as repre-

58 Ibid., 49-56.
59 Brodrick, *The Progress of the Jesuits*, pp. 263-267.

sentatives of the Holy See to hold conversations with the patriarch, Gabriel VII. Gabriel had been reported to desire to negotiate reunion of the Egyptian Church with Rome. This mission started with the appearance in the Eternal City of a genial Syrian named Abraham who, impressively armed with credentials, claimed to be spokesman for the patriarch in his desire to bring his flock into the Catholic Church. Pope Pius IV requested the Jesuits to undertake this delicate task. Laynez sent Rodríguez and Eliano to Egypt. All the fond hopes of repairing the damage done by Dioscorus in the fifth century suddenly withered with the discovery of the fantastic plot by which the patriarch, who had not the slightest intention of submitting to the pope, had issued the credentials to Abraham merely to facilitate the Syrian's realization of his strong desire to see the sights of Rome. With this strange episode the Jesuits became for the first time participants in the sad and baffling history of relations between Rome and the schismatic churches of the East.[60]

The mission to the Makaranga tribes in the southeastern part of the continent originated with an appeal for a priest by Gamba, chief of the country around Inhambane. Gamba's appeal was occasioned by contacts which his sons had made with the Portuguese at Mozambique. When word reached Goa, the Jesuits organized a party of three under a man of unusually severe penance and mortification, the thirty-four-year-old Portuguese, Gonçalo da Silveira. By February, 1560, the three were at Mozambique. Sickness forced one to return to India, but within a short while Silveira and Andrés Fernández had arrived at Otonguu where in seven weeks they baptized 450 natives.

Popular tales, which circulated among the Portuguese merchants, about a tremendous empire near the Zambesi, where palaces were built of gold, enchanted Silveira and caused him to dream of converting the Monomotápa (the head ruler) and leading all of south Africa into the Church. He left Fernández at Otonguu and after a frightful journey arrived at the kraal of the Monomotápa only to find, instead of a regal figure in a glittering palace, a dirty, half-naked ruler presiding in a rude hut of poles and grass. His disappointment, keen as it was, did not deflect him from his purpose, and in twenty-five days he had baptized the ruler and his mother. Soon he had brought the Christian population to three hundred.

Success begot its own destruction. Some Moslems in the kraal resented Silveira's presence and, working on the superstitions

60 Ibid., 260-262.

of the fickle emperor, they won him over to a plan to kill the priest. In the evening of March 15, 1561, Silveira prayed for several hours before his crucifix, then about midnight fell asleep. Shortly after, the conspirators had him strangled to death. At Otonguu, Fernández also felt the impact of resentment against success. The preaching of the Catholic faith was outlawed, and with his return to Goa, a wornout invalid, the short Jesuit enterprise was closed.

Two years after Silveira's death, two priests, Francisco de Gouveia and Agostinho de Lacerda, and two brothers entered Angola on the east coast of the continent. Almost from the beginning they met severe reverses. Lacerda soon died. Then the Angolese prince of Dongo, claiming that he could not live without Gouveia, held him captive for fourteen years, until the Jesuit died on June 19, 1575. Only four months before Gouveia's death did the first reinforcements arrive, when on February 11 two priests, Garcia Simoes and Baltasar Afonso, and two brothers landed at Luanda.

This new contingent enjoyed considerable success among the Angolese. After first learning the language, within three years they converted two hundred natives to Christianity. By 1593 they counted 8,000 Christians. They made the baptismal ceremony, a pivotal event in their apostolate, solemn and impressive. Afonso, writing of the seventy who were baptized on the octave of Easter, 1578, described the immense wonder of the Angolese as the new Christians marched in procession with lighted candles and palm branches in their hands. Describing one of his excursions up the Cuanza river, he told of a ceremony of six hours during which he baptized nearly four hundred. Then followed the general casting of idols into the flames as the natives raised their voices in demand that the devil depart from their land. Despite the promise of this mission, reinforcements were few. Only in February, 1580, did two more Jesuits arrive.[61]

In the western hemisphere the structure of the mission in Brazil, well-founded and strong, still had as its two main pillars *Brazil and Spanish America* Manuel da Nóbrega and José de Anchieta. In his *Chronicle of the Society of Jesus in the State of Brazil* (1663), Simão Vasconcellos, a seventeenth century Jesuit, included an attractive frontispiece, a cut showing, amid a border of Brazilian fauna and flora, a ship, which represents the Society, in full sail toward the New World. On the ship, among a group of Jesuits, stands

61 Rodrigues, *História*, I, ii, 556-558; II, ii, 505-515.

Manuel da Nóbrega, holding aloft the standard of the Society of Jesus. And on one of the sails appear the words: *Unus Non Sufficit Orbis* — One world is not big enough for them. Daring, mettle, optimism shine from the picture. And this was the spirit of the early Brazilian mission. The number of Jesuits grew steadily, but Anchieta warned them at Coimbra that fervent feelings were not enough to carry a missionary through the obstacles in Brazil. "You have to come with a bag full of virtues," he insisted.[62]

The broad scope of action continued to be twofold in nature: the seacoast towns and the deep forests. In the towns the schools carried on, and in some instances expanded. At Bahía in 1572 the college introduced philosophy into its curriculum; in 1575 it granted its first bachelor's degree; in 1578 it conferred five master's degrees. Important for the urban aspect of the colony was the year 1566. In August the Portuguese, by a momentous siege, wrested from the French a strong bastion which they had installed at Rio de Janeiro. Nóbrega and Anchieta were present during the siege and capture of this key installation. Nóbrega, in another instance of his vision, moved the Jesuit headquarters from São Paulo to Rio, erected a novitiate and house of studies on land overlooking the magnificent harbor, and became by his encouragement to the Portuguese colonists and his mollifying influence on the nearby Tamoyas the soul of the new settlement. Anchieta, by his ample and detailed accounts of its origins, wrote "the baptismal certificate of Rio." [63]

Among the natives of the forests the objective of the Jesuits remained basically simple: the settlement of the Indians in fixed communities, known as *aldeias,* where by life in a stable social body they could be weaned from their superstition, cannibalism and ferocity, and instructed in the faith. Anchieta made this transformation a joyful one as he kept up his amazing output of lively, vivid, and colorful religious plays and hymns. Indians learned to narrate, dramatize, play the flute. They sang their way into the Church. Even as he was molding the spiritual temper of early Brazil, Anchieta was laying the foundations for a national literature.

Tragedy struck the mission in 1570. On July 15, off the Canary Islands, French Calvinists murdered forty Jesuits who were sailing to Brazil. Ignácio de Azevedo had been visitor of the mission and, after personal experience of the vastness of the enterprise,

---

62 *MonBras,* II, 161-162.
63 Helen Dominion, *Apostle of Brazil* (New York, 1958), pp. 232-233.

returned to Europe for more men. On July 2, 1570, seventy-three Jesuits under his leadership sailed from Lisbon in three ships. The Huguenot pirate, Jacques Sores, overtook Azevedo's ship off the Canaries and butchered the superior and thirty-nine of his companions. In the short period of 1570-1571 twelve other Brazil-bound Jesuits fell victims of French corsairs. And in Brazil itself, in October, 1570, death took the great Nóbrega, only fifty-three years of age and after twenty-one years in the mission, including ten years of intelligent and inspiring guidance as superior.

This period closes with Anchieta as provincial. His long letters to Rome remain treasure chests of information about the country and its peoples. Keenly attentive to details of geography, climate, nature, he gave Europeans vivid descriptions of a fascinating variety of trees, herbs, foliage, streams, birds, flowers. As provincial this forty-three-year-old cripple had, within two years, gone from Bahía northward along the coast a thousand miles, back again, then another thousand miles south to São Vicente. His advice to his brother Jesuits at Coimbra was: "Work is medicine." Work was indeed the hallmark of the Jesuits on this vast mission.

The Spanish Jesuits were seventeen years behind their Portuguese brethren in missionary work in the western hemisphere. But once started, they moved rapidly. Beginning in 1566 they had within six years entered three major areas of New Spain: Florida, Mexico, and Peru. The mission to Florida failed; those to Mexico and Peru prospered wonderfully.

In 1566 the hard and ruthless founder of St. Augustine in Florida, Pedro Menéndez de Avilés, requested the Society to evangelize the natives of the land he depicted as nothing less than a luxuriant paradise. Three were assigned, Fathers Pedro Martínez and Juan Rogel and Brother Villareal. Lost in unfamiliar American waters in a vain search for St. Augustine, their ship wandered along the Florida coast, which by its dense wilderness, insect-infested shores, and primitive peoples in no way resembled Menéndez' land of flora. On October 6 Martínez went ashore to reconnoitre and was killed by the Indians, the first Jesuit martyr of North America.[64] Rogel and Brother Villareal stopped at a settlement called Fort Tequesta, and after a year's work with the natives could not point to a single convert.

---

64 F. Zubillaga, S.J., *La Florida. La Misión Jesuítica (1566–1572) y la Colonización Española* (Rome, 1941), pp. 239-244.

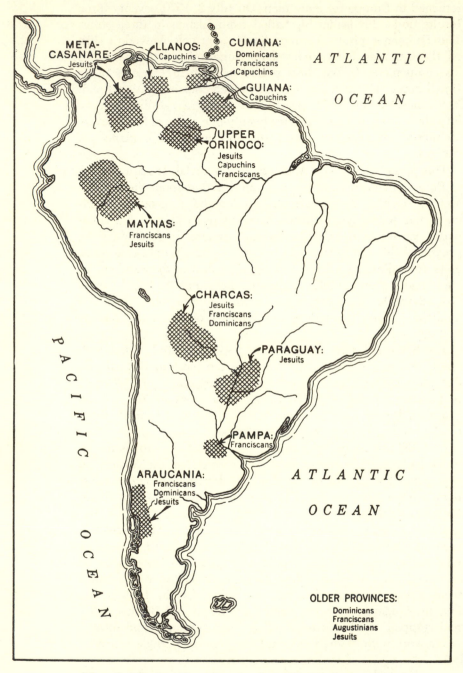

Map 2. Mission Frontiers in Spanish South America

Reproduced, by permission, from John Francis Bannon, S.J., *History of the Americas*. Volume I, *The Colonial Americas*, page 352. Copyright 1963 by the McGraw-Hill Book Company, Inc.

Soon six more Jesuits, including Juan Segura and Antonio Sedeño, arrived in Florida. Appalled by the frightful conditions they encountered, they withdrew to Havana to assess the situation. Florida's loss became Cuba's gain, for one result of this temporary retreat was the opening of a college at Havana. In September, 1570, Segura returned to the mainland, leading a group of seven other Jesuits in an expedition which ended in murder. Somehow or other — the sources are not clear — the Spaniards contacted an Indian, Don Luís, chief in an area called Ajacán, somewhere between the two rivers now known as the James and the York. At Don Luís' invitation Segura undertook a mission to Ajacán. He and his companions debarked on September 10, 1570, and settled at a point probably near the south shore of the York. Don Luís helped the missionaries to become established. Then he abandoned them. Starvation was imminent. On February 4, 1571, the chief and other Indians murdered two of the Jesuits who had gone to him for food. On the 9th he led the slaughter of the rest. This martyrdom of eight Spanish Jesuits, thirty-six years before the founding of Jamestown, has a vivid place in the dawn of Virginia's history.[65]

At Santa Elena three fathers and a brother, during an entire year, baptized only seven natives. Rogel and Sedeño advised the general, Francis Borgia, to send his men elsewhere, a suggestion which coincided with a request from Philip II for Jesuits to work in Mexico.

This deflection to Mexico was a happy one. Sedeño led the way, followed by Rogel and a fresh group of fifteen from Spain under Pedro Sánchez, who entered Mexico City on September 28, 1572. Within two years the Society had, with its church and school for six hundred boys in Mexico City and schools at Oaxaca and Patzcuaro, entered into the spiritual and cultural life of this important colony.

Meanwhile, to the southwest, five years before the transfer to Mexico, Jesuits from Spain opened a new mission. In 1567 the four provinces of Spain each assigned two men to the land made fabulous by Francisco Pizarro, Peru. In the steady flow of reinforcements to Peru were some exceptional priests who combined within them the dashing qualities of the explorer and the intellectual curiosity of the scholar. Alonso Barzana arrived in 1569, penetrated into the wilds of upper Peru, then into the eastern

---

65 C. M. Lewis, S.J. and A. J. Loomie, S.J., *The Spanish Jesuit Mission in Virginia, 1570-1572* (Chapel Hill, 1953), pp. 45-46.

valleys of the Andes, and produced as the fruit of his exploits a grammar, a lexicon, and a prayerbook in five Indian dialects. Diego Gonzáles Holguin became official interpreter for the colonial government in the Quechuran, Puquinan, and Aymaran languages, and with Diego de Torres Rubio, another master of the native tongues, wrote the basic works for the study of Peruvian dialects. José de Acosta, a young and gifted superior, gathered on his long journeys between Jesuit houses much information about the culture of the Indians and with this composed his monumental and authoritative *A Natural and Moral History of the Indies* (1590).

More enduring in influence than these individual Jesuits was the Society's college of San Pablo, founded in Lima in 1568. The oldest Jesuit school in Spanish America, San Pablo played a widely varied role, that of channel for the intellectual currents which came from Europe, nerve center for the Society's administration in the viceroyalty of Peru, mother of other Jesuit colleges, and research laboratory in medicine. For two centuries San Pablo sparked the cultural life of Peru.[66]

Conclusion   By 1580 Europe, Catholic and Protestant, could not but notice that a new spiritual force had entered the world. The Society then numbered 5,000. Two ministries especially forged ahead in their claims on Jesuit attention: the schools and the foreign missions. Jesuits conducted 144 colleges and wound about the world a band of mission stations which stretched from Japan, through the East Indies, Africa, and Latin America. A pattern for the future had been set. By this time it had become clear that the Society's fortunes would frequently depend on the temper of the political and social structure within which it lived. Its apostolic spirit threw it into the real, actual world of the current moment, and therefore such potent realities as the bureaucracy of Philip II, the Gallicanism of France, the Royal Patronages of Spain and Portugal shaped its day-to-day progress, setbacks, satisfactions, and frustrations. These augured an eventful future for the Society, assuring it that changes would always be just around the corner.

66 L. Martín, *The Intellectual Conquest of Peru. The Jesuit College of San Pablo, 1568–1767* (New York, 1968), pp. 145-146.

RAPID GROWTH AND FRESH ENTERPRISES

1580–1615

THE FIFTH GENERAL of the Society was Claudio Aquaviva, whose term of thirty-three years and. eleven months has been the longest in the history of the order. The Fourth General Congregation convened in Rome on February 7, 1581. Olivier Mannaerts, the vicar-general, and some other fathers visited Pope Gregory XIII to ask his blessing on the business of the congregation. Solemnly the pope addressed his callers: "Your holy order, and it is indeed a holy order, is spread throughout the entire world. Anywhere you look you have colleges and houses. You direct kingdoms, provinces, indeed the whole world. In short, there is in this day no single instrument raised up by God against heretics greater than your holy order. It came into the world at the very moment when new errors began to be spread abroad. It is all important therefore for the good of princes and peoples (and we desire to add, of Ourselves too) that this order increase and prosper from day to day, and above all that it be governed by good superiors. . . . Reflect that you hold in your hands a most serious business and that you are accountable to God for its outcome. Be sure of this: in the whole course of your lives you will not handle a business of such gravity and importance as this. . . ."[1]

The General, Claudio Aquaviva, 1581–1615

The congregation chose the thirty-seven-year-old provincial of Rome, who had been in the Society only fourteen years, Claudio Aquaviva. Son of the duca di Atri, educated in humanities, philosophy, theology, and law, ordained priest and well-placed in the inner circles of the Vatican, this highly intelligent man joined the Society in July, 1567, at twenty-four years of age. After his novitiate and a short period of teaching philosophy he was appointed successively rector at Naples, superior of the Neapolitan Province, then of the Roman Province.

1 Astráin, *Historia*, III, 209-210.

The problems which Aquaviva had to handle through the years were staggeringly complex: that of keeping pure and authentic the ideals and purpose of St. Ignatius as the number of Jesuits almost tripled, rising from 5,000 to 13,000; that of smooth organization as schools multiplied from 144 to 372, residences from 33 to 123, provinces from 21 to 32; that of the adaptation of the Catholic faith to the native cultures in China and India; that of the codification of Jesuit educational procedures; that of directing the expansion of the foreign missions.

Pre-eminent among the many accomplishments of this versatile superior was his preservation of the Ignatian character of the Society. A small group of disaffected Jesuits brought the Institute to the brink of destruction, but Aquaviva, by his clear grasp of the issues and his sure understanding of St. Ignatius' purpose, by his doggedness and skill, even though he reflected in his mode of governing the Roman milieu of increased legislative centralization, kept his inheritance intact. This struggle moreover had an ever broader significance. By bringing Aquaviva into direct confrontation with two of the most autocratic institutions in Europe, the Spanish monarchy and the Spanish Inquisition, it placed the general in the lists for the cause of freedom against arbitrary rule. Basically, the crown and Inquisition of Spain endeavored to restrain the Society's freedom to be what it wanted to be. In his courageous denial to them of their desired prey, Aquaviva scored a quite surprising victory for liberty within the Church.

The Society in Spain was the spawning ground of these troubles. There a few members, influenced in part by the strong spirit of Hispanicism stirred up earlier by Antonio de Araoz, attempted to alter radically the Society's *Constitutions.* Among the several changes which they envisaged, two were especially serious: a fundamental curtailment of the general's office, including the power to appoint provincials and rectors; and the creation of provincial chapters which would be invested with the right to make these appointments. These discontented men by their propaganda in Spain aroused the suspicions of the Inquisition, and by a series of slanted and unjust memorials to Rome stirred up uneasiness about the order in the minds of two popes, Sixtus V and Clement VIII.

Sixtus V concurred in a plan clandestinely evolved by the dissident Jesuits. These priests persuaded King Philip that what the Society in Spain needed was a visitation by a bishop. The royal diplomatic service worked with great secrecy, and Sixtus V appointed Jerónimo Manrique, bishop of Cartagena, as visitor. Dionisio Vázquez, one of the disgruntled Jesuits, recommended that the visitation be conducted according to the secret procedure of the Inquisition. Enrique Enríquez, another of this small band, urged that the visitor be invested with the faculty to change the Society's Institute. King Philip, shaping his instructions in accord with these recommendations, directed that the inquisitional method be adopted and that among the features of Jesuit life on which attention should be especially focused were the general's power to appoint local superiors and the dependence on Rome in government.

Aquaviva discerned the destructive purpose behind the respectable facade of an episcopal visitation. With skill and tenacity he carried out his defensive campaign. He directed each of the provincials of Spain and Portugal to draw up representations against the visitation, have them signed by the best known of the professed fathers, and then present them to the king, as forceful evidence for Philip to see where Jesuit solidarity truly lay and to recognize the agitators as the small but articulate minority they really were. Aquaviva added his own protest to Philip. He also went to Sixtus V and showed the pope that the visitation by Manrique could readily result in the removal of the Spanish Jesuits from the control of Rome by a powerful and jealous monarchy. Sixtus was impressed. But still he hesitated. Aquaviva then proposed a further argument. He pointed out the impropriety of a visitation being made by a bishop who in his youth had become the father of three bastards. That was enough for the bluff, reform-minded pope. He canceled the visitation. Aquaviva then filled the vacuum by designating three Jesuits, including the skilled missionary of many years experience in Peru, José de Acosta, as visitors to the provinces of Spain and Portugal.

Sixtus V however still had misgivings about the Society's structure and decided that the Roman Inquisition should examine the *Constitutions*. Aquaviva, knowing that no more eloquent defense of the Society could be voiced than by the bishops and princes with whom the Society was laboring throughout Europe, requested testimonials from them. Letters poured into Rome from all quarters, lavish in praise of what the Jesuits meant to the Church. Clearly and intelligently Aquaviva answered the difficulties which the inquisitors had about such points in Jesuit life as the omission of regular penances, the manifestation of conscience by the subject to his superior, the nature of the vows of the scholastics. Sixtus V was satisfied, save for one point, the title "Society of Jesus." For an order to bear the name of the Divine Master was, he felt, a sign of pride. He therefore instructed Aquaviva to address to him a formal request that the title be changed. Aquaviva did so. Sixtus placed the decree for the change on his desk for further examination. Death took the pope on August 27, 1590, the document never having been published. The following year Pope Gregory XIV issued two bulls confirming the Society's Institute.[2]

During the reign of Clement VIII (1592-1605) troubles rose again, and Aquaviva had to meet three major attacks on the essential structure of the Society. First, the Spanish malcontents demanded the summoning of a general congregation, in which they planned to strip the general of his powers. They committed the execution of their scheme to a man in whom Aquaviva had earlier placed his confidence, José de Acosta. Acosta, successful missionary in Peru and recent visitor in Spain, felt deep resentment because he had not been appointed provincial. He went to Rome, and unknown to Aquaviva had an audience with Pope Clement VIII, to whom he explained the unrest among the Spanish Jesuits as attributable to the worldliness of superiors and the vast power invested in the general. The remedy, he insisted, was in a general congregation. Pope Clement, a seriously conscientious man and genuinely disturbed by Acosta's story, ordered Aquaviva to summon a general congregation.

Aquaviva recognized the hidden objective to transform St. Ignatius' basic concept of the role and function of the general in the Society. Almost immediately this design met rebuff. In the provincial congregations, convened to elect delegates to the general congregation, no one of the alienated group was chosen. In another tactic, aimed at getting control of the conduct of the general congregation, the intriguers enlisted the sympathy and help of a Spanish Jesuit in Rome, the brilliant but dour theologian and critic of Aquaviva, Francisco de Toledo. With a view of putting the management of the congregation's machinery in Toledo's hands, Acosta suggested to Philip that he request Pope Clement to make Toledo a cardinal. Then the pontiff was asked to designate Toledo as presiding officer of the congregation. Clement gave Toledo the red hat, but Aquaviva by his superb tact convinced the pope to set aside the plan to have the new cardinal conduct the congregation.

The Fifth General Congregation, of such ominous origins, opened on November 3, 1593. The pope's message was sombre:

2 Ibid., 402-420, 434-448, 453-461, 471-475.

reports had reached him that the Society had fallen from its pristine fervor; he wanted the assembled fathers to provide a remedy. At Aquaviva's personal insistence, a committee, which gave a month to its work, examined his conduct as general. The report, aside from pointing out a tendency to overtenacity in his own judgment and an occasional manifestation of favoritism, completely vindicated Aquaviva. The Spanish ambassador at Rome, the duque de Sessa, presented a memorial which called for changes in the *Constitutions,* but by unanimous vote the delegates rejected the diplomat's intrusion.

Then the congregation decided to lay the ax to the root of the trouble. Of the twenty-seven Jesuits who composed memorials against the *Constitutions* of the Society, twenty-five were of either Jewish or Moorish descent. Feeling that in sheer self-defense the time had come for drastic action, the congregation stamped the disaffected Spaniards as "false sons," decreed their dismissal from the Society, and decided that henceforth Jewish and Arabic origins barred admission into the order.[3] By this severe legislation directed against Jews and Moors the congregation adopted the Iberian norm for respectability, *limpieza de sangre,* as an essential of Jesuit identity. This was utterly alien to the thought of Saint Ignatius. Gradually through the years later congregations eased this impediment to entrance into the Society, until finally in 1946 it was completely removed.

Toledo, Acosta, and Sessa made other sly but unavailing maneuvers, and when the congregation closed its sessions after two and a half months of business, the office of general remained intact and the loyalty of the Society to Aquaviva was beyond question. The meaning of this triumph was nothing less than the preservation of the Ignatian character of the Society. The chief architect of this victory was Aquaviva who, sure and steady in his grasp of Ignatius' thought, realized what was at stake. A less perceptive man might have compromised in the hope of buying peace. The forces ranged against him were, ultimately, among the mightiest in Christendom, the Spanish monarchy and the Spanish Inquisition. And a less intrepid man might have fallen back before the colossal force of the opposition. This victory had a dimension that went beyond the Society. It demonstrated that the shackles of a powerful institution within Christendom could be cut. Though he did not stand before Europe in the role of a pathfinder in humanity's press toward liberty,

3 Ibid., 516-531, 573-576, 580-597.

Aquaviva nevertheless won for the Society the freedom to determine its own character.

But the crises were not over. A second arose from the lingering doubts in the mind of Clement VIII about the wisdom of a lifetime term for the general. The pope indicated that an immediate solution for this problem, in so far as it personally touched Aquaviva, would be in his appointment as archbishop of Naples. Some Jesuits asked Cardinal Toledo, who boasted of his influence with Clement, to try to dissuade the pope. Toledo refused. Then João Alvarez, the Portuguese assistant, by a deft observation impelled Toledo to reconsider. He intimated that, if Aquaviva were made archbishop, the many princes who so admired the general would urge that he be made a cardinal. Toledo, distinctly unhappy at the thought of having Aquaviva as a companion in the Sacred College, went to the pope and proved that his boasts about his influence with Clement were not empty by persuading him to leave Aquaviva in the general's post.

A third crisis originated in the malice of an individual who had behind him the massive might of the Spanish court. Fernando Mendoza was a recalcitrant Jesuit who had become a friend of the conde de Lemos and was the confessor of the condesa de Lemos, the latter being the sister of the duque de Lerma, the power behind the throne of Philip III. Time and again Aquaviva tried to detach Mendoza from the court, only to meet with defeat. Then Mendoza took the offensive against his superior. Through Lerma he had Philip III invite Aquaviva to Spain. Aquaviva recognized the grim danger of falling into the hands of his willful subject and graciously declined the invitation. The king then asked Clement VIII to order the general to Spain. The pope did so. Under this severe pressure Aquaviva's health broke and he became seriously ill. Clement sent his own physician to check on the gravity of the sickness. The papal doctor concurred with seven others that travel was out of the question. By the time Aquaviva recovered Clement had died. The subject of the visit to Spain was dropped and the threat to the general's freedom removed. Mendoza meanwhile was named bishop of Cuzco in Peru.

Two events during 1608-1609, relieving these years of strain and tension, sent a refreshing breeze of peace and joy through the Society. In 1608 the Sixth General Congregation, called at the bidding of the congregation of procurators two years earlier, voiced its confidence in Aquaviva, and the following year, on July 27, Pope Paul V beatified Ignatius of Loyola.

In the preservation of the pristine spirit of the Society Aquaviva did more than just respond to the moves of his critics. Acting positively and constructively, he delineated and organized a practical tradition of spiritual practice based on the principles given by Ignatius. Convinced that the Society's effectiveness rested on the measure of each individual Jesuit's union and familiarity with God, he sent many letters to superiors and to the Society as a whole in which he reiterated, explained, reduced to practice the heritage left by Ignatius, and adapted it to the new circumstances of his own era. In his judgment the Society had fallen away from its initial fervor and impulse toward spiritual excellence. In 1604, and again in 1613, addressing superiors on this subject, he insisted that the cause was certainly not in a want of rules and instructions but in a "failure of execution" of those at hand, and that pious desires and ambitions are of little moment if not translated into deeds, the true sign of love. A subject to which he returned with frequency was "renovation of spirit," that periodic freshening of the interior life so necessary amid work and study. In 1587 he stressed that the preservation of the Society was dependent on a thirst for solid virtue, such as humility, obedience, and charity.[4]

Spiritual excellence faltered as members increased with startling rapidity. Ignatius recognized the possible although not necessary danger in large numbers, and the one reason for which he might have desired to live longer was to make admission into the Society more difficult.[5] To instill in the hearts of so many thousands of individuals the ideals meant by Ignatius for an elite was a formidable task which Aquaviva took on with energy and dedication.

A monumental letter was that of May 8, 1590, on the subject of prayer and penance in the Society. The deep chasm between those who identified the Society's spirit with long prayers and severe austerities and those who emphasized the essential place of apostolic activity was as wide as ever. Aquaviva decided to settle the question once and for all. With forceful directness, keeping clear the apostolic character of the Society, he laid down concise principles: the freedom of each Jesuit, whose formation is complete, to give to prayer and pious reading the time he has after the completion of assigned work; the liberty of those with long experience in mental prayer to choose under the action of the Holy Spirit the form and matter of their

---

4 *DeGuiJes,* pp. 232-233, 237-238.
5 *SdeSI,* I, 444; see also *Cons,* [142-144, 657, 658, 819].

prayer; the absence of constraint on the Jesuit that his prayer, even though directed toward apostolic service, always have an immediate practical aim; the readiness of the Jesuit to sacrifice during his free time the delights of contemplation for the toil of the apostolate; the need to acquire habitual prayerfulness in the midst of labor; moderation in the use of penance, striving for a middle path between neglect and excess in the use of this valuable means of holiness.[6]

Not in letters alone did Aquaviva endeavor to keep high the spiritual tone of the Society. In a little book of enduring value, *Helps to the Cure of Spiritual Sickness for the Use of Superiors in the Society,* he proposed precise and realistic applications of general spiritual principles, and demonstrated how to achieve that happy combination of "suavity and strength" which marked his own manner of governing.

Preoccupation with the preservation of the Society's spiritual heritage, therefore, stamped Aquaviva's long term of office. This concern produced, through the initiative of the general himself and three general congregations, a sizeable corpus of legislation. The general congregation of 1593 insisted on the full two-year period of the novitiate; that of 1608 decreed that each Jesuit must make the Spiritual Exercises annually for a period of eight or ten full days, and that a period of three days of special prayer should precede the biannual renewal of vows by those not yet completely formed. Aquaviva gave a definite and set form to the final year of the Jesuit's training, known as the tertianship.

This legislation flowed from a strong determination to keep the Ignatian ideal luminous and efficacious, but it also hazarded the danger of the formalism and legalism always inherent in the multiplicity of laws. Still more, it risked the loss of clear vision of basic purpose. Subtly this particular peril hurt the tertianship.[7] Aquaviva's instructions for the last year of formation molded this institution into a quasi-monastic pattern with detailed outline of external discipline and emphasis on the individual's dispositions of soul. He shifted from the earlier stress on apostolic involvement in the service of those in need of corporal and spiritual help, an involvement which was at once a probation and a schooling: a probation, in that it served as a final testing of an individual's aptitude for the energetic and labori-

6 *DeGuiJes,* pp. 238-242.
7 A. Ruhan, S.J., "The Origins of the Jesuit Tertianship," *WL,* XCIV (1965), 424-426; see also *ConSJComm,* p. 233, fn. 4 on *Cons,* [514].

ous work entailed in the Jesuit vocation; a schooling, in that it educated the individual in the *schola affectus,* the school of the heart, wherein he grew in the basic denial of self and in humility, so essential to the Jesuit way of life. The general congregation of 1965-1966, recognizing the need to break through to the older pattern, called for three years of experimentation in the several tertianships, after which a comparative study was to be made at a special conference. Guided by this study the general was to draw up an instruction on the last year of probation.

Besides his profound concern for the Society's interior spirit, Aquaviva gave much thought to the order's educational system. No single field of the apostolate so absorbed the energies of the Jesuits as the running of schools. A torrent of requests for colleges poured in on Aquaviva, and in his first three years of office he had to refuse sixty such petitions. By 1593 he had declined one hundred and fifty invitations throughout Europe. At the turn of the century, the Society was conducting two hundred and forty-five schools, and by the time Aquaviva had died the number had risen to three hundred and seventy-two.

The Jesuit Educational System

This conspicuous popularity of the Jesuit schools was another instance in history of an ideal entering into a receptive spiritual and cultural climate. The vogue of humanism had its part in the creation of this milieu. But not an exclusive part. Spiritual reform was also in the air. Since the end of the fifteenth century, the middle class lay people in the towns had been avidly reading the immense output of books about the interior life. A prolongation of the *devotio moderna,* this literature created, at least in part, the intellectual and spiritual dispositions that welcomed the Jesuit schools. In a striking example of historical continuity, the Society carried on the spirit of reform that had been welling up from so many and varied sources in the late Middle Ages.[8]

As important as this multiplication of schools was the completion of the *Plan of Studies (Ratio studiorum)* which Mercurian had inaugurated. This proved to be a slow, exhausting, and painstaking process. In 1584 Aquaviva delegated a committee of six to resume the task. After seven months of concentrated application the committee produced the *Plan and Arrangement of Studies (Ratio atque institutio studiorum),* a diffuse document which lacked the organizational touch of Ledesma and

8 Astráin, *Historia,* IV, 775; Dickens, *The Counter Reformation,* pp. 27-28.

Nadal and which emphasized the philosophical and theological aspects of the program, a reflection of the personal interests of the six committeemen. In 1586 Aquaviva sent it to the provinces for criticism. The committees in the provinces did their work thoroughly and expressed themselves candidly. Their reports, reflecting a wide divergence of opinion and a broad variety of national backgrounds, built up a Matterhorn of paper. Aquaviva kept his reviewers at the task of analyzing, correlating, and synthesizing the reports. A new document came forth in the form of rules for administrators and teachers of the different subjects and classes in the schools, decidedly different in its practicality from the discursive character of the preceding one. In 1591 Aquaviva sent it to the schools for a three-year trial period. Criticism was not so unsparing as that of the earlier edition, and there was hope that a fixed code was within reach. In January, 1599, Aquaviva was at last able to announce that a final document had been prepared. More compact, with 208 pages compared to the 400 of the 1591 edition, this *Plan of Studies* provided the Society's schoolmen with a curriculum and a coherent and graded set of objectives and methods from the class of grammar to theology. It integrated into a tight unity not only the more immediate committee work of fifteen years but also the more remote preparation done by St. Ignatius in the Fourth Part of the *Constitutions,* by Nadal at Messina, and by Ledesma at the Roman College. Through it flowed the wisdom and experience of half a century. The schools wherein the *Plan of Studies* was put into action, even though all did not have the higher faculties of theology and philosophy, became by their stress on the classical languages and their ideal of articulateness in Latin an important part of the European humanistic tradition.

More far reaching even than the schools was the Sodality of the Blessed Virgin Mary. From cities throughout the world flowed a stream of reports about the effectiveness of this instrument for the formation of a spiritual elite in all classes of society. It was common for a single town to have several sodalities, each designed for a particular craft or vocation or social class, artisans, magistrates, students, professional men. Aquaviva gave a decisive turn to the character of this movement.[9] Although Jean Leunis stamped the organization with its Marian character, making Our Lady the guardian of each member, Aquaviva went

9 J. Stierli, S.J., "Devotion to Mary in the Sodality," *WL*, LXXXII (1953), 17-45.

further, and taking a concept reminiscent of feudal fealty which had been grafted onto the original body by Frans de Costere, who had initiated the act of consecration to Mary, identified Our Lady in the Sodality rules of 1587 as the patroness of the sodalist. In a second contribution, Aquaviva obtained canonical recognition of the Sodality by the Holy See. In 1584 Pope Gregory XIII ratified the Sodality of the Roman College as the primary unit to which all other sodalities were to be affiliated, thus creating a world-wide organism which by its intense interior life and apostolic charity provided a higher way of life for thousands. During the two hundred years after the canonical erection of 1584, about 2,500 separate sodalities were affiliated with that at the Roman College.

The death in Italy of two Jesuits broke the last living links with that intimate fellowship formed by St. Ignatius in Paris in the early 1530's and left the destinies of the Society entirely in the hands of the succeeding generation. Alonso Salmerón died at Naples in 1585; Nicolás Bobadilla five years later at Loreto. Their Society of Jesus appealed strongly to the Italian youth, who continued to join the order in large numbers. During the term of Aquaviva the number increased from 1,689 to 2,763, over a thousand in thirty-four years. The colleges and residences rose from forty-two to seventy-five.

To this steady and gratifying development there was one serious check. Friction between the anti-clerical Venetian Republic and the Vatican had been mounting for years, and when in 1606 the breaking-point had been reached and Pope Paul V placed Venice under interdict, the Society, along with the Capuchins and Theatines, stood by the pope. For this loyalty they suffered the penalty of exile. Out of this conflict arose a celebrated debate in which Cardinal Bellarmine was one of the chief figures. Paolo Sarpi was the other. This clever, adroit Servite friar, articulate encourager of the government's anti-clerical program, despised both Rome and the Society and, anticipating the tactics of the rationalists of the Enlightenment, pressed for the ruin of the Society as a step toward the destruction of Rome. To the numerous writings of a team captained by Sarpi, Bellarmine by command of the pope had to make reply. Tediously the exchanges between the two sides went on. Paul V was anxious to restore peace, but the Venetians insisted, as one of their conditions, that the Jesuits should not return. The pope refused. The impasse seemed unbreakable when Aquaviva, with his characteristic breadth of view and sense of proportion, urged the pope not to allow the Society to be an impediment to the goal of peace. Paul acceded to the general, and in 1607 relations between the two states were restored. Another fifty years were to go by before the Society was allowed to reenter the Serene Republic.

St. Ignatius and his companions had themselves started the lively tradition among the Jesuits of popular preaching in Italy. Their successors in this period, especially Giulio Mancinelli, proved themselves worthy of their origins. Mancinelli took the influence of his energetic personality far beyond Italy by a strenuous campaign in dechristianized Dalmatia and a mission to Constantinople where, under the protection of the French ambassador, he reanimated the Latins in the Sublime Porte, inspired interest in reunion with Rome among the Orthodox, and brought solace to the Turks' Christian slaves.

In the field of learning the Roman College, drawing as it did on so many countries for its personnel, fitted perfectly the description given by Francesco Sacchini when he called it "a compendium of the world." Particularly striking was the presence of a number of very competent Germans who held important posts on the staff. Germany, no longer just receiving from the rest of the Catholic world, responded splendidly to the stimulus of the Catholic Reform and began to contribute in a major way to the vitality of the Church.

Among those sent to the Roman College to join Christoph Klau were two other Christophs, Grienberger and Scheiner, both astronomers. The presence of these three men in Rome coincided with the beginnings of the crisis of the Galileo affair. The central question, amid an array of related problems which aroused severe tensions between the cosmography of Aristotle and the recently discovered astronomical data, was the truth of the conclusions Copernicus presented in his *The Revolutions of the Celestial Orbs*. The Jesuit astronomers agreed with Galileo — up to a point. They confirmed the great man's discovery of Jupiter's moons and the phases of Venus; they were convinced that Aristotle's views on the unchangeability of the heavens and his system of crystal spheres had to be discarded; they were genuinely enthusiastic about this new frontier in knowledge; they gave Galileo a warm reception when he went to Rome in 1611. But they still looked for the compelling physical proof for his position on the objective validity of the Copernican proposition. The facts uncovered up to that time did not command the assent of their minds, and they therefore accepted the middle course of Tycho Brahe, which could at once keep the earth stationary at the center of the universe and still account for the new discoveries.

Since Galileo's claims seemed to be at variance with certain passages in Holy Scripture, the theologians became engaged. And in that age it was inevitable that Robert Bellarmine would be consulted. The old cardinal played a limited part in the lively debate, but it was enough to make manifest the limitations of his scholarship. Other theologians, including the Portuguese Jesuit, Bento Pereira, were more advanced than he in the interpretation of Holy Scripture, and Galileo himself anticipated better some of the teachings of Pope Leo XIII in his *Providentissimus Deus* of 1893. Backed by the advice of Grienberger, Robert counseled Pope Paul V that the claim of Galileo was a clever conjecture supported as yet by no convincing factual evidence. To him then fell the unpleasant task of communicating to Galileo in private the distressing decisions of the Holy Office of February 24, 1616. Galileo, to the end of his life, treasured a certificate signed by Bellarmine on May 26, 1616, that at this meeting he had not been asked to abjure any of his opinions or doctrines, and that he had received no penance.[10] With this Bellarmine's part in the involved business ceased. The famous trial of the great scientist took place in 1633, twelve years after the cardinal's death.

Meanwhile Bellarmine came to know among his Jesuit contemporaries in Italy two who in an exceptional way showed more concern for how to go to heaven than how the heavens go. One, the young nobleman from Mantua, Aloysius Gonzaga, repudiated the allurements of Renaissance life, gave himself with powerful single-mindedness to the Ignatian ideal, and finally as a young man of twenty-three, died in the service of the plague stricken on June 21, 1591. Usually known as the patron of youth, this catechist of Roman ragamuffins, consoler of the imprisoned, martyr of charity for the sick, just as appropriately and deservedly could be honored as a patron of the social apostolate. Bellarmine was his confessor. The other contemporary, Bernadino Realino, became by his sweet charity and unalterably benign manner through forty-two years the spiritual guide of the little Apulian town of Lecce. Bellarmine was his provincial for two years. In 1947 Pope Pius XII canonized Realino.

The novices at Sant' Andrea al Quirinale knew personally at least some of these renowned contemporary Italian Jesuits. Bellarmine spent the last year of his life with them. Through art

10 Brodrick, *Robert Bellarmine*, pp. 375-376.

they knew of other Jesuits, who died for the faith in distant lands. Martyrdom was one of the great spiritual themes of the Catholic Reform. On the walls of the novitiate there were paintings of Jesuit martyrs, each of whom had his angel who carried a palm and a crown, the symbols of victory. Louis Richeome described these paintings, now lost, in his *Spiritual Painting* (1611). With reverence and awe he wrote of them. There were Ignácio de Azevedo and his thirty-nine companions, slain off the Azores; Rodolfo Aquaviva and his four friends, butchered at Salsette in India; Paul, John, and James, crucified at Nagasaki in Japan; Abraham George, beheaded in Ethiopia; Antonio Criminali, pierced by lances at Cape Comorin in India; Edmund Campion, Alexander Bryant, Henry Garnet, Edward Oldcorne, and Thomas Cottam, executed in England. Richeome addressed the novices. "My dearly beloved, these are paintings of your brothers who were slain between 1549 and 1606. They are placed in this room not only to give honor to their memory but to provide you with examples." [11]

Spain and Portugal   Two streams of Jesuit history run through the Spain of this period, the one silt-laden and murky, its fountainhead a small group of disaffected religious, the other sparklingly clear and bright, its source the great majority of the Society's roster, devout and dedicated, including men of noble conquests in sanctity and in culture. Aquaviva's protracted struggle in Rome to preserve the Society's *Constitutions* originated, as we have seen, in Spain. There a group of about thirty or forty Jesuits, swayed by the current narrow nationalism and now turned hostile to their supernational Society, proposed to alter the order's institute.[12] Their strength, despite their small numbers, was formidable, founded as it was on two of the most powerful institutions in the country, the monarchy and the Inquisition. Four men especially, all with a background of bad relationships with their superiors, animated this movement. Dionisio Vázquez felt that he was not appreciated; Francisco Abreo went on personal begging tours for himself and wanted superiors to supply him with two brothers, one to be his secretary and the other to be

11 E. Mâle, *L'art religieux de la fin du xvie siècle* . . . (Paris, 1951), pp. 120-121.
12 Astráin, *Historia*, III, 352-369. G. Lewey, in "The Struggle for Constitutional Government in the Early Years of the Society of Jesus," *Church History*, XXIX (1960), 141-151, 157-158, interprets this episode as a rebellion against absolutism in the name of "constitutional principles." This is a clear instance of imposing a twentieth century viewpoint

his valet; Gonzalo González passed out literature against his rector among the students of the school; Enrique Enríquez slipped sixty uncensored pages into his otherwise properly censored book on moral theology.

The surest way for these men to vent their feelings was to arouse the suspicions of the Inquisition against the Society. They composed several memorials about their order, presenting the question of jurisdiction in a light calculated to arouse the jealousy of the inquisitors, so sensitive on the point of authority. They reckoned correctly, for on March 24, 1586, Antonio Marcén, provincial of Toledo, and another priest were taken by the Inquisition and disappeared into two years of mysterious silence. "We know no more about the imprisoned fathers," remarked the provincial of Castile, "than if they were in the Indies." Soon after, the jail door closed on two others.

The dissidents promptly seized their golden opportunity to widen their attack. Vázquez drew a picture that would chill the blood of any inquisitor: A Jesuit general with his vast powers, if ever he should lapse from the Catholic faith, could fill the world with error by the simple device of appointing heretical provincials and rectors. The obvious remedy was in trimming the general's authority and placing the choice of superiors in a capitular form of government. Vázquez also misrepresented the various grades in the Society as a source of discord, since they constituted "degrees of honor and dishonor." Enríquez described the *Ratio studiorum,* then being circulated among the schools, as a weapon in a campaign against St. Thomas. The Inquisition promptly called for copies of the Society's *Constitutions* and *Plan of Studies.*

This attack failed, especially for two reasons: in Rome Aquaviva skillfully presented the truth; in Spain the Inquisition blundered by overplaying its hand. The general took the case directly to Pope Sixtus V and demonstrated that the denunciations of Vázquez and Enríquez were but a tissue of lies. The papal secretary of state, Cardinal Girolamo Rusticucci, vigorously instructed the evasive general inquisitor, Cardinal Gaspar de Quiroga, that he was to return the documents demanded from the Society and that he was to halt the case of the four imprisoned Jesuits.

upon men of an earlier age. While it is true that what these men aimed to achieve would have resulted in a *de facto* decentralization of the order, their tactics, including recourse to the Spanish monarchy and the Inquisition, hardly manifested an esteem for constitutional principles.

The Inquisition spoiled its case by a show of brashness. Aquaviva called for volunteers to replace thirty Jesuits who had died of the plague in Transylvania. Of the many Spaniards who stepped forward, superiors chose six. Vázquez and Enríquez went directly to the Inquisition and exposed the insupportable cruelty to which these six Jesuits were to be subjected by being placed in the occasion of possible infection by heresy in Transylvania. Quiroga, with the approval of Philip II, ordered that all Jesuits be contained within Spain, and directed the Jesuit provincials, under pain of excommunication, to permit no subject to leave the country without the sanction of the Inquisition. The men chosen for Transylvania were stopped at the border. Sixtus V, sorely irritated for a number of reasons with Philip II, was infuriated. The papal nuncio severely reprimanded Quiroga and threatened to remove him from office. The Inquisition under this heavy pressure from Rome admitted the innocence of the four imprisoned Jesuits. Then followed, as has been seen, the abortive attempt to inaugurate an episcopal visitation of the Society in Spain, and the stern censures against Vázquez, Enríquez, and the others by the general congregations of 1593 and 1608.

The tension created by this dissension was further aggravated by serious criticism of the Society from another source. Four Dominicans leagued together with the objective of altering the Society's *Constitutions*, Domingo Bañes and Diego Peredo, who pleaded their cause from the lectern at the University of Salamanca, and Alonso de Avendaño and Gonzalo Romero from the pulpit. The attacks began in 1582 and continued for a little over ten years. Completely at variance with the general attitude of other Dominicans, this quartet struck hard at the Society. In the confessor of Philip II, their fellow religious, Diego de Chaves, they had an influential ally. Bañes, in a theological disputation, championed the proposition that, since it is the profession alone which makes one a religious, the spiritual and temporal coadjutors of the Society were outside the religious state. Gil González Dávila took up the Society's defense, and the Holy Office in Rome rejected Bañes' teaching. Peredo attacked the simple vows pronounced at the conclusion of the novitiate, teaching that the individual who pronounces these vows remains a layman who by study and pious exercises disposes himself to one day enter the Society. On February 1, 1583, Pope Gregory XIII in his bull *Quanto fructuosius* rejected Peredo's contention. The Dominican claimed that Gregory was speaking as a private doctor and not as supreme pontiff. The pope removed all doubts about his approval of the Jesuit *Constitutions* by another and even more explicit bull, *Ascendente Domino,* of May 25, 1584. Peredo retaliated with the charge that this bull was not issued in correct form. This allegation the Holy Office rejected. The open hostility to the Society's organization ceased only with the royal decree of February 4, 1595, insisting that peace must prevail between the two orders.[13]

The dissonance created by these conspirators can too easily distract from that other stream of Jesuit history, clear and bright like a silver cord, which runs through the Spain of this period. Among the majority of the Jesuits a creative and positive spirit was strongly at work, impelling them to extend their schools, to produce works of intellectual excellence which have placed them among the cultural leaders of western civilization, and to climb, under God's grace, the austere mountain of superior holiness. During Aquaviva's term the Society opened in Spain thirty-one new houses, most of them colleges. And when the general died, over 2,000 Jesuits in four provinces were working in eighty-seven communities.

Popular preaching was a ministry enthusiastically adopted by the Jesuits. In 1590 Aquaviva issued a directive, very far-reaching in its effects, that the provinces form bands of two or three men who were to penetrate the rural areas and preach the faith to the people of the countryside. But even before this instruction was issued, the colleges and residences had become hubs from which groups of preachers radiated. In 1584 eight priests from the professed house in Toledo spent an entire year going from hamlet to hamlet. That same year every Jesuit college in Castile sent out bands of home missionaries into the villages. To facilitate this large scale instruction of the people Diego Ledesma published a catechism entitled *Christian Doctrine,* which became very popular and was translated into several languages, including Polish and Lithuanian. Another renowned cathechist was Jerónimo Ripalda. Action crowned teaching. Epidemics ravaged Spain in the last three years of the sixteenth century. The Jesuits responded generously in this crisis, and in 1598, in Castile alone, over forty died in the care of the sick.

This vitality of the Society in education and the spiritual apostolate was only part of the varied richness of Spain's Golden Age. In the philosophical and theological areas of that wide cultural splendor the Jesuits had several distinguished leaders. With startling suddenness appeared a number of men of ex-

13 Astráin, *Historia,* III, 250-272, 278-287.

ceptional intellectual endowments, the Andalusian triad of Francisco Suárez, Tomás Sánchez, and Francisco de Toledo, and the Castilian triad of Gregorio de Valencia, Gabriel Vázquez and Luis de Molina. Leaning strongly toward speculation and metaphysics, these men made distinguished contributions to the body of scholastic thought. They represent one of the responses of the sixteenth century to the dissolution of the medieval synthesis. New intellectual problems, new forms of research, and a new cultural orientation exposed the aridity that had gripped scholastic thought during the "autumn of the Middle Ages." Humanism and Lutheranism were two responses to the need for renewal. Spanish theologians, especially Dominicans and Jesuits, met this challenge in their own way by a reanimation of the medieval approach and method. Modern in the sense that they introduced into their work a sense of history by the extensive use of scriptural and patristic sources, they nevertheless elected to follow the broad highway of scholasticism, and thus created what took its place in the history of western theology as the Spanish Scholastic Renaissance.

Toledo brought to his teaching and writing a clarity, elegance, and precision of the first order. Surpassed by others in the comprehensiveness of his thought, he was without equal in an incisiveness often tinged with irony. Sánchez, erudite and impressive in his authority on moral questions, won wide recognition particularly for his frequently re-edited *The Holy Sacrament of Matrimony* (1602). Supreme among the Spanish Jesuit thinkers of the age was Francisco Suárez, gifted with a tremendous breadth of intellectual interest and unusual keenness in the penetration of speculative problems. For over forty years this industrious, loveable, frail Jesuit lectured in Spain, Rome, and Portugal, turning out all the while his masterpieces of scholastic thought. The Venice edition (1856-1878) of his entire works runs to twenty-three volumes in folio. The chapel, the classroom, books, and pen, these made the texture of the undeviating life of this remarkable man.

The *Metaphysics* (1597) and the *Laws* (1612) are among the most celebrated of his writings. The *Metaphysics* flowed from a mind both traditional and original and, as the first complete and systematic presentation of scholastic metaphysics, was a modern event. Spain and Portugal did not contain its influence, for it moved northward and received an especially warm welcome in Germany where before 1620 six editions appeared.[14] With

14 Clare C. Riedl, "Suarez and the Organization of Learning," in *Jesuit*

this manifestation of a strong Spanish scholastic revival coincided the vast Iberian colonization overseas and the growing self-consciousness of the national states in Europe. These developments, abroad and at home, created speculative problems of the greatest magnitude and complexity, and Spain's best minds, led by Francisco de Vitoria and Suárez, tried to unravel them. Suárez endeavored to give a scientific and systematic articulation of international law for what was emerging as a community of nations. This he did within the framework of the natural law and the concept of the universal community of mankind, preparing the way for other great thinkers on the conduct of nations such as Hugo Grotius and Samuel von Pufendorf. This was one of Spain's several distinguished cultural contributions to the civilization of the West.

Of the three Castilians Gregorio de Valencia did the bulk of his work in Germany at the universities of Dillingen and Ingolstadt. Gabriel Vázquez, a native of Villaescusa de Haro, was the delight of his students. Insisting on a union of precise thought and lucid expression, he enlivened public disputations by his vast erudition, quick intelligence, and lively language. The contemporary theological world linked the two names, Suárez and Vázquez, and frequently they were the subjects of academic debate. At Salamanca students argued the question: to which, Vázquez or Suárez, shall we give the primacy of honor? Energetic and persistent in his manner, Vázquez always maintained an independence of thought in his search for truth. Two popes, Benedict XIV and Leo XIII, both men who appreciated intellectual achievement, paid special tribute to his scholarly endowments.[15]

Better known centuries later, largely because of an angry debate which he occasioned, was Luis de Molina. A subtle and acute thinker, Molina gave himself to the thorny problem of reconciling grace and free will. A double influence had conditioned him as he approached his task: first, a Jesuit's instinctive reaction against the denial of the will's freedom; and second, the teaching of one of the Society's most original, but surprisingly little known, scholastic thinkers, the Portuguese Pedro da Fonseca. As a Jesuit, Molina stood against the necessitarian theology of Luther and Calvin. St. Ignatius had written in his "Rules for

Thinkers of the Renaissance, ed. G. Smith, S.J. (Milwaukee, 1939), p. 2.

15 R. de Scorraille, S.J., *François Suarez de la Compagnie de Jésus* (Paris, 1911), I, 283-286, 313-314.

Thinking with the Church" in the *Spiritual Exercises,* [369]: "We ought not to speak nor to insist on the doctrine of grace so strongly as to give rise to that poisonous theory that takes away free will." As a student Molina had studied under Fonseca. Fonseca, in order to give a scientific vindication of the Tridentine doctrine of the fundamental integrity of man's free will while under the influence of efficacious grace, devised a solution called *scientia media.* This doctrine of "the divine middle knowledge" Molina adopted, and after thirty years of labor produced *The Concordance of Free Will with the Gifts of Grace.* His famous, if not particularly literary, opus appeared in 1588, an early salvo in what developed into one of the most acrimonious theological battles in the history of the Church. It promptly ran into the capable and vigorous opposition of the Dominicans who ranged behind their champion, Domingo Bañes. In this mighty contest of intellects the theologians, concentrating on the intricate problem of how to preserve the will's freedom while acting under the influence of efficacious grace, tred warily between the pitfalls of Pelagianism with its denial of the need of grace and Protestantism with its impairment of the will's liberty. The Dominicans, approaching the problem from the angle of the efficacy of grace, and the Jesuits, starting from the freedom of the will, locked in a general fray in which the difficult concepts of efficacious grace, sufficient grace, predestination, God's knowledge became the matériel of violent attacks and counterattacks. Both Molina and Bañes were hard hitters. Bad feeling, stirred up by the Dominican attack on the Jesuit *Constitutions,* spilled over into the theological arena. So violent had become the debate that in 1594 Pope Clement VIII ordered that the affair be brought to Rome for adjudication. There, for over ten years which were filled with reports, dossiers, tracts reaching mountainous proportions, and even with debates before Clement himself, the contest dragged on. It could have continued interminably except that Pope Paul V called an abrupt halt and, adopting a practical solution proposed by Cardinal Bellarmine ten years earlier, forbade both Jesuits and Dominicans to classify the doctrine of the other side as temerarious or heretical. A welcome peace descended on the doughty warriors, wounded and weary from the prolonged battle about the great mystery of God's action in the human soul. Among the casualties in this contest, smothered and hidden by the great clouds of dust which were raised, were the other works of Molina, his thoughtful reflections on the questions of church-state relationships and the economics of the age.

The same year Molina was born, 1536, another Castilian destined to ruffle the intellectual spheres came into the world. Juan Mariana, prodigious scholar of wide culture, yet irascible, haughty, and defiant, ranged in his writings over a wide number of subjects. In his *Change in Currency* (1609) he bitingly criticized the depreciation of money. The government confined him to a Franciscan convent on charges of disloyalty to the crown. Having had assignments to Rome, Messina, and Paris, he found ignorance of his country quite general. To rectify this he wrote twenty volumes on the history of Spain, not strictly critical in the modern sense of the word, but with an appealing energy and gravity of style. But as in the case of Molina, one work dominated all Mariana's others. In 1599 he published his famous *The Monarch and His Training*, dedicated to Philip III and designed to delineate the ideal character of a Christian ruler. In the course of the work he discussed the question of the lawfulness of tyrannicide, dispassionately proposing the pros and cons as quietly as he might discuss the number of angels on the head of a pin. He then supported the proposition that a tyrant should be removed from office, killed if necessary, except by poisoning, once the people have taken this decision, at least implicitly. This chapter caused not a stir in Spain, but it proved to be dynamite in France where Henry III had fallen beneath an assassin's knife. Aquaviva promptly condemned the work and in the sternest language forbade his subjects to entertain even the slightest favor toward tyrannicide.

These Jesuits shared in varying measure in the Spanish theological renaissance. Like the *conquistadores* who carved out a new world, the greater among these scholars opened up a new continent in the world of learning. Many components went into the making of this conquest: the fresh understanding of St. Thomas; the Erasmian enthusiasm for Holy Scripture and the Fathers of the Church; the sense of history with its appreciation of conciliar documents; the humanists' love of graceful language. Especially Maldonado, Toledo, Vázquez, and Suárez mastered this new continent. Each had his own distinctive emphasis, but the pattern was general: a new harmony of metaphysics, history, scripture, and patristics.

Two stars guided these Jesuits. The first was the legislation in the Society's *Constitutions*, which directed that the Jesuit in his formation was to study scholastic theology, positive theology, and Sacred Scripture. The second was the Dominican theological revival at Salamanca under the great Francisco de Vitoria. Vitoria by his own genius created in his teaching this attractive harmony and balance. Other sons of St. Dominic, especially Melchor Cano, Domingo Soto, and Pedro Soto took Vitoria's fire and kept it ablaze at Salamanca. It was there that Maldonado, Toledo, and Suárez did their early studies. Vázquez sat under the Dominicans at Alcalá. Through these Jesuits Spain helped Catholic Europe in two major ways: it sent them as couriers to the universities at Paris, Rome, Prague, Coimbra, Dillingen, and Ingolstadt, carrying the theological renaissance; it prepared the way for the future flowering of positive theology in the seventeenth century.

Matching in fecundity the theological and philosophical skills of these men was the spirit of holiness which bore fruit in both the lives and writings of Spanish Jesuits. For forty-six years, in the obscure post of porter at the college at Palma, Majorca, Brother Alonso Rodríguez lived a life of unusual sanctity, which has been officially recognized by his canonization in 1888. Brother Rodríguez, at the bidding of his superiors, wrote an autobiography and other small works which mark him as one of the great mystics of the Society. Among those who knew Alonso personally and drew inspiration from him was another saint of the Church, the young Pedro Claver, destined to be the apostle of the negro slaves at Cartagena in New Spain.

Among the authors, two still exercise a wide influence, one Luis de la Puente, and the other with the same name as the saintly porter of Palma. In 1605 with thirty years of Jesuit life behind him, including such posts as professor of theology, master of novices, rector, and visitor, La Puente began his distinguished career as a spiritual writer. Among his better known works are *Meditations on the Mysteries of Our Holy Faith* (1605) with its important preface on prayer, *A Treatise on Perfection* (1612-1616), and *A Life of Father Baltasar Álvarez* (1615). Ever the skilled and meticulous theologian, La Puente achieved in his writings a happy combination of ardent piety and doctrinal preciseness.

The year 1609 was a landmark in the history of spiritual literature. Then it was that there appeared for the first time *The Practice of Perfection and Christian Virtues* by Alfonso Rodríguez which has been translated into at least twenty languages. For forty years Rodríguez, a superior and master of novices, had given talks to his fellow Jesuits on spiritual subjects. Requested to organize and publish these talks, he produced a massive three-volume work marked by its sure and sound advice, its robust realism, its general good humor in the many catchy stories from the lives of the saints and fathers of the desert. Not in the least hostile to higher mysticism, Rodríguez nevertheless stressed the ascetical aspect of the spiritual life, thus rendering a distinct service to Aquaviva in his efforts to check the tendency toward a life of undisturbed contemplation among some Spanish Jesuits.

In Portugal the most delicate problem that faced the Jesuits arose from the Spanish conquest of their native land. To keep the patriotism of their subjects from breaking out in defiance of the conqueror, superiors had to maintain constant vigilance, and although generally successful, they suffered their moments of embarrassment. Between the Portuguese Jesuits and the Spanish monarch a fragile sort of amity prevailed. For his first visit to a religious house in Lisbon, during July, 1581, Philip chose the Society's professed house, and on his way back to Spain in 1583, passing through Évora, he stopped at the Jesuit college. Even though the monarch more than once voiced his praise for the Society, the Jesuits judged his words to be the tools of royal diplomacy rather than the expression of genuine affection. Their relations with the unwelcome monarch, ever proper, could hardly have become cordial.[16]

Spanish rule did not curtail the growth of the province. After the sharp drop in 1579-80 by the loss of about sixty-five men due to the plague of that year, the province moved forward quite rapidly. From 484 men in 1580, it increased to 570 in 1594, and to 665 in 1615. In 1610 there were seventeen houses. The College of Lisbon enjoyed wide popularity and in 1588 enrolled 2,000 students who under teachers of distinction, especially in the humanities, plunged into the lively, enthusiastic pursuit of classical studies.

To map the terrain of the Society's history during these thirty-five years is to undertake the charting of a territory, uneven, difficult, and of extremely sharp contrasts. This could hardly be otherwise since the violent, disruptive, and uncertain history of the country sucked everything else into the maelstrom. *France*

In 1580 a wide chasm, made by the rift between the king, Henry III, and the prestigious head of the Holy League, the duke of Guise, cut through the Catholic population. To both king and duke the Society owed much, and with each was associated as a friend and counselor a prominent Jesuit, Émond Auger with the Valois and Claude Mathieu with Guise. The mounting hostility between the two parties, where the very

16 Rodrigues, *História,* II, ii, 443-444.

destiny of the country could not but stir the heart of every Frenchman, carried the serious danger of disrupting the unity among the Jesuits.

Aquaviva's policy was to detach the French Jesuits from the political upheavals. He made his instructions precise: stay clear of politics; avoid in conversation even within the Society the public issues; keep guard against compromising remarks in the pulpit. He set about to remove Auger from the court and Mathieu from the League. Both Jesuits were obedient men, but resistance came from the king and the duke of Guise. Eventually, by steady and persistent effort, more necessary in the case of Guise, the general was able to assign both men to Italy. In 1587 he sent to France as visitor the tactful and prudent Venetian, Lorenzo Maggio, who for about a year, while checking on the religious spirit of the communities, helped to maintain calm in the ranks.

The years 1588-1589, highlighted by the murders of both Guise and the king and by the claim of the Calvinist Henry of Navarre to the throne of the realm, put Jesuit restraint to a severe test. In general they remained faithful to Aquaviva's instructions, but here and there individuals spoke out on the burning issue of the day. In December 1593, Jacques Commolet, a supporter of the League, publicly challenged the adherents of the Béarnais: "You say that the king of Navarre is a magnanimous prince, a fighter, a conqueror, benign and merciful. . . . But of religion you say not a word. Only give us assurance that he will maintain our faith. . . ." The next year at Dijon Christophe Clémenson vehemently urged the people to stand firm against Navarre.[17]

Henry's conversion to the Catholic faith and his coronation as king in 1593-1594 presented the Jesuits with a most embarrassing problem: to pronounce or not pronounce the pledge of loyalty to the new monarch. Nine years before, in 1585, Pope Sixtus V had declared Henry excommunicated as a relapsed heretic. Aquaviva in March, 1594, instructed the French Jesuits that, out of deference to the Holy See, they were to take no oath of allegiance to the king until the pope had lifted the censure of Sixtus V. If exile were the alternative, that should be their choice. In Paris their position quickly deteriorated. Enemies circulated stories about their disloyalty to the crown. The clergy of the city and the faculty of the Sorbonne took the oath. The papal legate judged it permissible. Under this steady pressure

17 Fouqueray, *Histoire*, II, 285, 445-446.

and guided primarily by the opinion of the papal legate, the provincial announced the readiness of the Jesuits to pledge their fidelity to Henry IV. Aquaviva promptly disapproved, and in the sternest kind of language. "I want you to know," he wrote, "that you have offended not only Catholics in general but also our own men. . . . Complaints have reached me from many provinces of different nations. . . . They regard your offer to take the oath as a dishonor to the Society." [18]

This rebuke opened the way for a long line of adversities which culminated, within a year, in the expulsion of the Jesuits from Paris. In May Jacques d'Amboise, rector of the University, revived the old campaign, now so familiar to the capital, with a request to Parlement that the Society be ejected from the country. Although not original, this case had a touch of freshness in the appearance before the bar, as the University's lawyer, of Antoine Arnauld. His speech, often called the "original sin" of the Arnaulds, was the opening salvo of the running battle which would engage the Society for many generations with one of the most unique and influential families of France. In a volcanic outpouring of his hostility, identifying Jesuits as founders of The League, agents of Spain, conspirators in the assassination of William of Orange, Arnauld excoriated the Society. But he also aroused a strong outcry of protest. Bishops, nobles, city governments, vigorously contested the lawyer. Parlement suspended judgment.

Parlement's indecision, however, was not for long. Six months later an event of startling suddenness shook Paris and gave the Society's enemies a fortuitous opening. On December 27, 1594, a demented law student, Jean Chastel, made an attempt on the life of the king. Investigation revealed that at one time he had attended lectures in philosophy at the College of Clermont. Nothing more was needed. Jean Guéret, the professor of philosophy, was clapped into jail despite Chastel's insistence, even under torture, that he had had no accomplices. The College of Clermont was searched. In the room of Jean Guignard, the librarian, they found books on the question of tyrannicide and in favor of The League. In a hurried and prejudiced process the courts rushed the unfortunate Guignard to the stake, and on January 7, 1595, he died in the flames. Parlement ordered the Society to quit Paris promptly.

This sharp blow, however, did not cut the thread of Jesuit continuity in France. The Parlements of Bordeaux and Tou-

18 Ibid., 348-349.

louse did not follow the action taken in Paris, and several of the Society's schools continued their work. The fortunes of the individual schools varied in relation to the tides of the religious wars. Those at Lyons, Dijon, and Puy-en-Velay were severely harassed. That at Bordeaux had to close in 1589. The University at Pont-à-Mousson suffered a sharp drop in students. But, on the other hand, the schools at Bourges and Nevers progressed smoothly, while in 1593 the Fathers added philosophy to the curriculum at Rodez and theology at Billom. Even some new colleges were opened, at Périgueux in 1592 and at Auch in 1593.

At Paris eight years elapsed before the Jesuits were able to return from exile. At the close of those years a dramatic change in the king's outlook on the Society took place, and hostility yielded to affectionate friendship. Aquaviva assessed the character of the king correctly and, feeling that given the light of truth Henry in his magnanimity and fairness would reverse the course of events, patiently set about to emancipate him from the yoke of mistrust placed on him by the anti-Jesuit bloc. He instructed the Jesuits in those provinces of France unaffected by the injunction of the Paris Parlement to conduct themselves as models of loyalty to the crown. Several well-known Jesuits, including Jacques Sirmond, Francisco de Toledo, and Antonio Possevino, requested the pope to lift the decree of excommunication against Henry. Alexandre Georges, who had been rector of the College of Clermont, in an audience with Clement VIII, played on the pope's name as he asked the pontiff "to open his arms of clemency to the king of France." Father Louis Richeome, a most charming and lovable man, wrote a telling work, *A Most Humble Remonstrance and Request of the Religious of the Society of Jesus addressed to the Most Christian King of France and Navarre, Henry IV* (1598).

Pope Clement, with a determination born of his anxiety about the sad state of religion in France, worked for the readmission of the expelled Jesuits. He even thought of making this a condition for lifting the sentence of excommunication. Aquaviva, however, with his characteristic catholic breadth of view, informed the pope that he would prefer to see the Society never return to Paris rather than delay, even for a few days, the reconciliation of Henry to the Church with its assurance of peace within France. Pope Clement gave absolution to Henry on September 17, 1595. A year and a half later, on January 20, 1597, he formally requested that the Jesuits be readmitted. But Henry still had serious misgivings about them as partisans of

Spain and fomenters of rebellion against the throne. Clement pressed the matter through a special legate, Orazio del Monte, who was accompanied by the knowledgeable Lorenzo Maggio. Henry received the two visitors in September, 1599, and was sincerely impressed by their appeal. He became less adamant. Then the last vestiges of hesitation and doubt were dispelled by one of the most personable Jesuits of the time, Pierre Coton. Maggio, in a decision of great consequence, summoned Coton to speak with the king. Sweet and winning of character, charming and courtly in manner, alert of intelligence, Coton had already vitalized the faith in Dauphiné and Languedoc by the force of his preaching. On May 29 Henry received Coton and another French Jesuit, Ignace Armand, at Fontainebleau. Up and down the corridors of the chateau the three men walked, chatting in an easy, affable way. The king asked Coton to preach. That sermon made the Jesuit a friend of Henry forever. Never had he heard "anything like it," remarked the king. The Society's case was won.[19]

Together with the king the two Jesuits worked at hammering out a formula which would set aside the act of 1594. Henry, a thorough political realist, knew the danger of outraging Gallican feelings, and therefore required that the formula both exact an oath of loyalty to the crown from the returning Jesuits and specify certain restrictions on the administration of the sacraments. On September 1, 1603, he issued the Edict of Reestablishment, known generally as the Edict of Rouen.

A clear, fresh dawn, full of promise of a glorious day, broke upon the Society. Within five months after the Edict thirty-two towns had requested Jesuit colleges. The king chose from the applicants, and soon eighteen new schools were being readied, from Caen and Rouen in the north to Cahors and Aix in the south, from Troyes in the east to Rennes in the west. But assessing, with his characteristic good judgment, the strength of the Gallicans and Parlement in Paris, he did not permit the opening of the College of Clermont. Of all these schools Henry made his favorite the one he started at La Flèche, near Angers. Converting the graceful and elegant Châteauneuf into a school, he envisaged it as "the most beautiful in the world." Within a year after its opening in January, 1604, over 1,000 students had been enrolled. Most famous of the early alumni was René Descartes.

Rapidly the Society grew. In 1605 two new novitiates, at Lyons and Rouen, were opened. In 1608 the French Assistancy, including the new Province of Toulouse, was created. In 1610

19 Ibid., 631-632.

there were over 1,300 men in forty-five communities. The king was delighted and told the Jesuits: "I am entirely yours."

As the Catholic nobles could not forget the presence of Huguenot swords within the realm, so the Jesuit writers and preachers could not put from their minds the enclaves of Calvinistic theology. As a consequence, much of their apostolate had a deep polemical coloring. It was in response to the immediate spiritual crisis that Jean Gontery wrote his *The Real Way to End Religious Differences* (1607), Guillaume Bayle his *A Catechism and Digest of Current Controversies* (1607), and Louis Richeome his *Huguenot Idolatry* (1608). The amount of this controversial literature was immense. In 1592 alone, the fathers at Lyons published one hundred and forty books and booklets of Catholic propaganda. In 1598, when Philippe Duplessis-Mornay, the "pope of the Huguenots", published his widely read work on the Holy Eucharist, a barrage of replies came from the Jesuits, notably Jean de Bordes, Fronton du Duc, and Louis Richeome.

For the Jesuit preachers a great preoccupation was the frightening ignorance of the faith found among the peasants of the countryside who, because of their nescience, were such easy prey for the Calvinist ministers. Pairs of Jesuits moved from village to village, mainly in the south. The chronicles of their work are stamped with an inevitable sameness of theme: instruction in basic truths of the faith, correction of superstition, rekindling the fervor of Catholic life, receiving crowds back to the sacraments. From these hardworking and forgotten teams came the first French martyrs of the Society. In February, 1593, Jacques Salez and Brother Guillaume Saultemouche, seized by Huguenots, met cruel and savage death while staunchly defending to the end the presence of Christ in the Holy Eucharist.

The tradition of excellence in sacred oratory, so firmly established by Émond Auger, continued worthily not only in Pierre Coton but also in the vibrant and grand-mannered Jean Gontery, who tended to be somewhat severe — Henry IV smilingly used to say that he preferred Coton's Hell to Gontery's Heaven — and in the cultivated and refined Gaspard de Séguiran, so versatile in humanizing the concepts of scholastic thought. The Jesuit preachers quite frequently used a unique device, the public religious debate with Calvinists, such as the three-day session at Meysse on the true church in which Jean Brossard and Imbert Boët participated.[20]

20 Ibid., III, 4, 162.

Over a land dreary and heavy with the monotonous exchange of theological argument passed the first breaths of the clear, fresh air of the new spirit of devotion and predilection for mystical experience. The Jesuits shared in this religious renaissance especially in two ways: by spiritual direction and by spiritual literature. Henri Bremond felt that behind most of the great spiritual enterprises of the first half of the seventeenth century in France was the inspiration of a woman.[21] Several new religious communities of women appeared, and frequently in a Jesuit they found a wise and practical counselor. Jean-Antoine de Villars and Jean Gentil guided Anne de Xainctonge in her care for the Ursuline group which she had founded at Dôle. De Villars also directed St. Jeanne Frémiot de Chantal toward her true vocation which flowered in her association with St. Francis de Sales and the foundation of the Visitandine nuns. Pierre Péquet of the Jesuit college at Avignon indirectly aided the Ursulines, for he had formed with exquisite finesse the ardent Provençal secular priest César de Bus, who in turn widened the apostolate of teaching for these nuns throughout the Midi. Jean de Bordes of Bordeaux assisted Jeanne de Lestonnac in establishing the Company of Mary, now known as the Order of Notre Dame, in order to complement the work of the Society. At Paris three Jesuits, Pierre Coton, Jean Gontery, and Charles de la Tour helped Madeleine de Saint-Beuve in the spiritual formation of the young women whom she had organized in 1607 according to the rule of St. Ursula. Later, Coton aided Françoise de Bermond in opening a house in Paris for still another Ursuline group which she had started in Provence.

In the movement known as Devout Humanism, stamped by the grace and charm of St. Francis de Sales, Louis Richeome, Pierre Coton, and Étienne Binet, broke new paths. With a taste for the beautiful and good things of life, with a lively imagination and a basic joy, Richeome gave in his writing a portrayal of his own attractive and lovable character. Coton, in his *The Interior Concern of a Devout Soul* (1608), comparable in so many ways to *Introduction to the Devout Life* (1608) of St. Francis de Sales, gathered together a collection of prayers, aspirations, and short meditations, which he developed according to the idea of generosity in one's gift of self to God in a strong and optimistic love. By this work, filled with such phrases as, "We must not allow other clanging sounds to drown out the

21 H. Bremond, *Histoire littéraire du sentiment religieux en France* (Paris, 1924-1936), II, 36.

voice of these chimes of prayer," Coton shaped the interior lives of a number at the French court.[22] Binet contributed greatly to this ardent milieu with such popular works as *Solace and New Life for the Sick and Afflicted* (1616), and *The Better Mode of Government: Rigorous or Gentle?* (1636), the latter directed to religious superiors.

The confident and prospering work of the French Jesuits received a rude blow on May 14, 1610. That was the day demented François Ravaillac assassinated Henry IV in the streets of Paris. Seven years of cordial friendship between the Jesuits and the most loved of all France's monarchs, who in his last letter had used the familiar phrase "my college of La Flèche" and who willed that his heart be entombed there, had come to a tragic end.

The king's murder was a signal for the Society's enemies to make a general advance. They tried to implicate it in Ravaillac's terrible deed. They failed. But Jesuits outside France by their writing unwittingly steeled the Gallican lances against their besieged brethren. In June, 1610, Parlement publicly burned *The King and His Formation* of Juan Mariana. As mentioned earlier, Mariana's section on tyrannicide, which caused hardly a ripple in Spain, had the makings of a violent tempest in France. As early as 1599 Richeome pointed out to Aquaviva the perils for the Society in France inherent in this passage. Aquaviva ordered that the offensive section be emended, and in July, 1610, in a solemn declaration he disassociated the Society in clearest terms from the least sanction of tyrannicide. But the damage had been done, and a convenient canard was for many generations at the disposal of the anti-Jesuits. The same year Robert Bellarmine, in refutation of William Barclay's defense of the divine right of kings, published his *Treatise on the Power of the Supreme Pontiff in Temporal Affairs*, vindicating papal claims to indirect power over princes in secular matters. Men of the regalist mentality were incensed, and Parlement broadcast its censure of Bellarmine's doctrine. One man excitedly wrote: "France, it is time for the tocsin to ring out strong and constant in the hearts of your children. . . ."[23]

---

22 Ibid., 76. L. Cognet, in *De la Dévotion Moderne à la Spiritualité Française* (Paris, 1958), pp. 67-68, tempers Bremond's enthusiasm and judges that a few Jesuits within the movement of Devout Humanism, such as François de Garasse, Antoine Sirmond, and even on occasion Louis Richeome, were disconcertingly optimistic in their portrayal of man's natural capability to act virtuously.
23 Fouqueray, *Histoire*, III, 241, 256.

In this emotional climate the Jesuits in Paris made a blunder of judgment. The king had hardly died when, contravening his political wisdom, they appealed to the sympathetic queen mother to reopen classes at the College of Clermont. Marie de Médicis issued the desired letters patent in August, 1610. And once more the Jesuits stepped aboard the tedious and exasperating treadmill of procuring Parlement's registration of the royal decree.

Parlement announced its judgment on December 22, 1611. The magistrates not only postponed the registration of the letters patent and explicitly forbade the Jesuits to teach, but also summoned them to appear in court and sign a declaration that they would conform their teaching to the doctrine of the Sorbonne. They then turned the screw even tighter. Making explicit their understanding of the doctrine of the Sorbonne and taking their cue from the sollicitor-general, Louis Servin, a specialist in Jesuit baiting, they called on the Society to affirm that below God the king of France has no superior in temporal affairs; to deny to any power on earth, even a general council of the Church, the power to release the king's subjects from their oath of fidelity to him; and finally to maintain by word and by pen the rights and liberties of the Gallican church.

Events seemingly had reached an impasse. The judiciary of Paris had summoned the Jesuits to repudiate openly the teaching of the Society's greatest scholars, especially Bellarmine, on papal power, and to acknowledge principles, under the general heading of Gallican liberties, unacceptable to the Holy See. Then a number of new developments enabled the Jesuits to ease themselves out of their uncomfortable situation. A lack of internal unity appeared in the ranks of Parlement. All the magistrates did not profess a Gallicanism of the same hardness, and some of them even sent their sons to Jesuit schools. Nor did the doctors of the Sorbonne enjoy unanimity in their repudiation of Bellarmine, since men like André Duval and Nicolas Ysambert showed sympathy toward Rome. And meanwhile the papal nuncio, Roberto Ubaldini, used his important office to soften Parlement's order.

From these factors resulted a formula greatly modified in two ways: first, the four specifically itemized points of Servin were dropped; second, to the words "Gallican liberties" was added the clause: "which have been always and from ancient times preserved and recognized in this kingdom," implying that Rome had at least tolerated them. On February 22, 1612, the provincial, Christophe Baltazar, Fronton du Duc, Jacques Sirmond, and others went to the registry office and declared that they conformed to the doctrine of the Sorbonne, even in that which concerned the sacred person of the king, the maintenance of royal authority, and the liberties of the Gallican Church "which have always and from ancient times been preserved and recognized in this kingdom." Aquaviva reacted with great displeasure at this refuge in fine distinctions and he sternly reprimanded the provincial, informing him that his action had caused the pope great sorrow and that it would have been better to close Clermont rather than sign such a document.[24]

Nowhere, save in France, had the Jesuits been forced to examine so explicitly their status in civil society. And under this pressure many moved away from the theory of Bellarmine on the indirect power of the papacy in temporal affairs. As Frenchmen they felt a bond of loyalty to their monarch; as Jesuits they could not forget their order's peculiar devotion to the Holy See. These obligations together placed a terrible strain on their conscience. In the turmoil after the assassination of Henry IV, when the enemies of the Society charged it with disloyalty to the crown, Coton, in an effort to refute the accusation, stated that the Jesuits were ready to sign with their blood these statements: it is heresy to believe that kings are given men by chance; the kings of France are the oldest sons of the Church, endowed with rare and signal privileges beyond the ordinary status of the other kings on earth; it is unlawful to refuse obedience [to the king]; he who resists the king earns damnation. Coton expressed nothing which formally contradicted Bellarmine and Suárez. But his words have a resonance which calls to mind the language of Bossuet at a later date.

These ideas appeared not only in writing. The Parisian Jesuits discussed among themselves the subject of the indirect temporal power of the pope, and Aquaviva received reports that they expressed such sentiments as these: confidence that the doctrine of Bellarmine on this aspect of papal power was not an essential point of dogma; annoyance that any Jesuit would uphold this doctrine as a matter of faith; the belief that the English Catholics, if the oath proposed to them by a heretical magistrate contained nothing more than a denial of this teaching, should not refuse it; the persuasion that those English Catholics who go to their death for declining to take such an oath are not martyrs

24 P. Blet, "Jésuites et libertés gallicanes en 1611," *AHSJ*, XXIV (1955), 168-170; J. Brucker, S.J., *La Compagnie de Jésus. Esquisse de son Institut et de son histoire* (Paris, 1919), pp. 232-233.

and cannot be said to have died for the faith. In December, 1610, Aquaviva sent stern admonitions about this kind of talk to the provincial, the superior of the professed house, and Coton.

As if the chastened Jesuits did not have their fill of anxiety, once more one of their fellow religious outside France caused an eruption of feeling against them. This time it was the gentle Francisco Suárez. In 1614, to contest the Oath of Allegiance of England's James I, he published his *Defense of the Catholic Faith*. The book offended the sensibilities of the regalists and a new storm broke over the Society. Parlement ordered the volume to be burned. The distracted superior in Paris wrote directly to the provincials in Spain and Italy: "I hope that you will put an absolute ban in your provinces on the publication in the future of any similar book.[25]

The real tragedy was that the French Jesuits, in the light of developments in the theology of church-state relations, were ahead of their times when they questioned Bellarmine's theory of the indirect power of the papacy in temporal affairs. Aquaviva's reprimands of 1610 and 1612 made them seem to be disloyal sons of the Church. Actually they were on the side of truth yet to be uncovered by the future probings of the theologians.

Bellarmine, brilliantly clarifying and synthesizing thinkers who had gone before him, taught that, while the pope as pope directly and immediately has no temporal power outside the Papal States, he does, by reason of his spiritual power, enjoy an indirect power in temporal things when spiritual values are at stake. This indirect power he extended in a practical way to the secular device of deposing a heretical ruler. Many current theologians question whether Bellarmine's conclusions about the use of such temporal means are consistent with his premise that the Church's power is in itself but one, and that solely spiritual. They challenge whether formally political acts, such as the deposition of a ruler, can be regarded as an extension of that single and solely spiritual power. The issue they raise against Bellarmine is not the right of the Church to defend herself and the faith; nor the right of the Church to meet moral issues; nor the right to somehow guide and correct the temporal order. It is rather whether the Church in the exercise of these rights may take hold of and use the procedures and processes of the temporal order, such as the deposition of unjust rulers. Not a few modern theologians affirm that consistency with the doctrine of the

25 Blet, "Jésuites Gallicans au XVIIe siècle?" *AHSJ*, XXIX (1960), 60-63.

Church's purely spiritual power demands that the Church may not adopt such secular processes. A modern French Jesuit, Henri de Lubac, has called Bellarmine's theory of the indirect power, in which he discerns a "lack of logic," a "bastard compromise." [26]

Bellarmine's difficulty lay in his failure to realize — as so many others failed — that the medieval world of the unitary society of the *res publica christiana* had passed and that the adolescent, immature political world of the Middle Ages, into which the papacy had to step as a contingent measure to preserve order and justice, was attaining to the maturity of the national state. In his discussion of the Church's right to depose unjust rulers, Bellarmine, speculating within the context of the historical circumstances that prevailed in the medieval era, made the mistake of raising to the absolute what was relative and contingent. He endowed details of a passing civil order with permanence. What he did not sense was that the national state was arriving at a consciousness of its maturity and adulthood, and that in its awareness of its own peculiar institutions to correct and direct its action it denied to the Church those secular acts the Church once performed, especially intervention against an unjust ruler. And a school of modern theologians affirm that this denial was valid.

The French Jesuits, in effect, were attempting to hold in practice what these modern theologians teach. The pressure of events made them sense that a new era in Europe's political development had dawned with the emergence of the increasingly mature national state. They did not think through the problem — indeed, it is yet to be intellectually exhausted — of the state with its own special finality and rights, but in their own particular agonizing perplexity they anticipated in the practical order what future theologians, who are more aware of the contingencies in historical development, have concluded, namely, that the pope does not enjoy the power to lay hands on the temporal power with such secular means as the deposition of unjust rulers. Out of harmony with a climate of opinion largely colored by hierocratic ideas of papal power and a limited theology of Church-State relations, they were heralds of a new age. But they paid a price in suffering. Through the years ahead their predicament would remain the same.

This antithetic stand of the French Jesuits toward Bellarmine's thesis cannot however diminish the genuine achievement of

26 John Courtney Murray, S.J., "St. Robert Bellarmine on the Indirect Power," *Theological Studies*, IX (1948), 501.

their Italian brother. In two ways Bellarmine contributed brilliantly to the thinking about the relationship of the sacral and the secular. With luminous clarity he, first, defended the distinction between the two powers, spiritual and temporal, and, second, the primacy of the spiritual and subordination of the temporal power. By the former he cleared the air of many of the exaggerated hierocratic ideas; by the latter he challenged in the name of man's spiritual freedom royal absolutism as it was expounded by James I of England. With these general principles the French Jesuits did not argue. But they did contest Bellarmine's practical conclusions about papal power. And for this reason they lived under a cloud.

Their difference with Bellarmine did not immunize the French Jesuits from the hostile forces released by the death of Henry IV. Over them hung a dark cloud of political hostility. Yet it was not entirely a period of unmitigated darkness. Several shafts of light broke through. Richeome published a most effective apology for the Society in his *Lament in Vindication of the Jesuits* (1615). Coton did the same in many brochures and in his *Statement on the Institute of the Jesuits* (1615).[27] In the Estates General, called for 1614, many of the cahiers from throughout the country sounded eloquent praise of the Society. Against their foes the Jesuits could match many friends.

In the empire and the dominions of the Austrian Hapsburgs *Germany and* the Jesuits by their schools created a movement such as, in the *Central Europe* judgment of Leopold Ranke, has never been seen in the history of the world. Initiative, growth, advance colored all Jesuit ministries of this age: scholarship, preaching, catechetics.[28]

When Aquaviva became general seven hundred Jesuits were responsible for nineteen colleges, besides other residences. When he died the number of Jesuits had reached almost 1,700 and the colleges had more than doubled. The enrollment in the schools was frequently very high. In 1582 the college at Cologne had 1,000 students. Vienna had the same number in 1590. In 1604 Dillingen had 700. At Munich the number rose from 600 in 1587 to 900 seventeen years later; at Würzburg from 700 in 1590 to 1,070 fourteen years later.[29]

The exuberance of school life continued to find a most colorful expression in the drama. Variety in form and technical aspects

27 Fouqueray, *Histoire*, III, 351-353.
28 L. von Ranke, *The History of the Popes* (London, 1847-1851), I, 415-417.
29 Brucker, *La Compagnie*, pp. 270-273.

continued to develop. Choruses and arias multiplied. Scenery became more elaborate with calm lakes and restless seas, star filled heavens and lovely landscapes, buildings and battlements. Mechanical devices in the forms of explosives, lightning, and flying machines became more sophisticated. Highly trained orchestras accompanied the actors. In Munich in 1643 an orchestra of thirty-two pieces assisted at the performance of *Theophilus*. And often, as in Munich in 1597, the play had a sweep and boldness of imagination that transcended the school walls. That year, to celebrate the dedication of the splendid Jesuit church of Saint Michael, the students presented *The Triumph of Saint Michael*, during which a chorus of nine hundred voices rang out with magnetic power and which concluded with a rousing scene as three hundred devils were cast into the flames of hell.[30]

The schools provided the atmosphere congenial to learning which helped the Jesuits to contribute to the cultural and scholarly life of the empire. A great teacher, renowned author of school dramas, and philologist like the Tyrolese Matthäus Rader; a prodigious author and scholar whose interests ranged from Greek grammar to archaeology like the Swabian Jakob Gretser; a widely respected Hellenist like the Bavarian Georg Mayr; a classicist of wide influence through his series of successful Latin textbooks like the Bohemian Jakob Spanmüller (Pontanus); all had their proper setting in the framework of the Jesuit college.

This predilection for the intellectual apostolate opened the way for the restoration of scholastic theology to a place of honor and dignity long since abdicated in Germany. A trio of non-German Jesuits, the Spaniards Gregorio de Valencia and Rodolfo de Arriaga, and the Dutchman Martin Van der Beeck (Becanus), brought Germany's higher learning into contact with the intellectual movements of other countries. Gregorio de Valencia, whose philosophical and theological works show a passion for order and clear method and who kept up a running polemic with the Protestants, taught at Dillingen and Ingolstadt for twenty-four years. Arriaga lectured at Prague and composed a commentary on the *Summa* of St. Thomas. Becanus, fairminded and versatile author of *A Summa of Scholastic Theology*, with

---

30 Purdie, in *The Oxford Companion to the Theatre*, 3rd ed., s.v. "Jesuit Drama," pp. 509, 512-513; Janssen, *History of the German People*, XIII, 202-203.

Gregorio de Valencia did most to place theological controversy about the authority of the Church on a methodic and scientific basis. The German Jesuits learned well from their masters and, as in the case of Adam Tanner, most illustrious pupil of Gregorio de Valencia, presented a worthy apology for the Church.

The school walls did not isolate the Jesuits of the empire from the people of the neighboring areas. As preachers and as catechists, priests and scholastics, whose reports read like lessons in the geography of the cities and their environs, radiated through the villages and hamlets. From Coblenz they preached in Andernach, Linz, Montabaur, Hachenburg, Leinburg; from Cologne in Oberwinter, Zulpich, Neuss. Among the people whom the Jesuits reached were some who had not received the sacraments in forty or sixty years. Typical of the catechetical reports are those of the college in Heiligenstadt for 1590 which record that catechism classes were conducted in fifteen villages on Sundays and feastdays and twice during the weeks of Lent. In 1594 Melchior Torites reported from Fulda that men of the Society had visited forty villages to teach catechism.[31]

The spirit of divisiveness reigned supreme in politically fragmented Germany, but no one difference evoked such acrid emotions as that of religion. A will for nothing less than complete and total victory over the other side spurred men to turn out an abundance of propaganda marked by the stiffest brand of intolerance. Toward the end of the sixteenth century this literature, often extreme in its language, reached a new low in harshness. Jesuits wrote against the Protestant position, and not always, as in the case of Sigismond Ernhoffer and Konrad Vetter, were they innocent of the unworthy and offensive language of their contemporaries. These Aquaviva reprimanded sharply.[32] With the turn of the century came a change as among both Catholics and Protestants some scholars searched for reasons to justify intellectually toleration of another religion. The Catholic theologian who was the first in Austria to try to clear the air in this dense and oppressive climate was Martin Becanus, who in 1608 published his *Keeping Faith with Heretics,* a distinguished move toward a rational appreciation of toleration.

As a body the Society could not be ignored by the Protestants. Their feelings covered a wide range, from the violent fear of Lu-

31 Duhr, *Geschichte,* I, 459.
32 J. Lecler, S.J., *Histoire de la tolérance au siècle de la Réforme* (Paris, 1955), I, 285, fn. 11.

kas Osiander, who saw in each Jesuit a son of Satan and a post-boy of hell set on converting Germany into a slaughterhouse of Protestants, through the begrudging praise of Andreas Dudith, who admitted the superior scholarship, culture, and virtue of the Jesuits, to the quiet confidence of Protestant parents who placed their children in Jesuits schools for the sake of a sound education. Some of the newer colleges, like those at Hildesheim, Worms, Erfurt, and Münster, were in areas where the Lutheran population was large, and for many a Protestant the patience, industry, and dedication of the Jesuits in the respected position of teachers created a new image of the Catholic. Converts were made. At Augsburg, between 1590 and 1600 the Jesuits converted twenty-nine to fifty-nine persons a year; in Regensburg forty-two in 1593, fifty-two in 1601; in Vienna between 1570 and 1610 seventy to two hundred and thirteen a year, three hundred in 1611 and five hundred in 1615. These typical statistics, while not staggeringly great, showed that the wall of religious division was not completely impregnable.[33]

At the conclusion of Aquaviva's term seventy-five years had elapsed since Pierre Favre was the solitary Jesuit in Germany. One man, more than any other, then became identified with the momentous changes that had taken place during that long period. From the time he joined Favre in the Society of Jesus in 1543, Peter Canisius, under five generals, saw the first tender saplings of the Jesuit apostolate break through the German soil and grow into a forest fair. To his faithful nurturing was due much of this gratifying growth. On December 21, 1597, at Freiburg in Switzerland this lovable, unwavering, childlike Jesuit saint died.

In Hungary another Peter, the third of the great trio of contemporary Peters, Canisius, Skarga, and Pázmány, saved his country for the faith of St. Stephen. Péter Pázmány, born a Protestant at Nagyvárad in 1570, converted at thirteen, entered the Society at seventeen. He studied in Rome under the prince among controversialists, Robert Bellarmine. The alert and zealous bishop of Nyitra, and later archbishop of Esztergom, Ferenc Forgách, faced by a desperate situation as with startling rapidity one noble family after the other deserted the Church, asked for the services of Pázmány. The Jesuit started his work in Hungary in 1601 and soon became the man of the hour. His writings and his sermons worked wonders and have become a landmark in the history of Hungarian literature. Creator of the philosoph-

33 Duhr, *Geschichte,* I, 485, fn. 2.

ical and theological language of Hungary in somewhat the way that Calvin, De Sales, and Pascal molded the French language, Pázmány, noting Protestant success in Germany and France through the use of popular idiom, did the same in his own country. In a more immediate way he did his most influential work among the great aristocratic families, more than thirty of whom he led back to the Church.[34] Other Jesuits moved in and bolstered his work by the colleges they opened at Thurolz, Klausenberg, Nagyszambat. Another region of Europe, seemingly lost to the Protestant tide, was reclaimed.

Two names reflect two aspects of Jesuit fortunes in Poland: *Poland* Piotr Skarga, the internal vigor of the Society; King Sigismund III, the benign attitude of the monarchy. Both set the tone for the circumstances under which the Society continued to prosper, so that in 1599 Aquaviva created out of the Polish Province of 11 colleges, 2 novitiates, and 432 men the Vice-province of Lithuania. Less than a decade later the general made it a full province.

Among the Poles the Jesuits found a stimulating response to popular preaching. Paced by the energetic Skarga, the priests of the Society spoke to thousands from the central area of the country to the border provinces. To listen to a Jesuit became one of the fashions of the day, so much so that even Protestants made a point not to become out of date in this respect. This intensive program of preaching had some notable cultural results. Careful to master the Ruthenian, Litt, and Lithuanian languages, the preachers by constant use kept these tongues alive, and especially in the case of Litt and Lithuanian warded off a real danger that they would disappear.[35] The Polish tongue received a fine elegance in Jakub Wujkc's translation of the Bible, and a vigorous freshness in Skarga's *Lives of the Saints* (1579), one of the nation's most widely read books, as well as in his *Sermons before the Diet* (1600), Poland's supreme literary achievement up to the time of the Triple Partition in the eighteenth century and an immense cultural and patriotic influence, especially in the nineteenth century.

On the national scene the person of King Sigismund III was a symbol of security for the Jesuits in Poland. There was, how-

---

34 É. Amann, *DTC* XII, 1, 97-100, s.v. "Pazmany"; M. P. Harney, S.J., "Cardinal Peter Pázmány," *Thought*, XI (1936), 225-237.
35 S. Bednarski, "Déclin et renaissance de l'enseignement des Jésuites en Pologne," *AHSJ*, II (1933), 200-202.

ever, one brief period when a storm of wrath and condemnation broke over them. And they had themselves to blame. The trouble originated in a sensitive area of the country's national life. A common judgment among the German and Russian neighbors was that eight centuries of history had not taught the Poles the art of self-government. Within Poland's social structure conflicting forces were often at the extremes of tension, and the squires, glorying in a constitution supposedly integrating the best of monarchy, aristocracy, and democracy, none of which they truly comprehended, spoke of their country's "golden freedom," which was in reality nothing more than a "thinly gilded" chaos. A reform movement which aimed to strengthen the monarchy developed, and with this the Jesuits, as true patriots, aligned themselves. The squirearchy reacted with indignation and rose up to break the pro-monarchical trend. The revolt of Nikolaj Zebrzydowski in 1606 was particularly strong. On the Jesuits fell a torrential outpouring of resentment and anger, forcing them to beat a hasty retreat from the political arena. The storm passed quickly enough, but they had learned the valuable lesson, that the surest way to jeopardize their future in Poland was to take sides in an uncertain political contest.

Like all Poles, they could not but be aware of the colossus on their eastern frontier. And the popes often dreamed of the day when the Third Rome of Moscow would enter into union with the First Rome. During this period the Jesuits participated in three distinct efforts to bring peoples of Eastern Europe within the fold. Twice they failed; once they gained partial success.

The first effort was the misson of Antonio Possevino, already seasoned by his discouraging experience in Sweden, to the court of Ivan the Terrible in 1581. Several popes had tried to establish relations with Russia but failed. Excitement ran high therefore when in February, 1581, three representatives of Ivan IV appeared at Rome. The Russian monarch, doing poorly in his war with Poland, sought papal intervention to mediate the dispute and offered the attractive assurance that he would open his country to the West. Pope Gregory XIII grasped this opportunity to break through the old barriers and exploit the possibility of uniting Russia with the Holy See and enlisting a powerful ally against the Turk. He decided to send a representative, and to this heavy and exacting responsibility he assigned Possevino.

On August 12, 1581, Possevino met Ivan for the first time. Then began an exercise in diplomacy which was bound to fail.

Behind his facade of goodwill Ivan hid his limited objective of halting Poland's military success. Nothing more interested him. The papal point of departure was the need of religious unity as a truly solid basis for any diplomatic accord, symbolized by a copy of the decrees of the Council of Florence which Possevino presented to Ivan. The Russian point of departure however was the basic exigency, before all else, of peace with Poland. The monarch drove a hard bargain and his terms were severe. He prevailed, and Possevino agreed to clear up the secular business first.

Possevino then approached the Poles, and at the small border village of Kiwerowa Horka he managed to negotiate a ten-year truce between the two great Slavic peoples. He then returned to Moscow. Ivan began to hedge on the religious question. February 21, 1582, was a date Possevino could never forget. On that day he and Ivan came to the crux of the papal mission, the question of church unity. Ivan erupted into a volcanic outburst of anger, scorn, and virulence. Over the Jesuit he brandished his sceptre with which he had killed his son not long before. Through it all Possevino stood up to the terrible monarch quietly and calmly. On March 14 he left Moscow for Rome, accompanied by a Russian envoy who had no real power to negotiate further. And so ended, in a mere exchange of gifts and diplomatic courtesies, his arduous efforts toward the inviting goal of religious accord between Rome and Moscow.

This diplomacy had its repercussions in Sweden, resulting in the exodus of the Jesuits who had remained there after Possevino had left in 1580. In dealing with the Russo-Polish differences, Possevino had to face the fact that Sweden had a strong interest in the developments in the Baltic area. Swedish arms had made notable conquests in Estonia, Livonia, and Ingermanland. But Poland laid claim to these same areas. Possevino expressed his sympathy for Poland's claims and thereby further alienated King John of Sweden. Despite the obvious damage to the Swedish Mission, he nevertheless had solid reasons for siding with Poland. First, the chance of winning the temperamental monarch to a positive stand for the Church was extremely remote; and second, it was part of the massive Catholic counter-offensive in the North to bring these disputed and predominantly Protestant areas on the south Baltic shores under the control of a Catholic power. John soon found occasion to display the full force of his indignation. In September, 1583, his Catholic queen died. He ordered the dismissal of the priests from the teaching staffs of the Royal College of Stockholm and two other

137

schools. In the early spring of 1584 the Jesuits quit Sweden. Their mission had failed.

The second Jesuit venture toward the East was in their encouragement of the pro-Roman movement among the Ruthenians. The Ruthenians, an important fraction of those Slavic peoples constantly pulled between Poland and Russia and whose center of equilibrium was Galicia, gradually became, despite their Byzantine rite and canon law, orientated toward Rome. To stimulate this sentiment became one of the prime concerns of Piotr Skarga. In 1577 he published a timely and persuasive book, *The Unity of the Church of God*. Not addressing himself to the topic of a universal reunion of all the Eastern Churches with Rome but confining his attention to the area of Poland and Lithuania, Skarga advised the Ruthenians that they could never find in their union with the patriarch of Constantinople, then dominated by the Turks, the energy to rise above their sad state of decadence of the previous century. This they could achieve only by union with the See of Peter. He assured them that within the Roman Church, a beautiful queen dressed in a glorious variety of colors, they would be able to retain their rite and liturgy. He also recalled the historical fact that the Ruthenians had participated in the earlier reunion with Rome enacted at the Council of Florence (1438-1445). Other Jesuits supported Skarga. Stanislaw Sokolowski published two works which encouraged union with Rome, and the fathers at Vilna, by sermons and instructions, created an intellectual atmosphere favorable to the Holy See. Indeed, never before had Ruthenian literary life been so active. Antonio Possevino persuaded Pope Gregory XIII to establish at Vilna a seminary for Ruthenians and to provide scholarships at the Jesuit colleges at Olomuc, Braunsberg, and Prague, as well as at the Greek College in Rome.

The Ruthenian bishops finally made a formal request for union with Rome, and on December 23, 1595, Pope Clement VIII announced that the Ruthenian Church was one with the Church of Rome. In October of the following year, at a moving ceremony held at Brest, with Skarga and other Jesuits in attendance, the Ruthenian bishops in a spirit of high spiritual exaltation solemnly proclaimed their ratification of the union of the churches. Known as the Union of Brest, basically a regional revival of the Union of Florence, it embraced the Ruthenians within the Polish-Lithuanian Commonwealth.[36] But a blight soon

36 O. Halecki, *From Florence to Brest (1439–1596)* (Rome, 1958), pp. 197-201, 331-333, 381-382.

fell on this memorable achievement. Fissures appeared in the Ruthenian body when some of the people decided to remain Orthodox. Sad days of embroilment lay ahead, and Catholic joy for the Ruthenians could not be complete.

The third Jesuit thrust to the East once again had Russia as its target. The results were bizarre. In the new venture the central figure was a Russian of mysterious provenance named Dmitri, who claimed to be the legitimate heir to the throne of Russia. In 1584 Ivan IV had died. Anarchy followed, and seven years later, amid great chaos, Dmitri, Ivan's young son, vanished. In 1603, almost twenty years after Ivan's death, while Boris Godunov was Tsar, a young man appeared in Poland claiming to be the missing Dmitri. The papal nuncio, Claudio Rangoni, believed him. King Sigismund decided to support his pretensions to the Russian throne. Rangoni introduced him to the Jesuit, Gaspar Sawicki. Dmitri expressed the desire to be a Catholic, and on April 17, 1604, Sawicki received the Russian's profession of faith.

A beautiful and entrancing vista opened up before the Polish king, the papal nuncio, and the Jesuits: the coronation of Dmitri as Tsar, followed by Russia's union with Rome under his leadership and inspiration. Pope Clement VIII reacted cautiously, but his successor, Paul V, was most enthusiastic. Dmitri collected an army in Poland, and with two Jesuits, Mikolaj Czyrzowski and Sawicki, as chaplains, moved into Russia. Victory marched with his troops, and on June 20, 1605, hailed by the people, he entered Moscow. The day of Russian unity seemed very near at hand. All the while, however, a strong tide, political and religious, was running with increasing swiftness against the new ruler. The presence of the two Jesuits, identified with the Latin liturgy and tradition, tended to alienate the people. In February, 1606, Czyrzowski warned Dmitri that a conspiracy against him was in the making. Not many days after Dmitri spoke to Sawicki of his plan to open a Jesuit school, on May 27, 1606, a riot broke out and some bajars assassinated Dmitri in the Kremlin. Certainly not the son of Ivan IV and most likely a tool of a group of bajars hostile to Tsar Boris Godunov, Dmitri took with him to his grave the extravagant and vain hopes of the Vatican and the Jesuits who as spiritual advisers, emissaries, and chaplains participated in the strange scheme. The prospects, breathtaking and enormous, were grounded however, on the weakest of bases, the ability of a single, unsteady ruler to turn an entire people from its traditional religious and ecclesiastical allegiance.

This period closes with a loudly dissonant note. In 1614 an ex-Jesuit, Heronym Zahorowski, resentful and vengeful, published *The Jesuits' Secret Instructions*. In this work, better known by its Latin title of *Monita secreta* and now long recognized as a clumsy forgery, he pretended to expose the hidden directives which guided the Jesuits in their malfeasance and trickery. A kind of archetype for anti-Jesuit literature, it has given direction to much that subsequent centuries, wittingly and unwittingly, have had to say about the Society.

The Low Countries, England, and Other Areas

In the Spanish Netherlands, after the havoc of the war of 1576, the Jesuits entered upon an energetic period of reconstruction. Guiding the work of a province returned from exile was a man of large vision, intense initiative, and eminent practical judgment, Olivier Mannaerts. By his careful attention to the formation of the young Jesuits, his clear aim to create eminent teachers, writers, and preachers, his encouragement of intellectual and scientific study, Mannaerts lifted the province he found in ruins to the heights of success. Aquaviva hailed this vigorous builder, who died in 1614 at the age of ninety-two, as "The Father of His Province."

The social milieu was congenial for Mannaerts' objectives. The vigorous and enterprising bourgeois of the Belgian cities responded wholeheartedly to the Society's humanistic approach to the apostolate and soon dotted their little corner of Europe washed by the Scheldt and the Meuse with schools. Twenty-five years after Mannaerts had set to work, 730 Jesuits operated twenty-eight colleges. In 1612 Aquaviva divided the province in two.

The vigor, solidity, and modernity of the schools were qualities which the Jesuits transmitted to their scholarship in the advanced branches of learning. Supreme among the theologians was Léonard Leys (Lessius) whose writing and teaching, characteristically concerned for its relevance to the present moment, bespoke a mind with the rare ability to see the application of unchanging principles in a changing world. His *Law and Justice*, a clear presentation of moral principles in view of the changing social structure of the sixteenth century, had immeasurable influence in the world of ideas. Lessius also inherited from Robert Bellarmine, whom he resembled so closely not only in brilliance of mind but also in amiability and humility of character, the theological contest with the school of Baius. A martial air hung over the field of theology in the 1590's, and Lessius felt the blows of battle in the censures passed on his writings by both the

University of Louvain and the University of Douai. The Holy
See intervened through Cardinal Ottavio Frangipani who, pre-
scinding from the doctrinal points at issue, instructed each side
to refrain from censuring the other. The Belgian Jesuits, dis-
satisfied with stopping at the threshold of the heart of the matter,
continued to ask Aquaviva to obtain a doctrinal decision at
Rome. The general pointedly replied to his impatient sons, "If
you think," he advised them, "that it is an easy matter to obtain
a victory in Rome, you are mistaken. The other side has its
patrons and champions, and these are most influential." [37] Soon
the Louvain dispute was swallowed up in the wider struggle
between the Dominicans and Jesuits on grace and free will.

In Holy Scripture Cornelissen van den Steen (Cornelius a
Lapide), insisting on the literal sense of the inspired word,
lectured brilliantly at Louvain for twenty years before his
assignment to Rome. In Patrology André Schott, assiduous
correspondent with the savants of the age, edited critical editions
of the Church Fathers. François d'Aguilon, author of a treatise
on optics remarkable for that period, and Odon Van Malecote
gained honored positions in scientific circles. But it was in historical research that the Belgians created their most enduring
institution. Héribert Rosweyde, struck by the hagiographical
riches in the libraries of the Low Countries, conceived the project
of producing scientific and critical editions of the old lives of the
saints. In 1603 he broached the subject to Mannaerts, who, with
characteristic breadth of wisdom, gave his approval. From this
simple origin grew the gigantic enterprise of the *Acts of the
Saints* still being produced by the world-famous Bollandists.

Two men especially distinguished themselves in a worthy line
of authors on spiritual subjects: the prolific Frans de Costere,
author of more than forty ascetical and polemical works, and
Jan David, excellent Flemish stylist and most popular for his
delightful persiflage and the joyous and original spirit of his
writings. The Flemings gave a warm reception to *A Candle-
snuffer for the Extinction of the Torches in Holland* (ca. 1607),
*The Christian Housekeeper with a Sponge to Wipe Away Bad
Habits* (1607), *The Christian Beehive* (1600), *The Flower Garden of the Church's Ceremonies* (1607), and other like titles.

In the direct apostolate of popular preaching, directing
Sodalities, organizing General Communions, the pattern among
the Belgian Jesuits closely resembled that in other provinces.

---

37 Poncelet, *Histoire*, II, 160-161.

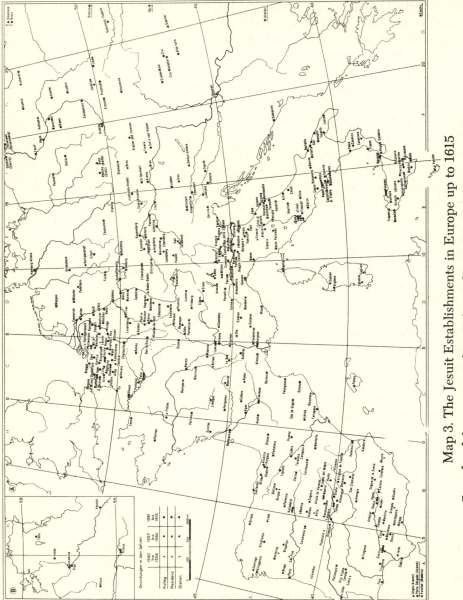

Map 3. The Jesuit Establishments in Europe up to 1615

Reproduced, by permission, from Hubert Jedin, K. S. Latourette, Jochen Martin,
Atlas zur Kirchengeschichte (Freiburg-im-Breisgau: Herderverlag, 1970), page 78.

One project of theirs, however, was unique. In 1587 Thomas Sailly met Alessandro Farnese, governor of the Netherlands, and from their conversation evolved the institution of an official chaplain corps for the governor's troops, which was confided to the Society and to which a dozen priests were assigned. Others enlisted, but when in 1600 the total reached twenty-four, Aquaviva, disturbed that so many were living outside community life, directed that the number be halved. Several of these chaplains, revered for their success in raising the spiritual tone among the Spanish troops, died on the field of battle, ten at the siege of Ostend and three in one day, July 2, 1600, at Nieuport. Reports of this gallantry deepened the enthusiasm of the Belgians for the Jesuits.

No priest in Belgium at this time could be oblivious of the seven northern provinces of the Netherlands which, under the control of the Calvinists and like a foreign mission field, challenged the zeal of the Catholics to enter upon a spiritual reconquest of Holland. Clement VIII in 1592 confided the Dutch mission to the Society. Cornelius Duyst and Willem Van Leeuw, in disguise and covertly bringing the Holy Sacrifice of the Mass, the sacraments, and counsel to the badgered Catholics, led the way for many Jesuits who were to follow in a highly successful enterprise.

Aquaviva, in recognition of the great achievements of the two Belgian provinces, saluted them with an exceptional tribute: "These provinces," he said, "are what I have ever held them to be, the flower of the Society." [38]

Across the channel the England of Queen Elizabeth held a special place in the heart of Aquaviva. He once had hopes of laboring there himself, and just seven months before his election as general, a personal friend of his, Robert Persons, had landed on the coast of Kent with Father Edmund Campion and Brother Ralph Emerson. The Society's mission in England during his generalate was small but brilliant. In 1593 it numbered seven men; in 1598, sixteen; in 1610, fifty-two, a numerical splinter compared to the large number of secular priests trained at Douai. When Persons and Campion arrived in 1580, Douai had already sent a hundred priests into England. During Elizabeth's reign four hundred seculars returned from the seminaries on the continent. But the Jesuit influence, in the persons of some of the finest men of their generation, was wider than mere numbers can indicate.

38 Ibid., 533-535.

Soon after their arrival in the summer of 1580, both Campion and Persons, clearly instructed by the general to attend exclusively to spiritual ministrations, started on their wide tours into the north and the west. Persons has left in his letters some beautiful vignettes of the Catholics, meeting with breathless fervor at secret places to attend Mass and receive the sacraments. The government soon realized that a new force, energetic and purposeful, had entered the land as from secret printing presses appeared several defences of the faith in a clear, virile, vibrant style.

A spy betrayed Campion, and after brutal torture and a biased trial on the charge of treason, this urbane, exquisitely refined "flower of England" was hanged, drawn, and quartered on December 1, 1581. Under Queen Elizabeth ten other Jesuits, including the charming and attractive poet, Robert Southwell, also went to martyrdom. Shortly after Campion's capture Persons returned to the continent so he could communicate more readily with Aquaviva about the English situation. Two hopes he had: to return to England, and there to die a martyr. Neither hope did he realize, but until his death in Rome in 1610 the English mission remained his dominant preoccupation. He begged money for it constantly; he routed fresh priests, both secular and Jesuit, across the channel; he wrote constantly. An early work, designed to provide spiritual reading for the benighted Catholics, was his *Christian Directory* (1582), which even the Protestants pirated, so powerful was it in its concrete, vivid, strong style. In other works Persons kept before the eyes of Europe a picture of the regime of oppression and denial of religious liberty under which Catholics lived.

In the England of the Tudors and the Stuarts the question of the relationship between the spiritual and temporal powers was especially complex. Many unusual incidents added to the complexity. Among these incidents were the Bull of Pope Pius V against Queen Elizabeth, the Spanish Armada, the Catholic raids on Ireland, the Gunpowder Plot, and the Oath of Allegiance imposed by King James I. English and Scots Jesuits felt the brisk repercussions from all of these.

Among some Jesuits a purely spiritual approach gradually yielded to considerations of international diplomacy. About 1582 Persons, having personally experienced the efficacy of the government's net spread for Catholics — he had several close brushes with the police — became convinced that the best Catholic hopes in England rested in the person of young James VI of Scotland. "On the conversion of Scotland," he wrote, "depends every hope, humanly speaking, for the conversion of England." [39] Indeed, for twenty years the handful of Jesuits, mostly Scots, on whom the papacy depended to keep Scotland within the Church, made James the keystone of the arch of their hopes. Their letters reflect in turn exalted hopes, bitter disillusionment, political naïvete, as they followed the fortunes of the Stuart along the road to the crown of England.

The Scots party was but one of the several groups into which the problem of how to save the Church in England splintered Catholics, both at home and abroad. Of the various disputes on policy and method none evoked such acrimony as that between the Jesuits and a small group of secular priests. A battle of books between the two groups went on for years in language crude and intemperate, to the scandal of Catholics and the delight of the government. One point of contention was an unusual institution created by the Holy See. Feeling that conditions in England were currently uncongenial for a hierarchy, the Vatican appointed a secular priest, George Blackwell, to the office of archpriest, empowered to be superior of his fellow seculars and instructed, for the sake of harmony, to consult the Jesuit provincial on major decisions. Protests arose that the Jesuits had executed a neat maneuver to obtain control of the entire mission, and Persons became in a long and distorted tradition of history the great opponent of a hierarchy in England. Recently published documents show that the establishment of an English episcopate had no warmer champion than this much maligned Jesuit.[40]

In the inauguration of the famous College of Saint-Omers Persons made another positive contribution to the English Catholic cause. On February 26, 1593, a bill "for reducing disloyal subjects to obedience" had its first reading in Parliament. One section of the bill, whereby the children of Catholic parents were to be taken at seven years and placed in the hands of Protestants for education in the state religion, and at the parents' expense, particularly incensed Persons. To rescue at least a few boys from this indignity he started a college at Saint-Omer, splendidly located within easy distance of Calais, Dunkirk, and Gravelines, channel ports nearest to England. With the school in Flanders he opened a rich spiritual and cultural tradition which is per-

---

39 *Letters and Memorials of Father Robert Persons,* S.J., ed. L. Hicks, S.J. (London, 1942), p. xl; Philip Hughes, *The Reformation in England,* vol. III, *True Religion Now Established* (London, 1954), 305-315, 318-334.
40 Brodrick, *Robert Bellármine,* p. 312.

petuated even today, after temporary locations at Bruges and Liège, at the Lancashire college of Stonyhurst.[41]

A person of genuine spiritual distinction associated with the English Jesuits in Saint-Omer was Mary Ward. This farsighted, courageous, and charming woman from Yorkshire, taking the Society as her model and relying on the spiritual guidance of Roger Lee, founded the Institute of Mary. She wanted her "English Ladies," or "Jesuitesses," as they became popularly known, to be a mobile and flexible group of religious, with neither cloister nor distinctive garb. In 1612 the bishop of Saint-Omer gave his approval. Seventeen years later the Congregation of Propaganda suppressed the institute. Mary Ward, too far ahead of her time, suffered much, even imprisonment, and only in 1877 did her community receive official recognition.

In England, about the time that she left home for the continent, two memorable affairs, which under James I kept the Jesuits before the government's mind, were the Gunpowder Plot and the great debate between the king and Cardinal Bellarmine. In 1605 a group of erratic Catholics planned to blow up the Houses of Parliament while King James was present. The government discovered the design and rounded up the conspirators. Henry Garnet, superior of the English Jesuits, had earlier learned of the scheme in confession and went through the agony of not being able to halt it. The government, discovering that he had had previous knowledge, arrested him, and tried him for treason. His defense, based on his obligation to keep the seal of confession, meant nothing to the state, and he went to the gallows on March 3, 1606. Arrested with Garnet, Father Edward Oldcorne and Brother Ralph Ashley went to the scaffold and Brother Nicholas Owen died in prison after brutal torture.

In 1606 Parliament passed an act which included an Oath of Allegiance to the king. A blend of both correct and controversial propositions, the oath in practice demanded of Catholics that they acknowledge it to be within the province of Parliament

---

41 L. Hicks, S.J., "The Foundation of the College of St. Omers," *AHSJ*, XIX (1950), 146-180. St. Omers was but one of Persons' educational enterprises. He founded, with the generous help of Philip II, English seminaries in Spain, visible signs to Elizabethan exiles of Spain's interest, which explained the Hispanophile tone in the attitudes of many English Catholics on the continent. See also Hicks, S.J., "Father Persons and the Seminaries in Spain," *Month*, CLVII (1931), 193-204, 410-417, 497-506; CLVIII (1931) 26-35, 143-152, 234-244; A. Loomie, S.J., *The Spanish Elizabethans* (New York, 1963), pp. 182-229, 235-236.

to decide what is heresy as well as to repudiate as heretical the common teaching of theologians through the centuries on the power of the pope in relation to temporal princes. The Catholic community was split. Blackwell, the archpriest, favored the oath. Richard Holtby, the Jesuit superior, opposed it. Pope Paul V denounced it. Cardinal Bellarmine wrote to Blackwell against it. King James learned of Bellarmine's letter to Blackwell, wrote a small volume against the cardinal and Paul V, and so started one of the most spectacular controversies in the intellectual history of Europe, which centered on two of the more thorny political issues of the day, the divine right of kings and papal power in temporal affairs. What began as a duel between a king and a cardinal expanded into a large scale battle. James called up his theologians. And lined up beside the cardinal was a formidable phalanx of his fellow Jesuits, Suárez, Van der Beeck, Pelletier, and Gretser. But, for all their lucidity and expertise as well as their denial to James' ideas the full possession of the field, they did not slow down, on the level of practical life, the steady turn of the mills as they continued to grind the Catholic community. The heroism of these days has found lasting memorials in several pieces of Jesuit literature, such as the autobiographies of two such disparate men, the unambiguous John Gerard, who described his brushes with the police and escape from the tower of London, and the self-effacing William Weston, whose pen was carried along by an elevated interior life; in the gracious and tender addresses by Edmund Campion to the Privy Council and Robert Southwell to the queen; and also in the contemporary accounts of the deaths of the eleven Jesuits who were executed under Elizabeth and the four under James I.

While these events unfolded in England, Jesuits were suffering and dying in the Celtic arc of Scotland to the north and Ireland to the west. At Glasgow Cross, on March 10, 1615, John Ogilvie met his death at the hands of the Calvinists with superb bravery, the first Scots Jesuit to die for the faith. He was beatified in 1929. In Ireland, handsome and well-bred Brother Dominic O'Cullane, with a background of military service against the Protestants under the Spanish and French flags, while helping the priests as they moved furtively through the land, was captured, and on October 31, 1602, went with deep prayerfulness to his execution at Youghal. O'Cullane was one of the impressive group of Irish Jesuits, organized under Irish superiors, which in 1609 numbered seventy-two men, eighteen of whom were in Ireland while most of the others were in training on the continent.

The essence of this mission was educational. Officials in the walled Anglo-Norman towns reported on the tenacity of the Jesuit school masters. Lord Burghley received information in 1595 that "every town is established with schools that have an idolatrous schoolmaster, overseen by a Jesuit." This Jesuit omnipresence checked the government's policy to make the towns Protestant, and no less a person than a modern provost of Trinity College, Dublin, Sir John P. Mahaffy, has judged that, "the Jesuits, by their vigorous and able action during the closing years of the sixteenth century, saved Ireland for the papacy." [42] Among this able group of educators two especially stand out: William Bathe, musician, linguist, and author of *The Door to Languages* (1611), a work immensely popular through Europe, and Stephen White, refined humanist who with his intimate knowledge of manuscripts in continental libraries opened up a wide view of Irish literature in Europe. Bathe, like Edmund Campion before him, had occasion to demonstrate his talents before Queen Elizabeth. The young Irishman came to the attention of Sir John Perrott, the Lord Deputy of Ireland, because of his ability to play several musical instruments, especially the harp. Perrott brought him to the English court. There he enchanted the queen with his music and his mnemonics. Even though Elizabeth gave him grants of land in his native Emerald Isle, Bathe, to avoid the Oath of Supremacy, went to the continent and entered the novitiate at Tournai in 1596.

To strengthen the Church in these saddened countries the Society undertook no more constructive enterprise than the foundation and management of seminaries on the continent for Englishmen, Irishmen, and Scots. Because of the vision and energy of English Robert Persons, Irish Thomas White, probably a brother of Stephen White, and Scots William Crichton, groups of high-minded young men studied at Rome, in Spain or Portugal or France, and then made their way home as priests, many destined to crown their gallant lives with martyrdom.

The Near East   The latter half of the sixteenth century might have become one of the golden ages in the history of the Church if Gregory XIII could have achieved his hopes in the Near East. This energetic pope, by his strong efforts to encourage the patriarchs of the Eastern Churches to unite once more with Rome, held open the door for millions of Orthodox, Nestorians, and Monophysites

42 Corcoran, *Clongowes*, 7.

to return to the one fold. For many of these delicate discussions Gregory depended on the Society.

In March, 1583, three Jesuits, counselors to Bishop Leonard Abel, left Rome to meet with leaders of the separated groups. These and other Jesuits who followed held conferences in many of the ancient cities of the Levant, but they were dealing with men who were custodians, and consciously so, of old and not readily discarded traditions which reached back to the days of Nestorius and Dioscorus. Success, which often seemed within their grasp, eluded them like a wraith. The patriarch of the Jacobites was willing to accept papal supremacy but not the decrees of the Council of Chalcedon; the patriarch of the Armenians made a profession of Catholic faith only to be haled to Constantinople and to have his decision reversed; conferences with the Melkites at Damascus broke down under pressure of the hostile Turk; the entourage of the patriarch of Jerusalem resisted his desire to renounce schism; in Egypt a new patriarch annulled the letter of submission to Rome sent by Gabriel VIII; the patriarch Elias VIII of the Chaldeans, after bringing the Jesuits to his country, informed them that there was nothing to change in his creed. Cairo, Mossul, Damascus, Jerusalem, Edessa, all became for the Jesuits scenes of blighted hopes.[43]

Through the years, under the gaze of the solemn Tower of *The Far East* Belem, which saw Francis Xavier leave for the Indies in 1541, groups of the saint's followers sailed down the Tagus for the Orient, Brazil, and Africa. To the Far East alone fourteen sailed in 1581, thirteen in 1583, twelve in 1585, fifteen in 1592, seventeen in 1597, twenty in 1599, twenty-four in 1609. These groups were typical in this steady flow to the Indies. Usually Jesuits of other nations made up part of these expeditions. In 1596, for example, of the nineteen, six were Italian, five Spaniards, the rest Portuguese. In 1614, however, all twelve were Portuguese. During the first fifteen years of the seventeenth century more than 130 Jesuits left for lands within Portugal's sphere of influence.

In India, aside from the far-flung Portuguese possessions where the missionaries continued to operate out of Goa, three areas especially presented enormous possibilities: the realm of the great Mogul, Malabar, and Madurai. At the court of Akbar, Rodolfo Aquaviva, despite four years filled with discussions, could not move the great Mogul beyond his vacillation. Recalled

43 Pastor, *History*, XX, 495-498.

at last by his provincial, Aquaviva left Agra in February, 1583. Five months later, while working at his new assignment at Salsette, near Goa, he was martyred with three fellow Jesuits by Hindus.

The priest who recovered the bodies of these martyrs was one of the most remarkable Englishmen who had ever gone to India. Thomas Stephens, native of Wiltshire and friend of Edmund Campion, landed in Goa in October, 1579. For nearly forty years, until his death in 1619, he worked on the Salsette peninsula. Padre Estevam, as he was known to the Portuguese, made a unique contribution to the mission by his literary achievements. His Konkani grammar was the first of an Indian tongue ever published. His Konkani catechism followed. By his Christian *Purâna* (1616) in the Marâthi language he attained literary immortality. Stephens, sensing that the Hindu *Purâna*, long poetical stories about the origin of the world and the exploits of the gods, exercised a strong fascination over the Hindu mind, composed a poem which related the story of the Old Testament and then the life of Christ. With vividness and beauty he created unforgettable passages full of oriental color. These have lived with the Catholics of India and have become part of their cultural heritage. As recently as 1935 a Protestant version, with distinctly Catholic passages deleted, was published. By the time of Stephens' death in 1619 the entire Salsette peninsula of some 80,000 natives had become Catholic. He was buried in the Church of Bom Jesus, near the incorrupt body of Francis Xavier.[44]

In 1584, the year after the death of the Salsette martyrs, Akbar again requested Jesuits. Three were sent, Fathers Jerónimo Xavier, grandnephew of St. Francis, and Miguel Pinheiro, and Brother Benito de Goes. In a remarkable test of endurance Xavier, through thirty years, stayed with Akbar and his successor, the Prince Jahangir, even on extensive tours into the Himalayas and Kashmir, ever hoping, as he said, that one day "the fish would bite." But the fish never did, and the grand scheme for the conversion through its leader of the "ladder into Asia" never materialized. In 1608 a discouraging task was made even more difficult. Ships flying the English flag entered Indian waters and Captains William Hawkins and Paul Canning received entrée at the court of the great Mogul. Protestantism, actively championed by the newcomers, only complicated the

---

44 G. Schurhammer, S.J., "Thomas Stephens (1549-1619)," in *Gesammelte Studien*, vol. II, *Orientalia*, ed. L. Szilas, S.J. (Rome, 1963), 367-376.

apologetic mission of the Jesuits. Both priests and seamen, in order to impress the august ruler, went beyond theology to make their point as when, to match the cornet player produced by the English, the Jesuits turned up with a Neapolitan juggler. In 1615 Jerónimo Xavier, sixty-five years old, returned to Goa after thirty years on the mission. Pinheiro also returned. Younger men replaced them, but Rodolfo Aquaviva's dream remained no more than that.

In the southwestern part of the great Indian peninsula, Malabar was a window opening upon a unique garden of singularly fair promise where lived some 200,000 Christians of the Syro-Chaldean rite, known as St. Thomas Christians. Contact through the centuries with the Chaldean Church of Mesopotamia and Persia tainted some of their liturgical forms with Nestorianism, and to bind with ties of affection and loyalty this large Christian community to the See of Peter called for wisdom and understanding of the highest order. But almost from the beginning difficulties plagued the relations between the Portuguese and the Christian Malabarese, and eventually a large segment of these Indians ended in a state of enmity with Rome.

Many threads went into the making of the fabric of a distressing story: the antipathy of some westerners toward a non-Latin liturgy; the incompetence of some Latin churchmen; the deviousness of men who held the key office of archdeacon in the Malabar Church. Differences among scholars only make the understanding of a complicated history all the more difficult.

Some of these differences center on the synod of 1599, called at Diamper by the archbishop of Goa, Aleixo de Menezes. Because this synod imposed a latinized discipline on the Syro-Malabar church, Eugène Cardinal Tisserant has called 1599 "a fateful date and one of the darkest in the history of relations between Latins and Orientals." Menezes, a zealous Portuguese who noted certain erroneous liturgical formulas and a rather loose ecclesiastical organization among the Malabar Christians, seemed to think that he should impose on the Indian archdiocese of Angamale the reforms which Charles Borromeo introduced into the Italian archdiocese of Milan. Yet, Domenico Ferroli, S.J., on the question of the liturgy, claims that Menezes "changed very little" and that "it is misleading to say that the Synod romanized the Malabar liturgy, or to any appreciable extent, assimilated it to the Roman rite." [45]

45 E. Tisserant, *Eastern Christianity in India: a History of the Syro-Malabar Church from the Earliest Time to the Present Day* (Westmin-

Diamper, and all the other related events, touched intimately the life of a scholarly and broad-minded Catalan Jesuit. Francisco Roz knew the Syriac and Malayalam tongues thoroughly and, like his fellow Jesuits at the seminary they conducted at Vaipicotta, approached the Malabar Christians with an esteem and understanding of their worship and organization. To him fell the delicate task of removing the Nestorian blemishes in the liturgical texts. In 1597 the Chaldean Metropolitan of India, Mar Abraham, died. Rome chose Roz as his successor and the first Latin bishop of Angamale. Roz, who won the affection of the Malabarese, noted with distress in 1604 how these people fled into the mountains at the appearance of a Latin priest.[46] To compound Roz' problems, within the structure of his church, which Pope Paul V raised to the dignity of an archdiocese in 1608, was a fatal flaw: the office of archdeacon. Through the centuries, when the bishops were Chaldeans, the archdeacon gradually acquired power to administer the church. The archdeacon under Roz, Jorge da Cruz, of the powerful De Campos family, resented the western impact on his people and the curtailment of his power by a European bishop. By 1618 he let his burning umbrage break out. Schism was not far off.

Madurai, beautiful city inland from the southeastern coast, was another focal point where Europeans demonstrated their inability to appreciate anything not of the West. Here it was not a liturgy that they depreciated but a social and cultural structure. For eleven years a zealous ex-soldier, Gonçalvo Fernandes, labored at Madurai without gaining a single convert. In 1606 the provincial, Alberto Laerzio, in a shift of strategy dispatched a twenty-eight-year-old member of the Roman nobility, the supremely intelligent Roberto de Nobili, to Madurai. So began one of the major breakthroughs in mission history.[47]

De Nobili soon discovered that the way to open the door of India to Christianity was to relinquish western social concepts and to adopt those of the subcontinent of southern Asia. With remarkable facility he learned Tamil. His studies opened his eyes to the set and rigid caste system wherein the high orders of Brahmins, Rajahs, and Vaisyas, in fear of ritual pollution by the despised foreigners or Parangis, avoided contact with that group. Portuguese authorities insisted that Indian converts dress and

ster, 1957), pp. 56-68, 166; D. Ferroli, S.J., *The Jesuits in Malabar* (Bangalore City, 1939), I, 193-194.

46 Tisserant, *Eastern Christianity in India*, pp. 70-75, 176.

47 Amann, *DTC*, IX, 2, 1704-1716, s.v. "Malabar (Rites)."

eat as Portuguese, and take Portuguese surnames. To the Brahmin the Indian Christian became one with the contemned Parangis. Fernandes, insensitive to this situation, would, in practice, force a convert to desert his social status and so become loathsome in the eyes of his own people. In this lay his failure to impress the influential people of Madurai. De Nobili, as an Italian nobleman, judged that his status corresponded to that of an Indian rajah. This he announced and soon gained the respect that Fernandes never received. He also acquired a social fluidity which enabled him to move not only among his own class of Rajahs but also among the Brahmins, the Vaisyas, and the Sudras, the latter a kind of intermediate stratum which embraced the greater part of the population.

He discovered further the high esteem in which the sannyasis, the men dedicated to the things of God, were held. With his provincial's permission he decided to become a sannyasi. Dressed in cloth of red-ochre, a triangular sandal mark on his forehead, high wooden sandals on his feet, he confined himself to a hot, steaming hut and ate only rice, fruit, and herbs. Terrible stomach and head pains did not deter him from his purpose. To master the Vedas, which alone could give him the inner meaning of his new life, he had to study Sanskrit. Within a year he could speak it fluently, the first European to master that language. He committed to memory whole passages of the Vedas in his amassing of information which might be of value in his efforts to tell the Indians about Christ and his Church. To explain to the many inquirers who came to his hut the Catholic understanding of such concepts as infinity, immortality, and personality was a most arduous task. But by 1609 the sannyasi from the West had sixty converts; by 1611, one hundred and fifty. Among the various problems which faced De Nobili was the question whether, because of religious reasons, he would have to forbid his Brahmin converts to wear ths signs of their caste, especially the sandal mark, the tuft of hair or kudumi, and the white cord stretching from the left shoulder to the right thigh. After study and with his provincial's approval, De Nobili judged that these signs could be understood in a civil sense, free of all religious superstition. A Catholic would not be forced to surrender his respectability in Indian society.

In 1610, even as he developed far-reaching plans for the Madurai mission, opposition began to appear. He hoped to see Hindus trained for the priesthood and Sanskrit adopted as the liturgical language of India, but fellow-Jesuits, offended by the newness of this approach, decided to bring his work to a halt.

Old Father Fernandes, disgruntled, sent his grievances to superiors. Nicolau Pimenta, visitor for Goa and Malabar, heard the judgment of two Portuguese theologians who condemned De Nobili's approach as superstitious, scandalous, and illicit. These charges did not go unchallenged. Laerzio, the provincial, rose to his subject's defense; Antonio Vico, a worthy Italian understudy of De Nobili, wrote a lengthy apology; De Nobili himself composed a thirty-nine page exposition of his methods. But in 1613 a new and unsympathetic provincial, the Portuguese Pero Francisco, ordered De Nobili and Vico to discontinue baptizing. In the midst of the deep darkness of disappointment created by men who were good and pious but incapable of setting aside Western molds of thought, a shaft of refreshing light broke through from Rome. In the last letter he sent to the Madurai mission, Aquaviva encouraged De Nobili, lifted the restrictions on his work except in the matter of the tuft of hair and the white cord, since at that moment they were under consideration at the Vatican. This vindication, even though not complete, greatly cheered the Jesuit sannyasi of Madurai.

Meanwhile, Japan was on the march to national unity under the military rule of three powerful leaders. It has been said that in the erection of the new Japan Oda Nobunaga quarried the stones, Toyotomi Hideyoshi rough-hewed them, Tokugawa Ieyasu set them in place. As had been the case with Nobunaga, Hideyoshi and Ieyasu drastically influenced the fortunes of the Society. Alessandro Valignano was the great Jesuit figure of this period, who visited Japan three separate times, 1579-1582, 1590-1592, and 1598-1603. This masterful Italian superior judged that, with the exception of the Chinese, the Japanese were the people most prepared to create the finest Christianity in the East. Deeply appreciative of the richness of Japanese culture, and convinced that when there was no compromise of Catholic dogma adaptation should be made to that culture, he directed the Jesuit priests to assume the status of Zen priests, the most respected of the Buddhist clergy; started a novitiate for native vocations to the Society and opened two seminaries. He removed from office the superior, Francisco Cabral, because of his policy of heavy-handedness and repression toward Japanese members of the Society. In 1602 two Japanese Jesuits were ordained; two years later the first native secular priest. Valignano had the highest esteem for the Japanese Jesuit brothers, because it was they, unimpeded by the language problem, who bore the heat of the day in catechizing and disputation.

The visitor expected great things, but three factors, culminating in a decree of expulsion in 1614, worked against success: the bad judgment of the Jesuit vice-provincial; a bitter controversy with the Franciscans; the influence of commercial interests, intensified by the arrival of the British.

Gaspar Coelho, the vice-provincial, disregarded Valignano's orders against Jesuit interference in local politics. In a colossal blunder Coelho promised Hideyoshi, who was planning an expedition against China, that he could procure not only the assistance of the Catholic daimyo of Kyushu but also Portuguese naval support. Coelho's rashness was quite possibly the first in a series of incidents which made Hideyoshi suspect that the Jesuits were spies preparing a western military assault on Japan. On July 24, 1587, the ruler issued a decree of expulsion of the Society from the country. Coelho reacted belligerently. He tried to organize a rebellion of the Catholic daimyo and sent requests to Goa, Macao, and Manila for troops. Valignano countered with sharp indignation. Only Coelho's death in May, 1590, saved him from a stiff punishment by the angry visitor. Drastic as the decree sounded, the government actually enforced it in only a half-hearted way. In the mind of Hideyoshi the Jesuits were of a piece with the Portuguese mercantile system, and harm to them might entail sanctions in the form of trade curtailment by Portugal. Valignano, eminent realist that he was, knew that the decree was held in suspension only because of the Macao trade, and explicitly admitted that the greatest incentive to conversion in Japan was the Great Ship of the Portuguese merchant marine. This trade affected not only the Japanese. To provide necessary funds for the mission, Valignano proved to the reluctant Philip II, Gregory XIII, and Aquaviva that the Society in Japan must invest in the commerce in silk. In 1598 he secretly went beyond the guidelines and received a reprimand from the general. This Jesuit mercantile activity became a target of Franciscan and Protestant criticism.[48] In 1590 he obtained an audience with Hideyoshi and by consummate tact secured the ruler's promise not to enforce the decree against the Jesuits if they did their work in a quiet and unobtrusive way.

During this uncertain truce a serious problem for the mission arose in the Philippines. There Spanish merchants and Spanish Franciscan friars eyed Japan as an inviting field for commerce and evangelization. The Portuguese merchants were determined to keep out the Spanish traders; the Jesuits were just as resolute to block the entry of the friars. Valignano argued cogently and

48 Boxer, *The Christian Century*, pp. 93-95, 117-121.

well for this seemingly selfish position of the Society. Rejecting all narrow jealousy and adopting the good of the mission as his norm of judgment, he included in his argument the point that the friars, in their distinctively different religious garb and by their different methods, would create the impression that Catholicism, like Buddhism, lacked unity and was merely a collection of "splinter sects." In his brief *Ex pastorali officio* in 1585 Pope Gregory XIII made Japan an exclusively Jesuit mission. The friars, refusing to be excluded, ignored the brief on the claim that it was obtained under false pretenses. They made strong representations to the Holy See, and finally, twenty-three years later, Pope Paul V officially opened Japan to them.

Valignano's fears were justified. The strong contrast between the Franciscan and Jesuit approach soon became evident as the friars, imitating their successful methods in Ibero-America where the indigenous cultures were primitive, tended to brush aside the mature civilization of Japan to which the Jesuits deferred with respect; the friars were free, but the Jesuits cautious, in the distribution of medals, rosaries, holy water; the friars concentrated on the poor, while the Jesuits worked among the influential classes. Great bitterness developed between the two groups, and their correspondence crackled with their stinging denunciations of one another. If the Franciscans condemned the sterile erudition of the Jesuits, the latter spoke of their critics as "the crazy friars." During this affray, his suspicions again aroused about the missionaries as a fifth column preparing an assault by Spain, Hideyoshi moved swiftly and brutally. At Nagasaki, on a cold winter's morning, February 5, 1597, he had twenty-six Christians, including six Franciscans and three Jesuits, crucified. These Pope Pius IX canonized in 1862. All, save the Franciscans, were Japanese. The three Jesuits were the scholastics Paul Miki, John Soan, and James Kisai.

Soon after, in September, 1598, Hideyoshi died. By adroit diplomacy and military success Ieyasu became dictator. His early actions encouraged the Jesuits, for he expressed an attitude of general religious toleration, employed João Rodrigues as his interpreter, and gave Valignano a gracious reception. Conversions were numerous, at least 70,000 from the spring of 1599 to the fall of 1600.

A strong undertow was, however, pulling against the Church. Buddhism was experiencing a renaissance, Ieyasu was himself a convinced Buddhist, suspicions about the Iberians were strong. Then in April, 1600, appeared the strongest omen of the mission's decline. At Bungo, with Will Adams acting as pilot, anchored the Dutch ship *Leifde*. Ieyasu, recognizing that he had a fine counterbalance against the Portuguese and Spaniards in the battle for trade, welcomed the newcomers. Will Adams supplanted Rodrigues as interpreter. The Protestant seamen spread anti-Catholic stories. Iberian influence declined, and with it the prestige of the Jesuits. Rivalry among the colonial powers of Europe became the wedge which eased the missionaries out of Japan. A tinder-box situation was aggravated by political scandals in which the names of Christians figured. The blow fell on January 27, 1614. Ieyasu ordered the expulsion of all missionaries and the return to some form of Buddhism of all Japanese Christians.

The decree worked havoc on the mission of one hundred and sixteen Jesuits, who with their catechists and helpers made up a staff of five hundred and thirty-four persons. On November 7-8, 1614, a small convoy left Nagasaki carrying all the Jesuits, save twenty-seven who one way or another managed to remain, away from the 300,000 Christians who were once the great hope of the Church of the Orient.

In the thirty years since St. Francis Xavier died on San Chian Island off the coast of China, twenty-five Jesuits knocked at the portals of the mighty empire, only to be rebuffed.[49] Preparing for the day when the law against foreigners would be lifted, the Society established a residence at Macao, the Portuguese enclave on a small peninsula in the Canton estuary. In 1578 Valignano stopped at Macao on his way to Japan.

As in India and later in Japan this perceptive, forward-looking priest left his impress on future Jesuit plans for China. For several months he stayed at Macao and studied as far as he could the culture of the Chinese. Convinced that the Society must disassociate itself from the image of the westerner as a marauder avid only for conquest, he formulated general principles for the missionaries: a deep sympathy and respect for the intellectual and spiritual values of the Chinese; the most perfect command possible of the language; the use of science as a step in the introduction of the faith; the development of the apostolate of writing and conversation; special concern for the cultivated classes on whom the government of the country depended; and the primacy of supernatural virtue. He assigned Michele Ruggieri to Macao to study the Chinese tongue. In 1582 Ruggieri received a companion, thirty-year-old, brilliant scientist and linguist, Matteo Ricci. In 1583 the two students of Chinese ways

49 D'Elia, Pasquale, S.J., in *Enciclopedia Cattolica*, III, 1659, s.v. "Cina."

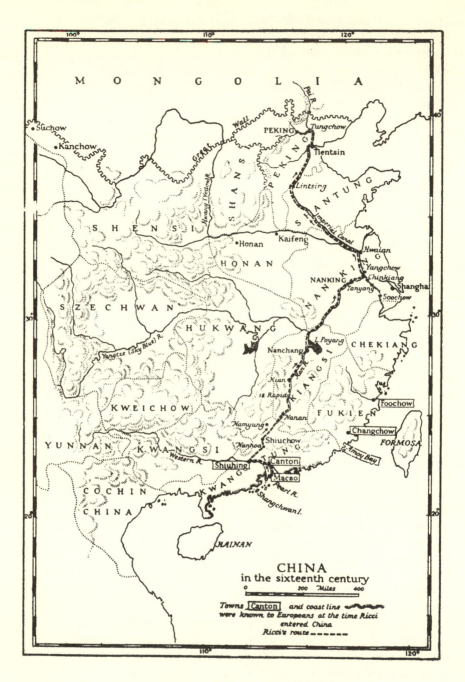

Map 4. The Journeys of Matteo Ricci

A map drawn by K. C. Jordan, in the book *The Wise Man from the West* by Vincent Cronin. Copyright, 1955, by E. P. Dutton & Co., Inc., publishers, and used with their permission.

received the long hoped for opportunity to reside within the empire. A mandarin, anxious to consult Ricci, about whose mathematical skills he had heard, gave them entrée. Ruggieri and Ricci obtained a site for a house at Shiuhing, which became a starting point for a mission which spread within twenty-five years to Nanking, Nanchang, Shiuchow, Shanghai, and Peking.

Ricci by his unusual gifts of mind and heart became the perfect embodiment of Valignano's principles in his appreciation for the dignity of Chinese culture and his flawless mastery of their language. Concentrating his efforts primarily on the conversion of the educated classes in whom the rule of the country was vested, and making the natural sciences the beginning of Catholic apologetics, he appealed to their ready intellectual curiosity by his exhibition of clocks, prisms, mathematical instruments, oil paintings, maps of the world. In 1594 he received permission to enter the elite social class of the mandarins, among whom his high intellectual prestige was magnified by his more than twenty works in Chinese on apologetics, mathematics, and astronomy, some of which have honored places in the history of Chinese literature. As a by-product of this unique apostolate he provided the solution to a riddle which had long baffled European cartographers, the precise location of evasive, inscrutable Cathay. Putting together disparate bits of evidence, he concluded that Cathay was nothing else than China.

The course set by Valignano, basically simple, was nevertheless beset with difficulties in its application. This Ricci discovered when he came in contact with the details of Chinese life. His conviction that Christianity did not necessitate the extermination of a non-European culture did not relieve him of the heavy responsibility of determining whether certain traditional Chinese practices, ceremonies in which the people honored their ancestors and Confucius, were compatible with divine revelation. The Chinese, in whom was rooted a strong filial piety and a close familial intimacy, included the deceased as part of the family as much as the living, and to the memory of their ancestors they erected in their homes commemorative tablets. On a national level they lived in a philosophical and ethical tradition which penetrated through the ages back to the studious and high-minded teacher of the sixth century B.C., Confucius, and him they honored in a ritual way. In order to comprehend the internal and essential significance of these customs, Ricci studied ancient Chinese literature, observed for many years the way in which certain of the educated class carried out the ceremonies, discussed the problem with Chinese scholars, and concluded that the rites, in origin and nature, were national and social forms devoid of religious significance. The recently deceased Pasquale d'Elia, S.J., eminent Riccian scholar and editor of the indispensable *Fonti Ricciane,* believed that Ricci judged the rites to be "certainly not idolatrous and perhaps not even superstitious." Widespread credulousness about the ceremonies however made Ricci's opinion difficult to prove, but he believed that with instruction converts could be taught to discriminate and remove the objectionable accretions of the centuries. He therefore gave countenance to the participation in the rites by the new Chinese Catholics.

Particularly troublesome was the problem of finding Chinese expressions for Catholic truths, a problem like the one which faced the early Christians who had at their disposal a vocabulary of a pagan civilization. After long and profound study of ancient texts and consultation with scholars, Ricci thought that *Tien,* "Heaven," and *Shangti,* "Sovereign Lord," described a Sovereign with the attributes of the God of the Christians.

In 1601 Ricci achieved his ambition to establish a Jesuit house at Peking, the imperial city. There for nine years, under the benign gaze of the emperor, he continued to hold the respect of the intelligentsia. Other Jesuits came to his help. Conversions began to multiply. By 1610 when Ricci died, twenty-five hundred Chinese, four hundred of whom were in Peking, had become Catholics. In the next five years the number had doubled. Ricci left devoted fellow-religious behind, but he also left doubts in the minds of some, especially Niccolò Longobardi, about his methods. This split presaged serious trouble ahead. Nevertheless, Jesuits who through the centuries followed Ricci into China found courage and inspiration in the memory of this kind, affectionate, and brilliant Italian priest, dressed in his plum-colored silk robes and tall black hat of the mandarins, riding in a palanquin or explaining a prism or solving a mathematical problem, all the while hoping to open the eyes of the Chinese people to Christ the Lord.

In one of the most amazing annals of Catholic missions, a Jesuit brother created an overland link between the India of Jerónimo Xavier and the China of Ricci. The Jesuits of India had heard many stories about the mysterious kingdom of Cathay and its supposedly great Christian population hidden somewhere behind the mountains of Central Asia. To contact these Christians, Jesuit superiors chose a forty-year-old, ex-soldier from the Azores, the energetic, chivalrous, and pious Brother Benito de Goes, companion of Jerónimo Xavier at the court of Akbar.

In March, 1603, Goes, disguised as an Armenian merchant, joined a caravan and started his trip "across the roof of the world." Over the plains of northern India he went, into the wild Himalayas to Kabul "in the bowels of the mountains," between high peaks and over a vast plateau to Yarkand, and then on to Karashahr. Here Goes solved the geographical enigma of Cathay. He met Mohammedan merchants who knew Ricci in China and who gave him information which led him to the same conclusion Ricci reached: Cathay is China. By slow, monotonous stages the Brother pushed on to the frontier fortress of Suchow where he arrived in February, 1606. He sent a letter to the Jesuits in Peking. Ricci dispatched a devoted Chinese convert, João Fernandes, to contact Goes. On May 31, 1607, Fernandes found the lonely, brave man, sick and bedridden. Eleven days later Goes died, four years after he had left Agra. Fernandes brought back to Ricci the Brother's few personal belongings and a single page from the Bible with St. Paul's boast that amid trials and dangers he had proved himself a true disciple of Christ. In his quest for Cathay Goes had found heaven, and in his lonely grave on the Chinese frontier formed a link between his brother Jesuits in China and in India.

In Africa, as during the previous period, four large areas *Africa* continued to engage Jesuit energies, Ethiopia, Mozambique, Angola, the Congo. To these was now added a fifth, Cape Verde. But, in contrast to the numbers who went to the Orient and Brazil, Africa received but a mite of the Jesuit manpower. Frequently in each mission the total of Jesuits could be counted on the fingers of one hand.

Ethiopia of this period raised missionary hopes to delightful heights. Despite the sterile results of the earlier mission of Andrés de Oviedo, the Society never ceased to try to keep some bridges open into that land. In 1589 two Spaniards, Antonio de Monserrate, a veteran missionary with experience at the court of the Great Mogul, and Pedro Paez, disguised as Armenian merchants, tried to enter, but the Turks captured them and kept them for six years in jail and in the galleys. In 1595 a Maronite, Abram de Guerguis, landed at Massawah, but was killed by Moslems. Three years later Melchior de Sylva managed to make his way to Fremona where he ministered to the Portuguese settlers.

The patience of years began to bear fruit in 1603. Paez, recently ransomed from the Turk, was received at the court of the Negus, Za-Denghal, who, deeply impressed by the personable and versatile Jesuit, very soon announced his intention of accepting the faith of the Roman Church. A rebellion broke out and Za-Denghal was assassinated. Paez won the respect of the new Negus, Socinios, but realizing that there was more than theology involved in the converting of a country where national pride could hardly admit that their ancestors had been in error for ten centuries, he moved with deliberate slowness. By quiet and steady instruction he implanted in the Negus' mind the deep conviction of the primacy of Rome and the obligation of its moral teachings. This spiritual evolution in the mind and heart of Socinios began to influence his court. Three other Jesuits came for theological discussions with the monks and intellectual leaders of the country. In 1614 Socinios felt that the time had come to promulgate the doctrine of the two natures of Christ. A wave of revulsion spread through the country and the Abouna became the center of a violent rebellion. Paez saw ten years of patient work brought to the brink of destruction as everywhere the cry resounded: "The faith of our fathers, Monophysitism."

In lower Africa Angola was the main mission. Yet the number of Jesuits was never large. Two arrived in 1580; four in 1584; six in 1593; two in 1596; one in 1597. The largest contingent, six priests and six brothers, arrived in 1602. But by 1607 all six priests had died. Of all these men the one who particularly stood out and whose large correspondence is a valuable source of Angola's early history was Baltasar Barreira, who worked in Africa for thirty-two years. Barreira reported a steady increase of Catholics among the natives. Less than a year after his arrival, he wrote about an Angolese prince named Songa whose son and brother received baptism. He described the son dressed in imperial red, with orange boots, a robe and round hat of white damask. The next year Barreira baptized Songa, also colorfully garbed. By 1590 converts had advanced to 20,000.

Two especially vexing problems affected this mission: war and slavery. Natives at times resisted and revolted against the Portuguese conquest. With the Portuguese troops went Jesuit chaplains, who, pressured by the governor and filled with patriotism, often overidentified themselves with the military. On February 2, 1583, the Portuguese won a particularly decisive victory. Barreira was with the troops and on the field of battle prayed for success. A letter of his and other sources gave a rather full picture of the conquest. They told of thirty men who went to the governor of the colony, each with a load of noses cut from the dead blacks. They pictured the procession of the Portuguese, garlands on their heads and palm branches in their hands, the Mass of Thanksgiving, and the foundation of a confraternity in honor of Our Lady of Victory. In 1596, the Jesuit visitor to the mission, Pedro Rodrigues, admonished, with success, the priests about their immoderate union with the arms of their nation.

The second problem was slavery. The slave trade in Angola was a major enterprise. At times Angolese chieftains gave the Jesuits, as they did to the other Portuguese, slaves as a tribute of their vassalage to the Portuguese crown. Portuguese colonists occasionally left slaves to the Jesuits in their wills. These developments reopened an issue that had troubled the Portuguese province from its early days: the use of slaves in Jesuit houses. Frequently Portuguese superiors asked for permission to have two or three slaves as domestics. Borgia, Mercurian, and Aquaviva refused. In Angola the relatively simple question of owning slaves escalated to the more difficult issue of selling those received as gifts. Some missionaries felt that this was a legitimate way to finance the mission. Jesuits in Europe were upset by this news. Barreira defended the practice and explained a device to avoid scandal: the use of a third person who would carry out the transaction and then turn the money over to the Society. Aquaviva rejected this expedient. And the provincial congregation of Portugal in May, 1590, insisted that the general's prohibition be seriously honored. They stated further that the missionaries, if in need, should rely on alms. These decisions scotched the issue in Angola for the time being.

Meanwhile the Jesuits broadened their apostolate. Through the munificence of benefactors they built a splendid church and an imposing college in Luanda. And during the four years, 1604-1608, the enterprising Barreira contacted local chieftains and set up mission stations in the Cape Verde Islands, at Cape Verde, and in Guinea, and Sierra Leone. But the debilitating climate of these lands, only fifteen degrees above the equator, inhibited the Jesuits and sent many of them to an early grave.[50]

In Brazil the Jesuits, assisting both spiritually and culturally the infant colony to take its first steps and to grow into a robust childhood, became more and more identified with the maturing of this vast settlement. Earlier in this century Joaquim Nabuco, Brazilian ambassador to the United States, remarked that one of the great formative elements in the creation of Brazilian unity

Brazil, Spanish America, and the Philippines

50 Rodrigues, *História*, II, ii. 520-527, 553-564, 575-596.

was the Society of Jesus. That his country had not been divided into three or four large segments, some Huguenot, some Dutch, he attributed to the binding cords of the Catholic faith. And those who most effectively built the Catholic Church along the coast and in the jungles, joining city and forest in a unity of religion, were the men of the Society. Perhaps overmagnanimous, the ambassador's judgment nevertheless has the merit of recognizing Brazil's immense debt to the Jesuits.[51] As in the Orient, here other nationalities gave valuable aid, such as the two Italians who joined the nine Portuguese who sailed in 1587. But the Portuguese, some fifty of whom went to Brazil between 1588 and 1609, always predominated.

Two events especially affected the Jesuits at this time: the transfer of the Portuguese rule to Philip II of Spain, and the thrust of the province into Paraguay. Spanish dominion brought a governor, Manuel Teles Barreto, who despised the Society. Barreto connived with an unscrupulous speculator, Gabriel Soares de Sousa, in building up at the expense of the natives a lucrative slave trade. Against this unholy alliance the usually gentle José de Anchieta hammered with all his strength. De Sousa tried to persuade the bishop, Antonio Barreiros, to believe that Indians were incapable of belief in God. Anchieta could point to the communities of natives who responded deeply and movingly to the truths of the faith. Despite his eloquent words, which remain a beautiful testimony to his belief in the dignity of the human person, Anchieta could obtain only a modified and limited action of the government against the slave trade.

In the years 1586-88 the Brazilian province made an important thrust into the interior. A few years earlier, at their provincial congregation, the priests took up the question of moving westward into Paraguay, and finally, in October, 1586, an expedition of five set out. On the way the English pirate, Robert Witherington, gave them moments of worry, but they made Buenos Aires. From Buenos Aires they moved into the interior to Córdoba. On August 11, 1588, the city of Asunción gave a rousing welcome to the three who finished the journey, Juan Salone of Catalonia, Manuel Ortego of Portugal, and Thomas Fields of Limerick, Ireland. They realized Nóbrega's old dream of a push to the West.

During this expedition, in 1587, José de Anchieta finished his term as provincial. The chief charge which critics brought

51 S. Leite, S.J., *Páginas de História do Brasil* (Rio de Janeiro, 1937), pp. 31-34.

against this sweet-tempered man was that he had been too lenient in the enforcement of the rules and *Constitutions* of the Society. One carper thought that his tender care of the sick was undignified. But the Jesuit visitor, Cristóvão de Gouveia, gave the more balanced judgment: "No provincial of Brazil will accomplish one-half as much." Ten years later, on July 9, 1597, the emaciated, wrinkled, little cripple died. In his last hours, still delightfully cheerful in spirit, he composed his last bit of verse. Staggering in its magnitude as was the record of his exploits, far more marvelous was his burning interior spirit which, breaking through his letters, revealed his sure grasp of St. Ignatius' objective for his sons, that of being "a contemplative in the midst of work." Christ Our Lord brought all his immense talents into focus. "We must," he wrote, "always have Him as our companion. . . . Even though we at times reject Him, He is ever knocking at the door of our hearts. His hope is to enter, live there with the Father and the Holy Spirit, and fill every tiny corner of our soul." In the soil of Brazil's spiritual origins Anchieta transplanted the ideal of "companionship with Christ" which he had learned in the *Spiritual Exercises* years before at Coimbra. With Nóbrega, he has ever remained a source of inspiration for all Jesuits who have followed into the land of the red wood.

In Spanish America, both to the north and to the south, the Jesuit apostolate was at once urban and sylvan. The great colonial towns in which the Society established schools could not be the place of ultimate interest since, as the general reminded his men, their prime purpose in crossing the Atlantic was to labor among the uncivilized peoples. The cities were therefore stepping stones between Old Spain and the wilderness of the American jungle and mountain.

In Mexico, by 1600, the Jesuits had opened seven colleges. In their first major enterprise among the heathen, they contacted the wild Chichimeco Indians, who were terrorizing the highway between the capital and the mines of Zacatecas. The transformation was astounding as they turned migrants and warriors into villagers and farmers. The man with the Midas touch, who brought the gold of peace where there had been brutality and ferocity, was Gonzalo de Tapia, one of the greater missionaries of the century.

Gonzalo, with Martín Perez, was the pioneer in the great northward push into New Vizcaya, which opened in 1591 and which in a two-columned movement advanced along the eastern and western sides of the jagged Sierra Madre. The pattern was the same. From canyon to canyon, river to river, valley to valley

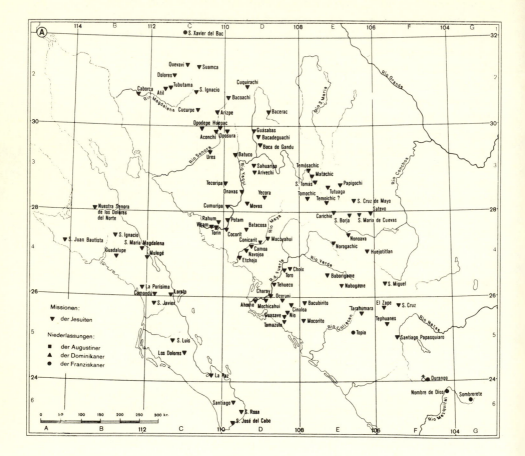

Map 5. Jesuit Missions North of Mexico City up to 1720

Reproduced, by permission, from Hubert Jedin, K. S. Latourette, Jochen Martin,
Atlas zur Kirchengeschichte (Freiburg-im-Breisgau: Herderverlag, 1970), page 84.

the Jesuits, as veritable spiritual *conquistadores,* pushed on, settling roving tribes into villages where they could learn crafts and cultural skills. Within six months after the advance started, several pueblos were formed and more than a thousand Indians were baptized. By 1600 the Jesuits had eight missions serving thirteen pueblos along the Sinaloa and Mocorito rivers. In the wake of the colorful soldier, El Capitán Hurdaide, the missioners added the whole valley of the Fuerte to the Church, and on the river Mayo brought 30,000 Indians into the fold. The vast area reaching from Mexico into the present southwest of the United States, incorporated into the Church by this prodigious and resourceful missionary drive, became known as Jesuit Land. Like the Portuguese Jesuits in the Far East, those in Spanish America welcomed their fellow Jesuits of other nations. In Mexico, for example, between 1572 and 1619, thirty-seven came from Italy, seventeen from Portugal, seven from France, five from the Low Countries, two from Denmark, one each from England, Ireland, Chios, Germany, Portuguese Africa, and the Philippines. These men, somehow or other, circumvented the policy of Madrid that none but Spaniards be allowed to go to the Spanish Indies. This policy threw responsibility for manpower, almost in its entirety, on the Spanish provinces, and as the seventeenth century unfolded a serious crisis developed. Economic pressure intensified the strain. Ample confidential documents, intended for the father general, pictured a life of need and hardship. In the *tercero* of 1600 all seven colleges in Mexico, save that of Guadalajara, ran at a deficit.[52]

In South America, in the cities like Cartagena, Bogotá, Quito, Santiago, along the great crescent of Spanish civilization which spread from the north in New Granada, along the swelling middle of Peru, to the south in Chile, the Jesuits established their colleges and churches. Of that arc of cities Cartagena, because of a particular social phenomenon and a remarkable priest, became tied in an unusually tender and human way to Jesuit history. Cartagena was a port of the slave trade and the mission station of Alfonso de Sandoval. At once an energetic apostle and scholar, Sandoval served by hand and pen the poor black wretches who were dumped like unfeeling cargo into the market of the city. With the arrival of a slave ship the priest went into

52 H. E. Bolton, "The Jesuits in New Spain," *Catholic Historical Review,* XXI (1937), 265; E. Burrus, S.J., "Pedro de Mercado and Mexican Jesuit Recruits," *Mid-America,* XXXVII (1955), 140-152; F. Zubillaga, S.J., "La Provincia Jesuítica de Nueva España. Su fundamento económico: siglo XVI," *AHSJ,* XXXVIII (1969), 164-167.

action, baptizing, consoling, washing, feeding the stinking chattel chained by neck and feet into groups of six, the living and the dead together. With the curiosity and intelligence of the competent scholar, Sandoval gathered from various sources data about the slave trade and wrote his *The Nature, Religion, Customs, Rites and Superstitions of the Negroes* (1627), still an essential source on the subject of slavery.

The heavy continental forests which pressed on littoral New Spain remained a constant reminder to the Jesuits of an uncompleted task. In them lived the millions of natives, variant in their degrees of primitiveness, some docile, others savage, whose conversions constituted the real frontier for the Society. Among the Ambobagacuas, Caronadas, and Cofanes, of eastern Ecuador, the hero was Rafael Ferrer, who in 1611 crowned by martyrdom his decade of labor during which he founded three Christian settlements. Among the Araucan Indians of Chile, the like of whose fierce and indomitable spirit the Spanish military had never before encountered, Luis de Valdivia and Gabriel de Vega had an uphill struggle, and in the turmoil of the conflict three of their fellow Jesuits lost their lives. Among the simple and childlike Guaraní of Paraguay Francisco Angulo and Alfonso Barzena baptized in the thousands.

Of all these individual missions, that among the Guaraní became the most memorable, for it was among these people that the missionaries developed the Paraguayan villages known as *reducciones*. A directive from Aquaviva gave the immediate impulse to these institutions. The general, realizing the danger of large-scale lapses from the faith among a roaming people who were without constant guidance, ordered that the Indians be gathered into permanent settlements. In 1610 Marcial de Lorenzana gathered some families, and about thirty-five miles from the northern bank of the Paraná and somewhat east of the junction of the Paraná and the Paraguay founded the village of San Ignacio. Further east, that same year two Italians, Giuseppe Cataldino and Simone Maccetta, organized for two hundred Guaraní the village of Nuestra Señora de Loreto. These modest beginnings were the mustard seed from which grew the impressive tree of the Paraguayan Reductions.

In the midst of the wide and varied activity of the Jesuits in South America appeared a particularly striking example of that harmonious union of prayerfulness and apostolic labor which St. Ignatius envisaged for his sons. Diego Álvarez de Paz went to Peru from Spain in 1584. His provincial, noting his decided attraction for the spirit of recollection and anxious about his ability to integrate this spirit with his apostolic labor, sought the advice of Aquaviva. The general instructed the provincial to be sympathetic to the young priest, since "the spirit of prayer, when it is not counter to obedience and the Society's ministries, is not alien to the Society but rather proper to it." The remarkable achievement of Álvarez de Paz as a writer, professor, and superior justified Aquaviva's confidence. His three volumes, *The Spiritual Life and Its Perfection* (1608), *The Extermination of Evil and Promotion of Good* (1613), and *The Quest for Peace* (1618), works of a man of deep speculative powers and ardent affections, mark him as an original theoretician on affective prayer.

From America the Spanish Jesuits made a long thrust into the Far East. In 1581 four of them joined religious of other orders in the creation of the only almost thoroughly Catholic people in the vast area of Asiatic paganism, the Philippine Islands. In this fresh enterprise the experienced Antonio Sedeño, who nine years earlier had founded the mission in Mexico, took the lead. Within a decade a hundred men of the Society were working on several of the islands of the vast archipelago. Schools began to rise with the foundation, in 1595, of the College of Manila and in 1601 of the seminary of San José, the educational institution with the longest continuous existence in the Philippines, and possibly in all Asia. In 1604 Pedro Chirino in his *An Account of the Philippine Islands* published one of the earliest detailed descriptions of the peoples and culture of this vast insular chain.

Far to the north of the Spanish possessions, at Port-Royal in Acadia and at St. Sauveur on the coast of Maine, two French Jesuits, Enemond Massé and Pierre Biard, made the first attempts of the Society to settle in New France. They stayed only two years, 1611-1613, forced to flee from the English who from Virginia ravaged the mission. But the beginning had been made, and with their return in 1632 the French Jesuits opened one of the most inspiring epochs in mission history.

All the impediments to progress on the missions did not originate with the native populations. Several thorny problems arose among the Europeans themselves and persisted until the suppression of the Society late in the eighteenth century. Two of the more important were the relationship of the missionaries to the system of the Royal Patronages; and then their relationship, as members of a religious order, to the bishops. The Royal Patronages (the Spanish *Patronato Real* and the Portuguese *Padroado Real*) were, in general, that combination of rights and duties

General Missionary Problems

which the monarchs of Spain and Portugal inherited in their capacity as patrons of the Church throughout the colonial world. The popes of the fifteenth and sixteenth centuries, preoccupied with the European balance of power and the Turkish threat, and not equipped to care for the new world which suddenly burst upon them, granted the Iberian monarchs the privilege of presenting bishops for vacant sees, administering the Church's tax structure, and supervising the clergy, in return for bearing the expense of sending priests to the missions, maintaining them there, and building churches. By mid-seventeenth century the popes realized that, as circumstances changed drastically through the years, the Royal Patronages had become a strong challenge to the authority of the Church. At the same time, throughout both colonial empires, legal and juridical issues were destroying the harmony of the missionary enterprise. One in their dedication to the Church, generous and self-sacrificing men scattered their energies and talents in nasty polemics on such questions as the extent of jurisdiction, the relationship of the several religious orders among themselves, and the legitimacy of the authority exercised by the hierarchy and the colonial administration. And frequently a clash of personalities only compounded the evil.

In this distasteful business the Jesuits had their share. At times the local government claimed the right to a voice in the transfer of individual religious from place to place. This pretension Aquaviva absolutely repudiated. An instance of this kind arose in the Philippines in 1598. The civil authorities demanded that they receive notice of changes among the religious. The Jesuits, in union with the other orders, informed them that if this were insisted on they would retire from the mission stations. The government backed down. Again, in 1629, Philip IV directed that superiors of religious orders submit on the occasion of a mission vacancy three names from which the civil authorities would choose one. As Aquaviva before him, Vitelleschi rejected this kind of interference.[53]

A second problem touched the relationship between bishops and Jesuits. A potential source of misunderstanding lay in the difficulty of reconciling the rights of a bishop to direct the missions in his jurisdiction and the status of the missionaries as members of a religious order. The individual religious was awkwardly situated between two authorities, the bishop and his

---

53 H. de la Costa, S.J., *The Jesuits in the Philippines, 1581-1768* (Cambridge, 1961), pp. 257-259, 271-272.

superior to whom he was bound by a vow of obedience. Conflicts, destructive of peace and concord, often arose when the bishop made his official visitation of the churches cared for by the Jesuits or priests of another order. In view of the dissensions which erupted in various areas of the Spanish colonies, Pope Gregory XV, in 1622, addressed a constitution to the archbishop of Mexico outlining a solution which honored the bishop's right to inspect the churches and examine the administration of the sacraments and the state of public worship, but which at the same time respected the religious as one answerable to his superior for his personal conduct.[54] These and other litigious issues dogged the missionaries down to the suppression of the Society.

Aside from these jurisdictional controversies, a problem of a more cultural nature pressed the Spanish and Portuguese Jesuits for a definite formulation of policy. It was the delicate question: should natives of the mission lands be admitted into the Society? Answers differed from area to area and frequently reflected the response to the wider question about the advisability of creating a native clergy. And this in turn depended on the cultural milieu from which the aspirant to the priesthood came. An educated convert from Nagasaki or Peking had greater initial potential than a native from the Sierra Madre mountains in Mexico or from the banks of the Amazon in South America.

The Spanish Jesuits quite naturally approached the problem within the framework of the experience and attitude of the Spanish colonial Church. As early as 1536 — four years before the Society of Jesus came into existence — Charles V, in response to urgent requests, civil and ecclesiastical, opened the College Santiago Tlatelolco in Mexico for the training of native priests as well as for the education of lay students. Franciscans headed the school. This enlightened step, however, failed in the wake of strong complaints that the Indians were not suited for the priestly vocation. This failure sent waves of hesitation and even resistance to a native priesthood which washed the farthest shores of colonial Spain. Ecclesiastical legislation solidified this negative attitude.

Certain important racial distinctions gave varying nuances to this legislation. There were the *indios,* pureblood natives; the *mestizos,* those of mixed European and native parentage; and the *criollos,* those born in the colonies of European parentage. In 1555, for example, the first Council of Mexico refused ordina-

54 De la Costa, *The Jesuits in the Philippines,* pp. 422-423.

tion to the *indios* and *mestizos,* because they resembled descendants of the Moors, and in 1591 the second Council of Lima
closed sacred orders to the *indios,* because they were only
recently converted. Legislation of this kind, prohibitive rather
than encouraging, disheartened any wide and deep aspiration
for a native Church.[55]

Within this context the policy of the Jesuits in colonial Spain
eludes any clear generalization. One of the outstanding Jesuits of
this era, illustrious not only for his exhausting activity in Peru
but also for his efforts to formulate a rationale for the existence
of the missions, was José de Acosta. Acosta's *The Apostolate
for the Eternal Salvation of the Indians,* written in 1576 but
published in 1588, is a masterpiece in this genre of literature.
He distinguished between principle and practice. Basic to his
thinking was the thesis that the priesthood was not locked to
the *indios.* Yet, for the moment, he felt that the principle
should be held in abeyance, not indeed because of any inherent
natural incapacity of the *indios* for so great a responsibility but
rather because of their want of education. Once trained, the
indios could worthily take their place at the altar. Acosta wrote
with hope, and for this hope he found a foundation in the story
of the Irish. A barbarous people, worse even than the *indios* of
America, the Irish, once they were patiently trained, evolved
from their uncivilized state into a fervent and cultured people.[56]

What could not in principle be denied to the *indios,* Acosta
insisted, must be held open to the *mestizos.* It could be, he felt,
that from among the *mestizos* would arise another Timothy, who,
though born of a Gentile father and a Jewish mother, did
excellent work in the infant Church. Yet here too a prudence,
based on the Church's ancient and traditional ideal of the
priestly dignity, influenced Acosta to defer, for the time being,
the advance of the *mestizos* to holy orders. With time these
people, already the masters of the Indian tongues, would match
this competence by the splendor and beauty of their lives.
Optimism colored Acosta's writing as he looked to the future.

Even before Acosta wrote his reflections on the creation of a
native clergy, Francis Borgia, as general, showed in the practical
order of administration his appreciation for vocations to the
Society from the mission lands. In a directive to Pedro Sánchez,

55 De la Costa, S.J., "The Development of the Native Clergy in the
Philippines," *Theological Studies,* VIII (1947), 226-231.
56 L. Lopetegui, S.J., *El Padre José de Acosta, S.I., y las misiones* (Madrid, 1942), pp. 383-386.

provincial in Mexico, while stressing prudence in the selection of native vocations, he excluded neither *criollos* nor *mestizos* nor *indios*. The catalogs of the Society's Mexican province pull back the curtain on local Jesuit policy and reveal a most interesting course of action in the light of the generally restrictive ecclesiastical canons. In 1585, of the 144 Jesuits in the province, thirty-seven were born in New Spain. Regrettably, the catalogs do not specify the race of these men. In 1592 sixty-one of the total of 216 were born in America; and in 1619, 121 of 348. Further study of the catalogs of other provinces in Spanish America may reveal a like picture. As for the Philippines, save for one brother, Alonso Sancho, received in Rome, there is no record of a single pureblood Filipino being admitted into the Society up to the year of the expulsion, 1768.[57]

Within the Portuguese sphere of influence the basic attitude, while it made room for distinctions, favored the cultivation of native clergies. In 1541, the year Francis Xavier left Lisbon for the Indies, Goa had a seminary for Indians. Several priests from Malabar had already been ordained. With its several training centers for native priests, India anticipated by twenty years the decree of the Council of Trent that each diocese of the Catholic world should establish a seminary. Alessandro Valignano, ever catholic in his view, shaped Jesuit policy with an eye to the encouragement of priestly and religious vocations among the peoples of the Far East. He argued strenuously for a bishop in Japan, but he did not want a European, stranger to language and customs. He hoped that the Japanese themselves would in time provide men who could take on that key responsibility. Impressed by the high level of culture in Japan and realizing the severe difficulty westerners had learning Japanese, he energetically advocated the training of Nipponese for the priesthood, both as seculars and Jesuits, and for the religious life as brothers in the Society. Because Francisco Cabral, the Portuguese superior, did not agree, Valignano, as visitor, replaced him with the sympathetic Gaspar Coelho. In 1590 there were seventy Jesuits in training. In 1602 the first two Japanese Jesuit priests were ordained; in 1604 the first secular.

Several adverse factors, however, slowed down Valignano's ambitious plans. Financial support for the projected seminaries did not arrive from Europe. Latin proved to be an obstacle to

---

57 Burrus, "Pedro de Mercado and Mexican Jesuit Recruits," *Mid-America,* XXXVII (1955), 140-152; De la Costa, *The Jesuits in the Philippines,* p. 234.

many students. What also may have checked him was the strongly critical judgment which João Rodrigues had of the Japanese. In February, 1598, Rodrigues wrote to Aquaviva that these people were irresolute and fickle, and that of the hundred or so brothers in the Society not one was fitted for ordination. Aquaviva took a firm stand in determining the aptness of candidates for the priesthood in the Society, and in 1610, four years after the death of Valignano, he forbade the ordination of any Japanese not forty years of age. Many of them resented this and became restive.[58] Then the expulsion threw all plans into disarray. In regard to certain other Asiatics Valignano was less optimistic, advocating the admission of Indians to the priesthood but not into the Society. When China was opened, the Jesuit missionaries, again making contact with a highly cultivated people, adopted as their own the attitude of Valignano toward the Japanese. In time, but much more slowly than in Japan, Chinese entered the Society and advanced to holy orders. The first was ordained in 1664. Through many storms in China the Jesuits kept as a guiding star the light set in the Asiatic skies by the great Valignano of the worth and dignity of a native clergy.

Conclusion   As the Society moved through the last years of the sixteenth century it displayed in a twofold way a remarkable internal strength and resiliency: first, it weathered an acute domestic crisis; and second, it manifested a fresh openness to human values in forms other than those of the West.

Matthias Scheeben, distinguished scholar of the nineteenth century, remarked of the Jesuit theologians of the sixteenth century: "The role of the lion fell to the recently established Jesuits." [59] Theology flourished in Bellarmine, Suárez, Toledo, Gregorio de Valencia, Molina, Vázquez, Fonseca, Becanus, Lessius, a Lapide. In the pre-suppression Society such a cluster of genius never reappeared. Only time will tell whether the age which has produced Émile Mersch, Henri de Lubac, Teilhard de Chardin, John Courtney Murray, Maurice de la Taille, Karl Rahner is as distinguished.

The creativity, strength, and enterprise, suggested by Scheeben's judgement, characterized many other fields of the Society's endeavor. Ricci and De Nobili spirited the noble essay in the

58 Boxer, *The Christian Century*, pp. 89–90, 219–220.
59 Le Bachelet, S.J., *DTC*, XIII, 1, 1044, s.v. "Jésuites."

adaptation of the faith to oriental cultures; Valignano brought new vision to the eastern missions; Gonzaga, Kostka, and Rodríguez, following Loyola, Xavier, Borgia, Canisius, Favre, continued the impulse to heroic holiness; Azevedo in the Atlantic, John, Paul and James in Japan, Campion and Southwell in England, Silveira in Africa walked in the tradition of martyrdom for the Church. Fresh streams of holiness and learning sprang from the fountain of the Society.

Chapter 4

CHALLENGES FROM NEW POLITICAL
AND CULTURAL HEGEMONIES
1615–1687

The Generals FROM 1615 TO 1686 SEVEN GENERALS headed the Society. The first of these, Muzio Vitelleschi, ruled for thirty years. During the next forty years the average term for the six men who followed was only a little over six and a half years, and some of these, quite old and unwell, did not bring to their task the energy and alertness which the burden of office demanded.

Muzio Vitelleschi, a fifty-one-year-old Venetian elected in November, 1615, guided the Society with intelligence, prudence, and a keen realization of his responsibility to the principles of St. Ignatius. Not so daring as Aquaviva, however, and tending to be preoccupied with the "dangers" which "menaced" the Society, he made *periculosus* a favorite adjective.[1] He died on February 9, 1645, in his eighty-second year. When the Eighth General Congregation convened, Pope Innocent X surprised the delegates by an unusual request. He asked them to set aside the established procedure of a congregation and consider, before they elected a new general, a series of eighteen questions he had drawn up. These questions, some of which aroused memories of the agitation during Aquaviva's rule, included such issues as the advisability of a regular convocation of a general congregation at set intervals, the designation of provincials by local congregations in each province rather than by the general, the personal visitation of the provinces by the general. For about a month the delegates thoroughly reviewed them. On the suitability of a general congregation meeting every nine years they were prepared to agree. Toward the other points they did not feel as well disposed. On January 1, 1646, Innocent, impressed

1 M. de Certeau, S.J., "Crise social et réformisme spirituel au début du XVIIe siècle: 'Une nouvelle spiritualité chez les Jésuites français,'" *RAM*, XLI (1965), 354-355.

by the sincerity of the deliberations, issued a brief, two points of which deeply affected the Society's administration. First, he ordered the convocation of a general congregation every ninth year; and second, he directed not only that the term of a superior, other than the general, be limited to three years but also that a period of a year and a half should elapse before a retiring superior could again be designated superior. The latter directive seriously hampered the Society's administration, since men with all the high qualities necessary for the wise guidance of a religious community were not always readily available. Six days after Pope Innocent issued his brief, the congregation chose as general sixty-one-year-old Vincenzo Carafa from the kingdom of Naples, highly regarded for his personal holiness and wide experience in the offices of novice master, rector, and provincial.

Then followed a quick succession of generals. Carafa, after a little over three years in office, died on June 8, 1649. The Ninth General Congregation elected in December of that same year the seventy-five-year-old Sienese, Francesco Piccolomini. Fatigued after leading three different provinces, Piccolomini lived only a year and a half and died on June 17, 1651. The Tenth General Congregation on January 21, 1652, elected the Roman, Luigi Gottifredi. While the congregation was still in session, Gottifredi, after a week's illness, died on March 12. Nine days later the delegates chose the seventy-year-old German from Juliers, Goswin Nickel.

In 1661, nine years having elapsed since the previous general congregation, another, the eleventh, was assembled in 1661. A serious problem faced the delegates. Nickel, eighty years old and seriously ill, was clearly incapacitated. He asked that he be given a vicar, and according to the conditions which the congregation would decide. The delegates asked Pope Alexander VII for the power to choose a vicar who would not only have the right of succession but would immediately enjoy the free and universal exercise of all the powers of the general. The pope consented. On June 7, 1661, the congregation chose Giovanni Paolo Oliva, a popular preacher and severely penitential member of the Roman province. According to the congregation's twenty-ninth decree, in which was formulated the norm of relations between Nickel and Oliva, the full power of general rested in the vicar, not *cumulative*, in such a way that both Nickel and Oliva possessed it by equal right, but *privative*, so that the vicar alone enjoyed it and Nickel could assume for himself none of it, with the consequence that any executive act of his would be illicit and invalid. Nickel was general in name only; Oliva in all but name.[2] Nickel lingered on for three more years until his death on July 31, 1664.

Oliva ruled for twenty years with distinction, gaining a tribute from Louis XIV, who saluted him as one of the most competent executives of the age. One of his first achievements, a great asset to smooth and efficient administration in the Society, was to obtain from Pope Alexander VII the repeal of the limitations set by Innocent X on the choice and term of superiors. He also asked Alexander to reverse Innocent's order for a general congregation every nine years, but the pope died before he reached a decision. A century was to elapse before the Society could revert to the original rules of the *Constitutions* in this important matter.

Oliva died on November 26, 1681. In July of the following year the Twelfth General Congregation picked the sixty-seven-year-old Belgian, Charles de Noyelle, in an election which uniquely resembled that in which St. Ignatius was chosen. With the exception of his own, De Noyelle received all the votes. He ruled for only four, but terribly agonizing, years. The Spanish Hapsburgs and the French Bourbons, making the office of the general one of the several focal points in which they tested their strength, crushed De Noyelle by their pitiless and unsparing pressure. Each power demanded that he pay a diplomatic visit to its own ambassador in Rome before that of the other. De Noyelle, fearful of offending either Versailles or the Escorial, was thrown into severe anguish. Through the correspondence between him and the confessor of Louis XIV, François de la Chaize, ran a deep current of his mental distress. De la Chaize was cold and adamant in his demands that the general see the French ambassador first.[3] Two months after his election De Noyelle yielded to France. Four months later Charles II forbade all communication between the government of Spain and the general.

That same year, 1682, Louis XIV, victorious in his campaigns in the Spanish Netherlands, revived an earlier request that the Gallo-Belgian province, embracing the area of his conquest, be transferred from the German Assistancy to the French Assistancy. In October and November, through letters which express his awe of the Sun King — "a prince so perfectly just will find our fathers submissive to his orders in every circumstance"; "in this, as in everything else, the Most Christian King will find us

2 Astráin, *Historia*, VI, 11.
3 G. Guitton, S.J., *Le Père de la Chaize* (Paris, 1959), I, 137-145.

178

completely obedient" — De Noyelle agreed to the transfer. But
he did not count on the Hapsburgs. When Spain heard of the
agreement, it demanded that Naples, Sicily, and Milan, all Spanish controlled, be transferred from the Italian Assistancy to the
Spanish Assistancy. This threw the perplexed De Noyelle into
an enervating state of indecision. His health began to fail.
Louis XIV, out of compassion for the distracted man, dropped
the matter for the time being.[4]

During the rule of these seven generals the Society continued
to grow, but in proportions which pointed to a serious internal
crisis. Through the fifty-three years from 1626 to 1679 its numbers increased by 2,000, from 15,544, to 17,655. This contrasted
sharply with the earlier increase of 2,000 within the ten years
immediately previous, the first ten of Vitelleschi's term. And still
more strikingly did it contrast with the fifteen-year-period,
1600-1615, when the numbers were augmented by some 5,000.
Sudden and pronounced easement therefore followed rapid
growth. The causes of this change were complex, but to a great
extent it was because of a voluntary reaction to a crisis induced
by a straitened financial situation. Resources for the support of
the scholastics did not keep up with the number of vocations
to the Society. Besides, many small colleges, accepted because
of the importunity of admirers, were not viable. Disaster, such
as in Germany during the Thirty Years War, struck many houses;
economic decline, as in Spain, sapped others. Most communities
struggled under the weight of heavy debts, and as general bank-
ruptcy became imminent, drastic action had to be taken. The
general congregation of 1615, troubled by the penury of the
schools, recommended that novices be admitted in limited numbers, only enough to sustain the life of the provinces. The general
congregation of 1645, returning to the same concern, not only
authorized the dissolution of several smaller colleges but also
prescribed that the general should determine the number of
novices each province might receive, even prohibiting, if necessary, the admission of any at all. Carafa, acting on this decree,
in July, 1646, ordered the provincials to keep the doors of the
novitiates absolutely closed to fresh recruits until further notice.
The general congregation of 1661, while authorizing Oliva, then
vicar-general, to discontinue poorly established schools, ordered
him to be chary about accepting new foundations. In 1664
Oliva checked with the provincials about the maximum number
of novices their resources would allow them to accept. True

4 Ibid., II, 79-81.

though it was that some provinces, such as the two in Belgium, prospered during this period, the picture in its broad lines distressed the generals greatly.[5] But their restrictive policies, dictated by the pinch of poverty, had a salutary effect. The Society could not have continued to grow at the pace it maintained from Ignatius to Vitelleschi without creating a serious threat to its internal spiritual unity. Curtailment had to come. Financial distress brought it about. The regression and stagnation which gripped several countries in Europe in the seventeenth century as they moved into the modern economic system left its mark on the Society.

During the fiscal anxieties of these several generals, great changes which could not but affect the Society were taking place in the intellectual world. Like the winds which sweep across the desert, turning the sand dunes into new shapes and forms, fresh ideas passed over the cultural terrain of Europe, reshaping older forces of thought and expression. The scientific movement, enlivened by the experiments of Galileo and others, contested with increasing self-assurance the age-old primacy of Aristotelian physics.

Many a Jesuit classroom necessarily echoed with the clash of the old and the new, since it was in the philosophy course that these matters were treated. Teachers found it difficult to take a stand because at first the issues were not too clear-cut and the way the battle would turn was not too obvious. But two men especially, René Descartes, who published in 1637 his *Discourse on the Method of Rightly Conducting Reason*, and Isaac Newton, who in 1687 published his *Mathematical Principles of Natural Philosophy*, hastened the day of reckoning. Widely alert and enthusiastic in their response to the scientific movement, save in Spain where interest was negligible, many Jesuits of Europe eagerly initiated a wide scope of experiments. By 1650 they were publishing for classroom use a series of scientific texts. Through the seventeenth century, in general astronomy alone — apart from special aspects of the field — they had produced at least fifty-six works. Long column follows long column of the volumes they wrote on physics, geology, botany, paleontology. These were the Schoolmen who participated in the transitional period between the discrediting of the Aristotelian physical system and the widespread recognition of Newtonian physics. This task of adaptation, difficult enough in itself, was made all the more complex by the appearance of the works of Descartes, whose influence

5 Astráin, *Historia*, V, 47-48; VI, 31.

reached far beyond the stimulus he gave to the careful and meticulously planned experiment. In his speculative writings, wherein he cast a prominent role for clear and distinct ideas, this brilliant alumnus of the Jesuit College of La Flèche challenged the traditional approach to philosophy and thereby brought hesitation, perplexity, and uneasiness to the ranks of his former teachers.

For a century these developments engaged the attention of one general congregation after another as the delegates endeavored to point the course the Society should steer across the shifting intellectual terrain. In the congregation of 1646 the Germans especially deplored the presence in some Jesuits of two qualities which should have no place in the thinking of the genuine philosopher: a withdrawal from reality, which some manifested in wasteful and empty speculation; and a certain naïveté, shown in a gullible and uncritical pursuit of novelty. In accord with a directive of the congregation of 1649, Piccolomini drew up a list of sixty-five propositions in philosophy and thirty in theology which Jesuits should refrain from teaching. Some of these reflected, even at this early date, the influence of Descartes. Others, such as: "It is within our power to touch a possible being even in its state of possibility," exemplified the arid sort of speculation repudiated by the delegates.[6]

Provocative as circumstances might have been, this particular approach to an intellectual situation carried within itself the question about its ultimate wisdom. Some sixty-five years earlier Salmerón, in somewhat analogous circumstances during the Molinist disputes, answered Aquaviva's request for advice on the question of unity of doctrine in the Society. He wrote at some length in a letter which breathed the spirit of freedom. One point he made was this: "I believe that we should not draw up a list of propositions which we may not defend. This has been done before and it has worked out badly. But if a catalog of this kind is actually composed, let it contain as few propositions as possible, lest the word go out that we wish to restrain the human mind within overtight limits and condemn by anticipation opinions and theses which the Church in no way has proscribed."[7] The old veteran of the Council of Trent, who could fall back on the experience of a long life in the intellectual world, insisted that difference of opinion was part of the advance of human knowledge and that the Society had sufficient limits

6 Ibid., V, 91-93, 283-284; Brucker, *La Compagnie,* p. 770.
7 *MonSalm,* II, 709-715.

traced out for the theological endeavors of its members in Holy Scripture and in the definitions of the popes and the councils.

While Aristotelian physics was capitulating before the discoveries of the new experimentation, Latin was surrendering her position as the honored and essential means of communication in the educated world. The vernacular tongues, more facile, more open to nuances, more subtle in the transmission of ideas, developed rich and superior literatures and, in a widespread cultural shift, gradually took the place of Latin. Protestants used the vernacular with great success in their appeal to the masses. The Society, understanding the situation, made a number of adaptations which, rather than violating a rigid and inflexible loyalty to Latin, flowed from the elasticity of official documents such as the Fourth Part of the *Constitutions* where St. Ignatius insisted that the scholastics learn the vernacular well, and the *Ratio Studiorum* of 1599 where translation into the vernacular in a well-turned style was recommended. In the classroom Latin maintained its primacy, but outside, in academies, the theatre, public functions, the national tongues gained in popularity and prestige. And even in the classroom, textbooks in the vernacular became more widespread.

During these years of change, another problem which engaged the generals was the hatred and antagonism which developed among certain groups within the Church against the Society. Two features of the Jesuits' apostolate especially provoked hostility: certain of their principles in moral theology, and their approach of adaptation to the native culture of the Chinese. This antipathy found vivid expression in two contemporary works, the *Provincial Letters* of Blaise Pascal and the *Old and New Controversies about the Mission of Great China* of the Dominican, Domingo Navarrete. Both became classical sources for the enemies of the Society.

Pascal was the eloquent voice of the stern and rigorous Jansenists, who denounced the Jesuits as the chief cause of the alleged laxity in the current teaching on moral questions. Among the Jesuits a professional interest in moral theology had always been great. Since in their apostolate they stressed the sacramental life nourished by penance and the Holy Eucharist, they received a particularly careful formation in the handling of moral questions so that they would be the skilled confessors called for by St. Ignatius in the *Constitutions*. Opposed to the rigor of Calvinism and inclined toward the imitation of Christ the Good Shepherd, they tended to favor liberty and to restrain the imposition of an obligation which was not certain. This attitude was of a part with that particular school of moral theology known as probabilism. In the latter part of the sixteenth century, in the long process of refining and clarifying older concepts, theologians, led by the Dominican, Bartolomé de Medina, formulated the doctrine of probabilism. According to this doctrine, when the lawfulness of an action is in doubt, one may follow the opinion favoring liberty so long as it is solidly and truly probable, even though the opinion favoring the law is equally probable or even more so. Jesuits in general embraced this doctrine. A few men, by their unreasonable use of it, brought discredit on the Society as a whole. And the Society's critics, not making the distinctions necessary for a balanced judgment, arrived at the sweeping indictment: A particularly potent and corrosive force, destroying the moral foundations of Christian life, was the Jesuit teaching in moral theology.

The intensity of this accusation caused the generals much concern. On July 4, 1654, Nickel, noting that "in these recent years scarcely does the list of prohibited books appear without listing a work by a Jesuit," urged that the priests assigned to the pre-publication censorship of books by other Jesuits be especially diligent. Three years later, returning to the same theme in the face of the violent criticism stirred up by Pascal, he stressed the responsibility each Jesuit carried for making sure he gave no occasion for bringing obloquy on the Society. Despite the precautions taken by the generals, moral laxity remained one of the favorite labels attached to the name Jesuit by the persistent and rigid Jansenists.

The *Old and New Controversies about the Mission of Great China* by Navarrete was an incisive and forceful indictment of the Jesuit missionary methods in China. The Dominican took this extraordinarily delicate question, which should have been hammered out by scholars in an atmosphere of quiet detachment, and made it a popular rallying point for enemies of the Society. In his book the Jansenists had an arsenal for their attacks on the Jesuits.

The question of the correct attitude toward the cultures of the East merged with another missionary problem, that of jurisdiction. The patronage systems of Portugal and Spain, becoming gradually more and more outmoded, conflicted with the new Congregation for the Propagation of the Faith (Propaganda), established in 1622, and the Jesuits, caught between the two in their rancorous contest, received buffets from both. Through the energy of Francesco Ingoli, the first secretary of Propaganda, this congregation began to throw out the cords designed to bind the missions to Roman control. Spain and Portugal, with memories of their generous support of the Church overseas and resentful of what they regarded as intrusion into their empires, tried to maintain their sway. For its purpose Propaganda used bishops who, in lieu of a national hierarchy, had titular sees and were known as vicars apostolic. The first vicars apostolic, aside from the threat to Iberian influence inherent in their office, fanned the fires of suspicion and contentiousness in the Far East because they were French. The individual missionary, dedicated to his supernatural ideals, became the prey of two, sometimes three, contending eagles. He stood alone, perplexed and afraid. The agonizing question was: With whom rests the local authority? In 1673 Pope Clement X decided that it was with the vicars apostolic. These then the Jesuits obeyed.

Yet from the vicars apostolic in Indochina came complaints, especially between 1673 and 1680, that the older missionaries, notably the Jesuits, showed insubordination. The responsible character of the men who presented these complaints intimated that the charges were not entirely without foundation. Propaganda asked Oliva to bring his men into line with a stern rebuke. The general presented to the Congregation the apologias drawn up by the missionaries. To these Propaganda did not react kindly. Oliva, reflecting that the withdrawal of the Society seemed to be the only way to satisfy the complainants, asked that the Jesuits be allowed to leave Indochina. Propaganda rejected this request.[8] These events left memories of tension between the Congregation and the Society, memories which lived on in a generally valuable but somewhat unfortunate book.

In 1677 Cardinal Urbano Cerri, secretary of Propaganda, drew up a report on the missions for the recently elected Innocent XI. So fine a panoramic view did it give, with its thumbnail sketches country by country, that Sir Richard Steele, anxious to alert Englishmen to the peril of the Roman Church "as a sort of universal spirit insinuating itself, as far as it can, into every particle of the universe," made a translation which he called *An Account of the State of the Roman-Catholick Religion Throughout the World.* In the section on Tonkin, Cerri recited the gravamina against the Society. Of the arrival of the vicars apostolic there he wrote: "The Congregation [Propaganda] knows how many oppositions they met with from the Jesuits, who being the first missionaries in those parts, could not well bear to find themselves subjected to the apostolical vicars. They

8 Brucker, *La Compagnie,* pp. 647-654.

thought they had lost in a great measure the esteem they were in, and that they should not be able to manage the Indians, as they had done before, that people being very sensible of the great virtue and disinterestedness of the vicars. The Jesuits began therefore to cry them down in public meetings, and even in their churches; and raising a damnable schism, exhorted the faithful by circular letters to deny their authority and to pay no obedience to them, making them believe with crafty insinuations that they were intruders and heretical bishops, and that all the sacraments administered by their priests were null." Balance and fairness do not ride with the sentences as they move along through the continuing account. The rationale of Cerri's partial report may be, in part at least, his uncomplimentary estimation of religious in general on the missions. On the problem of sending missionaries to areas not yet ready to receive a bishop he wrote: "It cannot be denied that secular priests will better succeed in such a ministry than the regular. When the former go upon a mission, they are transported with the zeal of living a more perilous and austere life than they do in their own country; whereas the latter take such an employment upon themselves to enjoy a greater freedom and to shake off the yoke of obedience." [9]

The missions were not the only area of the Church in which Roman officials, unfriendly to the Society, had interest. France too entered upon their horizon. A close advisor of Pope Innocent XI and friend of the Jansenists, Agostino Favoriti, joined a fantastic conspiracy which envisaged a general crusade against the French Jesuits by the closing of their schools and the revocation of their faculties to hear confessions, an assault to be crowned by a papal condemnation of the Society. Amid the dull haze of intrigue Oliva discerned the outline of what was the ultimate issue. "A plot," he said in July, 1681, "is in the making against us and our Institute." [10]

If the Society, absorbed in these insistent problems, was not insular, neither was it angelic. A group of some 17,000 men could not but feel the drag of human nature with its defects and failures. Repeatedly the generals issued letters addressed to the entire Society, many of which stressed the need, in view of

---

9 Urbano Cerri, *An Account of the State of the Roman-Catholic Religion throughout the World* (London, 1716), pp. ii-iii, 124-125, 184; Pastor, *History*, XXXIV, 78.

10 Guitton, *Le Père de la Chaize*, I, 66-67; Brucker, *La Compagnie*, pp. 587-588.

the damage that can result from routine, for renovation of spirit and awareness of the basic principles of St. Ignatius. For a while the feelings of nationalism and sectionalism created serious unrest in parts of the Society. In Sicily rivalry between Palermo and Messina, in the Spanish Netherlands between the Walloons and the Flemings, in Portugal between those north and south of the Tagus, hurried along the creation of new provinces. On the missions bad feelings developed between the recently arrived Europeans and the Creoles. The general congregation of 1649 enacted strong legislation against the men who seemed to have a mania for dividing provinces according to regional consciousness. Nickel attacked this divisive spirit with energy and skill, basing his appeal for unity on the spirit of the early Society when Ignatius had made a Frenchman first rector of the Roman College, a Spaniard the superior in Paris, a Fleming the rector of the College of Turin. During the wars between Charles V and Francis I, Nickel pointed out, in the College of Palermo, working with complete harmony of mind and heart, were a Fleming, a Lombard, a Castilian, a Frenchman, a Portuguese, a Piedmontese, and a Valtelline. This appeal to the origins of the Society aroused the sense of fraternal charity which gradually took the edge off the sharp local loyalties.[11]

Because of such action by Nickel and other generals, the spiritual state of the Society continued to be strong and vigorous. Nothing could more strikingly demonstrate the general intense and practical pursuit of holiness than the widespread desire to sacrifice self in hardship, discomfort, and loneliness among pagan peoples in the far away lands beyond the seas. Long lists of volunteers for the missions, including some of the most well known in Europe, such as Francisco Suárez and Luis de la Puente, rest in the archives of the Society as eloquent testimony to the high spiritual tone of the seventeenth-century Jesuit. Nicolas Trigault, veteran of the Chinese mission, visited several of the European provinces to tell his brethren about the waiting harvest in China. No less than four thousand responded in a vast desire to carry out what Ricci had started.[12]

A decade before the close of this period, in 1676, Oliva addressed the entire Society in a general letter. Jesuit generals have not been given to courting illusions about the state of the organization they headed, but on the basis of reports which he

11 Astráin, *Historia,* VI, 43-47.
12 F. Plattner, S.J., *Jesuits Go East* (Westminster, 1952), p. 104; *DeGui-Jes,* pp. 256-257. Lamalle, "La propagande du P. Nicolas Trigault en faveur des missions de Chine," *AHSJ,* IX (1940), 114.

received from the four quarters of the globe Oliva felt assured "that everywhere our rules are exactly observed and that by the divine mercy our Institute realizes a flourishing fulfillment in the purity of life of our men, their zeal for souls, prayerfulness, pursuit of learning, interior and exterior mortification, union of spirit, fervor for the missions." Defects there were, such as indulgence in a florid style of preaching, ignorance of Latin — "Hardly anyone writes it well," he observed — over-refinement of subtlety in philosophy, lapses in poverty occasioned by superiors who granted broad and general permissions. But from his vantage point he was able to give the well-grounded and balanced judgment that the Society of the late seventeenth century was generally faithful to the ideals of St. Ignatius.[13]

The Jesuit approach to the apostolate in Italy had by this time become an integral part of the religious and cultural life of the peninsula as the institutions such as the school and the sodality expanded and flourished. In 1621, for example, the Neapolitan Province of 596 men ran nineteen colleges; in 1626, the Sicilian Province of 690 men ran eighteen colleges; in 1635 the Venetian Province of 367 men ran seventeen colleges. In the development of this vigorous life of learning and devotion the pulse beat was particularly strong in scientific research and popular preaching.

At the Roman College, science continued to maintain through the distinction of its professors a place of honor. Grienberger died in 1636; Scheiner in 1650. But Germany again filled the ranks, this time with the versatile Athanasius Kircher. His hand in every facet of scientific investigation, this brilliant but erratic and peculiar genius, born in 1601, became known as "The Master of a Hundred Arts." Kircher holds an important place in the history of science. At once an ardent Aristotelian and a keen experimenter, he was one of the main links between medieval and modern science. Not equal to Clavius and Scheiner in the permanence of his work, he nevertheless by the universality of his erudition exercised a vast influence on the scientists of his day. The wide extent of his projects was memorialized in the Kircher Museum in Rome, one of the world's finest centers of scientific interest until the Piedmontese occupied the Eternal City in 1870.

Italian Jesuits in other parts of the country did not allow the Roman College to hold a monopoly in this field. At Ferrara and

Bologna Francesco Lana-Terzi performed some ingenious experiments in aeronautics; at Bologna Giovanni Riccioli did skillful work in astronomy; also at Bologna Francesco Maria Grimaldi discovered the diffraction and dispersion of light and suggested, one of the first to do so, its wave-like nature. Broad cultural and intellectual interests characterized, almost without exception, the background of these early Jesuit scientists who moved with competence and authority from one field of learning to another. Grimaldi, for example, before giving himself completely to science, taught literature for twenty-five years. Riccioli taught philosophy and theology for many years before he made astronomy his prime intellectual interest. As astronomers learned more about the craters on the moon, they gave them the names of renowned men. Two craters carry the names Grimaldi and Riccioli, and other lunar formations perpetuate the fame of thirty other Jesuits.

With Kircher at the Roman College were two other priests who brought in a special way distinction to its staff, Juan de Lugo, a theologian, and Sforza Pallavicino, a historian. De Lugo closed the impressive line of superior theologians whom the Spanish provinces sent to Rome. This native of Madrid, who taught at the Roman College from 1621 to 1643, when he was made a cardinal, left in his masterpiece, *Justice and Law* (1642), so highly lauded by St. Alphonsus Liguori, the imprint of his lucid reason and serene judgment. This work had a great influence on other theologians. Impelled to correct constantly and polish his writings, he published little of the vast amount of manuscript material he left behind.

Sforza Pallavicino succeeded him in the chair of theology at the Roman College but is remembered more for his *History of the Council of Trent* (1653) than for his theological works. To correct the hostile version of Trent presented by Paolo Sarpi, Pope Innocent X requested Pallavicino to write the Council's history. In five years, after access to secret archives in the Vatican as well as to previously collected data, he published his work in two volumes. Apologetic in tone and not entirely free of partiality and error, it nevertheless provided a good antidote to the bias of the bitter Servite.

While Kircher, de Lugo, and Pallavicino were at work at the Roman College, not far away artisans were building the massive church of San Ignazio. Cardinal Ludovico Ludovisi, wealthy and expansive nephew of Pope Gregory XIV, decided in 1626 to erect a church for the Jesuits. Six years later he died. Again, as in the case of the Gesù, the Society faced an acute financial problem, since the Ludovisi family were reluctant to defray the expenses. Only in 1642 was San Ignazio opened to the public, its interior simply whitewashed and undecorated. The general, Oliva, remedied this deficiency.[14]

Oliva, a refined and cultivated man, loved the fine arts. His generalate clearly and decidedly identified the Jesuits of Rome with the fullness of the baroque style. He actively sponsored three great artistic achievements: the completion of the church of Sant' Andrea al Quirinale; the decorating of the Gesù; and the painting of San Ignazio.

Since 1658, three years before Oliva became vicar general, the great Giovanni Lorenzo Bernini, then sixty years old, had been working on the new church of Sant' Andrea al Quirinale at the Jesuit novitiate in Rome. Bernini and Oliva were deep personal friends. Bernini provided a number of illustrations for an edition of Oliva's sermons. And Oliva gave the great architect a free hand at Sant' Andrea. So did principe Camillo Pamfili, nephew of Pope Innocent X, who supported the project with immense generosity. Bernini created one of the most handsome baroque churches in Rome. A simple but striking oval plan controls the rich marbles and varied decorations of Sant' Andrea. The rays of the sun, pouring from the lantern over the high altar and lighting up the gold of the dome, enhance the profound sense of unity. To Bernini Sant' Andrea brought a personal satisfaction he did not derive from any of his other works, and there he went when he sought interior peace and consolation.[15]

Oliva's second artistic project was the painting of the relatively bare Gesù. Oliva at first decided that a Jesuit brother, Giacomo Borgognone, should carry out the task. Difficulties however arose with the Farnese family, descendants of the church's original patron, Cardinal Alessandro Farnese, and these held up the work. Duca Ranuccio II di Parma hesitated about spending the money. His duchessa did not like Borgognone's plans. Oliva then turned to the widely applauded Giovanni Battista Gaulli. The two men signed a contract in 1672. Gaulli painted the dome, the pendentives, the tribune, and the left transept over the altar of Saint Ignatius. During the work Oliva and Bernini took an active interest, but it is impossible to unravel the parts they individually played behind the brush of Gaulli. Gaulli's fresco on the nave pictures the triumph of the Holy Name of Jesus

14 Haskell, *Patrons and Painters*, pp. 73-74.
15 Ibid., pp. 85-87.

189

and expresses the apostolic and missionary character of the Society. Gaulli finished his task in 1685, thirteen years after he had started.[16]

Oliva's third great artistic project was to get the decorating of San Ignazio under way. In 1680 he summoned to Rome the Jesuit brother, Andrea Pozzo. This was a decision of great import. Pozzo, a native of Trent, was then thirty-eight years old. Difficulties delayed Pozzo, and when he reached Rome Oliva was dead. But Pozzo realized Oliva's fondest hopes for San Ignazio. He made three distinct contributions to the church. He first took up the problem of the non-existent dome. Since the Ludovisi family did not contribute the necessary funds, the dome had not been constructed. This left a yawning gap. To fill this gap, Pozzo took a flat piece of canvas and by his peculiarly brilliant use of linear perspective created the illusion of a dome. This he finished in 1685.

Pozzo next addressed himself to the tribune and the apse. On these he did frescoes in which he depicted scenes from the life of St. Ignatius which reached their climactic point in the saint's vision at La Storta where he heard God say, "I shall be propitious to you at Rome." Pozzo here caught the spirit of vision and ecstasy which was one of the dominant notes of the art of the Catholic Reform. In his portrayal of the vision at La Storta, Pozzo joined the ranks of the other great artists who strove to express the radiance and mystery of a saint in deep union with the Living God.[17]

Pozzo reached the high point of his work with his fresco on the massive vault of the church. He took as his theme the missionary spirit of the Society as expressed in the words of Christ: "I came to cast fire upon the earth, and would that it were already kindled" (Luke 12:49). With luminous clarity he pictured God the Father sending forth a ray of light to the Son, who in turn transmits it to St. Ignatius, who then breaks it into four rays and sends them to Europe, Asia, Africa, and the Americas. With dazzling splendor Pozzo paid tribute to the zeal of his fellow Jesuits, who carried to men the light of God's love. He reached the climax of Jesuit identification with the baroque spirit in Rome.[18]

These elaborate churches, as a place for preaching the word of God, were symbols of a fresh flowering of Jesuit pulpit elo-

16 Ibid., pp. 78-83; Mâle, *L'Art religieux*, pp. 431-432.
17 Haskell, *Patrons and Painters*, 80-85; Mâle, *L'Art religieux*, 151-152.
18 Haskell, *Patrons and Painters*, pp. 90-91.

quence in Italy at this time. Paolo Segneri, Giovanni Pietro Pinamonti, Francesco de Geronimo, and Antonio Baldinucci made a powerful spiritual impact on their countrymen. Segneri, sometimes called the John Wesley of the seventeenth century, for twenty-seven years moved from village to village, especially in Tuscany and the Papal States. This reincarnation of the eloquence of St. Bernadine of Siena and Savonarola walked eight hundred miles a year, barefoot, and at times drew as many as 20,000 from the countryside on the occasion of a mission. For twenty-six years he had as a tireless companion, Pinamonti, a fine preacher in his own right but always in the shadow of the master. St. Francis Geronimo centered his energies on Naples where for forty years, starting in 1676, he remade the spiritual life of the town. His outstanding creation was the General Communion on the third Sunday of each month at the church of Gesù Nuovo. In the streets, on the squares, in every quarter of the city, he delivered short, snappy, forceful sermons which brought thirteen to fifteen thousand to the church each third Sunday of the month to receive the Holy Eucharist. This energetic, severely penitential priest made the entire city, with all its sorrows and needs, his vineyard. Unwed mothers, galley-slaves, debt-ridden poor, street waifs, all tasted of his wide mercy. Pope Gregory XVI canonized him in 1839. While St. Francis became identified with a single city, a contemporary ranged for twenty years far and wide through approximately thirty dioceses in the north drawing crowds that rivaled those gathered by Segneri. Antonio Baldinucci, a Florentine, used with powerful effect such dramatic means as the scourging of himself in public and the burning at the close of a mission of dice and cards in the town square. He was beatified in 1893.

Other Jesuits implemented the massive achievements of the popular missions by a prolific output of spiritual literature. Most of these men served their age well but lacked those exacting qualities which would place them in the company of the classical devotional authors. Among the best known were two future generals of the Society, Vincenzo Carafa and Giovanni Paolo Oliva. Carlo Rosignoli scored a great success with several works, reservoirs of colorful and amazing stories, which frequently had titles that began with the words, *The Marvels of* . . . Virgilio Cepari, whose extensive knowledge of the process of canonization Pope Benedict XIV, himself a classic author on that subject, highly appreciated, wrote the biographies of two Jesuit saints whom he knew intimately, Aloysius Gonzaga and John Berchmans. Berchmans was a Belgian scholastic who by his quiet

191

and unostentatious devotion to the pattern of a Jesuit's life during his course of studies attained a sanctity which the Church solemnly recognized in his canonization by Leo XIII in 1888. While a student at the Roman College he died on August 13, 1621.

What had been for the Society a period of general stability and tranquillity ended in the eruption at Rome of a great scandal. Devolving from the central figure of a Spanish secular priest, Miguel Molinos, who had been in the Eternal City since 1663, some seriously erratic ideas had made deep inroads among persons of prominence. This movement became known as Quietism. The tendency to exaggerate the aspect of passivity and repose in the spiritual life, which had turned up at various times in the Church's history, reappeared in Italy during the latter half of the seventeenth century with a strong orientation toward illuminism. In this milieu Molinos published in 1675 his *Spiritual Guide,* an aid to that state of complete abandonment to the divine will through the prayer of simple regard; and this form of prayer would exclude all other devotional means. The objective he placed before his reader was the reduction to a minimum of the volitional act by becoming like wax in the hands of the director. The Jesuits did not like the tone of this doctrine. Gottardo Belluomo published in 1678 his *The Excellence and Arrangement of Ordinary and Mystical Prayer* in which, without mentioning Molinos by name, he attacked his teaching. Molinos became uneasy and twice in February, 1680, wrote to Oliva, expressing, with his denial of error, a sincere respect for the *Spiritual Exercises.* Two years after the appearance of Belluomo's book, Paolo Segneri published his *Harmony between Effort and Repose in Prayer,* a sharp and incisive dissection of Quietist doctrine. To the defense of Molinos went the Oratorian, Pier Matteo Petrucci, bishop-elect of Iesi and author of several volumes on mysticism close in temper to the approach of the Spaniard. The conflict became intense in 1681. That year Petrucci wrote against Segneri. Segneri replied. Both *The Excellence and Arrangement* of Belluomo and the *Harmony between Effort and Repose* of Segneri, through the influence of Molinos' powerful friends, were placed on the Index. In a vague sort of way a party identified with Quietism took shape. Against it the Jesuits were hamstrung.

Then in July, 1685, to the stupefaction of Rome, the papal police suddenly descended on Molinos and arrested him. Evidence had piled up that the controversial spiritual director had been leading a double-life and had been teaching a doctrine even more extreme than that contained in his *Spiritual Guide*. From the maze of testimony it appeared that he had taught that a person in a high state of prayer, tempted to an obscene action, ought not quit this prayer to resist the temptation, and that such an act, if performed, was not matter for confession. This and other teachings brought the downfall of Molinos. A reaction set in. Petrucci, now a cardinal, had to retract fifty-four Quietist propositions taken from his writings, and Segneri was removed from the Index. Belluomo's work, however, was never removed from that list of prohibited reading. Although the ultimate and actual undoing of Molinos was precipitated by the police, the Jesuits had by their analysis of his ideas and tendencies alerted reflective people to this latest manifestation of an imbalance between ascetical and mystical theology.[19]

During the reigns of Philip III, Philip IV, and Charles II, the dust of fatigue and drabness gathered heavily on the Hapsburg coat of arms, which had shone so brightly during the Golden Age of Spain. Thousands of potential productive workers on the land and in the shop picked up a smattering of education, and in a rush for easy posts in the civil service cluttered with drones and incompetents the machinery of government. Several times the coinage was debased. A crippling system of taxation spread like a net over an inert people. Communications deteriorated; foreigners sapped the bulk of trade and rushed along the flow of money from the country. As this general malaise fell over Spain, the Society there could not avoid its stifling weight, and its colors, once full-blown in the age of Suárez and Molina, drooped and fell limp. The loss of earlier vitality and initiative showed itself in a number of ways: in the disappearance of superior talent among the theologians and philosophers, in the deep inroads gained by the atrocious literary taste of the age, in the pretentious and frequently credulous character of the literature.

Although by the end of Vitelleschi's generalship in 1645 the Jesuits were operating ninety colleges and seminaries throughout the country, this impressive figure does not give the true picture of the Society's condition. Statistics on manpower are a corrective. In 1616 there were 2,173 Jesuits in Spain. By 1652, thirty-six years later, the number had dropped to a little more than 1,800. Two factors in the national life chiefly accounted for

19 P. Pourrat, *Christian Spirituality* (Westminster, Md., 1955), IV, 129-134; *DeGuiJes,* pp. 407-410.

this drastic reversal of the steady growth: plague and poverty.[20] The periodic epidemics which swept through the country took a staggering toll: in the Province of Andalusia no less than 220 in nine years; in Seville sixty-five in two months in 1649. Among the deceased were those who gave their lives in the care of the sick, such as the sixteen in Murcia in 1648 and the seventy-seven in Andalusia in 1649. Poverty, which came in the wake of the country's economic recession, crippled the efficacy of the schools, and in some cases, by the sheer force of attrition, wore down the religious spirit of some individual religious. In accord with the directives from Rome previously mentioned, the novitiates turned away prospective novices because of the inability of the provinces to support them. Despite the harsh realities of inadequate lodging and poor food, rumors persisted that the Spanish Jesuits lived sumptuously on the wealth which they siphoned off the metal mines in their overseas missions. By 1673 they again numbered 2,000, but the plague and poverty made the growth slow.

Somewhat like the last brilliant burst of Spanish dramatic power in De Vega, Molina, and Calderón, and the splendid painting of Velázquez, Zurbarán, and Murillo, all of whom died after 1634 and some as late as the 1680's, the Society's ancient glory in theology did not disappear abruptly but faded gradually in a lovely sunset made by the light of three outstanding thinkers, Diego Ruiz de Montoya, Juan Martínez de Ripalda, and Juan de Lugo. Strikingly at variance with current Spanish absorption in speculation, stressing patristic sources and conciliar decisions in his work, Montoya started to publish only eight years before the end of his seventy years. Nevertheless he produced six books and received from Denis Petau the identical title so many have given to the Frenchman, Father of Positive Theology. He is a forgotten master. Matthias Scheeben, in his evaluation of Jesuit theologians, gave him the first place, superior even to Suárez for depth of thought and erudition, and judged his treatise on the Trinity as by far the best on that subject.[21] The Basque, Ripalda, with a penetrating mind of utmost delicacy in the distinguishing of concepts, composed *Supernatural Reality* (1634-1648), a work which has immortalized his name in the history of theology. Lugo brought to the lecture halls of Valladolid a memorable clarity of exposition and highly polished expression.

20 Astráin, *Historia,* V, 49, 127;VI, 37-40.
21 J. P. Grausem, *DTC,* XIV, i. 165, s.v. "Ruiz de Montoya, Diego."

By mid-century Spain had lost all three. Lugo was called to Rome in 1621; Montoya died in 1632, Ripalda died in 1648. With the departure of these three men the heavy shadows of dull monotony and endless repetition fell over the sacred sciences. Out of contact with developments in other parts of Europe in positive theology, mathematics, and the physical sciences, unaffected by the work of Bollandus, Van Papenbroeck, Tillemont, Mabillon, and the Maurists, preoccupied with perfecting the traditional scholastic approach, contented with what Aristotle or Cajetan had said, the Jesuit theologians expressed themselves in syllogisms and still more syllogisms. Disputations bogged down in the shaving of distinctions. Several times Vitelleschi, and after him Piccolomini, admonished the Spaniards to use their time more profitably than in the creation of subtleties.[22]

The literary decline began earlier and by mid-century the country had entered into the dark night of bad taste. Clear and direct writing disappeared before a tendency to envelop thought in complex metaphors and pompous periodic sentences, and to evolve enigmatic paradoxes and startling conclusions. These distortions invaded the Society, and priests who had wide experience in popular preaching warned the general about the danger to the apostolate of the pulpit. In several letters Vitelleschi instructed the Spanish provincials that they were not to tolerate gauche taste. In 1630 he told the provincial of Toledo that any scholastic who in his practice preaching in the refectory used an affected style was to be halted then and there, ordered to read a chapter from a devotional book entitled *Contempt of the World*, and then be given a severe penance.[23]

One name which has survived this heavy milieu and still appears occasionally in English translation is Baltasar Gracián. This native of Calatayud achieved a curtness of expression, in contrast to the current elaborateness, which reached its perfection in his *Exposition through Aphorisms of Ready Wisdom and the Art of Discretion* (1647), a collection of maxims which are generally vigorous, shrewd, true to their title, and in a way a landmark in Spanish literature.

Profuseness was the chief characteristic of the ascetical and spiritual literature of the Jesuits of this period. In numberless tomes and manuals the authors omitted no literary form — dialogues, soliloquies, collections of sentences — but in a style which was generally prolix and monotonous and aggravated by an

22 Astráin, *Historia*, V, 93-94.
23 Ibid., V, 112-113.

atmosphere of pious credulity and a penchant for the marvelous. Men like Luis de la Palma showed that the tradition of a La Puente was not entirely dead, but they were rare.[24] Of wide and immeasureable influence, at least by the sheer number of his works — he has fifty-six titles on many subjects — was Eusebio Nieremberg. To attempt to measure the influence of his *Time and Eternity* (1640) would be like trying to gauge the impact of *The Imitation of Christ* in the fifteenth century. As *The Imitation* was generally known in Spain as the *Gersoncito* — authorship being attributed to John Gerson — this work of Nieremberg became popularly known, from his Christian name, as the *Eusebio*.

The spiritual ministry in which a youthful energy and vitality continued was that of the popular mission. Jerónimo López, who joined to his forceful eloquence a flair for the dramatic which employed such devices as apostrophes to the crucifix and exposition of a corpse, spent years in the fatiguing work of moving from village to village. Succeeding López was an uncommon pair of preachers who worked together as a team from 1665 to 1672 and had no rivals in Spain in the art of conducting a home mission, Gabriel Guillén and Tirso González.

González reached a sharp turn in his life, which was to have wide consequences for the course of Jesuit history, when he was appointed to a chair of theology at Salamanca. In the course of his readings and his ministry he reached a conviction which became an insistent preoccupation for the rest of his life: the doctrine of probabilism was a source of laxity in morals and should be denied honor in the Society. His own preference he gave to the doctrine known as probabiliorism, according to which, when the lawfulness of an action is in doubt, one may follow the opinion favoring liberty only when it is more probable than the opinion favoring the law. He wrote a book in which, as the inflexible champion of probabiliorism, he attacked the learned men of the Society who favored probabilism. At Rome, by unanimous vote, the censors judged the work should not be published. In 1680 González wrote to Pope Innocent XI, asking the pontiff to urge theology professors to attack probabilism and support probabiliorism. Innocent, even though akin to González in his sentiments, was however not prepared to go quite that far. But seven years later the personal preoccupation of this Spanish preacher and teacher about the evil of probabilism became a matter of deep concern to the entire Society when the Thirteenth

24 Ibid., V, 94-95.

General Congregation, at the bidding of Innocent XI, elected him general.

Toward the close of this period the Society in Spain gained national attention, but of an unwanted kind. For three awkward years, 1666-1669, a Jesuit held high positions in the government. When Philip IV died and four-year-old Charles II succeeded as king of a petrified nation, the capricious and inept queen mother, Mariana of Austria, made her Austrian confessor, Johann Eberhard Nidhard, a member of the Council of State and the Junta de Gobierno, the inquisitor general, and then in effect the prime minister. This modest Jesuit, whose competence was in philosophy and canon law, did not have the qualities needed to set in motion again the becalmed ship of state. Nor did the people take kindly to an Austrian standing at the helm. Don John of Austria, handsome and popular bastard of the late king, whipped up a violent storm against the foreign priest. Factions formed, the *Nidhardistas* on one side, the *Austriacos* on the other. Fellow Jesuits, agonized at the prospect of a civil war occasioned by a member of the Society, urged Nidhard to leave Spain. On February 25, 1669, he quit Madrid, a gentleman to the end and true to his reserved and selfless character. In 1672 Clement X made him a cardinal.

With the opening of eight new colleges and an increase to a little over 700 men during this period, the Portuguese Province struck its roots more deeply into the nation's life. This steady growth coincided with the élan of patriotism which attended the overthrow of the Spanish monarchy in 1640. The Jesuits shared in these sentiments of patriotism and, as at no other time, pride in "The Little House of Portugal" colored the Society's apostolate.

Numerous books by Jesuits of this century, now closely guarded curiosities in library exhibition rooms, reveal a spirit vibrant with intellectual alertness, sensitivity to new impulses, and recognition of current problems. In two ways in particular did this sense of modernity express itself: first, in the development of the Portuguese language, and, second, in the assimilation into the philosophy program of the advances made in science. Despite exaggerations and artificialities in certain quarters, the Portuguese tongue achieved a character more malleable, more musical, more distinctly Portuguese. A group of Jesuit preachers energized this movement. Supreme among them, and indeed in the nation, was António Vieira. This speaker and writer of fecund intelligence, originality, and logical mind, brought the language to new heights of clarity and transparence by his vigorous, limpid, and harmonious style.[25] A Jesuit seventy-four years, he divided his time between Portugal and Brazil where he matched his eloquence by a most diversified zeal for the civilizing and sanctification of the natives. Born in Lisbon in 1608, he was taken to Brazil in his infancy. He entered the Society there in 1623. Motivated by a deep sense of patriotism, he placed his impressive spirit of magnanimity, breadth of culture, tenacity of purpose at the service of the crown. During his stay in Europe between 1641 and 1652 he ordered the commercial ties between Portugal and Brazil, founded a national bank, organized a commercial Brazilian Company, served with efficiency on diplomatic missions to France, Holland, England, and Rome. This patriotism betrayed him into a serious failure of judgment. With amazing credulity he let himself be hoodwinked by current prophecies and foretold a great millenium in which Portugal would, under the sceptre of a resurrected John IV, become the Fifth Empire of the World. Because of his writings in this vein as well as his strong appeals for toleration for the New Christians, the Inquisition at Coimbra sentenced him in 1667 to confinement within a Jesuit house. Earlier his varied activities had brought him trouble within the Society. Near the beginning of 1649 the general, Carafa, decided that Vieira should leave the Society and intimated to him through his provincial, Pedro da Rocha, that he should seek admission to another order. King John IV, for whom the tall, lean Jesuit was "o primeiro homen do mundo," offered him a bishopric. Vieira replied that his desire was to live and die a Jesuit. The king then blocked Carafa's plan. Carafa died on June 8, 1649, and on January 30, 1650, Rocha wrote to the new general, Francesco Piccolomini, that it would be to the Society's benefit to keep a man of Vieira's qualities.

Alongside the volumes of Vieira rest other contemporary works which show that among at least some Portuguese Jesuits there was a desire to join with their brethren north of the Pyrenees in establishing a new frontier in philosophy. Francisco Soares, for example, carried on an extensive correspondence with learned men of other nations, and in his works, such as the three-volume *Course in Philosophy* (1651), he cited all the important modern authors. *A Philosophical Survey* (1642) by Baltasar Teles was received with respect among the erudite.[26] In these faded pages

25 C. R. Boxer, *A Great Luso-Brazilian Figure: Padre António Vieira, S.J., 1608-1697* (London, 1957), pp. 3-4.
26 Rodrigues, *História*, III, i, 165-169.

come to life once more the voices of men alert to a world of changing ideas, who, while not of the stature of such predecessors as Fonseca, nevertheless showed a mind resolved not to terminate the advance of philosophy with the last page of Aristotle.

Dated as these philosophical encounters eventually became, in the popular apostolate one particular devotion, started in Lisbon in 1635, still retains a wide appeal. Marcello Mastrilli, an Italian on his way to the Indies, preached a series of sermons on St. Francis Xavier at the Jesuit church of St. Roque at Lisbon. He had launched the Novena of Grace which, at least until recent times, has enjoyed wide popularity.

The even tenor of these positive and constructive endeavors was jolted by a severe disruptive force: local feeling. With an inflated sense of local loyalty, bickering broke out among the Jesuits from different areas of the country. One particular group felt that others rode roughshod over them, kept them from positions of authority, discriminated against applicants to the Society from their region. They made these charges vocal. In 1653 the general, Nickel, under pressure also from King John IV, divided the province in two. Five years later he sharply admonished those whom he called "sowers of cockle," men who made the ruling of their two provinces more difficult than the entire rest of the Society. Oliva pointed out to the Portuguese Jesuits that they were contaminating a most flourishing area of the Society with their factionalism. Common sense eventually prevailed. António Vieira, who had been a proponent of the division, changed his mind. On July 24, 1662, the vicar general, Giovanni Paolo Oliva, in a beautiful tribute of confidence in Vieira which compensated for Carafa's intention to dismiss him, told him that he was relying especially on his prudence and wisdom to negotiate the reunion of the two provinces. In 1665 Oliva, amid expressions of universal satisfaction, brought the two provinces together.[27]

The threads which went into the making of the richly colored *France* tapestry of French culture and national life during the era of Cardinal Richelieu and Louis XIV were strong and vivid. Four especially assured the Society an important place in that striking fabric. They were: Gallicanism, Jansenism, a mighty wave of

27 Ibid., III, ii, 57-59, 62, 87; also F. Rodrigues, S.J., "O. P. António Vieira. Contradicções e Applausos. (Á Luz de Documentação Inedita," *Revista de História*, XI (1922), 88-91; Boxer, *A Great Luso-Brazilian*, pp. 9, 26).

religious fervor, and the cultural flowering of the Great Century.

Gallicanism, during this period of the mounting prestige of the French crown, increased in its intensity. The shift of the Jesuits, which began in the earlier period, toward a disavowal of Bellarmine's theory of the indirect power of the pope in temporal affairs became more pronounced. By the end of the seventeenth century, according to Hyacinthe Robillard d'Avrigny, all French Jesuits repudiated this theory.[28] A series of incidents during these seventy years compelled them to face squarely this thorny issue and enunciate more and more specifically their adherence to political Gallicanism.

Under Richelieu the most explosive incident was the Santarelli affair, another instance of a Jesuit outside France setting off an attack against his French brethren. In 1625 Antonio Santarelli published his *Treatise on Heresy, Schism, Apostasy, Sollicitation in Confession and the Power of the Roman Pontiff to Punish These Delicts*, in which he recited once more the frequently repeated doctrine of the pope's indirect power over princes in temporal concerns. The enemies of the Society sounded a call to arms. In a violent speech before the Parlement of Paris Louis Servin dropped dead of apoplexy. At the University the rector, Jean Tarin, strongly denounced the Society. Richelieu remarked tartly: "Maxims of this kind can ruin the entire Church of God. . . ." Pope Urban VIII, in a sharp rebuke to Vitelleschi, expressed his annoyance that Santarelli was allowed to raise such an explosive question. The Jesuits in Paris were exacerbated. It was so easy for a Spanish or an Italian Jesuit, in the tranquillity of his room in Madrid or Rome, to turn out a few pages which could bring about the destruction of the Society in France. Their letters to Rome were unanimous in their criticism of the imprudence of such writings as Santarelli's.[29]

The Parlement of Paris moved expeditiously. With Richelieu's approval the magistrates presented the Jesuits with three propositions which they had to accept. They were: disapproval of that evil doctrine in Santarelli's book which contravened the temporal independence of princes; conformity to the censure which the clergy of France and the Sorbonne would pass on Santarelli's work; profession of the doctrine commonly taught by the bishops, the universities, and the Sorbonne. It was a serious hour for the Society in France. Although a number of Jesuits judged that Santarelli's teaching was not a matter of dogma, they knew

28 Blet, 'Jésuites Gallicans?" *AHSJ*, XXIX (1960), 82.
29 Ibid., 62-63; Fouqueray, *Histoire*, IV, 144.

that their general would not allow them to disavow that teaching. Jean Suffren, the royal confessor, warned Marie de Médicis and Cardinal Richelieu that the Jesuits should not be expected to make an explicit denial of the pope's indirect temporal power. In anxious consultation, therefore, fathers from the professed house and the College of Clermont debated whether Parlement's conditions could be interpreted in a sense which would not be contrary to the faith. Each proposition was quite broad and open to a variety of distinctions. The teaching of Santarelli on papal power, for example, could be called evil in the sense that its proposal under circumstances then prevalent in France could result in civil disturbance. Pierre Coton advised: "Fathers, we must yield to the times." On March 16, 1626, the Jesuit spokesmen, having made a distinction on each of Parlement's demands and conditioning the entire act by the time-honored phrase used in similar circumstances in the past, *with deference to the decision of the Church,* signed the document. Although not an explicit denial of the pope's indirect power, for anyone who would so wish to interpret it this act was in reality a repudiation of that power.

So ended the Santarelli affair. And it marked a turning point in the relations between the Society and Parlement. The perennial campaign of hate subsided and the violent attacks ceased. In the years which followed a number of Jesuit writings appeared which paid tribute to the growing powers of the crown, the general temper of which could be synthesized in these sentences of Louis Cellot, professor of rhetoric at La Flèche: "Who is there who can worthily expound the privileges, liberties, immunities of the Gallican Church and the realm of the Most Christian King? What Catholic Frenchman will not defend them with vigor? [30]

Richelieu kept tight control of the Jesuit royal confessors. Gaspard de Séguiran, independent and free of all subservience, refused to conform to the designs of the cardinal. Richelieu, with increasing hostility, dinned into the ears of Louis XIII that De Séguiran was narrow and inflexible, and forced his dismissal. Jean Suffren succeeded in the post with the not too sanguine remark: "I shall not live long in this position." The minister hedged the new confessor in with severe restrictions and instructions, the general tenor of which was: "Do not go near the king unless summoned." Later the cardinal's displeas-

---

30 Blet, "Jésuites Gallicans?" *AHSJ,* XXIX (1960), 69; Fouqueray, *Histoire,* IV, 156-159.

ure fell with even greater impact on Nicolas Caussin. Caussin, in a plea for the termination of the Thirty Years' War, protested to Louis XIII about the sufferings which the conflict imposed on the people. Richelieu moved with precision. He banished the confessor to Quimper and blackened his name before his Jesuit superiors and the French government.

The same firmness of centralized power was magnified under Louis XIV, who assumed personal control of the realm in 1661. Up to 1689 three major incidents highlighted the trend among the Jesuits toward a greater adulation of the throne occupied by the Sun King. The first was the royal decree of 1673 on the question of what was technically known as "the royal right." According to an ancient custom, in dioceses of the north the king received the revenues and made appointments to benefices during periods when these dioceses were without a bishop. In 1673 Louis XIV extended "the royal right" to the dioceses in the south. In 1678 Innocent XI, a pope in the tradition of Gregory VII and Innocent III, sternly protested the king's action. Louis rejected the pope's remonstrance. Relations between the Vatican and France became tense. In the center, under pressure from both sides, stood the most renowned of Jesuit royal confessors, the amiable, moderate, peaceful François de la Chaize, who for thirty-four years was spiritual counselor of Louis XIV. In the controversy about "the royal right," De la Chaize did not concur with the adamant stand of the pope. Considering the wide benefits which the Church enjoyed through the benevolence of the Most Christian King, to him it did not seem quite correct to play the part of St. Anselm or St. Thomas Becket. He knew besides that, despite Innocent's sincere indignation, there was no point in trying to change Louis' mind once he was convinced that a particular question was a temporal affair. To Oliva he wrote: "May God keep me from believing that, as Your Paternity has insinuated, His Holiness cannot, without committing sin, dispense from such an unimportant regulation." [31]

The second episode was the Pamiers incident of 1681. A conflict arose in this southern town about the choice of a "capitular curate," one candidate being supported by the government and the other backed by a group of anti-regalists. On January 1,

---

31 Blet, "Jésuites Gallicans?" *AHSJ*, XXIX (1960), 73-74. What Père de la Chaize wrote of his own limited influence with Louis XIV confirms the judgment of Jean Orcibal that the royal confessor of the Sun King never participated actively in the formation of top level policy and had no part in creating the stern measures against the Huguenots between

1681, Innocent XI issued a brief confirming the designation of the anti-regalists' choice. The Parlement of Paris suppressed the brief on the pretense that it was of doubtful authenticity. This gave the enemies of the Society in Rome the opportunity they had been seeking. At the center of this Roman hostility was Agostino Favoriti, secretary for papal briefs. Favoriti's plan was simple: instruct the Jesuit provincials of Paris and Toulouse in the name of the Holy See to publish in France the papal brief which the Paris Parlement had recently suppressed. This would force the Society into an embarrassing confrontation with the government. Oliva realized that hostile forces were at work, and spoke plainly about a conspiracy against the Society. He described the predicament of the French Jesuits, pressed by the contrary forces of pope and king, as being placed between the hammer and the anvil. But Favoriti's plan misfired. The French authorities intercepted the copies of the papal brief. The Jesuits never received them.

Then occurred a most amazing scene. The Jesuits were summoned to the bar of Parlement, scene of so many condemnations in the past, and there heard that the magistrates had formulated an official decree which lavished praise on the Society in France. The magistrates clearly indicated what they interpreted the Jesuit position to be: if ever it came to a choice between the decrees of Parlement, the pope, or the general, the Jesuits would give precedence to those of Parlement. Not that the Jesuits were remiss in their duty to the Holy See in this episode. They never received the briefs and therefore could not publish them. But the magistrates, in their eulogy, showed that they were addressing Frenchmen of the same mind as themselves. In the beginning of 1681 De la Chaize very candidly explained to the general this attitude: royal ordinances, of the most ancient right, divine and human, natural and positive, oblige in conscience; the commands of the general, by virtue of religious vows, also bind in conscience; the execution of both will be fulfilled so long as there is no conflict. "But if, in consequence of contradictory orders, it should become necessary to disregard one or other command, let Your Paternity himself judge what it is incumbent on us to do." [32]

1676 and 1679, which measures were a prelude to the Edict of Fontainebleau of 1685 by which the Edict of Nantes was revoked. See J. Orcibal, *Louis XIV et les Protestants* (Paris, 1951), pp. 91-93.
32 Blet, "Jésuites Gallicans?" *AHSJ*, XXIX, (1960), 76.

The third episode was the announcement by the Assembly of the Clergy in March, 1682, of *The Declaration of the Rights of the Gallican Church*. Expressed in four articles this *Declaration* proclaimed the king's independence of the pope in temporal affairs, the superiority of a general council over the pope, the limitation of the use of papal authority according to the norms established by canons and the body of the Church. On the first article, which repudiated the theory of indirect papal power in the secular sphere, De la Chaize and a good number, if not all, of his fellow-Jesuits were in accord. But in Rome, De Noyelle dissented strongly. When Louis XIV ordered that the four Gallican Articles be taught in all colleges attached to universities, the general, feeling that the Society was at the brink of the greatest danger it had ever faced, was emphatic. "Never shall I permit," he announced, "a member of the Society to teach anything disapproved by the supreme pontiff." He instructed De la Chaize to request the monarch that the Society be excused from his order on the teaching of the four articles. A startling outburst of disapproval of Louis' decree at the Sorbonne, Douai, and Besançon, so general that it amazed the bishops, helped the Jesuits to extricate themselves from a taut situation. Louis granted De Noyelle's request. The general's action was straightforward and it achieved its objective.[33] But it could not erase the fact that his French sons, on the question of papal power over princes, were Gallicans.

A second thread in the tapestry of seventeenth-century France was Jansenism. In 1640 at Louvain was published a posthumous work entitled *Augustinus*, written by the bishop of Ypres, who had died two years earlier, Cornelis Jansen. The *Augustinus*, the fruit of Jansen's many years of study of Augustine, was one of the classics of that increasingly widespread interest in the Doctor of Grace which gave a distinctly Augustinian tone to much of the theology and spirituality of the seventeenth century. It also became one of the landmarks in the protracted struggle between the Jesuits and the Jansenists through the following century and a half.

Close collaborator with Jansen was the enigmatic, egotistic, yet magnetic, Jean du Vergier de Huranne, known more generally as the Abbé de Saint-Cyran. The theology they evolved followed in the tradition of Baius at Louvain, Calvinistic in

33 Guitton, *Le Père de la Chaize*, I, 150-151.

temper, pessimistic in its concept of an essentially perverted human nature, and exaggerated in its interpretation of divine grace. Deep animosity to the Society of Jesus attended its development, since both men, convinced that the decay in Christian living was due to the moral and ascetical teaching of the Jesuits, made no secret about whom they regarded as the enemy. The Belgian Jesuits tried, energetically but unsuccessfully, to halt the publication of the *Augustinus* at Louvain, and Saint-Cyran turned Paris into a theological arena by his own second edition of the work issued there in 1641. In that remarkable and singular religious community of Port-Royal, dominated by the amazing Arnauld family, he found a most receptive audience. Antoine Arnauld developed the ascetical aspect of this dour, rigorous movement in his popular *Frequent Communion*, a work in that impeccable French style which was then attaining its maturity and manifesting its subtle power to capture men's minds and hearts. In moving prose he discouraged the reception of the Holy Eucharist, even to the point of recommending abstention as a form of penance.

Several fine Jesuit scholars were among the first in France to criticize the *Augustinus*. Jacques Sirmond exposed its Calvinistic basis. Denis Petau called on his broad historical knowledge to augment his philosophical and theological arguments. François Annat called on the authority of St. Augustine, the Church Father whom the Jansenists claimed to be their own. Étienne Dechamps, probably the Jesuit longest in the arena of battle, published his *The Jansenist Heresy* (1654), a most exact presentation of the Jansenist idea and its theological destitution. The body of controversial literature developed to vast proportions. Arnauld wrote an attack on Jesuit moral teaching; the Jesuit François Pintherau replied; François Hallier of the Sorbonne rebutted Pintherau; Pintherau answered Hallier; Hallier again replied to Pintherau. Many others joined the recondite debate. People became surfeited with the arguments about grace. "Fie, fie, fie, on grace," Anne of Austria remarked in exasperation.

Perhaps the greatest weakness of the Jesuits was their failure, not indeed in every instance, to write their work in French. Many of their principal contributions in this crisis they did in Latin. Petau, master of an elegant and pure Latin style, did not achieve the same grace and power in French. In contrast to this deficiency of Petau's, it was a masterful command of the French tongue which elevated to eternal prominence the most effective figure during the entire controversy. And he was on the side of Port-Royal. Blaise Pascal, brilliant scientist and mathematician, pious and sensitive Catholic, published in 1656 and 1657 a series of letters, supposedly directed to a friend in the country, which became popularly known as *The Provincial Letters*. In these clever, trenchant, witty writings in which he took up one of the major issues of the day, the alleged laxity of the moral teaching of many theologians, Pascal cut sharply at Jesuit professors and authors. There was indeed a tendency among some scholars in the seventeenth century to replace revelation with dialectics as the source of morality, and in this Pascal had a deserving target. But his attack on the Society, for all its brilliance, was unjust. A very small number of his victims, such as Étienne Bauny and Georges Pirot, deserved the wounds they received from his slashing pen, but as Louis Bourdaloue observed, "The bad judgment of one man is put into the mouth of all. For the sound judgment of many not a single one receives credit."

The Provincial Letters won wide acclaim, and the erudite Jesuit contemporary, René Rapin, paid this tribute: "Nothing like this has appeared before in the French language." It meant little to Pascal's delighted audience that he cited a very limited range of authors; that he chose from these works admittedly bizarre examples and from these created a caricature of the Society; that he pronounced such an extravagant and unfair judgment as that the moral theologians, by watering down the stern doctrines of the faith, taught that Christ died in order to free men from the obligation to love God; that he had never studied a Jesuit book on moral theology save the handbook for confessors by the Spanish Jesuit, Antonio Escobar y Mendoza. So vicious were the shafts directed against Escobar that his name has passed into the French language, and *escobar* is a synonym for a quibbler, shuffler, prevaricator.

Several Jesuits, especially Jacques Nouet, François Annat, and Étienne Dechamps, all competent theologians, answered Pascal. Dechamps, for example, challenged his assertion that probabilism was practically an exclusively Jesuit moral doctrine. In his *Question of Fact* (1659) he listed ninety serious authors, including bishops, doctors of Paris, and religious of other orders, who held probabilism. Then there were Pascal's abundant references, supplied by Antoine Arnauld and Pierre Nicole. While these references were in themselves generally accurate, Pascal used them without precision, and they reflected the literary liberty which he, as well as other authors of the seventeenth century, assumed in their work. Many of his quotations, placed in italics, were not exact translations of the Latin originals but résumés, adaptations done in graceful French and generally quite remote from their sources. Literary excellence was cardinal. Even the originally French quotations Pascal felt impelled to adorn. Throughout *The Provincial Letters* there is probably not a single French citation of more than one line which did not feel a light *coup de pouce*. With formidable learning and vast erudition the Jesuit apologists endeavored to correct the false image of their Society, but those qualities of style, verve, sauciness, and wit, which might have made them a match for Pascal, they did not have. Unrelieved solidity of learning could not undo the damage of the inaccurate pleasantry.[34]

Pascal's propaganda found a colorful disseminator in one of the most unusual figures of the age, Armand de Rancé, reformer of the Cistercian community of La Trappe. This emotional and erratic man cast thunder at the Jesuits. Sinners went to La Trappe to find their way back to God, and De Rancé, in a wild flight from reality, attributed their moral perversion to "the casuists." D'Avrigny discerned part of De Rancé's problem, his ignorance. He wrote: "No one maltreated the casuists more, and judging from appearances, no one had read them less." [35] De Rance's Jesuit was the Jesuit he discovered in Pascal. Therefore he knew him not.

The Provincial Letters remain a monument in French literature. They commemorate both a failure and a success of Pascal. In his effort to upset the balanced approach of most Jesuits to moral questions he failed. Clearly and with serene authority the master moralist, St. Alfonso Maria de Liguori, spoke out in 1756, a century later: "The opinions of the Jesuits are neither excessively free nor excessively rigid but maintain a correct balance." Of the twenty-six post-Tridentine classical authors on moral problems listed by St. Alphonsus, over half, fourteen, were Jesuits. But in swelling a tradition of suspicion of the Society Pascal succeeded eminently. One of the most celebrated Jesuits of the nineteenth century, Gustave de Ra-

---

34 J. Brucker, S.J., *DTC*, IV, i, 175-176, s.v. "Dechamps ou Agard de Champs, Étienne"; M. Harney, S.J., *The Jesuits in History* (New York, 1941), pp. 283-284; J. Brucker, *La Compagnie*, pp. 545-549; Blaise Pascal, *Les provinciales ou les lettres écrites par Louis de Montalte à un provincial de ses amis et aux RR.PP. Jésuites*, ed. L. Cognet (Paris, 1965), pp. xxxviii-xlii. See also the review of J. Steinmann's *Pascal* (London, 1965), by J. Brodrick, S.J., in *The Month*, CCXXI (1966), 248-249.

35 H. Bremond, *The Thundering Abbot. Armand de Rancé Reformer of La Trappe* (London, 1930), pp. 144-145.

vignan, once recalled that as a young lawyer he felt a bias against the Society, due not only to the ancient antipathy of the Parlement of Paris but also to his readings in Pascal.[36]

The damage inflicted by *The Provincial Letters* extended far beyond the Society. In a strangely paradoxical role Pascal, even while he spoke for a hard and stern God, made his readers laugh merrily and thereby created an atmosphere of ridicule and derision for things sacred. This eloquent spokesman for a severe morality prepared the way for the skepticism of the eighteenth century. Destruction by eloquence was followed by destruction by philosophy.[37]

Paschalian scholarship is in a state of flux — perhaps it always shall be. A solid view of the present day judges *The Provincial Letters* as a collective work in which Port-Royalist theologians like Arnauld and Nicole, unable from a literary point of view to match the quality of their adversaries, used Pascal unfairly, almost as an instrument of their own polemics. Contentiousness stamped this famous contest of spirits, and in this, as in all polemics, lay the greatest tragedy, for each side ignored the positive values of the other. If the Jesuits failed to comprehend certain spiritual riches of Port-Royal, *The Provincial Letters* ignored the deep and solid tradition of sanctity in the Society. Mutual incomprehension ran like a thread through the entire encounter.[38]

Jesuit participation in the spiritual life of the country was not limited to a defense against Jansenism. The third thread in the tapestry of national life, in this era known for what has been called the "spiritual invasion" of France, was the extraordinary burst of spiritual fervor, exemplified in such persons at St. Vincent de Paul, St. Jean Eudes, Cardinal Pierre de Bérulle, Jean-Jacques Olier, Madame Acarie. The Society, in a great variety of ways, helped to create this aura of spiritual intensity. The Sodality of the Blessed Virgin Mary, established in the colleges

---

36 P. A. Ponlevoy, S.J., *Vie du R.P. Xavier de Ravignan* (Paris, 1862), I, 83.

37 A. Matignon, S.J., "Les Doctrines de la Compagnie de Jésus sur la Liberté. La Lutte contre Jansénisme," *Études*, VIII (1866), 12. Jean Steinmann (*Pascal*, p. 128), judging the issue from another angle, says that Pascal, while overstating his complaint, saw the dawning of the eighteenth century in an exaggerated reliance on reason and casuistry in Christian moral teaching, with the result of a "soft and accommodating religion."

38 Pascal, *Les provinciales*, ed. Cognet (Paris, 1965), pp. xliv-xlv.

of the Society, counted among its members, in France alone and
aside from the many canonized of other countries, Saints François de Sales, Jean Eudes, Jean François Régis, Pierre Fourier,
Louis Grignon de Montfort, and Jean Baptiste de la Salle. Individual schools were *ateliers* where were forged alumni of
genuine distinction. The university at Pont-à-Mousson made
some unusual contributions to other religious orders in Servais
de Lairuels, reformer of the Premonstratensians, Didier de la
Cour and Claude François, collaborators in the reform of Saint
Maur, and Philippe Thibaut, who brought a spirit of renewal to
the Carmelites.

The spiritual literature of the French Jesuits, prodigious in its
output, reflected a gradual falling away from the immediate influence of St. Francis de Sales and a turning to a fresh pole of
inspiration, Louis Lallemant. Étienne Binet continued to express in his delightful way the spirit of "devout humanism" until
his death in 1639, and the same sense of optimism and joy that
marked Binet's work stamped the several volumes by Nicolas
Caussin, Jean Suffren, and Paul de Barry. Louis Lallemant, who
entered the Society in 1605, became master of novices and instructor of tertians during a period when some French Jesuits
felt that the Society, with an exaggerated activity, had become
too thoroughly immersed in its works to the detriment of its
spiritual strength. Amid this tension between a demanding apostolic activity and a keen desire for a more profound interior
life, Lallemant, by reason of his position, influenced a group of
unusual men, notably Jean Rigoleuc, an author of steady sureness
of judgment, Vincent Huby, founder of several retreat houses,
Jean Joseph Surin, a brilliant and lucid writer who became
seriously disturbed in his role as exorcist of some nuns at Lou-
dun, and the impressive missionaries in Canada, Paul Le Jeune
and St. Isaac Jogues. He himself never published anything, but
in 1694 Pierre Champion edited some notes written by Rigoleuc
and Surin when they made their tertianship under Lallemant.
Champion entitled his work *The Life and Spiritual Doctrine of
Father Louis Lallemant*. Although this collection of notes
presents a literary problem of authorship, Lallemant's teaching
was faithfully reported and remains a classic in its forceful claim
for the supremacy of the spiritual in the life of an apostle.

Lallemant sensed the tension in a Jesuit's life, at once prayerful and apostolic, and in his overwhelming preoccupation with
the need for profound prayer in the formation of the perfect
apostolic worker he seems to have deviated from Ignatian doctrine by turning Jesuits from apostolic initiative. At times in

passages of the *Spiritual Doctrine* his thought seems to be groping in search of its own meaning, and, even from page to page,
to be contradicting itself as various texts lead to apparently
diverse conclusions. This air of uncertainty surrounded him even
in his lifetime, and Vitelleschi made inquiry about the nature
of the tertian instructor's teaching. What the general learned
seems to have put him at ease.[39]

The distinctive note of another grouping of influential authors
was the Christocentric emphasis of their teaching. In 1634 Jean
Baptiste de Saint Jure published his vast treatise, *Knowledge
and Love of the Son of God,* and was followed by many other
Jesuit writers with the same preoccupation, such as Nicolas
Roger in his *Mystical Incarnation, or Conformity to Christ*
(1649) and Jean Grisel in his *Mystery of the Man-God* (1654).
More extensive and more lasting than these books in its orientation toward the Person of Christ was the devotion to the Sacred
Heart of Jesus. A nun, who in 1671 had entered the Visitation
convent at the Burgundian town of Paray-le-Monial, was blessed
with visions of Christ in which the Divine Master, pointing to
his heart on fire with love for men, asked that reparation be
made for the coldness and indifference with which men returned
his divine charity. As spiritual director for Sister Margaret Mary
in the delicate mission of spreading devotion to the Sacred
Heart, Christ himself chose the Jesuit whom he called "My
Faithful Servant and Perfect Friend," Claude de la Colombière.
The Church has placed Sister Margaret Mary on the calendar
of saints and has beatified Colombière. In his appearance of
July 2, 1688, Christ designated the members of the Society of
Jesus as the propagators of the devotion to his Sacred Heart, and
the Society in several ways has responded to this special vocation, from the decrees of general congregations in 1915, 1923,
and 1966, reminding individual Jesuits of this responsibility, to
the various editions of the *Messenger of the Sacred Heart* and
the worldwide *Apostleship of Prayer.*

One particular facet of spiritual activity in the seventeenth
century which interested the government was that of the popular
missions, in which Jesuits, usually in bands of two, walked from
village to village and brought to the poor, the ignorant, and the

---

39 L. Lallemant, S.J., *La vie et la doctrine spirituelle du Père Louis
Lallemant, S.J. Introduction et notes par François Courel, S.J.* (Paris,
1959), pp. 29-33; *DeGuiJes,* pp. 353-355. Of Lallemant's *Spiritual
Doctrine* Henri Bremond (*Histoire littéraire,* V, 64), wrote, "It is one
of the three or four essential works of modern religious literature."

forgotten the streams of sacramental life. Louis XIII, deeply impressed by the achievements of these men, in 1634 assigned an annual sum of 4,000 livres for the support of these missions in Aquitaine, in which ten priests, two scholastics, and two brothers were engaged. Richelieu envisaged the establishment of a Jesuit group which would penetrate into every corner of the realm and in 1638 he guaranteed the sustenance of fifty Jesuits in this ministry through six months of the year.[40] Many a priest became well known for his wholehearted dedication to this monotonous work. In Montpellier, Sommièrs, Le Viverais, and Le Velay, the fondest memories were of Jean François Régis, the strong, gentle, enchanting priest who pushed through snow-filled valleys and harsh mountains in his quest for souls. Régis, who died in the course of his work at La Louvesc in 1640, is now a saint of the Church.

At La Louvesc two persons of wide influence in the spiritual life of France in the nineteenth century found inspiration. In 1806 St. Jean-Baptiste Marie Vianney, the curé d'Ars, made a pilgrimage to the tomb of St. Jean François to seek help in his studies for the priesthood. And there in 1826 Marie Victoire Thérèse Couderc, now a saint on the Church's calendar, founded the Religious of the Cenacle. In several ways she linked her group with the Society. She based her constitutions on those of St. Ignatius, and she made the presentation of the Spiritual Exercises to lay women a primary apostolic work.

For nearly four decades after Régis' death, Jean-Paul Medaille, who was formed in the saint's methods, carried on the labor of Christian instruction in the hamlets and villages of Auvergne, Velay, and Languedoc. He also assisted in the creation of the Congregation of the Sisters of St. Joseph, who made the rule of St. Ignatius the basis of their institute.

To the north, in the year that Régis died, another Jesuit, Julien Maunoir, began his amazing mission of forty-three years in Brittany. Himself a Breton, he reanimated an indifferent people and a careless clergy to that intense faith which remains so important a part of their culture. In each village he organized weeks of religious services, supplemented by colorful processions and dramatic scenes, so striking a feature of his amazing apostolate. He translated catechisms and spiritual literature into the Breton tongue, trained priests, opened at Quimper one of the Society's first houses for closed retreats where each year up to a thousand priests and laymen made the Spiritual

40 Fouqueray, *Histoire*, V, 262-264.

Exercises. In 1951 Pope Pius XII beatified Maunoir. Meanwhile thousands of miles from France, in the harsh wilderness of the new world, Isaac Jogues, Jean de Brébeuf, and others fell beneath the tomahawk of the Indians, adding martyrs to the list of Frenchmen who achieved outstanding holiness in that fervent era.

This high spiritual intensity and exalted aspiration did not, however, in the everyday round of practical business, erase misunderstanding and bad feeling. Although De Bérulle, a Jesuit alumnus, in his correspondence with men like Fronton du Duc expressed sincere cordiality, the Oratorians and the Jesuits had some disagreeable differences. De Bérulle excluded education from his venture, but by 1618 the Oratorians were running two schools, one at Rouen, the other at Dieppe. Rivalry broke out between these schools and those of the Jesuits, and this fed the tempers of hotheads whose indignant phrases still remain in the record to show human frailty in an age of a spiritual elite.[41]

Similar to this thread of spiritual fervor in its strength and beauty was the thread of cultural flowering. It touched in a special way theology, philosophy, and literature, all of which deeply involved the Society. The seventeenth century was a golden period in the study of church history, which permeated theological studies and, by recalling the beliefs and practices of the early church, demonstrated "the perpetuity of the faith." Several Jesuits by their sense of history and deep respect for factual erudition gave a new and fruitful direction to theological studies. Fronton du Duc helped fill a great gap by his critical editions of works of St. John Chrysostom, St. Gregory of Nyssa, and St. Irenaeus; Jacques Sirmond did prodigious work in editing texts, many of which have passed into the general editions of the councils by Labbe and Mansi and of the Greek and Latin Fathers by Migne.

Prince among these scholars was the native of Orléans, Denis Petau. Trained by his father in a milieu ardently Catholic and humanistic, by fifteen Petau had attained an excellent command of Latin and Greek. At seventeen he defended in Greek his thesis for the master's degree at Paris. After his entry into the Society he taught rhetoric at Reims, La Flèche, and Paris. Guided by Fronton du Duc, he read widely in history and became skilled in the use of texts and the determination of chro-

---

41 J. Lecler, S.J., in a review (AHSJ, VII, [1938], 302-304) of *Corespondance du cardinal de Bérulle*, I and II, ed. J. Dagens (Louvain and Paris, 1937).

nology. When assigned to lecture in theology, he brought to his task a preparation that was unique and that assured an approach distinguished by a fullness, depth, and scope far beyond that limited almost solely to metaphysics.

Petau has been called the Father of Positive Theology. In the strict sense of that term this is not precisely so, for he inherited an outlook which other Jesuits before him, especially Maldonado, Montoya, and even Suárez had already adopted. He joined them in their desire for that consummate and harmonious union of a strong metaphysics, a profound knowledge of Sacred Scripture, and a wide familiarity with the Fathers of the Church and councils. What was unique in Petau's contribution was his presentation in all its plenary majesty of the patristic and conciliar tradition. He ambitioned a theology *ad eruditae vetustatis expressa speciem,* formed according to the lines of the learning that perdures through the ages.[42] His *Theological Doctrines* — five volumes of the ten he contemplated — is without peer in that genre of theology. It is a wide hall in which the theologians and conciliar fathers of every era speak their reflections on God's revelation. On every page sounds the unending dialogue of century with century.

Petau recognized the special quality of his undertaking. He wrote to Vitelleschi about it. "In this treatise on things divine I have not followed the road trod by the old school. I have taken a new road, and I can say without pride, a road as yet untouched by any other. Putting aside that subtle kind of theology which meanders, like philosophy, through I do not know what labyrinths, I have created a simple, graceful venture, like a rapid stream, from the pure and original sources of Scripture, the councils and the Fathers." His death on December 12, 1652, not only brought this enterprise to an end, but also occasioned a tragedy in the intellectual history of Europe. The Jesuits at the College of Clermont gathered together the thousands of letters he had received, many from the scholars of the continent, and burned them. Only one remained, a message from Pope Urban VIII, found later between the pages of a book.[43]

Petau had lived in a period noted for its interest in the Church's history. One particular collection of the documents of

---

42 Denis Petau, S.J., *Dogmata Theologica Dionysii Petavii e Societate Jesu,* editio nova, J. B. Fournials (Paris, 1845), I, 1.
43 J. C. Vital Chatellain, *Le Père Denis Petau d'Orleans. Sa Vie et ses Oeuvres* (Paris, 1884), pp. 406-407, 447-448.

the councils recalls one of the century's greatest scholars, Philippe Labbe, historian, epigraphist, linguist, a man of tenacious memory and vast capacity for work. What Labbe left unfinished at death, the competent and versatile Gabriel Cossart completed. A worthy member of this company of men with a feel for the past, Pierre François Chifflet merited by his many publications this neat encomium from the Bollandists, "a man of utmost industry who deserves well of the saints."

The sense of assurance and certainty which carried the Jesuits along in their theological work failed them in philosophy. One of their own students, René Descartes, an alumnus of La Flèche, not only by his experimentation in physics but especially by his point of departure in philosophy, sent a wave of perplexity and dismay through their ranks. It took time for them to evaluate this challenge to their traditional philosophical framework, and reaction among them varied considerably. Pierre Bourdin objected, more by temper than solid argument, and brought disrepute to his own side. Descartes answered Bourdin in the 1642 edition of his *Meditations on First Philosophy*. In 1686, more than thirty years after Descartes' death, at his Alma Mater theses directed against his philosophy were defended in a public defense. Other Jesuits, however, in varying degrees, tried to work out a compromise by constructing a kind of combination of Cartesian physics and Aristotelian cosmology. Among those who leaned considerably in the direction of Descartes was Ignace Pardies, abreast of the times in his books on mechanics and mathematics and the first among the Schoolmen to concede victory to Newton. This gifted scientist, who corresponded with Newton on the subject of light, died of fever in his thirty-seventh year while caring for prisoners at Bicêtre. Descartes, therefore, had won over in one way or another several French Jesuits. But he sought a more complete triumph. Critical though he was of certain aspects of his education at La Flèche, he respected the Jesuits as the best teachers in the nation and hoped that they would adapt his *Principles of Philosophy* as a textbook in their schools. In this he was disappointed.

More luminous than the light created by the depth of theological research and the sharpness of philosophical speculation was the widespread brilliance of literary excellence which hung over France like the glow, created by thousands of lights, which spreads over a great city at night. In the cultivation of the literary finesse of the Great Century the Jesuits, especially through their popular schools, played an important part. In 1616 they conducted forty-six colleges. Sixty-three years later, 1679, they had almost double that number, eighty-three. In 1627, when 13,104 pupils were enrolled, the college at Rouen had the largest student body, 1,968, and Paris, La Flèche, and Rennes were not far behind. Numbers in the individual classes were sometimes killing. The class in humanities generally had about fifty students; the lower classes of grammar between 100 and 140.

The multiplication of colleges, by other religious as well as Jesuits, not only broadened the literary milieu of France but also created a social problem which worried the government. Sons of laborers and artisans in a mighty rush entered the colleges in order to learn Latin, the key to government positions, the liberal professions, and higher social distinction. Attracted by the free education, the poorer classes made up the majority of students in the Jesuit colleges. At Billom, for example, between 1610 and 1625, of the 1,500 students about 7% were of the nobility, 9% of the bourgeoisie, 24% of the minor official class, 18% of the merchant class, 27% of the laboring class, and 15% of the artisan class. At Châlons-sur-Marne, between 1618 and 1634, of the 650 students only 2% were of the nobility, 5% of the bourgeoisie, the rest of the artisan, official, merchant, and laboring classes. Various studies of the educational situation stressed a common theme: commerce and agriculture were suffering because of the wave of students moving towards the humanities. Cardinal Richelieu, disturbed by the implications of this development, devised a plan for the drastic reduction of the colleges. This scheme proved abortive, and later Colbert, with similar preoccupations, enjoyed no greater success than the cardinal.[44] The colleges continued to function and the movement from the lower classes to higher social distinction went on without serious check.

The Jesuit schools, maintaining as they did the classical tradition in a place of honor, turned the creative literary talents of students and professors alike to the composition of Latin poetry, which attained excellent form in several works by François Vavasseur and René Rapin. But valuable as was this concentration on the Latin masters in preparing youth to take their place in the most civilized country in the world, the Jesuits recognized the imperative need for greater attention to the explicit cultivation of their own tongue. This was the warning carried by the impact of Pascal's *Provincial Letters*. In Ranke's

44 F. de Dainville, S.J., "Collèges et fréquentation scolaire au XVIIᵉ siècle," *Population*, XII (1957), 470-472; 474-480.

words, the Jansenists "addressed themselves to the nation." And no more dramatic exhibition of the richness and beauty and power of the vernacular was there than the literary flowering of seventeenth-century France. In the Jesuit schools by the end of the seventeenth century, the Latin grammars were written in French, and on the stage, in the academies, in public celebrations French moved Latin to a secondary position. From these vibrant colleges, where some of the finest minds of the age were harbored and trained and where the feel for literary form and beauty was strong, passed men like Corneille, Bossuet, Molière, Buffon, to feed the great reservoir of French civilization.

As in other countries the Jesuits of the French schools richly developed the drama. This was especially so with the ballet and decor. Ballet had become so important in France that Claude Menestrier, a veteran teacher of literature at the Jesuit schools in Chambéry, Grenoble, Vienne, and Lyon, published in 1682 his *Ancient and Modern Ballets,* a work of great importance in this field. Sometimes the ballet was allegorical. In a tragedy about the fall of the Assyrian Empire, the Jesuits introduced a ballet called *The Dreams,* because the Empire's fall had been foretold in dreams. Sometimes the ballet honored a great public event. One celebrated the marriage of Louis XIV in 1660 and another commemorated the Peace of Nymegen in 1679. At Collège Louis le Grand in Paris many ballets honored the Sun King. In music and ballet the Collège rivalled the *Académie de danse.* Rich decor added to the splendor of the performances. The Jesuits took great care in choosing the costumes. And their scenery at Louis le Grand excelled in variety that of the Théâtre Français. Often the nobility attended and added to the brilliance of the occasion. Louis XIV and the exiled Charles II of England led the long list that included princes and princesses, dukes and duchesses, counts and countesses. Between the Jesuit drama and the cultural taste of the age there was a lively interplay. The extent to which one influenced the other is most difficult to determine.[45]

One of the masters of correct writing of his generation was Dominique Bouhours. Among the first, if not actually the first, to develop the idea of taste, he discussed this notion in his famous *La manière de bien penser dans les ouvrages d'esprit* (1687). In 1705 the first English translation appeared, done by a "Person of Quality," with the title *The Art of Criticism: or*

---

45 Purdie, *The Oxford Companion to the Theatre,* 3rd ed., pp. 511, 513-514, s.v. "Jesuit Drama."

the Method of Making a Right Judgment upon Subjects of Wit and Learning. From this work English critics seemingly learned to use the expression, the art of criticism, to mean the faculty of general literary appreciation. Dryden and Addison read the book, and Lord Chesterfield recommended it to his son. To Bouhours, friend of Nicolas Boileau, Jean de La Fontaine, and Jacques Bénigne Bossuet, Jean Racine presented his tragedies with the salute: "You are one of the supreme masters of our tongue." [46] Another Jesuit, known for his fine command of the French language, wrote himself out of the Society. Louis Maimbourg entered into a touchy field of scholarship when he took up writing the history of the French monarchy. His failure to maintain a cool reserve about Gallican liberties in his works on the medieval papacy summoned the lightning bolt which struck in the form of an order from Pope Innocent XI in 1681 that he be dismissed from the Society. Louis XIV provided him with a pension and lodging at the Abbey of Saint-Victor in Paris.

The holiness of France and the eloquence of France met in Louis Bourdaloue. For thirty-four years until his death in 1704, this saintly Jesuit priest instructed his countrymen by discourses which reached classical perfection in their balanced structure, sustained eloquence, richness of doctrine, through which he drove a Roman road of logic straight to the consciences of his hearers.

Thus, holiness and devotion in Régis, Maunoir, De la Colombière, Jogues, and De Brébeuf; learning and scholarship in Petau, Labbe, Pardies, and Bouhours; contention and strife in Jansenism and Gallicanism, made this one of the most complex periods in the history of the French Jesuits.

The first phase of the Thirty Years War started in Bohemia. *Germany and* With Silesia, Lusatia, and Moravia, three areas which it domi- *Central Europe* nated, Bohemia made a crazy quilt of languages, customs, and religions. Mutual suspicion ran through the Lutheran, Calvinist, Utraquist, and Catholic communities. In Prague, on May 23, 1618, the Protestants hastily formed a government against the Catholic Hapsburgs and threw two of the imperial officials from a window of Hradcany castle. On June 9 they exiled the Jesuits.

Ferdinand II, who was elected Holy Roman Emperor in August, 1619, knew the import of Bohemia as a unit of the

46 V. M. Hamm, "Father Dominic Bouhours and Neo-Classical Criticism," in *Jesuit Thinkers of the Renaissance*, p. 73.

empire. The Vatican realized its significance as a key for the religious control of central Europe. In the fall of 1620 armies under Duke Maximilian of Bavaria and Johann Tzerclaes, graf von Tilly, devout alumnus of the Jesuit college in Cologne, moved on Prague. On November 8, at the White Mountain, a broad elevation that overlooked the city, they defeated the Protestants. Prague surrendered unconditionally. To many Lutheran and Calvinistic gentlemen the religious implications of the Catholic victory were clear. These Protestants made their way about the city carrying either a breviary or a rosary.

The program of removing the Protestant faiths from the conquered area began almost immediately. The first targets were the preachers and ministers, who had the choice of conversion or exile. Cardinal Carlo Carafa, the papal representative, insisted on vigorous action. In his reports he was frank. Fear, he admitted, prompted many Protestants to receive instructions in the Catholic religion. "And since," he added, "little by little God purified their disposition, they embraced the Catholic faith." [47]

The second step in the program was the importation of priests. With Franciscans, Augustinians, and Capuchins, the Society moved into Bohemia. Almost immediately after the battle of the White Mountain, the Jesuits staffed their former church in Prague. They preached in other churches throughout the city; they distributed books. Knowing the Bohemian love of music, they composed catchy tunes for the catechism classes. They set up fifteen mission stations in Bohemia and Moravia. From Prague they moved into other towns; they opened colleges in Komotau, Krumau, Neuhaus, and Gitschin. In 1623 they assumed responsibility for the Caroline University in Prague. They rolled up impressive totals of converts to the faith: in 1622, 5,419; in 1623, 2,552; in 1624, 1,126; in 1625, 18,479; in 1626, 25,144. Between 1620 and 1632 they totaled 223,748. [48]

The Jesuit achievement in Bohemia, Silesia, and Moravia was striking, but a haze intrudes itself to rob the picture of complete lustre. The intolerance of the age, characteristic of Catholic and Protestant alike, moved with the civil commissioners and the soldiers of Ferdinand II into the towns and villages. And frequently with the civil and military authorities were the Jesuits. Yet often the priests by their sincerity and genuine devotion won the widespread love and confidence of the people, and in this way effectively divorced their mission from that of the gov-

47 Pastor, *History*, XXVII, 279.
48 Ibid., XXXVIII, 132-133.

ernment. At Glogau a Jesuit, most likely Matthias Nennichen, opposed the coercing of Protestants.[49] In 1629 at Schweidnitz, to express their objection to the rude tactics of the hoodlum soldiers trying to restore Catholicism, the Jesuits left town. Jesuit schools in Silesia, like the one at Glatz, which had an enrollment of three hundred students in 1627, and the one at Neisse with an enrollment of six hundred, were attended mainly by Protestants. Prisoners, the poor, the victims of epidemics received the tender care of the Jesuits. Genuine and deep devotion to the faith grew. In 1626, even though there were only 136 men, Vitelleschi erected the Province of Bohemia, which embraced Bohemia proper, Silesia, and Moravia. Within thirteen years the province numbered 624, almost a five-fold increase.

Time and the folly of the religious wars gradually wore down the old obduracy and hardness, and the spirit of toleration began to emerge slowly. Theologians also sought an intellectual and religious justification for the peaceful coexistence of different religions within a single state. In the Empire Martin Becanus took the lead among the Catholic theologians and gave his thought practical form in the advice he gave Emperor Ferdinand II. At the opening of the Thirty Years War, Ferdinand was anxious to detach the Lutherans in Lower Austria from an alliance with the revolt in Bohemia. The Lutherans demanded in return a formal guarantee of freedom to adhere to the Confession of Augsburg. Becanus assured Ferdinand that he was justified, in view of the grave situation, in meeting the Lutheran terms. Rome protested. Becanus, somewhat mischievously, replied that he failed to see how the toleration of Lutherans in Austria differed essentially from that accorded Jews in the Papal States.[50] He was, in this instance, simply carrying out in the practical order conclusions he had reached as early as 1605 when, as a professor of theology, he argued for religious toleration under certain circumstances. The religious wars sharpened his thought.

The maneuvering armies of Christian of Brunswick and Ernst von Mansfeld gave the Jesuits an early taste of the agony which the protracted war was to bring Germany. Christian moved

---

49 Duhr, *Geschichte*, II, ii, 350. Duhr identifies this Jesuit as Nerlich. I am indebted to Edmond Lamalle, S.J. director of the Roman Archives of the Society of Jesus, for the information about Matthias Nennichen. From a study of the catalogs of the Jesuit Bohemian province and other documents, he has shown that it could hardly have been either of the two Nerlichs, Wencelas or Paul, who made the protest to the emperor, and that most likely it was Matthias Nennichen.

50 Lecler, *Histoire de la tolérance*, I, 295.

from the north with blood-curdling threats. At Paderborn, where the Jesuits had one of their most northern communities, Protestant hostility mounted with the approach of the troops, and friends of the Jesuits advised them to flee. On January 22, 1622, about seventy left the town. Among these refugees was a scholastic, Athanasius Kircher, destined to become one of the most celebrated scientists of his day, who has left in his autobiography vivid descriptions of the cold, hunger, and weariness of tramping along open highways in mid-January.

Four years later, in 1626, Von Tilly launched his massive counter-offensive against Christian IV of Denmark. And three years after that, the Dane sued for peace. The Hapsburg troops held strong positions in the north. This was the supreme moment for the Catholic cause. With the encouragement of his Jesuit confessor, Wilhelm Lamormaini, Ferdinand II decided to undo the injustice against the Church since the Peace of Augsburg by restoring the bishoprics, parishes, and monasteries taken by the Protestants. For the Society this drastic turn of events was its greatest opportunity in Germany since it opened its first college eighty years before. Von Tilly took steps to found colleges at Lüneburg, Verden, and Stade. Albrecht von Wallenstein, the leader of a powerful free-wheeling army in the service of Ferdinand, encouraged the emperor to found others.

These plans and the need for buildings brought into sharp focus what had become an occasion of bad feeling between the Society and the older religious orders. With the approval of Rome, priories, nearly or completely deserted, were placed in the service of the Society, or technically "incorporated" into the new Jesuit schools. Publicly monks condemned the procedure. Also publicly the Jesuits defended it. So bitter did the animosity become that the Holy See imposed silence on both parties. Then, adding to the distress of this situation, the dream of thousands of young men, expertly trained in the faith, each year leaving their Jesuit schools and working as a yeast in the life of northern Germany, was soon rudely shattered. King Gustavus Adolphus of Sweden, aided by Cardinal Richelieu of France, invaded the Empire. Both sides fought desperately and left devastation in their wake. Jesuit chaplains moved with the imperial armies, and some of them recorded in their diaries detailed accounts of their work among the weary and sick troops. Kaspar Wiltheim described the awful scene as flames licked the roofs of the buildings at the terrible storming of Magdeburg where some 20,000 perished. Gustavus Adolphus moved swiftly and skillfully into the heart of Germany, and the course of his march can be traced by the location of Jesuit schools which were closed and often plundered. In September, 1631, the rector at Heiligenstadt sent his community to Göttingen. In January, 1632, superiors of the Upper Rhine Province reported that the men at Mainz had gone to Luxembourg, that the novitiate at Trier had been closed and the novices sent to other provinces, forty-one to France. In February, 1632, the Jesuits were forced out of Bamberg; in June, out of Erfurt. In February, 1633, they quit their college at Roesfeld, soon after plundered by Hessians; in August they were ordered out of Paderborn, in September out of Osnabrück where their church was used for Protestant services. All the letters reiterate the same grim tale: exile, the boom of cannon, plunder, devastation.

This terrible visitation of the three destroying angels, plague, famine, and war, made this an unforgettable period in the history of the German Jesuits. In 1623, during a severe shortage of food, those at Ingolstadt daily distributed bread to seven hundred and more of the poor. At Eichstädt, after the town had been sacked and burned, they sought out children cringing in cellars and feeding on the rats they had killed. In 1636, the community at Trier, once more back at the novitiate after its closing in 1632, fed each day as many as two hundred refugees who were fleeing before the invading armies.[51] Students in the schools were often extremely poor, and the college diaries are filled with instances of how the fathers gave assistance. At Emmerich, for example, in December, 1618, 130 needy students were measured for new shoes; in December, 1630, twenty-six talers were distributed among the indigent. Epidemics intensified the widespread misery. More than two hundred Jesuits gave their lives in the service of the sick during that dreadful first half of the seventeenth century. The rude dislocation of normal life by the ravages of war seriously curtailed the spiritual ministry. In 1630 the fathers of the Upper German Province distributed 600,000 Holy Communions. The next year the figure dropped; in 1643 it climbed to 978,000, only to fall sharply to 683,000 three years later.[52]

But war did not halt the printing presses from which circulated far and wide through Germany the devotional works of the most popular spiritual writer of the early part of the century, Jeremias Drexel. Especially successful in his combina-

---

51 Duhr, *Geschichte*, II, i, 398-407; II, ii, 157-179; C. V. Wedgwood, *The Thirty Years War* (New Haven, 1939), pp. 411-412.
52 Duhr, *Geschichte*, II, i, 596; II, ii, 28, 130-131.

tion of sound doctrine and the use of symbolism, which was then the fad, Drexel specialized in small tracts with such quaint titles as *The Christian Zodiac* (1622), *The Guardian Angel's Clock* (1622), *Heliotropium* (1627). These small volumes, richly decorated with their colorful symbolic characters, enjoyed a wide market. At Munich alone his editor had sold in twenty-two years 107,000 copies. After 1650, Jesuits produced an enormous number of small, practical, familiar works designed to sanctify each day of the year and each hour of the day. Very often, and this was probably more true in Germany than in any other country, the sodalities and congregations conducted by the Society determined the character of the devotional works by Jesuits, since it was often primarily for the sodalists that they wrote them. Not precisely a piece of spiritual literature but one which handled a prominent moral question of the day was the *Caution in Criminal Proceedings*, published in 1631 by Friedrich Spe von Langenfeld. One of the most depressing social ills of the times was the widespread mania for witch-hunting, which sent hundreds of poor, helpless old women to unjust trials and frightful deaths. Boldly and incisively Spe halted the national madness by exposing it for what it was, an amalgam of superstition, fear, malice, and injustice.

During this era of violence and crudity the Jesuit schools played a part not unlike that of the monasteries of seven hundred years earlier when, in an age of like rawness when the ancestors of Gustavus Adolphus fell on Europe, they preserved the tradition and dignity of learning. When the study of Greek declined and the Protestant schools dropped it from the curriculum, the Jesuit schools retained it. When a florid, pretentious Latin style threatened to supplant Cicero as the model, the Jesuits received a clear direction from Aquaviva in one of his last letters: "Cicero remains our exemplar." Those who succumbed to the current fashion incurred official disapproval when in 1655 the provincial congregation of the Upper Rhine Province insisted on a return to the classical style, and when in 1672 the congregation of the Lower Rhine Province did the same. The tradition of the drama lived on in the powerful and skillful plays of Jakob Bidermann, a student with Drexel under the great Rader. Scientific inquiry of a high order flourished in the astronomical investigations of Johann Deckers and Albert Curtz, who collaborated with the celebrated Johann Kepler. Poetic expression in themes of filial devotion to the Blessed Virgin, tender love for Germany and sorrow in her suffering received masterful form in the works of Jakob Balde, one of the greater poets of the age. In 1638 Balde published his best German poem, a piece he had created for the Sodality of the Blessed Virgin of which he was the prefect. Called *A Trophy for the Holy Mother of God (Ehrenpreis . . .)*, its tender and beautiful lines captivated Catholic hearts and soon were sounding in all the churches and chapels of Catholic Germany during devotions to Our Lady.[53] Greater in his poetical powers than even Balde, Friedrich Spe offset his unpleasant task of denouncing witch-hunting by some of the most delicate and melodious of German Baroque poetry. A keen observer of nature, finely attuned to harmonious sound, deeply sensitive to human feeling, this attractive Jesuit enriched his country's literature with some of its most lovely lyrical poetry.

Literature pointed toward religious controversy remained true to the tradition set by Bellarmine and Becanus. Although studies in dogmatic theology lacked originality and freshness, and although authors were generally content to reproduce in a more concise, methodical, and didactic form, adapted for classroom use, the works of their great predecessors, they at least kept alive in a period of cultural decline the memory of keen and penetrating minds of earlier years. In moral theology, however, a work of superior quality appeared. Hermann Busenbaum, gifted teacher at the University of Cologne, published in 1650 his celebrated *An Epitome of Moral Theology*. In this work, a neat, precise, and balanced summary of moral principles and the solutions proposed since the Council of Trent by the more solid authors to the cases of conscience most likely to come up in confession, Busenbaum produced the textbook preferred in those seminaries and universities which resisted the rigorist tide of the last half of the seventeenth century. St. Alfonso Maria de' Liguori admittedly leaned heavily on this widely recognized Jesuit authority. Despite Busenbaum's prestige, a strange myth has enveloped his name. To him, and frequently by association to all Jesuits, has been attributed the doctrine that the end justifies the means, be the means intrinsically good or evil. Most explicitly however Busenbaum excluded the use of bad means. But the myth perdures.

A normal consequence to prolonged havoc and destruction of war would be a cutback in the number of schools. But the peculiar political structure of the Empire set the tides in the opposite direction, and at the end of the Thirty Years War the Society was operating more schools than at its beginning. The

---

53 Ibid., II, ii, 120-121.

hundreds of small units into which the Empire was fragmented each wanted its own university, college, or academy, and they pulled the Society in every direction. Expansion spread manpower thin and necessitated the creation of large classes to be handled by a limited staff. In Augsburg in 1631, for example, one class had to be divided in two, and after the division one section numbered one hundred and eleven boys, the other eighty-two. Similar statistics for other schools all speak a eulogy for the hundreds of unsung heroes of the classroom during some of Germany's darkest hours.

While these men labored through the tragic events of the Thirty Years War and its sequel, in Hungary their brethren went on building up the Catholic restoration on the foundations laid by Péter Pázmány. In order to make this skilful organizer the Archbishop of Esztergom and Primate of Hungary, Pope Paul V in 1616 met the problem of the Society's refusal of ecclesiastical honors by transferring Pázmány from the Society to the Somaschi. The new primate continued, however, to rely heavily on his former fellow religious and committed to their care two colleges, a university, and a seminary. Protestants strenuously contested the Jesuit successes. In 1619 at Kaschau two Jesuits, Istuán Pongracz and Menyhért Grodecz, with the cathedral canon, Mark Crisinus, sealed their devotion to the faith with their blood when Calvinist soldiers seized them and by brutal beating and burning sent them to their deaths. The Church now counts them among her Blessed. Tenacious as were the Protestants in their hold on some quarters of the country, they could not halt the erection of a powerful Catholic bastion on the Danube.

Poland   During the eighteenth century Poland was a nation at bay. Across the borders of this distressed country poured Swedes, Turks, Russians, Transylvanians, Cossacks, who left behind sacked towns and a scorched landscape as memorials of their terrible visits. The Poles themselves, disorganized by an inherent tendency to political individualism and given to the peculiar political logic, "For lack of order Poland stands," were ill equipped to withstand the invaders.

A wide window onto the chaos and general debasement of cultural life in this period is provided by the letters and memorials, about one hundred and fifty of them between 1645 and 1740, which Jesuit superiors wrote concerning the colleges of Poland. Many of these documents, with their constant refrain about fire, pillage, hunger, cold, resembled in tone the letters of

German Jesuits during the Thirty Years War.[54] A typical year was 1626. Gustavus Adolphus of Sweden made a sweep of the Polish Baltic towns and expelled the Jesuits from Livonia, Braunsberg, and Marienburg. Another scarred year was 1647. The Transylvanian prince Rakocio and the Swedes left hardly a house in the entire Polish Province untouched. The college at Brest went up in flames, the college at Przemysl was devastated, the college at Sandomierz was twice pillaged. In the collapse of order and security the cultural standards of the Society's schools went into decline. Many Jesuits lost their esteem for teaching, especially in the grammar classes, and tried to avoid what they looked on as an arduous chore. The *Ratio Studiorum* lost its place of honor; prefects neglected to give time to the proper formation of young Jesuit teachers; Greek almost entirely disappeared from the curriculum; the philosophy courses became entangled in a mesh of subtleties. The average Jesuit resembled the rustic and pious gentleman, small in intellectual and spiritual aspirations. Superiors put the brake on this descent and prevented an even more serious deterioration as the calamities of the age multiplied and the men of the province were crushed by the weight of national disaster.

Strangely enough, amid this debris of war and this debasement of cultural values, appeared one of the most sensitive and distinguished classicists in the Jesuit humanistic tradition. Maciej Sarbiewski, whose delicately chiseled Latin poems awakened memories of the cadences and sharpness of ancient Rome's finest poetry, belonged by rights to an Augustan age. This Polish Horace — for so he was called — seems strangely out of place in this period of literary apathy.

Star differs from star in glory, and while Sarbiewski shone in academic circles by the clear light of his poetical sensibility, in the apostolate among schismatics Andrzej Bobola cast a glow on Poland by the noble way he met martyrdom. In an unhappy sequel to the Union of Brest of 1596, by which the Ruthenians acknowledged the supremacy of Rome, a faction of the schismatics refused to accept the decree. The patriarch of Moscow, subject to the tsar, and the patriarch of Constantinople, under the control of the sultan, by their political manipulations made a tense religious situation all the more taut. The restless and harsh Cossacks, aligned with the schismatics, harassed the Catholic Poles with terrible ferocity. In this explosive situation Bobola, a small, sturdy, genial, indefatigable man in his sixties, started

54 Bednarski, "Déclin et renaissance," *AHSJ*, II (1933), 199-223.

in 1652 to work among the poor people, mainly schismatics, in the dismal swamp lands around Pinsk. From cabin to cabin he moved, and by his gentle persuasiveness won great numbers for the Church. His remarkable success made him a prime target for the vicious Cossacks, who in 1657 descended on him at Jarrow and did their barbarous work by flogging, burning, dragging by horses, flaying. To all of this Bobola responded with an astonishingly sweet spirit of forgiveness, and on May 16 he died. Pope Pius XI canonized this martyr of Church unity in 1938.

St. Andrzej was not alone in the shedding of his blood for the faith. During this same period, between the years 1648 and 1665, the Cossacks took the lives of forty other Jesuits. A contemporary, Jan Zuchowicz, has left a solemn and subdued, yet vivid, account of each of these martyrs as they suffered amid the mad chaos of burning colleges, scattered libraries, and the perpetration of revolting atrocities on the Catholic population.[55]

During these dolorous decades, especially uneasy and distracted were the heads who wore the crown of Poland. Among the most dispirited of reigns was that of a former Jesuit. Jan Kasimierz, brother of King Ladislaus IV, entered the Society's novitiate in 1643. He left the order two years later, was made a cardinal in 1647, and in 1648 began his unhappy reign of twenty turbulent years, marked by civil and military reversals and concluded by his abdication.

Under one of Jan Kasimierz's successors, Jan Sobieski, Poland rose above its discord in a magnificent gesture of gallant sacrifice for the salvation of Christendom in a dark hour of crisis. A Jesuit played an important part in the designing of this memorable feat. In 1683 the Turks had moved on Vienna, and by September 11 only a few hundred yards separated them from the imperial palace. Pope Innocent XI, in whom still burned the crusading spirit of Urban II and Pius V, sent Carlo Vota to exhort Sobieski to throw Polish forces into the fight against the Moslem. This intelligent Piedmontese, who enjoyed great credit with the Polish monarch, carried out his mandate well, and by his persuasion, along with other factors the relative influence of which it is impossible to measure, he set him on the road to Vienna and one of Poland's most intrepid exploits. During the campaign which turned back the Turk, Vota attended Sobieski as his confessor.

55 Bober and Bednarz, "Relatio de caedibus . . . in Provincia Poloniae . . . 1665," *AHSJ*, XXIX (1960), 329-380.

Magnificent as was this feat, it had no more substance for Poland than a fitful momentary gleam of the sun in a cloud-filled sky. For the Jesuits, in this period of war and political anarchy, their endless task was to make new beginnings, always in the hope of the abilities of the next generation to establish order and peace.

In Antwerp stands the church of St. Charles, formerly in the hands of the Jesuits and under the patronage of St. Ignatius. Graceful and strong and dynamic in its lines, it is one of the thirty-seven churches built by the Belgian Jesuits in the early years of their province and a symbol of their energy, their vision, their élan. Before 1600 these churches were almost uniformly Gothic; by 1630 Baroque had become supreme. Both the rear-guard of the Gothic and the advance-guard of the Baroque, the Jesuits, even while receiving their inspiration from Italy, through the skill of men like Brother Pieter Huyssens, an architect of the first order, left on their structures a decidedly national imprint.[56]

This creative power molded their work in many other fields. In education, the two provinces by 1640 were running forty-two busy and thriving colleges; on the Dutch mission they had forty men by 1630, sixty-three men in 1634, eighty-two men in 1648, ninety-one men in 1654. In the publication of devotional literature they fed a popular desire to grow spiritually by such works as *Two Heavenly Keys* of Josse Andries, which sold 150,000 copies in a short time, and *The Divine Perfections* and *The Divine Names* of Léonard Leys (Lessius). In the field of catechetics many a priest received in his death notice the phrase "outstanding catechist," including Louis Makeblyde, whose influential work continued, with several modifications, into the twentieth century as the Malines Catechism. In the face of danger volunteers to serve the victims of epidemics were many, and of these, one hundred and seventy in the seventeen years from 1621 to 1638 made the supreme sacrifice. Of the Gallo-Belgian Province alone eighty-six men lost their lives in 1636 in the service of either the military or the sick, and in the two years, 1667-1668, eighty-two more. The growth of the Society in Belgium was the most extraordinary in the pre-suppression Society. In 1643, the Flemish-Belgian Province attained its maximum strength, 867 men; two years earlier the Gallo-Belgian

56 Poncelet, *Histoire,* I, 575-580.

Province reached its top number, 856. These 1,700 men had been only 154 sixty-four years before.

Of all the creations of this dynamic drive the most celebrated has been the Society of Bollandists. The enterprise, begun in 1603 by Héribert Rosweyde to produce critical editions of the vast manuscript material on the lives of the saints, experienced its first major success in 1616 when Rosweyde published his *Lives of the Fathers*, the foundation stone of the mammoth *Acts of the Saints (Acta sanctorum)*. Jan von Bolland, whose name has given the internationally respected group of scholars their popular identification, carried on where Rosweyde left off, but changed the original plan of leaving the critical apparatus to the last two volumes of a projected eighteen by presenting the apparatus with the *acta* of each saint. In 1659 Daniel Van Papenbroeck, one of the greatest of the Bollandists and the hero of such great moderns as Hippolyte Delehaye, joined the staff. Van Papenbroeck brought his critical sense, sound judgment, ready pen, and love of work to this exacting task. But even before his arrival, in 1643 two volumes of the *Acts of the Saints* for January appeared. As the scholarly enterprise moved forward, its importance for the Church received special recognition from Pope Alexander VII. "Never had there been undertaken up to that time," said the pontiff, "any work more useful or more glorious to the Church." [57]

Besides their *Acts of the Saints*, a perennial member of the republic of scholarship with that character of permanence and continuity which makes it fit naturally into subsequent centuries of the Society's history, the Belgian Jesuits produced another memorable volume, more a work of the moment, yet more expressive of the wide sense of optimism which the Society felt in the early seventeenth century as the massive wave of the Catholic Reform moved onward. *A Portrait of the First Century (Imago primi saeculi)*, a ponderous work of 952 pages, elaborately adorned with emblems and published in 1640, commemorated the first centenary of the establishment of the Society. From between its covers sounds, loud and clear, the confident melody of a triumphant spirit. On each page hangs the flag of victory. A few examples. At the top of one page is a large engraving, in elaborate baroque style, of a tall candle, resting on the land against a wide vista of city and country and diffusing its light in every direction. Over the candle is the inscription: *The spread of the Society of Jesus*. Beneath is the

---

57 Ibid., II, 459-468, 480.

sentence: *Once lighted, it fills the world with its glow.* Another engraving represents a large rotund fountain from which flow several streams of water. Over it are the words: *Freely does the Society pour itself out for the solace of its neighbors,* while below is the reading: *All you who thirst, come to the waters; come and make purchase with no price to be paid.* Still another emblem shows a broad expanse of the sky with a multitude of stars illumining the night. Above are the words: *In its contempt for honor the Society attains greater distinction,* and below: *In darkness the stars glitter the more brightly.* Under several of these engravings are lengthy Latin verses which elaborate on the engraving's particular theme. Militancy, self-assurance, the spring in the march of an army on the road to certain victory permeate the text. The Society's achievements through its first hundred years were truly eminent. Gratification was understandable. But *A Portrait of the First Century* can rest only uncomfortably in the presence of the Jesuit *Constitutions* and St. Ignatius' humble attitude in regard to "this least Society of Jesus." From the general Vitelleschi it evoked a stern rebuke for the Belgian Jesuits, and a little later it provided Blaise Pascal with some choice barbs against the Society.

Two major developments, the one theological, the other military, intruded on the Jesuits, to distract and divert their energies from these positive achievements. They were Jansenism and the campaigns of Louis XIV.

In a theological atmosphere still infected by the ideas of Baius, Cornelis Jansen produced his celebrated work on the thought of St. Augustine, the *Augustinus.* He intimately confided that his objective was to make an apology for Baius. The Belgian Jesuits quickly discerned the subtle danger and, relying generally on the Tridentine decrees and the Church's condemnations of Baius and arguing that Jansen's doctrine, in the manner of Calvinism, obliterated the difference between the natural and the supernatural and destroyed man's internal freedom, attacked the *Augustinus.* Nonetheless Jansen gained an immense following. The papal internuncio to the Low Countries, Andrea Mangelli, felt that it was because of the Jesuit attack rather than despite it that Jansenism won such popularity. He reasoned that the scholars at the university, embarrassed by their loss of intellectual primacy to the dynamic and enterprising Jesuits, threw their sympathy and support to a movement that had the Society as an enemy. In such wise, the papal diplomat philosophized, does evil become mingled with good in life.

What started as an incidental skirmish broadened into a far-reaching battle. The disciples of Jansen found influential defenders not only at the University of Louvain but also in the archbishop of Malines, Jacques Boonen. They dueled with the Holy See, hedging, dodging, procrastinating in the face of Rome's decisions against them. Among all the religious orders the Jesuits alone contested them. In 1653 no religious, save the Jesuits, spoke out in support of the bull *Cum occasione* of Innocent X in which the pope condemned on May 31, 1653, the famous five Jansenist propositions.

Hatred for the Society was among the imports the Jansenists carried into Holland for distribution among the Catholics. French Jansenists found asylum there and gained ascendancy over the minds of many Dutch priests. As in Belgium, with Jesuits clearly opposed to the theology of the *Augustinus* and others ardently in support of it, the Catholic community was deeply split. Jan Neercassel, influential Dutch priest who closed his life as archbishop of Utrecht, professed a deep veneration for Port-Royal, and when he died in 1686 the way had been prepared for the tragic schism of Utrecht and the consequent crushing of the several successful Jesuit missions in Holland.

Besides this bitter theological conflict which diverted so much precious Jesuit energy from positive and constructive ventures, war with its disorders, unrest, and uncertainty fell upon the Netherlands as in 1667 the armies of Louis XIV began their long campaign of aggression.

In England this period, including the execution of Charles I, the protectorate of Oliver Cromwell, the restoration of the monarchy, was an age of drastic change. But amid these shifts in government, constant and unaltered remained the legal status of the Society of Jesus as a proscribed and treasonous group of men. Enforcement of the law varied with foreign policy and domestic politics, but the shadow of the scaffold was never entirely erased.

Early in this century the English Jesuits had the good fortune to be ruled for twenty-one years by a knowledgeable man, akin to Claudio Aquaviva in the delicate harmony he preserved between determination and gentleness, Richard Blount. The tree planted by Campion and Persons, Blount watered. In 1623 when the English Jesuits numbered 218, of whom a little over a hundred were in the homeland, Vitelleschi erected the Province of England and sanctioned the opening of a novitiate in London. To assure orderly and systematic procedure Blount divided the country into districts, such as the London district under the patronage of St. Ignatius, the district of South Wales under St.

Francis Xavier, the district of Worcestershire under St. George, the district of Lincolnshire under St. Hugh.

Through the restless years the reports from these districts, like those from the German houses during the Thirty Years War, reveal in specific detail the circumstances under which the Jesuits brought the sacraments and the word of God to the Catholic people. From 1641 to 1644 the fathers in the Oxford-shire district of St. Mary reported large scale confiscation of the property of Catholics and the consequent difficulty in finding a place to hide. In 1637 the Jesuits of the Durham district noted that the rigorous exaction of fines was deterring some Protestants who wanted to become Catholics, and that it was a difficult task to keep faltering Catholics from conforming to the established Church. Conversions were made — in the Sussex district, twenty-eight in 1635, fifty-two in 1636, one hundred between 1638 and 1640; in the Durham district, ninety in 1635, fifty in 1636; in the Devonshire district, eleven to twelve a year between 1645 and 1659 — but these typical numbers could not begin to compensate for the vast leakage which reduced the Catholics to about ten per cent of the population at the close of the rule of James II.[58]

Prolonged into this period from the earlier one were two themes, the one, lofty and inspiring, of heroism to the point of death; the other, drab and dispiriting, of tension in relations with the secular clergy. The splendor of Campion lived on in men like Henry Morse, priest of special dedication to the victims of the plague, who in 1645 went gallantly to the scaffold with a prayer for England on his lips, and Thomas Holland, who at Tyburn in 1642 gave a final example of his graceful eloquence as he spoke in his sweet, strong voice until silenced by the halter. Under Charles I seven English Jesuits went to the gallows, and one under Cromwell. Under Charles II occurred the monstrous lie of Titus Oates. This degenerate, twice expelled from Jesuit schools abroad and refused admission into the Society, spread the story that the Jesuits were engineering a plot to overthrow the king and turn the country over to the Catholics. In the excitement churned up by his mendacity, eleven Jesuits, including the provincial, Thomas Whitebread, were executed. Several, including Claude de la Colombière, chaplain to the Duchess of York, were imprisoned. Besides the eleven victims of the Oates plot, five other Jesuits were killed under Charles II. On October

---

58 *Records of the English Province of the Society of Jesus,* ed. H. Foley, S.J. (London, 1877-1882), III, 122, 400-404; IV, 615-617, 668.

25, 1970, Pope Paul VI canonized forty martyrs of England and Wales, among whom were nine Jesuit priests and one Jesuit brother. Edmund Campion, Alexander Briant, Robert Southwell, and Henry Walpole died under Elizabeth I, Thomas Garnet, Edmund Arrowsmith and Brother Nicholas Owen under James I, Henry Morse under Charles I, and Philip Evans and David Lewis under Charles II.

These martyrs came from a Catholic community in which tension had placed heavy strains on the bonds of unity. Among some of the secular clergy dislike of the Society was intensified because the Jesuits, through their Sodality of the Blessed Virgin which attracted souls who aspired to a more holy way of life, won a special place in the affections of many English Catholics. This unhappy situation worsened with the arrival in England of two bishops in rapid succession. William Bishop, consecrated in June, 1623, and instructed to compose the differences between the secular and regular clergy, gave the impression that he thought that this could be achieved by the removal of the Society from England and the termination of Jesuit control of the English colleges in Rome and Spain. He died on April 14, 1624, only eight months after his arrival from the continent. Richard Smith succeeded him as the titular bishop of Chalcedon. Like a terrible blight, personal and official tragedy descended on his six years in England as relations between the Jesuits, other religious, and himself deteriorated. The central problem focused on the source of jurisdiction by virtue of which the religious administered the sacraments, particularly penance. The Jesuits claimed that they had received faculties to hear confessions through their superior in Rome. From the long tedious pages of correspondence arises the mist of ambiguity, even about the episcopal position of Smith, whether he was really more than a vicar apostolic. Pope Urban VIII intervened on May 9, 1631, with his brief *Britannia,* in which he upheld the regulars in the matter of hearing confessions. This brief, while paying tribute to the great gifts of Smith, rebuked him as a fomenter of disagreement and a destroyer of charity.[59] The year the *Britannia* arrived Smith left England and lived in quasi-retirement until his death in Paris twenty-four years later, a

---

59 Philip Hughes, *Rome and the Counter-Reformation in England* (London, 1944), pp. 378-407. Smith claimed that the regulars, including of course the Jesuits, were determined to have him removed, not because of himself personally, but because they were determined not to have a bishop in England (ibid., p. 336).

man who perhaps — it is extremely difficulty to assess blame — misused a splendid opportunity to bind the dangerous wound in the Catholic body of England.

All this acrimony might have dropped out of memory in the joy and brightness of a new age opened by the ascent to the throne of the Catholic duke of York as James II. The Jesuits, showing their elastic organizational efficiency at its best, opened twelve schools. Two of these were in London and enjoyed immediate success even among Protestants. The first, in the Savoy, soon had an enrollment of 400, over half Protestants. The second, on Fenchurch Street, included in its *Rules* some directives which reflected unique credit on the Society in that era of religious bias. Three of the rules tell their own story.[60]

> III. And altho' Youths of different Professions, whether *Catholics* or *Protestants*, come to these Schools; yet in Teaching all, there shall be no distinction made, but all shall be Taught with equal Diligence and Care, and every one shall be promoted according to his Deserts.
>
> IV. There shall not be, either by Masters or Scholars, any tampering or medling to persuade any one from the Profession of his own Religion; but there shall be all freedom for every one to practise that Religion he shall please, and none shall be less esteemed or favored for being of a different Religion from others.
>
> V. None shall upbraid or reproach any on the account of Religion; and when any Exercise of Religion shall be practiced, as hearing *Mass, Catechising,* or *Preaching,* or any other; it shall be lawful for any *Protestant,* without any molestation or trouble, to absent himself from such Exercise, if he please.

The promise of these schools was short-lived. James II did not match the stature of political acumen, tact, and discretion — perhaps no one could have — required of a Catholic ruler in a country so virulently biased against the Church. Close to the monarch were two Jesuits, John Warner, his confessor, and Edward Petre, his confidant and counselor. An exact and precise evaluation of Petre's influence in the formulation of the king's self-defeating and unrealistic policies evades measuring, since most contemporaries who wrote of him were unfriendly. Terriesi, envoy of Modena and a moderate Catholic, observed: "The king seems determined to push on in religious matters as far as he possibly can, and the Jesuit Petre, who controls him, is just

---

60 J. H. Pollen, S.J., "A Jesuit 'Free School' in London 1688," *Month,* CXXVIII (1916), 264-267.

the man to do it, without a thought for the future until it is in on him." [61] Some contemporaries felt that he was a mere tool in the hands of a much more subtle man, the earl of Sunderland. The king himself, in a show of political naïveté, contributed in large measure to the whispering that surrounded his Jesuit friend. He made Petre a member of the Privy Council. He persistently sought to have him appointed to the College of Cardinals, seemingly oblivious of the resentment that this would naturally foment among the secular priests. Petre himself certainly did not seek this honor. In 1688 the Glorious Revolution closed this brief chapter in English history, and, as the invasion of Gustavus Adolphus killed Jesuit hopes in northern Germany, the landing of William of Holland at Torbay did the same in England. Once more, after three short years of easement, the Jesuits became "a people who fled the light of day." James's opinion of Petre varied with the times. Right after his flight the king remarked that his Jesuit counselor had given him nothing but good advice. Later, when he wrote his memoirs, he altered his earlier generous statement, saying that Petre "was indeed a plausible but weak man, and had only the art by an abundance of words to put a gloss upon a weak and shallow judgment." [62] A just appraisal must await further scholarly study.

In Scotland a handful of Jesuits, usually six to a dozen at one time, tried with even fewer seculars to keep alive the darkening embers of the faith. In 1628 John Macbreck wrote to Vitelleschi that the Scots mission was "almost, not to say quite, the most arduous and difficult one in charge of our Society," an opinion formed in the awareness of the peculiarly pitiless hatred of Presbyterians for the Catholic Church. As in England, the turn of the political wheel opened or closed opportunities for the priests, but usually they lived like hunted animals. In 1630 William Leslie reported to the general that it was difficult to find a haven, since the Scots Catholics faced a choice which meant either the shipwreck of their faith or exile; and Robert Valens, in view of this persecution, wrote: "I now say my breviary in the fields, or lurk all day in the hills dressed like a peasant." In 1639 another outburst of anti-Catholic feeling prompted Thomas Rob to report: "There is a general panic, so that the people who used to afford us shelter and lodging for a night will not now let one

61 J. P. Kenyon, *Robert Spencer, Earl of Sunderland, 1641-1702* (London, 1958), p. 134.
62 F. C. Turner, *James II* (London, 1948), p. 305.

of our Society come near them." [63] After the Restoration a wave of fervor spread through the land and washed both Catholics and Protestant alike. In 1663 one Jesuit reported over a hundred conversions, mainly nobles. Gentlemen made eight-day retreats and led penitential lives. To the general went an earnest plea from the nine men on the mission for help, since nothing was holding back wavering Catholics from an open profession of faith "except the want of priests to instruct them, and the insufficiency of our numbers." But to the Protestants, who sounded the alarm that "the pest of Popery," as they called it, was spreading, came the windfall of the Titus Oates affair in England. Rumors and calumnies fed ignorant minds. About 2,000 people were sent to prison. James Forbes related to Oliva in 1679 the terrible setback the Society's work suffered because of Oates' lie. "It is remarkable what a revolution this has occasioned in the entire condition of our affairs. Before this happened, the Catholic cause was in so flourishing a state that never was there a time since heresy began to move forward in this country when the crop seemed to be ripening more quickly for the harvest." Scotland was not to be like Hungary and Poland, a land re-won for the Church by the Society. Perhaps the best summary of the Jesuit achievement in that northern land was the brief phrase in one of the annual letters, "Our men have kept the faith from being completely crushed." [64]

In the background of this recital of genuine heroism sounds the same kind of dissonance that mars English Catholic history of this period: misunderstanding and strain between the secular priests and the Jesuits. One special irritant was the question of vocations. The Scots colleges on the continent, in Rome, Douai, and Madrid, were designed to train secular priests for service in Scotland. At one time or another all were under Jesuit supervision. Many of the young seminarians, attracted to their masters' manner of life, entered the Society. The Scots College at Madrid, under the Society from 1633 to 1767, provided an example in the extreme, since during those years twenty-three became Jesuits, one a Franciscan, and only three secular priests.[65] Disappointment and chagrin among the seculars, a

63 W. Forbes-Leith, S.J., *Memoirs of Scottish Catholics during the XVII and XVIII Centuries* (London-New York, 1909), I, 11, 76-79, 190.

64 Ibid., II, 55, 138-139.

65 V. A. McClelland, "Scots Jesuits and Episcopal Authority 1603-1773," *Dublin Review,* No. 507 (1966), 124.

most understandable reaction, grew out of this unbalanced situation.

The fortunes of the Irish Jesuits, thirty-eight in their native land in 1617, rose and fell with the baffling political turns of this turbulent century. The Catholic Confederation of Kilkenny opened in 1642 an all too brief period of freedom during which they followed the scholarly bent of their apostolate in twelve schools and residences. Cromwell's armies terminated this. Jesuits dropped to only twelve in number. Two died in the blood bath at Drogheda. Cromwell instructed his government in Dublin that, "Whereas the poorer sorts of Irish in Ireland doe, as well as the rich, abound in children," these children "att the age of tenn yeares and upwards bee taken from their Parents and bound Apprentices to religious and honest people in England or Ireland. . . ." Against Catholic schoolmasters the government legislated that they "be secured and put on board of such ship as is bound for the Islands of the Barbadoes." In this climate of oppression James Forde built a cabin in the Bog of Allen and there, between 1652 and 1656, managed to carry on a program of elementary and advanced general education. Under Charles II, despite the grim policy of the Puritans, "those men of sourest leaven," who controlled educational policy in Ireland, the Jesuits were able through thirty years, 1660-1690, to open schools at New Ross, Drogheda, Cashel, and Dublin. Blessed Oliver Plunket, who invited the Society to Drogheda, wrote to Oliva in 1672: "I have three Fathers in the diocese of Armagh who by their virtue, learning, and labors would suffice to enrich a kingdom." [66] In this school some forty Protestant children were enrolled. Thus the school remained the distinctive Jesuit contribution to the presence of the Church in Ireland.

The Far East   In its responsibility to the mission world the Portuguese province was caught between the two arms of a strong vise: on the one side, the staggering vastness of the foreign lands which made help from other European nations imperative; on the other, the sensitivity of the Portuguese government on the question of the Padroado, which frequently created difficulties, even to the point of closing the sea lanes to foreign Jesuits. Official documents of the seventeenth century swing between admission and exclusion of non-Portuguese within the area of the Padroado. In 1664, for example, Alfonso VI denied sailing per-

66 T. Corcoran, S.J., "Early Irish Jesuit Educators," *Studies*, XXIX (1940), 550-551; XXX (1941), 73-74; Corcoran, *Clongowes*, p. 32.

mission to subjects of other lands. To Goswin Nickel, the general, he complained of the number of non-Portuguese Jesuits who managed to get to the Orient, much against his royal will.[67] But frequently the fleets carried with official approbation some foreigners among the groups of their Jesuit passengers. Some characteristic examples of the steady movement to the Orient follow: in 1629 forty-one, of whom twenty-four were Portuguese, sailed; in 1635, thirty-three, of whom ten were Portuguese, twenty-one Italian, and two German. In the first ten years after the restoration of the Portuguese monarchy in 1640 fifty-nine, of whom thirty-three were Portuguese, sailed. In the ten years, 1672 to 1683, there were eighty-two. These figures, limited to the men who actually left Europe, do not reveal the full missionary zeal of a province whose gaze always ranged beyond the horizon of the ocean seas. In 1618, for example, at Coimbra alone seventy of the community volunteered for foreign duty.

In India the Jesuits carried on their work within the organizational framework of two provinces, that of Goa, which included Mysore in the interior of the country, and that of Cochin or Malabar, which embraced Madurai of the hinterland. In 1626 the Goa Province numbered 320 men; the Malabar Province, 190.

Most of these men concentrated on the schools and catechetical stations already initiated. A handful in Mysore — there were never more than seven fathers at a time during the seventeenth century — adopted the approach of Roberto de Nobili in his unique effort to win the influential classes. But the early misgivings in some quarters about this Jesuit sannyasi because of his sympathy and respect for an Oriental culture blossomed into a storm of opposition rasied by men unable to conceive of the Church in anything but western cultural forms. This opposition culminated at a conference of theologians in Goa in 1618. There De Nobili heard the archbishop, Cristóvão de Sá cry out: "A Father of the Society of Jesus has gone over to paganism, and he asks me to connive in his apostasy." The majority of the theologians at the meeting voted against De Nobili. The case went to Rome, and with it a classic on the principle of adaptation, the harassed Jesuit's *Answer to the Objections Raised against the Method Employed in the New Madurai Mission.* Five years later Pope Gregory XV in the Apostolic Constitution *Romanae Sedis* of January 31, 1623, upheld De Nobili against the constricted position taken by his critics. Cautioning against all traces of superstition, he approved the use by the Brahmin

67 Rodrigues, *História,* III, ii, 133-135.

Christians of the cord, the sandal, and the ablutions. In 1654, nearly blind and a fragile man of sixty-eight, on his provincial's orders, De Nobili quit Madurai for Mylapore where others could care for him. He left his heart in the city where in 1605 he had found not a single Christian and where after thirty-nine years of extraordinary study and mortification he left 4,183 who professed Christ.

De Nobili realized that the form of his vocation demanded unique qualifications of intelligence and virtue which few men could meet. He understood the problems created by the severance of the sannyasi from the poorer classes in Indian society. He therefore developed a plan for a group of Jesuit missionaries who would as pandarams adopt the rule of Hindu ascetics of the Sudra class and who therefore could with certain precautions establish contact with the pariahs or so-called outcasts. They were known as pandaraswamis, a title which denoted religious teachers. The first Jesuit whom De Nobili chose for this intermediate role was Baltasar da Costa. Wearing golden earrings and a yellow tunic, Costa journeyed through the kingdoms of Madurai, Tanjore, and Sathiyamangalam, and baptized 2,500 adults. Most of the converts were of the tainted classes, although some few were Sudras. This success delighted De Nobili. The superior of the Malabar Province, Manuel de Sousa, outlined this plan in 1651 for the general, Francesco Piccolomini. Most Jesuits preferred this group. Some even expressed doubt about the profit gained from the exacting life of a sannyasi. Others twitted the Jesuit sannyasis as a species of canons living in an aura of glory. Actually only five Jesuits followed De Nobili in the fullness of his role, and after 1675 this vocation died out.[68] But De Nobili's life carried a forceful and even dramatic lesson, that of accomodation in the missionary venture. Jesuits who became pandarams kept this principle alive, and in such a way that the care of the pariahs was assured. But there remained a problem which in the next century would develop to the point of crisis: how build up Christian unity if Indians of the higher classes and lower classes could not be brought together for worship under one roof. The principle of universal Christian love faced the ancient Indian social structure of castes.

The Jesuits who followed De Nobili cultivated Mysore, Marava, and Tanjore as well as Madurai. The bright and enthusiastic Italian Leonardo Cinnami founded the mission in Mysore in 1648. As a pandaraswami, in the role envisaged by De Nobili,

68 Amann, *DTC,* IX, 2, 1717-1718.

a Portuguese of aristocratic origins, João de Brito, began in 1674 a distinguished missionary career in Madurai. After twelve years there, he moved into Marava where between May and July, 1686, he baptized 2,070 natives. Arrested and severely tortured by men who resented his impact on the people, he was expelled. Then, chosen to make a report on the mission, he sailed to Europe. Martyrdom awaited his return to India.

The letters from this select group in the De Nobili tradition revealed two things: first, the cold facts and figures of their official reports; and second, the great warmth of spirit which the Ignatian ideal generated in their hearts. Only with a minutely detailed atlas can one follow the steps of these men to Xirangapattanao where in 1674 there were three hundred and sixty Christians; to Bassuapura with its two hundred Christians; to Canacanali with its four hundred; and to Quelamangala with its four hundred and twenty. Men after the heart of Ignatius, they felt the way Cinnami did when he outlined for his brethren in Europe three reasons why a Jesuit should deeply desire to go to Mysore: the intense poverty and suffering entailed in the life of a sannyasi; the wide field for the conversion of souls; the well-grounded prospect of martyrdom. "The bravest and most generous among the soldiers of Christ will seek the place of greatest danger. . . . I value this life more than the empires of the entire world. . . . The model and captain of this mission is St. Francis Xavier. Now God showed him all the sufferings he had to endure. He was not frightened, but cried out, 'Even more, Lord, even more.' " [69]

These letters, written during the century when the enterprising Dutch were wresting from the Portuguese their vast oriental empire, went beyond a narrative of conversions, baptisms, catechetics, and also told the harsh story of naval battles, military sieges, bombardments, and the sacking of cities. In 1622 Manuel Roiz sent to Europe a most dispirited letter in which he diagnosed the rapid decline of Portuguese colonial power which nothing could halt. The missions soon felt the repercussions of this international conflict. Priests, no longer receiving the modest stipend of the Royal Patronage from viceroys absorbed in war, felt the pinch of destitution. The Dutch blockade turned once prosperous towns into depressed areas. In 1648 the six Jesuits at Mylapore barely subsisted in a city of distressing poverty as shipping moved to Pulicat. In 1658 the Fishery Coast fell to the Dutch; in 1662, Cranganore; in 1663, Cochin. From several of

69 D. Ferroli, S.J., *The Jesuits in Mysore* (Kozhikode, 1955), pp. 57-58.

these areas the Calvinist conqueror expelled the Jesuits. In others they made life miserable for them. The boom of the cannon of the men from Amsterdam, Groningen, and Haarlem sounded the requiem for much of the apostolate started by Xavier, Berze, and Valignano.

Meanwhile, among the Malabar Christians, a parallel history of setbacks and defeat developed. The archdeacon, Jorge, as has been seen, openly contested the rule of Archbishop Roz. This rebellion mushroomed, during this period, into schism. Besides this split on jurisdictional lines between Roz and Jorge, other potions went into the making of the heavy drink of revolt: tension between Propaganda and the Portuguese Padroado, resentment among the Syro-Malabar Christians at the intrusion of the Latins, strain between Jesuits, Dominicans, and Carmelites. Roz died in 1624, leaving memories of a noble, intelligent, broadminded man, one of the great figures in Jesuit mission history, whose views, if they had prevailed, might have saved the religious unity of these people.

His successor was the Portuguese Jesuit, Cristóvão de Brito. A poor choice because his ignorance of Syriac raised a wall between him and his people and offset his instinctively great charity and kindness, Brito was found wanting particularly in his failure to rule. Hoodwinked by the archdeacon, he virtually abdicated all his powers to him. The death of Jorge in 1637 presented Brito with another occasion to blunder terribly. To try to win the allegiance of Jorge's powerful family, the Campos, he appointed as the new archdeacon the immoral, ignorant Tomás de Campos, not yet thirty years of age. He died in 1641, leaving his office, in its power, practically insolvent.

Another Jesuit, Francisco Garzia, succeeded to the see. A scholar of Syriac, he stressed the study of this language among the seminarians at Vaipicotta. Despite his laudable attempts to take the reins of the archdiocese into his own hands, Tomás de Campos spirited a widespread secession in 1653. Rome sent Carmelites to try to heal the schism. They did not succeed. As Garzia lay dying he implored the archdeacon to return to the Church, and even suggested that he be carried to Tomás' house if there were any hope of making peace. The end came to the old bishop on September 3, 1659. Just sixty years had passed since the synod of Diamper. Chaos reigned where once there had been great promise of a Catholic bridgehead in India.[70]

70 Ferroli, *Jesuits in Malabar*, II, 45-49; Tisserant, *Eastern Christianity in India*, pp. 75-82.

Early in the seventeenth century Japan drastically reshaped her foreign policy, and this brought disaster to the Catholic Church. By 1638, in a gesture of contempt for Europe, after locking her gates to the powers of the West save for a small entrance for Dutch merchants, first at Hirado, then at Deshima, the Land of the Rising Sun had become a *Sakoku*, the Closed Country. To supplement this policy the emperors turned to the extermination of that vivid vestige of the West, the Church of Christ. Iron purpose stamped the anti-Catholic program of Tokugawa Hidetada, whose determination was surpassed only by the savagery of the intelligent but sadistic Tokugawa Iemitsu.

These men struck the stone of Japanese Catholicism and set a spark which turned into the beautiful white flame of fidelity to the faith even to death. Reliable documents record, up to midcentury, 4,045 martyrdoms. And these prescind from the famous Shimabara insurrection. At Shimabara, in 1637-1638 the poor peasants rose up in sheer exaspiration against pitiless exploitation. This social problem became a religious one when the Catholics were promised forgiveness if they would apostatize. From 35,000 to 37,000 went to their death by decapitation, leaving not a single Catholic in Arima, which had been up to 1612 an entirely Christian community. More than thirteen percent of the Catholic population of 300,000 gave their lives for the faith, a record probably without equal in the annals of the Church, and a beautiful tribute to the training given by the Jesuits, who had concentrated on the area of northwestern Kyushu where, in the Arima fief alone, they had in 1613 seventy churches. On the honor roll of martyrs the Society has eighty-seven names, of whom forty-four were Japanese.[71]

The ways in which the Jesuits met death were revolting in their cruelty. Some died, as did Carlo Spinola, Brother Leonardo Kimura, and seven scholastics, by being roasted at the stake; others, as did Manuel Borges, Brother Nicolau Fucanaga and two novices, by being hung head-down, the body tightly bound, in a stinking pit filled with excrement and other filth; others by being tied to a board and with head hanging back a bit having water continually poured over the face so that only by frantic efforts could they breathe. Marcello Mastrilli, by his two days of endurance, set the record for the length of this water torture.

Human nature shrinks before the fierceness of such barbarism,

---

71 Laures, *The Catholic Church*, pp. 177-179; Boxer, *The Christian Century*, pp. 334-335, 448.

and all the Catholics did not rise to the heights of heroism which it demanded. And as the years passed and priests became fewer — in 1623 there were only twenty-eight Jesuits, twelve friars, and one native secular priest — an increasing number of Catholics deserted the faith, especially those who received baptism simply to follow the example of the Christian daimyos. Here and there, however, groups of Catholics formed, amid the vast sea of pagan civilization, little islands where they preserved through the centuries some features of their religion and which put into the hands of missionaries of the nineteenth century, who returned with the abandonment of the closed-door policy, a thread of history which led back to Francis Xavier. Among those who failed the supreme test were a few Jesuits. In 1643, for example, five of them, four Europeans and a Japanese, accompanied by five Chinese and Japanese catechists, were captured off the coast of Chikuzen where they tried to penetrate the cordon erected against westerners. Subjected to merciless torture, all ten weakened and denied the faith. Some Dutchmen saw the four European Jesuits at Yeddo, "their eyes and cheeks strangely fallen in; their hands black and blue, and their whole bodies sadly misused and macerated by torture," and heard them boldly say to the interpreters that they did not freely apostatize but only because of the intolerable pain. One promptly retracted and soon died in prison. The failure which created wide dismay was that of the aged and ailing vice-provincial, Cristóvão Ferreira, a veteran of twenty-three years on the missions, who in 1633 surrendered after hanging six hours in the pit. Two other provincial superiors, after Ferreira, also apostatized.[72]

In the correspondence of the Jesuits and Franciscans of this period the heated criticism of one another continued. Each side charged the other with lack of cooperation. Feelings of resentment spilled over among the laity, invited rivalry among the confraternities conducted by the two orders, and crippled Catholic unity when it was most needed. In the shadows of twilight over the underground Church both heroic charity and human frailty met and played their parts.

In China developments were more promising. When Ricci lay dying at Peking in 1610, he remarked to Sabatino de Ursis: The door was opened to great opportunities but also to great danger and labor. How the opportunities unfolded, the statistics on converts and missionaries tell. By 1627, 13,000 Chinese had been received into the Church; by 1636, 40,000; by 1640, 65,000; by

72 Boxer, ibid., pp. 391-393, 445-446.

1651, 150,000. In 1617 eight priests and six Chinese brothers manned the mission stations; in 1623, eighteen priests and six brothers; by 1627, the priests had increased to twenty-six; by 1664, to about thirty in forty-two stations.

Dangers, as Ricci predicted, did arise. But they came from two sources he could not have foreseen: first, internal political convulsions, the Manchu invasion, and the change of the imperial dynasty; and second, the arrival of the Dominican and Franciscan friars and their adverse critique of his missionary methods. The impact of change at the court of the emperor a group of foreigners could not escape. Between 1617 and 1622, under the inspiration of the mandarin Shen Ch'ueh, in a drive to prevent the infiltration of a foreign cult, a persecution descended on the Catholics, and the missionaries went into hiding. In 1644 the ageless Chinese witnessed another changing of the guard as one dynasty took over from another. The Ming line, which had ruled since 1363, fell as the troops of the Manchus poured through "The Pass between the Mountains and the Sea" at the eastern end of the Great Wall. The Ch'ing emperors were to hold sway until 1912. One of the first of the new dynasty, K'ang-hsi, was in his early teens when between 1664 and 1669, during the period of his minority, the regents attacked the Church and placed the missionaries under house arrest at Canton.

In each instance of persecution a learned Jesuit did much to turn the tide and restore to Catholics a position of relative security, Johann Adam Schall von Bell in 1622 and Ferdinand Verbiest in 1669. Both men strengthened the tradition of the Jesuit missionary-scientist which Ricci had started in China. Longobardi, disagree as he did with Ricci on the issue of the rites, nevertheless heartily endorsed his reliance on the scientist for the Christian cause. In November, 1610, he wrote to Father General Aquaviva that the most effective way to help the Chinese mission would be to send capable men, especially mathematicians. Two years later he repeated his request. "To us," he wrote, "it is certain that mathematics will open up our objective." The same year he sent Nicolas Trigault to Europe to collect a science library and obtain two astronomers.[73]

The response of the European Jesuits was generous. With Trigault twenty-two missionaries sailed on April 16, 1618, from Lisbon. Schall was one. Other scientists were the Italian Giacomo Rho, the Bohemian Wenceslaus Kirwitzer, the Austrian Johann

---

73 P. D'Elia, S.J., *Galileo in China* (Cambridge, Mass., 1960), pp. 22-23.

Alberich, and the Swiss Johann Terrenz Schreck, who brought with him a science library of about 7,000 volumes and very probably the first telescope to arrive in China. Alberich and four other Jesuits died during the journey.

Schreck (frequently referred to by the Latinized form of his middle name as Terrentius) was the link between Galileo and China. An enthusiastic friend and admirer of Galileo, he shared with the great astronomer the honor of being a member of the distinguished Accademia dei Lincei. He composed the first treatise in Chinese on the telescope, and with Longobardi worked on the correcting of the Chinese calendar. Probably his deepest disappointment arose from his failure to enlist Galileo's help. During eight years he mailed requests to his old friend for assistance on certain problems, but the great Pisan, possibly piqued by his disagreements with two Jesuits in Europe, Horazio Grassi and Christoph Scheiner, declined to answer, and at the end of eight years curtly remarked that he had nothing to offer.

In mathematics and astronomy therefore there was "an encounter of cultures." On the Jesuit side, the missionaries brought to China a superior mathematics in geometry and the new algebra as well as advanced European techniques in the manufacture of astronomical instruments. They did not however present a united front on the question of a geocentric or heliocentric universe. While a number of the second generation of the missionaries, men like Schreck and Kirwitzer, were ardent Copernicans, the news of the Roman condemnation of Galileo in 1632 reversed this trend and restored the Ptolemaic view which Sabatino de Ursis had clearly expounded in Chinese as early as 1611. On the Chinese side, the scientists of the ancient empire had developed through the centuries a cosmology and an astronomy which was not so backward as some Jesuits believed. Even Ricci did not realize the fundamentally correct thrust, in contrast to the Aristotelian doctrine, of the Hsüan Yeh teaching about the floating heavenly bodies in infinite space. And Schreck in his *Brief Description of the Measurement of the Heavens,* which he published in Chinese in 1628, while explicating the telescopic discovery of sunspots, failed to indicate that the Chinese knew of the blue-black umbrae on the sun a dozen centuries before Europeans ascertained them. Almost a century passed before the Jesuits found to their own profit the vast store of celestial data recorded by the Chinese. Very likely they failed in this strange way because their arrival in China coincided with the cultural decadence of the dying Ming dynasty when earlier scientific achievements were not so evident. Despite these deficiencies on both sides, the encounter of the Chinese savant and the Jesuit scientist reached conspicuous accord in 1635 in a monumental compendium of scientific learning, the joint project of Hsü Kuang-Chhi, Li Chih-Tsao, Li Thien-Ching, and the Jesuits Schreck, Schall von Bell, Rho, and Longobardi.[74]

In this specialized approach to the apostolate of the missions Schall von Bell and Verbiest were vital additions. Schall, a democratic German, easygoing but intolerant of humbug, arrived in China in 1622 and went to Peking to assist Longobardi and Schreck in their work on the Chinese calendar. This master of flawless Chinese, constructor of cannons and derricks, builder of astronomical instruments, author of 137 treatises in Chinese, predictor of solar and lunar eclipses, rose to the dignity of president of the Mathematical Tribunal and Mandarin of the First Class. Verbiest arrived in China in 1659. This resourceful Belgian deeply impressed the intelligent K'ang-hsi. For five months he daily taught the emperor the latest developments in mathematics and astronomy. In 1669 he undertook the refitting of the famous Peking observatory. Scientific competence in the persons of these missionaries evoked in imperial circles an evolving attitude of respect, then esteem, and then kindness toward the Church.

The Society sent many other men of unusual gifts into China. Cartographers like Giulio Aleni and Michal Boym created professional maps of the empire. Craftsmanship of this kind reached a high point in the handsome volumes of the great sinologue, Martino Martini, who published in 1665 his *New Atlas of China,* containing seventeen large maps and a full commentary. Besides Martini, Michel Trigault and Prospero Intorcetta excelled in the understanding of Chinese culture, customs, and history. Ricci had called his own work, "clearing the brush." These followers widened the clearing immensely.

They gave a striking demonstration of their appreciation of non-Western culture when they requested the Holy See that the Chinese be allowed a liturgy in their own tongue. In 1615

---

74 Ibid., pp. 28-32. J. Needham, *Chinese Astronomy and the Jesuit Mission: An Encounter of Cultures* (London, 1958), pp. 2-3, 8-11. See F. A. Rouleau, S.J., in a review of *Science and Civilization in China.* Vol. III. *Mathematics and the Sciences of the Heavens and the Earth.* by J. Needham (Cambridge, 1959) in *AHSJ,* XXX (1961), 299-303, for a carefully nuanced judgment of Needham's conclusions about the Jesuits' failure to appreciate ancient Chinese scientific data.

and 1616 Pope Paul V granted permission for the translation of the Bible and for the native priests to offer Mass and recite the breviary in literary Chinese. For some uncertain reason, very probably because the Jesuits did not have the translations prepared, the matter hung in abeyance. Luigi Buglio, one of the most accomplished sinologists of the century, took twenty-four years to complete his translation of the missal, breviary, and ritual into elegant Chinese. Around 1665 the missionaries again raised the question of the use of the vernacular. Technically, since the decree of Paul V had never been revoked, they did not have to approach the Holy See again, but, probably because of the long lapse of time, they judged it prudent to do so. But never were they able to obtain a reiteration of the earlier decree. Several times the newly established Propaganda, to which the popes referred the request, gave a negative answer. Pope Alexander VII and Pope Innocent XI favored a Chinese liturgy and recommended approval to Propaganda, but the Congregation in each instance decided negatively, and the popes did not choose to reverse the ruling.[75]

A problem, closely related to that of a Chinese liturgy, was that of admitting into the Society Chinese as candidates for the priesthood. The many memoranda sent to Rome by individual Jesuits indicated a general consensus that a radical program for the creation of a native clergy was imperative. Realization however lagged far behind the ideal. One major obstacle was the practical impossibility to find in a small Christian community, enveloped by a massive pagan society, candidates who gave solid assurance of moral integrity and stability in an exacting vocation. In Coimbra, in 1665, Cheng Ma-No Wei-Hsin (Emmanuel de Siqueira) was ordained a priest in the Society, the only one through the entire century since the Jesuits first penetrated the Middle Kingdom. Twenty-four years later, August 1, 1688, three Chinese Jesuits, the first to be ordained in China itself, received Orders at Nanking. These three were all over fifty years of age and managed to memorize enough Latin phonetically to get through the Mass in a tortuous manner.

Serious detriment to the growth of the Church as was the insistence on Latin, it did not contain the explosive power inherent in the problem of the ceremonies practiced by the Chinese in honor of Confucius and their ancestors. On this perplexing question disunity prevailed among the Jesuits, some fol-

---

75 G. H. Dunne, S.J., "What Happened to the Chinese Liturgy?" *Catholic Historical Review*, XLVII (1961), 1-14.

lowing the insights of Ricci, others opposing all accommodation, and still others steering a middle course. Niccolò Longobardi, the most important Jesuit spokesman for the rejection of the Ricci approach, wrote a treatise which Francisco Furtado, the vice-provincial between 1641 and 1650, ordered to be burned. The arrival of the friars, two Spanish Dominicans in 1631, and two Spanish Franciscans in 1633, complicated an already sensitive situation. Some of what they saw, such as Jesuits wearing silk garments, they did not like. In general, unenthusiastic about the introducing of Christianity through the media of clocks and prisms, they chose to work first with the poorer classes and then upward into the higher social echelons. Yet some of the friars conceived a positive respect for the ancient civilization they encountered. Among these latter was the intelligent and dedicated Dominican, Fray Domingo Navarrete.

Navarrete was a major exponent of the essential arguments against the school of Ricci. Alert to the contemporary scene, aware of the atheistic or idolatrous influence of neo-Confucian commentators, fearful of the strong pull toward syncretism, he judged that the current nature of the rites — not what they were in their origins centuries before — demanded that Catholics discontinue their practice.[76] His preoccupation was the present, not the past. Those Jesuits who championed a policy of accommodation did not deny that among some people, not all, superstition had infiltrated the ceremonies, but they contended that with time and education they could remove the idolatrous overtones. They explicitly said that they counted on time. Jacques Le Favre, whose cause for beatification was introduced in 1903-1905, appealed to the example of St. Augustine who, amid another pagan civilization, moved gradually in the eradication of superstition from the practices of his flock.

Although some Jesuits and some Dominicans found themselves in complete agreement, the failure to achieve universal unity of thought snowballed into a major dispute of intense bitterness which opened a nasty split between the two orders. Basically the popular preacher and the scholarly sinologist could not agree. Snide remarks did nothing to cushion the collision between the two groups. Domingo Navarrete, who could coin a phrase, drew a similarity between Xavier's failure to enter China and the difficulties which the Friars were experiencing in entering the Empire. In Xavier's case the devil himself kept him out;

76 D. Navarrete, O.P., *The Travels and Controversies of Friar Domingo Navarrete*, ed. J. B. Cummins (Cambridge, 1962), I, lxiv-lxxi.

in the present situation the devil was using the Jesuits as his instruments. For him China was not a nest that had room for both white birds and black birds.[77]

To halt the participation of Catholics in the rites the Friars appealed to Rome. In 1643 the Dominican, Fray Juan Morales, who acted as their agent, described the rites in a way that could only evoke condemnation. This censure Rome issued in 1645. The Jesuits sent their own representative to Rome. Martino Martini, thorough and profound sinologist, presented the problem in the light of Jesuit studies of Chinese civilization. In 1656 Pope Alexander VII through the Holy Office decided that the ceremonies as described by Martini were "a purely civil and political cult," and therefore undeserving of blame. Both sides now had a papal document of approbation.

In 1664 began the five-year period of persecution of the Catholics during the revolt against young K'ang-hsi. For a while it seemed that this tribulation would hammer the missionaries into a unity. Placed under house arrest, fourteen Jesuits, three Dominicans, and the only Franciscan in China at the time lived under the same roof. Making good use of this enforced leisure, in a series of forty meetings which ended in January, 1668, they endeavored to formulate a uniform method for their apostolate. They drafted a document of forty-two articles which included, in the light of the decree of Alexander VII of 1656, recognition of the Ricci approach to the problem of the Chinese rites. All signed it with the possible exception of the Franciscan.

Shortly after, Fray Navarrete expressed his misgivings. He discussed his perplexities with several Jesuits, including the competent Prospero Intorcetta and Jacques Le Favre. Satisfied, he wrote out a statement of his concurrence. The same year he quietly left Canton and made his way to Europe. Back in the West, in a wide range of accusations from double-dealing to suppression of Catholic doctrine, he attacked the Jesuits in China and condemned the Ricci approach to the question of the rites. Even though he believed that some accommodation was possible, he was not prepared to move as far forward as certain Jesuits. In June, 1676, he published a volume of 518 pages, divided into seven units and entitled *Treatises on the History, Politics, Ethics, and Religion of the Chinese Monarchy.* In this he frequently indicted the Jesuits in China. Within a year, by March, 1677, he completed another work of wider influence among the Society's enemies, *Old and New Contro-*

77 Ibid., lv, lviii.

versies about the Mission of Great China. In 1679 Jesuits in Spain heard that this work was going through the press. They obtained some sheets from the printer. What they read prompted them to complain to the Inquisition about the author's bias against the Society. A complex internal struggle brought the printing to a halt at page 668. The manuscript of the unprinted pages is in the Biblioteca Nacional, Madrid. Copies of the incomplete book reached the Jansenists and members of the Paris Foreign Mission Society, for whom it became a kind of Fifth Gospel. In June, 1689, Antoine Arnauld, at the age of seventy-seven, began to learn Spanish so that he could read Navarrete in the original. He based the sixth volume of his *Moral Practice of the Jesuits* on the Dominican.[78]

The works of Navarrete made it difficult for the Jesuits to see behind the pen an author who could appreciate any positive contribution to the Church by the Society. Yet Navarrete praised the apostolate of the Jesuits in other areas of the world. "They will," he said, "go to death for the faith." The story of the tension between this doughty Dominican and the Society had an improbable détente. In 1677 Navarrete, recently designated archbishop of Santo Domingo, reached his see. A survey of the situation there revealed that the only reliable and capable priests he had were the Jesuits. In letters to King Charles II of Spain he lavished praise on them and their apostolate. Twice he wrote to the monarch criticizing the men of his own order, whom he found poorly educated and conducting a university which was an educational absurdity.[79] But his cordiality in Santo Domingo did not alleviate in Europe the hostility to the Society which his writings aroused.

The area of Asia second only to the Philippines in its widespread acceptance of the faith was Indochina, especially in Cochin China, Annam, and Tonkin. Following the Dominicans and Franciscans, the Society's pioneers, Francesco Buzoni and Didacus Carvalho, arrived in Cochin China in 1615. Once Japan had been closed to Westerners, the Japanese Province with headquarters at Macao, in a broad shift of frontier from the northeast to the southwest, shunted many missionaries to this area so responsive to the faith. Within twenty years the Jesuits baptized 12,000 natives. To the molding of this Catholic appendage of pagan China France contributed one of the most effective Jesuit missionaries of all time. Alexandre de Rhodes,

78 Ibid., cvi-cx.
79 Ibid., lxxviii-lxxxiii.

native of Avignon and of Jewish Spanish descent, genial, affectionate, superb linguist, most adroit amid shifting exigencies, did gigantic work in building a Church which through three and a half centuries of turbulent history, including internecine strife, French domination, and Japanese occupation, numbers those who have died for the faith in the hundreds of thousands, a record for protracted martyrdom with few, if any, parallels in the annals of Christianity. De Rhodes arrived in Cochin China in 1625, and two years later went to Tonkin. There he remained until his banishment in 1630. He gave tremendous impetus to the onward sweep of the Church, and by 1658 the converts in Tonkin numbered 100,000. To the Holy See he made strong appeals for a hierarchy and the development of a native clergy. Back in the area of Hue and Danang in 1640, he labored there until 1645. In 1660 he found his final resting place in Ispahan, the capital of Persia, deeply respected and mourned by the shah. That his noble heart belonged to Indochina breaks through the simple, moving narrative of his mission reports. Today, as the shadow of the North Vietnamese falls across that sorrowing country, one of the significant questions is whether the work of De Rhodes and his heroic followers, such as the nineteenth century bishop of the Paris Mission Society, Jean-Théophane Venard, will survive.

While De Rhodes labored in Indochina, some 1,800 miles to the northwest another Jesuit was making missionary history of another kind. Antonio de Andrade, prompted by rumors of Christians living beyond the mighty Himalayas, made a momentous journey into the land of the Lama monasteries. He plunged through deep gorges, plowed through chest-high snow drifts, crossed the dizzy heights in their blinding white cover, scaled to the top of Mana Pass, eight hundred meters higher than Mt. Blanc, the first European to gaze toward the mountain world of Tibet from the pinnacle of the Himalayas. In a book published in Lisbon, Andrade opened the eyes of Europeans to the peculiar religious community he had found in Tibet. Other Jesuits followed, but due to shifting and unstable circumstances had to abandon their plans to make a permanent settlement among the Lamas.

A serious problem which set off another series of journeys by Jesuits was the distance between Rome and Peking. Business transactions dragged on for years. At Macao on October 10, 1589, Alessandro Valignano wrote a letter which reached Rome in 1606, seventeen years later. In 1660 Schall reported to the general that one of his letters took five years to be delivered.

Giovanni Francesco de Ferrari wrote to the general in June, 1661; the general replied in April, 1664; Ferrari received this answer in October, 1668. Seven years had elapsed. Piccolomini and Nickel were especially anxious to discover whether a land route would be more practicable than the usual course by sea. To make a systematic reconnaissance of the Persian caravan route and the possibilities of entering India through Persia, Heinrich Roth and Franz Storer, disguised as Armenian merchants, left Smyrna early in 1651, traveled with a caravan to Ispahan, then through parched, lonely country to Binder-Abbas on the Persian Gulf, whence they took ship to Goa. Starting from the other direction, Johann Grueber, after a failure in a west to east attempt, left Peking in April, 1661, and by way of Su-Chou, Lhasa, Agra, and Smyrna, arrived at Rome in February, 1664, almost three years after he had started out. Weighing all the practical elements involved, the Jesuit superiors decided to continue to use the sea lanes between Europe and Asia. Besides, the Portuguese government, sensitive on the question of the Royal Patronage and the status of Lisbon as the point of departure for Asia, made protest against any deviation from this traditional honor.

In sub-Saharan Africa, of the three Jesuit missions, Cape Verde, *Africa* the Congo, and Angola, only the last survived through the century. At Cape Verde a duel went on between the debilitating climate and the Jesuits. And the climate won. The Portuguese Jesuits, among whom the missionary spirit was high, felt little enthusiasm for Cape Verde, and replacements therefore were few. Sebastião Gomes, a veteran of twenty-two years in Africa, diagnosed the sentiments of his fellow Jesuits: they detested Cape Verde where deadly diseases had carried off so many. Finally, in 1653, after forty-nine years of effort, the Jesuits withdrew, to be replaced by Capuchins.

The second Jesuit venture into the Congo — the first was between 1548-1555 — lasted for almost a century, from 1581 to 1674. The initial labors gave great promise. The enterprising Baltasar Barreira, from his base in Angola, made an exploratory trip through the Congo in 1581. He baptized 1,500. Four years later, Baltasar Afonso, also from Angola, entered the Congo to fortify the faith of the Christians there. In 1619 two unusually fine missionaries, Duarte Vaz and Mateus Cardoso, arrived. Cardoso did especially effective work in translating prayers into Congolese. He wrote in 1625: "In the hundred and fifty years since the faith entered the Congo nothing has been comparable to what the Society has achieved in one year." An important part of that achievement was the erection of a college in São Salvador.

Within fifty years, however, the attrition of nationalism, rebellion, and the shortage of Jesuits wore down this great promise. In 1645 Spanish Capuchins arrived at São Salvador. They received a warm welcome. But in 1651 the cathedral chapter in São Salvador wrote to Pope Innocent X that the Capuchins were trying to woo the Congolese from their alliance with Portugal to an alignment with Spain. The Portuguese Jesuits concurred in the accusation and denounced the friars as partisans of Spain. Soon after this serious break in Catholic harmony came the disintegration of civil order as the Congolese broke out in rebellion. To this unhappy scene increasingly fewer Jesuits came. The last lingering hope that replacements would arrive died by 1675. The structure raised on Barreira's foundations ninety-four years earlier collapsed.

The mission in Angola was more durable. The Jesuits divided their forces between teaching grammar and literature at their college in Luanda and the more elementary catechizing among the native tribes. Men from other nations began to join the Portuguese. In 1623 four Italians arrived, and in 1629 another Italian and a Fleming. But in general the numbers never were great. Over the years, probably the greatest continuing frustration which the Jesuits experienced was their inability to open a seminary for the training of Angolese priests. Frequently the project came to the fore, but in 1623, in 1627, in 1679, and again in 1684, for one reason or another, the project was aborted.

Between 1641 and 1648 the mission suffered a serious setback. On August 24, 1641, twenty ships, the strong arm of the expanding Dutch seaborne empire, entered the harbor of Luanda and captured the city. The Portuguese retreated and settled in the hinterland. On August 15, 1648, the Portuguese navy returned and retook Luanda. The governor, his officials, and three Jesuits marched through the streets to the Society's church and there made a public act of thanksgiving to God. Again the Jesuits took up the work of the mission which was to last until the Society's suppression in Portugal in 1759.[80]

In Ethiopia the period of this chapter (1615-1687) opens with the widespread rebellion against the Negus Socinios, who, profoundly influenced by the personable Pedro Paez, had an-

---

80 Rodrigues, *História*, III, i, 374-381; III, ii, 193-235, 237-244, 280-284, 323-334, 348-360.

nounced his intention of uniting the Abyssinian church to Rome. Socinios put down the uprising, requested Rome for a patriarch, received the sacraments of penance and Holy Eucharist from Paez. Having seen the fruit of almost twenty years of toil in the remarkable conversion of the Negus, Paez died in May, 1622.[81] Disaster followed his passing. While in broad outline the Ethiopian Church seemed one with the Catholic Church, many knotty problems about liturgy, the validity of holy orders of the Ethiopian priests, and the calendar of feasts remained. The man whom Pope Urban VIII sent as patriarch and on whom devolved the responsibility of solving these problems, the Portuguese Jesuit, Afonso Mendes, lacked the flexibility, historical perspective, and cultural breadth to appreciate the liturgical traditions of the Ethiopian Church and to distinguish between essentials and non-essentials. Compounding the difficulty, the government imposed the edict of union with violence and cruelty. Each priest had to swear, under pain of death, adherence to the Catholic faith; the Roman liturgy, Lenten fast, and date of Easter had to be observed. From hamlet to hamlet emotions ran high. Intrigues multiplied; Socinios grew weary of putting down rebellion. Five years after his arrival, in 1629, Mendes made three concessions: return to the ancient liturgy; the weekly fast on Wednesday instead of Saturday; recognition of the Ethiopian calendar. These only stimulated rebellion. In 1632 the Negus, now a tired old man, gave his restive people a choice between the two churches. On September 16 he died, professing himself a Roman Catholic. And with him passed the hopes of the Catholic Church in Ethiopia, for the new Negus, Basilides, forbade contact with the priests of Rome. Two Jesuits were stabbed to death, five others hanged. Mendes quit the country for Goa in 1636.[82]

For much of the tragic outcome the government's cruelty was certainly responsible; so was Mendes' rigidity. But far deeper than the level of either governmental or ecclesiastical policy lay an even more powerful irritant: the intransigence of Catholic moral teaching in the face of legal concubinage. Pretended descendant of Solomon, Socinios, despite the great hopes which he had given, claimed that he was free to imitate his illustrious ancestor and keep his harem. Polygamy, aggravated by adultery, ran unchecked among the country's leading men, in

81 J. B. Coulbeaux, *DTC*, V, i, 953-956, s.v. "Éthiope (Église d')."
82 Ibid., 958-960; C. Beccari, S.J., ed., *Rerum Aethiopicarum Scriptores Occidentales Inediti* (Rome, 1907-1917), VIII, xiii-xvi.

253

whom the prospect of Ethiopia's adherence to an exacting code of morality aroused the fiercest opposition.[83]

This mission took through the years a heavy toll of Jesuit lives. Just in travel to Ethiopia, between 1554 and 1639, of the fifty-six who tried to enter the country twenty were either captured by Mohammedans or perished in one way or another. In 1650 Franz Storer received orders to reconstruct the mission. Disguised as an Armenian surgeon, he made his way to the capital. Only three letters were received from him. In 1662 he died, how and where unknown. Silence fell over the Jesuit venture in Ethiopia, one of St. Ignatius' fondest concerns.[84] And today, three centuries later, near Lake Tsana, in mute testimony to the patient labors of Paez, remain the ruins of a once beautiful and superb mission station.

Brazil,
Spanish America,
and the
Philippines

In Brazil five new colleges gave tangible evidence of the growing stability of the Jesuit enterprise to which, through the seventeenth century, 258 Jesuits journeyed from Europe. In 1615 superiors created the area of Maranhão a vice-province which, born in the blood of martyrs, was always to exact the greatest kind of ruggedness of the missionaries. In 1607 Luís Figueira, who rose magnificently to the awesome challenge, moved into Maranhão. Natives slaughtered his companion, Francisco Pinto. For thirty years he doggedly held on against all the revulsions he found among a barbarous people. Then in 1637 he returned to Portugal to recruit helpers. In April, 1643, he sailed with fifteen fellow Jesuits. His high hopes foundered with the ship when it grounded on the Brazilian coast. Only three of the missionaries were saved. Two were drowned; the ten others, including Figueira, made Marajo Island on a raft where the natives seized and devoured them.[85] Then into this harsh mission stepped a giant, not only of Jesuit history but also of that of Brazil.

Born in Lisbon in 1608 and moved to Brazil as an infant, António Vieira gave his unique talents of eloquence, linguistic comprehension, human sympathy, and organizing power to the peoples of Maranhão and along the Amazon. On the two continents which made his stage he played his part with superb skill. In Europe, as has been seen, the classroom, the pulpit, governmental business, diplomacy occupied him. But the work

83 J. B. Coulbeaux, *Histoire Politique et Religieuse d'Abyssinie* (Paris, 1929), II, 220-224; see also A. Brou's review in *AHSJ*, I (1932), 376.
84 Plattner, *Jesuits Go East*, 85, 169-172.
85 Rodrigues, *História*, III, ii, 178-179.

of his predilection was among the Amerindians. With them he spent three different periods of his priestly life, at the beginning but a year, 1640-1641; then nine years, 1652 to 1661; and finally sixteen years, 1681 to 1697. He founded more than fifty villages, translated the catechism into native languages, taught the skills of peace and civilization. But he served them best by his greatest gift, his eloquence. With burning words he exposed and denounced the terrible injustice of the European slave traders. He proclaimed that in a period of forty years, in the region of the Amazon alone, Portuguese mistreatment of the Amerindians caused the death of two millions. Like the great Dominican, Bartolomé de Las Casas, he exaggerated, but as the forceful spokesman of the only religious order in Brazil which had a consistent tradition of upholding the natives' freedom, he did induce a hesitant government to protect the Amerindians from at least the worst abuses.[86] Usually vacillating Lisbon ended on the side of Vieira and his fellow Jesuits, but the animosity of the profiteers matched his eloquence and twice they drove him and the other Jesuits from the area. With characteristic vividness Vieira called Maranhão-Pará Portugal's La Rochelle. In 1661 his enemies forced his exile to Portugal. But in 1681 he returned. On July 18, 1697, at Bahía, the voice of Portugal's noblest orator was stilled forever. This giant of the seventeenth century, worthy successor of the two pioneers of the previous century, Nóbrega and Anchieta, died in his ninety-first year and, almost to the day, on the first centenary of the death of Anchieta.

In the vast Spanish lands which stretched from Sonora to Chiloé Island the Jesuits made a twofold division of their apostolate: the work, largely educational, in the cities, and the continuing penetration into the unknown interior. In the towns like Quito, Lima, and Mexico City they transplanted from the old world the civility and urbanity of Spanish culture. Along the great rivers, the Amazon, the Marañón, the Orinoco, and in the depths of the dark jungles between these waterways, they sought out the primitive peoples.

The sheer vastness of this staggering enterprise, magnified by responsibility to the Philippines and the Marianas, accentuated a crisis in manpower which fell upon these missions in the seventeenth century. In 1626 there were about 1,300 Jesuits in colonial Spain. But they were not enough. As poverty gripped the home

---

86 Boxer, *António Vieira*, p. 21; C. R. Boxer, *The Golden Age of Brazil 1695-1750* (Berkeley and Los Angeles, 1962), p. 277.

provinces, necessitating a curtailment of the number of novices received into the Society, it became extremely difficult to meet the quota of missionaries allowed by the Council of the Indies. Aggravating this unhappy situation was the official ban on all non-Spanish missionaries. In moving language the Jesuits in Mexico asked their general in 1653 to try to persuade the Council of the Indies to allow Jesuits of other nationalities to join them. The next year Spain reaffirmed her ban. But ten years later Oliva managed to obtain a concession as Spain agreed to endorse Jesuit missionaries from lands ruled by the Austrian Hapsburgs.[87]

All the while a mighty reservoir of missionary aspiration was building up in Germany. In just the two years 1615-1616, and from Ingolstadt alone, the general received forty letters from young Jesuits seeking assignment abroad. But Germans, the "heresy-infested northerners," were those most suspected by the Spaniards. Between 1600 and 1670 only thirty-three "northerners" managed to get to the Indies, Spanish and Portuguese. They would have to wait for the eighteenth century when they could move in a mighty column to the ports of embarkation in one of the supreme mission endeavors in the Society's history.[88]

Of all the cities where the Jesuits settled, one was unique by reason of the vast scale of its violation of justice and Christian charity. Cartagena, with the dubious distinction of being the chief slave market of South America, had not heeded the protestations of the great spokesman for the dignity of the enslaved Negro, Alfonso de Sandoval. Then came, in 1610, a scholastic, the Catalan, Pedro Claver, to be trained by Sandoval and, in a striking example of the pupil overshadowing the master, to win a privileged niche in the history of man's compassion for his fellowman. After ordination Claver, binding himself by vow to be the slave of the slaves forever, during almost forty years met the slave ships, descended into the stinking holds filled with poor, frenzied, distressed Negroes, brought physical relief by his practical nursing in a spirit of tenderness, and with a sweet patience opened their minds to the truth of Christ. Some 300,000 wretches received baptism from this compassionate man, canonized by Pope Leo XIII in 1888.

While St. Peter labored at the dock side, other Jesuits worked in the jungle. Two characteristics marked the Society's aposto-

87 De la Costa, *Jesuits in the Philippines,* p. 437; Astráin, *Historia,* V 47-49, 263-264, 278.
88 A. von Huonder, S.J., "German Jesuit Missionaries in the Seventeenth and Eighteenth Centuries," *WL,* XXIX (1900), 473-474.

late in the interior of the southern continent: movement and
stability. Priests and brothers never ceased to be in perpetual
motion in their penetration into the mysterious recesses of the
unknown land; others halted to form stable, permanent communities of Indians. Of all these communities those in Paraguay,
usually called Reductions, became the most widely known.

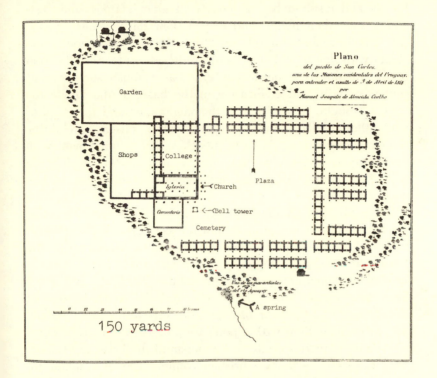

Map 6. Plan of a Typical Paraguay Reduction

Reproduced, by permission, from Pablo Hernández, S.J., *Misiones del
Paraguay. Orgánización social de las doctrinas guaraníes de la Compañía de
Jesús* (Barcelona: G. Gili, 1913), Vol. I. page 104.

From the time of their earliest contacts with primitive peoples,
the Jesuits recognized the need of a settled and ordered way of
life in order to raise up in their midst a mature and enduring
native church. Anchieta created communities in Brazil; Tapia
in Mexico; and in 1610 Jesuits in Paraguay did the same. In
the latter place these units attained an unusual degree of
spiritual and cultural perfection. From a central plaza, pointing
north, south, east, and west and built of the material of the area,
even stone and adobe, spread the homes of the people, who

sometimes numbered up to 10,000. Close by stood the assembly of workshops with tools for carpentry, masonry, metal work. Behind the homes stretched the fruit orchards, the pasture land for cattle, the farms which provided wheat, rice, sugar cane, and cotton. In the church, the noblest edifice of all and center of the community's life, the Indians, instructed in the dignity of the liturgy and inspired by the beauty of altar, statues, and vestments, sang their hymns and played their musical instruments. On feastdays they turned out for religious processions, gala affairs with flower and song, and produced, under the direction of the missionaries, mystery plays. To establish such vibrant centers of faith and civilization in the heart of the jungle the Jesuits brought, in addition to the sacraments and the word of God, their skills as metallurgists, cattle raisers, architects, farmers, and masons. These talents they had to implement with an enormous measure of patience because of the hard battle with the natural indolence and nomadic tendencies of the natives.

The expression Paraguay Reductions has its ambiguities. The Spanish civil unit of Paraguay did not correspond to the boundaries of the present republic of Paraguay. Neither did the Jesuit Province of Paraguay. The latter, from 1625, comprehended the present states of Argentina, Uruguay, and Paraguay, the frontier zones of Bolivia, and the southern area of Brazil. By 1767, the year of expulsion, this Jesuit province had fifty-seven reductions with a population of 113,716 natives. Some historians are more specific and understand the Paraguay Reductions to mean the thirty Christian communities of Guaraní Indians settled in the central and upper regions of the Paraguay and Uruguay rivers, stretching westward to Corrientes at the confluence of the Paraná and Paraguay rivers and eastward toward the city of Porto Alegre. Only eight of these thirty communities were in the territory of present-day Paraguay. Fifteen were in Argentina, and seven in the region of Río Grande do Sul of Brazil.[89]

The creation of these reductions was a major religious and social achievement in the history of the Society. Great as was this feat in itself, it attained even finer distinction in the obstacles overcome, obstacles from the natives themselves and

89 G. Kratz, *El tratado Hispano-Portugués de límites de 1750 y sus consecuencias* (Rome, 1954), pp. 6-7.

from European fortune seekers. The natives, not always docile, at times rose against their friends. In 1628 they killed Roque González de Santa Cruz, Alonso Rodríguez, and Juan del Castillo. Pope Pius XI beatified these three priests in 1933. In 1635 the natives slew Cristóbal Mendoza, and in 1645 Pedro Romero.

The worst kind of discouragement, however, originated in the highland of São Paulo de Piratininga. Adventurers in quest of wealth through trade in slaves started from that high plateau — therefore they were known as *paulistas* — paddled up the great waterways, descended on the reductions, ravaged them for booty, and bound the natives in couples for the long trek to the slave market. The aged and infirm they tied together and threw into a huge fire. They began their incursions on a small scale in 1611. With the years the attacks grew in intensity. One of the most fierce was in 1628 when the raiders devastated the area of Guayrá and left intact but two of the eleven reductions and 12,000 of the original population of 100,000. The Jesuits led their people deeper into the forests. The *paulistas* followed. In 1652 one of the missionaries, Francisco Díaz Taño, estimated that over 300,000 natives had been lost in the raids.

To halt these onslaughts, one of the finest men on the Jesuit staff, Antonio Ruiz de Montoya, went to Madrid in 1637 and obtained permission to arm the Indians. He returned to Paraguay in 1640. Trained by a brother, who had been a soldier, the natives met the enemy in 1641 and performed gallantly. Their action brought respite to the reductions. But it also evoked an image of a potentially rebellious army and sent a tremor of fear through the royal government in Spain. In 1661 Philip V ordered the withdrawal of firearms from the reductions. Once more the villages were reduced to helplessness. But once more, eighteen years later, necessity compelled the crown to restore shot and shell to its defenseless subjects.[90]

Aside from the contemporary problem of the predatory incursions of the *paulistas*, the reductions, by the nature of their organization, harbored the seeds of future tension which would

90 R. García-Villoslada, S.J., *Manual de Historia de la Compañia de Jesús* (Madrid, 1954), pp. 323-325; Astráin, *Historia*, VI, 670-679. A recent article, too late for me to use extensively, is "Antonio Ruíz de Montoya and the Early Reductions in the Jesuit Province of Paraguay," by J. E. Groh, *Catholic Historical Review*, LVI (1970), 501-533.

in part be responsible for the suppression of the Society. A self-enclosed social structure, each village gradually began to assume the image of a challenge to the authority of the king and the royal governors, a kind of *imperium in imperio*. When the winds of secularism would grow in strength, as civil society moved toward the perfection of its own legitimate aspirations, they would beat with force against such institutions as the reductions. This particular violence was still over the horizon of time, and selfless men, unaware of the cruel fate that awaited their successors, continued to write one of the noblest pages in Jesuit history.

While this venture in the construction of the South American church moved forward, the search for more and more tribes continued. There were always others to be found. In his accounts about the Mojos people, in the northeastern area of present day Bolivia, Antonio de Orillano drew a vivid picture of the heat and humidity of the jungle, the burning fevers which crippled men for months at a time, the loneliness and desolation of the unknown, the discomfort from beasts and insects. For the expedition among these people, called by Orillano "a novitiate in patience," superiors in Peru chose three men: Fathers Pedro Marabán and Cipriano Barace and Brother José del Castillo. In 1668 they started the slow, tedious task of weaning the pagans from the practice of infanticide and the cult of the moon, and of leading them to settlements such as Our Lady of Loreto where on March 25, 1682, 600 Mojos received baptism.[91]

Up and down the Marañón River Lucas de la Cueva, one of the greater Jesuit missionaries of all times, moved for thirty-four years, and even as a septuagenarian continued to sail up tributary streams in search of other tribes. While this intrepid priest added year to year of labor, others, far younger, went to early graves. Phucas Majano went blind under the constant racking of fevers and died but three years after his arrival on the mission; Raimundo de Santa Cruz, scarcely forty years old, drowned; Pedro Sánchez, only twenty-seven, fell under the lances of hostile Abijoras.

In the Philippines, island-hopping far and wide marked the Jesuit apostolate there. Sometimes the missionaries joined the civil government's incursions into new areas, as when in 1637 Marcello Mastrilli, famed for his propagation of devotion to St. Francis Xavier, accompanied the expedition to Zamboanga. The whir of movement reverberates in the annual catalogs of the

91 Astráin, *Historia*, V, 550-557.

province where, in a baffling way, new houses appear and then disappear from year to year.[92] The number of men in the province fluctuated, 111 in 1615, 127 in 1632, 96 in 1651.

The greatest single island hop was to the Marianas, some 1,500 miles to the east. These islands, called the Ladrones by Magellan because of the predatory instincts of the natives, aroused little interest among the Spaniards because of their poor natural resources. Diego Luis de Sanvítores, however, decided to give them his attention. With the aid of the queen regent in Spain, Mariana of Austria, in whose honor he named the islands the Marianas, Sanvítores with five other Jesuits landed on Guam, June 16, 1668. There he found 20,000 people scattered in 180 small villages. Soon he dispatched some of his companions to Tinian and Saipan. The natives responded readily to the teaching of the missionaries, and in one year, on Guam alone, some 6,500 received baptism, while practically all the others were catechumens. Within three years, however, troublemakers aroused sharp opposition to the Jesuits and turned the Marianas into the most dangerous mission of the Society. By 1685 less than twenty years after Sanvítores' arrival, twelve Jesuits were killed. The first was Luis de Medina who, after baptizing some 600 on Tinian, fell under the lances of some natives of Saipan. The second was Sanvítores himself. Only forty-five years old and four years in the Marianas, he was cut down by an apostate on Saipan.[93] Native unrest, uprisings increased; decadence set in; dark days lay ahead for this difficult mission.

In North America, with the exception of two abortive attempts by the French, the missionary venture of the Jesuits had been an exclusively Spanish enterprise. But sixty years after they entered Mexico City, others from France, in 1632, settled in Quebec. And two years later others from England settled at St. Mary's City, Maryland. Segments of these three cultures, Spanish, French, English, from which grew the rich variety of the Church in the northern continent, were eventually to be brought together within one political unity by the creation and expansion of the United States of America.

The spiritual élan which permeated the Society of seventeenth-century France and which was made incarnate in St. Jean François Régis and the Blesseds Jacques Salez, Guillaume

French and English America

---

92 Ibid., 671.
93 Ibid., VI, 812-820.

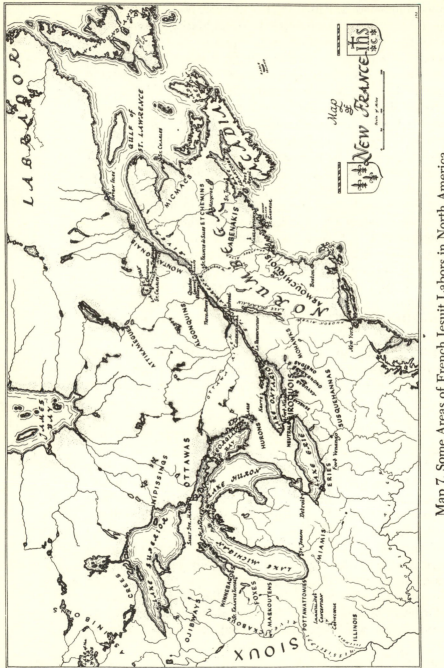

Map 7. Some Areas of French Jesuit Labors in North America

Reproduced, by permission, from John H. Kennedy, *Jesuit and Savage in New France.*
Copyright 1950 by Yale University Press.

Saultemouche, Julien Maunoir, and Claude de la Colombière, crossed the ocean with the many other Jesuits who sailed out of Brest and Le Havre for the colonial city at Quebec on the St. Lawrence in Canada. In 1632 they made a third attempt to settle in the New World. This time they stayed. Three years later, at Quebec, they opened the College of Our Lady of the Angels. Four years still later they welcomed the Ursuline, Marie de l'Incarnation, who at their invitation had come to join their mission among the Hurons. This nun, gifted with extraordinary mystical graces, founded at Quebec the first school for the education of young women in North America.

Soon after the Jesuits settled in Canada, twenty-three priests and six brothers staffed the mission. From their center at Quebec, under the intelligent and far-seeing leadership of Paul Le Jeune, they started their penetration of the country's interior which in the decades ahead took them 500 miles to the east and north, 1,500 miles to the west, 1,700 miles south on the Mississippi. To the west, occupying the great peninsula between Lakes Huron, Erie, and Ontario, and bordering on Georgian Bay, were the Hurons. Under the direction of Jérôme Lallemant, the missionaries discerned the valuable geographical position of the area for contacts with other peoples and attempted, as their brethren in Spanish America were doing, to arrange the country around a central village. But they never achieved the success of the Paraguay Reductions, for the docility of the Guaraní did not mark the Huron character. And then, in the terrible years 1648-1649, over Huronia fell the silence of death brought by the fire and tomahawks of the Iroquois. During the short period of fifteen years some twenty-five priests worked there.

Others pressed the thrust to the west. René Ménard, a veteran among the Hurons and the Cayugas, tried to reach the Dakotas beyond Lake Superior but sometime in 1661 he became lost in the forest and was never heard from again. Between 1665 and 1689 Claude Allouez, rugged and tenacious, covered some 3,000 miles as he traveled through the area of the Great Lakes, instructing more than twenty Indian nations. To the north, among the Algonquins along the Ottawa River, twenty-four Jesuits labored between 1640 and 1682. Southeast toward the Atlantic and the British colonies, among the docile and impressionable Abnaki, Gabriel Druillettes, lean and weather-beaten, had a major part between 1646 and 1652 in the creation of what was unique among the Indians, a people entirely Catholic.

Among the stories which the Jesuits and the French colonists heard from the Indians was one about a mighty river, somewhere toward the west, which rolled southward. Jean Talon, first intendant of New France, dedicated to the expansion of the French domain, resolved to investigate this story. In 1672 he enlisted the service of a daring explorer, Louis Jolliet. A Jesuit, Jacques Marquette, also was interested in the mighty river as a possible gateway to many other Indian nations. The initiative of Talon, the courage of Jolliet, and the Christian zeal of Marquette merged to form the famous French exploration of the Mississippi River in 1673.

Marquette was ordained a priest at Toul, France, on March 7, 1666. Described by his superior as a man of "wonderfully gentle ways," he had been in New France since September 20, 1666. Through seven years, during which he gradually moved some 1,500 miles westward by way of Sainte-Marie-du-Sault to La Pointe du Saint-Esprit on Lake Superior, he acquired a vast knowledge of the country and the Indians. Between 1671-1673 he was at the mission station of Saint Ignace, directly opposite Mackinac Island. From there he wrote to his superior in his mission report for 1672-1673 that he was preparing "to seek toward the South Sea new nations that are unknown to us, to teach them to know our great God, of whom hitherto they have been ignorant." He, Jolliet, and five companions left Saint Ignace on May 17, 1673, and a month later entered the Mississippi from the Wisconsin River. In mid-July they reached the mouth of the Arkansas River. By then they had concluded that the Mississippi did not flow toward Florida or Virginia into the Atlantic but southward into the Gulf of Mexico. Along the route, which had taken them nearly 1,700 miles from Saint Ignace, they had contacted several Indian nations. On July 17, exactly two months after they had started, they turned back. They had reached approximately the same degree of latitude which, some 1300 miles to the west, Eusebio Kino, coming out of Mexico, would touch two decades later.[94]

George Bancroft's ringing sentence, "Not a cape was turned, not a river entered, but a Jesuit led the way," is overgenerous because frequently the actual pioneers were the fur traders. But the priests were not far behind. Numerous tribes through the vast expanse of the continent, instructed by these Jesuits, passed on from generation to generation loving memories of their teachers. In 1821 a report from America to Propaganda

94 J. P. Donnelly, S.J., *Jacques Marquette: 1637-1675* (Chicago, 1968), pp. 112, 183, 209-226, 338-340.

made this observation about the Indians: "They have a great veneration for the Black Robes (so do they call the Jesuits). They tell how the Black Robes slept on the ground, exposed themselves to every privation, did not ask for money.[95]

These Frenchmen left an imposing memorial of their American missions in the accounts which they sent home. Each year between 1632 and 1673 the superior of the mission, using material he had obtained from the individual missionaries, drafted a report, or *une relation,* for the provincial in France, who then published them in a series of duodecimo volumes which have become known in the English speaking world as *The Jesuit Relations.* The *Relations* aroused wide interest in France and were awaited with keen interest. Starting in 1896, Reuben Thwaites, a professor in the University of Wisconsin, published an English translation of these documents, as well as of letters and journals of the missionaries, in an invaluable series which reached seventy-three volumes. From these pages, written in a simple and direct style, rise up vivid pictures of the cultivated and refined Black Robe squatting in a circle of filthy savages, or paddling his canoe across a wide windswept lake, or sleeping in a smoke-filled hut, or standing as an object of derision before jeering Indians. The gold of Christian charity which shines through these volumes is some of the brightest and purest in the history of Christianity.

But 1673, a year which historians can recall only with a sigh, ended these published *Relations,* and the full flow of documentation suddenly became a mere trickle. Pope Clement X, in an effort to ease the acrimony of the debate on the Chinese rites, by his brief *Creditae nobis coelitus* of April 6, 1673, forbade the publication of any literature on the missions without the approval of the Congregation of Propaganda. The terms of the brief were severe. Violation of it brought excommunication reserved to the pope. A religious also incurred removal from office and loss of all canonical voice in his community. Although the permission of Propaganda could have opened the way to the renewal of publication, the French Jesuits were not able to employ this device, because France, ever conscious of her Gallican liberties, refused to recognize within her boundaries the jurisdiction of the Roman Congregation.[96] Therefore, as far as the

95 T. Hughes, S.J., *History of the Society of Jesus in North America, Colonial and Federal* (London, 1907-1917), II (text), 262.
96 L. Pouliot, S.J., *Étude sur les Relations des Jésuites de la Nouvelle-France (1632-1672)* (Montreal, 1940), pp. 12-15.

public was concerned, an almost complete silence fell over the work of the Jesuits in New France. Among themselves and their brethren in Europe they kept up a lively correspondence; and some of these letters survived the pillaging of the Society's archives at the time of the suppression and found their way into Thwaites' *The Jesuit Relations and Allied Documents.*

The high point of their charity was reached in martyrdom. Several fell under the blows of the Iroquois, then a cruel and aggressive confederacy of five nations located between the French and English territories, who pressed like a sharp thorn into the growing body of Christian Indians along the St. Lawrence. In 1642 Isaac Jogues and Brother René Goupil were captured by the Mohawks, one of the five Iroquois nations, and taken to Ossernenon, the present day Auriesville in New York State. There Goupil fell under a tomahawk. Jogues, held as a captive for thirteen months and brutally tortured, was rescued by the Dutch of Fort Orange. In 1646, now accompanied by Jean La Lande, a dedicated lay helper of the Jesuits, he voluntarily returned to the Mohawks on a peace mission. At Ossernenon both met the fate of René Goupil. Two and three years still later the Iroquois fell on the Hurons, decimated them and killed Antoine Daniel, Jean de Brébeuf, Gabriel Lallemant, Charles Garnier, and Noël Chabanel. In 1930 Pope Pius XI canonized these eight martyrs. Others too made the supreme sacrifice in the service of the mission, losing their lives in the rushing waters of the rivers and the great drifts of snow.

What these men did flowed from profoundly spiritual interior lives. Some of them, in recording the sentiments of their hearts, revealed how intensely they had grasped the Jesuit ideal of apostolic service for Christ. Paul Le Jeune wrote in 1635:

> Three forceful thoughts console a good heart which is in the infinite forests of New France or among the Hurons. The first is: "I am in the place where God has sent me, where he has led me by the hand, where he is with me, and where I can seek him alone." The second is, in the words of David: "When worries throng my heart, your consolations are my soul's delight." (Ps. 93:19). The third is that we never find crosses, nails, or thorns in the midst of which, if we look closely, we do not find Jesus Christ. Now, can any person be evil when he is in the company of the Son of the Living God?
>
> I do not know what the country of the Hurons is, to which God in his infinite mercy is sending me, but I do know that I would rather go there than to any earthly paradise, since I see that God has so ordained. How strange it is. The more crosses I see prepared for me there, the more my heart rejoices and flies thither! What happiness it

is for me to see nothing but savages, crosses, and Jesus Christ. Never in my life in France have I understood what it was to distrust self entirely and to trust in God alone — really alone, without the presence of any creature.

In 1646 Isaac Jogues wrote to a fellow Jesuit as he was preparing to leave for the Mohawks, who had treated him so savagely four years earlier.

> My heart tells me that if I have the blessing of being sent on this mission, *Ibo et non redibo:* I shall go, and shall not return. I shall be happy if our Lord wills to finish the sacrifice where he began it. May the little blood that I shed in that land be a pledge of what I am willing to give him from all the veins of my body and from my heart. Indeed, that nation is as "A spouse of blood to me" (Ex. 4:25). May our good Master who has acquired that nation by his Blood, open to it, if he will, the door of his Gospel, as well as to the other four nations, its allies and neighbors. Farewell, dear Father; beg God to unite me inseparably to him.[97]

Sentiments of this kind explain the Jesuits' response to the Iroquois cruelty as they continued to dispatch more men to the valley of the Mohawk River. In 1654 Simon Le Moyne, followed by others of rare missionary ability, went among the Onondagas, the first Europeans to do so. This priest of wide knowledge of the Iroquois character and traditions, and of consummate skill in interpreting Iroquois eloquence and diplomacy, also worked among the Mohawks, who almost killed him in 1661. Plagued by the colonial hostilities of the French and English, the mission to the Five Nations had to close down in 1686. One settlement alone, Caughnawaga, on the St. Lawrence and opposite Montreal, found a measure of stability and security. It remains today an Indian town, still served by the Jesuits, and honored by the presence of the bones of Kateri Tekakwitha, the Indian virgin known as the Lily of the Mohawks, who, in a step toward beatification, was declared in 1943 to have been of heroic virtue.

Twelve years before Jogues gave his life at Ossernenon and forty years after Gonzalo de Tapia was killed in Sinaloa, on St. Clement's Island in the Potomac River, Andrew White of the English Province offered the Holy Sacrifice of the Mass. With about 320 Englishmen including two other Jesuits, John Gravener, alias Altham, and Brother Thomas Gervase, White landed there on March 25, 1634, to form under the leadership of

---

97 F. Roustang, S.J., *An Autobiography of Martyrdom* (St. Louis, 1964), pp. 71, 268, quoted with permission of B. Herder Book Company.

Leonard Calvert, brother of Cecil, the second Lord Baltimore, the English colony of Maryland as a haven for persecuted Catholics and the principles of religious toleration and pluralism. White also gave to American colonial history one of its classic documents in his *An Account of the Journey to Maryland,* which he wrote in Latin and in which he described the Potomac as "the sweetest and greatest river I have ever seen, so that the Thames is but a little finger to it." Extending the area of this mission beyond St. Mary's City, the Jesuits instructed the nearby Indians. In 1637 White made his residence among the Patuxents. More Jesuits came from England, and within ten years after White's arrival they had converted 1,000 natives and most of the Protestants among the colony's founding fathers. In St. Mary's County White laid the cornerstone on which was built the impressive structure of the American Church. The history of the first century and a half of that Church is practically identical with the history of the Society's Maryland Mission.

In 1644 a mighty wave of the rabid anti-Catholic animus, which was to batter Maryland periodically until the American Revolution, broke over the settlement. Protestants, invading from Virginia in the ship *Reformation,* burned St. Mary's City, decimated the Indian mission, bundled White and Thomas Copley off to England in chains. Three priests, not yet forty years of age, Roger Rigby, Bernard Hartwell, John Cooper, disappeared from history in the welter of fire, plunder, and bloodshed.

Leonard Calvert, however, soon returned, and the Jesuits began to replace the ruins of their labor. During 1683-1684 two developments threw a light of hope on the future: first, Robert Brooke of Maryland entered the Jesuit novitiate at Watten in Belgium, the protonovice of the vocations which the sterling Catholic families of the colony were to give to the Society; and second, in New York, Thomas Harvey, with the encouragement of the Catholic governor, Thomas Dongan, began, probably in 1684, a school which was financially based on King's Farm where Trinity Church now stands, at the corner of Wall St. and Broadway. The prospects in New York fascinated John Warner, the English provincial, who proposed to the general that the mission in Maryland be made an appendage of the city on the Hudson. But Dongan's departure from office in 1687 terminated, very probably, the Jesuit school. And the failure of the Stuart cause made mockery of Warner's fine dreams. The heavy yoke of Protestant bigotry fell on the Church along the Atlantic seaboard, and the Catholics became a people fey.

As in the earlier period, disputes of a legalistic nature continued to mar the work of the missionaries. Organizations, designed to establish and preserve order, often had the inverse
effect in the acrimony of debates about the possession and
extent of authority. Two developments of this kind stand out
in this period: one, the affair of Bishop Palafox of Puebla de
los Angeles in Mexico; the other, the entrance of the Paris Foreign
Mission Society into the area of the Portuguese Padroado.

The issue on which Bishop Palafox y Mendosa and the Society
met head on concerned faculties or authorization to preach and
hear confessions in the Jesuit churches of Puebla de los Angeles.
For seventy-five years the Jesuits of the Province of Mexico
had carried on their work, all the while enjoying the faculties
granted by Pope Gregory XIII and confirmed by Gregory XIV
and Paul V. Bishop Palafox, an energetic builder and genuinely
apostolic-minded man, with lightning suddenness in 1647, forbade the Jesuits of Puebla to preach or hear confessions and
ordered that they present their faculties within twenty-four
hours for his inspection. The Jesuits had recourse to their provincial. So began a weary and protracted story of litigation
which eventually enveloped the colonial civil power, the Council of the Indies, the Spanish king, and the pope. A number of
statements by Palafox, sometimes self-contradictory and gradually
unveiling an enigmatic strain in his character, added further
circles to a deep labyrinth of perplexities. But what gave this
case a meaning beyond its mere juridical aspect was the ammunition it provided the Society's enemies in Europe in the
form of widely inaccurate and unfair reports made by Palafox.
With little discernible concern for exactness, this holy and zealous
prelate made seriously imprecise statements about Jesuit wealth
and the income from their haciendas. Actually, shortly after
Palafox became bishop, in 1644 the total debts of the houses of
the province far outweighed the income, 438,520 pesos to
117,700.[98]

The second development, the inauguration of the apostolate
of the Paris Foreign Mission Society, had wider repercussions.
This Society began its history with two French Jesuits, Alexandre
de Rhodes and Jean Bagot. De Rhodes, one of the greatest of
Jesuit missionaries, returned in 1650 to Europe from what proved
to be in all Asia one of the areas most responsive to the faith,

98 F. J. Alegre, S.J., *Historia de la Provincia de la Compañía de Jesús de
  Nueva España,* ed. E. Burrus, S.J. and F. Zubillaga, S.J. (Rome,
  1956-1960), III, 3*.

Indochina. Some 300,000 natives had by this time received baptism. Since the civil authorities had taken a hostile attitude toward Christianity and would expectedly resent an influx of numerous European priests, De Rhodes asked the pope to assign a few bishops who could instruct and ordain a native clergy. In 1652 Pope Innocent X requested the Jesuit to find some secular priests who were equipped for such an undertaking. In Paris De Rhodes met Bagot, a spiritual director of distinction, who had among his devotees a group of diocesan priests. From this meeting of the two Jesuits came the seed of the Paris Foreign Mission Society which the seculars formed.[99] In 1658-59 Pope Alexander VII acted on De Rhodes' proposals. He divided the Far East into several vicariates apostolic, appointed François Pallu to that of Tonkin and Pierre Lambert de la Motte to that of Cochin China, and directed that they be responsible to Propaganda. It was De Rhodes' broad vision which inspired this new missionary orientation: the creation of vicars apostolic aided by secular priests, directly under the Holy See and independent of the Portuguese colonial ecclesiastical system. The Congregation of Propaganda instructed the new vicars apostolic to respect as far as possible the customs of the natives and to avoid in their travel Portugal and her dependencies.

Portugal responded with decision. The first vicar apostolic of Cochin China, Pierre Lambert de la Motte, arrived in Siam in 1662. He escaped arrest by the Portuguese only by taking refuge with Dutch merchants. Two of his fellow priests however were seized and died in jail after a long captivity, guilty of having entered their assigned mission without the authorization of Portugal. The years ahead yielded some of the most acrimonious dealings of Catholic with Catholic in the history of the missions. Two powerful institutions met in conflict. And caught in the middle was the individual missionary, often a Jesuit. Allegiance to one invited the umbrage of the other.

In 1673 Pope Clement X confirmed the authority of the vicars apostolic and ordered the missionaries to submit to them. This the Jesuits promptly did. Domingos Fuciti, on September 4, 1677, expressed his acquiescence with great nobility of spirit. Manuel Ferreira said simply: "Causa finita est." But Ferreira was wrong. In a letter of 1682 to the general he told of the distress of the individual missionary. "If I obey the king," he said, "Propaganda excommunicates me. If I obey the pope I am stripped of my Portuguese nationality." The same year Juan

99 Brucker, *La Compagnie*, pp. 647-651.

Bautista Maldonado wrote in a like vein: between them Rome and Lisbon were crushing him.[100]

Two years earlier Oliva had transmitted startling news to the Jesuits in the Far East: those in the areas concerned were, in virtue of their third vow, to take an oath of obedience to the vicars apostolic. In 1678, Innocent XI, on the recommendation of Bishop François Pallu of Tonkin, had drawn up a constitution by which the missionaries were obliged to pronounce such an oath. Actually he did not publish the document but arranged that the superiors of the religious orders would order their subjects to swear their submission *in virtute sanctae obedientiae.* The Jesuits obeyed Oliva's command. In other quarters however opposition arose. At Canton the Augustinians and the Franciscans refused. Some Dominicans who took the oath earned a reprimand from their superiors. Louis XIV forbade Frenchmen to make such a promise as a violation of Gallican liberties. The situation became an unconscionable botch. Propaganda eventually yielded in regard to the oath and in 1688 abolished it. Then the Congregation evolved a wise and farsighted policy which has generally prevailed to this day: first, in areas served by religious the vicars apostolic were selected from the religious; and second, territories were so divided that specific areas were assigned to but one religious family.[101]

It had been a sad story. On the level of planning, Propaganda had sagaciously adopted the design for the creation of the vicars apostolic, since the Padroado had been declining in its efficacy and since it was only proper that the Church's action should be freed from secular control. Yet, estimable policy that it was, it brought, on the level of execution, poignant pain to unselfish and dedicated men far from their homes. Changes of program, which should have been thrashed out by Rome and Lisbon, actually evolved through a series of distressing incidents in far-away lands, and on the head of the poor missionary poured the hot coals fired by the strife between two strong powers. Legalism and litigation once more clouded a beautiful page of heroism in mission history.

This unnecessary and avoidable dissension did not strike the only dissonant note. Saddest of all was the contention between the Friars and the Jesuits, not indeed in doctrinal matters, but mainly about methods of evangelization. Nor did António Vieira

---

100 F. Rodrigues, S.J., "Nas missões do extremo-oriente. Quatro missionarios do padroado português," *Brotéria,* XX (1935), 301-315.
101 Pastor, *History,* XXXII, 458-460; Brucker, *La Compagnie,* pp. 654-655.

advance good feeling by his notorious remark which ran through the Portuguese court that, "the Dominicans lived off the Faith while the Jesuits died for it." [102] From the outer edges of Portugal's empire to the rim of Spain's came the complaint of Jesuits about what Vieira called their "continual and cruel war" with the Friars, a strange product of men whose lives were professedly guided by the sweet charity of Christ.[103]

Conclusion   Jesuit history became more and more identified with the history of nations. The Society's fortunes rose and fell with the broader successes and failures, the wider prosperity and suffering of the countries in which it was established. The ravages of Germany's Thirty Years War, the élan of the Sun King's France, the decadence of Philip IV's Spain, and the scorched earth policies of Poland's invaders deeply affected the tempo of Jesuit life in these lands.

The Society's history also became increasingly associated with the intellectual thrusts of the age. The spirit of the earlier period perdured as men of superior talent continued to animate the world of learning: Lugo, Ripalda, Lessius in speculative theology; Petau, Sirmond, Labbe, and Du Duc in positive theology; Van Papenbroeck and Henschen in historical research; Bouhours, Rapin, Balde, and Bidermann in literature. The new challenges of the century, Jansenism, Cartesianism, and Newtonianism caught up Jesuit scholars and teachers in the sharp debates which they initiated.

On the missions the ardor of earlier decades retained its intensity. The wide frontiers of the unknown liberated the deep natural and supernatural resources of great missionaries: Cinnami, Verbiest, De Rhodes, Vieira, Schall, Claver, La Cueva, Sanvítores, Jogues, De Brébeuf, Andrew White.

Next to the banners of success storm signals began to appear. In China and India other missionaries decried the attempts at accommodation; throughout the East the Protestant Dutch and English whittled down the Portuguese empire; in Europe Port-Royal deplored Jesuit theology; in Propaganda certain ecclesiastics envisaged the destruction of the order; Descartes and Newton shook the older categories of philosophy and troubled minds in the schools; the vernacular challenged the supremacy of the classical curriculum. The world into which the Society had been born was yielding to a new order.

102 Navarrete, *The Travels,* I, lv.
103 Boxer, *The Christian Century,* p. 231.

CONFRONTATION WITH
THE AGE OF REASON
1687–1757

DURING THE NEXT SEVENTY YEARS five generals headed the *The Generals*
Society. Many of their more pressing problems were developments of the perplexing issues which in their incipient stages
confronted Aquaviva a century earlier: the overwhelming power
of the French crown; the diffusion of Dutch and English imperialism; the authoritarianism of the Spanish and Portuguese Royal
Patronages; the established status of the vernacular tongues in
western culture; the mounting rapidity of the scientific advance;
the harsh interpretation of the Society's attempt to strike an
accommodation between the Catholic faith and the cultures of
China and India. In the course of the century since Aquaviva
began his term, like streams that increase in force even as they
run, until they meet to form a mighty rushing river, these problems expanded to overwhelming proportions. From new and
fresh sources other streams poured their waters into the expanding river: the renaissance of Jansenism under Pasquier Quesnel;
the antipathy to the ultramontane character of the Society
among modern states of northern Europe growing in awareness
of their own identity, each with its own peculiar brand of
"Gallican liberties"; the aversion among regalists for the Suarezian doctrine on the origins of civil authority. But by far the
most crushing was the Enlightenment, that period in western
history which was personified in men like Locke, Diderot,
Hume, and Voltaire, and which Crane Brinton and Paul Hazard
have called a revolution, and Peter Gay has identified with the
rise of modern paganism. The Enlightenment swelled to flood
tide the waters that swept away the old order. Among the more
considerable victims was the Society. As it moved into this new
era its numbers grew in moderate measure. In the thirty years,
1680-1710, it increased by about 2,500 to reach just short of
20,000 men. In the next forty years it advanced by another

2,500 to arrive at 22,500 men. But even as the Society grew, its roots were being washed loose by the rushing waters of the new age.

The first general of this period was Tirso González de Santalla. The circumstances of his election were unusual and his rule of eighteen years advanced under almost continual storm clouds. In June, 1687, the delegates of the Thirteenth General Congregation convened in Rome. Among those from Spain was González, a skillful preacher, professor of moral theology at Salamanca, and zealous champion of the moral system of probabiliorism which placed him at odds with nearly all other Jesuit moral theologians, who followed the doctrine of probabilism. He had never been a superior.

The spiritual climate of the Church in those closing years of the seventeenth century was heavy with a preoccupation about moral theology and the variety of its systems. Frequently used words in the theological vocabulary were "laxism" and "rigorism." In 1676 Pope Innocent XI, an austere man whom Pope Pius XII beatified in 1956, condemned sixty-five propositions which favored laxism in moral theology. Four years later he issued a decree in defense of the probabiliorism of Tirso González. When the Thirteenth General Congregation assembled in 1687, the pope made it very clear that he wanted two things: first, the election of González as general; and second, a decree stating that Jesuits were free to defend probabiliorism. The congregation did as the pope wished.[1]

Innocent, despite his good intentions, impaired the Society by his choice of González, because he set it on a course that was to take it through eighteen years of severe distress and tension. Very soon after González' election a struggle developed between him and his assistants. The question at issue was a book.

The new general brought to his post a deeply rooted obsession that the extinction of probabilism within the Society was a duty of pressing importance. Innocent XI, he claimed, said that he was elected precisely to root out laxity in the Society, and he personally felt that he would be guilty of serious sin if he did not wipe away the stain of what was the common teaching of Jesuit moral theologians. To his last days, as an old man over eighty, he tenaciously kept this goal before him.

Four years after the congregation had disbanded, the troubled general, noting that not a single Jesuit had lifted his pen to defend probabiliorism, decided to do so himself. The assistants

1 Astráin, *Historia,* VI, 228-230. See fn. 2 on 230.

advised against this project, since they felt that it would be a public scandal to have the general attacking the principles advocated by most Jesuit teachers of moral theology. González decided to evade the opposition by having his book printed secretly at Dillingen in Germany. He envisaged this volume as a kind of digest of the more extensive work which he had in manuscript form since 1672 when the Society's censors rejected it for publication. He found two Jesuits who shared his views and appointed them censors. In August and September, 1691, the book of 587 octavo pages came off the press in Dillingen. González entitled it *A Short Treatise on the Correct Use of Probable Opinions.*[2]

In this work the general enumerated the reasons why he had entered the lists in the debate about probabilism and why he hoped to see it uprooted from the Society of Jesus. Probabilism was the source of a pernicious laxity in morals and license in personal habits; it weakened the teaching of the Gospel; it was the occasion for many sins; it was contrary to the mind of the popes and would likely soon be condemned. The general in effect dressed nearly every Jesuit moral theologian with a sanbenito. He then drew attention to the eighteenth decree of the Thirteenth General Congregation which elected him in 1687. According to his interpretation, the congregation proclaimed that the Society of Jesus does not embrace as its own the moral system of probabilism. Actually, the eighteenth decree simply stated that in the past the Society had not prohibited, nor now prohibits, the defense by a Jesuit of the moral system of probabiliorism. González' presentation reflected a noteworthy failure in accuracy and precision on his part.[3]

News of the Dillingen book reached the Jesuit curia in Rome. All the assistants, repeatedly and with great earnestness, by word and in writing, asked the general to keep the book from appearing in public. On November 9, 1691, González thanked them for their zeal and vigilance, told them that the printing was already completed, and that he was prepared to let the volume appear, not indeed with his name on the title page but as the work of an anonymous member of the Society of Jesus. Two days later, the assistants declared that this would not do. The book should be suppressed. At their request the pope, the recently elected Innocent XII, expressed the wish that the entire edition be brought to Rome and deposited with the Master

2 Ibid., 242.
3 Ibid., 243-244.

of the Sacred Palace. Then communications among the concerned parties became tangled. The assistants informed the provincial of the Upper German Province, Benedikt Painter, of the papal order. At the same time González, appealing to a permission which he had received from the papal secretary of state, insisted that the books must be sent to himself. Shortly after, the pope directed that for the time being the books remain in Germany under close custody.[4]

In February of the following year, Paolo Segneri came to Rome as the papal preacher for the Lenten season. He had extended meetings with Pope Innocent, and he tried to persuade González to surrender his views. With amazing candor he reminded the general that his obligation was to rule, not write books. He drew attention to the numerous authorities in moral theology, the professors at the Roman College, the assistants, all of whom favored the doctrine of probabilism. With a deft plunge of the rapier, he pointed out that the immense breadth of this phalanx of opinion made the safer and more likely system that of probabilism, and that González was conquered by his own principles. But to no avail.

In June, 1692, the assistants approached the pope with another suggestion. They proposed that the release of the book be held up until the regular triennial meeting of the congregation of procurators, scheduled for November, 1693. Although business of this kind was not the normal concern of a congregation of procurators, nevertheless, because of the unusual circumstances, it might be wise to request the advice of the delegates. On June 14, Innocent agreed. This delay of another year and a half did not make González very happy.

Then the general took another tack. He resurrected his manuscript of 1672, *The Foundation of Moral Theology*, and thought that if he omitted the offensive elements of his *A Short Treatise on the Correct Use of Probable Opinions*, he might at long last have his older work published. On June 30, 1693, Pope Innocent consented on condition that González would shelve his Dillingen book and that *The Foundation of Moral Theology* would receive the approval of the censors. The general proceeded to remove the objectionable features of the *A Short Treatise*, but, fearful of trouble with censors outside the Society, requested that the examiners be Jesuits. Innocent asked him to submit a list of ten priests qualified for this task. This González did. The assistants presented eight names. From the two lists the pope

4 Duhr, *Geschichte*, III, 9.

chose three, Bartolomé Carreño, a Spaniard, André Semery, a Frenchman, and Christoph Zingnis, a Tyrolese. With the exception of some details to which Zingnis objected and which were then deleted from the text, the book received the approval of the three examiners. By February, 1694, *The Foundation of Moral Theology. A Treatise on the Correct Use of Probable Opinions* appeared on the market. Very soon it appeared in several cities of Europe, and in a little more than a year twelve editions were printed. The natural curiosity of the theological community made it a best seller, but soon, because of the inherent limitations of the work, interest waned and it joined the long column of undistinguished and unread books.[5]

The *Foundation of Moral Theology* is a confusing work with annoying lapses in clarity and precision. To his usual arguments in favor of probabiliorism González added a new one. He pictured the Supreme Judge of mankind appearing garbed in the ideas of a probabiliorist. The Judge summons before the divine tribunal a man who had in life followed the more lenient opinions, and demands an account of his stewardship. The man presents a list of the weighty authorities whose judgments made probably licit the opinions he followed. Without more ado, the judge sends the poor probabilist into eternal damnation. St. Alfonso Maria de' Liguori, alluding to this passage, observed: "Let this be our greatest solace, that we must stand not before the tribunal of probabiliorists but of Christ."[6]

The volumes under lock and key in Germany had an even more inglorious end. They seem to have vanished from the face of the earth. Antonio Astráin, industrious researcher and author of the magisterial history of the Spanish Assistancy, saw during his investigations but one copy, that in the Biblioteca de San Isidro in Madrid, a gift from Eusebio Truchses, the German assistant, to Ambrosio Ortiz.[7]

Meanwhile, during the immediate preparations for the publication of *The Foundation of Moral Theology*, the congregation of procurators assembled in November, 1693. By this time the problem of the general's books had been practically solved but not without disrupting the arrangements for the congregation. González, who spoke of the "damned nationalism" which harmed the missions, churned up national feeling by turning the private Jesuit dispute about the Dillingen book into an international epi-

5 Astráin, *Historia*, VI, 320-323.
6 Ibid., 333-334.
7 Ibid., 320.

sode. To gain support he appealed to the Hapsburg courts of
Spain and Austria. Madrid, excited by the general's claim that
behind the objections to his work lurked the maneuverings of
the French cardinals, became especially sensitive, and Charles
II, alerted by rumors that a move was on to choose men for the
procurators' congregation who would vote for the summoning of
a general congregation with a view to the removal of the Spanish
general from office, ordered royal officials in Spain, Sicily,
Naples, Sardinia, and Milan to observe closely the provincial
congregations and to make known to the elected delegates the
king's concern for his Spanish subject in the general's office in
Rome. Spanish honor demanded the protection of González.[8]

Free though it might be from the need to review the general's writings, the congregation soon became enmeshed in a
complex legalistic wrangle about its own rules of procedure.
On November 19 the delegates proceeded to take up the main
business of their meeting: to decide whether a general congregation should be convened. A majority, one vote above half the
total, was required to decide the question. Thirty-three votes
were cast, seventeen in favor of convening a general congregation, sixteen against. No one doubted that the former had prevailed. That evening, however, the secretary of the Society,
Egidio Estrix, had a doubt. Half of thirty-three is sixteen and a
half; seventeen is only a half beyond this; therefore, because
a full vote beyond half of the total was wanting, a general congregation should not be convened. So started six months of
dispute. González, who personally opposed the calling of a
general congregation, drew up a twenty-one page defense of
this position. The Holy See finally took over the case and submitted it to a committee of five cardinals. By a vote of three to
two the cardinals decided against the convocation of a general
congregation.[9]

Even though a general congregation had been forestalled
amid the legalistic dispute of 1693-1694, one had to be called
three years later in accord with the fifty-year-old decree of
Innocent X which called for such a meeting every nine years.
When the Fourteenth General Congregation assembled in 1696,
Pope Innocent XII exhorted the members to do their work in a
spirit of charity. *Recedant vetera, nova sint omnia*, the pontiff
urged. The delegates complied. To clarify what had become a
source of doubt, they decreed that a vote for a general con-

8 Pastor, *History*, XXXII, 624-625.
9 Ibid., 625-631; Astráin, *Historia*, VI, 306-315.

gregation by the congregation of procurators had to have a majority of at least three votes. They closed their business in an atmosphere of tranquillity and goodwill.

But González returned to his old obsession. In 1702, convinced that the question of probabilism meant life or death for the Society, he sent a memorial to Clement XI requesting that the pope proclaim what should be the right moral norm in avoiding the extremes of Rigorism and Laxism. There was no doubt what González had in mind. The pope, however, did not act. The general was then eighty years of age and his energies had noticeably failed. Advised by his assistants to appoint a vicar to assist him, he chose Michelangelo Tamburini. Nevertheless he had the energy to send another memorial to the pope asking for a condemnation of probabilism. Once again the time drew near for the novennial general congregation, and it was called for January, 1706. Anxiety about the superior who tried so relentlessly to impose his personal ideas on the entire Society hung heavily on the hearts of the delegates as they prepared to leave for Rome. Death, however, removed this burden by taking the general on October 27, 1705.

If it were possible to quarantine the issue of probabilism, the record of González would be most commendable. He fostered the foreign missions with devoted attention. He encouraged the genuine religious spirit that animated the Society. He fought strongly when the honor of another was at stake, as when the Spanish Inquisition issued its ridiculous condemnation of some of Daniel van Papenbroeck's work in the Bollandist enterprise of *The Acts of the Saints;* he halted a similar censure at Rome. In his niche as a father general of the Society he stands, a figure for the most part admirably chiseled but with certain incongruous and conflicting lines that destroy a total harmony of impression. His vicar-general succeeded him when, on January 31, 1706, the Fifteenth General Congregation elected Michelangelo Tamburini to head the Society.

Tamburini, a fifty-eight-year Modenese, received early in his term of twenty-four years the full impact of a concerted campaign of slander and vilification against the Society. Serious trouble began when the Society's enemies seized upon the resurrected question of the Chinese rites. In China, during the latter years of González' generalate, Charles Maigrot, vicar apostolic of Fukien and member of the Paris Foreign Mission Society, forbade within his jurisdiction in 1693 the use of *Tien* and *Shangti* as terms to express God, as well as participation in the ceremonies in honor of Confucius and ancestors. In his determination to reopen the issue at Rome, he claimed that the situation as presented there by the Jesuits through Martino Martini was not true and, therefore, that the subsequent approbation of Pope Alexander VII in 1656 had no bearing on the real situation in China.

In 1697, the Holy Office took under consideration the issues raised by Maigrot. Slowly, carefully, with attention to both sides, the inquiry went on through seven years. The Jesuits reenforced their case by transmitting to Rome a declaration of the Emperor K'ang-hsi that the Confucian and ancestral ceremonies were solely civic in character. As an issue which affected so closely in a practical way the approach of the Church toward an Oriental civilization, it was one of the most difficult and delicate ever considered by the Holy See. On November 20, 1704, Pope Clement XI confirmed the decision of the Sacred Congregation of the Holy Office: a prohibition against the use of *Tien* and *Shangti* to designate God and against participation by Catholics in the Confucian and ancestral ceremonies. This decision did not pass judgment on the contention of the Jesuits that the rites in themselves were non-religious in character but, looking rather to the actual situation, found that among so many of the people had superstition become entwined with the ceremonies that they could not be tolerated. Basically it repudiated the conviction of the Jesuits that education and instruction, as used by the early Christians who adopted pagan practices and feasts, could disassociate superstition from the rites. The pope withheld promulgation of the decision in Europe until 1709 but commissioned his legate, Carlo de Tournon, and the vicars apostolic to enact it in China.[10]

Unfortunately this momentous issue did not remain confined to the conference rooms in Rome but readily became a rallying point for enemies of the Society. When calm reflection, deep knowledge of Chinese civilization, and exact scholarship should have prevailed, partisan feeling, intense hatred, and violent bias triumphed, and a brand of literature marked by viciousness and crudeness devastated the reputation of the Society, especially of the men who were expending themselves for the faith in China. On September 11, 1704, two months before the papal decision, a Jesuit veteran of the Chinese mission, Kaspar Kastner, remarked to Clement XI that the Society's enemies were less concerned about the purity of worship in China than the dis-

10 Pastor, *History*, XXXIII, 423-424; Brucker, *La Compagnie*, pp. 708-710.

grace of the Jesuits. The pope agreed.[11] Robert Streit, O.M.I., one of the fathers of scientific missiology, pointed to many of the writings about the missions in the mid-eighteenth century as a genre of literature which, for superficiality and unscrupulousness, has no parallel in history.[12]

Two of the more effective groups in the campaign of vilification were the Jansenists and the Paris Foreign Mission Society. The Jansenists proclaimed that the fire of division in the Church could only be quenched by the extinction of the Society. One of them, Michel Villermaules, published between 1733 and 1742 a massive collection of libels in his seven-volume work *Anecdotes on the State of Religion in China.* The Paris Foreign Mission Society sponsored Villermaules' work. Charles Maigrot, one of its members, authored an essay in which he depicted the Society of Jesus as the checkmate of every papal move in China, bringing disaster upon the Chinese Church, and the general as the pope of China, empowered to teach the gospel of Confucius. Antoine Arnauld in his pamphlets against the Jesuits emphasized that he drew some of his material not only from the Dominican sources in Paris and Rome but also from the archives of Propaganda, some of whose officials regarded the Society with deep hostility. Domenico Perroni, the procurator of Propaganda in China, gave the measure of the depth this animus could reach. Somewhat like Cato with his *Delenda est Carthago,* he expressed his feeling bluntly: "Let us uproot them utterly. They must be eradicated." When Antonio Laghi, the Franciscan vicar apostolic of Shansi, protested, Perroni repeated: "Let us uproot them utterly. They must be eradicated." Further protest brought the same response: "Let us uproot them utterly. They must be eradicated." [13]

Pen sketches augmented the literature of vilification and swelled the torrent of biased feeling. One of these depicted the Jesuit visitor to China, Filippo Grimaldi, enthroned among the mandarins and turned with scornful eye toward the other missionaries. Swathed in these vile slanders which in many uncritical histories still cling to them, the Jesuits stood before the gaze of Europe as repulsive traitors to the Church who subordinated Christ to Confucius, permitted Catholics to worship as pagans, and amassed large fortunes. The Eighth Commandment seemed to have dropped out of the Decalogue. In

---

11 Pastor, *History,* XXXIII, 422.
12 Ibid., XXXVIII, 477-478, fn. 1.
13 Ibid., XXXIV, 80, fn. 2.

China other missionaries avoided contact with the Jesuits; in Rome bishops discovered that it was unpopular to defend the Society and that they could expect only a loss in prestige at the Vatican if they did so. In a judgment that presaged a viewpoint which was to gain wide acceptance in the decades ahead, Cardinal Girolamo Casanata, speaking of the Society as the quondam right hand of the Church, suggested that the general good can at times call for the amputation of a hand.

No general since St. Ignatius faced an attack of the proportions which Tamburini had to meet. Fierce as was the assault endured by Claudio Aquaviva, it seemed like a local skirmish compared to the wide front of this onslaught of the early eighteenth century. Through the smoke and din of this mortal battle the one position to which Jesuit superiors held tenaciously was that of obedient submission to the Holy See. The general in Rome and the visitor in Peking, as will be seen more in detail in the section on China, unreservedly voiced their acceptance of the pope's decree.

These protestations however did not silence the persistent cant of the Society's enemies, but what perhaps grieved the Jesuits most was the *volte-face* of the papal legate, Carlo Mezzabarba, who was sent to China in 1719 to investigate the tangled situation there. This thirty-four-year-old diplomat granted a series of eight concessions in regard to the rites — later revoked by Pope Benedict XIV —and manifested a general appreciation of what the Society had attempted. Before he quit China he solemnly assured the Jesuits that he would support them at Rome. To three of the superiors who, on their knees, asked his frank criticism if in any way they had done wrong, he replied that all he had seen of the Jesuits merited only the highest praise, and he encouraged them to be of good heart because he intended to withstand their calumniators. Back in Rome he joined the chorus of condemnation of the Society.[14]

Pope Innocent XIII took action. He instructed the Congregation for the Propagation of the Faith to issue a brief to Tamburini. The time for the amputation of the limb of which Cardinal Casanata spoke seemed to have arrived. Under date of September 13, 1723, the Congregation indicted the Jesuits in China for disobedience, remissness in duty by refraining from the administration of the sacraments, and artful obstruction of orders from the Holy See. Tamburini they accused of official negligence by failure to insist on his subjects' obedience. The

14 Ibid., XXXIII, 81-82.

punishment threatened for failure to rectify these breaches of duty amounted to a condemnation of the Society to slow death. No more novices were to be received; nor were more men to be sent to the Far East. Three years were given the general to prove his own and his subjects' obedience. The stern phrases of this brief, exactly fifty years before the suppression, gave the measure of the strength and the determination of the Society's enemies.

Actually the sharp edge of these threats was blunted almost immediately. Pope Innocent XIII acknowledged that the brief had been formulated on the solitary claims of those opposed to the Society and that Propaganda had in the severity of its expression gone beyond his personal intentions. He asked Tamburini to present the Society's side of the story and eased the harshness of the penalties by declaring that they should be regarded as merely "intimated."

This unpleasant affair between the pope and the general was cast against a background of earlier tension between the Society and Innocent when he was still Cardinal Michelangelo de' Conti. When Conti was nuncio in Lisbon, he and the Jesuits had a protracted disagreement about the financial problem of the annates. The Jesuit Cardinal Alvaro Cienfuegos spread unfavorable reports about Conti's work in Portugal. During the conclave of 1721 the Jesuit royal confessor at Madrid, Guillaume Daubenton, persuaded King Philip V to send a royal veto against Conti. The veto arrived too late, shortly after Conti's election as Innocent XIII. This news from Madrid soured somewhat the pope's view of Spain and the Society.[15]

Tamburini was not embarrassed by a paucity of evidence for the Society's defense. With an impressive array of documents he demonstrated that he had sent orders to the Jesuits in China to observe the Church's decree; that he had each year reported to the Holy See on the mission situation in the Far East; that the Society's missionaries had tried, even at personal peril, to persuade the people to submit to the decree on rites; that he had called to order the priests who because of scruples refrained from administering the sacraments; that these same priests had again taken up their ministry. This defense he submitted to Innocent, who died soon after, on March 7, 1724; then to Innocent's successor, Benedict XIII. He reenforced his argument with extracts of letters from Jesuits in China and with

---

15 Ibid., XXXIV, 24, 28, fn. 4, 83-86; F. P. della Gattina, *Histoire Diplomatique des Conclaves* (Brussels, 1866), IV, 12 fn. 1, 14-15, 18.

statistics on the number of times they had administered the sacraments. He won his case and Benedict XIII removed the ban on the reception of novices and the dispatch of men to the Far East.[16] But the victory was only a partial one. Tamburini's evidence convinced the pope but it did not halt those who were intent on the ruin of the Society. At his death on February 28, 1730, Tamburini left the Society intact but unsure.

On November 30, 1730, the Sixteenth General Congregation chose Frantisek Retz, a native of Prague, to head the order. This fifty-seven-year-old Bohemian received all but two of the seventy-eight votes cast, his own and another, and so missed by only one vote the distinction of a unanimous election, previously attained by St. Ignatius and De Noyelle. During his twenty years as general commenced one of the more important pontificates of the century. Benedict XIV, known for the breadth of his learning, reigned from 1740 to 1758. Within two years he closed the controversies about the Chinese and Malabar rites.

On July 5, 1742, Benedict issued the constitution *Ex quo singulari* in which he rejected the Chinese rites, advised the missionaries that conversions were due to God's grace, urged them to preach the faith in its purity, encouraged them to martyrdom, and commanded that they take an oath of obedience. What especially distressed the Jesuits in China was the indictment made against them in *Ex quo singulari* that they were disobedient and contumacious. One of these troubled Jesuits, Valentin Chalier, wrote to Retz on November 5, 1743, that he and his fellow religious were conscious of no act of disobedience. A Vincentian, Teodorico Pedrini, known for his opposition to the Jesuits, wrote to Propaganda from Peking on November 1, 1743, a defense of the Society's fidelity to the decision of the Holy See.[17]

On September 12, 1744, Benedict issued the constitution *Omnium sollicitudinum* in which he finalized the papal policy in regard to the issue of a selective apostolate in India. Jesuits, in deference to the Indian social structure, avoided open contact with the pariahs lest they be rendered unacceptable to the influential Brahmins. Benedict decided against this practice. Retz, anticipating an adverse judgment, insisted as early as 1739 that, once the Holy See had spoken, the problem reduced itself to one of obedience even though it meant the collapse of the mission.

16 Pastor, *History*, XXXIV, 197.
17 J. Krahl, S.J., *China Missions in Crisis: Bishop Laimbeckhoven and His Times 1738–1787* (Rome, 1964), p. 35, fnn. 20 and 21.

Four years after Benedict's decree the general recorded his joy in the reports he received that the Jesuits in India had obeyed.[18]

After Retz died on November 19, 1750, two very short generalates followed. Ignazio Visconti, sixty-nine-year-old Milanese, was elected on July 17, 1751, by the Seventeenth General Congregation. He died four years later, on May 4, 1755. On November 30 of the same year the Eighteenth General Congregation chose the sixty-nine-year-old Genoese, Luigi Centurione, who died less than two years after, on October 2, 1757.

Through the first half of the eighteenth century the decrees of the congregations, as those of the latter part of the previous century, register the changing temper of the world of thought. The delegates showed a constant preoccupation with the widening popularity of scientific experimentation and the mounting influence of Descartes, Gassendi, and Malebranche. Wisely they sought a via media that would recognize the just claims of metaphysics and the natural sciences. The Sixteenth General Congregation, 1730, felt that concord could prevail between peripatetic thought and "that more attractive kind of learning," modern physics, mathematics, and experimentation. The Seventeenth General Congregation, 1751, thought the same. However, the legacy of Aristotelian physics, already discredited in so many ways, weighed heavily on the spirit of innovation, for both congregations decreed that the Society's teachers should adhere to Aristotle not only in metaphysics and logic but also in physics. This specific legislation revealed on the official level a serious failure to stay abreast of current intellectual advances.[19]

Among individual Jesuits interest in and appreciation of the scientific movement varied considerably. In the *Philosophical Transactions* of the Royal Society of London, chartered in 1662 by Charles II, for "the promoting of physico-mathematical-experimental learning," appear the names of many Jesuits, a standing testimonial to their scientific ingenuity, imagination, and excellence.[20] Some of them were official correspondents, Francesco Lana-Terzi, for example, being designated as such on the same list as Huygens, Leibniz, and Newton. Others, although not so honored, nevertheless communicated with the Royal Society, which published their letters. Sample titles from the

18 Ferroli, *Jesuits in Malabar,* II, 443-445, 450.
19 Astráin, *Historia,* VII, 13-15, 22; Rodrigues, *História,* IV, i, 340.
20 C. Reilly, S.J., "A Catalog of Jesuitica in the 'Philosophical Transactions of the Royal Society of London,' (1665-1715)," *AHSJ,* XXVII (1958), 339-360.

catalog of the *Transactions* reveal a wide range of interest: *Reflections made by P. Francesco Lana, S.J., on the Observation of Signor M. Antonio Castagna, concerning the Formation of Crystals; A Letter of the Learned F. Linus to a Friend of his in London, animadverting upon Mr. Isaac Newton's theory of light; A Letter from Father Bourzes to Father Estienne Souciet Concerning the Luminous Appearance Observable in the Wake of Ships in Indian Seas.* On the other hand Rudjer Josip Bošković lamented the lack of up-to-date instruments at Collège Louis-le-Grand and the blindness toward Newton of some Jesuits who regarded his views as heresy. To the credulous rector of the college at Sens, who showed him among the school's treasures a piece of Aaron's rod and a rib of the prophet Isaiah, he suggested, in the interest of truth, that they be thrown away.[21]

The intellectual temper of the age, however, penetrated far beyond the border of science in the strict sense of that word. Western Europe became a vast atelier in which men at odds with their Christian past hammered out a new age. Their masterpiece was the Enlightenment. Different in personality, talent, individual intellectual interests, and practical approach to current issues, they shared a common mentality. Alienated from the spiritual tradition of the Middle Ages and the reform movements, Catholic and Protestant, of the sixteenth century, and imbued with a sense of their own personal independent wisdom, they entered into a common pact for the destruction of revealed religion. They spoke with many voices, but there was one Enlightenment.[22]

This alliance, one of the most powerful of its kind in the history of western civilization, used a variety of weapons: banter, caricature, ridicule, serious criticism, and learned treatises. In diaries, correspondence, pamphlets, and books the savants of the Enlightenment convulsed the life of Christendom. In this general melee the Society suffered severe wounds. Voltaire, Diderot, D'Alembert, and other master spirits of the age were willing recruits for the forces which made the destruction of the Society a point of honor.

The victory which the men of the Enlightenment were in the course of gaining underlined what was perhaps the Society's most serious failing in its encounter with a changing world.

---

21 Elizabeth Hill, "Biographical Essay," in *Roger Joseph Boscovich: Studies of His Life and Work on the 250th Anniversary of His Birth*, ed. Lancelot Law Whyte (London, 1961), pp. 55-56.
22 P. Gay, *The Enlightenment: An Interpretation* (New York, 1967), I, 3.

Since the *Ratio studiorum* had been issued in 1599 there had never been a general revision. The *Ratio* was a document of its time, an age when, in reaction to the Protestant reform, the centralizing tendency at Rome grew stronger and legislation took on the quality of immutability and the stamp of *in perpetuum*. A measure of flexibility the *Ratio* did have. Yet, as a document tied to the generalate of Aquaviva, it did not measure up to the spirit of adaptation so characteristic of the Society's *Constitutions*.

After Aquaviva the generals usually regarded the *Ratio studiorum* as a heritage to be preserved in its original form. They insisted on fidelity to its directions. Accommodations to new cultural conditions they conceded with reluctance. Historical changes they yielded to in silence. Change seemed to denote decay. By the opening of the Age of Reason, the time had come and gone for a thorough reappraisal of the curriculum and pedagogical methods. Not only was science on the move, but the articulate Latinist was losing his status as *le beau idéal* of the cultured man. While several of the general congregations tried to make accommodation to the mounting scientific impulse, they shared with the generals the failure to initiate a complete and specialized review of the Society's educational apostolate. The revision of the *Ratio* which was carried out in 1832 was at least a century and a half late.

In the four provinces which ranged from the Alps to Sicily the Jesuits of this era continued to cut the furrows started in earlier generations. In the classroom, the pulpit, and the confessional they inherited at the turn of the century a rich legacy of erudition, culture, and holiness, to which with varying degrees of success they remained true. In the 133 colleges and 22 seminaries the tradition of Latin eloquence lived on and occasionally flowered in the tragedies, produced with a flourish and elaborate scenery, of a man like Giuseppe Carpani. More scholarly in his approach, Girolamo Lagomarsini dedicated his energies to the critical examination of the texts of classical authors, especially in the thirty volumes he envisaged of the entire works of Cicero to be annotated with various readings. He collected vast numbers of manuscripts which eventually made his project unwieldy. Working in a field before German scholars had evolved the principle of using as few texts as possible while at the same time covering the entire field, he, made immobile under the mountain of manuscripts, left behind some eighty volumes of material now resting in the Vatican Library.

287

At the Roman College the faculties of philosophy and theology lived in the shadow cast by the majestic forms of an earlier period, Suárez, Bellarmine, Toledo, Lugo. Gian Battista Faure, despite his penetrating mind and lucidity of exposition, never composed a work of significance beyond his short polemical tracts and notations on the work of others. Winds which troubled the intellectual writers of Italy came from across the Alps in the form of the older Jansenism and the newer rationalism of France. The most articulate Jesuit against these new currents was Alfonso Muzzarelli. In a wide variety of titles touching devotional, dogmatic, and moral topics of the day, such as the severely criticized devotion to the Sacred Heart, Muzzarelli in a lively Italian style presented the Catholic stand. In his *Émile Undeceived* (1782) he gave a critique of Rousseau. His chief work, *The Sound Use of Logic in Religious Matters* (1785), grew with each new edition, three volumes in the first, six in the second, ten in the third.

In science the Roman College could boast of one of the greater scientists of all time. There, through twenty years, 1740-1760, Rudjer Josip Bošković (Roger Joseph Boscovich) lectured in mathematics, physics, and astronomy. This native of Ragusa (Dubrovnik) in Dalmatia, elegant Latinist, original thinker with the ability to free himself from current patterns of thought, as a young Jesuit earned this eulogy from Orazio Borgondi, his learned Jesuit professor of mathematics: "He starts where I leave off." In the twenty-four years between 1736-1760 he published some sixty books or opuscula on scientific subjects. After years of reflection he published in 1758 his masterpiece, in which he anticipated many developments of atomic physics, *Theory of Natural Philosophy*. From an absolutely new point of departure in physics, he conceived the material world as made up of individual non-extended points which are centers of action, while the action, be it attractive or repulsive, between the points is a function of the distance which separates them. Originality, lucidity of expression, versatility characterize other aspects of his scientific thought and mark him as a precursor of much of modern theory, including that of relativity. Always an excellent religious, although at times irritable and aggressive and not suffering fools gladly, Bošković served the Society well, especially in eradicating the notion in some quarters that Jesuits were closed to new ideas. Today the appreciation of his contribution has been greatly intensified. The University of California at Berkeley recently purchased a sizeable quantity of archival material relating to him, which includes over one hundred and eighty manuscripts and about two thousand pieces of correspondence. Historians of science have honored this amazing polymath in the past ten years or so, not only by serious books and articles but also by making him the subject of three international congresses.[23]

During their labors in higher studies the Jesuits never lost touch with the common man, especially in the vibrant tradition of preaching. The year this chapter opens, Giovanni Battista Scaramelli was born in Rome. He carried on in a superb way the work of men who were active when he was a boy, Segneri who died in 1694, De Geronimo who died in 1716, and Baldinucci who died in 1717. Master not only of the spoken but also of the written word, he became a reliable and popular guide in the field of spiritual literature through his *Directory in Asceticism*. He had also written a *Directory in Mysticism*, but superiors, afraid lest amid the rising criticism of the Society an inexact expression might draw lightning from the Holy Office, permitted only the publication of the section of the Discernment of Spirits. A Venetian printer, Simone Occhi, managed to obtain a copy of the complete manuscript, published it on his own authority, and had the pleasure of issuing a popular success. Not only did the book not incur the disfavor of the Holy Office but became, during the greater part of the nineteenth century, the classic work in mystical theology.

Writing of this kind sent a fresh breath of encouragement through the Church. The Molinos scandal had threatened, by the timidity and fear of heresy which it engendered, to stamp out interest in genuine mysticism. But in still another writer the Society forged a strong link with its spiritual literature of the past. Manuel de la Reguera, a Spaniard who spent many years in Rome, took the small work, *The Practice of Mystical Theology*, of Miguel Godínez, heavily medieval in content, and amplified it by scholia and notes, providing thereby a rich mine of patristic, scholastic, and scriptural sources of mysticism. This he published at Rome as *The Practice of Mystical Theology* in 1740. Fifty-four years had passed since Molinos had been arrested in the same city.

Spain turned an important corner in her history in 1700 when the Bourbon, Philip V, grandson of Louis XIV of France, was

23 T. F. Mulcrone, S.J., "Boscovichian Opportunities in the History of Science and Mathematics," *Bulletin of the American Association of Jesuit Scientists*, XLIII (1966), 1-4.

willed the throne by Charles II. The new dynasty released the country from the doldrums of over half a century which saw shipping between Spain and the Indies in 1700 seventy-five per cent less than in 1600, and which witnessed the crown, in 1692, declare itself bankrupt for the third time. The War of the Spanish Succession evoked the old Iberian pride in arms and gave to a dull, formal, and ostentatious nobility a new self-respect. Philip V, by his personal bravery — before he drifted into senility — assisted in lifting his people from their lethargy, and Elizabètta Farnese, his masterful Italian wife, by her ambitious drive through thirty-two years, galvanized them into action.

This new orientation of the nation brought fresh life to the Society no less than to the other institutions of Spain. During the last three decades of the seventeenth century superiors in their correspondence with the general reflected the malaise which had blanketed the nation. They lamented the lack of zest for teaching, the decline of intellectual standards in the schools, the indifference about the upkeep of libraries, the waning fervor of the sodalities. With the advent of the Bourbons a different spirit, enthusiastic and joyous, sparked the reports on the apostolate as a reawakened fervor among the Jesuits broke through their lethargy and launched new spiritual and cultural ventures: special schools for nobles; retreats for priests; devotion to the Sacred Heart of Jesus; a National Royal Academy.[24]

In 1727 the Society started for the first time in Spain a unique kind of institution, similar to those initiated in Vienna and Graz seventeen years earlier. It was the Royal School for Nobles. Members of the aristocracy, noting the increasing spirit of democracy at the Jesuit Imperial College of Madrid, wanted an establishment where their sons would be removed from the bourgeois and poorer pupils who made up the student body of a typical school of the Society. Philip V therefore founded this Royal School of Nobles and placed it under Jesuit direction. Young noblemen flocked to its halls and an enthusiastic aristocracy hailed it as a great success. Twelve years later the Society opened a like school in Barcelona, and in 1752 another in Calatayud. These elite institutions concretely revealed the Jesuit involvement in the polarization that had been taking place within Spanish society through the seventeenth and eighteenth centuries. By this specialized education the Jesuits contributed to the preservation of the political and social ascendancy of the

24 Astráin, *Historia,* VII, 40-45, 109, 119-128, 195-200.

nobility, to which the crown, somewhat ingenuously, turned as to a reservoir of talent for running the machinery of government. Even before the establishment of the Royal College of Nobles in Madrid, the staff of the Jesuit Imperial College wrote of the priority that should be given to the education of "the sons of princes and nobles, because they are the principal part of the state." [25] Yet, despite this statement, the few Colleges of Nobles, in contrast to the hundred other traditional Jesuit colleges in Spain, represented but a small fraction of the Society's Iberian apostolate.

In the encouraging of an intellectual renaissance the recently created Royal Academy led the way. Two Jesuits, Bartolomé Alcázar and José Casani, both teachers at the College of Nobles in Madrid, founded in 1713 with five other scholars the Royal Academy. Alcázar was particularly active in mathematical and literary circles. Casani, probably the best known Jesuit in Madrid because of his flair for the dramatic and the flamboyant, had an extraordinary power of invention in staging pageants, organizing colorful processions, erecting triumphal arches, creating pompous inscriptions. Both priests and the other members of the Academy achieved mixed results in their effort to lift the nation from its prostrate state. They awakened interest in cultural ideas but uncovered no geniuses. Spaniards cultivated literary expression but did not attain sublime heights. There was no dearth of poets but what was missing was poetry. The outstanding satire in Spanish literature of the eighteenth century, *A Journal of Learned Men*, came from the pen of a Jesuit, Luis de Losada. Another Jesuit, José Francisco de Isla, became the center of a tempest in literary circles by his *Story of the Famous Preacher Fray Gerundio de Campazas* (1758), a biting criticism of the bad taste in the sacred oratory of Spain, not because the work enjoyed any superior literary qualities — it is actually slow-moving and incapable of sustaining interest — but because it was the only novel printed in Castilian in the eighteenth century. It did, however, have a good effect on public taste, and even today among men of letters the terms *Gerundiano, Gerundianismo, Gerundiada* are used to designate the literary profanation of the Spanish pulpit of this era.[26]

Among the embers of cultural ambition the fire of most dis-

25 Ibid., 45; J. Simon-Diaz, *Historia del Colegio Imperial de Madrid* (Madrid, 1952), I, 165; J. Lynch, *Spain under the Habsburgs* (New York, 1969), Vol. II, *Spain and America, 1598-1700*, 130-131.
26 Astráin, *Historia*, VII, 205-213.

ciplines flamed up fitfully. In theology, hampered by a monotonous repetition of the same arguments in the same form, no one made a breakthrough or provided new insights. Philosophy had the same uninspired tale to tell. But in history the taste and love for the documents of the past which animated secular historians of this period passed over to church historians, who began to conduct great mining explorations in the dusty archives of cathedral centers. The affection for erudition which Ruiz de Montoya manifested in the early 1600's did not infect his fellow Spanish Jesuits until a century later when a few men like Andrés Burriel appeared. In 1749 Burriel was on the point of sailing for the California mission when King Ferdinand VI, learning of his vast erudition, summoned him back to undertake the awesome task of filing the vast and rich archives of Toledo. Ferdinand hoped to dig out arguments from history to support the regalist ideas and royal pretensions of the eighteenth century. Whether Burriel realized the king's purpose is not known, but he did a colossal piece of work in raising from oblivion rich treasures of church history. In only four years he examined more than 2,000 documents, made copies from old missals, breviaries, acts of the saints, martyrologies, legal codes, diplomas, the works of St. Isidore.

Jesuits who engaged in writing historical literature, however, did not show the same competence. Bartolomé Alcázar, in his *Chronology of the Society of Jesus in the Province of Toledo* (1710), displayed a like love for documents and citations from letters, but he vitiated his work with the pious purpose of edifying his fellow Jesuits, which led him to suppress important facts and to give infantile explanations of others. Alvaro de Cienfuegos, later a cardinal, published a widely read life of St. Francis Borgia, for a time hailed as the last word in scientific history on the saint. But a comparison of documents quoted by Cienfuegos and the originals casts doubt on the scholarly integrity of the author, who clothed the fruits of his labor in a befittingly deplorable style.[27]

In the spiritual apostolate the Jesuits opened up a new avenue with the retreat movement among priests. Prince among the popular preachers of the era, Pedro de Calatayud, a tall and striking man with a sonorous voice and noble simplicity of style, and a religious of a most austere and selfless life, moved for forty years up and down Spain. In 1739 he had finished at Burgos a brilliant mission at which 5,000 received Holy Communion

27 Ibid., I, xli-xlii; VII, 218.

when the archbishop requested that he give an eight-day retreat to his priests. This he did to 450. Other dioceses took up the idea. In 1753 Calatayud gave two retreats to some 1,200 ecclesiastics. The deeply spiritual personal life of this priest reflected the fervor which then permeated the Spanish provinces.

His name is also prominent in the diffusion of one of the most formative devotions of the age, that to the Sacred Heart of Jesus. This devotion entered Spain along two different avenues, the court and private piety. King Philip V, requested in 1725 by Joseph de Gallifet, the French assistant, to use his influence in obtaining from the Holy See permission for a Mass and Office in honor of the Sacred Heart, became very interested. Two years later the Spanish Jesuits, influenced by De Gallifet's book, *Devotion to the Sacred Heart of Jesus* (1726), began to practice this devotion privately. Gradually it spread. In 1732 at Lorca, Calatayud founded the first Spanish congregation in honor of the Sacred Heart. Many others followed. The spirit of the devotion caught fire among Jesuits and lay people, and it soon became an important feature of the Society's apostolate. Inspired by it was another in the long line of Spanish mystics, Bernardo de Hoyos, who wrote a sensitive account of his supernatural experiences.[28]

In spiritual literature a new trend appeared, a kind of pious moralism which flourished in the eighteenth century. Francisco Garau, gifted with no small measure of originality and ease of style, announced the new fashion with his *The Wise Man Instructed in Human Goodness through Forty Moral Axioms* (1675) and *The Wise Man Instructed in the Life of Grace through Various Maxims and Evangelical Ideas* (1688).

Behind these spiritual and cultural activities rumbled the jarring notes of political complications. The Bourbons, on their entry into Spain, introduced the Jesuits to the role of the king's confessor in that country. Guillaume Daubenton, sent by Louis XIV to accompany Philip V, was the first to assume that powerful post. He served from 1700 to 1705 and from 1716 until his death in 1723. In contravention of the norms for Jesuit confessors of secular rulers drawn up by Aquaviva, Daubenton advised on secular affairs in the government. Especially in the last three years of his life, when Philip V became increasingly withdrawn and there was a dearth of outstanding statesmen, he helped guide the king on political and economic matters. Another Frenchman, who served under Philip V and Ferdinand VI from

28 Ibid., VII, 109-113, 122-128.

1746 to 1747, Jacques Antoine Fèvre, embarrassed the Vatican by his resolute regalistic stance against Rome. The papal secretary of state, Cardinal Silvio Valenti Gonzaga, called him "the dangerous man." The nuncio at Madrid, Cardinal Enrico Enriquez, classified him as "a mortal enemy." Pope Benedict XIV regarded him as an importer of Gallican principles into Spain and as a hostile critic who interpreted the Holy See's rights in Spain to be "swindles on the part of Roman priests." Fèvre's successor, probably the most famous of these royal confessors, was the Spaniard Francisco de Rábago. Rábago supported Ferdinand VI in his contention that the Spanish Inquisition, by reason of earlier papal privilege, enjoyed independence of the Roman Index of Prohibited Books; he assisted in formulating the concordat of 1753 which severely humiliated the Holy See; he helped prevent the implementation of a number of directives from Benedict XIV. In July, 1754, amid internal political maneuvering, the marqués de Ensenada, a friend of the Society, fell from power. Two months later, after seven years of service, Rábago was removed from his post and informed that the inquisitor general would assume the duties of royal confessor. Because the enmity he gained for himself became attached to the Society, many Jesuits were relieved to see him leave office. As one of them expressed it: if thirty men sought a benefice, only one received it, and the royal confessor made twenty-nine enemies not only for himself but also for the Society. Rábago in fact felt the same way himself.[29] While priests like Pedro de Calatayud were lifting their country from its spiritual malaise, the royal confessors were abetting a philosophy of monarchy which within two decades was to turn on the Society and destroy it.

Portugal   For some sixty years a great growth characterized the life of the Society in Portugal. Then in the decade 1750-1760 occurred a series of political convulsions which with startling suddenness left not a single Jesuit free in the land.

Hand in hand with the moderate and steady growth — in 1709 the province numbered 770 men, and forty years later 861 men, with twenty colleges — went an impressive cultural productivity, especially in philosophy, literature, and history. António Cordeiro had the reputation of a philosophical adventurer whose works had certain Cartesian nuances. He enjoyed

---

29 *Ibid.*, 153-157, 165-169; Pastor, *History*, XXXV, 63-66, 367-368; García-Villoslada, *Manual*, pp. 448-451.

a prominent place in *Mercurio filosófico* . . . , the engaging booklet by Francisco António lengthily entitled *A Philosophical Broker, a Work Directed to the Philosophers of Portugal and Designed for the Establishment of Perfect Peace between Ancient and Modern Philosophy* (1752). Ignácio Monteiro, a vigorous and independent thinker, refused to submit to the despotism of older authors. He highlighted the opinion of many Jesuits who, convinced of the need to acknowledge new scientific data, petitioned John V to alter the old statutes of the University of Coimbra which closed the door to anything deviating from traditional doctrine. Despite this petition, in 1746 the king forbade the introduction of any opinions opposed to Aristotle. To mathematics the Jesuits brought fresh vigor. During his generalship Tamburini encouraged in their mathematical work Ignácio Vieira and Giovanni Battista Carbone, an Italian who worked in Portugal. In 1754 Visconti lavishly praised Eusébio de Veiga for his contributions to the same discipline. In the humanities several men, such as José Caeiro, who composed a monumental Latin-Portuguese dictionary which eventually supplanted Bento Pereira's celebrated prosody, went beyond older achievements. Caeiro made another valuable cultural contribution, this time in his historical accounts of the Society's suppression in Portugal wherein with a fine critical sense and a genuine objectivity, in a style both magisterial and free of affectation, he recited the story of the Society's destruction.[30]

This intellectual movement and productivity of the Jesuits had its counterpart in their spiritual counseling which grew in awareness of the rich depths in the devotion to the Sacred Heart of Jesus. This devotion, which had been known in Portugal before 1728 only in an obscure sort of way, received its great impulse from the Far East. In China José Anselino met the remarkable Alsatian missionary, Roman Hinderer, who made the Sacred Heart the central force in his life. Anselino wrote about this devotion to his two brothers, both members of the Order of St. Jerome in Portugal. The Hieronymites spread the news. Other religious communities took it up. In a special way the Jesuits responded to it and incorporated it into the spiritual direction they gave others.

In the apostolate of the Spiritual Exercises the turn of the century was a slackwater time, but Tamburini, by his exhortations to his Portuguese sons, started the flow of the stream again. Two foreigners led the way in popularizing the retreat move-

30 Rodrigues, História, IV, i, 286-293, 337-338.

ment among priests, the widely known Spaniard, Pedro de Calatayud, and the popular Italian of thirty years service in Brazil, Gabriele Malagrida. Soon statistics such as these began to be recorded: 700 ecclesiastics made a retreat in Braga at the Jesuit Church of São Paulo; 300 did so for ten days at Valença; 370 priests made a retreat at Ponte de Leima; 240 at Melgaço; 228 at Guirmarães; 178 at Vila do Conde.[31]

The religious spirit among the Portuguese Jesuits was healthy. Superiors, speaking candidly and without inhibition in their reports to Rome, such as that of the provincial in 1733, gave a detailed picture of fidelity to the Society's ideals. Two works evoked their religious spirit in an especially pronounced way: the service of victims of epidemics and the foreign missions. Up to 1712, 143 had given their lives in the care of the sick. And year after year down the Tagus sailed groups of missionaries, frequently augmented by those of other nations, for China, India, Africa, and Brazil. At mid-century, in 1749, 893 Portuguese Jesuits were laboring in the field afar.[32]

Within five years this vibrant and healthy body was done to death. One man especially achieved this extraordinary feat of destruction. In 1750 Sebastião José de Carvalho e Mello became minister of foreign affairs and war and soon gained the ascendancy in the royal cabinet. A competent, energetic, and ruthless man, with diplomatic experience at London, where he observed the state-controlled church, and at Vienna, where he imbibed the spirit of the Enlightenment, he brought to his service at Lisbon the peculiarly narrow and doctrinaire mentality of the rationalists. Quickly gaining the confidence of the young monarch Joseph I, and thereby assuring his freedom to advance from his "enlightened" encampment against the Church, he determined that among the first ramparts to be taken were those of the Society of Jesus.

Initially Carvalho's relations with the Jesuits at court were cordial. The French ambassador even reported that the new minister owed his office to the influence of the king's Jesuit confessor. But a change came rapidly enough. Two major events in Portuguese history, one foreign and the other domestic, erased Carvalho's warmth and courtesy and arrayed the Society before him as an enemy to be destroyed. The first, the War of the Seven Reductions, which will be seen in detail in the

31 Ibid., 105-106.
32 F. Rodrigues, S.J., "A Companhia de Jesus em Portugal e nas Missões. Esbôço Histórico," *Revista de História*, X (1921), 162.

section on South America, gave him the opportunity to spread
through Europe fantastic stories — so fantastic that the sophis-
ticates of the Enlightenment ridiculed them for their crudity —
about Jesuit machinations. The second, the preaching of the
popular Jesuit, Gabriele Malagrida, after the disastrous earthquake of 1755 in Lisbon, touched a sensitive nerve. In Malagrida's
proclamation that the calamity was the just judgment of an
angry God on a sinful people, Carvalho resented the implication
that his conduct of the government merited censure. Within
five years he had Malagrida executed and all Jesuits either
imprisoned or exiled from Portuguese soil.

The four provinces of France — almost 3,000 men operating in   *France*
1749 eighty-nine colleges and thirty-two seminaries — were
among the most vibrant of the entire Society. Yet they were
among the first to disappear in the gradual destruction of the
order.

Three significant modifications in the life of France, probably
more than anything else, facilitated the Society's downfall: the
change in the intellectual climate effected by the Enlightenment; the rupture in the tradition of a strong central authority
under Louis XIV by the comparatively indolent rule of Louis
XV; the infiltration of a resurgent Jansenism into several of the
parlements of the country.

Though England and France battled through the eighteenth
century in the massive struggle for colonial supremacy, the
intellectual leaders of the two countries entered into a kind of
informal *entente cordiale*. The coinage of Sir Isaac Newton,
John Locke, Matthew Tindal, John Toland, and David Hume
found an avid market in France. Then Frenchmen, while respectful of the English models, issued a currency of their own
with its peculiarly distinctive cut and size. Denis Diderot, the
baron d'Holbach, Jean le Rond d'Alembert, and Voltaire altered,
with shattering completeness, the intellectual landscape of the
nation. The venerable fidelity to the Catholic faith, the luminous
ideal of personal holiness, the deep belief in the supernatural
life of union with God were cut away to make room for a
cynical skepticism, a rather thin and superficial deism, and
even a refined species of atheism.

The saving of France's religious heritage the Jesuits regarded
as a mandate. But they entered the conflict with a severe
handicap. Effective as the author's pen might be, the most
sensitive sounding board for new ideas had moved from the
university lecture hall to the elegant salon of the gracious host

297

or hostess. With exquisite charm women like Madame du Deffand, Madame d'Épinay, and Madame Geoffrin received the *philosophes* into their drawing rooms, which tinkled with fresh opinions formulated in vivacious, witty, and refined language. The baron d'Holbach, knight-errant of atheism and publicly committed to the destruction of religion, in his splendid country and city homes reigned as monarch in the realm of the salon. Often enough the Jesuits were the victims of the barbed quip. The Neapolitan Abate Ferdinando Galiani, a jack-in-the-box personification of perpetual motion, told his delighted hearers about his study of military tactics and how he personally believed that soldiers on the attack would be more effective with longer bayonets and shorter rifles, like the Jesuits, who lengthen the creed and shorten the commandments. And a round of laughter must have gone through Paris at Voltaire's mischievous lines about René-Joseph Tournemine, one of his Jesuit teachers:

> C'est notre Père Tournemine
> Qui croit tout ce qu'il imagine.[33]

In 1722 the duchesse d'Orléans, "Madame," wrote that she did not think that there were a hundred people in Paris, clerics as well as laymen, who believed in Christ.

But private homes did not monopolize the ranks of the *avant-garde*. Throughout the country, clubs, cafés, academies, *sociétés de pensée* were the pegs which held over France the broad web of the Enlightenment. Amid the murmur arising from so many quarters the leaders of this novel intellectual trend stood over their planning boards, traced their grand strategy, and formulated as one of their objectives the prompt eviction of the Jesuits, not indeed as their ultimate goal but as an essential step toward the more ambitious design of the complete eradication of the Catholic Church from the soil of France. Determined on an internal revolution which would snap the links between the kingdom and the traditional faith, and realizing that they encountered the greatest obstacle in the Society of Jesus, they openly announced that the Jesuits had to be crushed. Voltaire, a pupil of the Jesuits, despite a certain nostalgic admiration for his former masters, judged that they had to be sacrificed. To Claude Adrien Helvetius he wrote: "Once we have destroyed the Jesuits we shall hold a good hand against the detestable thing." Despite their powdered wigs,

---

33 P. Hazard, *European Thought in the Eighteenth Century* (New Haven, 1954), pp. 228-229. A. Desautels, S.J., *Les Mémoires de Trévoux et le mouvement des idées au XVIIIᵉ siècle* (Rome, 1956), p. 9.

delicate minuets, cultivated language, the men of the eighteenth century could be brutal, vicious, and inhumane.[34] The Jesuits faced an implacable enemy, one of the strongest cultural movements in the history of western civilization.

The second significantly sharp change in France took place at the court. Following the strong authoritarian rule of Louis XIV, that of Louis XV, who became monarch at the age of five, was marked by incompetence and absence of initiative. The period of this chapter embraces the last twenty-eight years of the reign of the Sun King and the first forty-two of his successor. Both monarchs placed the Society in peril, Louis XIV by the abuse of authority as the active engineer of a potential schism in the body of the Society, and Louis XV, with a natural dislike for government, by his failure in energetic and imaginative leadership, which opened the dikes to the onrush of forces which were to sweep away the Society ten years before the end of his reign. Every school boy knows his famous evaluation of his own reign: "Après moi le déluge."

Louis XIV confronted Tirso González with a difficult problem soon after his election. This problem arose from the conquests the monarch made in the lower area of the Hapsburg Netherlands which, in the Society's organization, belonged to the German Assistancy. He requested that the Gallo-Belgian Province be transferred to the French Assistancy. Earlier, during the latter part of De Noyelle's term, he had made this request but did not press the ailing and distracted general. But with the election of González he reopened the question. De la Chaize warned the general: "We have to treat with a king who, while extremely devoted to the Society, is nevertheless most tenacious in holding to his decisions." [35] González hesitated. Louis moved with dispatch. On April 25, 1689, he ordered the French assistant, Paul Fontaine, and all Frenchmen in the Society's curia to quit Rome and return to France. He allowed no contact with the general.

A sense of doom fell over the French Jesuits. González judged that he did not have power to delegate a superior for the Society in France unless the superior enjoyed free and open communication with him. This decision left an acephalous body of men. Fontaine found wide criticism of the general among the French Jesuits, haunted by the fear that they, even though unwillingly, were slipping into schism. During these dark hours

34 A. Sorel, *Europe Under the Old Regime* (New York, 1964), p. 69.
35 Guitton, *Le Père de la Chaize*, II, 81.

De la Chaize kept alive their hopes and aspirations that they be able to preserve their union with the rest of the Society. In August, 1689, Louis ordered De la Chaize and Fontaine to convoke the five provincials and "other delegates" to elect a vicar-general for France. De la Chaize felt that this delicate situation could best be handled by restricting the numbers at the meeting. He therefore limited the "other delegates" to four ex-provincials, including himself as former provincial of Lyons.

Through October and November these ten men, who did not want to elect a vicar-general on their own responsibility, discussed their agonizing problem. They finally decided to appeal to Pope Alexander VIII. They wrote the pontiff that they felt that the solution rested with one of several possibilities: either the pope could oblige González to accede to Louis' wishes about the Gallo-Belgian Province; or he could himself delegate a vicar for France; or he could give power to the French Jesuits to elect a superior; or finally, he could adopt some other method he himself might devise. In a kind and sympathetic answer to De la Chaize, Alexander chose the first suggestion, compliance with the desires of Louis XIV. González promised prompt obedience. The road between him and the French Jesuits was opened. On June 10, 1690, Fontaine was back in Rome. Negotiations followed, the colleges in conquered Belgian territory were attached to the Province of Champagne, the rest of the Gallo-Belgian Province remained in the German Assistancy but under the direction of a Frenchman as provincial. It was a happy outcome of a desperate situation in which some of the finest provinces of the Society were pushed by the strong arm of the king to the brink of severance from their general.

De la Chaize, whose understanding, moderate spirit and tact did so much to ease the French Jesuits through this crisis, at the same time helped to relieve the great tension which had built up between the papacy and the French crown. When Pope Innocent XI died on April 12, 1689, thirty-five sees in France were vacant. He had refused to confirm the appointment as bishop of any priest who took part in the Assembly of the Clergy which issued the Four Gallican Articles in 1682. The two succeeding popes, Alexander VIII and Innocent XII, wanted to end this feud. In the vast correspondence between Rome and France which unfolds the intricate negotiations wherein both sides made concessions, including the royal annulment of the decree that the Four Gallican Articles must be taught in the seminaries, the pacific, irenic, moderate voice of De la Chaize constantly speaks up for the calm use of reason and charity.

Where Louis XIV endangered the Society by his initiative and headstrong action, Louis XV did so by his natural disinclination to stay at the helm and fight his way through a political tempest. A contemporary remarked of him: "A void is ruling France." This was not completely just, because Louis, not the utterly apathetic and indolent ruler that some would picture him to be, could at times summon up the steel-like resources of the best of the Capetian line. Besides, at his side for nearly twenty years stood his beautiful, intelligent, and adroit favorite, Jeanne Antoinette Poisson, marquise de Pompadour, whose desires and inclinations guided strategic decisions of state and court. To determine the degree of influence, if any, which *la favorite* exerted on the precise issue of the Society's presence in France is most difficult. The Encyclopedists she protected; among the *philosophes* she found congenial company; with delight she received the sprightly verses with which Voltaire hailed her. Yet, despite her obvious predilections and her easy entrée to the king's mind, Louis in several crises of state resolutely placed the crown on the side of the Jesuits. He acted with personal conviction but without that measure of grit which might have carried him to victory.

The third significant change in the structure of France was the installment of an energetic and ardent Jansenist spirit in the Parlements of the country. Reanimated by the engaging and subtle ex-Oratorian, Pasquier Quesnel, the Jansenists not only stirred up new flames from the embers of past controversy but also shifted drastically the terrain of the conflict. Where Arnauld, professing loyalty to Rome, had contended that the thing called Jansenism was merely a bogey invented by the Jesuits, and that therefore papal denunciations of this fiction did not apply to him and his associates, Quesnel directly challenged the extent of papal power and its claim to obedience. Still more, in a style which combined unction and violence, he lifted Jansenism out of the restricted circle influenced by Port-Royal and brought it to large segments of the middle and even lower classes.

This extension of Jansenism widened the field of animosity toward the Society. In the late seventeenth century and in the eighteenth it took root in Champagne where the bishops of several important sees, Sens, Reims, Troyes, Châlons-sur-Marne, made a militant show of their Jansenist convictions, notably Gaston de Noailles, bishop of Châlons-sur-Marne from 1695 to 1720, who placed the Jesuits under interdict. Burgundy too entered into the heritage of Port-Royal. This Jansenist presence made itself felt on the enrollment at some of the Jesuit schools.

Although statistics are not sufficiently precise to give an exact demonstration of the relation between Jansenist hostility and the drop in the number of Jesuit students, it is noteworthy, for example, that the Society's records for 1727 show that where the Jansenists were strongest the enrollment in the colleges dropped most radically. And in 1761 the Jesuit reports indicated that the Sodality of the Blessed Virgin had been prohibited in the same dioceses.[36]

The Jansenists scored a particularly great strategic success by the conversion of strong groups, and in some cases the majority, in the Parlements to their creed and spirit. The implications of this success became especially clear when the branch of Jansenism was grafted to the ancient trunk of Gallicanism. This new combination forced the clarification of the stand of the French Jesuits toward Gallicanism, highlighting the distinction between their repudiation of its theological form and their adherence to its political expression. Two events in 1713 elucidated this distinction: first, the appearance of several Jesuit superiors before the Parlement of Paris; and second, the promulgation of the constitution *Unigenitus* by Clement XI against the Jansenists.

In March, 1713, the provincial of the Province of France, the rectors of the professed house, the college, and the novitiate presented themselves in the chambers of the Parlement. As had happened a century earlier, a Jesuit published a book which aroused murmurings in Gallican circles and which forced the fathers in Paris to explain their position in regard to the prerogatives of the French monarch. In 1710 Joseph de Jouvancy (Juvencius), one of France's most distinguished pedagogues, published the fifth volume of his *History of the Society of Jesus,* in which he narrated the story of the Society's expulsion from France in 1594 and the condemnation by Parlement of Bellarmine, Suárez, and Santarelli. His presentation tipped the scales on the side of the Society and against the Parlement. Storm clouds began to gather, but on March 23, 1713, the Jesuit superiors in Paris went to the court of law to express their views on De Jouvancy's *History.* It was with sorrow, they said, that they saw the publication of a work in which the author was so clearly at fault in his sympathy toward theologians "so justly condemned by your decrees of the years 1610 and following." They spoke

36 F. de Dainville, S.J., "Effectifs des collèges et scolarité aux xviie et xviiie siècles dan le nord-est de la France," *Population,* X (1955), 470–472.

clearly: "We are convinced that this court . . . will give us the justice of believing that we are far removed from adopting such sentiments, that we hold it a great honor to appear here, that no one could be more submissive than ourselves nor more inviolably attached to the laws and maxims of this kingdom concerning the regal rights and power which in temporal affairs depends neither directly nor indirectly on any other power on earth, God alone being above it." They simply reiterated that political Gallicanism already a century-old among them.[37]

Despite this clearcut dedication to their king they were regarded as militantly loyal to the pope. The Jansenist controversy proved that. In September 8, 1713, Pope Clement XI issued his constitution *Unigenitus,* a condemnation of Jansenist teaching as contained in one hundred and one passages extracted from Quesnel's *Moral Reflections on the New Testament.* In a stinging riposte the Jansenists hit back, and Quesnel denounced the *Unigenitus* as a work of iniquity and Clement as a doctor of lies. The Jesuits accepted battle on this new terrain of direct assault on the papacy and with energy defended Clement's action. This allegiance to Rome earned for them the name "Ultramontane." True sons of the Church, they remained true sons of France. Papal in the realm of the sacral, they nevertheless professed Gallicanism in the realm of the secular.

Three important changes, therefore, the intellectual climate of the age, the temper of the royal court, and the character of the Parlements made the Society's tenure in France a precarious one. But the Jesuits did not lack resources in their struggle for survival. For over a half-century, between 1701-1762, they published a monthly magazine, *Journal de Trévoux,* which served as a mouthpiece against the *philosophes.* Conceived by Jacques Philippe Lallemant and Michel Le Tellier and backed financially by the Duc du Maine, natural son of Louis XIV, the *Journal* was first published at Trévoux, capital of the duke's principality of Dombes. At first largely bibliographical in nature, presenting abstracts of current noteworthy books and limiting critical comment to those works which attacked religion, it gradually broadened its purpose to include an evaluation of all the intellectual contributions of the age.[38]

37 Blet, "Jésuites Gallicans," *AHSJ,* XXIX (1960), 81-82.
38 Desautels, *Les Mémoires,* pp. vi-xvi; G. Dumas, S.J., *Histoire du Journal de Trévoux* (Paris, 1936), pp. 1-20. The complete original title was *Journal de Trévoux. Mémoires pour servir à l'histoire des sciences et des arts.* Occasionally scholars refer to the *Journal* informally as *Mémoires de Trévoux.*

If it were at all possible to span the gap between the thought of the Enlightenment and the Catholic faith, the *Journal de Trévoux* would have been that unique bridge. The *philosophes* and the Jesuits had many common interests in the widening intellectual world, of which one central and dominant preoccupation was the idea of human nature. In the protracted debate with the Jansenists the Jesuits, while denying their opponents' position that human nature had been essentially vitiated by original sin, affirmed the integrity of man's natural powers, and in their humanistic tradition they positively cultivated them. This esteem for the nature of man was part of the intellectual inheritance which the *philosophes* received from the earlier century, and because of this mutual interest the Jesuits were the one group in the Church which had the capacity, if it were at all possible, to hammer out an accommodation to the new trends of thought.

The Jesuit reaction to the appearance of Diderot's *Encyclopédie* gave the measure of the Society's openness to an intellectual enterprise of this kind. The first issue of the *Encyclopédie* appeared in July, 1751. In the October number of *Journal de Trévoux*, Guillaume Berthier, the editor, greeted the new publication and wished it well. He composed a full and careful synopsis of d'Alembert's *Discours préliminaire,* and suggested that the editors of the *Encyclopédie* indicate their sources and use quotation marks when directly citing other works. In November, Berthier saluted the *Encyclopédie* as a noble and mighty enterprise and prophesied that the editors would, on the completion of their work, be able to quote Horace's *Exegi monumentum aere perennius.* In 1752, through the first three months, he followed up his earlier suggestion on the acknowledgement of authorities, and revealed some interesting fruits of his personal research. In the first volume of the *Encyclopédie* appeared over a hundred articles which, either in whole or in part, had been extracted word for word and without acknowledgment from other works, especially technical maritime and commercial dictionaries. He also revealed that some parts of the *Encyclopédie* had been lifted directly from the writings of the Jesuit, Claude Buffier, who had died fifteen years earlier. Diderot's claim that he and his colleagues were pioneers sagged somewhat before this proof of plagiarism. Berthier, despite the results of his detective work, remained open to the positive contributions of the *philosophes.* He supported the experimental method in science, intellectual curiosity and the use of reason, and the idea of progress in human society. Against the critics of Descartes, Gassendi, Newton, and Leibniz he wrote, "Is it not these philosophers who have perfected astronomy, geography, navigation, and most of the arts?" In his conviction that philosophy had worked for the world's enlightenment against "ignorance, heresy and enthusiasm," Berthier worked for an understanding with the intelligentsia of the age.[39]

Gradually, however, the possibility of harmony between the Jesuits and the *philosophes* dissipated. Against open hostility to the idea of the supernatural, divine revelation, and the mysteries of the Catholic faith, the Society had to take a strong stand. Even the central ideas of the integrity of human nature and the dignity of human reason, which might have marked out an area of friendly contact, became distant poles of separation. Deeply involved in the advance of the sciences and absorbed in physical phenomena, the *philosophes* thought in terms of empiricism. Many Jesuits also valued the data of science, but insisted on something more, a strong metaphysics. The *philosophes* could not allow for the supernatural. The Jesuits could. A mighty struggle therefore developed. The Jesuits wrote in defense of the faith staunchly enough but on a level of style that did not match the verve, smartness, and wit of Voltaire. They presented their arguments intelligently and with a breadth of erudition and understanding, but under Voltaire's withering scorn the prestige of their journal shrank and its editors lost much of their original optimism.[40]

In a way more fundamental than style the Society did not rise to the full measure of the serious challenge of the age. The theological questions raised by the deists called for ingenuity to discover new approaches and new ideas, but in general the Jesuits relied on the older ways devised by earlier generations who faced very different problems. Becoming more tied to the textbook, theology became atrophied. There were exceptions,

39 Robert R. Palmer, *Catholics and Unbelievers in Eighteenth Century France* (Princeton, 1939), pp. 18-19. The Jesuit defense of the essential integrity of human nature against the Jansenists was branded by them as an alliance with the Enlightenment. One Jansenist dictum was: Molinism and Deism are twin brothers. See John N. Pappas, "Berthier's Journal de Trévoux and the Philosophers," *Studies on Voltaire and the Eighteenth Century*, ed. T. Besterman (Geneva, 1957), III, pp. 3, 198, 217. For a list of articles on metaphysics in the *Encyclopédie* taken in whole or in part from the works of Buffier, see Kathleen S. Wilkins, "A Study of the Works of Claude Buffier," *Studies on Voltaire and the Eighteenth Century*, ed. T. Besterman (Geneva, 1969), LXVI, p. 178.
40 Desautels, *Les Mémoires*, pp. xiii-xiv.

notably Jean Hardouin. This litterateur, linguist, historian, philosopher, and theologian received a commission from the Assembly of the Clergy in 1687 to reedit the councils of the Church. In his eleven-volume edition he produced one of the most solid and erudite works of the early eighteenth century. A prodigious worker and the soul of generosity, Hardouin frequently found himself in trouble because of his somewhat bizarre and extremely original opinions, but his intellectual oddities appear tiny against the great mass of his work. One critic made the observation: "For forty years he labored to ruin his reputation but without succeeding."

In philosophy the faculties in the colleges generally ranged themselves against the Cartesian influence, which had touched so much of France's thinking. But Malebranche, who gave a certain religious tinge and attractive literary form to the currents of philosophy, aroused a sympathy among a number of Jesuits. Adventuresome Yves André pronounced: *Hors Malebranche et Descartes, en philosophie, pas de salut.* The general congregations of 1687, 1696, and 1706 voiced concern about the impact of modern authors on scholasticism, and they proscribed a number of propositions. Nevertheless, in theses printed in the colleges and in notes dictated in class which advocated clear and distinct ideas as the norm of certitude and which sedulously avoided such consecrated scholastic terms as "substantial form," the spirit of the distinguished alumnus of La Flèche was present.[41] But the general trend of Jesuit thinking found a synthesis in Gabriel Daniel's critical *A Trip through the World of Descartes,* published in 1699. In the form of an imagined conversation with a dyed-in-the-wool Cartesian, Daniel cleverly pressed his dialogist about the world as conceived by Descartes. By this device he criticized the Cartesian hypothesis of vortices as being neither accurate nor widely accepted. Pleasant and engagingly presented, *A Trip through the World of Descartes* went into several editions in English, Spanish, Italian, and Latin.

In this conflict for the mind of France, even more substantial than the resources which the Society had in the *Journal de Trévoux* was the wide network of schools. Here the classical tradition held the ascendance and shared in the final flourish of the Great Century. Bouhours lived for two years in the eighteenth century; De Jouvancy, nineteen years. Teachers kept up the flow of new editions of the classics. Gabriel Le Jay and Charles Porée continued the brilliance and panache of the Jesuit

41 Brucker, *La Compagnie,* pp. 775-776.

dramatic tradition by their Latin comedies and tragedies, marked by verve and originality. Le Jay also created several ballets. To answer critics of the Society's theatrical activities, Porée composed a didactic ballet in 1726 entitled *The Education of Man through Drama*. The Jesuit dramatic efforts in the French language, however, did not match in liveliness and sparkle the Latin works. Save for those of Joseph Antoine de Cerceau, the plays in the vernacular did not rise above the mediocre. In another area of literary creation, Claude Buffier published *A New French Grammar* (1709). The French Academy adopted it as the best then in existence.

Despite the impressive strength of the educational edifice, cracks began to appear. One was the rigidity of the syllabus. Between 1687 and 1716 occurred the famous and far-reaching "Conflict between the Ancients and the Moderns." Inspired by the fecundity of the literature of "The Great Century," fatigued by the constant return to the themes and imagery of the Greek and Roman classics, impelled by the ideal of progress which the onward movement of science had injected into art and literature, the intelligentsia turned against tradition and authority. Imitation of the ancients as a literary principle fell into disrepute. The guidance of literary taste moved from the hands of the scholar into those of the social elite, including women. The salon replaced the lecture hall as the judgment seat of literary merit. The most influential works of the eighteenth century placed art at the service of science in a great movement of *vulgarisation*. During the first sixty years or more of the century, this cultural tide ran strong and sustained a steady enthusiasm, on the popular level, for reading in the humanities and especially the descriptions of new inventions and machines. Through the years 1730-1760, probably more than any other thirty years in French history, the bourgeoisie became of a sudden an educated class, taken up with literature in which the style was light and agreeable in contrast to the solemn tomes of the professionally learned. Many Jesuits, hailing this great corpus of readable and informative literature, spoke, as did the deists, of living in an age "so enlightened as ours." [42]

But the Jesuit class in humanities continued on the beam that was transmitted by the *Ratio studiorum* of 1599. In 1703 De Jouvancy firmly asserted what the generation formed in the atti-

---

42 R. R. Palmer, "The French Jesuits in the Age of the Enlightenment," *American Historical Review*, XLV (1939), 54-55.

tudes of the Moderns would never accept, that no man, unless he be an expert in Greek, is educated. Educational experience through the centuries, distilled in such a Jesuit assembly as the International Conference on the Apostolate of Secondary Schools, held in Rome in 1963, heightened the limitations of De Jouvancy's inflexibility. This Conference stated: "The concept of humanism is not itself identified with any specific category of subjects as such. It implies a connection with permanent human values even if the forms of these values differed, for example, in the sixteenth, eighteenth, or twentieth centuries." [43] In 1763, sixty years after De Jouvancy's pronouncement, the Jesuit emphasis on Latin came under severe fire by Louis René de la Chalotais, who growled that hardly ten out of a thousand alumni, even with a full course in the humanities and philosophy, could write a good letter. "The work given them," he said, "is so monotonous that it inevitably leads to idleness and boredom. Always Latin and composition!" Sensitive to the strong stratum of truth amid the layers of De la Chalotais' immoderate language, Claude Buffier, in a spirit of innovation at Collège Louis-le-Grand, sought from 1701 on a freer and wider curriculum. [44]

This fresh approach by Buffier and others notwithstanding, the Jesuit schools did not graduate, with the exception of the learned Breton, graceful writer, and founder of *Année littéraire*, Élie Fréron, any outstanding lay champions of the faith, who by their erudition, modernity, and articulateness could command the attention of the nation and expose the many chinks in the intellectual armor of the rationalists. Among the thousands of Jesuit lay alumni, the men of the Enlightenment, rather than meeting effective contenders, found some of their own more influential leaders, such as Voltaire and Charles Auguste de Ferriol, comte d'Argental, from the Collège Louis-le-Grand in Paris, Denis Diderot from the Collège de Langres, and Jean Antoine Nicolas de Caritat, marquis de Condorcet, from the Collège des Bons Enfants in Reims.

43 "International Conference on the Apostolate of Secondary Schools, Rome, September 2nd to 4th, 1963," *Jesuit Educational Quarterly*, XXVII (1964), 57-58.

44 J. W. Donohue, S.J., *Jesuit Education: An Essay on the Foundations of Its Idea* (New York, 1963), pp. 64, 89; Wilkins, "Claude Buffier," pp. 31-63. In physics, mechanics, and mathematics in eighteenth-century France the Oratorians gave the best instruction. See J. N. Moody, in a review of *The Development of Technical Education in France, 1500-1850* by F. B. Artz (Cambridge, Mass., 1966) in *The Catholic Historical Review*, LV (1969), 476-477.

For a wide variety of reasons the enrollment in several schools dropped drastically through the eighteenth century. The college at Châlons-sur-Marne, for example, had 400 students on its register in 1629, only eighty-five in 1737, and 100 in 1761; the college at Reims had 924 in 1629, seventy-five in 1743, and seventy in 1761; the one at Dijon had 860 in 1629, 480 in 1734, and 294 in 1761. The twenty-one colleges of the entire Jesuit Province of Champagne (the civil provinces of Champagne, Burgundy, Lorraine, Barrois, and Alsace) dropped from 5,678 students in 1629 to 3,021 in 1761. Epidemics, famine, and war, especially in the frontier towns, accounted for many of the decreases. So did fluctuations in the cost of living in relation to the wheat market. And in some areas Jansenism contributed its own peculiar erosive influence.[45]

Bound as they had become to a formalized kind of classicism in the schools, and sharp as was the drop in the numbers of their students, outside the classroom and in the field of spiritual literature the Jesuits preserved a freshness and vitality. The condemnation of Quietism brought on a reaction which led in general to a constrained and timid piety and dry asceticism, but among the French Jesuits it did not rupture their ties with the exalted spiritual temper of the seventeenth century. In the celebrated controversy which involved Bossuet, Fénelon, and Madame Guyon they had no considerable part, although in the *Journal de Trévoux* they could not conceal their sympathies for the cultivated and personable bishop of Cambrai, without accepting his Semi-Quietist doctrines, rather than for the authoritarian and unaccommodating bishop of Meaux. And then they produced some exceptional writers on spiritual subjects. Claude Judde (1661-1735) not only showed no trace of anti-mysticism but revealed an enthusiasm for Jean Joseph Surin. Although he himself did not publish, after his death one of his novices, Jacques Lenoir-Duparc, issued his works in seven volumes. A contemporary of Judde, Jean Croiset, continued with abundant literature the propagation of devotion to the Sacred Heart. The most famous of all, and the one who still exercises a wide influence, was Jean Pierre Caussade. Alive to the milieu in which mysticism had become a bad word, Caussade applied his pen directly against this antipathy for anything that suggested higher prayer. But his memory remains primarily because of his teaching on abandonment of the soul to Divine Providence. In the nineteenth century, Henri Ramière gathered Caussade's letters

45 De Dainville, "Effectifs . . . ," *Population*, X (1955), 456-472.

to Visitation nuns in which he developed the principle of trustful abandon to God, and organized them for the sake of order into a treatise entitled *Self-Abandonment to Divine Providence* (1861). A wide success, it today remains a spiritual classic of great popularity. Dom David Knowles judges that a place would have to be found for Caussade in a list of the ten greatest spiritual directors since St. Bernard.[46]

Germany and Central Europe   Central Europe at this period resembled a kaleidoscope, so varied were the patterns of cultural and political life. There was the growth of state absolutism, perfected by Joseph II; the decline in classical studies; the ascendancy of French culture; the beginnings of enthusiasm for the German tongue after 1760; the skepticism of the Enlightenment and the rationalism of Leibniz and Wolff; the distaste for theological polemics and the rise of pietism; the hollowness of university life around 1680 and the impulse for freedom of research and thought centered at Halle after 1720; the series of important wars, that of the Spanish Succession, the Austrian Succession, and the Seven Years. All of these, intruding themselves in one way or another into the Society's history, make a perfectly focused picture difficult to attain.

Three influences were especially important: state control of education; the drastic shift in the intellectual and cultural milieu; the geometric mold of philosophy as propounded by Christian von Wolff. Through the reigns of Charles VI, Maria Theresa, and Joseph II the Austrian state widened its hold on education. On October 2, 1770, Maria Theresa, proclaiming a principle which Joseph II applied even more rigorously than she, said that "the school is and remains a political matter." Austria set the tone for the other Catholic German states, and its autocratic procedure, of which the educational reform program of 1772 was an instance, was carried on the four winds, producing a bewildering harvest of directives about methods, textbooks, and procedures.[47]

Control of the universities was a prime objective. Under Maria Theresa, in the decade between 1750 and 1760, Gerhard

46 J. P. de Caussade, S.J., *Self-Abandonment to Divine Providence* (London, 1959), p. v.
47 Duhr, *Geschichte*, IV, ii, 29, 37-38; Charles H. O'Brien, "Ideas of Religious Toleration at the Time of Joseph II. A Study of the Enlightenment among Catholics in Austria," *Transactions of the American Philosophical Society Held at Philadelphia for Promoting Useful Knowledge*, new series (LIX) Part 7 (Philadelphia, 1969), p. 31.

van Swieten gradually tied higher education to the state. Behind him stood a strange alliance of Jansenists and advocates of the Enlightenment. The Jansenists in the Hapsburg lands, far removed from the old theological preoccupations of Antoine Arnauld and Blaise Pascal, espoused a secular, humanitarian, and even Erastian outlook which linked them to the Austrian *Aufklärer*. Behind their intellectual congeniality Cardinal Bartolomeo Pacca discerned another common bond: their hostility to the Society of Jesus.

This hostility was impressively effective. Professors formed in the mentality of the Enlightenment, such as Paul Joseph von Riegger, Karl Anton von Martini, and Joseph von Sonnenfels, replaced the Jesuits in the university chairs of law. Simon Ambrosius Stock, Jansenist auxiliary bishop of Vienna, headed the theological faculty at the University of Vienna from 1759 to 1772. He dismissed the Jesuits and installed Jansenists. Victories of this kind the Jansenists recorded in their *Nouvelles ecclésiastiques*. A story for November 12, 1760, for example, related that Maria Theresa had decreed that two chairs of theology be given the Dominicans and the Augustinians in all universities of her states, determined as she was "to wipe out the corrupt doctrine spread abroad by the Jesuits." Stock's successor at the University of Vienna was the influential Benedictine abbot of Braunau, Franz Stephan Rautenstrauch, also a Jansenist and an exponent, albeit in a moderate way, of the Austrian government's anticurialist position. His theological reform, in several ways a progressive one, postdated the Society's suppression.[48]

Outside Austria the most influential churchman was Johann Nikolaus von Hontheim, who in 1763 published under the pen name Justinus Febronius his widely read *The Church and the Legitimate Power of the Roman Pontiff*. Almost immediately the Jesuits in Trier, the see where Von Hontheim was auxiliary bishop, felt the impact of this forceful work. A year after its appearance they were removed from their positions on the faculty of theology. Benedictines replaced them. Then university after university, Cologne, Freiburg-im-Breisgau, Mainz, Würzburg capitulated to the state-orientated theology, removed the Jesuits, and sanctioned a cisalpine frame of mind which gradually isolated the German Church from the Holy See. Then followed the terrible chasm between the papacy and the three

48 M. U. Maynard, *The Studies and Teaching of the Society of Jesus at the Time of Its Suppression, 1750–1773* (Baltimore and London, 1855), pp. 143-146; O'Brien, "Ideas of Religious Toleration," pp. 31-33, 53.

archiepiscopal electorates of Cologne, Mainz, and Trier, which widened through the years up to the French Revolution.

Contemporaneously with these external setbacks, the interior state of theology in the hands of the Jesuits, while solid, lacked originality and breadth of vision. This was the age of the epigones, those scholars who devoted their energies to the condensation of the masters of the past and pounded their doctrines into formulae and formats manageable in the schools. The manual burgeoned and in the process unhappily came between the students and the original writings of the Church's great thinkers. This new style reached man's estate in the set of fourteen volumes published between 1766 and 1771 by professors at Würzburg. Three Jesuits, Heinrich Kilber, Thomas Holzklau, and Ignaz Neubauer, responded to the request of the bishop of Würzburg and produced a valuable work, at once a skillful analysis and synthesis, the *Dogmatic-Polemical-Scholastic-Moral Theology* in fourteen volumes (1766-1771), popularly known as *Theologia Wirceburgensis.* This formidable achievement represents the most important cooperative theological work by the Jesuits of this age.

Among individual theologians two Jesuits best reflect the modern intellectual currents. Vitus Pichler and Benedikt Stattler answered the need for a fresh kind of apologia for the Church and its teaching. Apologetics, understood as an accounting for, a justification and defense of the Church, has always been, even from apostolic times, a task for Christian intellectuals. Its mode has changed with the spirit of each age. Pichler and Stattler gave clear accentuation to a fresh approach by constructing, in the face of the Enlightenment, a demonstration of the possibility and fact of divine revelation. Pichler, the successor at Cologne of one of the Society's greatest canonists, Franz Xaver Schmalzgrueber, has been saluted as the father of the tract known as Fundamental Theology. This new feature dominated Catholic theology for the remaining years of the eighteenth century and the early part of the nineteenth. Stattler, more enterprising and intellectually engaged on a wider scale, attempted what many Catholics desired: a renewal of Catholic thought and adaptation to current needs. He put aside what he called "the yoke of scholasticism" and endeavored to take account of scientific progress and modern metaphysics. Because of what were judged to be concessions to Wolff and Febronius, a number of his works were listed on the *Index of Forbidden Books.* Not at all the least fascinating of the persons of his age, Stattler represented an important period in the history of the Church's apologia.

Other scholars deepened the well of positive theology. The valuable *Collection of the German Councils* (1759) is a monument to the industry of Gaspar Hartzheim, known as the Labbe of Germany, of Aegidius Neissen, and Hermann Scholl. The same kind of valuable work for the understanding of the Hungarian Church came from the scholarship of Károly Peterffy in his edition of *The Sacred Councils of Hungary* (1741).

The absolutist thrust of the Austrian government inevitably affected the Jesuits in the colleges as it had done in the universities. This occurred during a period of important shifts in the intellectual and cultural climate of Germany. Subtly new aspirations infiltrated German life as the older ideal of the learned man whose refinement was largely measured by his competence in Latin prose and poetry lost its hold on the imagination of the people. With French civilization forming lively centers in the numerous courts of Germany, each seeking to be a miniature Versailles, classical studies by the turn of the century had gone into serious decline. In Protestant schools the teachers of poetry and rhetoric joined Catholics in loud lament over the decadence of Latin.

The Jesuit colleges became fields of combat in an Austrian version of "The Conflict between the Ancients and the Moderns." From Rome, speaking for tradition, and from Vienna, representing innovation, they received disparate directives. On June 16, 1731, the general, Retz, while recommending history for the curriculum, advised the Austrian provincial that he wanted Latin and Greek retained. A little more than twenty years later, on July 22, 1752, Visconti suggested that each teacher be provided with a copy of *For Christian Teachers of Literature. A Way to Learn and Instruct* (1691), written in Latin by one of the most articulate Jesuit advocates of the classical languages, Joseph de Jouvancy. The Jesuits throughout Germany and Austria responded energetically and endeavored with fine new dictionaries and further editions of Virgil, Horace, Ovid, and Cicero to keep their Latin program fresh and vigorous. Greek, which had fallen on desperately bad days, they tried to restore to a place of prestige with new volumes which bore dates between 1730 and 1750. But it was an autumnal sunshine that vanished with the Society's suppression.

At the same time the Austrian government in its own successive programs for secondary education was determined to stress the importance of mathematics, science, and history in the curriculum. The Jesuit response was unenthusiastic. On February 7, 1733, Retz wrote to the royal confessor asking that he obtain

313

for the Society's schools freedom to pursue their own syllabus. In 1751 the Austrian Jesuits in their provincial congregation expressed their discontent with the government's directives. But the next year the government insisted on compliance. During these uneasy years a reaction had set in against French culture as an alien plant, and the Germans, at first hesitatingly and then with confident strides, moved toward the cultivation of their own tongue. The Jesuits moved with the tide. As early as 1735 Franz Wagner developed a plan for fostering German expression. The next year Franz Xaver Kropf did the same. In 1755 Georg Herman explicated the idea of written exercises in German. And this new interest continued through the succeeding years.[49]

Sensitive as were the Jesuits to national influence in language studies, they reacted with more crucial and far-reaching results to changes in the field of philosophy. In the early part of the century on the German university scene appeared Christian von Wolff. In an atmosphere of tension between the old peripatetic school and the champions of the new science, Wolff, looking to Euclid as his model, set out to devise a method to dissipate the common vagueness in terminology by arriving at distinct and fixed concepts. Under the influence of Leibniz, who made the primacy of essence the core of his metaphysics, he brought this central preoccupation into his theory of method. In this system, in which metaphysics became a kind of geometry of being and deduction was supreme, he lined up a chain of definitions, link after link, derived from clear and distinct concepts. In his textbook he gave German rationalism a local habitation. Several German Jesuits were among the first to be duped by Wolff. While criticizing the inventor on certain points of doctrine, men like Sigmund von Storchenau and Benedikt Stattler organized their manuals according to his method, format, and arrangement of matter. The Austrian Jesuits broke with the old organization of philosophy and adopted the new. The significance of this change extended far beyond the immediate precincts of the later eighteenth century, for the Jesuits became, among others both Catholic and Protestant, the channels by which German rationalism penetrated much of philosophy in the nineteenth and current centuries.[50]

49 Duhr, *Geschichte*, IV, ii, 5-6, 19-21, 75. A. Fauchier-Magnan, *The Small German Courts in the Eighteenth Century* (London, 1958), pp. 40-41.

50 J. Gurr, S.J., *The Principle of Sufficient Reason in Some Scholastic Systems* 1750-1900 (Milwaukee, 1959), pp. 48-53.

In other works the Society continued along the roadways opened in earlier years: scientific studies, spiritual writing, popular preaching, catechetics. Astronomy still retained a peculiar attraction for some of the best Jesuit talent. For thirty-six years, starting in 1755, Maximilian Hell, as court astronomer, directed the observatory in Vienna and produced thirty-five volumes of his observations. At Prague Joseph Stepling and at Mannheim Christian Mayer and Johann Metzger kept their skilled eyes trained on the skies. These men, usually excelling in mathematics, frequently made, as did Stepling at Prague, important advances in that field of study. As her court mathematician Maria Theresa chose the Milanese, Antonio Lecci, an extensive author on hydrostatics. The wide diversity of Jesuit scientific interests appeared in the eight-volume work, *Numismatics,* by Joseph Eckel, custodian of the imperial cabinet of medals; in the treatises of the naturalist, Franz Wulfen, on the valleys and mountains of the Alps; and in the dikes at Lake Rofner-Lise by which the engineer, Joseph Walcher, saved the countryside from floods.

The German Society made an invaluable contribution to the history of the missions in the work initiated by the Bavarian Joseph Stöcklein. Stöcklein, who spent most of his Jesuit life in Austria, inaugurated the massive collection of Jesuit mission reports dispatched between 1642 and 1726 known as *Recent World News* (*Der Neue Welt-Bott*), which appeared from 1728 to 1761. This assembly of documents is one of the indispensable quarries from which mission history of the seventeenth and early eighteenth centuries is still being cut.

Jesuit spiritual writing at this time received a unique and distinctive stamp. The drama had always enjoyed a favorite place in the Society's schools, and it now widened its scope to include spiritual literature. Franz Lang, moderator of the Marian Sodality at Munich from 1692 to 1706, directed his sodalists in staging meditations and contemplations from the four weeks of the *Spiritual Exercises.* These he published in 1717 under the title *The Drama of an Ascetical Retreat,* and then *The Drama of Human Passions* and *The Drama of Sorrow and Love,* on the Passion of Christ. A tradition of publishing such works grew up in Munich. Among the several Jesuits who followed Lang's example the most celebrated was Franz Neumayr, who produced in two large volumes, under the title *The Drama of Asceticism,* the productions of the Munich Sodality staged annually between 1737 and 1750. Neumayr, an indefatigable rhetoric teacher, preacher, and moderator of sodalities, also published more than a hundred other works, chiefly on spiritual subjects. Generally precise and to the point, somewhat dry but always practical, his writings carried at times such engaging titles as *Melancholy's Remedy* (1757) and *The Uprooting of Sloth* (1755). More personal than Neumayr was the widely influential Joseph Pergmayr. During his life he only published a short account of Venerable Philipp Jeningen, but after his death his other writings were gathered together and issued in five volumes in 1778-1779. True to the large basic principles of the *Spiritual Exercises,* he nevertheless showed, undoubtedly because of his experience as director of the Visitation nuns in Munich through twelve years, a distinctly Salesian touch in his development of such topics as the love of God and abandonment to God.[51]

This awareness of the Christian's call to high holiness expressed itself not only in writing but also in action. In 1754 Johann Adolf von Hörde, the vicar-apostolic in northern Germany, writing to Pope Benedict XIV about his jurisdiction, highly praised the zeal and industry of the Jesuits. He was referring to the northern missionaries of the Lower Rhine Province. In the early eighteenth century men of this province had stations in Hanover, Schwerin, Hamburg, Lübeck, Bremen, Copenhagen, and Stockholm where, in the heart of the Protestant north, they cared for the pockets of Catholics and tried to augment them. At Lübeck, for example, in 1709, there were only fourteen Catholic families and sixty Catholics in the entire city. Fifty-three years later the number had risen to a mere 150 Catholics. Conversions were hard to make, only five in 1731, two in 1764. In Bremen the Happy Death Society, organized by the Jesuits, especially interested the Protestants from whom three to twelve converts were made yearly. At Copenhagen, in 1723, the priests gave Holy Communion to about 4,000. From there they made excursions into Seeland, Laaland, Sweden, and Norway. Statistics from all the northern centers gave testimony to the same fact: the extreme patience needed to bring the people of northern Europe back to the ancient faith.[52]

In 1758 the superior of the Upper Rhine Province, Kaspar Hoch, told the general of the fine religious spirit in his jurisdiction. That reliable barometer of the spirit of self-sacrifice, the desire for the foreign missions, substantiated Hoch's claim, for over seventy men of his province were laboring in other continents. From all the German-speaking provinces a host of dedi-

51 Duhr, *Geschichte,* IV, ii, 125-126.
52 Ibid., IV, i, 100, 115-118, 123-124.

cated and industrious men joined the zeal of central Europe to the zeal of those two veterans of missionary expansion, Portugal and Spain. In the century before 1770 some eight hundred crossed the seas to foreign lands.[53]

The provinces which supplied this great flow of men to the missions experienced a steady growth, and this despite the torments of war in Germany. With the invasion of the Palatinate by Louis XIV in 1688, the German Jesuits once more, as they looked on the columns of refugees fleeing from villages swept by smoke and flame, provided food for the hungry and clothes for the naked. And so on through the Wars of the Spanish Succession, the Austrian Succession, the Seven Years. The Lower Rhine Province of 709 men in 1700 had become 830 in 1753 but dropped to 799 in 1772. The Upper Rhine Province, between 1717 and 1773, increased from 402 to 503. The Upper German Province generally ranged about 1,000 men. From this unit Ricci formed in 1770 the Bavarian Province of a little more than 500 members. The seizure of Silesia from Austria by Frederick the Great made the creation of a Silesian Province, even though small, a practical necessity. In 1742, therefore, Retz separated that area from the Bohemian Province. In 1770 it numbered only 144 men. Largest of all was the Province of Austria which expanded from 1,242 members in 1705 to 1,819 in 1773. At mid-eighteenth century the Society in Germany, Austria, Bohemia, and Hungary was operating 126 colleges and sixty-six seminaries, aside from residences, houses of probation, and missions.

Poland, during this period, had an experience somewhat like *Poland* the emergence of western Europe from the stark state of siege of the tenth century into the glow of the twelfth-century Renaissance. War had continued to be the dreadful scourge. Repeatedly the Jesuits saw the fruit of years of labor disappear in a few hours before the torch of an invading army. They tried, for example, to carry on at Vilna, a city whose chronicles list the following episodes: 1702, pillaged by the Swedes; 1705, ravaged by Saxon and Russian armies; 1706, a major fire and famine; 1710, an epidemic which took 35,000 lives; 1715, a terrible fire; 1733, invaded by Russians; 1734, three-quarters destroyed by fire. With the reign of Augustus III (1734-1763), however, a relative quiet settled over the torn land, and once more the culti-

---

53 Ibid., IV, i, 127-128. Huonder, "German Jesuit Missionaries," *WL*, XXIX (1900), 472.

vation of heart and mind received its honored place in the national life.

Two developments in particular sparked the Jesuit renaissance of the mid-eighteenth century: the stimulus of the Piarist schools, and contact with great teachers outside Poland.[54] Around 1755 the Piarist Fathers opened schools which were in touch with the currents of intellectual life in other European countries. One of their number, Stanislaw Konarski, a vibrant man with dynamic ideas, breathed new life into the educational efforts of Poland. The Jesuits, prodded by these lively new arrivals, snapped to attention and once more took on the smart look of elite troops. At this time they also established contact with great teachers in other countries, especially in Prague, Vienna, France, and Italy. To Josef Stepling at Prague and Maximilian Hell at Vienna, both distinguished scientists, went several gifted Poles to be formed in the latest mathematical advances. These students, especially Tomasz Zebrowski and Marcin Poczobut, returned to their native land as firebrands, inciting a love for learning and giving their nation, by reason of the superb astronomical observatory they established at Vilna, an enviable international reputation. Piotr Rogalinski studied at Paris when Noël Regnault lectured at Collège Louis-le-Grand; Mikolaj Kussowski and Jerzy Kowminski worked under Laurent Beraud at Lyons. Then in public exhibitions, which the Polish populace attended with avid enthusiasm, these and other Jesuits demonstrated the latest successes in science, especially physics, astronomy, and mathematics. They did a great deal to fix Polish terminology in the mathematical sciences. In 1766 at the University of Vilna they undertook the king's project of surveying the entire country in preparation for the construction of a map of Poland, a work rudely halted by the First Partition in 1772. Philosophy shook off its dullness as the teachers, aware of these scientific advances and using French and Polish in place of Latin as a medium of instruction, worked out a lively and relevant transformation of their matter.

This Jesuit renaissance manifested itself in several other ways: in the mastery of other languages, in journalism, in oratory. Many men mastered other European tongues. Starting around 1740 and extending to the Suppression of 1773, the number of Jesuits who knew French and Italian tripled. Libraries, nurtured with special care, expanded. New journals made their appearance. From 1759 five publications at Warsaw and three at Vilna

---

54 Bednarski, "Déclin et renaissance," *AHSJ*, II (1933), 206-207.

came from the presses. In the schools the study of Polish literature, fortified by a deepened knowledge of Polish history, rounded out the traditional classical program of studies. Oratory developed into a sort of national specialty as Poland, democratic and parliamentarian in character with its Diet and Senate and smaller local diets, became a large rostrum where eloquence had a political and social import. Rhetoric's status as a civic ornament sent sharp repercussions through the schools and raised oratory to a place of high distinction in the curriculum. Because of the sharp civic orientation, the Jesuits wove into the forensic training at their schools the study of the nation's history and institutions, and so produced a politico-rhetorical amalgam distinctly Polish.

Another vehicle which raised the nation's cultural taste was the national theatre, first created in 1765. Toward the buildup of a repertoire Franciszek Bohomolec, who drew considerably on Molière, contributed many individual dramas. King Stanislaus II Augustus (1764-1795) established the custom of "The Thursday Dinners," those gatherings where under the royal encouragement men of intellectual interests discussed literature and presented their own compositions. Besides Bohomolec a most familiar figure at these select assemblies was the lyric poet, Adam Stanislaw Naruszewicz, whose odes on nature combine in a contemplative mood Horatian terseness and the rich imagery of the psalms.[55]

On these Polish scenes so full of promise a dark night descended with abruptness. In 1772 started one of the greatest predatory actions in Europe's history, the extinction of Poland as a nation. A year later the Society was suppressed.

No country more than Belgium gave proof of the baneful effect international diplomacy could have on the Society's fortunes. The two Belgian provinces, once among the most vibrant and fertile in the Society, dropped drastically in numbers as the people, atrophied and writhing under Spanish and Austrian governors, felt the harrow of war cut across their land during the campaigns of Louis XIV and Louis XV. The Flemish-Belgian Province, with 801 men in 1626, dropped to 559 in 1717 and to 542 in 1749. The Gallo-Belgian Province, with 743 men in 1626, dropped to 434 in 1710, and then rose a bit in 1749 to 471.

---

55 Ibid., 213-217; W. Borowy, "Polish Literature in the Eighteenth Century," *The Cambridge History of Poland from Augustus II to Pilsudski (1697–1935)*, ed. by W. F. Reddaway et al. (Cambridge, 1941), pp. 179-182.

In Holland too both the Church and the Society suffered reverses. Against the Church, recalcitrants created the Schism of Utrecht; against the Society, enemies induced the civil authorities to decree banishment. In both these setbacks the Jansenists were the victors. The disciples of Jansenius, such as Johannes Neercassel, an Oratorian, gained high positions in the Church. As vicar-apostolic and titular archbishop of Utrecht (1663-1686) he welcomed several French Jansenists, including Arnauld and Quesnel, who gradually gained ascendancy over the minds of many Dutch priests. Pieter Codde, also an Oratorian and a Jansenist sympathizer, succeeded Neercassel as vicar-apostolic in 1686. Storm clouds gathered when two Jesuits, Norbertus Aerts and Frans Verbiest, in collaboration with a secular priest, Van Wijk, published an exposé of Codde's faulty theology. Another Jesuit, Louis Doucin, by his French translation of the work guaranteed it a wide circulation. Pope Innocent XII summoned Codde to Rome. In 1702 Clement XI suspended him and in 1710 removed him from office. Back in Utrecht, Codde became a center of rebellion, and people openly insulted the pope. In 1723 the cathedral chapter at Utrecht, with the approval of the Estates General, elected as archbishop Cornelius Steenoven. Benedict XIII excommunicated him. Steenoven defied the pope and the Schism of Utrecht was born. Before this the civil governments in a number of provinces had expelled the Society, and in 1720 the Estates General pronounced the Society to be the author of all the mischief in Holland's religious life.[56]

In England too reversal and discouragement keynoted this period. The revolt of 1688 against James II and the accession of William III and Mary II open the most dismal period in the history of the modern English Church. Intensified penal legislation pressured many Catholics to capitulate, excluded them from positions such as that of barrister and attorney, made them incapable of property inheritance, imposed on them the onus of double taxation. Names of families, long loyal to the faith, disappeared from the Catholic community: Shelly, Mordaunt, Teyham, Roper, Gascoigne, Giffard, Swinburne. These were grievous losses, since the priests who lived with these families kept the faith alive in neighboring areas.[57] The Catholic population dwindled, until in 1714 it was about five percent of the total

---

56 Pastor, *History*, XXXII, 334, 655-656.
57 B. Hemphill, O.S.B., *The Early Vicars Apostolic of England 1685-1750* (London, 1954), pp. 83-84.

population, and it continued to diminish. Timidity and apology became the marks of a people drained of spirit and initiative.

In keeping with this general background of depression resounded the baleful sounds of discord between secular priests and regulars which had begun over eighty years before. Further dissensions between the new vicars-apostolic and the regulars, particularly on the question of the source of jurisdiction for the regulars to administer the sacraments, whether from the bishop or from the religious superior, exacerbated a sore situation. In 1745 the complaint was made that the divisions "have come to that excess as to make it doubtful whether ye administration of the sacraments is truly and validly observed." Following the advice of the esteemed secular priest of the nineteenth century and distinguished critical historian, John Lingard, that the truth must be told, a bishop and a Jesuit, both English, concurred in the judgment that these dissensions had seriously wounded the Church in England. Bernard Ward, first bishop of Brentwood, wrote that "it was this more than anything else which led to the loss of the faith in this country," and the Jesuit, John Morris, said that "the blood of martyrs was shed in vain because of 'the awful dissensions that prevailed between seculars and regulars . . . God's blessing could not rest on the work of men amongst whom such animosity was found.'" [58]

Eventually Propaganda decided in favor of the vicars-apostolic, and in 1745 Pope Benedict XIV confirmed this decision. Cornelius Murphy, superior of the Jesuits in the London district, requested a delay in enforcement until he could receive instructions from Rome. Propaganda, however, in letters to the superiors general of the religious orders involved, insisted on immediate compliance with its decree, while allowing for future representation. The Jesuits, unlike some others, submitted without condition. On May 30, 1753, after hearing the objections of the religious, Benedict XIV in the brief *Apostolicum Ministerium* granted the vicars-apostolic practically all they desired. That same year Bishop Richard Challoner wrote a warm encomium on the Jesuits' diligence in England, their courtesy, respect, and ready disposition to help in any way they could.

On one point however he registered his displeasure. The seminaries in Spain under the Society's care were sending but a handful of secular priests back to England. In this displeasure other vicars-apostolic concurred. But if the stream of newly ordained priests had almost dried up, so had the spring from

58 Ibid., pp. viii-ix.

which it ultimately flowed, the Catholic population of England. Reduced almost to obliteration, timid and fearful, it no longer produced vocations as in earlier centuries. Besides, where in 1590 no religious order had a novitiate especially designed for Englishmen, in 1750, absorbing some of the currently few vocations, seven communities of men on the continent were operating novitiates of this particular nature.

Aside from the decrease in numbers, however, these seminaries had lost the momentum of their pristine drive. Tarnished by routine and the hardening of education into stereotyped forms, they no longer produced the priest prepared to meet the peculiar English situation. The Jesuit provincial, after his visitation of 1656 at the English College in Valladolid, severely criticized the theology program, heavily scholastic and of little or no relevance to England's needs. Equally serious was the loss of facility in the English tongue. Having entered the seminaries quite young, listened to lectures in Latin, and spent several years in a foreign land, the priests returned home speaking a faulty English. Andrew Poulton, in his sermons at the Savoy Chapel during the reign of James II, spoke his mother tongue haltingly. This vivid deficiency un-Englished these priests and marked them as foreigners.[59]

In Scotland, as in England, the fall of James II had calamitous results for the Church. González, general of the Society, could not understand the dire and somber tone of the reports from the Scots Jesuits. Bishop Thomas Nicolson explained this to him: "You would not wonder if you understood the predominance in Scotland of the terrible Calvinist sect of the Presbyterians. Their hatred of us is stolid and implacable." [60] The familiar pattern of loss and gain among Catholics in proportion to the severity or relaxation of persecution continued. Into every word of their reports the Jesuits breathed a spirit of endurance, especially during what became known as the Ill Years, the six or seven years of famine starting in 1696. In 1702 Alexander Macra reported the terrible poverty of his 700 Catholics and their love for the Mass. "In the summer time," he wrote, "we all live upon butter, cheese, and milk. I am fortunate if I get a little oat-cake, not always well baked." In 1702 John Innes related

---

59 Ibid., pp. 96-97. M. Trappes-Lomax, *Bishop Challoner* (London, 1936), p. 122; J. H. Pollen, "English Colleges in Eighteenth Century Spain," *Month,* CXIX (1912), 190-193; A. C. F. Beales, *Education under Penalty* (London, 1963), pp. 154-157.
60 Forbes-Leith, *Memoirs,* II, 158.

how he traveled by night and hid in caves and forests. "I have had to lie down without food or drink in barns or stables among the brute animals, upon a little straw, or sometimes on the hard, bare earth. . . . What disguises have I not worn, what arts have I not professed! Now master, now servant, now musician, now painter, now brass-worker, now clockmaker, now physician, I have endeavored to be all to all, that I might save all." [61] Reports from other priests were in like vein.

The Jesuits did not escape sharing the price which Catholics had to pay for the failure of Prince Charles at Culloden in 1746. Three priests, John Farquharson, his brother Charles, and Alexander Cameron were captured and exiled. Cameron died at sea. The brothers Farquharson were shipped to Holland. But before long, with wonderful resilience, they were back in their native land. With them in this dogged determination to stay with the mission was James Innes, who needed three successive banishments to convince him that it would be wiser to stay on the continent.

In Scotland, no less than in England, the creation of vicars-apostolic presented the problem of their relationship with the religious orders. While in 1711 Bishop James Gordon wrote to Tamburini that he could not give too great praise to the Scots Jesuits for their zeal and piety, in 1750 Bishop Alexander Smith sent to Propaganda a bitter indictment of them, alleging that they manifested hostility to him and refused to follow his instructions on the administration of the sacraments. Three years later, however, when Smith, as well as Bishop Hugh Macdonald, that ardent Stuart supporter who blessed Prince Charles' standard before Culloden, expressed the desire that the regulations issued by Benedict XIV for England be applied to Scotland, the Jesuit superior concurred.

The Irish Jesuits shared with their English and Scots brothers the pain of reversal brought by the fall of James II. The Puritan-spirited Church and state, true to its Cromwellian legacy, harassed the Catholic population with relentless perseverance. From 1690 to 1782 especially, the government pressed drastic penal legislation. But earlier, in 1673, Oliver Plunket revealed how this restrictive legislation was changing the character of the Anglo-Norman towns. "It is now expected," he wrote, "that no Catholic will be allowed to live in the cities." Under King William and Queen Anne the cities were quite thoroughly cleared of Catholics. This made it even more imperative to keep Catholic edu-

61 Ibid., 194-196.

cation alive. Generally about twenty in number — twenty-eight in 1755 — the Jesuits responded to this need with spirit. In 1694 Anthony Knoles, superior of the mission, wrote to González: "Very great is the diligence of our adversaries, and it is now most intense, to prevent members of the order from giving education to boys. But their zeal is enough to urge them to face the work and its dangers with courage; they toil in secret." In 1717 he wrote to Tamburini: "Father Michael Murphy is taking the risks of giving education to young people at this time in the capital of the country. He has taught Greek and Latin throughout the last five years, and is doing so at present." [62] It was in the capital where the need was greatest because of the aggressive proselytism of the Protestants, including Jonathan Swift, dean of St. Patrick's Cathedral. The Jesuits dug into the lanes and alleys of oldest Dublin and kept their schools going. Especially hallowed was the memory of John Austin, who in 1750 opened a classical school at Saul's Court, off Fishamble Street, and of Thomas Betagh, the last Irish survivor of the suppressed Society, living until 1811, who was remembered sitting, at the age of seventy-three, in a cellar in Dublin hearing the lessons of his furtive students.[63] The school no doubt was a major reason why the Irish Jesuits achieved a success denied the Society in England and Scotland.

The Far East   The form of the missions, especially those of Spain and Portugal, changed noticeably through the years as new tinges of color, some material and others spiritual, altered the general aspect of the apostolate overseas. Because Portugal, losing much of her empire to the Dutch, and Spain, draining her treasury in her wars against Louis XIV, could not always honor the pledge of financial support, the physical upkeep of the mission posts suffered and the missionaries themselves often felt the pinch of extreme poverty. Then, spiritually, fresh nuances modified the older and more familiar procedures. The idea of guiding the secular clergy through the Spiritual Exercises caught on and spread widely. Replacements from Europe brought with them a powerful new force which they inlaid into the older framework, the devotion to the Sacred Heart of Jesus. And among these replacements were particularly large numbers of Germans. Between 1670 and 1770 some 800 went overseas. They had always taken pride in that St. Francis Xavier, personally experienced in the

62 Corcoran, *Clongowes,* pp. 32-33.
63 Ibid., pp. 37-38.

severe privations of mission life, recommended especially the sturdy Germans and Belgians for that apostolate. St. Peter Canisius, as German provincial, despite the desperate need for priests in Germany, offered some of his men "as the first sacrifice of our province." But Alonso Salmerón, then vicar-general, refused this generous offer, because Germany's dire straits ruled out the possibility of sparing any men for the missions. But the fire for work among pagans burned intensely in the hearts of the German Jesuits. In a single year 1615-1616 forty petitions for mission work went to the general from Ingolstadt alone. Zeal of white heat intensity inflamed the letters sent by such distinguished men as Friedrich Spe von Langenfeld and Athanasius Kircher. On one of Kilian Stumpf's appeals Tirso González added his own comment: "A beautiful letter! Great hope must be held out to this man of obtaining permission to go to the Indies." [64] Once the Treaty of Westphalia had proved that the religious struggle in Germany had reached a stalemate, the generals began to release this pent-up fervor in what became the first major migration of Germans overseas.

These German Jesuits by a rare combination of versatility and application made a valuable contribution to their new undertaking. On the Spanish missions men from the countries of Haydn, Handel, Mozart, and Beethoven taught the natives the harp, the clarinet, the flute, the violin, the cornet, the organ. In Santa Fe and Buenos Aires churches echoed with the sweet strains of beautiful orchestral Masses produced by German-trained natives. Around 1740 every Reduction in Paraguay boasted a choir. But the darlings of these missions were the German and Dutch brothers. Portuguese and Spanish superiors lavishly praised these goldsmiths, woodcarvers, cabinetmakers, bellfounders, architects, clockmakers. One Spanish superior wrote: "The mainstay of the misssions in the West Indies are the German Brothers." [65] Sometimes a special skill projected a brother into national prominence, as in the case of Brother Josef Zeittler, who organized at Santiago and Concepción the only two dispensaries in all Chile.

Other countries paralleled Germany in helping Spain and Portugal. The Italians were always generous, and at the time of the Society's suppression there were ninety-three of them in the Spanish missions alone. Not to be outdone by the continent, poor benighted Ireland, in the finest tradition of Brendan and Columban, sprinkled Jesuit missions throughout the world with her

64 Huonder, "German Jesuit Missionaries," *WL*, XXIX (1900), 475-476.
65 Ibid., 481.

sons. Between 1574 and 1773 more than forty Irish Jesuits became "exiles for Christ." [66] Belgians, ever since Francis Xavier's intrepid contemporary, Gaspar Berze, had given the missions generously of the powerful initiative and alert intelligence of their people through men like Verbiest and Trigault. In Paraguay alone, from 1608 to 1767, including a few Frenchmen, they numbered forty-five. Without missions of their own until the nineteenth century, they shed martyr's blood in lands for which other nations were responsible: four in the Marianas, one in Japan, one in China, and three in South America.[67]

António Franco, an eighteenth-century historian of the Portuguese Province, observing the great number of Jesuits who were going to the foreign missions, interpreted this as a clear sign of the abundance of the Holy Spirit which God was pouring out on that province. These men went fully briefed on what to expect; loneliness, discomfort, disease, destitution, fatigue. The letters from the veterans with their vivid portrayal of their experiences saw to that. Human nature of itself could never have sustained such a steady flow of men eager to make of their lives a complete kenosis for God's greater glory.

The Orient continued to attract the greater number. In 1735 superiors opened a novitiate outside Lisbon for the training of young men destined for India. In 1701 nineteen sailed to the East; in 1702, nine; in 1708, thirty-two; between 1730 and 1740, 146; in the three years between 1751 and 1754, ninety-two. Many Italian names appeared on the roll call, as well as a growing number from German-speaking lands.[68] In 1736 an especially talented group of four of the latter sailed: Florentine Bahr of Silesia, who during his more than thirty years in China was to achieve a flawless command of that country's tongue; Anton Gogeisl of Bavaria, a fine astronomer and inventor, who for twenty-six years was to be assessor of the mathematical tribunal at Peking; Augustin von Hallerstein of Carniola, who eventually became president of that same tribunal; and Gottfried Xaver von Laimbeckhoven, ingenious and enterprising apostle who was made bishop of Nanking. The periodic difficulties raised by the

---

66 A review by P. de Leturia, S.J. of J. Mac Erlean, S.J., *Irish Jesuits in Foreign Missions from 1574 to 1773* (Dublin, 1930), in *AHSJ*, I (1932), 156.

67 P. Delattre, S.J. and E. Lamalle, S.J., "Jésuites Wallons, Flamands, Français missionaires au Paraguay, 1608-1767," *AHSJ*, XVI (1947), 98-176.

68 Rodrigues, *História*, IV, i, 165-166, 188, 201-202.

Portuguese government about foreigners working within the area of the Padroado still put sand into the cogs of the missionary machine. In 1702, for example, Peter II severely chided González because some Jesuits failed to go through Lisbon on their way to the Far East. To add to Portuguese aggravation, France expanded her colonies in India with settlements in Bengal and the Carnatic. French Jesuits joined their fellow nationals and by the middle of the eighteenth century numbered twenty-two men there. Besides, in only the fifteen years before 1702, about forty had reached China.[69]

Despite Portugal's generous contribution of men to the Orient, the two provinces in India lost much of the original thrust given by the pioneers. The Province of Goa, which in 1626 numbered 820, dropped to 219 in 1717 and to 150 in 1749. The Province of Malabar, with 190 men in 1626, fell sharply to only sixty-seven in 1717 and to forty-seven in 1749. Several reasons, whose individual influences it is hard to estimate, conspired to create this reversal: the loss of men at sea; the ascendancy of England and Holland over Portugal as colonial powers; the quarrels between the Padroado and Propaganda; the challenge to the Jesuit program of adaptation to Indian culture. The last was especially serious.

Missionaries of wide talent, in their sympathetic effort to understand intimately the civilization of India, took their cue from Roberto de Nobili. Firmly fixed as one of the greatest figures in the Catholic mission among the Brahmins of Madurai was Giuseppe Costanzo Beschi from Castiglione. This priest of quick intelligence and impetuous nature — fellow Jesuits judged him because of a lack of prudence as unqualified to be a superior — filled his thirty-six years in India from 1710 to 1746 with the production of grammars, dictionaries, ascetical works in Tamil, all of which he crowned with a classic of rare beauty of language, *The Unfading Garland* (1726), a Tamil Divine Comedy of 3,615 stanzas. Johann Ernst Hanxleden of Hanover, lovable and mild scholar, by the rare imagery and meter of his poems, *Mishiàda Pana* on our Lord's life, composed in 1728, and *Nála Parvam* on the four last things, made important contributions to Malayalam literature. In Pazhayur in 1932, on the second centenary of Hanxleden's death, amid great pomp a library was opened to perpetuate the memory of this German priest and scholar.[70]

69 Ibid., III, ii, 144; IV, i, 214-215; Plattner, *Jesuits Go East*, p. 223.
70 Ferroli, *Jesuits in Malabar*, II, 319-322, 330, fn.

The French Jesuits settled at Pondicherry in 1689 and opened a school soon famous, especially for its scientific studies. Gaston Coeurdoux gathered invaluable data on the common origins of Sanskrit, Latin, and Greek, which he sent to the French Academy.

Coeurdoux had discovered a new continent in the sea of learning, but by one of history's strange tricks the Jesuit's achievement has been overshadowed. Scholars often make the starting point of Indo-European philology and comparative linguistics the "Third Anniversary Discourse to the Asiatic Society of Bengal," delivered by Sir William Jones in January, 1786. Jones advanced the theory that Latin, Greek, and Sanskrit had "sprung from some common source, which, perhaps, no longer exists." A just and humanitarian administrator in India, an intellectual whose achievements included the mastery of at least twenty-eight languages, Jones won acclaim for this insight into the relationship of Latin, Greek, and Sanskrit. But almost twenty years before Jones' famous address, Gaston Coeurdoux wrote to the Abbé Barthélemy of the Académie des Inscriptions et Belles-Lettres about the striking similarity of Latin, Greek, and Sanskrit, drew up illustrative word lists, expatiated on the grammatical and phonological relationship of the words, and concluded that these languages had a common origin. Coeurdoux had further correspondence with Barthélemy. These letters the Abbé turned over to Anquétil Dupperon, a scholar of the Académie. Probably because of the turmoil of the French Revolution, they were not published in the *Mémoires* of the Academy until 1808. Coeurdoux had died nine years earlier, in 1799, at the age of eighty-eight, probably never aware of the place his insight had merited for him in the history of philology.[71]

Other priests went to Madurai to study Tamil and the methods of the Brahmin missionaries. One of the first of these Frenchmen to become vibrant transmitters of the De Nobili tradition, Venance Bouchet, during twelve years at Trichinopoly, baptized 20,000 Indians. To Portugal went the honor of giving to India a canonized saint. In May, 1691, João de Brito, almost murdered in the Marava five years earlier, returned there from Lisbon where he had been sent to report on the Mission. Once more this untiring priest, who lived on boiled rice and herbs, plunged into a land which was at once a wilderness of beasts, a medley of swirling rivers, and a battleground of fighting rajahs and

71 John J. Godfrey, S.J., "Sir William Jones and Père Coeurdoux: a Philological Footnote," *Journal of the American Oriental Society,* LXXXVII (1967), 57–59.

poligars. Within eight months in 1691, on the border of Madurai, he baptized 8,000 catechumens. This success aroused hatred of some pagans, and in January, 1693, De Brito was seized. From his prison, anticipating a violent death for the love of God, he wrote with charcoal to a fellow Jesuit: "The hope that I would gain this happiness has twice drawn me to India." [72] On February 4, 1693, scimitar and hatchet brought this sannyasi the crown of martyrdom. In 1947 Pope Piux XII canonized him.

Around the turn of the century the basic missionary approach of these Jesuits received a serious challenge, and a critical controversy arose about what were known as the Malabar Rites. Distinct from the De Nobili dispute of the first quarter of the century, it nevertheless resembled that earlier quarrel in the identity of the basic issue, that of accommodating the Catholic faith to the cultural forms of India. Certain practices of Jesuit missionaries beyond those specifically approved by Gregory XV in 1623 aroused the misgivings of other European priests. Again two groups of men, sincere and dedicated, clashed in their fundamental approach to the mission issue, and a memorable controversy was born. One group believed that accommodations opened the door to the conversion of India; the other group feared that accommodation cultivated abuse. The trouble started in the mission of the French at Pondicherry. The Capuchins of the area, who had been there before the Jesuits arrived, disturbed by what they regarded as concessions to heathenism, in 1703 filed complaints at Rome. That same year, in November, an ecclesiastic of great importance arrived at Pondicherry. Carlo Tomasso Maillard de Tournon, a Piedmontese, was on his way to China, appointed by Clement XI as apostolic visitor and *legatus a latere* "for the East Indies, the Chinese Empire, and neighboring Islands and Kingdoms." He carried the additional title of patriarch of Antioch. The legate's broad commission embraced the problem of the rites in the Orient, but the supreme objective of the pope was the establishment of regular diplomatic relations with China. For this delicate mission Clement XI chose the cultivated De Tournon and personally consecrated him bishop on his thirty-third birthday.

The legate's departure from India was more memorable than his arrival. He spent eight months in Pondicherry. Two days before he embarked for China, he presented the Jesuits, much to their consternation, a list of sixteen points which had to be ob-

The Malabar Rites

---

72 Ferroli, *Jesuits in Malabar*, II, 85-87.

served under pain of ecclesiastical censure. Among these points two practices on which he insisted especially appalled the missionaries. They concerned the rite of baptism and visits to sick pariahs in their homes. Since to use saliva and to breathe on a person were repugnant to the Indians, the Jesuits, in administering baptism, omitted these parts of the ceremony. De Tournon insisted on their restoration. Since the Jesuits were pandarams, or ascetics of the Sudra class, which status by this time precluded contact with the pariahs, they avoided open visits with the outcasts. De Tournon required that the missionaries attend sick pariahs in their huts. This clash of viewpoints indicated the change in the social position of the Jesuit pandarams since the time of Roberto de Nobili. Earlier the pandarams had been able with certain precautions to have contact with the pariahs, but with the passage of time and the shift of social customs they became a specialized group, known simply as "the Brahmins' missionaries," who were excluded from association with the outcasts.[73]

In arriving at his decisions De Tournon violated a canon of responsible diplomacy, the acquirement through factual evidence of a full and balanced understanding of the situation. Indisposed and confined to bed most of the eight months, he could make but limited observation. What information he gathered he received in large measure from the Capuchins, who, in addition to their opposition to the Society, were ignorant of Tamil — the bishop of Mylapore noted that after twenty-five years in the misson only one Capuchin had some knowledge of Tamil — as well as from Jean Jacques Tessier de Quéralay of the Foreign Missionary Society of Paris. Tessier, influenced by the Jansenist propaganda in France, collaborated with the Capuchins and some disgruntled Hindus in the composition for the education of the legate of a dossier of 551 pages against the Society. Only cursorily did De Tournon speak with the Jesuits. He included on his list of prohibited practices certain things which the Jesuits had never allowed or had never head of. He forbade the marriage of children. This the Jesuits did not tolerate. He banned the use of pagan names at baptism. This the Jesuits never permitted. He prohibited the cord of one hundred and eight threads dyed in saffron. This the Jesuits never heard of.[74]

73 Amann, in *DTC*, IX, 2, 1734.
74 Ferroli, *Jesuits in Malabar*, II, 428-435; Adrien Launay, *Mémorial de la Société des Missions-Étrangères* (Paris, 1912), I, 20-21; II, 538-539.

Overnight the Society's work in Malabar, Mysore and the Carnatic was caught up in a crisis. Since his directives on baptismal ceremonies and visits to the pariahs threatened the existence of the mission, the Jesuits went to De Tournon and pleaded with him to recall the decree. The meeting was tense. In the decree the legate ascribed certain statements to the French Jesuit, Venance Bouchet. Under oath Bouchet affirmed that he had never made the statements. Finally the Jesuits won a stay. De Tournon allowed them three years to discover the mind of the Holy See on these problems.

Then began a protracted correspondence and a series of embassies between Rome and India that went on for forty years. One major issue was purity of religious practice. Another, more searching, was that of Christian charity. Critics accused the Society of diluting Catholic belief by the toleration of superstition, and of violation of the supreme commandment of Christian love by their cooperation with the social structure of castes. Through these forty years the Jesuits tried to clarify their position. In their judgment an ancient civilization like that of India could not be changed overnight, and the pursuance of De Tournon's prescriptions meant the ruin of the mission. Time, patience, education were essential.

In 1706 Pope Clement XI through the Holy Office confirmed his legate's action. The bishops of Goa, Cranganore, and Mylapore protested. Venance Bouchet and the Portuguese Jesuit, Francisco Laines, went to Rome and tried to demonstrate what they thought to be the shortsightedness of De Tournon's position. The pope then modified his stand. On July 23, 1708, by an *oraculum vivae vocis* he told Bouchet that the legate's decrees should be observed except where in the judgment of the missionaries there would be detriment to God's glory and the salvation of souls. This unusual procedure started a wave of wide confusion. Rumors, which a precisely worded document could have restrained, spread through India. In the south people told the story that the pope had abolished the legate's decree. This Clement denied. In the brief *Non sine gravi* of September 17, 1712, he made it clear that he supported De Tournon.[75]

In 1720 another Jesuit, Antonio Brandolini, went to Rome and presented to the Holy See a critique of De Tournon's decree. He pointed out the document's unreliable sources, since the information was obtained from persons who knew almost nothing of Malabar's interior. He indicated its cultural illiteracy, since

---

75 Amann, in *DTC*, IX, 2, 1726.

it allowed for no differences between customs along the coast of Malabar and customs in the interior. He demonstrated its divorce from reality, since it did not take into consideration the fragile condition of the infant Church surrounded by Hindus.

In the Italian Dominican, Luigi Maria Lucino, Laines and Brandolini met an energetic opponent, whose reasoning however suffered from the serious flaw of forcing oriental problems into a European context. Lucino claimed, for example, that repugnance for the use of saliva in baptism savored of Calvinism, since Calvin had called this rite a stupid and dirty ceremony. He felt that to grant a dispensation from this part of the ritual might open the door for the request of Lutherans to be dispensed from the adoration of the cross. Very cogently he argued against the divisiveness fostered by the caste system against Christian unity in love. He condemned those who tolerated the divisions by caste as the new Pharisees. Christ rejected the Pharisees. So the followers of Christ must repudiate the Brahmins. The Jesuits admitted that in principle Lucino was right. But, as Brandolini pointed out, the missionaries were dealing not with abstractions and intellectual distinctions but with men and women living within the structure of an ancient civilization that could not be abruptly changed. Laines tried to put the Indian abhorrence for saliva within its cultural milieu. He explained that Indians felt this distaste in the way Europeans felt a repugnance for the "holy urine" and "holy cow dung" of the Hindus.[76]

The Holy See basically rejected the Jesuit representations. On August 24, 1734, Clement XII in the brief *Compertum exploratumque* ratified De Tournon's decree of thirty years before, although he modified some of the irritating language. On May 13, 1739, in the brief *Concredita nobis,* the same pope required an oath of the missionaries to keep the decrees of the Holy See. The climax came on September 13, 1744, in the bull *Omnium Sollicitudinum* of Pope Benedict XIV. In regard to the use of saliva and the insufflation at baptism, in view of the harm which these allegedly would do, Benedict granted permission to omit them for a period of ten years. About the lock of hair and the cord, approved in the time of Roberto De Nobili, he said nothing. But on the problem of association with the pariahs, he insisted that the Gospel must prevail and repudiated social distinctions within the Church of God.

Five years before Benedict issued his bull, Father General Retz, who knew the anxieties and forebodings in the hearts of the

76 Ferroli, *Jesuits in Malabar,* II, 433-434.

Jesuits in Malabar, recalled in a letter to their provincial that before all else the Jesuit gives obedience to the Holy See no matter what the cost. Again, in 1742, stressing the love of the cross in a spirit of obedience, the general wrote that if the mission suffered harm it would not be the fault of the Society. The Jesuits responded generously. Four years after *Omnium Sollicitudinum*, in 1748, Retz communicated his pleasure to the provincial of Malabar. "Words do not come easily to express the joy and consolation which your letters have aroused in me as I read of the submission and exact obedience with which the fathers have complied with the decree of the Holy See." [77] After the suppression of the Society, members of the Foreign Missionary Society of Paris moved into Jesuit posts. They acknowledged that they found only the slightest traces of superstition among the Christians. And with time they came to recognize the need of some adaptation.[78]

At the time that Benedict XIV made his conclusive decision, he approved a suggestion put forward by Retz toward the solution of the caste problem. The general, prompted by some missionaries, proposed the creation of a special unit of Jesuits who would be devoted principally to work among the pariahs. Several priests, fully realizing that association with these poor and abject outcastes meant social severance from their fellow Jesuits in the Sudra class, volunteered for the new enterprise. In the Carnatic Gaston Coeurdoux reported that "a noble rivalry arose" among the Jesuits there. By 1747 four fathers had donned the garb which marked them for pariah service. The annual letter of 1747 from Malabar contained an apostrophe to these men: "According to the words of the Apostle you are 'the dregs of humanity,' but the Society regards you as her noblest glory, and the Province of Malabar looks upon you as her most precious ornament." Over the whole project, however, hung a great fear: discovery by the pagans that the men of the pariah mission were of the same organization as the men of the Brahmanic mission with the inevitable disrepute and collapse of the latter. In the face of this awful possibility Angelo de Franceschi epitomized the Jesuit feeling: "But if God in his inscrutable wisdom should call for the disappointment of our hopes, in tears and affliction of soul we shall submit and never fall from holy obedience." [79]

77 Ibid., 450.
78 Ibid., 466.
79 Ibid., 452-455.

Sentiments of this kind could not offset the damaging image created by one of the classics of anti-Jesuit literature. In a two-volume work that appeared in France in 1744, the year of the *Omnium Sollicitudinum,* a Capuchin, Pierre Curel Parisot, whose name as a religious was Father Norbert, gathered together a formidable collection of calumnies. This work, his most famous, was entitled *Historical Memoirs Presented to the Sovereign Pontiff Benedict XIV on the Missions of the East Indies in Which it is Disclosed that the Capuchin Missionaries were Right in Separating from Communion with the Jesuit Missionaries Who had Refused to Submit to the Decree of Cardinal de Tournon, Legate of the Holy See, against the Malabar Rites.* Father Norbert withdrew from the Capuchins and in 1760 assumed the name Abbé C.P. Platel. From the powerful Portuguese minister of foreign affairs, Sebastião José de Carvalho e Mello, he received encouragement in his literary endeavors to achieve what he admitted was his purpose, the ruin of the Society.

In 1748 there were about 300,000 Christians in the area affected by the *Omnium sollicitudinum.* By 1840 they had dropped 60,000 to 240,000. What losses can be ascribed to the decision of the Holy See cannot be measured, since war, famine, pestilence, and the removal of the Jesuits by the suppression all took their toll. Mid-eighteenth century marks a turning point. Till then the number of Catholics mounted. After that point it declined.

China   In China the fortunes of the Jesuit mission during the earlier and latter parts of this period contrast with all the sharp difference between black and white. Where in 1687 there had been bright hope, in 1757 there was distress and lament. The one development which, more than anything else, brought about this change in mood was the Church's stand that Catholic Chinese might not participate in the ceremonies in honor of their ancestors and Confucius.

Through the years the Society maintained among its missionaries the high standards in scholarship and the understanding of Chinese culture set by Ricci. On January 29, 1688, Ferdinand Verbiest died. Ten days later five French Jesuits arrived at Peking. This group was the great Belgian's last service to China, for they were the answer to the appeals for help which he had been sending to Europe and which Colbert and de la Chaize brought to the attention of Louis XIV. With the help of "The Sun King" the French Jesuits set out for the work in which they were to bring honor to the faith by their superior proficiency in science, art, and medicine and which would be a worthy complement to the achievements of their fellow religious of other nations.

These men studied their new home widely and carefully, and found a channel to send their knowledge to Europe in the famous collection, *Lettres Édifiantes et Curieuses,* letters from missionaries throughout the world, which between 1703 and 1776 reached thirty-four volumes and did much to stimulate popular interest in Europe about things Chinese. Some of what the Jesuits had written about China, however, did not reach European eyes in its original form, for at his editorial desk in France Jean du Halde occasionally touched up the manuscripts, much to the annoyance of the authors.

Some of these Frenchmen, for all their zeal, compromised the Ricci approach to Chinese civilization. These enthusiastic students carried on the researches of earlier Jesuits who tried to discern in China evidence of Judaic origins and who, even around the mid-seventeenth century, claimed to have found among the Chinese forty Hebrew ceremonies — this was Domingo Navarrete's report — as well as evidence that Confucius had foreseen the Messiah. Known as Figurists, this tiny group of Frenchmen claimed that the Chinese classics adumbrated the Old and New Testaments, the mysteries of man's fall and redemption, and even our Lady's Immaculate Conception. This line of thought terrified other Jesuits, as well as the Friars, in a land where the tendency toward syncretism ran strong and where some converts attempted to align Christianity with Confucianism, Taoism, and Buddhism.[80]

Alongside these French Jesuits, those from Portugal, especially men like Tomás Pereira, José Suares, and João Mourao, scarcely remembered today because of general unfamiliarity with the abundant Portuguese records, brought distinction to Peking by their wide correspondence with the Royal Society of London, the Royal Academy of Paris, and the Imperial Academy of Russia. A Portuguese Jesuit and a French Jesuit made possible the first treaty China ever made with a European power. In 1689 the empire signed an agreement with Russia. At Nerchinsk Tomás Pereira and' Jean François Gerbillon, acting as interpreters, by their personal suggestions saved from almost certain breakdown the consultations between the Chinese and the Russians, and so helped create between the two powers a peace

---

80 Navarrete, *The Travels,* I, lxviii.

which lasted more than two centuries. The official copy of the treaty was in Latin. Jesuit influence became especially evident when the emperor, putting aside the traditional attitude of China's superiority to other countries, directed Pereira and Gerbillon to see that the principles of the western Law of Nations be observed.[81]

K'ang-hsi was delighted with his Jesuits and imperial pleasure reached a high point in 1692. That year the emperor granted what the missionaries had been hoping for, a decree which granted them freedom to preach throughout the extent of the realm and to receive into the Church anyone who desired to become a Catholic. Behind this remarkable document was the suasive influence of the Portuguese Jesuit, Tomás Pereira, who four years before at Nerchinsk had performed so skillfully in the art of diplomacy. In 1700, of a population of fourteen millions, 300,000 were Christians. The Jesuits, fifty-nine of them in 1701, dreamed of K'ang-hsi as the Chinese Constantine. They shared the care of two hundred and fifty churches and chapels with twenty-nine Franciscans, eight Dominicans, six Augustinians, and fifteen seculars, mainly of the Paris Foreign Mission Society.[82]

But China was not to have a Constantinian peace. The Roman decision of November 20, 1704, against the toleration of the rites, among other factors, changed the mood at the imperial court. Though slowly and carefully arrived at, this judgment by its nature was bound to cause distress and resentment. Lack of tact in its promulgation in China and the mutual distrust among the missionaries magnified the difficulty. A storm broke about the person of the papal legate to China, Carlo Tomasso Maillard de Tournon.

De Tournon left Pondicherry for China in June, 1704. He arrived at Peking on December 4, 1705. This embassy was the first time in modern history that the Holy See directly approached an oriental monarch. In Europe K'ang-hsi enjoyed the reputation as a statesman of superior intelligence. At Peking, through conversation with the Jesuits at court, the emperor conceived an esteem for the vicar of Christ. De Tournon carried with him a carefully drafted letter to K'ang-hsi from Clement

---

81 J. Sebes, S.J., *The Jesuits and the Sino-Russian Treaty of Nerchinsk* (Rome, 1961), pp. 103-122.

82 J. de la Servière, S.J., *Les anciennes missions de la Compagnie de Jésus en Chine* (Shanghai, 1924), p. 55; F. Rouleau, S.J., "Maillard de Tournon, Papal Legate at the Court of Peking . . . ," *AHSJ*, XXXI (1962), 264-323, esp. fn. 65 on 299.

XI in which the pope thanked the emperor for his benevolence toward Christians, praised him and his people, and expressed the hope for his conversion. The legate's central objective was the establishment of formal diplomatic relations between Rome and Peking. This grand plan envisaged the residence at Peking of a Catholic prelate of distinction and at Rome of an imperial Chinese ambassador.[83]

On December 31, 1705, K'ang-hsi received De Tournon with a splendor never previously afforded a visiting dignitary. Crowds stood in awe as mandarins and colorfully dressed foreign officials escorted the visitor from the West, carried in his sedan chair. With utmost graciousness and exquisite courtesy K'ang-hsi arranged the meeting in the private garden house. For about two hours the papal legate and the "Son of Heaven" were together.[84]

The promise of that cordial reception never materialized. The year that followed was a general disaster. With the glow of this imperial reception about him, De Tournon had planned to visit the Catholic mission stations throughout the provinces, a project that would have enhanced the prestige of the Church in the eyes of the Chinese people. The nagging illness that kept him bedridden in India, probably an acute duodenal ulcer, plagued him in China and forced the cancellation of the tour. Among some of the missionaries he found strong hostility to the Society. Members of the Foreign Mission Society of Paris, zealous priests influenced by the Jansenist propaganda in France, pressed for the recall of the Jesuits from China. The procurator of Propaganda in China, Domenico Perroni, succinctly expressed his opinion about the Jesuits: "Eradicandi sunt." De Tournon confided to Charles Maigrot, a member of the Paris Foreign Mission Society and a vicar-apostolic, that the evil in China which had to be cut at the root was the Society of Jesus. Provoked no doubt by his debilitating sickness, he acted offensively toward Chinese mores, became excitable under strained circumstances, and lost his poise as a diplomat. On January 2, 1706, the Bavarian Jesuit, Bernhard Kilian Stumpf, pleaded with De Tournon to consult with Chinese authorities on Chinese issues. The legate replied that the only Chinese evidence acceptable to him were books. Living Chinese had no interest in the truth. This unusual principle had another adherent in the Jesuit, Claude de Visdelou.

83 Rouleau, "Maillard de Tournon . . . ," *AHSJ*, XXXI (1962), 269-275.
84 Ibid., 310-311.

De Visdelou broke with his fellow religious and furnished the legate with the Chinese texts which seemed to run counter to the Jesuit position in the debate about the rites.[85]

It was this problem more than anything else that lurked behind the papal embassy like a terrible specter. That one reason for the legate's presence in China was to handle this divisive issue no one doubted. Rumors were rife. These reached K'ang-hsi, who remarked to one of the Jesuits at court, Jean François Gerbillon, that De Tournon ought to realize that the prohibition of the ancestral and Confucian ceremonies would mean the desertion of the faith by the Catholic Chinese. On June 29, 1706, the emperor received De Tournon a second time. Curtly he warned the legate that he would not allow any interference with ancient customs of the realm. In October of the same year he dispatched two Jesuits, António de Barros and Antoine de Beauvollier, to Rome with a critique of De Tournon's actions. Both priests, in separate ships, were lost at sea when their vessels were wrecked in a storm in sight of the Portuguese coast on January 20, 1708.[86]

The intense differences among the missionaries brought disenchantment about Christianity at the court. Men in De Tournon's entourage maligned the Society. Kilian Stumpf listed no less than twenty-five accusations. This defamation replaced with suspicion and wariness the trust and respect which K'ang-hsi had toward the Jesuits. Exasperated by the attitude of western superiority toward the culture of his people among the anti-Jesuit priests, K'ang-hsi acted with finality. On December 17 he issued an order by which all missionaries, in order to avoid banishment, had to file a request for a diploma granting permission to preach, a document to be issued only to those who promised not to assail the rites. The same month he deported Charles Maigrot and two other vicars apostolic.

De Tournon reacted sharply. Now in possession of the secret decision taken in Rome a little over two years earlier, he ordered the missionaries on January 25, 1707, under pain of excommunication to answer, if questioned by the authorities, that in Chinese custom and doctrine were many things against divine law, especially "the sacrifices of Confucius and ancestors" and the words *Tien* and *Shangti* as expressions of the true God of the Christians. K'ang-hsi ordered the legate out of the country. On

---

85 Pastor, *History*, XXXIII, 434–437.
86 Ibid., 438; Rouleau, *AHSJ*, XXXI (1962), 265, fn. 2.

June 30, 1707, De Tournon arrived at what he called "this tiny hovel of Macao."

Clement XI gave De Tournon his complete support. When the first radiant reports about the legatine mission reached Rome, the pope conferred on his friend the red hat, which reached the sick and disillusioned man only six months before his death when only forty-one-years old, at Macao on June 8, 1710. In March, 1709, this just and courageous pope promulgated the carefully weighed decision of the Holy Office which prohibited participation in the rites by Catholics. On September 25, 1710, he, ever one with his legate, confirmed De Tournon's action, enjoined observance of his directives and rejected appeals from China. On October 11 the Holy Office informed Tamburini of this denouement. The same day the general replied with the assurance of the Society's submission and his personal determination to see that each Jesuit gave complete obedience. The next year, in November, the congregation of procurators met. On the 20th Clement received the general, the assistants and the delegates, who had gone to the Quirinal to affirm in solemn manner the Society's adherence to the decision of the Holy See.[87] Tamburini, not the merciless man that his language might suggest, fell into some excited rhetoric. "But if, nevertheless, there should be anywhere on earth, which heaven avert, any one of Ours who should be of other sentiments, or use or or be likely to use other language — for where there are so many subjects, no human prudence can altogether prevent or hinder such a contingency — the general declares, asserts, and professes in the name of the whole Society, that he here and now reprobates and repudiates that man; and that such a one deserves punishment, and is not to be acknowledged for a true and genuine son of the Society. The Society will hold him, as she has ever held and now holds such persons, for degenerate and no child of hers; and to the extent of her power will ever restrain, repress, and crush him." [88]

Despite these protestations, Pope Clement felt that obedience was not complete and spoke of "difficulties, tergiversations, subterfuges, and pretexts" which continued in China. Determined that all toleration of the rites be annihilated, he followed up his earlier condemnation with the brief *Ex illa die* of March 19, 1715, in which was formulated, in language which was crystal

87 Brucker, *La Compagnie*, p. 710; Pastor, *History*, XXXIII, 455-456.
88 J. Rickaby, S.J., "Clement the Eleventh and the Chinese Rites," *Month*, LXXIII, (1891), 76.

clear and allowed for no loopholes, an oath of obedience to be taken by each missionary.

The impression of obstructionism given by some of the Jesuits in China arose, in part at least, from a critical problem of conscience. Kilian Stumpf, visitor to the vice-province, approached the bishop of Peking, Bernardino della Chiesa, and expressed, despite his apprehension for the mission, his acceptance of the Church's ruling. But what the Jesuit superior acceded to, the Chinese Catholics in large numbers rejected. Unable to comprehend why they had to become less Chinese in order to be Christians, they refused to surrender this important feature of their social and national life. This created a delicate problem for the priests: could they in conscience administer the sacraments to these people? Stumpf, respecting the consciences of his subjects, informed them that they were free, if they wished, to leave the mission. He asked them however to stay, place their trust in God and told them to refrain from priestly activity until a solution to the knotty question was found. In Rome these priests fell under heavy criticism, charged with impeding and embarrassing the Holy See. Tamburini incisively instructed them to continue the administration of the sacraments. The Bavarian Jesuit, Ignaz Kögler, wrote to Lisbon in November, 1724, "While we weep over these pitiful ruins, while we hope for some comfort from Europe, all we get is a letter from our general, written by order of Propaganda, which leaves us prostrate with grief and almost kills us." The benighted missionaries, pressed between sincere doubts and the reprehension of their general, gradually worked their way to a solution to ease their consciences. Again they resumed their sacramental work.[89]

This charge of obstructionism was but one of the long list filed against the Society. De Tournon blamed the Jesuits for the dreary outcome of his mission. Maigrot laid the disaster to the Chinese church at their door. Stumpf, distressed by the way quarrels were crippling the Church's strength, preferred to have the Society withdraw from China than to see the cause completely ruined. A man of magnanimous stamp, like the true mother before Solomon faced with the violent division of her child in two, Stumpf expressed his willingness to surrender to the Society's critics rather than see everything lost. At this crucial moment the official roster of the Society listed in the vice-province four colleges, two of which were at Nanking and

89 Pastor, *History*, XXXIII, 458, 462–467; XXXIV, 85.

Peking, and thirty-seven residences; and in the French Mission twenty-eight residences.

Despite Stumpf's readiness to leave, it was the continued presence of the Jesuits at Peking which held the greatest hope for the Chinese Church. Among the pagans distrust of Christianity fed on their resentment of the decree on the rites, which they interpreted as western contempt for their culture, and the high tribunals of the empire issued decrees of banishment against the missionaries. These decrees K'ang-hsi confirmed in 1717. Actually he did not enforce them, but his two successors, Yung Ch'eng (1723-1736) and Ch'ien-Lung (1736-1796) did so with determination. Darkness fell over the Church in China. In one place a candle of hope burned through the bleak years. At Peking the three emperors, in their admiration of and respect for the learning of the Jesuits, allowed them to remain and even keep a church open for the Christians there. K'ang-hsi had a predilection for the Frenchmen. Dominique Parrenin, in collaboration with five other attentive observers like Jean Baptiste Régis, constructed the famous "Jesuit Map" of China, Manchuria, and Mongolia which was published in Paris in 1735. Under Yung Ch'eng, even while priests, including thirty-six Jesuits, were being rounded up and collected at Canton for shipment to Macao, Ignaz Kögler presided in Peking as president of the Tribunal of Astronomy, and Parrenin and Antoine Gaubil taught Latin at the new school for diplomatic interpreters, founded to train civil servants for the negotiations with western powers. In 1735 Kögler published ten volumes of updated astronomical tables which incorporated the work of such celebrated European astronomers as the Englishman John Flamsteed and the Frenchman Jean Dominique Cassini. His collaborator was the only English Jesuit on the China mission, André Pereyra, whose original family name was Jackson and who was raised and educated in Oporto. Under the temperamental and moody Ch'ien-Lung nothing but heroic devotion to Christ could make these men persevere in what one of them called "their chained slavery," as they pursued their work in art and science, "tied to a chair from one sun to the next," in order to make the emperor well-disposed to the faith.[90] In 1743 at Peking nine priests and three brothers of the Chinese vice-province lived in two residences; the French Mission had six fathers and

---

90 De la Servière, *Les anciennes missions,* pp. 64-65; SMV, VI, 498; Needham, *Chinese Astronomy and the Jesuit Mission,* p. 12, fn. 17; Plattner, *Jesuits Go East,* pp. 246-247.

four brothers. A dozen Chinese priests rounded out this unusual group of men who used their talents at the royal court as painters, engineers, sculptors, musicians, astronomers, workers in glass and enamel. Outstanding were two superb scholars, Joseph de Prémare, one of the greatest sinologists of all time, and Antoine Gabriel, superior to all the great Chinese savants of the day in his understanding of the literature and history of their people.

This policy of silent service, based on the hope of softening the imperial intransigence toward Christianity, met the severest kind of criticism from non-Jesuits in other parts of the empire. To missionaries, caught up in the daily ordeal of living like hunted animals, the Peking Jesuits appeared as servants of a Nero, thriving amid material luxury. These critics, living heroically themselves, failed to recognize another kind of spiritual prowess in the imperial city. Despite this unselfish service of the Jesuits to the emperor, another Edict of Milan never came, but here and there, amid the bulk of Jesuit reports, appeared passages which gave a glimmer of hope for the Church. Some of the more inspiring came from the pen of one of the most admirable Jesuits who ever labored in China, the great-hearted Austrian, Gottfried Xaver von Laimbeckhoven. This native of Vienna left home as a young priest at the age of twenty-seven in 1735 and died in 1787 at Tangkiahsiang after nearly fifty years in China and thirty-five as bishop of Nanking.

Because of his abilities as a mathematician Laimbeckhoven seemed destined for the class of mandarins, very possibly the only Jesuit in history whom superiors considered for mathematical service at three imperial courts, in China, Cochin China, and the realm of the Great Mogul. Laimbeckhoven, however, personally preferred a direct apostolate among the people, since he did not see the value of making a long overseas journey in order to be a slave of a pagan ruler. Superiors honored his preference, and in 1739 he began in Hukwang his long Chinese apostolate.[91]

His letters, with their moving accounts of the fidelity of the Christian peasants during persecution, have a spiritual resonance like that of the messages of Robert Persons during his journeys in England in 1580-1581. The home of the missionary was either on the mountain, or in a boat on a lake, or in a cave, or on a deserted beach. "Leave me with my neophytes whom I love from the depths of my heart," he wrote a fellow Jesuit,

91 Krahl, *China Missions,* pp. 4, 23-25, 82-83.

"and let me die among them. To expire among them will be the greatest consolation of my deathbed." In the first four years he converted 1,700, mainly peasants and fishermen.[92]

In 1754 Laimbeckhoven received the greatest shock of his life. Pope Benedict XIV confirmed his designation by the king of Portugal as the bishop of Nanking to succeed the Portuguese Franciscan, Francisco de Santa Rosa de Viterbo, who had died four years earlier. Three years later he received another heavy burden. On May 26, 1757, the Jesuit bishop of Peking, Policarpo de Sousa, died. Before the end, De Sousa designated Laimbeckhoven as the administrator of the diocese. For twenty years, while the see remained vacant, Laimbeckhoven had to carry the responsibilities of Peking as well as Nanking. And they were years of calamity for the Church, presaged by the martyrdom between 1746 and 1748 of two Jesuits, António José Henriques and Tristano de Attimis, and five Dominicans. The disappearance of religious liberty left a melancholy prospect for Étienne Guillaume Le Coulteux, who saw the position of respect formerly held by the Church lost forever. "Never," he wrote, "can the damage which has been done be repaired." Ignaz Kögler told of how he wept "over these pitiful ruins." [93] Laimbeckhoven confirmed these reactions. In 1724, before the persecution, Nanking had been a flourishing diocese of about 100,000 Christians. It had a cathedral, and the province of Kiangnan alone had thirty parish churches. Laimbeckhoven saw this vigorous community dwindle to about a third with about two dilapidated chapels. Pessimistically he reflected that naught but a shadow remained of the former splendor of his wonderful diocese.[94]

Within the Jesuit ranks a lack of harmony aggravated this distressing situation. The Portuguese, far overstretched by the eighteenth century in their generous commitments to the missions, were not able to supply enough qualified men and needed the assistance of other countries. Usually the Jesuit visitors were German, Italian, or Austrian, although the vice-provincial was generally a Portuguese. The meeting of these men of diverse provenance sometimes resembled the meeting of flint and steel. Sparks flew. In 1698 a report to the papal secretary of state from the nunciature in Portugal about a Jesuit detachment to the

92 Ibid., p. 25.
93 H. W. Hering, "A Study of Roman Catholic Missions in China—1692-1744," *New China Review,* III (1921), 106-126, 198-212; Pastor, *History,* XXXIV, 85.
94 Krahl, *China Missions,* pp. 138-139.

missions observed that the genius of the Portuguese and that of the Italians did not seem to mesh very smoothly. In 1750 António Gomes, the vice-provincial in China, in an especially sour mood observed that only patience kept him from wishing a plague on the one who sent so many Germans to China. Acidly he added: "But since they are here I have no remedy for the situation except patience. But for the future, let them stay in Europe." [95] The presence on the royal tribunals of Germans like Hallerstein and Gogeisl, profound scholars in the fields of mathematics and astronomy, annoyed the Portuguese. Laimbeckhoven noted that young Jesuits from Portugal were arriving in China without sufficient moral and intellectual formation. Friction could only result from the attitude represented by two young Portuguese Jesuits, Felix da Rocha and José Simois, who saw it as their duty to keep "foreigners" from gaining the ascendancy in Peking.

To add to the distress brought on by nationalism came stories from Europe of alleged Jesuit disobedience in China. St. Ignatius had once written that he desired obedience to so characterize the Jesuit as though the whole good of the Society depended on this. Rarely had this obedience been so insistently tested as in China during the early eighteenth century. Others, including two officials of the Franciscans, testified to the fidelity of the China Jesuits to the Ignatian tradition. What hurt particularly, therefore, was the news that in Rome disobedience was one of the charges made against them. In November, 1724, Ignaz Kögler wrote from Peking to the confessor of the queen of Portugal of his grief, his amazement, his curiosity: grief that men who sacrificed so much to be missionaries should be accused of such enormities as heresy and disloyalty to the Holy See; amazement at the senseless repetition of requests each year for testimony to the obedience of the Jesuits in China; curiosity as to whether these testimonials were being suppressed in Europe. Kögler did not appreciate the nature of the opposition in Rome. A short time earlier, on October 28, he and the other Jesuits in Peking addressed a poignant letter to Father General Tamburini in which they clearly expressed their acceptance of the papal decisions, their deep sorrow because of the enormous scandals imputed to them, and their interpretation of this crisis as a unique occasion to become more like to Christ in his sufferance of calumny. [96]

95 Rodrigues, *História*, III, ii, 136.
96 Pastor, *History*, XXXIV, 85–86, 539–545.

The Jesuits loved the China mission, and superiors dispatched some of their most gifted men despite the staggering losses over the horrible shipping lanes. In 1673, for example, Prospero Intorcetta, who had returned to Europe to obtain recruits for China, sailed with twelve companions in the fleet that left Lisbon in March. When he reached Macao only one had survived. Two among the dead were the promising mathematicians, Adam Aigenler and Beatus Amrhym. Both priests, up to their final sickness, kept detailed accounts in which they recorded the terrible details of stifling heat on a becalmed sea under an equatorial sun, gasping for breath in an ovenlike hull, drinking putrid water, seeing sick men die in agonizing convulsions.[97] In that same year the Angola mission lost seven men when their galleon went down. In 1684 Philippe Couplet, a Belgian, destined to die by drowning in 1693, told Philippe Avril, a Frenchman who would lose his life in a shipwreck the same year, that of the six hundred Jesuits selected for China in the century since Ricci had entered the Empire only about a hundred arrived there. Thieves, pirates, sickness, shipwreck took the others. Couplet's figures may need some checking, but he was well-versed in this aspect of Jesuit history and in 1687 published a catalog with a *curriculum vitae* of each of the Society's priests who worked in China during the century after 1581. The Jansenists in France knew the reason for the enormous losses in the Jesuit ranks: an angry God was wreaking vengeance on a body of despicable men.[98]

Adverse to the Church's fortunes as had been the decision on the rites, it was nevertheless not the all decisive factor against religious freedom in China. The two emperors who followed K'ang-hsi and other high officials in the government opposed on national and cultural grounds the presence of Christianity. As early as 1640, in a work called *A Collection of Writings of the Sacred Dynasty for the Countering of Heterodoxy,* members of the Chinese intelligentsia argued, from the Buddhist as well as the Confucian viewpoint, against the theological doctrines of the western missionaries. Almost certainly, regardless of the rites issue, they would have followed the same course. Then the suppression of the Society, the French Revolution, and the political convulsions in the rest of Europe closed the reservoir of man-

97 Plattner, *Jesuits Go East,* pp. 110-113.
98 M. Hay, *Failure in the Far East* (Philadelphia, 1957), p. 155, fn. 2; SMV, I, 706; II, 1562-1566.

power, automatically condemning the missions to decline and death.[99] In the collapse of Ricci's great enterprise ended, amid the rush of many forces, one of history's noblest and most charitable efforts by men of one culture to appreciate the positive values of another.

A century and a half later the westernization of China brought about a staggering social change: the secularization of the rites. The spread of experimental science removed Confucius from his semi-divine status, and the laicization of life in general drained away the religious elements in the veneration of the dead. In the light of this fundamental revolution of attitudes, and assured by the affirmation of the Republic that the rites were devoid of religious significance, Pope Pius XII in 1939 lifted the ban of 1704.[100]

During the religious turmoil in China after De Tournon's visit, in the land north of the Himalayas a Jesuit filled some of the more fascinating pages in the history of travel. In September, 1714, Ippolito Desideri started from Delhi and arrived at Lhasa, the Dalai Lama's capital, in May, 1716. The first European to look on the holy mountain of Meru and crystal-clear Manasrovar, "the most beautiful lake in the world," he recorded vivid descriptions of his extraordinary mountain journey. For five years he lived with the monks in a Lama monastery, discussed with them and wrote for them an explanation of Christianity. In 1721 Tamburini ordered him to leave because of a jurisdictional dispute with the Capuchins. He returned to Europe and provided the West with a detailed study about the monk-governed state hidden behind the highest mountains of the globe.

In Africa, of the several Jesuit essays, the solitary mission to strike roots and grow was Angola. There, through the eighteenth century, the staff at the colleges in Luanda numbered about ten priests and seven brothers, the group which appears in the register for 1700. The Dark Continent therefore outmatched the Jesuits of the pre-Suppression Society in what was perhaps their greatest mission failure. It remained for their followers of

99 K. S. Latourette, *A History of the Expansion of Christianity. Three Centuries of Advance, A.D. 1500–A.D. 1800* (New York, 1951), III, 355-356; also, Latourette, *A History of Christian Missions in China* (London, 1929), pp. 153-154; Douglas Lancashire, "Anti-Christian Polemics in Seventeenth Century China," *Church History*, XXXVIII (1969), 218-220.

100 A. Brou, S.J., "Le point final à la question des rites chinois," *Études*, CCXLII (1940), 275-288.

the nineteenth century to alter this discouraging record by their creation of some of the most vigorous bodies of the modern African Church.

Brazil, like the missions in the Orient, always remained un- *Brazil and* finished business. Despite steady advances of the missionaries, *Spanish America* no end of Amerindians awaited the Gospel. The figures of departures from Lisbon show that there was no slack in the Society's response to the call from Brazil. In 1705 twelve sailed; in 1717, ten, of whom nine were Portuguese novices; in 1729, thirteen. In 1727 Tamburini made Maranhão an independent vice-province. For this area, between 1703 and 1721, sixty-nine sailed; between 1750 and 1756, thirty-seven. Two new colleges, at Parnaguá and Bahía, and three seminaries added to the consolidation of the Brazilian enterprise.[101]

In general the Jesuits in Spanish America followed the directions taken by earlier generations. In 1750 some 2,300 men were stationed there. The strength of the provinces varied from area to area and provided some vivid contrasts, such as the sharp increase of the Chile Province, from sixty men in 1626 to 242 in 1749, and the somewhat static condition of the New Granada Province, for the same years dropping from 200 to 193. But the trend was generally toward augmentation. Here and there fidelity to the exacting programs of formation for the young Jesuits lapsed. Tamburini and Retz admonished superiors of the Province of Ecuador for their carelessness on this score, and the same two generals checked the Province of New Granada for deficiency in the humanistic training of the scholastics, a prerequisite for success in higher studies. "What good is a multitude of men," asked Tamburini, "if they do not have the capacity to serve the Society's aims?" Religious spirit was high and gained from the archbishop of Lima, Antonio Zuloaga, the somewhat embarrassing tribute that they were the only ones who worked with seriousness of purpose among the Indians.[102]

On the mission roster, almost completely Latin in its make-up, more and more German names appeared. These additions from north of the Alps brought valuable qualities of endurance, concentration, and tenacity to which there remain many testimonials, such as Adam Gilg's grammar of the Pima and Eudeve tongues, Johann Gummersbach's series of ascetical works in the

101 Rodrigues, *Historia*, IV, i, 218-220.
102 Astráin, *Historia*, VII, 331-332, 445; García-Villoslada, *Manual*, p. 553.

Mexican tongue, Franz Inama von Sternegg's writings in natural science, Jakob Baegert's account of Lower California, and Brother Johann Steinefer's widely published *A Medical Anthology* (1712). The correspondence of the German Jesuits, probably packed with fresh insights into the mission history of New Spain, awaits its editor. Four letters of Anton Benz, a Bavarian who went to Mexico in 1749, give a clue of what might be expected. Containing important and interesting information found nowhere else, they adumbrate the untouched archival secrets which have much to tell to round out the story of the Jesuits in Spanish America.[103]

The Province of Mexico received one of the most illustrious of these non-Spaniards. Eusebio Kühn, usually known in the United States as Eusebio Kino, born in 1644 near Trent in the Tyrol, trained as a Jesuit in the Province of Upper Germany, a vigorous, perceptive, and magnetic personality, dominated for the twenty-five years before his death in 1711 the religious history of the Sonora-California-Arizona frontier. Starting from the lengthy chain of Jesuit missions which extended along the Sierra Madre, he forged new links along the Sonora-Arizona boundary and the San Ignacio, Sonóita, and Santa Cruz rivers. Indefatigable rider, he seemed to live in the saddle. Great lover of the Indians and provident for their well-being, he started cattle ranches and introduced European cereals and fruits. Superb cartographer, he created maps which are witnesses to his precise and keen observation. Assiduous diarist, he penned accounts of the mission which illumine the stirrings of Christianity and civilization in that frontier land. In 1965 the State of Arizona dedicated a sculpture of Kino in Statuary Hall in the Capitol at Washington, D.C., where seventy years before the State of Wisconsin paid the same honor to Jacques Marquette.

One of the many Jesuits inspired by Kino was the clearheaded and iron nerved Juan Salvatierra, a son of Italy from Milan, who found his great challenge in Lower California, that long finger of land, sterile, arid, and inhabited by indolent and dull yet cruel and treacherous natives. Salvatierra first offered Mass there in 1697 at the mission post of Our Lady of Loreto and at his death twenty years later left a string of missions through the length of the peninsula, a monument to his refusal to be overwhelmed by the opposition of man and nature. The natives added to the

103 P. Dunne, S.J. and E. Burrus, S.J., "Four Unpublished Letters of Anton Maria Benz, Eighteenth Century Missionary to Mexico," *AHSJ*, XXIV (1955), 336-378.

list in the Jesuit martyrology by murdering in 1734 Lorenzo Cananzo and Nicolás Tamaral. Through the sixty years until the Society's suppression fifty-six Jesuits labored in Lower California.

This hard mission comes to life again in the *Observations in Lower California* (1771) of the gruff, blunt Alsatian, Jakob Baegert. He opens with the unpromising sentence: "Everything about California is of such little importance that it is hardly worth the trouble to take a pen and write about it." Then for some two hundred pages he talks about the country's people, their customs, revolting weaknesses, rudimentary culture, diseases, and languages, a down-to-earth panorama of mission life devoid of all sentimental illusions.

Of wider scope than Baegert's *Observations* was the *History of the Society of Jesus in New Spain* by Francisco Alegre. His record spanned the period from 1572 to 1766, the year before Spain exiled the Jesuits from its realms. Only in 1841 was his work first published. Alegre, a native of Vera Cruz and a highly competent historian, produced a lively, colorful, richly documented, and eminently readable account, one of the three classics of Jesuit history in New Spain, ranking with *The History of the Triumphs of Our Holy Faith* (1645) by Andrés Pérez de Ribas and *Data on the Temporal and Spiritual Conquest of California* (1757) by Miguel Venegas.

On the lower continent the mysterious waterways which passed through the darkness of the interior still called on the ingenuity and zeal of the missionaries. Among the Mojos Cipriano Barace continued to be the great inspiration. During his twenty-seven years among these people, of whom he baptized some 40,000, he instructed them in the knowledge of agriculture, manual arts, and in the construction of churches which in beauty and splendor rivaled those in the cities of Peru. In 1702 he began to branch out among other tribes, the Guarayes, the Tapacuras, and the Baures. From group to group he moved until on September 16 a shower of arrows cut him down, crowning with martyrdom one of the most indefatigable men in the entire history of the Society in South America. Co-workers and successors of Barace included men whose *curriculum vitae* leaves one amazed that a human being could for so long endure the enervating humidity and withering heat of the pest-ridden jungle. Pedro Rado died at the age of seventy-eight after forty-three years on this mission; Diego Fernández at the age of eighty after fifty-two years among the natives.[104]

104 Astráin, *Historia,* VI, 570-571; VII, 370.

Along the banks of the Marañón the mantle of the great La Cueva fell on the worthy shoulders of the intrepid Bohemian, Samuel Fritz. In 1704 Fritz became superior of the mission based on Ecuador when its manpower had been sadly depleted, reduced in 1706 to only eight men. Fritz went to Quito, described the desperate situation to the provincial and returned with ten reinforcements from the many who volunteered. In a sweeping move to expand the mission further to the east, he sailed along the Marañón and the Amazon from the slopes of the Andes to the area of Pará, charting the great river and composing an account replete with descriptions of the invasion of mosquitoes and insects and the yelping of beasts in the wilderness. But his dauntlessness earned for him a broken heart. The Portuguese, to whom his journey brought him close, tracing the route taken by Fritz, sailed out of Pará, up the Marañón, plundered the villages organized by the Jesuits and retired with booty and prisoners in a nightmarish reproduction of what the "paulistas" had done to the reductions of Paraguay in the previous century. In 1725, after forty years of work along the Marañón and the Amazon, Fritz died. The village where the Jesuits of this mission made the deepest penetration into the jungle with a successful community life for the Indians was that of San Ignacio, sixty leagues to the east of the confluence of the Napo and the Amazon. So it remained until the suppression of the Society.[105]

Only with the gravest difficulties did the poor and under-manned Province of New Granada establish a mission along the banks of the Orinoco. Twice begun and twice abandoned, a village finally began to prosper about 1731 under the care of José Gumella, who by his clever craftsmanship as carpenter, mason, architect, and painter won the hearts of the Indians. To build up this straitened province Spain, despite a great tragedy in 1716, gave generously of her own manpower. In 1716 the entire party of twenty-three missionaries was lost when the ship *Sagronis*, hardly outside the harbor of Cadiz, went to the bottom during a storm. In 1723 thirty-six men sailed; in 1735, fifty-six; in 1743, twelve. Other expeditions followed in subsequent years. By 1735 throughout the vast plains within the area of the province, the Jesuits had created eight villages in which resided 5,931 domesticated and christianized natives.[106]

Chile remained the area where the Indians most energetically withstood conversion. The Araucans, resistant as ever, exacted

105 Ibid., VII, 401-415.
106 Ibid., VII, 439-440, 454-466.

from the missionaries the greatest patience before they could administer the 112,296 baptisms which they did in the thirty years 1732-1762.

The Province of Paraguay, distinguished by its reductions, did not rest but, in a constant outward movement, widened its perimeter in several directions. To the west, from the Paraguay River to the first foothills of the Andes, stretched the wide prairies of the Chaco. Into this vast territory plunged José de Arce, who, with his genius for convincing the natives of the value of a settled life, managed in 1690 to organize the village of the Presentation of Our Lady. Three years later enemy Indians descended on the colony and wiped it out. But Arce began again and within a decade he, aided by fellow religious, had established four reductions for 3,000 converts. The number of men in this province oscillated strangely through the years. The 269 of 1710 rose to 352 in 1735, dropped to 303 in 1749, then rose to 400 in 1756. Epidemics largely explained the drastic setbacks. During one of these, forty men died. Assistance from Spain accounted for sharp increases. In 1717 fifty-seven men sailed for Paraguay; in 1726, sixty; in 1733, fifty-eight; in 1745, sixty-eight.[107]

During this steady advance, exactly at midcentury, occurred an international event which initiated the complete destruction of the Jesuit achievement in Spanish and Portuguese America. In 1750, on January 13, Spain and Portugal affirmed a treaty for the exchange of territory in America. Not a momentous pact in itself, it nevertheless had sombre significance for the Society, propelling as it did a series of reactions which, with other causes, led to the suppression of the Society in 1773. The main theatre of combat against the Society was in several of the capitals of Europe, but this Boundary Treaty of 1750 was a kind of Sarajevo.

By this agreement Spain and Portugal sought to end a protracted period of litigation about the borders of their respective domains. Spain ceded to Portugal a large area east of the Uruguay River, which today is a considerable part of the Brazilian state of Rio Grande do Sul. To Spain, Portugal yielded the district of San Sacramento on the north bank of the Rio de la Plata across from Buenos Aires. The Jesuits were drawn into this international business, because in the territory east of the Uruguay they conducted seven reductions with 29,191 natives. Enforcement of the treaty led to a series of military engagements,

107 Ibid., VI, 704-710; VII, 480-483, 497, 737.

known as The War of the Seven Reductions, and catastrophe for the Indians.[108]

By virtue of the agreement the natives in the seven reductions were called on to migrate west of the Uruguay. To Portugal were ceded their homes, churches, buildings, and land. For each village they were offered 4,000 pesos. The smallest reduction was worth more than a million pesos.[109] Against this injustice the Jesuits protested strongly.

Several of the missionaries met in conference at which sixty-eight out of seventy judged the transfer of so many natives to be impracticable. But beyond the question of practicability they stressed the violation of the natural rights of life, liberty, and property, and this they represented to their fellow Jesuit and royal confessor in Spain, Francisco de Rábago. The Indians, they admitted, owed allegiance to the king, but in return "he owes them protection in all their rights." With natural and divine law the missionaries could not reconcile this particular human legislation.[110] This problem also reached the desks of two generals, Frantisek Retz and Ignazio Visconti, but neither superior seemed to sense the deep moral implications of the treaty as they urged the missionaries to comply with the royal desires. Visconti wrote with particular acerbity and absence of fatherly understanding. On each of the missionaries he imposed an order in virtue of holy obedience and under pain of mortal sin not only not to resist directly or indirectly the transfer of the land but also to use his influence that the Indians comply.[111]

The unpleasant task of informing the natives of their fate fell to the veteran missionary Bernhard Nusdorffer. For a month, from March 9 to April 10, 1752, he made the circuit of the seven reductions. The inhabitants received the news with dismay but promised their Jesuit friend that they would obey. Nusdorffer then dispatched fifteen expert missionaries and some Indians from each reduction to search west of the Uruguay for land suitable for new communities. They found none.[112]

Events reached an impasse. The Jesuits, despite the uninviting terrain, tried to get the emigration started. Some natives became obstinate. Others censured the missionaries. Still others

108 Ibid., VII, 640-642; Kratz, *El Tratado*, pp. 23-25.
109 Astráin, *Historia*, VII, 642-643.
110 Kratz, *El Tratado*, p. 52. G. O'Neill, S.J., *Golden Years on the Paraguay* (London, 1934), pp. 218-219.
111 Astráin, *Historia*, VII, 644-647; O'Neill, *Golden Years*, pp. 220-221.
112 Kratz, *El Tratado*, p. 58.

cooperated for a while, but then returned. Their qualities of instability and fickleness came to the fore. Into this painful situation, two years after the enactment of the treaty, stepped the delegate of Father General Visconti, Lope Luis Altamirano, a man probably nonpareil in the history of the Society. He announced at least twenty-four precepts in virtue of the vow of obedience with penalties that included dismissal from the Society, suspension of priestly faculties, and excommunication reserved to the general. Altamirano's abrasive policy only deepened the recalcitrance of the Indians. It took two military expeditions, in 1754 and 1756, before Spanish and Portuguese troops seized the reductions and dispersed the natives.[113]

This colonial debacle in America became a key position in the diplomatic checker game of the new minister of foreign affairs in Lisbon, Sebastião José de Carvalho e Mello. Carvalho, who assumed office only a few months after the signing of the Boundary Treaty of January, 1750, disapproved of the agreement, described it as an obstacle to peace, and suggested that his government cancel it. The Portuguese monarch, feeling that such an action would be incompatible with the royal word of honor, refused.[114] With his administrative finesse Carvalho adjusted to the situation, took the disturbances in the seven reductions, and molded them into an effective instrument against the Jesuits. In March, 1755, he directed his brother, Francisco Xavier Mendonça Furtado, governor of Grão Para and Maranhão, to move the Portuguese Jesuits, under any convenient pretext, from the Spanish border and to intercept their correspondence with the Spanish Jesuits. In his program of harassment he undertook negotiations with Spain to supplement the Boundary Treaty of 1750 with what seemed to be the broader purpose of completely removing the Jesuits from all the missions in Portuguese and Spanish America.[115]

In Portugal, Carvalho pressed his campaign of libel against the Society. He published a sixty-eight page pamphlet called *A Brief Account of the Republic Founded by the Jesuits in the Spanish and Portuguese Dominions of the New World and Their War against the Armies of the Two Crowns*, (1757). The title suggests the contents: responsibility for the war in the reductions fell not on the Indians but on the Jesuits, their avarice, and disloyalty to Spain and Portugal. Between 1757 and 1759

---

113 Ibid., pp. 76-78; O'Neill, *Golden Years*, pp. 232-233.
114 Kratz, *El Tratado*, p. 39.
115 Ibid., pp. 131, 198, 223-225.

translations appeared in Italian, French, Spanish, and German.[116] A former Jesuit, expelled from the Society in May, 1757, Bernardo Ibañez de Echávarri, later supported Carvalho's defamation with a work entitled *The Jesuit Kingdom in Paraguay,* (1770). These writings wove into the popular imagination, like bewildering arabesques, fantastic stories of Jesuit machinations in the Americas. In 1759, two years beyond the cutoff date of this chapter, Carvalho exiled all Jesuits from Portugal and its overseas possessions.

The same year, in Spain, Charles III succeeded Ferdinand VI. The new monarch expressed Spanish disenchantment with the Boundary Treaty of 1750. He authorized the dispatch of sixty-eight more Jesuits to the Province of Paraguay. Pedro Ceballos Cortés y Calderón, governor general at Buenos Aires since November 4, 1576, investigated the issue of the reductions, exonerated the Jesuits of all blame, and recommended their continuance in the missions. On February 12, 1761, Portugal and Spain signed an agreement to annul the eleven-year-old Boundary Treaty.[117] In about two years the Jesuits had resettled about 14,000 natives in the evacuated reductions. The original treaty, which might have passed into history with no more significance than just another instance of the human suffering which often follows in the wake of pacts between nations, carried an ominous meaning for the Church. It presaged the banishment of the Society from the two great Iberian empires and the malaise that would then fall over many of the mission lands.

The Philippines   As in Spanish America, the Jesuits in the Philippines divided their attention between town and country. In 1726 they were operating four colleges, at Manila, Cavite, Cebu, and Iloilo, San José Seminary in Manila, and eight residences. Including their posts in the uncultivated areas of both the Philippines and the Marianas, they were in 1755 caring for the spiritual needs of 130 communities with 212,153 Catholics. Especially because of the Marianas, the Philippine mission exercised a strong fascination on the Jesuits of Europe. In large numbers they sailed there

116 Ibid., pp. 5, fn. 19; 133, fn. 27. These accusations were the culmination of a tradition of denigration of the Society among some earlier colonists, allegations which "were either wholly false or grossly exaggerated . . ." Carvalho reaped where others had sown. See Boxer, *Golden Age,* p. 289.

117 Ibid., pp. 240-241, 279-281.

— twenty men in 1708, forty in 1717, twenty-four in 1722, thirty-four in 1730, and so on. But the province somehow resembled a broken cistern. The manpower kept draining off. A high mortality rate — thirty-three died in the five years, 1735-40 — was one large crack. In 1710 the province numbered 165; thirty-nine years later it had dropped to 126. Among the fresh arrivals, as in the rest of the Spanish domain, were a considerable number of non-Spaniards.

Two who stood out in a special way were Pavel Klein and Brother Jirí Kamel. Klein, a Czech, of wide learning, published in Spanish and Tagalog. In the latter tongue he composed a series of reflections entitled *Hell Laid Open to the Christian, that He may be Advised Not to Enter Therein* (1713), and made a translation of Dominique Bouhours' *Christian Thoughts for Each Day of the Month* (1714). In Spanish he published a kind of medical catchall, *Simple Remedies for Various Complaints* (1712), which enjoyed wide popularity. Klein also directed Ignacia del Espíritu Santo, the holy woman who founded the first Filipino religious order of women, the Religious of the Virgin Mary.

Kamel, also a Czech, operated the celebrated pharmacy at the College of Manila, which served not only the school but also the city and far beyond. He communicated with the Royal Society of London, to which he sent neat descriptions and specimens of insects and plants, called attention to the St. Ignatius bean from which strychnine was derived, and received from the celebrated Carl von Linné the honor of having the *thea japonica,* or *camellia,* an oriental shrub of the tea family with evergreen leaves and roselike flowers, named after him. Some 300 drawings done by Kamel to illustrate his writings lie in the British Museum and the Louvain archives of the Society awaiting their editor and publisher.[118]

Sometime shortly after 1720 the Jesuits, with the Dominicans, made a major breakthrough in the islands. For some time they had discussed means to train natives to be secular priests, and finally in the 1720's they realized their hopes in the ordination of the first Filipinos, some of whom studied at the Society's San José seminary. By 1750 the project was well under way and an encouraging supply of priests was coming forth. But the obstacles remained crushing in their force. There was the hardcore opposition of nearly two centuries to a native clergy, so vividly

118 De la Costa, *Jesuits in the Philippines,* pp. 507-508, 556-558.

epitomized in the Augustinian Fray Gaspar de San Agustín. If God did not erase the emerging Filipino priesthood, "what abominations will result from it!" exclaimed the friar in 1725. Still more, there was the structure of the Church in the Philippines, which of its nature discouraged vocations to the secular priesthood. In 1750, of the 569 parishes and missions in the Islands, religious held 427 — the Jesuits had ninety-three — and the native priests held 142. The Royal Patronage system shored up this structure, favoring as it did the religious, who in turn tended to regard the Filipino seculars as a threat to their existence. The Filipino seminarian for his part, looking at this formidable organization, frequently had no better prospect than to become an assistant to a religious pastor.

Several Jesuits wanted to cure this case of ecclesiastical lock-jaw and felt that the Society should surrender at least some of the parishes, especially the better developed ones. They could not forget that the Society's *Constitutions* ([324, 588]), in order to preserve Jesuit mobility, ruled out the stable administration of parishes. An intramural debate gained momentum, and in 1687 the provincial congregation sent two priests to Rome, one supporting the withdrawal from and the other advocating the continuance in the parochial apostolate.

Another hoary issue rose out of the past, and in its resolution by Rome tied the Jesuits to the parishes until the suppression. It was the vexatious problem of episcopal visitation of parishes under the care of religious. In late 1697 the new archbishop of Manila, Don Diego Camacho y Ávila, started an official inspection of the parishes in his jurisdiction. He began with the Dominican church of San Gabriel. Within a week the provincials of the religious orders withdrew their subjects from over a hundred towns within the archdiocese. Camacho, with only fifty-three secular priests, could do nothing but surrender. The case went to Rome. In 1705 the Sacred Congregation of the Council judged, rightly and justly, that the archbishop had the right to investigate the state of the pastoral care of souls and the administration of the sacraments. But the Congregation also declared that the religious orders could not resign parishes and missions without incurring "censure, forfeiture of goods, and other penalties." This solved the Jesuits' dilemma. They stayed in the parishes. But the Congregation's decision did more. It checkmated the natural and free development of a Filipino clergy. In 1898, when the American conquest of the Islands broke the power of the Spanish Royal Patronage, the archbishop of Manila had genuine control of only twelve of 350 parishes in the appointment of pastors. Spanish friars directed the others.[119] A brief glance back over the centuries to September 17, 1581, when the Jesuits first entered Manila, gives a graphic picture of how forces and events outside the Society shaped the course of its history.

Still dependent on the Philippines, the Marianas, because of seemingly endemic internecine strife, reached a nadir of decadence. The Spanish military government, taking drastic action to keep the natives under surveillance, began in 1695 a mass transplantation of populations, moving them from several islands to Guam and Rota. Pedro Murillo-Velarde in his *History of the Philippine Province* (1749) detailed the discouraging handicaps of this mission, the loneliness, isolation from news, the sterile earth under a melancholy sky, the periodic fury of wind and sea. Another group of islands, the Palaus, which Pavel Klein called "the new Philippines," offered on their discovery a further incentive to the Jesuits, who proceeded forthwith to make gallant but frustrated efforts to reach their peoples. Tragedy dogged their every attempt. In 1710 Jacques Duberon and Joseph Cortil were clubbed to death by the natives of Sonsorol. The next year Andrés Serrano, Ignacio Crespo, and Brother Étienne Baudin died in shipwreck. In or about 1731 Antonio Cantova was murdered. These Pacific Islands lived up to their reputation for danger and disaster.[120]

This period closes on the eve of the death of New France. *French and English America* Through the years of the mammoth struggle between England and France in which this vast mission field of Canada was one of the greatest prizes at stake, the Jesuits, inheriting the skills and experience of the pioneers, carried on the work among the Red Men. Along the St. Lawrence, up the Saguenay, on the Kenebec, Lake Superior, Lake Michigan, Green Bay, the Illinois, they maintained in 1710 nineteen posts with several auxiliary stations. Ever since 1632 they had worked out of Quebec, but in 1700, with no diminution to the importance of Quebec, they approached the interior from another direction. That year Paul du Ru, on January 8, arrived at Fort Maurepas, the first capital of the new French colony, across the bay from Biloxi. A few months later he built the first chapel in Louisiana with the help of the Bayagoulas Indians at present day Bayou Goula.

---

119 Ibid., pp. 516-517, 525-529; see also *Theological Studies*, VIII (1947), 234-238, 248.
120 De la Costa, *Jesuits in the Philippines*, pp. 549-551; Astráin, *Historia*, VIII, 762-781.

Eighteen years earlier Robert Cavelier de La Salle had claimed for France the area about the delta of the Mississippi, and in 1699 Pierre le Moyne d'Iberville started the settlement at Fort Maurepas. For twenty-seven years after Du Ru's arrival a few Jesuits made sporadic visits to the colony. In 1727 Nicolas de Beaubois, a vivacious, imaginative, practical, and impatient man, arrived at New Orleans with six other Jesuits. These early years in Louisiana made another now familiar page in the mission history of that era with its strange amalgam of heroism, contention between religious orders, and wearisome jurisdictional conflicts. Capuchins and Jesuits tangled with one another. Caught in the skein of this dismal quarrel, De Beaubois, even as he contributed to the material welfare of the colony by the construction of a cotton mill, the manufacture of indigo, and the planning of a canal, was with his fellow Jesuits under ecclesiastical interdict.[121]

North of New Orleans, the initial experience of the priests who moved among the Yazoos, the Arkansas, the Alibamons, the Illinois, and along the Wabash resembled the bleak and discouraging earlier experience of their predecessors in Canada. They found it nearly impossible to break through the tough resistance of the Indians to all their efforts at conversion. One priest reported: "Nothing is more difficult than conversion of these savages. . . . We must first make men of them, then Christians." Paul du Poisson observed about the Arkansas: "By human standards no great good can be accomplished among them, at least initially." [122] This same Du Poisson was the first Jesuit of this Louisiana mission to shed his blood for the faith when he fell, on November 28, 1729, during a rising of the Natchez Indians. Jean Souel met the same fate two weeks later, on December 11, at the hands of the Yazoos.

Through the first half of the eighteenth century the Jesuits who worked in the proximity of the English colonies felt the repercussions of the great international conflict between England and their native country. In two areas especially, in Maine among the Abnacki and along the Mohawk among the Iroquois, they troubled and disquieted the English. Blocking England's purpose to eradicate French influence from Maine stood the Abnacki, Catholic and sympathetic to France, especially at the mission of Nanransouock, near the Kenebec and staffed since

121 J. Delanglez, S.J., *The French Jesuits in Lower Louisiana, 1700-1763* (Washington, D.C., 1935), pp. 297-298.
122 Ibid., p. 380.

1693 by Sébastien Rasle. Marked by the British for liquidation, this versatile priest and fine linguist eluded his pursuivants for years until the fatal day of August 23, 1724, when the enemy surprised Nanransouock in a raid and with a musket volley felled the grand veteran of twenty-five years on the Kenebec.

Earlier the Iroquois had been for England's colonies a convenient buffer state which contained French influence. With apprehension, therefore, the English observed the mounting influence of the French Jesuits who, even as they made Catholics of the savages, won friends for France. Thomas Dongan, Catholic governor of New York (1682-1687), fostered a plan to convert the Iroquois and yet keep them on the British side. He sent an appeal to England for English Jesuits, but when in 1687 James II joined New York to the Dominion of New England, he was relieved of his office. In 1709, enveloped in the bitter conflict of Queen Anne's War, the mission among the Five Nations came to an end. Opposite Montreal, however, the Catholic village of Caughnawaga remained as a kind of northern star guiding the Iroquois to the place where they could find the message taught by the Black Robes. Through the years many filtered northwards.

The Jesuits who went among the Indians did not go blindfolded. The veterans warned them, without mincing repulsive details, about what to expect. François de Crépieul, who spent twenty-six years in Canada, 1671-1697, drew up a document entitled: *A Memorandum for Future Missionaries*.[123] Among the less obnoxious items he mentioned were: sleeping, dressed, on the icy ground or in the snow; eating from dishes rarely washed; the cramped huts, filled with smoke so dense that one cried and felt as though salt had been thrown in his eyes. He drew a graphic picture of the vast atelier of the missionary: the deep snows, thick forest, frozen lakes. "Suffering and distress," he wrote, "are the appanage of these laborious and melancholy missions."

As did their Spanish and German brethren far to the southwest in Pimería Alta, Arizona, and Lower California, the French Jesuits rounded out their missionary effort by their published reflections, studies, and critiques. On the basis of his *Customs of the American Savages* (1724), a work of keen observation and understanding gained through many years of study of the Iroquois, mainly at Caughnawaga, Joseph François Lafitau has

123 C. de Rochemonteix, S.J., *Les Jésuites et la Nouvelle France au XVIIᵉ siècle* (Paris, 1895), III, 419-420, fn. 2.

been recognized as the Father of Cultural Anthropology. Another Jesuit, a year older than Lafitau, was the widely traveled François Xavier Charlevoix. His *History and General Description of New France* (1744), despite its inaccuracies and limitations, remains basic for the study of Canadian origins.

Despite these cultural landmarks, the eighteenth-century mission of New France, in contrast to that of the seventeenth, suffered in the full telling of its story because, as has been noted, Pope Clement X banned further publication of mission reports, and what the missionaries accomplished is known chiefly through the private correspondence which survived destruction during the period of the Society's suppression. But far more important than the external events of which these aging sheets of paper tell is the intense spirit they reveal, a spirit which shows that the eighteenth-century Jesuit minted a coin every bit as valuable and genuine as that of the Jesuit of the 1600's.

The nine Jesuits in Maryland and New York, like their English brethren, felt the rude shock of the arrival in England of King William and Queen Mary from Holland. The revolution of 1688 spurred new anti-Catholic legislation and opened the flood gates of that mean spirit which hunted down Catholics in every corner of life, political, social, economic. Enemies of the Jesuits honored them with the title: "the terror of the whole Protestant world." So began in Maryland the dispiriting existence of living under penal law, summed up so laconically in the Jesuit records: "In Maryland the priests had to face many difficulties. Still they remain, lending assistance as best they can to those unfortunate Catholics." [124]

One of the most important ways in which they rendered this assistance was with their traditional instrument, the school. Because of the absence of records, only meagre and fragmentary information remains to throw light on the earliest educational ventures in Maryland. Around 1742, at Bohemia Manor, deep in the wilderness near the Pennsylvania border, in order most likely to avoid the attention of the Protestants, they started classes. Among the first boys to enroll were two future Jesuits and archbishops of Baltimore, John Carroll and Leonard Neale.

As the suffocating social atmosphere of Maryland became worse and social ostracism more stringent, the Jesuits looked to the freer atmosphere of Pennsylvania. There a number of Catholic German farmer immigrants needed priests, and about

124 T. Hughes, *History*, II (text), 155.

1732 Joseph Greaton opened the chapel of St. Joseph in Philadelphia. To give further care to these immigrants the general, Retz, deflected German Jesuits from the Indies. Theodor Schneider and Wilhelm Wapeler in 1741 founded stations at Goshenhoppen and Conewago amid the gentle hills of southern and eastern Pennsylvania. Nine others soon reenforced them. Among the new priests was Ferdinand Steinmeyer (Farmer), who traveled widely in Maryland, Pennsylvania, New Jersey, and New York City, where as early as 1758 he celebrated Mass, all the while keeping a lifeline of the faith open to the small settlements between the Chesapeake and the Hudson.

Europe had entered upon one of the great spiritual battles of *Conclusion* its history: the contest between the Church and the Enlightenment. In their assault on the traditional faith Voltaire and his entourage made the Society a primary target, and thus they delineated the Society's place in the eighteenth century: the major portal of the citadel which was marked for total demolition.

The Jesuits had lost the initiative which distinguished their earlier history, and on many fronts they fought a defensive action. Desperately needed were profound and perceptive thinkers who could discern behind the hostility of the *philosophes* a quest for the positive values of freedom and toleration and a drive toward an ideal of justice, truth, and human dignity, an ideal which in time would contribute to reform in the Church. But no theologians of the stature of Bellarmine, Suárez, Vázquez or Petau appeared, and the era of the epigones had come as constructive thought in philosophy and theology yielded to the repetition and condensation of the masterpieces of earlier days. The tide of the Enlightenment swept over a large area of Europe, especially France, and left the Jesuits struggling amid the rising waters of skepticism, deism, and atheism. Overseas their missions started on the sharp decline to destruction that was their destiny. In China the venture in accommodation was thwarted; in India it was maimed; in South America the Portuguese government began the work of demolition; in North America the Protestants blighted the Catholic colony of Maryland. At headquarters in Rome, Tamburini almost became the general destined to preside over the Society's dissolution as its enemies, a full fifty years before the actual suppression in 1773, came within a hair's breadth of obtaining from the pope the death sentence of the order. Around their rekindled fires the Jansenists gathered and held their councils of war.

The lacerations inflicted on the Society came therefore from several enemies. Of all the foes the most effective and relentless was the phalanx of the *philosophes*. When they captured key positions in the European courts, victory was in sight. Lisbon, Paris, Madrid, Naples, Parma, and Vienna were the pegs which held the strands of the broad web of their conspiracy.

Chapter 6

EXILE, SUPPRESSION,

AND RESTORATION

1757–1814

ON MAY 21, 1758, THE NINETEENTH GENERAL CONGREGATION *Lorenzo Ricci,*
elected the fifty-five-year-old Florentine, Lorenzo Ricci, to head *General,*
the order. Ricci had been a teacher of rhetoric, philosophy, and *1758–1773*
theology, in which role he manifested a quick and clear intelligence. He had also been secretary of the Society for two and
a half years, but never a superior. A man therefore of wide
academic background, he brought to his new responsibility no
practical administrative experience.

Ricci was elected during the apogee of the Age of Reason,
when the governments of the major Catholic powers, penetrated by the spirit of the times, were placing the Holy See under heavy siege. In Portugal Sebastião José de Carvalho, in
France the duc Étienne François de Choiseul, in Spain Pedro
Pablo Abarca y Bolea, conde de Aranda, in Naples the marchese
Bernardo Tanucci took the lead in a concerted drive to humili-
ate the Church. Giving strength to their position was a forceful
hostility to the older forms of the ecclesiastical-state relationship. In the long history in Europe of the mutual concerns of
the sacral and the secular, the conflict between the papacy and
the *philosophes* was no mere isolated incident. Rather, it was
a stage in the difficult movement of leaving behind the medieval world and moving into a new and dissimilar era. Some of
the master spirits of the Enlightenment, intent on the lodestar
of human dignity and freedom, and critical of ecclesiastical
restraint, were the protagonists in the advance by which civil
society, in its reach for maturity, was sloughing off the forms
of the Middle Ages and was driving toward a clarification of its
own internal values. To Caesar they would give the things of
Caesar. But this worthy objective they compromised. For to
God they denied the things of God.

The governments of Europe quite naturally focused on this
issue of church-state relations. This was their peculiar concern,
and they now had the positions of power from which they could
move against the papacy. A great bulwark of their policy was,

as seen in the previous chapter, the alliance of Europe's cultural leaders whose vision embraced a horizon wider than diplomacy and politics. Their deeper purpose was the eradication of the Christian faith. José Nicolás de Azara clearly expressed the Enlightenment's proposition: "to shake off the yoke which in the centuries of barbarism had been imposed by the court of Rome on the childish credulity of princes and peoples."

Before a pitiless fire many in the Christian ranks, Anglican, Lutheran, Calvinistic, and Catholic, felt an acute crisis of religious confidence. Several ecclesiastical leaders, justifying change by the premise that the church must be abreast of the times, and bending to the winds of "reasonableness," muted the sterner truths of Christianity, preached a bland piety and, in an atmosphere of misty language about the golden rule of human conduct, taught a more tender brand of moral obligation. To be *au courant,* even monks demolished treasures of medieval art. This rage for modernity has been called "the treason of the clerks." [1]

The eighteenth century had its saints. St. Paul of the Cross founded the Passionist Fathers; St. Alfonso Maria de' Liguori founded the Redemptorists. But their holiness and fervor did not mold the general character of their age. The craze for the contemporary vogue and the quest for the secular became passports to an irreligious Europe. Vocations to the diocesan clergy steadily declined in Austria, France, Spain, and Italy. Religious orders and congregations, except the Carthusians, Trappists, Capuchins, and congregations of women, which remained constant, went into a sharp decline. During the century before the French Revolution, the Benedictines throughout Europe dropped some fifty percent. By 1789 over fifty monasteries of the Cistercians of Common Observance had no more than three monks. In contrast, the Society increased by 2,500 in the forty years from 1710 to 1750. On a landscape dotted by the prostrate ruins of earlier spiritual glories, it still stood as a strong pillar. [2]

---

1 Gay, *The Enlightenment,* I, 336-357; Pastor, *History,* XXXVII, 310-311. Gay, who judges that "the most effective French modernists were the Jesuits," seems to say, in language that is somewhat ambiguous, that they were attempting the impossible task of preserving their tradition of Christian humanism, and as a consequence "the treason of the clerks was forced upon them" (pp. 354-355). Paul Hazard judges that the fall of the Society was due to "the spirit of the times, the age of philosophy, of 'enlightenment' " (*European Thought,* p. 108.)

2 H. Daniel-Rops, *The Church in the Eighteenth Century* (London, 1964), pp. 262-266.

The *philosophes* gave tribute to the Society's religious vitality by the animus with which they sought its destruction. In the
mortal contest between them and the Church, one important
salient on which the fighting raged concerned the very existence of the Society of Jesus. Whether this body, so distinctly
ultramontane, was to be or not to be became one of the essential
issues. The papacy lost the battle, one of the greatest reversals
on the humiliating road which led to the death of Pius VI in
exile at Valence and the imprisonment of Pius VII at Fontainebleau by Napoleon Bonaparte.

Ricci headed the Society when the Church suffered this sharp
defeat. Several generals before him, especially Aquaviva and
Tamburini, experienced long periods of anguish because of
bitter opposition to the Society, but none endured, in intensity
or duration, the affliction felt by Ricci as through fifteen years
he saw the Society gradually dismembered and eventually
crushed. Pope Clement XIII gave Ricci the key to his strategy:
prayer and penance. To this the general remained true. In a
series of letters he kept before the Society a clear understanding of the basic issues and the primacy of the spiritual resources
on which a Jesuit must rely. In November, 1763, for example,
he issued a letter, *On Fervent Perseverance in Prayer;* in June,
1769, another, *On Greater Fervor in Prayer;* in February, 1773,
still another, *On a New Incentive to Prayer.*

Giulio Cordara, a Jesuit witness of these events, voiced the
opinion that the pockets of hostility in Rome rather than the
pressure of the Bourbon courts accomplished the suppression of
the Society.[3] Enmity at Rome of the most virulent kind there
certainly was. Ever since the last quarter of the seventeenth

---

3 Pastor, *History,* XXXV, 379. Cordara was a personal friend of Lorenzo
  Ricci, for whom he had a great affection but who, he thought, was not
  the man to meet the Society's problems of that day. He commented
  on Ricci's election: "I would have judged him most competent to
  guide the Society on a quiet and tranquil sea. But because of his gentle
  nature I felt that he was less well equipped to be at the helm amid
  violently tossing waves. I believed that to handle misfortunes of an
  uncommon nature uncommon means should be employed, and, since
  this was the character of the times, I was convinced that exceptional
  daring was essential and that not an inch of ground should be yielded.
  Others held a vastly different view. Nothing save silence and patience,
  they said, should be pitted against the rising storm. Resist but a bit
  and all would deteriorate even more. This judgment prevailed" ("Julii
  Cordarae de Suppressione Societatis Jesu Commentarii," *Atti e Memorie
  della R. Academia di Scienze Lettere ed Arti in Padova,* Nuova Serie,
  XL [1923-1924], 61).

century the Jansenists held strong positions among curial officials. Cardinal Domenico Passionei, who identified himself as
leader of the Roman Jansenists, hobnobbed with the stars of
the Enlightenment; Francisco Javier Vázquez, general of the
Augustinians, argued vigorously for the triumph of Jansenistic
wisdom and the death of Jesuitical ignorance; Guido Bottari,
prefect of the Vatican Library, opened his house to weekly anti-
Jesuit meetings, attended by Cardinal Neri Corsini, Vázquez,
Prospero Buttari of the Oratory, and Scipio Ricci, a nephew of
the Jesuit general. The Oratorians also played host to meetings
of this kind at their house at Chiesa Nuova. In Florence the
learned Giovanni Lami, most articulate of Jansenist thinkers in
Italy, expounded at the Biblioteca Reccardi a program of literary assault on the Society designed to lead to its eventual obliteration. Others, infected by the rancor aroused by the debates
on the Chinese and Malabar rites, thickened the atmosphere of
hostility. Pope Benedict XIV remarked that certain leaders in
the Church glowed in their detestation of the Jesuits, and Pope
Clement XIII confided to the general, Ricci, that the greatest
enemies of the Church and the Society were in Rome.[4] These
testimonies enhance the judgment of Cordara, but they were
expressed before the Bourbon juggernaut moved into the final
stages of its crushing assault on the papacy. Once Spain, France,
and their satellites began to advance in a solid phalanx, amid
insinuations of possible schism, they, more than the Roman
enemies, it would seem, were the ones who crushed the bewildered final protestations of Pope Clement XIV.

When Clement capitulated before the threats and warning of
reprisal, Ricci could do no more. The papacy was the main
citadel of defense, and when that fell the cause was lost.
Through the long and hard campaign Ricci gave his sons a most
inspiring example of fortitude, even unto death as a prisoner
in Castel Sant' Angelo.

The execution of the Society did not occur with one swift
stroke. Moving successively, Portugal acted first, in 1759; then
France, in 1764; then Spain, in 1767; then Naples, later the
same year; then Parma, the next year. The papal suppression
throughout the world came in 1773.

Portugal   Portugal lead the way. The chief engineer was Sebastião José
de Carvalho, who had gained the complete confidence of the
king, Joseph I. This tall, imposing figure, with a face full of in-

---

4 García-Villoslada, *Manual*, pp. 527-529.

telligence, demonstrated his power of decision and endurance when he raised Lisbon from the ruins of the disastrous earthquake of November 1, 1755. These great natural gifts of leadership, adorned by diplomatic experience in London and Vienna, he turned ruthlessly against the Church. Cardinal Bartolommeo Pacca made this assessment of Carvalho: a man of the Enlightenment intent on the humiliation of the Church; an advocate of disbelief and a devotee of regalist philosophy; a molder of a Church subordinate to the state, differing little "from the system of the Anglican Protestant Church." [5]

The precise point of departure of his attack on the Society is not clear. There was the War of the Seven Reductions which, as has been seen, occasioned a flood of propaganda which placed the responsibility for the chaos and bloodshed on the Society. There was also the pamphlet of Gabriele Malagrida, *The Real Cause of the Earthquake that Ruined Lisbon on November 1, 1755* (1756), which was bound to wound the sensibilities of a man of the Enlightenment. Whatever the cause which tipped the scales in favor of taking action, Carvalho's strategy was simple: to convince the Holy See that the Society in Portugal was so honeycombed with corruption that its extinction was imperative.

On September 19, 1757, Carvalho moved with dispatch. Pleading the defense of the king against an organization so hostile to the crown, he ordered the Jesuit confessor to quit the palace, and on the following day prohibited the appearance of any Jesuit at court. A few months later, early in 1758, he peremptorily demanded of Pope Benedict XIV the end of Jesuit disobedience to the Church, lust for gold, thirst for power, and avarice for land. The Holy See, not duped by these wide and general charges, requested specific evidence. Carvalho ignored this request. The Portuguese ambassador at Rome and cousin of Carvalho, Francisco de Almada e Mendonça, used strong language with Benedict, then a dying man, and insisted that he take drastic action against the Society. On April 1, 1758, the pope appointed Cardinal Francisco Saldanha to make a canonical visitation of the Portuguese Jesuits.

The brief, by which the pope authorized this visitation and in which he insisted on canonical procedure, justice, and charity, became an instrument of destruction of the Society. Saldanha, a good-natured man of no exceptional competence or

5 S. Smith, S.J., "The Suppression of the Society of Jesus," *Month*, XCIX (1902), 118.

endowments, owed to Carvalho his entrance into the College of Cardinals. On May 31, 1758, he opened his visitation at the professed house of São Roch in Lisbon. He met the community and left immediately. Five days later, on June 5, he issued an edict in which he disclosed his frightening discovery that every Jesuit house under Portuguese rule, in Europe, America, Asia, and Africa, was a center of scandalous commercial transactions. The papal nuncio, Filippo Acciaioli, congratulated Saldanha on what was an excellent document save "for one slight omission," the evidence. And without evidence, continued the nuncio, it could be classified only as calumny.[6]

During this period of tense relations between Portugal and the Vatican Lorenzo Ricci was elected general, on May 21, 1758. Earlier the same month, on the 3rd, Pope Benedict XIV died, and his successor, Clement XIII, gave early evidence of his attitude toward the Portuguese business when he announced that he wanted Saldanha's visitation carried out properly and charitably because of the Society's great contribution to the Church. In this mild pontiff, steeled by his resolute secretary of state, Luigi Torrigiani, Carvalho met a kind of eighteenth century Hildebrand.

What might have developed into a protracted and immutable impasse between Clement and Carvalho received a sudden jar on September 3, 1758. That night an attempt was made on the king's life. The monarch survived, but Carvalho had found his golden opportunity. Mystery surrounded the attack, and rumors only deepened the mystery. One story linked the assailant to the noble family of De Tavora. A government official and lackey of Carvalho, Ignácio Ferreira, accused the Society. After three months, on December 13, 1758, the police arrested several members of the De Tavora family and troops surrounded all Jesuit houses in order, as Carvalho announced, to protect the residents from the fury of a people who believed that they had shared in the crime against the king.

The new year, 1759, opened ominously. On January 11 ten Jesuits, accused on the basis of statements extracted under torture from the duque de Aveiro and others, were arrested as conspirators against Joseph I. Two days later twelve of the De Tavora family and household, after a trial which offended legal procedure, were publicly and barbarously executed. Six days later the king ordered that all Jesuit property be confiscated.

The sweeping and general accusations against the Society

6 Pastor, *History*, XXVI, 297.

did not convince the Vatican. The nuncio tried and failed to extract precise and clear information from Saldanha. Luigi Torrigiani, secretary of state under Clement XIII, had no more success. The pope requested an official report of Saldanha's visitation. But the cardinal had no report to give because, since the time he was appointed visitor, he had only twice entered Jesuit houses, and only for a brief time. In March he informed the pope that he had decided, in view of the corrupt state of the Society, to invoke the secular power.

Three months after the decree of confiscation of property came the order of expulsion. On April 20, 1759, Joseph I wrote the pope that he was ordering the eviction of the Society from his realm. For all his loud demands for action Carvalho did not show the smooth and quick competence which the Spanish government displayed eight years later, and he took five months before he placed the first exiles aboard ship. On September 17 one hundred and thirty-three priests were moved out of Lisbon down the Tagus. On October 5 the king declared the Jesuits rebels and traitors. The same day Saldanha in a pastoral letter warned the faithful to have nothing to do with them, announced the failure of his visitation since they, rather than reform, continued to deteriorate, and called on the people to join him in prayer that the degenerates receive the grace of conversion. On October 24 the first batch of exiles were put ashore at Civitavecchia in the Papal States.

Carvalho and Saldanha both hoped to separate the younger men from the Society. The king announced that he would allow those who had not yet pronounced their final vows to remain in Portugal if they requested Cardinal Saldanha for release from their first vows. Only a few capitulated. Then the resolute, including the novices, were gathered together in the colleges of Évora and Coimbra, allowed to mix with their relatives, and once more enticed by the royal offer. Their constancy was striking. Of the one hundred and forty-five scholastics at Coimbra only three gave in. Including the men overseas in the missions, about six-sevenths of the 1,700 members of the Portuguese Assistancy remained true to the Society. The government carried out the great expulsion in stages, and eventually about 1,100 Portuguese Jesuits reached Italy.[7]

The sustenance of these men became a staggering problem. Somehow or other the Italian Jesuits found lodging for them. Friends were generous with their contributions, but with the pas-

7 Ibid., 333, 337.

sage of time the Jesuit communities had to cut their food allowance, then sell their paintings. Ricci, at first determined to stand fast by the Society's rule not to accept stipends for Masses, finally asked the pope to be dispensed.

Carvalho almost immediately showed that he intended the expulsion of the Society to be but a phase in his general assault on the authority of Rome. On June 15, 1760, he ordered the papal nuncio to leave Lisbon without delay and to be out of the country within four days. Less than a month later, on July 7, the Portuguese ambassador at the Vatican, Francisco de Almada, retired from Rome. Carvalho had moved closer to his goal of a schismatic Portuguese Church.[8]

He then crowned his campaign against the Society with a crude exhibition of barbarity. For two and a half years he held in prison, first in Belem Tower and then in a dungeon of Junqueira, Gabriele Malagrida, one of the ten Jesuits arrested in connection with the attempt on the king's life. During his confinement the old veteran of thirty years on the missions became a source of dispute among his fellow prisoners. He performed frightfully severe penance; he claimed that a voice bade him to undertake even greater mortification; he spoke to angelic hosts in the darkness of the cell. To him was ascribed a work — some authorities deny his authorship — *The Heroic and Wonderful Life of the Glorious St. Anne* (1753) in which it was asserted that St. Anne had taken the vows of religion in her mother's womb and that she had, while building in Jerusalem a sanctuary for devout girls, used angels disguised as bricklayers. At the Inquisition's trial of the old man, Carvalho's brother, Paulo, presided. Broken and confused, Malagrida insisted that he had actually spoken with St. Ignatius Loyola, St. Philip Neri, and St. Theresa. A Dominican member of the tribunal protested against the brutality of the questioning, and thereupon received orders to accept a bishopric overseas. Found guilty of heresy, deceit, and other outrages, Malagrida was led on September 20, 1761, to Rossio Square and there brutally strangled and burnt at the stake.[9]

Another Carvalhian savagery was not so speedy. The Portuguese penal system boasted a series of underground dungeons, the most celebrated of which were those of São Juliano. Into these tight underground chambers, dark, gloomy, and damp, Carvalho stuffed about one hundred and eighty Jesuits from the

8 Ibid., 346-352.
9 M. Cheke, *Dictator of Portugal* (London, 1938), pp. 152-157.

missions, including some of other nations. The French and Austrian governments obtained the release of their subjects, but the Portuguese, poorly fed, deprived of the sacraments save at the hour of death — and then a physician had to swear that death was imminent — rotted away through the years. Seventy-nine died in the dungeons; others went mad. Only in 1777, on the death of Joseph I, did about sixty survivors emerge after over fifteen years of confinement. During this perversion of justice the monarch, in 1770, honored Carvalho with the title of Marquês de Pombal.

Carvalho's victory was a strange act of self-mutilation. The great Portugal of the sixteenth century had come upon hard days, and by the time Pombal had gained power the nation had lost to England and Holland many of the conquests of her superb sea captains of an earlier age. These wounds on the body of the empire were grievous, and at a time when a leader would presumably seek to foster whatever could contribute vitality and endurance, Carvalho, with the peculiar blindness of the Enlightenment, banned a group of men who, besides their literary, scientific, and spiritual creations, were conducting twenty colleges in Portugal and thirty in the colonies. Almost 850 he either jailed or ejected from Portugal. Even though Peking and Nanking technically lay within the sphere of the Portuguese Padroado, the viceroy of India, Manuel de Saldanha de Albuquerque, highest Portuguese authority in the Orient, received instructions not to touch the Jesuits in China because they behaved "more like gentiles than religious" and were not easily replaceable. But from other mission fields made sacred by some of the greatest apostles in history, from the India of Francis Xavier, Roberto de Nobili, and João de Brito, from the Macao of Alessandro Valignano and Matteo Ricci, from the Brazil of Manuel da Nóbrega, José de Anchieta, and António Vieira, from the Africa of Gonçalo da Silveira, Baltasar Barreira, and Pedro Paez, his ships, carrying on their crowded, unhealthy decks some 850 men, plied the ocean seas to Europe. Of the 142 who sailed from Goa on two ships, pious in name, *Nossa Senhora da Conceição and São Vicente Ferreira,* but dreadful in harsh reality, twenty-three died en route. Of the 119 who reached Lisbon only forty-six were able to continue to Italy. Inspired by the Enlightenment, Carvalho seriously impoverished the subjects of the Portuguese crown.[10]

His sweeping action had a significance that went far beyond

10 Krahl, *China Missions,* pp. 129-131; Plattner, *Jesuits Go East,* pp. 248-

the borders of Portugal. To a continent aware of the magnitude of the Society he proved that it was vulnerable. Sure in the knowledge that he was a leader and the tutor of Europe, he said with pride: "I shall show the Bourbons how to negotiate with Rome." This he did by more than just his example. An enormous work of three volumes, entitled *Chronological Deduction*, appeared over the name of José Seabra de Silva and, circulating through Europe, planted seeds of suspicion about the terrible spectres that were abroad throughout the land. The theme was simple: Portugal was enjoying a tremendous prosperity at the time the Jesuits entered the country; with their coming began the great decline; behind each national disaster lay the nefarious Society of Jesus. With his remarkable command of the Portuguese language in which he had few peers, Carvalho revised the entire work and introduced some sections of his own. It was his literary contribution to the Bourbon project which tasted its first success in France.[11]

France The second country in which the Society was destroyed was France. This period opened with an attempt on the king's life by Robert François Damiens, who had been a servant at the Jesuit Collège Louis-le-Grand twenty years before. Amid the furor some tried to link this act to the Society. They failed and the storm passed. Not swept away by the passions of a mob, nor bludgeoned by the crude use of naked force as in Portugal, in France the Society was gradually strangled by the cords of legalism and juridical manipulation. On the mountain side of French civilization and poised ominously over the Society in the valley below rested several immense landmasses of the national life: the reanimated Jansenists, the Gallican-minded Parlements, the skeptical and rationalistic intelligentsia. The loosened stone which dislodged these landmasses and started the avalanche of disaster was the rash and reckless conduct of a single Jesuit. Antoine Lavalette, superior of the mission in Martinique, became involved in financial difficulties, and the Society was haled into court. Once the Parlement of Paris had the Jesuits at the bar of justice, Jansenists and Gallicans united and with the weapons of jurisprudence and legal technicalities brought the Society to destruction. The whole process, from Lavalette's setback until the king's decree of suppression, took nine years.

255; Rodrigues, *História*, IV, i, 5-6; "A Companhia," *Revista de História*, X (1921), 162.

11 Cheke, *Dictator*, pp. 216-217.

Antoine Lavalette, an engaging, enterprising man with a flair for practical affairs, volunteered for the mission of the Lesser Antilles of the Paris Province. Sent in 1741 at the age of thirty-four to Martinique, he schooled himself in the social conditions of the country, the techniques of administering plantations and the processes of trade between the Caribbean and Europe. In time he became treasurer of the mission, and then superior. In order to relieve the heavy debt on the mission he developed plantations and shipped the produce, sugar, coffee, and indigo to France where they were sold. Acting well within the limits on business by clerics set by canon law, he gained a fine reputation for commercial skill both at Martinique, at Marseilles, and other port towns in France. Then he began to take risks. Without the knowledge of his superiors in France and Rome, giving full play to his instinct for business, he borrowed heavily in order to purchase more land. Ability to meet payments depended on his success in selling the produce of the plantations. In 1755 Lavalette fell a victim to the international rivalry between France and Britain which soon developed into formal war. Off Bordeaux, English corsairs took heavy shipments of his sugar and coffee, valued at 600,000 livres. Then they swooped down on thirteen Dutch ships which he had hired. Only one of his cargoes reached Cadiz.

Even before the second disaster at sea the trading house of Lioncy and Gouffre, to which he owed a million and a half livres, went bankrupt. Superiors in France acted quickly to forestall further damage. They sent strict instructions to Lavalette to desist from further borrowing; they appointed in quick succession five visitors to investigate the situation in Martinique; through Jean Pierre Dominique de Tiremois de Sacy, treasurer for the missions, they made strenuous efforts to raise the money needed to meet the payments. Because the Franco-English war made the sea lanes unsure, the letters may never have reached Martinique. Certainly only Jean François de la Marche, fifth appointee as visitor, managed to reach the island, but too late to halt disaster. Then more bills, in excess of the originals, came in.

Superiors, including Ricci, sent more orders to Lavalette to desist from further financial transactions. The embarrassed man ignored these instructions, and in a desperate effort to save the situation began, in violation of canon law, to manipulate some trading agreements with Dutch merchants at St. Eustache and Curaçao. Ricci gave permission to the French Jesuits to try to raise 200,000 livres in order to meet fresh demands of creditors, but the provincial of Paris, Pierre Claude Frey de Neuville, decided, in the light of the traditional legal interpretation in France that each religious house was alone responsible for its financial status, to take a firm stand against further payments. Creditors, however, brought action against the Society, basing their complaint on the contention that the French Jesuits as a body were answerable for Lavalette's debts. Lower courts in Marseilles and Paris upheld the complainants. The Jesuits took the case to the Grand Chamber of the Parlement of Paris on appeal. On May 8, 1761, Parlement sustained the lower courts. It also granted a year of grace to settle the debts.[12] But within the year other developments pushed this particular problem into the background.

The initial issue of the Society's financial liability before the law soon broadened into the much wider question of the Society's right to exist in France. While the lawsuit was still in the hands of the Parlement, Abbé de Chauvelin, a sour and fierce-tempered man, in whom burned a flaming spirit of militant hostility to the Society, addressed the magistrates and, while pointing out that the Jesuits were in part arguing their case for the separate financial responsibility of each house on the grounds of their *Constitutions*, developed a sombre picture of those same *Constitutions* as the mysterious guide to their reprehensible conduct. Asserting the approbation of regicide as an example of Jesuit morality, he expounded his theme with such a rising tide of emotion and described with such vivid pathos the attempt on the king's life in 1757 that he brought tears to the eyes of his listeners. Even though the periodic review of the *Constitutions* by Parlement since as early as 1660 made nonsense of De Chauvelin's oratory, the judges ordered the Jesuits to submit a copy. This Antoine de Montigny did immediately.[13]

Then the king stepped in, and on May 30, in a resolute show of strength, informed Parlement that he reserved to himself the study of the Society's *Constitutions*. These he turned over to a special commission of the Royal Council, and thereby created another incident in the long series of disagreements between the crown and the Parlement. From the reign of Louis XI (1461-1483) tensions of a grievous kind began to drive the monarch and the judiciary apart. The emergence, during the reign of Francis I (1515-1547), of the magistrates as *la noblesse de la*

12 J. Egret, "Le procès des Jésuites devant les parlements de France (1761-1770)," *Revue Historique*, CCIV (1950), 3; Smith, *Month*, XCIX (1902), 351-353.
13 Egret, *Revue Historique*, CCIV (1950), 4.

robe, with all its implied quest for authority, accentuated the potential for division within the realm. Where Richelieu and Louis XIV bridled the restive judges, the presence of a weak or a young king Parlement interpreted as an invitation to break the grip of royal constraint. Under the frequently languid Louis XV, what had started as a narrow contest between the Parlement of Paris and the Society took on the added dimension of a constitutional struggle between the monarch and the judiciary. The Society's fate was swept into the larger stream of France's political life.

Three months after its judgment against the Society on the question of financial liability, Parlement, again boldly taking the initiative, on August 6, 1761, ordered that the works of twenty-three Jesuits, including those of Bellarmine, Toledo, and Lessius, be publicly burned as destructive of Christian morality and that the Society, in view of its evil effects on the education of youth, no longer receive any novices. Further, it decreed that in towns where there were other schools the Society should close its colleges by October 1, 1761; in places without other schools, by April 1, 1762. Again the king intervened. He enjoined that this resolution of Parlement be suspended for a year, until August 6, 1762. Parlement replied with another gesture of defiance. With sugared language about their love "for the sacred person of the Lord King and his concern for public peace," the magistrates proclaimed that they would brook no delay. With this expression of most respectful disobedience they formally registered Louis' letters patent, but on condition that the suspension demanded by him be cut to less than the desired year. They assigned April 1, 1762, as the date for the execution of their decree.[14]

During the next eight months before this hour of doom, the royal council made several inept attempts to save the Society. In one elaborately contrived essay, striking the note of patriotism, they highlighted the Jesuits as deeply loyal sons of France. They drew up a Declaration which they asked the Jesuits to sign. This document contained a disavowal of tyrannicide, a profession of the Gallican Articles in the Declaration of the French clergy of 1682, a submission in all respects to the laws and ordinances of the realm, and assurance of refusal, even if commanded by the general, to do anything contrary to the points made in the Declaration. A document of this sort, containing a vast mixture of theology, political philosophy, and ethics, was in

14 Ibid., 5-7.

its impreciseness open to many and varied distinctions. The political brand of Gallicanism which stressed the dignity of the French crown had not been unpalatable to the French Jesuits for a century and a half, but the Gallican Articles of 1682 contained a principle on which Rome was particularly sensitive, the superiority of a general council over the pope. Here, however, Étienne de la Croix, the provincial of Paris, applied a distinction. Since these Articles were so widely taught in France, he felt prepared to acknowledge them, not indeed as articles of faith but as theological opinion. He changed the text a bit, but not substantially, and then with other Jesuits signed the Declaration. For all this tightrope walking he not only did not save the Society but received a scathing reprimand from Ricci. The general lectured the French Jesuits that they had jettisoned their reputation for special attachment to the Holy See, warned them that those who signed had to stand before the judgment seat of God, advised that it would be better that the Society perish than survive by sinful means and that, having come into being as an instrument of service to the Holy See, it should close its life in the same way. On these hapless Jesuits also fell the indignation of Pope Clement XIII, who voiced his irritation at their solemn profession of opinions which he termed as "contrary to the rights and authority of the Holy See." Never had the Society in France been so isolated and desolate, under sentence of obliteration by the Parlement and severely rebuked by general and pope.[15]

In January, 1762, the crown, in its mood of appeasement, tried a fresh approach: that of altering the Society's character by the mutilation of its *Constitutions*. The duc de Choiseul, who shaped the foreign policy of the government, peremptorily advised Ricci that the only hope for saving the order in France was for him to renounce his authority as incompatible with the laws of France and to appoint a French vicar-general who would rule the French provinces according to the statutes of the realm. He insisted on immediate action under threat that otherwise the crown would throw the Society to the parliamentary lions. Ricci clearly perceived not only that what De Choiseul asked exceeded his powers but also that it would place the French provinces in peril of developing an individual spirit alien to the main body of the Society. He rejected it outright. Pope Clement XIII supported him completely. The papal nuncio at Paris, Pietro Pamfili-Colonna, recognized that this plan, even if adopted, would not

---

15 Smith, *Month*, XCIX (1902), 499-502; Pastor, *History*, XXXVI, 421-423.

halt Parlement in its determined drive to achieve nothing less than the Society's extinction.[16]

Two months later the king's counselors made a fresh attempt to mollify Parlement. Again the purpose was to alter the structure of the Society, but this time by unilateral action of France through a royal decree and independently of the pope and Ricci. In March Louis issued an edict of eighteen articles. One of these articles, all of which contained ideas repugnant to the Society's *Constitutions*, gave particular offense: the delegation of the general's powers to the five provincials. Parlement scorned the proferred olive branch. It simply refused to register the king's edict. To augment this show of insolence the magistrates on March 28 sent to the monarch a thick volume entitled: *Extracts from the Dangerous and Pernicious Assertions of Every Kind Maintained at All Times by the So-Called Jesuits,* an ensemble of lies which placed in the mouths of Jesuits at least seven hundred and fifty-eight quotations falsified by omissions, additions, and alterations in wording and punctuation, and which Johann Ignaz von Döllinger, one of the greater historians of the nineteenth century, called so barefaced a fraud that he was at a loss at which to wonder most, "the dishonesty or audacity" of the authors.[17] And on April 1, the date which they had set the previous August, they closed all the Jesuit schools within their jurisdiction. The Paris Parlement had scored a double victory: over the crown and over the Society.

Four months later, on August 6, 1762, this same Parlement announced that the so-called Society of Jesus, obnoxious to civic order, violator of the natural law, destroyer of religion and morality, perpetrator of corruption, was barred from France. Several particular directives implemented this general decree: each Jesuit had to withdraw from his community and sever connections with the Society elsewhere; further, each Jesuit had to refrain from university studies, abstain from positions of teaching and civic responsibility unless he first took an oath by which he repudiated the Society's rules, disavowed its moral teaching as expressed in the *Extracts* and accepted the Gallican Articles of 1682. All the Society's buildings and estates were declared confiscated.[18]

Normally the Parlement of Paris was the bellwether for the twelve parlements of the provinces — or *conseils souverains* as

16 Smith, *Month*, XCIX (1902), 509-510; Pastor, *History*, XXXVI, 440.
17 Smith, *Month*, XCIX (1902), 362, 367-368.
18 Pastor, *History*, XXXVI, 451-452.

they were called in some towns. (Nancy received a parlement only in 1775.) In the action against the Society, however, the provincial magistrates did not follow Paris with lockstep and in neatly ordered ranks. Excepting the Parlement of Rouen, which actually anticipated the proceedings in Paris, the others moved quite gingerly. In Toulouse, Pau, Rennes, and Grenoble the Society had many friends, alumni of their schools, members of their sodalities of the Blessed Virgin, men who came to know them in the daily business of their lives. The courts of Bordeaux, Perpignan, and Metz manifested no enthusiasm. In Aix, the Parlement of Provence, even though peopled with intransigent Gallicans, met strong opposition from its own president, a former naval officer, Alexandre J. de Boyer, marquis d'Éguilles. This resistance it managed to overcome, and D'Éguilles was banished from France *à perpétuité*. The courts of Besançon, Colmar, and Douai definitely declined to join the line of march.[19]

What seems to have worn down the reluctance of the provincial courts was class consciousness, the sense of union among the French magistrates as they joined in a great collective act. For some of the lesser known courts it was an opportunity to let the rest of France know of their existence. At the end of the judicial year of 1763-1764, the decrees against the Jesuits had the appearance of a crazy quilt, so disparate were their particular formats. Four parlements, those of Paris, Rouen, Toulouse, and Pau, banished them from France. The courts in Dauphiné, Guienne, Burgundy, Provence, and Brittany declared them suppressed but allowed them to remain. Alsace, Franche-Comté, and Flanders took no action against them.[20]

The king, again refusing to be muffled, decided to equalize the situation. By an edict in November, 1764, he established a general norm for all of France. While he reluctantly proscribed the Society throughout the country, he nevertheless allowed the former Jesuits to remain in the kingdom on the condition that they live as "good and faithful subjects" under the spiritual authority of the bishops. Further, he erased any demand that they take an oath that would embarrass them. A year earlier he had insisted on a yearly allowance, modest though it be. Angry and exasperated because the Parlements forced his hand, Louis exclaimed: "I have no overwhelming love for the Jesuits, but every heresy has made them an object of contempt. This is to their honor. I shall say no more. If for the peace of my kingdom

19 Egret, *Revue Historique*, CCIV, (1950), 11-19.
20 Ibid., 12-13, 22-23.

I unwillingly dismissed them, I wish at least that it not be believed that I concurred in all that the parlements did and said against them." [21]

In Toulouse the first president, François de Bastard, addressed the members of his own parlement after its decree of Feburary 26, 1763, against the Society. "Gentlemen," he said, "you have just given a baneful example: an act of suppression. You in your turn will suffer the same fate." Eight years later, in 1771, De Bastard's prediction came to pass. A king, irritated by "the scandalous spectacle of a challenge to my sovereign powers," through the Chancellor René Maupeou broke the tight grip of the judicial oligarchy. Maupeou peremptorily declared all offices vacant and organized a new judicial body. Unable to drive from their minds the bogeyman of the Society of Jesus, some of the *chassés* claimed that they discerned in the glove of Maupeou a revenging Jesuit fist.[22]

Revenge or no revenge, the royal initiative of 1771 could not alleviate the overwhelming catastrophe of 1764. Without roof, food, or work, 2,900 former religious faced destitution, Frenchmen denied by Frenchmen the freedom of trying to save for *la belle France* one of her dearest heritages, her Catholic faith. Ricci tried to settle them outside France, but several governments, anxious not to offend France in the checker game of international diplomacy, canceled the general's efforts. Some of the homeless men sailed for the foreign missions; others received haven in other religious communities in France; still others found harbor in private homes when it became a fashion of the day to house an ex-Jesuit. Voltaire received Antoine Adam as his guest, an event which attracted international attention and which caused the watchful James Boswell to exclaim, "What a curious idea!" [23] Because the scholastics and brothers experienced special difficulty in the day to day struggle for existence, Ricci transmitted to the provincials power to release them from their vows. Many took advantage of this, but others, such as the fifteen scholastics who went to Poland, refused to surrender to the enervating circumstances.

During the period before the king abrogated the offensive oath required of a Jesuit if he would obtain ecclesiastical, official, or educational status, some few capitulated. The solicitor-general, Omer Joly de Fleury, estimated that, of the 1,200 Jesuits

21 Ibid., 23-27.
22 Ibid., 27.
23 G. Dumas, S.J., "Voltaire's Jesuit Chaplain," *Thought*, XV (1940), 17.

within the jurisdiction of the Parlement of Paris, only one hundred and fifty took the oath. In general, complete figures were not kept, and even Ricci, who interpreted the exodus as a purification of the Society, could not learn the identity of those who yielded.[24]

The disaster that fell on the French Jesuits had a serious secondary effect in so far as it deeply concerned the English members of the Society. The most important single work of the latter was the college which they operated at Saint-Omer. It came as a great blow that Parlement not only included them in the decree of dissolution but also arranged that their property be turned over to the secular clergy. Feeling ran high among the English Catholic laity, who hotly debated the merits of the case. The students, loyal to their masters, went with them to Bruges in the Austrian Netherlands on October 19, and when the new administration arrived at Saint-Omer they found an empty building.

One obvious result of the legal engagement between 1760 and 1764 was the rise to preeminence, if only temporarily, of the Parlement of Paris. The defeat of the Society had, however, a deeper significance than a triumph of the judiciary of the nation because, behind the facade of juridical decrees and legal jargon, several influences were at work: Gallicanism, rationalism and Jansenism. The last was possibly the most intense. For well over a century the Gallicans in the Parlement of Paris, content with the Jesuits' loyalty to the prerogatives of the crown, did not harass them. But when the spirit of Port-Royal, reanimated by Quesnel, took hold in a variety of subtle theological and political ways upon several of the magistrates, the Jesuits were prejudged. The Arnaulds had their revenge at long last.

The *philosophes* recognized this. Without a grain of love for what Quesnel stood for, they delighted in the denouement, not because the Jansenists were gratified but because their own work was being done for them. In 1761 D'Alembert wrote to Voltaire: "Let the Jansenist rabble rid us of the Jesuit blackguards. Do not put anything in the way of these spiders gobbling one another up." A year later, still the delighted onlooker of the struggle, he again commented to Voltaire: "There is nothing sluggish in the way the parliamentarians are doing their job. They think that they are of assistance to religion, but unwittingly they are serving Reason. They are filling the role of

24 Egret, *Revue Historique*, CCIV (1950), 21, fn. 7; Pastor, *History*, XXXVI, 492-493.

executioner of high justice, employed by Philosophy from whom, without realizing it, they take their orders." In 1764 D'Alembert pulled his observations and judgments together in *The Fall of the Jesuits in France*. With the disappearance of the Society, the nation, he felt, had grown in its enlightenment and had removed from the scene the greatest champion of superstition. Next to go were those other devotees of religious fanaticism, the Jansenists. "The Jesuits were the regular troops, recruited and disciplined under the standard of superstition. They were the Macedonian phalanx which it behoved Reason to see broken up and destroyed. The Jansenists are merely the Cossacks and the Pandours whom Reason will make cheap work of once they have to fight alone. . . ." [25]

Elated as were the Jansenists in their chant of victory, they failed to realize that it was incredulity that triumphed, not their Augustinianism. By entering into an alliance with the Gallicans, whereby they crossbred their theology and the teaching of Edmond Richer, they lost their original identity and created a doctrine known as *jansénisme richériste*. But even if this strange hybrid had not come about, Port-Royal had entered battle for a cause already lost, since it attempted, with an archaic Augustinianism, to run against the grain of the prevailing humanism which was in strong flow from the headwater of the Renaissance. Mère Angélique would have recognized neither the Jansenists of 1764 nor the banner under which they achieved victory.[26]

During this struggle the Society did not want for champions. Bishops, in the Assembly and as individuals, protested with almost complete unanimity aganist the policy of Parlement. In December, 1761, of fifty-one bishops assembled, forty-four addressed the king in favor of the Society. Of the minority, only one unreservedly advocated its suppression. Again, in May, 1762, they sent a candid message to Louis XV, urging him to prevent the injustice planned by Parlement. In eloquence, outspokenness, and clear reasoning the bishop of Grenoble, Jean de Caulet, excelled. What frightened him was the arbitrary conduct and disdain for justice of the magistrates. "If a fellow citizen of mine has been condemned without a hearing . . . what security," he asked, "have I that I shall escape the same fate?" Simon-Pierre de la Corée, bishop of Saintes, lamented

---

25 Smith, *Month*, XCIX (1902), 272; CII (1903), 172; Pastor, *History*, XXXVI, 375.

26 L. Cognet, *Le Jansénisme* (Paris, 1964), pp. 121-122.

"the mortal blow" to the apostolate of retreats, sodalities, schools, spiritual counseling; Henri de Fumel, bishop of Lodève, told the king of his alarm, and on a prophetic note cautioned him that the enemies of the Society of Jesus "are your enemies and the Church's enemies"; Jacques-Marie de Condorcet, bishop of Lisieux, wrote: "Of the designs of the Lord I am ignorant, but I tremble. Such is the common experience these days of all who have a true love for religion." [27] Most striking and impressive of all the episcopal protestations was that of the archbishop of Paris, Christophe de Beaumont. Parlement, in a spasm of violent indignation, summoned the archbishop to its chambers. To save him from this indignity the king ordered him to disappear to the Cistercian monastery of La Trappe in Normandy. Echoing the sentiments of the French hierarchy, Pope Clement XIII in solemn and moving phrases appealed to the king to save the Society.

These protests were like so many voices lost in a vast desert. Pierre Claude Frey de Neuville said that the bishops' praise of the Society "will at least make a fine epitaph for us." It amounted to nothing more than an epitaph because, in the absolutist political structure of France, order and justice depended ultimately on the person of the king. And Louis XV, in his languid, irresolute way, abdicated his authority. What Henry IV or Louis XIV would never have countenanced, Louis XV succumbed to. France's great tragedy during this century was that she was denied as monarch the promising duc de Bourgogne, Louis XV's father. This humble, generous, hardworking prince died before his time, in 1712. As the funeral party turned from St. Denis, Saint-Simon remarked: "We have been burying France." Among the many institutions of France that followed the duke into the earth before the century was over, the Society of Jesus was the first.

At the time of the decree of suppression the French provinces had one hundred and fifty-two men in the foreign missions, twenty-seven priests and brothers in the territory from Quebec to Louisiana, seventeen priests, including five Chinese, and three brothers, including one Chinese, in China, and the others in the West Indies, the East Indies, Greece, Guiana, Syria, and Egypt. The decree affected these men in different ways. Those in French colonies had to leave. Those in other sovereignties re-

27 G. F. X. de Ravignan, S.J., *Clément XIII et Clément XIV* (Paris, 1854), pp. 106-107, fn. 1; also *Volume supplémentaire. Documents historiques et critiques*, pp. 196-197, 204-209, 213.

mained. Several, because of the sudden and drastic shifts in colonial supremacy, found themselves under foreign flags. By the Treaty of Paris, negotiated a year before the Society's dissolution in France, the fleur-de-lys no longer flew over Canada, which had been ceded to the British. Although Louisiana had been turned over to Spain in 1762 by a secret treaty, French officials, due to complications in the transfer of sovereignty, remained for a time, and these ordered the thirteen Jesuits there, save the seriously ailing veteran, Michel Baudouin, to leave. In Canada the new English administration, honoring their pledge to respect the religion of the conquered population, left the Jesuits free in their work. In Boston, however, members of "The Society for Propagating Christian Knowledge among the Indians" planned to exploit the achievements of the Jesuits, but the outbreak of the revolution of the colonies in 1775 deflected their proselytizing aspirations. For the missions of the *outremer* the main significance of the Society's death in France was the gradual desiccation of a rich stream of competent, versatile, and devout priests and brothers, with the consequent inevitable shriveling of a ministry that had ever been marked by youthful freshness and vibrancy.

Spain was the third country to suppress the Society. Avoiding *Spain* the wearisome legalistic maneuvering in France and the fuss and stir of the ecclesiastical visitation in Portugal, the Spanish government moved quietly and expeditiously. The control tower from which many of the directions were received was in Naples. There the marchese Bernardo Tanucci, who knew Charles III intimately as king of Naples before he became king of Spain in 1759, followed with avid interest the policies of his former protégé and lavished on him his advice.

A thorough regalist and a forceful anti-papal doctrinaire, he filled the pages of his correspondence to Spain with extravagant expressions of his intense aversion for the Society. Representing the Jesuits as a group of intriguers, whose aim was a wealth and a power limited only by the boundaries of the earth and whose tactics were the devices of hell and the principles of Machiavelli, he dedicated himself to the extinction of this monstrous enemy of the civilized world. "I shall regret," he exclaimed, "having to pass into the next world with the knowledge that I was leaving behind me this poison in the house of my honored lord." [28] In the royal entourage several men who shared Tanuc-

28 Pastor, *History,* XXXVII, 38.

ci's feelings toward the Society gained positions of influence: the marchese Geronimo di Grimaldi, the minister of Italian origin who was in charge of foreign affairs; Pedro Pablo Abarca y Bolea, conde de Aranda, who was a tough soldier, a friend of French deists, and the president of the Council of Castile; and Manuel de Roda y Arrieta, who was an agent at Rome for Spain and who was strongly influenced by the Jansenist party there. One's attitude toward the Society became a norm for promotion or embarrassment in public life. Alumni of Jesuit colleges were excluded from governmental posts. Officials were secretly scutinized to discover their viewpoint on the Society.

These extravagant symptoms of an autocratic state did not go unchallenged. Throughout Spain and her colonies, in the Jesuit schools, masters carried on the teaching of Francisco Suárez on the origins of civil authority. The voice of this magisterial figure, one of Spain's most brilliant minds, still sounded far and wide within the lands of Iberian culture, advancing the doctrine that rulers do not receive their authority directly from God but through the mediation of the people. The government revealed its sensitivity to the influence of this intellectual heritage in its sweeping decrees, once the Jesuits were exiled, whereby it tried to eradicate Suarezian political ideas.[29]

The mood of the absolute state, on the other hand, found an articulate voice in Pedro Rodríguez, conde de Campomanes. For Campomanes, who postulated that all energies of the nation be at the disposal of the crown, an organization with the international character of the Society was intolerable, and its presence, threatening as it did the life of the state, called for drastic action. Either the Society had to be uprooted or Spain would succumb. It was this intransigent regalism which vitiated his other laudable aspirations for Spain. With his personal knowledge of the works of European scholars like Grotius, Mabillon, van Papenbroeck, Baronius, and Muratori, Campomanes had a just grievance against the stagnant scholasticism and Aristotelianism identified, as has been seen, with the uninspired Jesuit colleges of the second half of the seventeenth century. Intent on the study of the vernacular and the new critical methods in history and natural science, he called for the eradication of what he oversimply lumped together as "doctrina jesuitica." But regalism and Febronianism distorted his crusade for a cultural renais-

29 G. Furlong, S.J., "The Jesuit Heralds of Democracy and the New Despotism," in *The Expulsion of the Jesuits from Latin America*, ed. M. Mörner (New York, 1965), p. 44.

sance, seemingly blinded him to the current Jesuit intellectual renewal, so much a fulfillment of his own aspirations, and influenced him to become a colleague of Aranda, Roda, and Grimaldi.[30]

Strongly entrenched in high places, these regalists held their greatest prize in the person of the king. Fifty years of age in 1766, of fairly good judgment and irreproachable personal life, Charles III, maintaining the tradition of Philip IV and Ferdinand VI as defenders of Spanish rights against the encroachments of Rome, fell under the spell of Tanucci and his constellation in Spain. In the Society of Jesus, Charles, looking through the eyes of these counselors, saw a terrible bugbear.

As had happened in Portugal, a dramatic event gave this feeling against the Society a focal point of action. On March 26, 1766, a riot broke out in Madrid against the government. Among the royal officials, Leopoldo de Gregorio, marqués de Esquilache, the Sicilian minister of finance, was particularly unpopular. His fiscal policies and his foreign provenance irritated the people. A rise in food prices exasperated edgy tempers. Then the government attempted to regulate men's dress. It issued a decree against the popular long cloak and the wide-brimmed sombrero in favor of the French wig and three-cornered hat. Stirred to indignation the people of Madrid poured into the streets. They made Esquilache their special target. They raided his house but he escaped. Before this popular fury the king fled to Aranjuez. Jesuits with other priests moved among the people in order to calm them.

The government opened a secret investigation of the disturbance. In none of the documents appeared a single incriminating line against the Society, but before long interested parties had converted an eruption of social unrest into a Jesuit strike against the crown. In a special court known as "The Extraordinary Council of Castile," wherein secrecy shrouded judges, witnesses, and procedure, the Society's enemies worked out their design. The Jesuits sensed that something ominous was astir. Yet, on January 11, 1767, forty of them sailed with royal assent from Cadiz for Pará and Chile. The papal nuncio, Lazaro Opizio Pallavicini, discerned the implications of the secret inquiry and informed Cardinal Luigi Torrigiani, the papal secre-

30 Furlong, ibid., pp. 44-46. R. Krebs Wilckens, *El pensamiento histórico, político y económico del Conde de Campomanes* (Santiago de Chile, 1960) pp. 151-155; see also his "The Victims of a Conflict of Ideas," in *The Expulsion*, pp. 50-52.

tary of state, that Spain was on the eve of a conflagration which threatened to consume the Society.[31]

From Naples, Tanucci plied the Spaniards with urgent exhortation. He prompted them, in imitation of "the two shining examples" of Portugal and France, to grasp this propitious moment to eject the fomenters of rebellion. In September he repeatedly warned that the Jesuit schools, wherein the supremacy of the Holy See was exalted and Spanish citizens were changed into slaves, must go or the state would pay the terrible price of the eradication of royal power, the impoverishment of the country, and the death of arts and science. On November 22, 1766, he sent his pious encouragement that God would bless Manuel de Roda with the perseverance and energy "to bring this glorious work to a successful conclusion."

Tanucci's application received its reward. On January 29, 1767, the Extraordinary Council reached its decision: the Society of Jesus should be banished from the realms of Spain and its property confiscated. The tediously familiar cant about avarice and lawlessness terminated with the new charge that the Jesuits, sensing that power was slipping from their hands, incited the people to riot against the crown. On February 20 a special commission, after examination of the Extraordinary Council's proposal, recommended its adoption and suggested that the king add the enigmatic statement that he was locking within his royal breast certain other reasons for his decision. Charles concurred and on February 27, 1767, issued a secret decree ordering the banishment of the Society and the seizure of its property.

Then began a process memorable for its thoroughness, efficiency, and secrecy. The conde de Aranda, appointed to supervise the operation, had copies made of the royal decree and of his own specific instructions for its execution. On March 20 these were on their way in sealed packets to the officials of cities where there was a Jesuit house. In Madrid and environs the packets were to be opened at midnight of March 31-April 1; in other areas at midnight of April 2-3. At the Jesuit communities throughout the kingdom the procedure resembled what took place at the Imperial College at Madrid. At midnight troops pounded at the college door; they assembled the awakened Jesuits in the refectory and then read the royal decree of exile; they directed them to leave immediately, taking with them only the clothes they wore, their breviaries, a prayer book, any snuff, chocolate, and small change they might happen to

31 Pastor, *History,* XXXVII, 101, fn. 6; 104-105.

have. Before dawn all two hundred Jesuits in Madrid were out of the city and on the road to exile. Two days later some 2,700 were marching to ports of embarkation, those of the Province of Castile to Santander, those of the Province of Andalusia to Jérez de la Frontera, those of the Province of Toledo to Cartagena, those of the Province of Aragón to Tarragona.[32] In anticipation of popular resentment, the king declared any public demonstration of protest to be an act of high treason. Within a year's time some 2,300 Jesuits from Mexico, South America, the Philippines, saw the lands of their labor for God's glory drop beyond the horizon as the ships into which they were inhumanly herded pointed their prows toward Europe. And 188 colleges and 31 seminaries, both at home and abroad, were emptied of their masters.

In the camp of the Enlightenment the cup of joy overflowed. Tanucci hailed Roda as the "Spanish Hercules;" Francisco Vázquez, general of the Augustinians, calling for a hymn of praise to God, who was glorified in Spain by that country's purification from the Jesuit reptiles, gloated over the thought of the exiles sailing over the waters to the Papal States where he impatiently awaited them with their overthrown household gods of avarice, ambition, slander, and regicide. As had happened in Portugal, the Spanish government next moved openly against the Church. The next year Charles III issued a Pragmatic Sanction decreeing that all papal bulls, briefs, and edicts destined for the Spanish realms, save in cases of conscience, had to be submitted before promulgation to the Council of Castile. Governmental circles encouraged the development of Gallican overtones in canon law and hastened the spread of translations of Febronius' *The Church and Legitimate Power of the Roman Pontiff*. Roda, in a letter to De Choiseul, expressed his government's mood: "We have killed the son. Now nothing remains for us to do except to carry out like action against the mother, our Holy Roman Church." In a message to José de Azara, member of the Spanish embassy in Rome, he sounded the note of the Enlightenment's triumphalism. On April 14, 1767, he wrote that the whole of Spain had recently undergone a cesarian section and that soon he, Azara, could expect a handsome gift of thousands of Jesuits.[33]

In one unexpected way Pope Clement XIII, grieved and deeply shaken by the events in Spain, upset the Spanish pro-

32 Smith, *Month*, XCIX (1902), 632-633.
33 Pastor, *History*, XXXVII, 124-127, 202; Garciá-Villoslada, *Manual*, p. 546.

gram. Charles' government planned to land the Jesuits in the Papal States, and on May 13, 1767, thirteen transports with 570 men anchored off Civitavecchia. The pope refused to admit the exiles. His policy, neither arbitrary nor heartless, was based on solid reasons: Spain's wanton disregard of international relations by a unilateral decision to place exiles in the territory of another prince; the lack of accommodations in the Papal States already burdened with the Portuguese Jesuits; the problematical character of the pension — each priest was to receive 100 pesos annually — cessation of payment being threatened if a single Jesuit throughout the world spoke or wrote in criticism of the king.

The Spanish officials then opened negotiations to deposit their unwanted cargo on Corsica. It was a tangled and involved process, since the French, the Genoese, and some Corsican insurgents were all making a bid for control of the island. On May 22 the ships arrived at the port city of Bastia. War and the lack of lodging kept the Jesuits from landing immediately. For more than a month some had to live in crowded quarters aboard ship, from which they found some little relief in a bit of daily exercise on the shore. Less fortunate were others, members of the Province of Toledo, who had to live aboard ship for five months. Eventually the exiles found accommodations, a few in regular dwellings, but most in barns, stables, and old chapels. Food was poor and scanty; household furniture and table cutlery were wanting; books were scarce; vestments and altar supplies were inadequate to allow each priest to say Mass daily. Many fell sick. In five months sixteen of the Castilian Province alone died. Time only magnified the discomfort and suffering, because in the late summer of 1767 and in early 1768 some 1,800 men, the first batches from the colonies, began to arrive, bringing with them another irritant, the friction, often just below the surface and now uncovered by the nauseating sea voyage, between those from Spain and those born in the colonies. Seventy-eight died during the voyage.[34]

The same noble ideal started these men on the road of the religious life. As novices they had gone in spirit to Manresa and there with St. Ignatius showing the way in the *Spiritual Exercises* they professed their desire for dishonor with Christ dishonored, poverty with Christ poor, humiliation with Christ humiliated, when this would be to God's greater glory. In this hour these resolutions were being tested in the fiery furnace of adversity. Some of the refugees must have sincerely and calmly judged

34 Pastor, *History*, XXXVII, 118, 163-173.

that God could be served more efficaciously by severance from the Society. Others however simply crumbled before the privations and ran away from the challenge to their spirit of sacrifice. Stranded on a foreign shore and discouraged by no visible prospect of a change, several, in disguise and finding transportation to the mainland in fishing boats, fled the monotony and rudeness of Corsica, went to Rome, obtained release from their vows, and returned to Spain. In one day thirty members of the Andalusian and Toledo Provinces disappeared from Corsica in this way. The provincial of Andalusia advised his men to fend for themselves.[35] Spanish officials in their correspondence between Rome and Madrid made frequent references to those petitioning for release from the Society, and by November, 1771, four and a half years after the banishment, the government had listed seven hundred and nineteen. Some of these, freed from the discipline of religious observance and made giddy by the wonders of a great metropolis, carried on in a shameful manner, much to the distress of Ricci, who wondered at the ease with which the Roman Penitentiary granted its dispensations. The shadow of these defections only heightened the bright glow of the heroic fortitude of those who persevered.

The destitute colony was able to hold together only about a year. In May, 1768, France purchased the Genoese rights on Corsica. The French commander received orders to collect the refugees, place them aboard ships, land them at Sistri, from where each man could fend for himself. Soon a batch of 800 men stood on Italian soil, in tattered clothes, without money and with no place to go. Confronted by these harsh developments, Pope Clement lifted the ban against entering the Papal States.

During these months of trial these Spanish Jesuits had in their midst one who with supreme skill, strength, and sweetness imposed order on their torn and scattered group. José Pignatelli, grandee of Spain and native of Saragossa, of fine intelligence, delightful urbanity, and aristocratic graciousness, was only thirty years old and fourteen years a Jesuit when he went into exile with his brethren. The provincial of Aragon, by an unusual act, invested him with his own authority and commissioned him to act as his right-hand man during the emergency. With serenity and refined charity Pignatelli was a strong pillar of support for his fellow exiles. Amid the general chaos on Corsica he searched

35 Ibid., 172-173.

out lodgings, gathered food, organized academies in history, mathematics, and oriental languages. At the expulsion from Corsica, with energetic administrative skill, he settled in three weeks almost a thousand fellow religious at Ferrara. For twenty-four years, remaining ever for ex-Jesuits a spiritual, intellectual, and financial pillar of strength, he labored at Bologna, Parma, Naples, and Rome until his death in 1811. In 1954 Pope Pius XII canonized this apostle of the ruins of the Society of Jesus.

Overseas the withdrawal of the Jesuits seriously weakened the colonial church. In South America and Mexico, aside from the uncounted numbers in the cities dependent on them for their spiritual and intellectual formation, they left behind some 305,000 Christian Indians. In the Philippines and the Marianas they left behind a Catholic population, for which they were responsible, of about 213,000. Other religious, despite fine efforts to fill in the open ranks, could not cope with this overwhelming situation which broke on them with such suddenness. The natives of the Reductions began to drift back to old ways of life. By 1797, thirty years after the decree of expulsion, in the reductions of Paraná and Uruguay alone there were only 15,000 persons. The jungle gradually reclaimed the enclaves of civilization as the acalias, the cedrelas, and the rosewood took root where chapel, shop, and house once stood, and as a tangled mat of brush covered cultivated pastures. For Spanish America this sudden loss of so many Jesuit priests and brothers opened a new era. A depressing malaise fell over the Church. And into the intellectual vacuum rushed unchallenged the anti-Christian ideas of the Enlightenment.[36]

An aspect of this story of exile, rarely noted by historians, was the cultural renaissance which the Spanish Jesuits carried with them to other lands. From Madrid, Cervera, and Valencia especially, professors and students brought a sensitivity and enthusiasm for fresh expression in philosophy, literature, mathematics, and music. Scholastics studied under men like Mateo Aymerich, intimate associate of José Finestres y Monsalvo, who in many ways turned the University of Cervera into a fountainhead of Spain's eighteenth-century renaissance, and Bartolomé Pou, refined Latinist, whose history of philosophy was the first of this genre to appear in Spain. Cultural germs planted in

36 Ibid., XXXVIII, 476–477; De la Costa, *Jesuits in the Philippines*, p. 581; Garciá-Villoslada, *Manual*, p. 554.

Italian soil grew into plants of fascinating variety, and after 1773, when the Society was suppressed, former Jesuits moved with greater freedom to the intellectual centers like Padua, Bologna, and Rome.[37]

Archives in these and other Italian cities contain Jesuit papers and correspondence which give a unique insight into the cultural history of this period. Lorenzo Hervás y Panduro, the father of modern comparative philology, whom Navarro Ledesma called the world's last humanist and first philologist, spoke with his fellow Jesuits from Asia and the Americas who had mastered the languages of those regions. He called the assembly of former missionaries a forest of learning. In his correspondence, preserved in the Vatican Library and in the National Library in Rome, he frequently expressed the hope that some Spanish linguist would profit from this "forest of learning" before American scholars from Yanquilandia would defoliate it. Cardinal Alessandro Mattei presented Luciano Gallissà y Costa, librarian at the University of Ferrara, to Pope Pius VI as "hombre más erudito de Europa." Menéndez y Pelayo judged *The Revolution in Italian Musical Drama* by Esteban de Arteaga as one of the most beautiful works of the eighteenth century. Juan Andrés, spearhead of the movement of literary criticism, was the world's first author to trace out in broad lines a synthesis of all literary history.[38]

Even though harshly treated by their king and his government, several of the Spanish Jesuits looked back with affection for the culture of their country. Among the most articulate were Catalans like Juan Francisco Masdeu, who wrote the impressive *A Critical History of Spain and Spanish Culture* (1783), and Valencians like Antonio Conca y Alcaraz, who published much on Spanish art. Masdeu's two brothers, José and Baltasar, also Jesuit exiles, brought to Italy with them a renewed scholasticism

---

37 M. Batllori, S.J., "La irrupción de Jesuítas españoles en la Italia dieciochesca," *Razon y Fe*, CXXVI (1942), 113-114.

38 Ibid., 115-116, 124-129. A number of the younger Spanish Jesuit exiles, while loyal to the Church, nevertheless fell under the influence of either the rationalism of the French encyclopedists or the sentimentalism of Jean Jacques Rousseau. The more notable of these were Juan Andrés, Lorenzo Hervás y Panduro, and Antonio Eximeno. Their weak formation in philosophy during an ebb tide in Spanish philosophical and theological studies most likely accounts for their failure to discern the substantial defects in the thought of the encyclopedists and Rousseau. Gerald A. McCool, S.J., "Rouseau and the Spanish Jesuits," WL, LXXIV (1945), 329-338.

which blossomed into the Thomistic revival of the nineteenth century. The missions also contributed to this cultivated Spanish-speaking diaspora, especially in the Chilean, Juan Ignacio Molina, who composed the valuable *An Essay on the Natural History of Chile* (1782) and the Mexican, Francisco Javier Clavijero, whose *Ancient History of Mexico* (1780) has an essential place in the bibliographies on Spanish America. Other treasures of this Spanish culture in exile await their rescue by scholars probing into widely scattered Italian archives.

Naples and Parma   The Kingdom of Naples was the next to banish the Society. Marchese Bernardo Tanucci, by an intensive program of propaganda through brochures and pamphlets which were placed in shops, coffee houses, and barracks, prepared the public for the approaching coup. No incident, however, such as the riots in Spain and the attempt on the king's life in Portugal, occurred to serve as a pretext. He therefore took his cue from France and fell back on the "reasons of state" enunciated by the Parlement of Paris. With pretentious rhetoric he lauded the magistrates of France as "the most learned and pious men seen in three centuries," guided by the soundest of reasons in ridding their country of "those noxious people." To Roda in July, 1767, he expounded the diplomatic syllogism he had evolved: What Spain and France have done Naples should do; but Spain and France have suppressed the Society; therefore, Naples should suppress it also. In sixteen-year-old and unconvinced King Ferdinand I, Tanucci met a disconcerting obstacle. He therefore created a "Commission on Abuses," staffed with political satellites, who obediently parroted the minister's favorite charges against the Society and called on the king to imitate his father, Charles III of Spain. Ferdinand gave in. On November 20, 1767, troops surrounded the Jesuit houses in Naples. Fortitude in the Neapolitan Province was not so distinguished. Faced by a choice between exile or severance from the Society, only three hundred and eighty-eight of six hundred and thirty-one took the way to exile. The first of this number were landed at Terracina on November 26th. News of the expulsion reached Sicily a few days later. Even less than that of the Neapolitans was the stability of the Sicilian Jesuits. Some theologians circulated an opinion which shook morale considerably, that a member of the Society was not bound to measure up to the heroism exacted by a life in exile. Of seven hundred and eighty-six men only three hundred and fifty-two, including nine scholastics and fourteen brothers, went into exile. And within five years seventy-two of these, including five former rectors, withdrew from the Society.[39]

The little Bourbon state of Parma could not afford to be out of step with the greater members of the royal family. Guillaume du Tillot, correspondent of Voltaire, intimate of Roda, admirer of Carvalho, and chief minister to sixteen-year-old duca Ferdinando, could not bear that Parma should not reflect the policies of Spain. Troops therefore, on the night of February 7-8, 1768, took positions around the Jesuit houses, assembled the communities, and marched them, about one hundred and seventy, to the border. Most made their way to Bologna.

In this general calamity the Society had no more vigorous defender than Pope Clement XIII. More than fifty times he took action in one form or another to forestall the suppression in France alone. To Charles III of Spain he poured out his deepest feelings. "Of all the blows of fortune which have befallen Us . . . none has pained Our fatherly heart more than Your Majesty's decision to banish the Jesuits from your realm. . . . We testify before God and man that the Society as a whole, its Institute, and its spirit are completely guiltless, and not merely not guilty, but pious, useful, holy, both in its objectives and in its rules and principles." [40] These and other encomiums of the Society by Clement XIII were to be a serious embarrassment to his successor, and they show, in their ineffectiveness, the low state to which papal prestige had fallen in this rationalistic age.

One of the most curious documents of the history of the Society's suppression was a pen sketch called "The Jesuit Tree" (Arbre Géographique contenant les Établissements des Jésuites par Toute la Terre et le Nombre des Sujets). The duc de Choiseul and Parlement sponsored this work, allegedly based on a catalog, or register, sent from Rome in 1762, and meant to present to the nobility and judiciary in a compact way information about the Society. Jacques Crétineau-Joly, famous "chouan of the writing desk" of the nineteenth century, published it in the fifth volume of his *Histoire Religieuse, Politique et Littéraire de la Compagnie de Jésus* (1845). The larger branches of "The Jesuit Tree" represented the different countries, the smaller branches the provinces of the Society, and the leaves the towns and cities in which Jesuit communities were located.[41]

The General Suppression

39 Pastor, *History*, XXXVII, 222-241.
40 Ibid., XXVII, 152-154; Brucker, *La Compagnie*, pp. 819-820.
41 Crétineau-Joly, *Histoire religieuse, politique et littéraire de la Compagnie de Jésus* (Paris, 1844-1856), V, 278-279.

By 1768 the Society's enemies, having cut away several of the branches, then laid the ax to the roots of the mighty trunk. This they did by the application of steady pressure on the pope in order to force him to suppress the Society throughout the world. The diplomats of Portugal and the Bourbon courts forged a united front against the papacy. Eventually all the Catholic powers became involved, if not, as in the case of Spain, France, and Naples, in the actual demand for the Society's extinction, at least, as in the case of Austria, in acquiescence to the deed. For six years before 1773 the status of the Society preoccupied the chanceries of Catholic Europe, not as what at first glance might seem to be a compact and isolated episode in diplomatic history, but as a single strand in the web of international negotiations which covered other issues of the day, such as the Franco-Spanish unity against the England of William Pitt, France's seizure of the papal enclaves of Avignon and Venaissin, and Naples' occupation of the papal territories of Pontecorvo and Benevento.

The duc de Choiseul, of wide experience at Rome, Vienna, and Paris in the execution of French foreign policy, and a creature of Madame de Pompadour, broached the idea of a concentrated drive in which the Bourbon courts together would "urge and force the pope" to dissolve the entire Society. Carvalho, thinking even more broadly, ambitioned the incorporation of Lisbon and Vienna in this overwhelming coercive assault against Rome. On April 21, 1767, De Choiseul wrote to the marquis d'Aubeterre, French minister at the Vatican: "If the pope were prudent, enlightened, and strong, he would come to but one decision, to suppress this Society entirely. . . ." [42] Clement XIII however, although by nature a timid and indecisive man, reflected the strength of his secretary of state, Cardinal Luigi Torrigiani, and committed himself to the preservation of the Society. For this stand he suffered greatly in the last year of his life, January, 1768, to February, 1769.

An incident, initially unrelated to the Jesuit question, brought matters to a head. The duke of Parma issued a series of ordinances directed against the Church. Pope Clement, in a brief of January 30, 1768, pronounced these decrees to be null and void. The Bourbons interpreted this as a papal attack on temporal princes, and in view of the Family Compact of August 15, 1761, they banded together to defend the small member of

42 Pastor, *History,* XXXVII, 315-320; Smith, *Month,* C (1902), 264-265.

their alliance. De Choiseul sounded the call to arms: "The dignity of the monarchs who are members of the Family Pact demands that we allow no prince of this royal house to suffer insult with impunity." [43] Six months later France and Naples made reprisals against the pope. Neapolitan troops took the papal towns of Benevento and Pontecorvo while Avignon and Venaissin fell to French arms. Diplomats recognized that in these conquests the Bourbons held valuable cards in their game to win from the pope the suppression of the Society. Through January, 1769, in a coordinated series of distressing interviews, the Spanish, Neapolitan, and French ambassadors presented Clement with peremptory and vigorous demands that he surrender to the royal desire of their princes. With magnificent courage the seventy-six-year-old pontiff answered with a blunt "no," remarking that he would rather have both his hands cut off than suppress the Society. A few days after he had received D'Aubterre in audience, this dogged fighter succumbed to a heart attack on February 2, 1769.

The Jesuit question overshadowed the conclave which opened thirteen days later. After minute and careful analysis of various cardinals, during which the Bourbons made a candidate's attitude toward the Society a basic norm for determining his acceptability as pope, attention finally focused on the person of Giovanni Vincenzo Antonio Ganganelli. As a friar of the Conventual Franciscans he took the name Lorenzo. A man of good intelligence, scholarly, kind, and charming, he twice declined when elected to the generalate of his order. Ganganelli did not bind himself to suppress the Society as the price for his election, but in a general sort of way he remarked that, if canonical requirements were not violated, the abolition of the Jesuits could in his eyes be considered a possibility, and even as something worthwhile. On May 18, 1769, Ganganelli was elected and took the name Clement XIV.

For four years, 1769 to 1773, when he finally dissolved the Society, Clement suffered terrible mental anguish, made the more acute by the merciless taunts and buffeting by the Bourbons. On the papal throne with its universal view of the world, and realizing that he was pope not only of the realms of the Bourbons but also of lands where the Society enjoyed favor, he saw the enormity of suddenly demolishing an organization which his immediate predecessor had defended so staunchly. One thing became immediately clear: he was not going to be pre-

43 Pastor, *History*, XXVII, 271.

cipitous in giving the Bourbons what they demanded. In his conversations with the diplomats he urged patience, kept asking for time, confided that he had to regard his conscience and his honor. Cardinal de Bernis, witty frequenter of Parisian salons, subtle diplomat, and since 1769 the French ambassador at Rome, perceptively observed that Clement had looked too long at the deep chasm over which he had to jump.[44]

The Bourbons, however, remained determined to get Clement across the chasm. Yet, curiously enough, despite their determination, they did not always push their diplomacy at top speed. Other problems modulated the pace. De Choiseul in general advocated a slow and gradual pressure on the pope. Thinking of papal Avignon held by French troops, he feared that Clement might suggest a deal whereby France, in return for the suppression of the Society, would give back her conquest. But the longer France held Avignon the more plausible would be her claim to it. He therefore advocated a cautious pace. He also, in his hierarchy of values, gave priority over the abolition of the Society to the strength and efficacy of the Bourbon Family Pact in its confrontation with William Pitt and his design for British imperialism. He complained that the Jesuits had become so great an obsession with Madrid's diplomats that Spain was ignoring "the greatest and most essential of national interests." "The Jesuits," he told De Bernis, "are at the moment nearly driving me daffy . . . To the devil with them." Yet Spain's fervor was not always at white heat. At one time France became aware of a sudden slow-down in the Spanish harassment of the pope. The confessor of Charles III, anxious for the canonization of the Spanish nun, Maria de Agreda, and a dogmatic definition of the Immaculate Conception of the Blessed Virgin, persuaded the king to relieve the pressure on the Vatican, at least for a while.[45]

On November 30, 1769, Clement faltered and formally promised Charles III, in writing, that he would suppress the Society. Yet he continued to stall. He spoke of a tedious mosaic work he had to do. In varied ways he deliberately embarrassed the Jesuits and then pointed to this as evidence of his sincerity. He authorized a visitation of the Roman Seminary, in charge of the Society. The financial investigators went over the books for two centuries and then announced that the Society had embezzled

44 Ibid., XXXVIII, 167; M. Cheke, *The Cardinal de Bernis* (London, 1958), p. 243.
45 Pastor, *History*, XXXVIII, 153, 181-182; Cheke, *The Cardinal*, pp. 241-242.

five million gold scudi. The appalled Jesuits pointed to the heavy debt which they carried, but the pope removed the seminary from their care. He did the same with the Irish College. The non-Italian Jesuits in the Papal States he deprived of jurisdiction to hear confessions. "You see," he told De Bernis, "that when I am trusted and allowed to act, all goes well." But this procrastination could not go on forever.

July 4, 1772, was an ominous date for Clement. On that day a new Spanish ambassador, José Moñino y Redondo, arrived in Rome. He and De Bernis worked out a crafty plan for their business with the pope. Moñino was to take the hard and ruthless line; De Bernis was to adopt the air of a friendly counselor, gently advising the pope that wisdom called for the acceptance of the Spaniard's demands. Rightly disturbed by the presence of Madrid's deceptively suave diplomat, Clement dreaded his tactics. Moñino defined his objective simply: to disentangle the Jesuit question from all others and obtain its early resolution. In a little more than a year he achieved his purpose. Through July, August, and September, in his audiences with the now terribly distracted and distraught pope, this slick tactician, by such insinuations as the likelihood that all religious orders might be consumed in a great conflagration, finally forced the pope to agree to the preparation of a document of suppression. Clement entrusted this task to Francisco de Zelada, a Spanish priest at the Vatican. Zelada followed the pattern of thought as dictated by Moñino. From that moment Zelada entered the inner circle of those who prepared the suppression.

The most substantial hope for the Society was at the court of Vienna where a positive and clear stand against the suppression by the powerful and pious Empress Maria Theresa, who esteemed and liked the Jesuits, would have given Clement XIV a superb argument against the Bourbons. This Moñino realized. "If Vienna resists," he observed, "the pope will do nothing." But Vienna did not resist. Absorbed in arrangements for the marriage of her children into the royal families of other European powers, particularly that of Princess Marie Antoinette to the dauphin of France, Maria Theresa trod carefully lest she offend these other powers. Giving priority, as was natural, to imperial policy and Hapsburg prestige among the royalty of Europe over the defense of the men she truly admired, she informed Charles III in April, 1773, that she would place no obstacle in the way of the Bourbon program. With that vanished the pope's hope for Austrian support.

The denouement came quickly. In June, Moñino heightened

his offensive. To hasten the pope's decision he bribed two of Clement's close advisors, the Conventual Franciscan friar Innocenzo Buontempi, who was his secretary and confidant and whom the diplomats regarded as a kind of Gray Eminence, and the author of the document of suppression, Francisco de Zelada, who had received the cardinal's hat in April, 1773. For Buontempi Moñino arranged a gift of 10,000 scudi, for Zelada, 8,000. The Spanish government, in gratitude to "his most useful Eminence," also awarded Zelada two canonries in Seville and Córdoba.[46] In a two-hour interview with Clement, Moñino so bullied the sick and nervous man that the pontiff begged the pitiless Spaniard not to frighten him so. Completely held in bonds by the tightening cords of Bourbon diplomacy, the pope finally capitulated, and on June 8 signed a brief suppressing the Society throughout the entire world. He entitled this brief *Dominus ac Redemptor*. By a second brief, *Gravissimis ex causis*, Clement erected a special commission of five cardinals to whom he entrusted the duty of informing the Jesuits of their fate and of handling the many procedural problems which were inevitably part of so vast an operation. On August 9 the pope met with these cardinals and set August 16 as the date for the enactment of *Dominus ac Redemptor*.[47]

Secrecy completely enveloped these preparations. Clement bound the five cardinals to the strictest silence under pain of excommunication reserved to himself. On the 16th, according to normal procedure in the promulgation of a brief, the document should have been announced in the Campo di Fiori and copies placarded at the gates of the Vatican. In this instance neither action was taken. Rather, in the evening of the 16th, the secretary of the commission, accompanied by soldiers and police, went to the community at the Gesù where the general resided. To Ricci and the other Jesuits he announced that the Society was no more. Immediately and without protest the general submitted. The next day the Jesuit churches in Rome were closed, save the Gesù, San Ignazio, and San Appolinare, and these were under the care of the Capuchins, the Minorites, and seculars.

On the 18th the president of the commission of cardinals, Andrea Corsini, sent a letter to all bishops, informing them about

---

46 Pastor, *History*, XXXVIII, 275-276.
47 Smith, *Month*, CI (1903), 401-403, 505-506. The brief in its final form carried the date August 16, but Clement XIV signed the minute on June 8 (ibid., 401, fn. 4).

the developments in Rome, and ordering them to "proclaim, publish, and intimate the briefs *Dominus ac Redemptor* and *Gravissimis ex causis* to the Jesuits assembled in every one of their houses, colleges, or residences, or wheresoever any of the individual members were to be found" within their episcopal jurisdiction. This unusual manner of proclamation, in the presence of the Jesuits assembled in their communities, and the failure to promulgate the *Dominus ac Redemptor* at Rome *urbi et orbi* opened a Pandora's box of perplexing canonical difficulties.

The *Dominus ac Redemptor* is a lengthy document. It has forty-five paragraphs, some quite long. In the first paragraph Pope Clement sounded the keynote: Our Lord and Redeemer had come to earth as the Prince of Peace. This mission of peace, transmitted by Christ to his apostles, Clement felt was his responsibility to preserve in the Church, a responsibility which he had to carry out not only by the encouragement of institutions which fostered peace but also by the eradication of institutions which impeded peace. The brief has two main divisions, a recitatory part in which the pope reviewed the reasons which in his judgment called for the extinction of the Society, and a functional part in which he pronounced the actual sentence of suppression and dictated various provisions for its execution.

In the first part Clement, recalling incidents in the history of the Church, enunciated the principle that not only guilt of serious crime but also, on an even wider and broader basis, the interior harmony and tranquillity of the Church is justification for the dissolution of a religious order. He enumerated a long list of charges against the Society but avoided passing judgment on the validity of these charges. Looking back into the Society's history, he recalled that its institute, encountering severe criticism, occasioned grave discord, but he did not claim that this criticism was justified. He recalled the distress of earlier popes at the dissension among Catholics in regard to Jesuit doctrinal teaching, but refrained from affixing blame to the Society. The *Dominus ac Redemptor* suppressed the Society but without condemning it. Yet, reflecting strongly the influence of Spain, the brief recited in its historical flashback only those unpleasant episodes which evoked memories of discord and contention, and studiously ignored the long procession of Jesuit martyrs and confessors, thus deliberately creating an image of the Society as nothing more than a perennial fountainhead of evil in the Church. The voice of Moñino sounded in all its

399

phrases, and for his reward in this sordid victory he received from his king the title of conde de Floridablanca.

One immediate and great good came from the disappearance of the Jesuits. On April 10, 1769, between the death of Clement XIII and the election of Clement XIV, De Choiseul advised De Bernis that, if the former pope had reigned another ten years, a schism would most likely occur in the Church. "Without question," he wrote, "the pope must be a man with understanding of the spirit of the Courts and the mood of our age, so completely different from that of the previous century." [48] De Choiseul's advertence to schism was not mere idle talk. That Portugal, Spain, and France might take to the road opened up by Henry VIII of England caused well-grounded trepidation at Rome. The sacrifice of the Society, removing as it did a serious irritant to Bourbon relations with the Vatican, helped to keep important countries linked to the Holy See until a better day. Even in their death the Jesuits continued true to their vocation of service to the Church.

In this final act of service they paid a price of intense physical and spiritual suffering. Twenty-three thousand men who had entered on a way of life sketched for them in the opening phrases of the Formula of the Jesuit Institute, approved two hundred and thirty-three years before by Pope Paul III: "Whoever desires to serve as a soldier of God beneath the banner of the cross in our Society, which we desire to be designated by the name of Jesus . . . ," suddenly felt torn within them all those intimate and human ties of affection which bound them, one to another, in a spiritual brotherhood, and saw disappear all those familiar landmarks by which they daily steered their course to eternity: the Society's *Constitutions*, the rules, the schedule of work, the guidance of superiors. Far more painful than the loss of roof and table was this spiritual dispossession. The novices were dismissed; so were the scholastics and brothers. The priests were free to live as secular clergy or to enter another religious community. Personal grief found many expressions. One was that of Francisco Puig, who concluded his journals about the Jesuits exiled from the Philippines with a phrase suggested by Psalm 136 and which he read in one of the letters of Francis Xavier. "If I ever forget you, O Society of Jesus, may my right hand be forgotten as well." [49]

---

48 Pastor, *History*, XXXVIII, 27.

49 N. P. Cushner, S.J., *Philippine Jesuits in Exile. The Journal of Francisco Puig, S.J., 1768-1770* (Rome, 1964), pp. 154-155.

Soon the fields were astir with animals clawing away at the carcass. With dispatch the governments closed in on the Jesuit holdings. Tanucci cynically observed that the cardinals' commission on the suppression was more eager to track down Jesuit money than Jesuit offenses. Portugal, France, and Spain had already acted. Clement XIV reserved the Society's property for the Church, but governments, such as Austria, dissented so vigorously that the pope backed down. A group not often adverted to in the story of the suppression and which had eyed Jesuit holdings for some time were the planners of a state-controlled educational system. For this enterprise they counted on the Society's property to provide the financial foundation. Although Pombal was enabled to start the first school system in Europe maintained by the nation, other European statesmen were disappointed in their treasure hunt, for many a Jesuit staff lived in severe privation, and they could not realize on any grand scale their bureaucratic dreams. Tanucci's search for Jesuit wealth in the Kingdom of Naples unearthed a debt of 200,000 ducats.[50]

Each Jesuit library had its unique history. Many volumes and manuscripts traveled far and wide. Gerard Meerman, an avid book collector of the eighteenth century, acquired a rare scholarly treasure in the block of manuscripts, *codices Claramontani*, taken from the old Collège de Clermont. In 1824 the most famous of all harvesters in the field of books and the organizer of the British Museum, Sir Thomas Phillipps, purchased at least some of these. By 1841 his collection included Jesuit block-books from China. Some of the Society's library in Tours appeared at an auction in 1825 at Sothebys in London. In South America the library of more than forty thousand volumes of San Pablo college in Lima was transferred to the stacks of the rival Dominican University of San Marcos. The Dominicans had asked King Charles III for this favor. This the monarch granted, and "as a gift from his liberal hand" also the books in the other Jesuit houses of Lima. Hundreds of volumes have come to rest in havens like the British Museum and the Bibliothèque Nationale. Others are still on the circuit, each a souvenir of the mighty spiritual contest of the eighteenth century.[51]

50 H. Hans, "The Dissolution of the Society of Jesus in the Eighteenth Century and Its Financial Consequences," *Education and Economics: The Year Book of Education* (1956), 138-140; Pastor, *History*, XXXVII, 241-242.
51 A. N. L. Munby, *Portrait of an Obsession. The Life of Sir Thomas*

Ricci ended his days as a prisoner in Castel Sant'Angelo. Moñino, intent on a solemn vindication of the deed he had engineered, constrained the pope to confine the general and the assistants and to prosecute them for criminal action. On September 23, 1773, the gates of Castel Sant'Angelo closed on Ricci, then seventy years old. He left only in death, two years later. His keepers refused him permission to write, boarded up his windows, posted an armed guard, deprived him of even a little fire during the winter, denied him the consolation of celebrating Mass. A mean-minded functionary cut his food allowance in half. In several secret sessions, until January, 1774, officials interrogated him about the Society and especially about the alleged cache of fifty million scudi. In reply, Ricci pointed to his inability to support the Portuguese and Spanish exiles, and showed that what money he sent abroad was destined for the foreign missions and could be checked in the Society's books. No evidence presented against him stood up. Yet the investigators stalled and refused to render the verdict which justice demanded. Ricci then appealed to the commission of cardinals concerned with the Society's dissolution. They enigmatically replied, "Providence takes care." When Pius VI was elected in 1775, Ricci, in terms of moving simplicity, appealed to him for justice. The new pope was determined to give him and the assistants their freedom, but the Bourbons through Floridablanca protested that the honor of their royal houses was at stake. Despite the fulminations of Spain, Pius released some of the assistants in July and August, but before he could do the same for Ricci, the general died on November 24, 1775.

A few days before his death Ricci received Holy Communion. As the priest held the Blessed Sacrament before him, he read a grave and solemn statement, announcing that, in full awareness of his proximate appearance for eternal judgment before the throne of the God of Truth, the Society had given no reason for its suppression and he none for his imprisonment. So closed one of the cruelest of tragedies in the old fortress on the Tiber.

The execution of the *Dominus ac Redemptor* did not follow a uniform pattern throughout the world. In several countries and principalities the governments refused to allow the brief to be carried out with completeness and in every detail, insisting that the priests of the dissolved order continue to live in community and run their schools. A number of factors accounted

Phillipps, *The World's Greatest Book Collector* (London, 1967), pp. 13, 19, 23, 39; Martín, *The Intellectual Conquest,* p. 96.

for this resistance to the papal action: a wide sympathy for the Jesuit apostolate; the realization of the religious and cultural void which the scattering of the religious would create; apprehension at the wide popularity of the secular philosophy of the Enlightenment. In two major countries, Prussia through three years, and Russia indefinitely, the rulers rejected the brief outright.

Local governments, therefore, each with its own peculiar approach denied the suppression a universal consistency and uniformity. In Switzerland, for example, at Lucerne, Fribourg, and Solothurn, in Germany at Düsseldorf, Düren, Jülich, Münstereifel, Ravenstein, Augsburg, and the Palatinate, because of the remonstrances of the civil authorities, which gained Rome's dispensation, the former Jesuits carried on as secular priests, living in community and conducting their schools and churches.[52] But at best this was but a temporary expedient, since time would deplete the ranks of those teachers who were denied the power to train successors. In Austria, Maria Theresa retained them in the schools for the humanities, mathematics, and physics. In Belgium the officials acted with harshness. For about a month they closed off all the former Jesuits from contact with other people, and for two years they kept the Flemish provincial in jail even though they had to admit that they could produce no evidence of misbehavior against him. From the Jesuit houses they seized about thirty valuable paintings by Rubens, Van Dyck, Breughel, and De Crayer, and shipped them to the imperial galleries in Vienna. With appalling boorishness they gutted splendid libraries. Of some 500,000 volumes, they classified three-quarters as theological rubbish and sold them for their value as waste paper.

Through nearly twenty-five years the Bollandists endeavored to continue their internationally known enterprise. Two major obstacles brought on their demise: the bureaucracy of the Austrian government and the wars of the French Revolution. In 1775, when the professed house in Antwerp, where the Bollandists lived, became by order of Maria Theresa a military academy, the scholars moved to the abbey of Caudenberg in Brussels. In 1786 Joseph II suppressed this abbey and ordered the Bollandists to move to the Theresianum, the former Jesuit college in Brussels. Two years later, Joseph, unhappy because the scholars did not meet his imperial desire that they issue a volume a year, and because he felt that their work was "of little

52 Pastor, *History*, XXXVIII, 347-357.

interest to really educated men," decreed the dissolution of their learned society. In 1789 he approved the purchase of the Bollandist library by the Norbertine abbey of Tongerloo. The Norbertines graciously welcomed five of the ex-Jesuit scholars, who still hoped to carry on despite the imperial disapproval. But the armies of the new French Republican invaded the Netherlands. Some of the treasures of the rare library went up in flames. Some were smuggled out of the country. And so came to a bitter and sorry close one of the greater scholarly enterprises in the history of Western civilization.

The national disaster which visited Poland as she was wiped from the map of Europe in the famous Triple Partitions of 1772, 1793, and 1795 intensified the suffering brought by the suppression. The papal nuncio to Poland, Cardinal Giuseppe Garampi, reported to the Holy See that the ex-Jesuits were wandering about the country in distress and want. Eventually 270 of them found employment as teachers in schools and tutors with families. The English Jesuits received the news of the suppression at their continental school at Bruges. The prince bishop of Liège rescued them from dispersion by his invitation to move with their students to his see. In 1776 Pope Pius VI approved the arrangement whereby, living together as secular priests, they continued their classes. This went on for twenty years. In Ireland the sixteen Jesuits formed, through 1774-1776, a voluntary and unofficial association wherein they pooled their resources against the day when the Society — *Societas Resurrectura* they called it — would once more live.[53]

Throughout the world, therefore, former Jesuits entered into other channels of the Church's life. Many continued their early interests as teachers, scholars, writers. Some twenty-five were destined for martyrdom during the violence of the French Revolution. Forty-six were chosen by the Holy See to be bishops, including John Carroll, the first bishop and archbishop of Baltimore. Two others in the United States were so honored, Lorenz Grässl, a Bavarian who died in Philadelphia in October, 1793, two months before Rome named him Carroll's coadjutor, and Leonard Neale, also designated coadjutor in Baltimore.[54]

In most areas, even though not always permitting the brief's execution in every precise detail, the civil or church authorities nevertheless allowed its promulgation with relative promptness.

53 Ibid., 377-378; Corcoran, *Clongowes*, p. 40.
54 W. Kratz, S.J., "Exjesuiten als Bischöfe, (1773-1822)," *AHSJ*, VI (1937), 185-215.

In Prussia this was not the case. By his conquests in Poland and Silesia Frederick the Great had absorbed into his realms thirteen Jesuit colleges and seven residences, staffed by about two hundred and twenty men. For about three years, determined not to lose such competent scholars, he firmly forbade the promulgation of the brief *Dominus ac Redemptor*.

Frederick was a late convert to the cluster of European admirers of the Jesuits. Before 1768 he kept pace with any of the apostles of the Enlightenment in his contempt for the Society, the abolition of which "noxious vermin" he warmly advocated. But his preoccupation as a child of the Age of Reason with the worth of education transformed his attitude toward these experienced teachers. His military and predatory policies brought him into contact with Jesuit schools, and with his sense of statesmanship he recognized their contributions to the culture of his realms. In 1769, just before the election of Clement XIV, suspecting the inevitability of the suppression, he announced to D'Alembert that it redounded to his personal honor to preserve some fragments of the Society, and warned the Frenchman that his country would one day regret its action against the Jesuits. Through his Roman agent he advised Clement XIV that, regardless of developments elsewhere, he intended to keep the Society intact in his states. When Tanucci heard this, he could not believe it.[55]

Frederick was at Breslau when the brief arrived. He made his policy absolutely clear to the bishop, Moritz von Strachwitcz: the document was not to be published. He informed the provincial of the Jesuits in Silesia, Franz Gleixner, about his directive to the bishop, and ordered that the Jesuits continue their work. So began three years of mental disquiet for the Jesuits in Silesia and Ermeland. Frederick's order threw them into a quandary, raising as it did a technical but important point of canon law. Gleixner judged that correct canonical procedure for the promulgation of *Dominus ac Redemptor*, as distinctly delineated in the instruction of the cardinals who were supervising the suppression, demanded that the notification of the brief be given in each Jesuit community by the local bishop, and that, until this was done, no Jesuit could feel free of his obligations as a religious of the Society. All Jesuits did not agree with Gleixner. The rector of the college at Braunsberg, speaking

55 Pastor, *History*, XXXVIII, 418-421, fn. 2 on 421. A recent work which I was unable to consult is H. Hoffmann, *Friedrich II von Preussen und die Aufhebung der Gesellschaft Jesu* (Rome, 1969).

for those in Ermeland and West Prussia, could not see how he could allow a canonical technicality to stop him from following the widely broadcast desire of the pope that the Society be dissolved. Serious misunderstanding arose from this uncertain situation. Cardinal Giuseppe Garampi, the nuncio to Poland, criticized the Jesuits who stayed at their posts as recalcitrant in the face of the known wishes of the pope. Gleixner, aware of these accusations and realizing that his logic, for all its canonical correctness, did not alleviate the awkwardness of a survival which was due to the frustration of papal policy by a secular ruler, requested the bishop of Ermeland to petition the pope for approbation of the Society's continuance in the realms of Frederick II. Repeatedly he told the royal minister at Breslau that for the Society to continue the pope's permission was indispensable. "Of one thing there is no doubt," he said as he reiterated his readiness to comply as soon as notified of the brief by proper ecclesiastical authority, "We are not rebels." Garampi brushed this aside as mere lip service.[56]

If Gleixner looked to Rome for an easement of this thorny problem, so did Frederick. Initially Prussia and the Vatican faced each other with intransigence from two rigid positions, but gradually, through about two years of diplomatic exchange, both sides eased their demands and moved toward a reasonable solution. From a baffling maze of details the central issue which emerged was whether the Society should retain its character as a religious order. By the end of 1775 Pope Pius VI and Frederick arrived at substantial agreement. Pius was willing to allow the Jesuits to continue their corporative work in church and school, even to accept recruits, but on condition that they function not as members of a religious order but as individuals under the jurisdiction of the bishops. Frederick, for his part, while unable to grasp why the pope was so adamant on depriving the Jesuits of their character as religious, received what he basically wanted, the guarantee of their presence as educators.

On January 3, 1776, the king issued orders that the Society of Jesus be dissolved in his realms. Six months later, to this new, somewhat anomalous corporative unit, he gave the title: Priests of the Royal Schools Institute. This Institute lasted twenty-four years, until 1800, when under Frederick William III a Catholic School Board, designed for control of the Catholic schools in Silesia and opening teaching positions to laymen, replaced it.

56 Ibid., 433-434.

Overseas, most of the Jesuit missions, situated as they were within the Portuguese and Spanish empires, had been dismantled before the final action of Clement XIV. In the main, therefore, the brief of suppression touched those countries whose governments were not sympathetic and were even hostile to the Church: the English possessions in North America and China.

In 1773, from Maine to Georgia, the English colonies were but two years from Bunker Hill and Lexington and the beginnings of the great rebellion against England. Twenty Jesuits worked in Maryland, Pennsylvania, New Jersey, and New York. Together, the suppression of the Society and the Revolution brought the tiny American Church of 30,000 Catholics to the most perilous state in its entire history. Propaganda had given little attention to this mission. The London vicar apostolic, Richard Challoner, within whose jursidiction it presumably fell, frankly expressed the desire to be free of the responsibility. For all practical purposes the Jesuit provincial in England had been the only overall director. The suppression broke the tie with him. And the Revolution severed the very fragile link with Challoner. The ex-Jesuits, by their fidelity to their posts from Maryland to New York, saved the Church from disaster.

In this crucial period there emerged the impressive figure of John Carroll, former member of the Society, an aristocrat of polish and social ease, but above all a man of vision who not only sensed a great future for the young United States of America but also divined, because of the freedom it enjoyed, a vigorous Church. He took the initiative in rallying his fellow ex-religious in order to guarantee three things: first, an organization of former Jesuits to hold the mission lands against the day when the Society would be restored; second, a college which would be a source of an intelligent Catholic laity and probably of priestly vocations; third, some sort of definite connection with Rome. In 1784 the Holy See appointed Carroll prefect apostolic in the United States, and in 1789 designated him as the first bishop of Baltimore. Despite financial worries and the frustrations created by human misunderstandings, he never gave up his dream of a college, which in 1789 he finally started at Georgetown on the Potomac River and placed in the hands of the ex-Jesuits. Himself trained in the Society's course of studies, he vested in Georgetown, with its syllabus of humanities and philosophy, his "hope of permanency and success to our H. Religion in the United States." This wise churchman had correctly interpreted the history of his times, and in his creation of the mother of the long line of Catholic colleges and universities in the United States, he supplied one of the essential needs of the young American Church.

In Canada the French Jesuits, after the English conquest, tended a dying mission. They tried to enlist the help of fellow Jesuits from other lands, but the governor, Sir Guy Carleton, following the policy shaped by the British government, forbade the entry into Canada of the hoped for reinforcements. Nor did he permit the admission of Canadian youths into the order. In 1772 Bishop Joseph Briand of Quebec petitioned King George III to allow the Jesuits and the Recollects to receive novices, but the monarch refused. Then came the *Dominus ac Redemptor*. On the advice of Carleton and lest a public pronouncement reawaken the claim of Lord Amherst, Canada's conqueror, to the Society's property, Briand informed the Jesuits of their suppression in strict secrecy. He was happy to keep these apostles of the Indians in Canada. He could not however halt the attrition of time. As the years passed and death took its toll, the missionaries gradually disappeared, laid to rest in places filled with Jesuit memories, Quebec, l'Assomption-des-Hurons, Montreal, Prairie du Rocher. The last to die was Joseph Casot, in 1800. The Iroquois had given Isaac Jogues the name Kenwenteshon, "The Day that Knows no Waning." It was not a name that could be given this once brilliant mission. During the seventeenth and eighteenth centuries, three hundred and twenty French Jesuits had served in North America. About one hundred and forty-four of the English Province had done the same.[57]

Throughout the Orient, as in Canada, the lamentation was the same: a once vital mission was withering because it was denied reinforcements. From India the Carmelite, Paulinus of St. Bartholomew, wrote deploring the torper and inertia which had replaced the fervor and enterprise on the departure of the Jesuits. The archbishop of Cranganore, Salvatore dos Reys, in a moving plea to Propaganda, begged for priests for Madurai and Mysore where the missions were on the brink of ruin.[58]

In China the Society died amid a cacophony of claims to jurisdiction, excommunications, and nationalistic vindications. The arrival of the news in China of the suppression of the Society raised the question of who had jurisdiction to publish the *Dominus ac Redemptor*. Bishop von Laimbeckhoven, still administrator in Peking and represented there by the Austrian Carmelite Josef Max Pruggmayr — his name as a religious ap-

---

57 T. Hughes, *History*, II (text), 597–598, 704.
58 Pastor, *History*, XXXVIII, 496; XXXIX, 397–402.

pears in Propaganda's archives as Giuseppe M. a S. Teresa —
maintained his jurisdictional power and received the backing of
Propaganda. The Portugese vice-provincial, José Espinha, in
a strange gesture, sided with the recently appointed bishop of
Macao, Alexandre da Sylva Pedrosa Guimarães, who also
claimed jurisdiction in Peking. Sylva arrived in Macao on August
23, 1774, a creature of Pombal, who demonstrated his want of
wisdom by his first episcopal act. With a facade of learning,
behind which lay a not particularly bright intelligence, he
issued a pastoral message on the suppression of the Society of
Jesus, twelve pages in length with 210 footnotes to document
his calumnies and allegations. This imprudent man, whose
position on jurisdiction in Peking Propaganda rejected, linked
up with Espinha in a Portuguese alliance.[59] To acerbate this
problem of the true seat of authority in the Chinese capital, the
Jesuits, as they did in Prussia and White Russia, split on the
question of the need for formal promulgation of the brief in
Peking in order that it be effective. Behind these differences
pulsated the intense feelings of nationalism, characteristically
expressed by Joseph Amiot of the French Mission after the
suppression had been accomplished: "No longer are we Jesuits,
but Frenchmen we still remain." Espinha promulgated the
Dominus ac Redemptor on September 22, 1775. Pruggmayr did
so on November 15 of the same year.[60]

For the next decade internal strife tore the Chinese Church.
Legalism, fed by nationalism, ran rampant. In 1780 Giovanni
Damasceno Salusti, a secular priest, was consecrated bishop
of Peking, but a year later, under a burden that demanded a
patience and prudence which he did not have, he broke and
died. Peace came only in 1785 with the arrival of the Franciscan
bishop, Alejandro de Gouvea, who found the religious spirit of
the Chinese Church so choked by the tight cords of juridical
formalism that practically every priest in Peking, for one reason
or another, was under excommunication. On the subject of the
disposal of Jesuit property, so little was it by 1775 that Laimbeckhoven expressed his amazement to Propaganda that the
question was even raised. He exclaimed: *Seges est ubi Troia
fuit.*[61] Eventually the bishop of Peking took over the holdings
of the vice-province, while at the request of Louis XVI in 1783

59 Krahl, *China Missions*, pp. 213, fn. 7; 214.
60 Ibid., p. 268, fn. 15.
61 Ibid., p. 221, 287; Pastor, *History*, XXXIX, 412.

Propaganda made the Vincentians the inheritors of the French possessions.

Under Emperor Ch'ien Lung (1736-1796), an intellectually alert and culturally curious man who enjoyed the company of the Jesuits at court, the men of the dismantled Society continued their intellectual apostolate at Peking. The twilight of Ricci's great endeavor was a beautiful one, richly colored by Michel Benoist's remarkable general map of the Chinese Empire, as well as by the erudite literary work called *Memoirs on the History, Sciences, Arts, Customs and Usages of the Chinese,* in the composition of which, with other Jesuits, Benoist had collaborated. In the provinces, where Ch'ien Lung for all his genuine admiration of the ex-Jesuits did not check the persecution of Catholics by the high tribunals of the empire, a handful of the former Society preserved amid danger and dire poverty contact with the Christian communities. In 1784-1785 the persecution reached high intensity. Thirty missionaries were lost in one way or another. Not a single European missionary of Propaganda remained in the countryside. The dogged old bishop of Nanking, Gottfried von Laimbeckhoven, carried on until quietly at Tang-kiahsiang on May 22, 1787, this beautiful flame of Christian life fluttered and went out. The last member of the vice-province to die was Simão d'Almeida, in 1805; the last of the French mission, Louis Poirot, in 1814.

In 1835, on a wall of a house outside Peking, a French Vincentian missionary, Bishop Martial Mouly, came upon the epitaph of the Jesuit mission to China written by Joseph Amiot. By his own admission not a very tender man, Mouly nevertheless confessed that the reading of Amiot's words moved him deeply and brought tears to his eyes. He included a copy of the Latin original in one of his mission reports which was published in 1837 in the *Annales de la Propagation de la Foi,* the successor to the famous *Lettres édifiantes.*[62] It reads:

In the Name of Jesus
Amen.
Long unshaken but overcome at last
By so many storms,
It has fallen.
Traveler, stop and read.

Reflect for a few moments on the inconstancy of things human. Here lie the French missionaries of that very renowned Society which taught and spread abroad in all its purity the worship of the true

---

62 *Annales de la Propagation de la Foi,* X (1837), 101-103.

God; which, while imitating amid pain and toil and as far as human weakness allows Jesus whose name it bore, lived virtuously, helped the neighbor and, making itself all things to all in order to gain all, for two flourishing centuries and more gave to the Church martyrs and confessors. I, Joseph-Marie Amiot, and the other French missionaries of the same Society, under the patronage and protection of the Tartar-Chinese monarch and with the support of the arts and sciences which we practice, still forward the divine cause. While in the imperial palace itself, amid altars of false gods, our French Church shines with a true magnificence, we, secretly grieving even to the last of our days, have erected here amid burial groves this monument of our fraternal affection. Go, traveler, continue on your way. Felicitate the dead; weep for the living; pray for all. Wonder, and be silent.

In the year of Christ, 1774, on the 14th day of October, in the twentieth year of Ch'ien Lung, the 10th day of the 9th moon.

A fitting epitaph for the whole Society! Traveler, stop and ponder over the inconstancy of human affairs.

The whole story is yet to be told. Many documents in many archives await their editor. Periodically some of this buried information appears in a learned journal and illumines a bit more another phase of a very complex history. Such, for example, happened in the study of the papers of Rolland d'Erceville, president of the Parlement of Paris at the time of the Society's suppression, redoubtable enemy of the Society, and an active agent in the liquidation of its resources. In 1890 D'Erceville's great-grandson, an alumnus of the Jesuit college of St. Geneviève in Paris, gave some of his ancestor's papers about the seizure of the Society's assets to a Jesuit. And these have illumined how the suppression was executed in French Guiana. Many other mosaic pieces of this kind wait to be put in place.[63]

Despite these yet unearthed pieces the picture in its general lines is clear and will not be essentially altered. Through the sixteenth, seventeenth, and most of the eighteenth century the Church sent through the world one of the mightiest waves of missionary zeal in its long history, a wave which broke on two disastrous rocks, the suppression of the Society and the disarray of Europe by the French Revolution and Napoleon. During those nearly three hundred years thousands of men, including some of the most gifted in Christian history, left Europe to

General Conclusion on the Missions

---

63 C. Larère, S.J., "La suppression de la mission de la Guyane Française (1763-1766)," *AHSJ*, IX (1940), 208-226.

bring Christ and his Church to unbelievers. Yet, at the end of this immense expenditure of energy and heroic dedication, very few stable, vigorous, self-supporting churches had been created. Judged by this norm, today commonly accepted by theologians as the purpose of the missions, the Church had failed. And the Society shared in that failure.

In Africa, at the suppression, the Society left only faint vestiges and memories of its several ventures. In Japan and China Catholics begotten in the tradition of Xavier and Ricci were a *gens lucifuga*. In Latin America and the Philippines there was an ecclesiastical organization, but in the unhealthy state of almost complete dependence, even after so many centuries, on Spain and Portugal. In Canada the Church looked to France for hierarchy and priests. In the south of India tough little Catholic communities carried on, but supported for the most part from the outside. No fresh self-reliant Churches formed of new ethnic groups had taken their place beside the venerable Churches of Spain, Portugal, France, and Italy. After three centuries Christendom remained Christendom, namely Europe, and the mission lands remained mission lands.[64]

This failure suggests a blazing contrast with the immense success in church-building among the Germanic peoples in the early Christian centuries. Within a little more than a century after St. Augustine landed in Kent, the Anglo-Saxon Church produced a Bede, a Willibrord, a Boniface. Failure to do the same in modern times raises the question: why? Reasons are many and complex and vary from area to area. Persecution, especially strong in Japan and China, made organization impossible; the expansion of the Protestant colonial powers, England and Holland, enveloped and often submerged Catholic communities; a narrow mentality, unable to envisage a Christianity outside western and Tridentine forms and intensely hostile to adaptation to native cultures, blocked important breakthroughs, especially in China and India; the extremely low and barbarous level of culture of some of the pagan peoples, making it impossible, for example, to conceive a Bede or a Boniface arising shortly from the Iroquois of New York, resisted the basic elements of civilization; jurisdictional friction and disputes, splintering a united front, arose between the Royal Patronage system and the Congregation of Propaganda; the vast distances, to which distances in Europe were not remotely comparable, made

64 Adrian Hastings, *The World Mission of the Church* (London, 1964), pp. 24-29.

communication with Rome most difficult, and this at a time when the centralizing tendency of Propaganda left less and less room for individual initiative and freedom in the mission areas; and possibly the most cogent of all, the failure on the part of the missionaries, especially in the areas of the Royal Patronages, to build vigorous native churches led by indigenous hierarchies. Very few Asiatics were consecrated bishops until the twentieth century. Not that the missionaries, in many areas at least, were averse to native vocations, but in a kind of failure of confidence, they did not envisage as an imperative goal the transfer of the local churches to their own peoples. The early authoritative voices of the Italian Alessandro Valignano, the Frenchman Alexandre de Rhodes, and the Spaniard José de Acosta had lost the ring of persuasiveness as the years turned into centuries.

These circumstances, some beyond their control, others born of limited personal vision, inhibited the Jesuits on their missions, so that, when the ties with Europe were broken by the Society's suppression and the disruption of Europe in the era of the French Revolution and Napoleon, no solid structure was left standing on the foundations of native rock. Jesuit charity, industry, fortitude, imagination, intelligence, gallantry there were without measure. But with these luminous qualities the harvest reaped by the end of the eighteenth century was not commensurate.

For a long time the ancient abbey of Monte Cassino, repeatedly destroyed and rebuilt, has used as its device the words *Succisa Virescit:* Even thought cut down, it blossoms. These words might be applied to the Society of Jesus and its experience in White Russia. There, because of Russia's share in the First Partition of Poland, two hundred and one Jesuits in four colleges and two residences of the Polish and Lithuanian provinces suddenly found themselves under the rule of Empress Catherine the Great. And there the Society continued to exist until 1820. Two factors especially created this situation: first, the intransigence of the empress who, appreciating the Jesuit contribution to the cultural advance of her dominions, refused to allow the publication of the brief of suppression; and second, the gradual, hesitant willingness of Pope Pius VI to let Catherine have her way.

The *Dominus ac Redemptor* arrived in Poland in mid-September, 1773. Catherine directed that it be treated as nonexistent, and the governor of Mogilev ordered that all copies of the document be turned in to him. The Jesuits, no less acutely

Survival in White Russia

than their fellow religious in Prussia, felt the harsh pressure of the vise in which they were caught. Here again it was the delicate question of whether the brief's efficacy depended on correct canonical promulgation. Heading the Jesuits was the rector of the college at Polotsk, Stanislaw Czerniewicz, a Lithuanian who shortly before the publication of the brief in Poland had been appointed vice-provincial of the Jesuits in White Russia. Czerniewicz wrote to Cardinal Giuseppe Garampi, papal nuncio to Poland, for advice, exposing to him the delicacy of the situation: recognition of the brief would displease the empress and probably bring a storm down on her Catholic subjects; disregard would be tantamount to disobedience to the pope. Garampi did not answer.[65] Toward the end of 1773 the Jesuits explained to Catherine that failure to acquiesce to the brief burdened their conscience with a sense of guilt, and therefore they requested two things of her: first, that she approve their surrender of the name of Society of Jesus; and second, that she petition the pope to permit them to live in community life. On January 13, 1774, the autocrat issued a ukase, instructing the Jesuits to alter nothing. She counseled Czerniewicz that he was over-scrupulous.[66]

Differences in the interpretation of the canonical status of the Jesuits aggravated the situation. Garampi, with diplomatic deftness, gave back with one hand what a moment before he had taken with the other. He judged that the brief, since it was a matter of common knowledge, obliged in conscience. However, since positive law does not obligate to do the impossible — and such was the practical situation of the Jesuits — he felt that they could continue their work. He elaborated this opinion with the claim that the Jesuits were obliged to press Catherine energetically for liberty to obey the pope.

Hemmed in on all sides by perplexity, Czerniewicz turned to Pope Pius VI. He explained the interpretation of the canon lawyers, who held that the Jesuits in White Russia, because the brief was not promulgated, were bound in conscience to continue to observe their religious vows and the *Constitutions* of the Society. Further, he pointed out that, despite this interpretation, some of his subjects were uneasy in mind and others even felt obliged to withdraw from the Society. Through Cardinal Carlo Rezzonico he asked the pope kindly to give some

---

65 Pastor, *History,* XXXIX, 211-213.
66 Ibid., XXXIX, 214; P. Dudon, S.J., "The Resurrection of the Society of Jesus," trans. G. McCool, S.J., *WL*, LXXXI (1952), 321.

indication that he was not displeased with them. On January 13, 1776, the pope replied enigmatically: "May the result of your prayers, as I foresee and you desire, be a happy one." [67] He indicated that he was looking toward White Russia with eyes that did not see. The Jesuits there continued to run their schools and their churches.

During the three-year period, 1780-1783, three events took place which enhanced the growth and endurance of the Society in White Russia: the opening of a novitiate, the election of a vicar-general, the verbal approbation of Pius VI. As time went on the need for a house of training for aspirants to the Society became more evident. By February, 1777, less than three years since the issuance of the *Dominus ac Redemptor,* the number of Jesuits had dropped one fourth because of deaths and withdrawals, from two hundred and one to one hundred and fifty. Czerniewicz informed the Russian authorities that the Jesuits could not continue their work in the schools without replacements. Since he felt that the permission of the pope was necessary for a novitiate, he suggested that Catherine might intimate to the Holy See that this permission would be a gratifying return for the benevolence she had shown Catholics in Russia. The empress, with her usual assurance, and entertaining no doubts whatsoever about the outcome, told Czerniewicz to begin construction.[68]

Then followed one of the strangest episodes in the Church's diplomatic history, as a sly, ambitious bishop, subservient to the Russian government, fooled and embarrassed Vatican authorities. One of the key figures in the long, tedious, and complex correspondence between Rome and St. Petersburg on the question of the Jesuit novitiate was a Lithuanian nobleman, Stanislaw Siestrzencewicz, first incumbent of the new "Bishopric of White Russia," with his see at Mogilev, for the care of all Latin Catholics in the Russian Empire. Siestrzencewicz suggested to Rome that he be given authority over all religious orders in White Russia. Officials at the Vatican, frustrated by Catherine's resistance to the brief of suppression, grasped at this suggestion as a way to erase the Jesuits, for with the powers of official visitor the bishop by a simple fiat could do so. Siestrzencewicz received the powers of visitor for three years. Catherine gave her imperial *placet* to the Roman document on March 13, 1779. Soon after, the Vatican learned how it had been duped. At Catherine's

---

67 Pastor, *History,* XXXIX, 230.
68 Ibid., 240-241.

direction, Siestrzencewicz by virtue of his new powers, issued a pastoral letter granting the Society permission to open a novitiate. Cardinal Lazaro Opizio Pallavicini, papal secretary of state, flew into a rage. Pius VI protested and demanded retraction. Cardinal de Bernis, a sensitive observer, remarked that actually the pope was not so displeased as he seemed.[69]

The new novitiate became something of an international issue as the diplomatic dispatches of the Bourbons burned with indignation. Moñino, in an energetic use of pressure, warned Catherine that the Jesuits were enemies of the state and that Catholic merchants would feel obliged in conscience to quit Russia. Catherine refused to be intimidated and, asserting her position as mistress of her own house, repudiated outright all Bourbon interference in what she regarded as a domestic problem. By November, 1782, she became nasty, threatening to abolish religious freedom for the Catholics in White Russia and to convert them to the Orthodox Church. The Bourbons retreated. One factor that contributed to Catherine's triumph was the war in the American colonies. During this conflict Russia followed a policy of neutrality. So strenuous had Catherine's expression about the novitiate become that the Bourbons, allies of the Americans, feared that they might push Catherine away from her position of neutrality into the English camp. Versailles, therefore, sent instructions to De Bernis to moderate his demands at Rome on the novitiate question, and to persuade Grimaldi at Madrid to do likewise. Meanwhile, on February 2, 1780, the novitiate opened at Polotsk with eight novices.[70]

The second event which solidified the Society's position in White Russia was the election of a vicar-general. Among the Jesuits the question had arisen about the wisdom of assembling a general congregation and electing a superior. They presented the problem to Karol Korycki, the former assistant for Poland. After consultation with others, including two other former assistants, he advised that they proceed with an election, not in virtue of the power of the Russian ruler but in virtue of the Society's *Constitutions,* rights, and privileges, still intact and not touched by the unpromulgated brief of suppression. On October 17, 1782, the delegates chose Czerniewicz as vicar-general. The ambitious bishop Siestrzencewicz tried to influence the members

69 Ibid., 249-250; S. Zalenski, S.J., *Les Jésuites de la Russie-Blanche* (Paris, 1886), I, 311-329.
70 Pastor, *History,* XXXIX, 257-260, 268-270; Zalenski, *Les Jésuites,* I, 327-346.

of the congregation to designate him as a superior general, but they very politely, yet firmly, rejected his pretensions. Catherine assured Czerniewicz that she sided with him in this episode.

The news of the election stung the Bourbons like the lash of a whip across the face. Moñino, Grimaldi, and De Bernis, with a firm united front, concentrated their diplomatic fire on Pius VI and demanded that the election be abrogated. For a while the pope held out against them. But early in 1783 he gave way and on January 29 sent briefs to Madrid and Versailles in which he pronounced null and void what had taken place in White Russia, and declared as still in force the *Dominus ac Redemptor*. The worried pope had more than the Bourbons to trouble him, for over the Vatican fell the shadow of Catherine's threat to take into the Orthodox Church the Catholics of her realms. Cardinal Pallavicini, therefore, demanded that the Bourbon courts compromise and keep secret the briefs recently sent them. They, at the moment fearful of antagonizing Russia, did so.[71]

The third event which gave stability to the Society in White Russia was the positive approbation given by Pope Pius VI. Only a month and a half after he had issued the briefs reaffirming the action of Clement XIV, Pius practically retracted the assurances he had given Spain and France. The provocation came from Russia. The Empress Catherine sent Jan Benislawski, former Jesuit and now a canon in Vilna, to Rome, bearing three requests to be made of the pope, one of which was for papal confirmation of the Society and approval of each step the Jesuits in Russia had taken at her command. Three times Pius received Benislawski and discussed with him the Russian demands. At the last audience, on March 12, 1783, he acceded to Catherine's triple request. On the point of the Society's continued existence in Russia, he three times said, "I give my approval." [72] Ten years had elapsed since Clement XIV had issued the *Dominus ac Redemptor*, and Catherine received the reward of her decade of intransigence as Rome and St. Petersburg had reached at long last accord on the irksome issue of the Society of Jesus.

Catherine with positive determination encouraged the Society's increase. In her farewell to the Portuguese envoy on his departure from Russia, she expressed her defiance of the Catholic powers which fought for the Society's dissolution, boldly stating that White Russia was the most fortunate province of her empire since its youth were trained by the Jesuits. On July 18, 1785,

71 Pastor, *History*, XXXIX, 281-286.
72 Ibid., 286-290; Zalenski, *Les Jésuites*, I, 384-389.

Czerniewicz died, leaving with the one hundred and seventy members of the Society the memories of his wise, tactful, and intrepid guidance through twelve unsure years. On his shoulders had fallen the frightening responsibility of guiding a group of men whose consciences were disturbed by a sharp conflict of opinions about the force of the brief *Dominus ac Redemptor*. He fully realized that for a while he was walking a canonical tight-rope, but unswervingly he kept his eyes focused on the one thing that eminently mattered for him as a Jesuit, the will of the Holy Father. That attitude remained fundamental. What transpired in the heavy and complex correspondence between the European chanceries — for example, about the Siestrzencewicz affair — with its neat tilting and furious blasting, he could not possibly have known save in an occasional and imprecise way. Only dimly at first could he discern what gradually became clearer: that Pope Pius VI countenanced the existence of the Society in White Russia. He acted not only with integrity but with correct judgment. On October 8, or September 27 according to the Julian calendar still used in Russia and the two hundred and forty-fifth anniversary of the approbation of the Society by Paul III, the thirty members of the congregation chose Gabriel Lenkiewicz, sixty-three-year-old Lithuanian as vicar-general.

Through the twenty-nine years from Lenkiewicz' election in 1785 until the restoration of the Society throughout the world in 1814, there were four superiors. Two years before the death of Lenkiewicz on November 21, 1798, the unfailing protector of the Society, the Empress Catherine, had died, but any anxiety about a change of official policy dissolved with the benign and encouraging gestures of the new ruler, Paul I. On February 12, 1799 (dates are according to the Gregorian calendar), Franciszek Kareu, sixty-four-year-old native of Lithuania, was elected vicar-general, and one year later the czar turned over to the Society the Church of St. Catherine in St. Petersburg and gave approval to start a college there. In 1801 Pope Pius VII directed that Kareu and his successors be known as general of the Society, and no longer merely vicar-general. Kareu died on August 11, 1802, and was succeeded by a man who by his versatile talents as linguist, physicist, and architect, and by his engaging personality had earlier won the admiration of Paul I, Gabriel Gruber, sixty-one-year-old Austrian from Vienna. Tragedy cut short a term of office which promised great things. After less than three years of rule, on April 7, 1805, Gruber was burned to death when fire broke out in his residence. On September 14 Tadeusz Brzozowski, fifty-six-year-old Pole, was elected general. To this

418

office, which he held up to the universal restoration of the Society in 1814 and beyond to his death in 1820, this warmhearted man brought an intimate knowledge of the Society's problems gained as secretary to the three previous superiors.

Almost from the first moment of the suppression voices rose to demand, in one form or other, the restoration of the Society. Many men realized that they had lost a mighty seawall against the restless, pounding waves of godlessness which were inundating them. In France an influential Carmelite nun championed a plan to allow the ex-Jesuits of the country to organize as secular priests. Soeur Thérèse de Saint Augustin, daughter of Louis XV and member of the St. Denis convent, had a sympathetic listener in her father and an interested cooperator in the archbishop of Paris, Christophe de Beaumont. De Bernis and the duc d'Aiguillon, the minister of foreign affairs, were deeply disturbed by this project, but were relieved when Clement XIV, on March 9, 1774, cut it short by his order to the French hierarchy that it refrain from all action contrary to the *Dominus ac Redemptor*. By 1787 the bishops of Belgium wanted the Jesuits back. The secularistic policies of Joseph II had inflicted deep wounds on the Belgian Church and made the absence of the Jesuits all the more conspicuous. Throughout the Catholic principalities of Germany a relaxed morality and confused thinking among youth, excited by the ideas imported from revolutionary France, spurred parents to clamor for the return of the old masters. In the domains of the Hapsburgs, Cardinal Christof Anton Migazzi, archbishop of Vienna, took the lead when in 1793 he petitioned Emperor Francis II to sponsor the restoration of the Society. Klemens Wenzeslaus, elector of Trier, backed Migazzi. So did the papal nuncio at Cologne and future Leo XII, Annibale Della Genga. In Poland, before it passed from the map of Europe, several provincial diets passed resolutions, to be introduced at the national diet, requesting the return of the Jesuits. Cardinal Ercole Consalvi, one of the most perceptive, clear-minded, and practical churchmen of the nineteenth century, appreciated what the Jesuit contribution could be in those perilous times. He wrote to Gaetano Albani, nuncio at Vienna: "You do me wrong, great wrong, when you think that there ever was a time when I was not strong in my belief that the Jesuits must be reestablished. As God is my witness, that has always been my firm conviction. . . . There was a time when, even though I backed them, it seemed a little on the fanatical side to say that the Church could not live without them since she had

419

lived without them for so many centuries. That, however, is an error of which I had been disabused long before the French Revolution when I learned what the true nature of Jansenism was. I believed then, and I believe now that the Church lives very badly without the Jesuits. If I were master, I would re-establish them tomorrow." [73]

Two definite essays to give these sentiments a clearly organized form attained a measure of success, although neither reached particularly imposing proportions. One was the Society of the Sacred Heart of Jesus; the other, the Fathers of the Faith of Jesus. In 1794 two French seminarians from St. Sulpice in Paris, Eléonor de Tournély and Charles de Broglie, desirous of creating a community shaped according to the Ignatian ideal, founded at Antwerp the Society of the Sacred Heart of Jesus. The constant maneuvering of the French armies — it was the period of the French Revolution — forced them to take refuge at Hagenbrünn, near Vienna. Dominant among the priests attracted to this group was Joseph Varin d'Ainville, of a nature buoyant and optimistic. Varin became superior after the death of De Tournély on July 9, 1797. Using the *Constitutions* of St. Ignatius as his model, Varin formed the structure of the new institute. From Florence, on his way into exile under the custody of French arms, Pope Pius VI sent him a warm message of encouragement. By the end of 1799 this society numbered forty ardent and single-minded men.[74]

The Fathers of the Faith of Jesus — first called the Fathers of the Holy Faith — was the design of Nicolò Paccanari of Trent. On August 15, 1797, with nine companions this erratic and showy priest pronounced the vows of religion at the chapel of Caravita in Rome. José Pignatelli, naturally alert to any rebirth of St. Ignatius' ideals within a new religious community, early discovered fundamental flaws in Paccanari's program. The old ex-Jesuit interviewed Paccanari and inquired about his adherence to the Institute of the Society of Jesus. Paccanari admitted that he had made some alterations. Quite bluntly Pignatelli told him that he did not have, nor could he hope to have, the Ignatian spirit. Nevertheless, a year later, Pope Pius VI, at Siena and during the same journey into exile on which he blessed the plan of Varin, gave Paccanari a gracious audience, encouraged his endeavor, and gave him the privilege of reciting the Breviary as had been used in the Society of Jesus. The pontiff also made

73 Dudon, *WL*, LXXXI (1952), 336.
74 Ibid., 340.

420

a suggestion of great import. He advised that the Fathers of the Faith of Jesus and the Society of the Sacred Heart of Jesus unite.

In April, 1799, Varin and Paccanari held a series of discussions at Hagenbrünn on the project of consolidation. Although Varin's group outnumbered Paccanari's — about forty to nineteen and although Varin was better equipped to guide such a lofty enterprise, Paccanari was elected superior and the united society was named the Fathers of the Faith. The new organization met early disaster, and the rock on which it splintered was the superior himself. In the minds of many of his subjects he raised serious doubts because of his histrionic and affected demeanor and his reluctance to commit himself to eventual union with the Society in Russia. Not three years passed since the union of 1799 at Hagenbrünn before several of the priests deserted him and made their way to Polotsk. In 1804 Varin and others planned to break with Paccanari and organize their own association in France. Varin spoke with Cardinal Giuseppe Spina, who was in Paris negotiating with Napoleon. Spina advised a break. Then Pope Pius VII, in Paris for the coronation of Napoleon, gave his approval. From that date an independent unit of the Fathers of the Faith — they kept the name adopted in 1799 — carried on in France under Varin.

In 1807 Paccanari, cited before the Holy Office on charges of scandalous living, received a ten-year sentence of imprisonment. Freed two years later by French troops who occupied Rome, this strange, unstable man passed into oblivion, followed by a variety of dubious accounts on how he ended his days.[75] Despite the ignominy of the superior, the Fathers of the Faith during their brief existence kept alive, at least in a general sort of way, the memory of the Jesuits. More important still, they, and the Society of the Sacred Heart of Jesus before them, recruited several excellent men, like Anthony Kohlmann, Jean Louis de Leissègues Rozaven, Joseph Varin d'Ainville, and Giuseppe della Torre, who were to carry heavy responsibilities in the restored Society.

During this growing interest in the re-creation of the Society, three factors especially hastened the day when the decision of 1773 would be reversed: first, the breakdown of the Bourbon united front; second, the gradual shift of Pius VI from a cautious and tremulant sanction to a clearly enunciated desire for the Society's reestablishment; and third, the steel-like determination of Pius VII to effect that reestablishment. The first

75 Ibid., 341-342.

great crack in the Bourbon wall appeared in France. In September, 1792, the Legislative Assembly decreed the abolition of the French monarchy, and four months later Louis XVI went to the guillotine. In 1793 Ferdinando, duca di Parma, now a wiser and more reflective ruler, deserted the other Bourbons and, in a dramatic reversal of his decree of expulsion, sought the return of the Jesuits to his duchy, asking Catherine the Great and Lenkiewicz for a handful of what he called "the precious seed" stored in Russia. When he appealed to Pius VI for his sanction of this move, the pope, still menaced by Spain and Naples, in a secret reply, enveloped his ratification in general and broad language about the good of souls taking precedence over all else. Soon three Jesuits had left Polotsk for Parma.[76]

The duchy became the homing ground for José Pignatelli, the hero of the Spanish dispersal. He joined the arrivals from Russia and on July 6, 1797, renewed his vows as a Jesuit. Two years later they opened with the pope's approval a novitiate at Colorno. Soon five novices from Bergamo, including the future distinguished Cardinal Angelo Mai, and one from Bologna, began their training under Pignatelli, now in the new role of a living link between the old and the new Society of Jesus.

Ferdinando, not content with a limited reestablishment of the Society, pressed Pius VI for a more expansive policy. An amazing flow of letters went between pope and duke on this question. In language that would have startled Moñino, De Bernis, and Tanucci, he told the pontiff that an earlier restoration of the Jesuits would have prevented the current miserable state of Europe, and that if the request for their return had to come from a Bourbon, he, a Bourbon of the Bourbons, was making that request. Ferdinando's candor and sincerity unlocked the guarded convictions of Pius, who confided that he too personally disapproved the extinction of the Society but that Spain's inflexibility had taken away his freedom of action. Still the duke persisted. Pius encouraged him to turn his rhetorical powers on his relative, Charles IV, the king of Spain, who had succeeded to the throne in 1788 and felt a filial obligation to be true to his father's anti-Jesuit program. Ferdinando followed Pius' counsel, and in forthright letter after forthright letter, assuring Charles that God's blessings would descend on Spain if he would open the gates to the sons of St. Ignatius, he called on him to disown his father's legacy. But Charles remained adamant

76 Ibid., 329–330.

and wrote Pius VI that the atrocities of the French Revolution sprang from "the teaching and impure hands" of the Jesuits.[77]

For his part the pope, in 1798, dropped somewhat his circumspect and chary attitude. On February 20 French troops seized the eighty-two-year-old pontiff and set him on the road to exile. During this journey into France Pius received a dispatch from Lorenzo Litta, papal ambassador extraordinary at St. Petersburg, presenting several reasons for a clear pronouncement of papal recognition of the Society of Jesus in Russia. On March 2, 1799, the pope instructed Litta that the Russian court, the hierarchy, and the Jesuits themselves should file formal petitions for such a statement. Six months later, however, on August 29, 1799, death came to the pope at Valence on the Rhône and took from him the opportunity of speaking freely and openly the convictions of his mind and heart.[78]

The third important factor which reversed 1773 was the resolute determination of the new pope, Pius VII, to reestablish the Society in any country from which came requests. On May 8, 1800, Barnaba Chiaramonti was elected pope in Venice. *March 14* While he was still in the city of the lagoons, he received in audience Luigi Panizzoni, one of the Jesuits at Parma. He told Panizzoni that he concurred with Ferdinand's advocacy of the Society's restoration, and delegated him to convey the apostolic blessing to Polotsk and give to Kareu relics of the true cross.

In Russia, meanwhile, the attitude of the new monarch toward the Society matched in benevolence and interest the position taken by the new pope. Early in 1799 Kareu sent the personable and cultivated Gabriel Gruber to St. Petersburg to request the explicit approval of Paul I. Gruber spoke to the czar about the suggestion, made by Pius VI shortly before his death, that Russia formally request the Vatican for explicit and formal sanction of the Society. Paul, attracted by the intelligent and erudite Jesuit and with memories of the gracious reception Pius VI had given him when he visited Rome in 1782, demonstrated his good will in a series of significant actions: by founding an imperial Jesuit college at St. Petersburg, by entrusting to the Society the Church of St. Catherine in the same city, and by sending on August 11, 1800, a personal, handwritten message to Pius VII petitioning explicit ratification of the Society in his empire.[79]

77 Ibid., 330-334.
78 Ibid., 335-336.
79 Ibid., 345-346; Pastor, *History*, XXXIX, 328-329; Zalenski, *Les Jésuites*, II, 84.

Spain reacted promptly and heatedly. In the stick-waving tradition of Moñino, the Spanish ambassador at Rome painted for the pope a picture of "the immense evils" which would visit the Vatican if it should yield but a fraction on the Jesuit question. Quietly but determinedly Pius informed Charles IV that he intended to pronounce his formal sanction of the Society in Russia. This he did on March 7, 1801, in the brief *Catholicae Fidei,* and so laid to rest the latent fears of several good men about the canonical correctness of the organization centered at Polotsk.

Two developments were especially pronounced during the decade after *Catholicae Fidei:* first, a wave of petitions for affiliation with the Society in Russia poured into Polotsk from individuals and groups in Europe and the United States; and second, a great surge of missionary zeal moved through the Jesuits in Russia. In a two-way movement, inward and outward, the Society at Polotsk gave as well as received.

News of *Catholicae Fidei* turned toward Russia the eyes of the aging survivors of the suppressed Society as well as young men who felt attracted by St. Ignatius' ideals. Pope Pius approved manifold requests for affiliation with the Russian group, and rapidly pockets of Jesuits formed in Switzerland, Belgium, and Holland. In an England considerably less hostile since the era of Edmund Campion and Robert Persons two hundred and twenty-five years before, priests who had fled from their school in Liège before the French armies conducted a school at Stonyhurst, a Lancashire estate donated by Mr. Thomas Weld. On May 27, 1803, by appointment of the general Gabriel Gruber, Marmaduke Stone, who had been in the Society six years when it was suppressed, became provincial. About thirty-five men of the pre-suppression Society reentered; an equal number declined to do so. Four months later at Hodder, a mile from Stonyhurst, Charles Plowden, a bluff, candid, and vigorous man of exacting standards, opened the novitiate. He started with twelve novices and initiated in the province a tradition of excellence which remained through the century. United with the English in their request for readmission into the Society, Richard O'Callaghan, an Irishman who had entered the Society fifty years before, in 1753, tied the old, gallant Irish mission, now in the evening of its life, to the dawn breaking in Russia.[80]

Nowhere did there occur a more amazing and colorful demon-

80 J. H. Pollen, S.J., "An Unobserved Centenary," *Month,* CXV (1910),

stration of the new turn of affairs than at the Church of the
Gesù in Naples on August 15, 1804. In the presence of the
sovereign who had expelled them thirty-seven years before, and
of his queen, Marie Carolina, the Jesuits in a solemn ceremony
took possession of their old church. Ferdinand, shaken by the
events of the French Revolution, had reshaped his attitude toward the Society and petitioned Pius VII for its return to
Naples. Gruber chose José Pignatelli to head this restoration
and named him superior of the Italian Province. Very soon Pignatelli met a delicate situation. Ferdinand wanted the Jesuits —
but with a difference. He conceived a kind of Neapolitan Society
of Jesus which would exclude any dependence on a superior
outside Naples. Pignatelli, however, persuaded the king to dis-
card his plan and respect the *Constitutions* as evolved by St.
Ignatius. The Neapolitan enterprise had hardly struck root when
in late 1805 Joseph Bonaparte received the kingdom from his
all-powerful brother. Expelled by the new ruler, Pignatelli led
his thirty or so Jesuits to Rome where they settled near the Colos-
seum. Within a short time he had formed the structure of a
regular Jesuit province with a novitiate at Orvieto, a quasi-college
at Tivoli, a tertianship and inchoate professed house at Rome.

Overseas a modest but important restoration took place in the
new republic of the United States. Vague rumors of *Catholicae Fidei* of March 7, 1801, had reached America. Bishop John
Carroll and his coadjutor, Bishop Leonard Neale, both ex-Jesuits
and intensely concerned about the future of Georgetown College,
tried to clarify these reports. On May 25, 1803, they wrote a joint
letter to Gruber and reported that there were thirteen ex-Jesuits
in the United States. "Most of them," they wrote, "solicit with
ardent desire to end their days in its [Society of Jesus] bosom."
On May 12, 1804, Gruber replied. He welcomed the applicants,
outlined the procedure to be followed, and authorized Carroll
to appoint the superior. By May, 1805, death had reduced the
number of ex-Jesuits to ten. Of these, five decided to reenter the
Society. The two bishops and three others decided not to do so.
On June 21, 1805, Carroll appointed Robert Molyneaux as
superior. On August 18 Molyneaux, Charles Sewall, and Charles
Neale, at St. Thomas Manor, Charles County, Maryland, pronounced their vows. John Bolton and Sylvester Boarman did so
in October. These five men repaired the broken strand of Jesuit

459; B. Basset, S.J., *The English Jesuits from Campion to Martindale*
(New York, 1968), pp. 366-368; Corcoran, *Clongowes*, pp. 40-41.

history that reached back to Andrew White and the origins of Leonard Calvert's colony in 1634.[81]

Molyneaux, a Lancashire man, sixty-three years old, amiable and cultivated, but indolent, without initiative and physically debilitated, did not give a very inspired leadership, but nevertheless, with additions from other provinces and with American vocations, the tiny band expanded. In 1805 two Englishmen arrived. In 1806 Brzozowski sent three priests from Russia, including the versatile Anthony Kohlmann. That same year at Georgetown, Molyneaux opened a novitiate which included among its first aspirants to the Society the two Fenwick brothers, Enoch and Benedict, the second of whom became bishop of Boston in 1825 and founded Holy Cross College, Worcester, in 1843. In 1810 the Americans received an invaluable addition in the brilliant Giovanni Grassi, native of Bergamo, who had been trained by Pignatelli at Colorno, made rector at Polotsk at twenty-nine years of age, and who by his initiative and purposefulness raised the stature of Georgetown College and gave it the ordered curriculum and discipline it sorely needed. With its Americans, Englishmen, Italians, Germans, this little group of Jesuits became a melting pot of nations, anticipating the destiny of the young republic which had become their new home.

Through the twelve years before 1814, therefore, the authority of Gruber and Brzozowski gradually broadened and extended through Europe and across the Atlantic. Slowly they began to put together, piece by piece, the body of the former Society. Meanwhile, in Russia, the pre-1773 characteristic trait of apostolic service recurred to stamp the Jesuits of the new era. In two ways especially, aside from the schools, does the ring of the annals of these years chime with records of the sixteenth, seventeenth, and eighteenth centuries: first, in the zeal for the missions, and second, in the supreme sacrifice made in care for the sick. From White Russia Jesuits penetrated into Odessa, the Caucasus, and Siberia. In 1803 the Bavarian, Aloys Landes, headed eight Jesuits to work at Saratov on the Volga among a large colony of German immigrants.[82] And in Russia itself, in 1812, when thousands of Napoleon's frozen soldiers were captured during the bitter retreat from Moscow, fourteen Jesuits, while assisting the sick and the wounded, gave their lives.

81 E. I. Devitt, S.J., "The Suppression and Restoration of the Society of Jesus in Maryland," *WL*, XXXIV (1905), 215-225.
82 Pastor, *History.* XXXIX, 307.

The year 1812 marked at once the flood tide of the Society's success in Russia and the beginning of the ebb tide of failure. On March 1 the ministry of education published the Czar Alexander's ukase of December 22 of the previous year by which the Jesuit college at Polotsk, despite the vigorous opposition of the University of Vilna, was raised to the rank of an academy with the same rights as the University.[83] The same year a Scot, John Paterson, received the sanction of the Czar to form the Russian Bible Society. It was this organization which occasioned a strong flow of events against the Society's position in Russia.

The Russian Bible Society was the outgrowth of the British and Foreign Bible Society, founded in England in 1804. This English organization originated a worldwide movement "for the wider distribution of the Scriptures, without note or comment." Prince Aleksandr Nikolayevich Golitzyn, the Russian government's minister in charge of foreign religions, saw in the Russian Bible Society a facile means to elevate the educational level of the orthodox clergy. A friend of Alexander I from boyhood, he shared the Czar's idealism and vision of peace founded on the revealed word of God. Enthusiasm, earnestness, and conviction pervaded his correspondence on this subject. To Noah Worcester of Brighton, Massachusetts, he wrote that he esteemed the object of the Massachusetts Peace Society as of almost equal importance as that of the Bible Societies, "for it is only in proportion as the divine and peaceable principles of the Gospel of Jesus Christ prevail in the hearts of men, that lasting and universal peace can be expected. A blessed period is promised in the word of God when men shall learn the art of war no more." [84] To John Shore, the first Baron Teignmouth and first president of the British and Foreign Bible Society, he expressed his belief that the work of Teignmouth's organization was the work of God. "It is truly pleasing to observe, how rapidly a most earnest desire to read the words of eternal life, spreads in our country . . . In one word, it is impossible not to see that the work of the Bible Society is supported from on High, and it is not the work of man . . ." [85]

Prince Golitzyn was a personal friend of Father General Brzozowski. To gain the support of the nobility, who esteemed

83 Zalenski, *Les Jésuites*, II, 161-163.
84 *Correspondence of the Massachusetts Peace Society with the Emperor of Russia and Prince Alexander Gallitzin* (London, 1817), p. 3.
85 *Extracts of Letters from the Rev. Robert Pinkerton on his Late Tour in*

the Jesuits, he asked the general to throw the Society's prestige behind the scriptural movement. Brzozowski was in an awkward position. The attitude of the Church toward vernacular translations of the Bible, set in a negative and defensive cast since the first papal index of Paul IV in 1557, and further solidified by the later prescriptions of Pius IV, Sixtus V, and Clement VIII, was the only position which he knew. He therefore declined, explaining that the Society could not encourage a translation not approved by the Holy See. He was correct. Golitzyn however insisted. Brzozowski remained adamant.[86] The desire for the scriptures spread rapidly throughout the Russian realms as bishops avidly sought copies of the recently printed Bible. Brzozowski had offended the altruism of an important official in the government, and now stood alone, isolated in his fidelity to the policy of the Holy See. On March 3, 1814, he wrote, "Our Prince Golitzyn is no longer what he used to be."[87] The Society's ultramontanism invited enmity in western Europe before 1773. Now in its Russian asylum the same ultramontanism changed official friendship into enmity.

The final act of universal restoration came with suddenness. Napoleon had brought Pope Pius VII to Fontainebleau as his captive in 1812. Even while the emperor, defeated and cornered, bade farewell to the Old Guard in April, 1814, the seventy-four-year-old pontiff was on his way back to his own city. He reentered Rome on May 24, 1814. As part of his effort toward the religious reconstruction of the continent, in turmoil and chaos after the collapse of the Napoleonic Empire, he determined to restore the Society throughout the world. He told Cardinal Bartolommeo Pacca that he would like to do so on July 31, the Feast of St. Ignatius. Difficulties in the composition of the bull, however, delayed its completion beyond that date. Several cardinals, consulted about the text, debated such delicate problems as the apportionment of blame for the suppression, the sensitivities of civil governments, the measure in which the Society should be lauded, the possible alteration of the Society's Institute, the general temper of the document. Through the energy of Cardinal Pacca the bull was ready for the Octave of St. Ignatius' feast, August 7.

Russia, Poland, and Germany; to promote the Object of the British and Foreign Bible Society. Together with a Letter from Prince Alexander Gallitzin, to the Right Honourable Lord Teignmouth (London, 1817), pp. 63, 66.

86 Zalenski, *Les Jésuites*, II, 212-213.
87 Ibid., 213.

On that day, at the altar of St. Ignatius in the Gesù, Pius VII offered the Sacrifice of the Mass. Then in the chapel of the Sodality of Nobles and in the presence of an immense crowd, which included cardinals, royalty, and about one hundred and fifty members of the suppressed Society, Monsignor Cristaldi read aloud the bull *Sollicitudo Omnium Ecclesiarum*. It was considerably briefer than the *Dominus ac Redemptor* of Clement XIV, only fourteen paragraphs. Pius gave the key to his thinking in the opening paragraph: his pastoral office impelled him to use the means provided by God to care for the spiritual needs of the faithful throughout the world. After a short review of his relations with Kareu and his approval of the Society's existence in Russia, and then in the Two Sicilies, he returned, with deep solemnity, to the seriousness of his pastoral obligation to the Church, affirming that he would be guilty of a capital crime if he neglected to employ the skilled rowers for the storm-tossed bark of Peter which the Society could provide. To the Jesuits themselves he gave a word of exhortation, urging them to be true to St. Ignatius and his legacy.[88]

When Cristaldi finished, Pius gave the bull to Panizzoni. Then one by one the aged men who had experienced the sorrow of the suppression knelt before the pope. To each the gracious and smiling pontiff said a few words. Then amid cheering crowds he returned to the Quirinal. Among those in Rome that day who did not attend the ceremony were the two monarchs of Spain, King Charles IV and Queen Maria Luisa, expelled by revolution from their country. Some days later, however, they visited the Gesù. The Spanish Jesuits in the city gathered to pay their respects. The son of the king who had expelled the Society from Spain wept. This scene symbolized peace in the forgiveness of past injury. But it also symbolized, somehow, future trial and affliction, because it pictured the Society turning in sympathy to the old regime when a new world of democracy was being born.

During the two centuries before the Suppression, the Jesuits *Conclusion* had become an important part of the fabric of the society of Catholic Europe and the Catholic colonies. They were a prominent landmark on the road of history between the Reformation and the American and French Revolutions. Exaggerated as it is to say that Europe of the twelfth century had become one great Citeaux, this judgment nevertheless highlights the pervasive in-

88 Dudon, *WL*, LXXXI (1952), 353-354.

fluence of the Cistercians. Again allowing for obvious overstatement, it might be said that between 1570 and 1760 the Catholic world had become one great Jesuit school.

In neither case did the honored ascendancy last. As the history of the Church unfolded, the developments of the Twelfth-century Renaissance and the arrival of the friars terminated what have been called the Benedictine centuries. In the late eighteenth century the Enlightenment closed what can appropriately be named the Jesuit centuries.

Between the Society's suppression and restoration Europe experienced the convulsions of the French Revolution and the rule of Napoleon Bonaparte. And so it happened that, apart from the tiny fragment in White Russia, the Society, invariably engaged in the thick of the Church's conflicts, was absent from the scene of one of her most agonizing battles. At one of the great turning points of history the Jesuit presence in the world, so cogent and robust for over two centuries, was missing. Across this period dominated by Mirabeau, Danton, Sièyes, Talley-rand, Bonaparte, is written a provocative question: how successfully, if it had not been dissolved, would the Society have weathered the storm during those decades of revolution? Any answer can never be more than problematical.

But at the two points that mark the lacuna in its existence, the suppression and the restoration, the Society shared intimately in the Church's life and fortunes. Clement XIV signing the brief of suppression in 1773 and Piux VI dying in Valence on the Rhône in 1799 were parts of the same profound humiliation. Pius VII returning to Rome from Fontainebleau in May, 1814, and his promulgating the bull of restoration a few months later were segments of the same beginning in the reconstruction of a broken Church.

On the interior force of the Society's ideal the years between the suppression and the restoration threw a revealing light. These years demonstrated how intimately this ideal had been part of Europe's — and the world's — history as it endured and found expression, in varying degrees of faithfulness to the original, in a number of institutions. It still was a power. Through the decades of revolutionary chaos it continued to have the fire to capture the hearts of youth, and these young men were on hand, when the day of reestablishment dawned, to give assurance to the aged survivors of the catastrophe that the Ignatian vision would live on.

ACCOMMODATION TO A NEW POLITICAL, SOCIAL, AND COLONIAL WORLD
1814–1914

THE SOCIETY WAS BORN during one of the great transitional periods of European history, the Renaissance. It was reborn during still another important era of change, that of the democratic and industrial revolutions of the nineteenth century. Adaptation did not come with the same ease in each case. In 1540 the Renaissance had been running its course for some two hundred years and was in unquestioned possession of the field. The Jesuits, fresh and unhampered by memories of the medieval world, embraced the predilection of the modern world for the literary traditions of Greece and Rome and, in one of the more conspicuous instances of adaptation in history, placed these traditions at the service of the Church. In 1814 and the years which followed, the Society was not so successful. Filled with recollections of a world of national monarchies and accustomed to the intimate association of altar and crown, the Jesuits as a whole — there were exceptions — found it a painful, anxious, and uneasy experience to adjust to the nineteenth century.

The Generals

One factor especially, among several, made this so: a philosophy, bequeathed by the French Revolution, which aimed at the dechristianization of the state. With the overpowering force of a flood this philosophy purposed to draw all institutions within its own pale, create an all-pervasive unity among citizens of a state, and place the spiritual power at the service of the political. Alexis de Tocqueville discerned that the modern European state of his century was not really a break with the old monarchies in their quest for power but was actually their fulfillment. The City of Man supplanted the City of God as the ultimate reality. A new spiritual community, the republic one and indivisible, became the ultimate value. Such was the trend of political thought and action within the world into which the Society was reborn.[1]

1 J. C. Murray, S.J., "The Church and Totalitarian Democracy," *Theological Studies*, XIII (1952), 526-528.

This philosophy did not remain in the minds of theorists, finding as it did its fulfillment in organizations committed to the radical transformation of traditional Christian society. Toward the close of the century Pope Leo XIII singled out the Masons as especially active in a "vast conspiracy" which aimed at the control of governmental machinery and the destruction of the Church in its entirety.[2] Thinkers of the Enlightenment produced a progeny who carried their thoughts into action. At the hands of these laics, over and over again, in Europe and Latin America, the Society suffered the loss of home and country. For the Jesuits the nineteenth century was a century of exile.

These hardships begot some unfortunate results for the Society. First, they blinded it to the rich and positive values in the concepts of freedom spread abroad by the Revolution; and second, they so maneuvered it that it became boxed into the corner of identification with a political order rapidly passing from the face of Europe. Pope Paul VI, with the quiet detachment that historical perspective can give, spoke of the basically spiritual nature of the aspirations of the era of the French Revolution. These the Society, in the midst of the turmoil, did not discern. Ever on the defensive and often in exile, it did not find it easy, amid violence, disorder, and injustice, to focus clearly and sharply on these spiritual values. Consequently, unlike men such as Charles Forbes, comte de Montalembert, and Ludwig Windthorst, it did not distinguish itself in the creation for the Church of an aggiornamento in the area of political thought. A greater failure was to allow itself to become identified with the ancient and passing monarchical order. This was an understandable lapse. Even though born anew in 1814, the Society in a very real sense was an old institution through whose history were tightly woven the thousand threads of thinking and sentiment which made it of a piece with the world of the absolute monarchies. To friend and foe the Society represented the values of ante-1789 Europe. The Austrian Emperor Francis I, thoroughly educated in the tradition of Josephinism with its inherent animosity to the Society, made a volte-face in 1821 when, frightened by the momentous events in France, he welcomed the Society into his domains as any ally in the fight against the spread of revolutionary principles. Joseph de Maistre reflected that, against the offspring of a revolution which was nothing less than satanic, stood an alliance, most natural, of pope, mon-

2 J. C. Murray, "Leo XIII on Church and State: The General Structure of the Controversy," *Theological Studies*, XIV (1953), 3-7.

archs, and Jesuits.[3] This experience was largely a European thing.

The major exception was the Society's growth and expansion in the United States. In a nation where the government did not image the totalitarian kind of European democracy and where the constitutional principle of the separation of church and state gave religion a freedom never enjoyed under the Catholic monarchs, the American Society developed into the most vital organ of the whole Jesuit body.

Spontaneity, therefore, sureness, and above all, freedom from the past with which the Society moved into the sixteenth century, did not stamp the European Jesuits of the nineteenth century. But differences between the pre-suppression period and the restoration period did not rest there. In the former, at least initially, the Jesuits were preoccupied with the blueprints of their enterprise and the nature of the works they should undertake; in the latter they picked up the thread of their history where it had been cut and, guided by the legal documents as they stood in the mid-eighteenth century, they moved quite naturally into the classroom, the pulpit, the writer's desk, the confessional, and the foreign mission field. In the former, St. Ignatius, by his personal and intimate direction, imparted to a few key men the authentic spirit of the Society; in the latter, the transmission of this spirit encountered formidable difficulties because of the peculiarly different backgrounds of the 600 men who made up the Society in 1814: some, old men who had been Jesuits before 1773; others, men who went to White Russia and became part of the living link with the old Society; others, former members of the Fathers of the Faith; and still others, secular priests only recently admitted.

During these first six critical years, when this internal fragmentation made a strong cohesive force imperative, the most striking feature of the Society's structure was the absence of the general from Rome. The Russian government rejected Brzozowski's repeated requests to go to Rome and held him until his death in 1820. Brzozowski gave wide powers to a vicar-general, Mariano Petrucci, but this was inadequate, and in the first general congregation after Brzozowski's death the diversity of spiritual provenance among the men erupted into a nasty internal struggle.

3 Pope Paul VI, *Il primo saluto,* An Appeal to the Laity, given at Frascati, September 1, 1963, in *The Pope Speaks,* IX (1963), 176-177; E. E. Y. Hales, *Revolution and Papacy 1769-1846* (London, 1960), p. 229.

In Russia after 1814 the Society's prestige rapidly declined. Several factors contributed to this radical transformation of official benevolence into official hostility. Freemasons, whose lodge in St. Petersburg enjoyed Czar Alexander's protection, sounded their disapproval of the general restoration of the Society by Pope Pius VII. The old conniving archbishop of Mogilev, Stanislaw Siestrzencewicz, now an octogenarian, sponsored the idea that it would be dangerous for the Russian state if the Society's leader lived outside Russia. The czar, an emotional man filled with a sense of mission to create a common religion for all, saw in Prince Golitzyn's biblical enterprise an instrument for his own religious purpose. He too, like Golitzyn, resented Brzozowski's refusal to cooperate. Hostility to the Society displaced his former friendliness.[4]

Late in 1814 the atmosphere of rancor became even more intense. In the thirteen years of its existence the Jesuit college in St. Petersburg never had among its students a convert from the Orthodox Church to the Roman Catholic Church. The instructors had carefully observed the government's legislation against proselytism. But toward the end of 1814 one of the students announced his decision to become a Roman Catholic. And he was a nephew of Prince Golitzyn. Since 1812 two of Golitzyn's nephews had been enrolled at the college. In 1814 the elder, Aleksandr, aged fourteen, probably influenced by the lucid teaching of the French Jesuit, Jean de Rozaven, revealed at Christmas dinner his intention to be a convert. Prince Golitzyn had both nephews removed from the college and placed under instructors of the Orthodox faith. On January 15, 1815, Brzozowski wrote, "A great tempest has been raised here because a nephew of Prince Golitzyn has categorically declared his intention to be a Catholic." [5]

Late in 1815, on December 20, Czar Alexander issued a ukase ordering the banishment of Brzozowski and the other twenty-six Jesuits from St. Petersburg. Under military escort their carriages rode out of the city and took the road to Polotsk. On August 31, 1816, Brzozowski again asked permission to go to Rome. The czar refused. The general remained at Polotsk until he died on Feburary 5, 1820. His death foreshadowed the end of the Jesuit presence in the Russian empire, since on March 13 of the same year an imperial order of banishment was issued, and some 350

4 Zalenski, *Les Jésuites*, II, 210-211, 222, 242-248.
5 Ibid., 215-216, 437-438.

Jesuits gradually withdrew from Polotsk, Mogilev, Riga, Odessa, Saratov, Astrakhan, and Caucasia, and started their trek to new labors in other lands.[6]

The harvest of Brzozowski's captivity was reaped in the general congregation summoned by the vicar-general, Mariano Petrucci, to meet in Rome on September 14 of that same year. This congregation, somewhat like the long prelude before the first assembled after Ignatius' death, experienced sharp internal dissension. A group, inspired mainly by the fractious Sicilian, Luigi Rezzi, and aiming to delay the start of the congregation until they could control the votes and then make some changes in the *Constitutions*, questioned the status of some delegates by challenging the validity of the vows pronounced in Russia. Rezzi drew the aged Petrucci into his camp and enlisted the sympathy of Cardinal Della Genga, the future Leo XII. The energetic, clearminded Frenchman, Jean de Rozaven, with the backing of eighteen delegates fought for and won a free election. He appealed to the secretary of state, Cardinal Ercole Consalvi, who took the protest to Pope Pius VII. The pope directed the congregation to assemble and, in order to remove any doubts about the validity of the balloting, he ratified the canonical correctness of the vows taken in White Russia. On October 18 the delegates chose the seventy-two-year-old Veronese, Luigi Fortis. Rezzi they expelled from the Society.

The decrees of the congregation reflect the major preoccupation of the delegates and the nature of the work of reconstruction to be undertaken by Fortis. Three basic problems emerged: first, the preservation of the spiritual and juridical character of the Society; second, the training and formation of the Society's members; third, the efficiency of the important apostolate of the schools. These the congregation attended to by proclaiming that all the legislation and ordinances of the suppressed Society remained intact, by insistence that the novitiate and the tertianship be done in their entirety, and by a decree that the *Plan of Studies (Ratio Studiorum)* be revised in accord with modern needs. Helped by these guidelines, Fortis, with kindly insistence, applied himself to the vast program of reconstruction. Nine years later he died, on January 27, 1829.

On July 9 of the same year the Twenty-first General Congregation elected the forty-four-year-old Dutchman, Jan Roothaan, the youngest general chosen since Claudio Aquaviva. Like his great predecessor, Roothaan, during his twenty-four years in

6 Ibid., 223-227, 235-248.

office, exercised a decisive influence in the Society's development. A native of Amsterdam, he entered the novitiate in Dünaburg in 1804 when he was nineteen, studied and taught in White Russia, became rector in Turin and vice-provincial of Italy. An intense and single-minded man of decidedly serious nature, not unrelieved however by occasional flashes of good humor, he committed himself thoroughly to the objective of making the Society worthy of its honored traditions. In three principal ways he achieved this: by his insistence on an accurate understanding of the *Spiritual Exercises;* by the revision of the *Ratio studiorum;* and by his encouragement of the missionary spirit.

Roothaan's firm stand about the strategic place of the *Spiritual Exercises* in the life of a Jesuit rested on the rock of a deep interior conviction. His personal retreat notes during his years as general, 1829-1852, reveal an intense desire to be faithful to the thought of St. Ignatius. On December 27, 1834, he issued a general letter to the Society, certainly one of the most important in its entire history, on the study and use of the *Spiritual Exercises.* Indicting some retreat masters for improvisations which departed from the spirit of St. Ignatius, he insisted that the men of the Society acquire a precise and full understanding of the text. To facilitate this, he issued a more accurate Latin translation of the Spanish original. Because of the urgency of these directives, the retreat plans published by some Jesuits of the nineteenth century manifested an adherence to the text far more strict than those by Jesuits of the two earlier centuries — some far too narrow and to the point of dryness — but the general had scored a sound point in making his subjects keenly aware of the fount of their spirituality.[7]

In the revision of the *Ratio studiorum* Roothaan took up a work Fortis had not been able to carry through to completion. The general congregation of 1820 had directed Fortis to appoint a commission to work out an adaptation of this code for the educational needs of the post-French Revolution world. Fortis, besides naming the commission, sought the opinion of individual Jesuits throughout the Society. Many reports indicated new trends: greater attention to vernacular languages; wider stress on mathematics, history, and geography; a more alert appreciation in logic and metaphysics of modern philosophical currents; a comprehensiveness in projecting a program for the natural sciences. Since Fortis had not finished the work, the general

7 *DeGuiJes,* 467-468, 540-541.

congregation of 1829 instructed Roothaan to act immediately. The task was done expeditiously, and under date of July 25, 1832, Roothaan issued his revised *Plan of Studies* on a temporary and trial basis. This new code continued as an experiment during his generalate, but it never received the official approval of a general congregation. The revolutions in France and the rest of Europe, in North and South America broke the social and political framework within which a single plan, as in 1599, could have operated. Modern states made education the specialized interest of government and frequently dictated the details of the curriculum. The old era of Jesuit educational uniformity had passed. Yet, Roothaan's *Ratio* did help toward unity of endeavor in the educational apostolate of the Society as it strove to make the necessary accommodation to the needs of a new age in its history.[8]

With the schools in Europe the missions across the seas had been a chief apostolate of the Society before 1773. Under Fortis some Jesuits went to North America and the Aegean Islands, but Roothaan, in a decisive and momentous letter of 1833, took up the thread of missionary zeal and wove it into the fabric of the new Society. In this letter he outlined a plan of action, pointed to the fields white unto the harvest, excited missionary ambitions, and asked provincial superiors to be generous in support of the work overseas.[9] Soon names so familiar in the Jesuit annals of the sixteenth, seventeenth, and eighteenth centuries began to reappear: Madurai, Nanking, Ceylon, Brazil, Argentina, Chile, Colombia. New names were added, St. Louis, Oregon, San Francisco, Santa Fe.

Roothaan therefore by his emphasis on the *Spiritual Exercises,* by the updating of the *Plan of Studies,* and by opening the floodgates of missionary zeal forged strong ties with the old Society. These he made even stronger by his other letters in which he sought to inculcate the Ignatian spirit. No general used the epistle to the extent Roothaan did to keep the Society true to its ideals.

In 1848 he had occasion to experience personally what so many of his sons throughout Europe had felt, the discomfort and sorrow of exile. During March the antipathy of the republicans in Rome rose to open hostility, and Pope Pius IX suggested that the general withdraw from the city. In disguise Roothaan

---

8 William McGucken, S.J., *The Jesuits and Education* (Milwaukee, 1932), pp. 130-131, 135-136.
9 *DeGuiJes*, pp. 466-467.

left Rome and sailed to Marseilles. He did not return until April 20, 1850. Death closed his influential term as general on May 8, 1853.

On July 2 of the same year the Twenty-second General Congregation chose as his successor the fifty-eight-year-old Belgian of wide experience, Pieter Beckx. In his character Beckx blended an even measure of firmness and kindness which marked his long term of thirty-one years. The breakdown of order in so many areas of Europe under the stress of so many revolutions made him especially anxious, because the community life of thousands of Jesuits was repeatedly disrupted. Aside from the expulsions before he became general, in 1859, 1860, and 1870 the Society was dispersed in Italy; in 1850 and 1859 it was expelled from New Granada; in 1868 from Spain; in 1871 from Guatemala; 1872 from Germany; in 1880 from France; in 1881 from Nicaragua. The pain of exile he himself and his curia experienced when a hostile government made it impossible for them to remain in Rome. In 1870, when the Piedmontese entered the city, he witnessed the theft of the Society's colleges, museums, libraries, and observatories. In 1873 he was ejected from the professed house. In October of the same year he moved to Florence for what he trusted would be a brief absence from Rome. Then he moved to the ancient monastery of San Girolamo in Fiesole where the hoped-for short stay lengthened to twenty-two years. These disruptions he met with his eminently fine qualities of quiet steadiness and patience.

Despite this constant harassment in clear view of the whole world, the old legend about the Society's mighty political force lived on in the imaginings of many. A most fantastic scheme, inspired by this popular misunderstanding, originated in the strange mind of Auguste Comte, the father of sociology. Comte, who inscribed the names of Loyola, Xavier, and Bourdaloue on the positivist calendar and in whose eyes the Jesuit general had been the true head of the Catholic Church for the past three hundred years, sent a personal copy of his *Positivist Catechism* to Beckx. He unfolded before the general a plan whereby he himself and Beckx would join forces in an alliance designed to wipe Protestantism, Deism, and Skepticism from the face of the earth. The pope, he proposed, should reside at Paris with the title of prince-bishop of Rome.[10] Beckx had all he could do to hold the Society together without thinking about the fantasies of others about Jesuit power.

10 A. Guillermou, *Les Jésuites* (Paris, 1963), pp. 90-91.

In the midst of discouraging reports from all quarters the general led the Society in a unique act of devotion on January 1, 1872. On that day all the provinces consecrated themselves to the Sacred Heart of Jesus. Aside from the fact that the Society had received from Christ Himself a special commission to propagate devotion to the Scared Heart, this consecration was in keeping with the devotional life of the age when the faithful sought in various ways union with the suffering Savior. Monsignor Maurice d'Hulst suggested that the century be known, in spiritual terms, as the century of the Sacred Heart.[11]

In September, 1883, Beckx, now eighty-eighty years old, convened the Twenty-third General Congregation and requested a vicar. A lull in the political turmoil enabled the congregation to convene in Rome. The delegates chose the sixty-four-year-old Swiss, Anton Anderledy, with the right of succession. Beckx then wished to resign, but Pope Leo XIII requested that he remain in office at least a little longer and seek support and counsel in Anderledy. On January 24, 1884, Beckx transferred his authority to the vicar except for, as he expressed it, "some little reservation to myself." But his fast failing energies made even this compromise difficult, and on May 11 of the same year he announced his resignation. Three years later, on March 4, 1887, he died.

Anderledy, who had been a missionary at Green Bay, Wisconsin, for a short period, remained at Fiesole. Sudden death brought his short term to an end on January 18, 1892. So uneasy and taut was the political life of Italy at the time that the members of the curia feared to bring his body to Rome for burial lest they thereby create a public disturbance.

For the same reason Pope Leo judged that the general congregation should be convened outside Italy. In September, 1892, the delegates therefore assembled at Loyola, Spain. On October 2 they chose as general the forty-eight-year-old Spaniard, Luis Martín. They recommended that the general change the Society's headquarters from Fiesole to Rome as soon as possible. This Martín did two and a half years later, in January, 1895. Twenty-two years had passed since Beckx had been forced to quit the city. A man of great energy and quick decisiveness, Martín launched one of the most valuable ventures of the modern Society, the production of scholarly editions of documents which touch on Jesuit origins and history. To date, this enterprise has reached one hundred volumes of the *Monumenta His-*

---

11 R. Aubert, *Le pontificat de Pie IX (1846-1878)* (Paris, 1952), p. 465.

torica Societatis Jesu. For the general student of history this project is a rich source of insight into a past age, and for the Jesuit a sure way to a deeper appreciation of his vocation. To supplement this undertaking, Martín encouraged the writing of the Society's history in various countries. Some fine work resulted, especially that on the Spanish Assistancy by Antonio Astráin, that on Germany by Bernhard Duhr, that on the Portuguese Assistancy by Francisco Rodrigues, and that on Italy by Pietro Tacchi Venturi. In 1905 a sarcoma appeared on Martín's right arm. Surgeons performed several operations and finally amputated the limb. This affliction the general bore with fortitude, and on April 18, 1906, died.

On September 8 of the same year the Twenty-fifth General Congregation elected the sixty-four-year-old native of Württemberg, Franz Wernz. In the precise and directive nature of his letters to the Society, such as on the manner of making the tertianship, in contrast to the broader and more hortatory type of his predecessor, Wernz showed his background as a canon lawyer. Less than three weeks after the outbreak of World War I he died, on August 19, 1914, only a few hours before Pope Pius X, and twelve days after the centenary of the restoration of the Society.

Italy   Italy of the nineteenth century experienced two risorgimentos, the one national which culminated in the country's unification, the other religious which blossomed in the first Vatican Council. Both concerned the Society deeply.

In the mighty contest between the heirs of the Enlightenment and the traditionalists of the old order, men of the stamp of Cavour, Mazzini, and Garibaldi made the Society one of their initial targets. Through these hundred years hardly an area of Italy allowed the Jesuits a continually free and undisturbed existence, and the date of a revolution usually meant for them another expulsion. The leaders of the new movements, with a fright that was amazing, regarded the Society as the bugbear of modern governments. Camillo Benso, conte di Cavour, wrote: "Woe to the country, woe to the class that should confide to them the exclusive education of youth! But for fortunate circumstances, which destroy in a man the lessons of his childhood, they would make in a century a bastard and brutalized race. . . ." And Giuseppe Mazzini, in retreat in a small Swiss village with nothing to distract him but to look out on the deep snows and the crows strutting below his window, had this simple joy spoiled for him because the crows, solemnly black, reminded him of the Jesuits.[12] And action followed sentiment. The great Piedmontese push in 1859-1860 swept the Society before it. To Victor Emmanuel Beckx protested, in vain, against the seizure of fifty-seven houses, including colleges. In 1873 the Parliament of the recently unified Kingdom decreed the nonexistence of all religious orders. With their legal status as secular priests the Jesuits continued on a modest scale their former educational work. The government, by periodic leniency in applying the law, gradually opened the door to greater freedom. The Jesuits entered, and in a gratifying way grew. By 1914, within a framework of five provinces, they numbered 1,600 men.

To voice their critique of the turbulent and fluid civil order they had an influential sounding board in their journal *La Civiltà Cattolica*. In 1848 Carlo Curci, a born polemicist, felt that the Society should publish a bimonthly magazine of general cultural interest, addressed to the laity and dedicated to the restoration of Christian principles in the intellectual, social, familial, and political life of the country. Roothaan, fearful of the political implications in such sensitive areas, did not approve. Pope Pius IX however supported the project and paid for the first issue which came out in April, 1850. Animated by the energetic pen of Curci, the circulation soon rose from 4,200 to 12,000.

A point of dispute which the editors could not avoid was the onward march of the European aspiration toward democracy and political freedom. They professed respect for all forms of legitimate government, representative included. But very early they began an implacable criticism of constitutional governance and modern democracy as being infected with heterodoxy. While they gave excellent service to the Church by keeping before Catholics many truths which could be dulled and even completely forgotten, they failed to capture with any deep degree of perception the positive values in the spirit of freedom and made the serious mistake, in an attitude both negative and inflexible, of tending to identify the Christian order with the old regime. They were guilty of that confusion of thought which De Montalembert noted in so many Jesuits and about which he complained to his friend, Gustave de Ravignan, their "confounding with the aberrations of the revolutionaries that invincible movement which is carrying the modern world to the point of substituting for absolute monarchy the principle and practice of

12 W. R. Thayer, *The Life and Times of Cavour* (Boston, 1911), I, 78; E. E. Y. Hales, *Mazzini and the Secret Societies* (New York, 1956), p. 163.

national sovereignty." The French nobleman expressed his violent wish to cleave in two the editors "who each day make it their business, while defending the Church and the Holy See, to outrage reason, justice, and honor." [13]

At Malines in 1863 De Montalembert delivered an eloquent plea for freedom of conscience. *La Civiltà Cattolica* printed a critique which could only have aggravated him the more. Here for the first time appeared a distinction which was destined to become classic.[14] It was the distinction between "thesis" and "hypothesis." *La Civiltà Cattolica* maintained that freedom of conscience and of the press, considered as universal principles, are to be condemned. This was the "thesis." But under certain circumstances and among certain peoples these freedoms could be legitimate and could therefore be defended by Catholics. This was the "hypothesis." This distinction acquired greater and wider fame in the interpretation which some theologians gave the *Syllabus of Errors* of 1864.

The general tendency of the Italian Jesuits toward a conservative kind of political thinking made them, in the eyes of many patriots, allies of Austria and enemies of national unity. No one wrote with more venom than Vincenzo Gioberti, who denounced the Society as the chief obstacle to the civic and religious salvation of Italy and to the harmonious fusion of religion and modern civilization. By private intervention the Jesuits tried to persuade Gioberti to desist from his waspish campaign. Unsuccessful, they answered him publicly. Gioberti responded with his famous *The Modern Jesuit,* a work most unworthy of his capabilities and critical of all post-Tridentine Catholicism. During this barrage of words about loyalty to Italy several Jesuits clearly manifested their sympathy for the neo-guelf movement, which envisaged a unified nation, but in the form of a federation of the individual Italian states, each with a constitution and all tied together in their recognition of the presidency of the pope. Ironically, this plan was in essence that proposed by Gioberti in his *Moral and Civil Primacy of the Italians* (1843).[15]

Of the Jesuits absorbed in Italy's current problems, none was more articulate than Luigi Taparelli d'Azeglio, one of the clear-

13 Aubert, *Le pontificat,* pp. 39-40, 252, fn. 1; Pietro Pirri, S.J., "Civiltà Cattolica, La.," *Enciclopedia Cattolica,* III (1949), 1759-1762.
14 Aubert, *Le pontificat,* pp. 24-25, 226, 260.
15 Ibid., p. 25; E. Hocedez, S.J., *Histoire de la théologie au XIXᵉ siècle* (Paris, 1947-1952), II, 167-170.

est Italian political thinkers of the day and an editor of *La
Civiltà Cattolica.* As he wrote in 1852 to his celebrated brother,
Massimo, his golden dream, *sogno dorato,* was to see a union of
Catholics and a liberalism freed of anti-religious animus. A
thinker, devoted to the Church and yet ambitious for national
unity, a discerning observer of how tightly tied together were the
threads of national aspiration and anti-clericalism, he dared to be
a pioneer and risk the chance of mistakes in an attempt to undo
the knot. Among his publications the most famous were those
on nationalism. He knew that nationalism was one of the burning
issues of the day. To help in the clarification of this issue, he
discussed it in a scientific way and in the light of the general
principles of morality. His intention was theoretical, not political.
He attacked the idea of nationalism as an absolute value in itself,
independent of moral restraint. The nation cannot, for example,
turn falsehood into truth; nor can freedom ignore eternal truth;
nor can the nation intrude on the rights of the family. As a son
of Italy he aimed, not at undermining the cause of national unity
but at placing it on a secure foundation. Not entirely successful
in his plumbing the depths of the modern freedoms, and bound
somewhat by older patterns of thought, he nevertheless took
positive steps forward.[16]

Nowhere more than in his correspondence does he manifest
his desire to participate in his country's *risorgimento.* To
Roothaan he wrote in February, 1847, urging that the Society
encourage a liberalism cleansed of anti-religious sentiment. "If
liberalism," he said, "can today be regarded as an opinion admis-
sible among Catholics, the consequence for us is important.
We should not only not speak unfavorably about this trend, but
show *in a positive way* that, once its anti-Christian hostility has
ceased, our resistance also ceases." Roothaan replied with caution. Not only was the political arena no place for the Society,
but the fruits from the tree of liberalism, as already tasted in
some countries, were far from sweet. "I approve," the general
wrote, "neither the adulation of some for princes nor the exaggerated aversion of others for all that pertains to liberalism. But
if one considers that, in substance, liberalism tends of its very
nature toward liberty, or rather toward a freedom from any
and every kind of restraint, and that up to the present its fruits
in those regimes that have a constitution are bitter rather than
not, (I am speaking of those countries which until recent times

16 S. Messineo, S.J., "Il P. Luigi Taparelli d'Azeglio et il Risorgimento
  Italiano," *La Civiltà Cattolica,* XCIX (1948), 492-497, 501-502.

have been monarchical), I do not wonder that only with difficulty can one become a partisan of it." [17]

About twenty-five years later Curci was caught in a storm which blew strong winds of nationalism across Italy. In 1874, only four years after the Piedmontese troops had taken Rome, he felt that an entente would eventually develop between the Holy See and the young Italian Kingdom. In a memorial he presented his ideas to Pope Pius IX. The *Rivista Europea* published the text of the memorial. Curci did not disown it, and in 1877 he was dismissed from the Society. He then wrote several brochures on the same subject. They were placed on the Index, and he himself was suspended. Eventually he submitted, and shortly before his death on May 29, 1892, he was readmitted to the Society.

Twenty years after Curci's death the Italian Kingdom celebrated the fiftieth anniversary of its proclamation in 1861. *La Civiltà Cattolica* recalled that the *risorgimento* was the achievement of many violations of the moral order. It stigmatized the celebrations as copies of the frenzy of fifty years earlier when international freemasonry was aroused to the ambition of making the ancient capital of the Catholic world the seat of neo-pagan Italy. Yet, despite the intensity of the language of *La Civiltà*, new currents of feeling were running through Catholic Italy and no one seriously expected to see the papal gendarmes once more on the streets of Rome.[18]

To the theological *risorgimento* the Society made impressive contributions. At the Roman College, given once more to the Society by Pope Leo XII in 1824, in the creation of a pro-papal atmosphere the professors aroused dispositions of favor toward the doctrine of the pope's infallibility. Students like the future archbishop of Munich, Karl August von Reisach, formed in the principles of Bellarmine and Suárez on papal prerogatives, returned to their countries and helped spread a spirit of ultramontanism. At the same time the faculty acquired a fine staff of scholars in the field of positive theology. Giovanni Perrone, prefect of studies at the college for many years, led the way. His most brilliant student, Carlo Passaglia, built up a broad knowledge of scriptural and patristic sources, complemented by an intimate familiarity with post-Tridentine theology, especially of Petau and Thomassin. Passaglia in turn inspired Klemens

17 Ibid., 498-500.
18 A. C. Jemolo, *Church and State in Italy 1850-1950* (Oxford, 1960), pp. 110-111.

Schrader, an Austrian, somewhat narrower in spirit and more scholastic by bent. Entering into the fullness of this tradition, Johann Franzelin, a Tyrolese, brought his solid understanding of texts and monuments as well as a wide knowledge of the advances made by the German historical school.

Two theological peaks during the reign of Pope Pius IX were the decree on the Immaculate Conception of the Blessed Virgin Mary and the definition of papal infallibility at the Vatican Council. Toward both, Jesuits contributed their scholarship. The pope, animated by a personal desire, shared by many throughout the world, to declare the Immaculate Conception of Mary a dogma of the faith, relied to a great degree on Perrone and Passaglia. After the encyclical *Ubi primum* of February 2, 1849, in which Pius sought the advice of the hierarchy on the advisability of such a definition, Perrone prepared the first draft of a bull incorporating the theological foundations of this doctrine. It was not entirely satisfactory. Passaglia, with Dom Prosper Guéranger, submitted in 1852 a second draft. It too failed to win complete approval. The same year Pius gave the task to a commission of theologians. By November, 1854, five more drafts were prepared. In the work of the commission Passaglia, because of his wide patristic knowledge, was a leader. In November, 1854, the seventh draft and the first to be entitled *Ineffabilis Deus* was ready. Between November 20 and 24 the bishops, who had arrived from different nations for the ceremony of promulgation, met together and presented their criticism of various arguments and expressions. Passaglia was among the theologians present to answer objections. Finally, on December 8, 1854, Pius, in the presence of more than two hundred cardinals, archbishops, and bishops, solemnly defined the Immaculate Conception of the Virgin Mary to be an article of faith. Only five years after this sacred occasion in which he had been a leading architect, Passaglia left the Society because of friction with superiors. He took the chair of moral philosophy at Turin, became absorbed in the cause of Italian unity, and in 1862 secured the signatures of 8,943 priests to a petition, addressed to Pius IX, which requested that the pope, for the sake of peace, renounce the papacy's temporal power.[19]

19 Aubert, *Le pontificat*, pp. 187-188, 278-279; E. E. Y. Hales, *Pio Nono* (London, 1954), pp. 146-149; J. J. Hennesey, S.J., "A Prelude to Vatican I: American Bishops and the Definition of the Immaculate Conception," *Theological Studies*, XXV (1964), 409-411, 417-418; also

Immediately before and during the Vatican Council the issue of widest interest was that of papal infallibility. In February, 1869, ten months before the Council opened, *Civiltà Cattolica* published an article under the title *A Letter from France* which gave wide offense.[20] The article divided the Catholics of France into two categories: those simply called "Catholics," and "Liberal Catholics." The hallmark of true Catholics, in contrast to the Liberal Catholics, was the hope for a proclamation in positive form of the doctrines of the *Syllabus* and for the definition by acclamation of the doctrine of papal infallibility. This distinction caused consternation among theologians and bishops, who were shocked at the possibility of so delicate a question as papal infallibility being proclaimed without prior conciliar debate and the refinement of terminology. *La Civiltà Cattolica* sent a tremor of anxiety through the Church.

This preoccupation with the excitement about papal infallibility did serious disservice to one of the finer theological movements of the nineteenth century. Perrone, Passaglia, Schrader, and Franzelin made, with the secular priest Matthias Scheeben, an illustrious line of theologians who, absorbed in the mystery of the inner life of the Church, studied the invisible aspect of her nature as well as the juridical and hierarchical. The most influential pioneer of this rediscovery of the riches of the Church's inner life after centuries necessarily concerned with her visible structure was the secular priest, Johann Adam Möhler, who died in 1838. Möhler, himself influenced by romanticism and its love of history, found some of his basic inspiration in the priest, eventually bishop of Regensburg, who by his intense charity and prayerful union with God is said to have taught rationalistic Germany to pray again, Johann Michael Sailer. Sailer had been in the Society three years when it was suppressed. By their writing and teaching, Perrone, Passaglia, Schrader, and Franzelin scattered abroad the theological treasures opened by Möhler and so gave impetus to the movement which continued to the encyclical *Mystici corporis* of Pope Pius XII and culminated in the Dogmatic Constitution of the Church, *Lumen Gentium*, of the Second Vatican Council. Schrader doubtlessly drew up the original *schema* on the Church in the First Vatican Council. He entitled his first chapter: *Ecclesia est Corpus Christi Mysticum.* Political turmoil in Europe shortened the Council

his "National Traditions and the First Vatican Council," *Archivum Historiae Pontificiae,* VII (1969), 504.

20 Aubert, *Le pontificat,* p. 316.

and erased the opportunity to draw a more complete picture of the Church's nature.[21]

On the precise issue of papal infallibility, most Jesuits associated with the Council seem to have favored, with varying degrees of expression, the definition. Perrone helped to draw up the first draft. On the other hand, Franz Quarella, prefect of studies at the German College and counselor of Bishop Wilhelm von Ketteler in his opposition to the definition, edited the bishop's *Quaestio*, which was circulated among the conciliar fathers and in which he proposed the thesis of Bossuet that papal infallibility depends on the collaboration and approval of the bishops. Cardinal Paul Cullen, who contributed so effectively to the definition in its final form by removing any suggestion of possible papal intervention in the political realm, a concept which disturbed some governments, invited the scholarly advice of Franzelin and Josef Kleutgen. Jesuits had important roles in the formulation of initial dogmatic drafts on other subjects. Perrone and Schrader, for example, worked on the draft which treated the relationship of church and state. In this they showed their blindness to the passing of political power from the absolute monarch to the masses by their harking back to a bygone era and championing an ideal adjustment of church and state in the juridical union of the two.[22] Like Salmerón, Laynez, Jay, and Canisius at Trent, these men did their most persuasive work in the hidden and arduous task of scholarship, the influence of which it is often impossible to decide with precision.

Nor is it possible to take exact measure of the Society's weight at the Vatican during the long reign of Pope Pius IX. By temperament Pius did not like the Jesuits, but in them he recognized that he had loyal warriors in the combat against the revolutionary ideas of the age and in the development of the ultramontane movement. Strong as was the union between the papacy and the Jesuits in Rome, it did not deserve the exaggerated observation, made after Pius' death, that his rule was a kind of occult government composed of Jesuits and *La Civiltà Cattolica*, a judgment shared by some American Protestants. One of the latter felt that Pius had started his pontificate as a

21 P. Riga, "The Ecclesiology of Johann Adam Möhler," *Theological Studies*, XXII (1961), 563-565; H. de Lubac, S.J., *The Splendour of the Church*, (New York, 1936), pp. 61-63; Hocedez, *Histoire*, I, 253; II, 353-356; III, 319.
22 Aubert, *Le pontificat*, pp. 326-327, 340-341; J. J. Hennesey, S.J., "James J. Corcoran's Mission to Rome: 1868-1869," *Catholic Historical Review*, XLVIII (1962), 177-178.

"Protestant pope," but the Jesuits had "transubstantiated" him.[23]

The rich theological developments under Pius shared the field of Catholic intellectual interests with a robust renaissance of Scholasticism. In 1879 Pope Leo XIII issued one of his more memorable encyclicals, *Aeterni Patris,* in which he called on scholars to return to the wisdom of St. Thomas and to adapt his thought to modern needs. *Aeterni Patris* actually was a papal blessing on a movement which had begun in Italy three quarters of a century earlier and which received its main impetus from the Jesuits. Shortly before the suppression of the Society in Spain, Catalonian Jesuits joined other cultured men in a local literary and philosophical reawakening, which included a fresh appreciation of scholastic thought and method and which had as a key center the Jesuit Colegio de Cordellas in Barcelona. Among the Jesuit exiles from Catalonia who settled in Piacenza were the gifted brothers, José Antonio Masdeu, a theologian, and Baltasar Masdeu, a philosopher. At the Jesuit Collegio de San Pietro in Piacenza both communicated their scholastic enthusiasm to Vincenzo Buzzetti, who became a secular priest and professor at the seminary in Piacenza. In the seminary two who absorbed Buzzetti's ardor for St. Thomas were brothers, Domenico and Serafino Sordi. When the Society was restored in 1814, the Sordis became Jesuits and the wellspring within the order of a lively neo-scholastic movement.[24] Through the years this movement either prospered or faltered in the measure of the intellectual powers or limitations of its more articulate spokesmen, the Italians Matteo Liberatore and Camillo Mazzella, the German Joseph Kleutgen, and, probably, the most brilliant of all, the Frenchman, Louis Billot, whom Pope Leo XIII personally summoned to Rome to teach at the Gregorian University. The Spanish apostles of the Enlightenment gave valuable assistance to the papacy of the nineteenth century when they shipped the Masdeu brothers and the other Spanish Jesuits to Italy.

In *La Civiltà Cattolica* several of the Jesuits in this movement found a medium to carry their enthusiasm beyond the lecture hall. By creating in the intellectual world an awareness of this fresh appreciation of the thought of the Angelic Doctor, this

23 Aubert, *Le pontificat,* p. 286; Hales, *Pio Nono,* pp. 150-151. James H. Symlie, "American Protestants Interpret Vatican Council I," *Church History,* XXXVIII (1969), 460.

24 Aubert, *Le ponitficat,* pp. 188-189; T. J. McMahon, "Joseph Anthony Masdeu, S.J. A Distant Herald of the Aeterni Patris?" *Theological Studies,* III (1942), 163-188; Hocedez, *Histoire,* II, 350; III, 370-371.

journal prepared the way for several of the encyclicals of Pope Leo XIII and his analysis of the political order and its natural finality. This was one of its positive, forward looking contributions to the Church as it moved into the modern world.

Besides the rise of Thomism there appeared at the Roman College a spirit of eclecticism in philosophy, manifested especially in the persons of Salvatore Tongiorgi and Domenico Palmieri. These two original professors, highly sensitive to the advances of science which they tried to incorporate within the structure of their thought, showed to what inferior state Aristotle had fallen. Supplementing this speculative thought, other Jesuits did important work in astronomy and archaeology, especially Pietro Angelo Secchi, internationally known for his comprehensive spectral classification of the stars, the first of its kind, and Giuseppe Marchi, meticulous investigator of the catacombs in Rome, a field of study in almost complete oblivion since the twelfth century save for labors of Antonio Bosio in the early seventeenth century. Marchi initiated a new era in Christian archaeology and trained the expert Giovanni Battista de Rossi, who gained the deserved respect of Mommsen and other German scholars. Scriptural studies received a great impulse when in 1909 Pope Pius X founded the Pontifical Biblical Institute and placed it in the care of the Society.

German scholars in general, absorbed in their highly critical historical studies, had little regard for what Italy was producing in the world of learning. The doctor in Rome is a jackass in Germany, they used to say. In 1846 the future Cardinal Guillaume-René Meignan complained that Roman theology was inattentive to what was going on in the world about it. Echoes of this complaint were heard in the pontificate of Pius IX. But these criticisms, general and too simplified, failed to evaluate at their genuine worth the real contributions of Perrone, Passaglia, Franzelin, and others.[25] While these scholars gave their specialized kind of service to the Church, others carried on as teachers in the colleges, staffing the twenty-five such institutions which were in operation in Italy at the close of this period.

For Spain the nineteenth century was a century of tragedy. Abroad, in the earlier years, this land of the conquistadores lost in rebellion most of her American colonies, and, in the latter years, she went down in defeat before the arms of the United States at Manila Bay and at Santiago de Cuba. At home deep

Spain and Portugal

25 Aubert, *Le pontificat*, pp. 185-187; Hocedez, *Histoire*, II, 349-350.

fissures ran through the nation as the champions of constitutional government challenged an autocratic monarchy, and as the monarchists themselves split in a bitter contest between Carlists and the line of Ferdinand VII. Aggravating the Spanish version of the mighty European political contest between tradition and modern aspirations were strong underlying forces of social and economic imbalance. Not "the unchanging Spain" depicted by the literary travelers of the Romantic movement, the country experienced several drastic, though sporadic, social and economic transformations.[26] Jesuit history entered into this complex and violent Spanish experience. During the hundred years, starting in 1815, for a little less than a third of this time, they were dispersed.

There were three distinct diasporas. The first and shortest was between 1820 and 1823. Only five years earlier, in 1815, the first Jesuits returned to Spain, 112 priests and 10 brothers, at the invitation of Ferdinand VII. It was an invitation to disaster. Ferdinand, not the hidebound knave of republican propaganda, could, when exigency demanded, play the pragmatist and desert the role of the autocrat. Despite his capacity to trim, rebellion broke out in various parts of the country and carried twenty-five Jesuits to their death. Ferdinand accepted a constitution, and the new government, true to its anti-clerical spirit, expelled the Society. Three years later however, within the framework of Metternich's Concert of Europe, the French armies broke the back of the constitution and restored Ferdinand to his former position. Again the Jesuits returned. During the next dozen years they increased to 350 men, who conducted colleges at Madrid, Alcalá, Loyola, Majorca, Manresa, and Valencia, and opened residences as well in Manresa and Barcelona.

These institutions hardly appeared when they were erased. King Ferdinand died in 1833. His brother Don Carlos tried to deprive Ferdinand's daughter Isabella of the throne. Civil war broke out. María Christina, the queen mother, to gain support for Isabella against the Carlists, made concessions to the liberals. During this time of uncertainty cholera spread through some of the provinces. It struck Madrid in the summer of 1834. Many died in mid-July. On the 17th the agitated Madrileños turned on the religious communities and started a massive assault by breaking into the Jesuit Colegio Imperial. More than forty Franciscans, eight Mercedarians, and seven Dominicans

---

26 R. Carr, *Spain 1808-1939* (Oxford, 1966), pp. 1-3.

were killed. The murdered Jesuits numbered four priests, eight scholastics, and three brothers. A year later, almost to the day, the government decreed the dispersion of the Society. The novices and juniors went to Nivelles in Belgium; forty-two of the province went to Argentina within a year; others scattered throughout the country; in five years about twenty-five left the Society.[27]

On March 16, 1851, the government of Isabella II, in which generals succeeded one another with whirlwind rapidity in the office of chief minister, negotiated a concordat with the Holy See. Article 29 was vague and imprecise. Under cover of this legal obscurity the Jesuits and other religious orders returned to Spain. The article allowed the reentry of the Vincentians and the Oratorians and one other order approved by the Vatican. The Spanish bishops interpreted the phrase "one other" to mean, not one for the entirety of Spain, but one for each diocese. The Jesuit beginnings were modest, with residences at Durango, Bilbao, Tudela, and Santander, but soon there was a rush of novices and in ten years the Society had three novitiates, one at Loyola with 120 men, one at Puerto de Santa María with 75, and one at La Selva with about 90. In 1863 Father General Beckx divided the province of 860 men in two.[28]

Then once more revolution struck the country. In 1868 General Juan Prim drove Queen Isabella from the throne. The ruling junta put the Jesuits once more on the road to exile. The liberals formed the First Republic in February, 1873. The second president, Francisco Pi y Margall, sounded its theme: "Catholicism is dead in the conscience of humanity and in the conscience of the Spanish people." But the republic was shortlived. In January, 1875, the monarchy was restored in the person of Isabella's son, Alfonso XII, who insisted, in his reconstruction of internal order in a chaotic country, that the concordat of 1851 be respected. Again therefore the Jesuits returned. During the stability of the Bourbon restoration they made notable progress. In 1910 they started their monthly journal *Razon y Fe*. By 1914 they numbered 3,200 men in three provinces. But in this country of distorted history they were burdened with their own

---

27 Ibid., 120; L. Frías, S.J., *La Provincia de España de la Compañía de Jesús 1815-1863* (Madrid, 1914), pp. 42-52; also his "La Compañía de Jesús Suprimida en España hace un Siglo," *AHSJ*, V (1936), 203-208.

28 E. A. Peers, *Spain, the Church and the Orders* (London, 1939), pp. 80-83; Frías, S.J., *La Provincia de Castilla de la Compañía de Jesús desde 1863 hasta 1914* (Bilbao, 1915), pp. 11-23.

peculiar "black legend." For all their advances they could not outstrip the image created by their enemies of the Enlightenment, and they entered the twentieth century appearing to many of their countrymen as wealthy titans who operated steamship companies and Moroccan mines. Like a deep underground river ran this stream of virulent anti-Jesuit feeling, to break forth again in the decree of exile of 1932.[29]

For Portugal, as for Spain, the nineteenth and early twentieth centuries were periods of political torment and immaturity, the repercussions of which intimately touched the Society. Harassment, spoliation, and exile hampered the Jesuit effort at restoration in a country humiliated and debilitated by the loss of Brazil in 1889. It was 1829 before the government authorized the Society's return. Five Frenchmen led the way. But five years later, in the wake of a revolution, they went into exile. In 1858 they were able to return, and during the relative freedom of a half-century until the revolution of 1910, they started seven colleges, reached in 1880 the status of a province with 120 men, and in 1902 launched their learned journal *Brotéria*. But the expulsion of Manuel II and the advent of the republicans in 1910 put them once more on the road to exile. In 1914, scattered to Spain, Belgium, and Holland, the province numbered 360 men. Only in 1933 did the adoption of a new constitution by Portugal allow them to return home.[30]

France   Through these hundred years the course of the Society's history in France was extremely uneven, deeply affected as it was by the drastic changes in government from the Bourbon Restoration, through the July Monarchy, the Second Republic, Second Empire, and Third Republic. Its origins centered about an eighty-year-old survivor of the old Society, Pierre de la Clorivière. This man of profound union with God and of exquisite eloquence in his writing about spiritual subjects brought to the task of restoration memories not only of the Society's suppression but also of the violence of the French Revolution, which took the lives, in Paris alone, of some twenty-five of his fellow ex-Jesuits, and of the Napoleonic dictatorship which put him in the Temple for five years. Designated provincial of France by Brzozowski, he started on January 3, 1815, the long retreat for sixty novices, of whom thirty were priests.[31]

29 Peers, *Spain*, p. 89; Carr, *Spain*, p. 468.
30 García-Villoslada, *Manual*, pp. 624-627; J. Burnichon, S.J., *La Compagnie de Jésus en France: 1814-1914* (Paris, 1914-1922), I, 486-488.
31 Burnichon, *La Compagnie*, I, 63.

From all quarters the Jesuits received requests to take up the work of education. In the first quarter century eighty-seven appeals to run minor seminaries, nine to run major seminaries, thirty for colleges, and fifty-five for residences poured in on them. But they could accept only a tiny fraction, and during the Restoration they confined themselves, save for the short-lived college at Billom, to work in minor seminaries. By 1826 they had undertaken the charge of eight.

What started so auspiciously ran into trouble through the 1820's when the anti-clericals went on a publicity rampage against the Society. With extravagant language they portrayed this insecure body of 300 men, who were still trying to consolidate themselves, as enormous battalions storing up ammunition against the day when they could lead France back to barbarism. In 1828 they pressured Charles X into approving an ordinance by which all teachers had to sign a declaration that they were not members of an unauthorized teaching body. This was aimed directly at the Society, for the Jesuits had decided, lest they arouse old hatreds, not to press for official recognition but to base their work on the general principle of freedom as enunciated in the Charter of 1814-1815. But their enemies, ever adept in their legalism, skirted the Charter by the ordinance they forced on Charles. In September, 1828, not one Jesuit stepped into the classroom. Then came the July Revolution of 1830. Menacing crowds moved about the Jesuit houses. Superiors moved the novices to Spain and Italy. Only fifty-six priests and a few brothers, scattered and in disguise, remained in France. Others started "exile colleges" in Savoy, Spain, Switzerland, and Belgium.[32]

The character of these events during the first fifteen years following the Bourbon restoration foreshadowed the cast of the French Society's history until the First World War. In the nation where the contest between the Church and the secularists was protracted and especially virulent, the Society's fortunes advanced or retreated with the flow of the battle. A major focal point of dispute was the control of the University of France, that centralized structure, created by Napoleon in 1806 and 1808, which regulated through the minister of national education and his subordinates the schools at all levels, university, secondary, and primary.

32 Ibid., 466-468, 492-497, 500, 514-527; Adrien Dansette, *Religious History of Modern France* (New York, 1961), I, 201; J. W. Padberg, S.J., *Colleges in Controversy. The Jesuit Schools in France from Revival to Suppression, 1815-1880* (Cambridge, Mass., 1969), pp. 64-70.

During the early stages of the July Monarchy of Louis Philippe, when an attitude of religious indifference prevailed in the government, the Jesuits returned and reorganized their communities. But in 1843 another storm broke. The Catholics had mounted a campaign to break the hold which the secularists then had on the University of France. They made secondary education the specific salient in this campaign, and highlighted the Church's freedom to teach. The anti-clericals did not meet the issue squarely and honestly. At a time when the Society did not run a single school, with deft tactics they shifted public attention from the real point of controversy and propagandized the terrifying menace of a Jesuit take-over in the field of secondary education. As this Jesuit phantom rose over the schools of France, Léon Gambetta's future anti-clerical aphorism was anticipated by: "The Jesuit, there is the enemy." The comte August Arthur Beugnot remarked, "I admire the University. It has chosen the word most apt to fire spirits, irritate them, inflame them for the cause." [33] At the Collège de France Jules Michelet and Edgar Quinet demeaned their lectures by turning them into diatribes against the Society. With ludicrous histrionics Michelet pictured himself as another Petrus Ramus, massacred by the Jesuits on a future St. Bartholomew's Day. By his novel *The Wandering Jew* Eugène Suë set the popular imagination ablaze with wrath against the Society. In June, 1845, Roothaan advised his French sons to reduce the numbers of the larger communities where antagonism was strongest. Those in Paris scattered to at least eight different houses; others moved the novitiate from Avignon to Nice; some thirty left Saint-Acheul; forty scattered from Laval. The general's directive was sensible. He cautioned that it was no time for a show of bravado. The disappearance should be carried out quietly and "sans éclat." [34]

Then after five years came the Second Republic of Louis Napoleon Bonaparte. Then the Second Empire and almost a quarter century of peace and progress for the Society. In March, 1850, the National Assembly passed the famous Falloux law which granted the religious congregations freedom to conduct schools. Under this Edict of Nantes for Catholics 251 schools opened within a year of its enactment. In the first three and a half months the Jesuits received at least fifty-two requests for colleges. They undertook eleven before the close of the year.

33 Burnichon, *La Compagnie*, II, 136-138, 462-464.
34 Ibid., 654-655.

By the end of the Empire in 1870 they were running eighteen as well as teaching in six major seminaries.

After the fall of Emperor Napoleon III in the Franco-Prussian War, and during the bloody episode of the Paris Commune when Frenchmen fought Frenchmen for control of the capital, five Jesuits, including the superb teacher of history, spiritual director, and preacher, Pierre Olivaint, fell before either the firing squad or the savagery of the mobs. During the early years of the Third Republic, while the monarchist trend still ran strong in the Assembly, the Society surged forward in a burst of expansion and opened twelve new colleges between 1871 and 1880.[35]

Then the pendulum swung the other way, and the secularists gained the ascendancy. Since the Enlightenment and the Revolution the anti-Catholic tide was running strong in France, and from the beginnings of the Third Republic after the Franco-Prussian War the Freemasons took pride in their organization as a spearhead in the dechristianization of the country. The engagement between revealed religion and the secularist spirit of the age of reason had moved into the nineteenth century, and men like Jules Ferry and Émile Combes carried on the mission of the duc de Choiseul and Jean d'Alembert. During the Third Republic the irreligious tide reached a high water mark when the republicans gained control of the Chamber of Deputies and in 1879 passed legislation that denied the Jesuits, the Marists, and other "unauthorized" religious groups the freedom to teach. Jules Ferry, a cold and hard man, led the attack. He symbolized the doctrinaire secularism and republican authoritarianism that denied, in the name of state unity, educational pluralism. The next year, on March 29, 1880, the government accepted a motion by the Chamber of Deputies and ordered the dissolution of the Society within three months. On June 30 the police entered the thirty-seven Jesuit houses throughout France and evicted the religious, who then found refuge in England, Switzerland, Spain, and Belgium. Pope Leo XIII felt that the French Society had received the *coup de grâce,* and only hoped that the other orders and congregations could be saved.[36]

Gradually, however, as the government relaxed its enforcement of the Jesuit dispersion and Leo XIII tried by his flexible diplomacy to ease the tension between the Church and the Republic, the exiles returned and even began to teach once more.

35 Ibid., III, 375; IV, 314, 408.
36 Dansette, *Religious History,* II, 37-38; 40-44.

But by 1899 another crisis had developed. First, under the moderate Pierre Waldeck-Rousseau, and then under the crusading Émile Combes, the republicans carried on their drive against the Church. On July 9, 1901, new legislation directed against the religious teaching orders became law. The Jesuits left their twenty-four colleges, two minor seminaries, and two special technical schools, and once more sought refuge abroad. These abandoned colleges epitomized a weakness and a strength of the Jesuit presence in France during the nineteenth century. In contrast with the creativeness which sparked other Jesuit activities, especially in the missions, the colleges had felt a restraint imposed by a middle and upper class student body and by an attitude of fear, even hostility, toward modern educational change. Yet, against the claims of an omnipotent state, they had stood solidly for the principle of freedom to determine their own character, the supremacy of spiritual values, and the worth of the older traditional humanistic formation.[37]

These educational reverses issued in great measure from adverse political circumstances. But the Society also faced other problems more specifically philosophical and spiritual. A recent one was the philosophy of Félicité Robert de Lammenais; another, far older, was the piety and theology of Jansenism. For some fifteen years, starting around 1820, many French Jesuits were captivated by the doctrine of De Lammenais on the criterion for certitude, which placed it basically in the universal consent of mankind or the "Common Sense." With meticulous care Père Jean Rozaven, the French assistant, whom Bishop Félix Antoine Dupanloup hailed as France's most competent theologian since Bossuet, tried to turn the tide. To avoid public conflict he wrote lengthy letters to the many Jesuits involved. In 1834 the Encyclical *Singulari* of Gregory XVI terminated the controversy. Roothaan then requested the Jesuit champions of De Lammenais to sign a renouncement of his teaching. This they all did. The older problem of Jansenism refused to be scotched so easily. The Jesuits met their old enemy in many of the priests who had been trained in the rigid and moral teaching of Louis Bailly, a French secular priest, whose *Dogmatic and Moral Theology* (1789) was a standard manual in the seminaries of France for nearly a half-century. To combat this they stressed the frequent reception of the sacraments of Penance and the Holy Eucha-

37 Ibid., II, 193; Padberg, *Colleges*, pp. 273-280.

rist, and in the widely distributed *Compendium of Moral Theology* of Jean Pierre Gury they had an effective antidote.[38]

Overriding all these issues which engaged the Society was the dilemma which faced the nation: to remain true to the old regime, or to join in the creation of a new world of democratic freedom. In the early days of the century most Jesuits, from families which tried to preserve the older values, inclined toward the traditional fidelity to the crown. Among them however rose voices which challenged their rigidity. A Belgian Jesuit who worked in France, Philippe Delvaux, spoke proudly of the liberal institutions in his own country. To Roothaan in May, 1841, he wrote about liberty in the United States. "Close to ten years ago Father de Rozaven wrote me that, on the whole and after the experience of recent centuries, liberty as realized in America is better for the Church than the protection of the absolute monarchies." [39]

Études, the monthly magazine of the French Jesuits, also spoke in a positive way about liberty. Founded in 1856 by the Russian nobleman and member of the Society in France, Jean Gargarin, it first had the more ample title *Études de théologie, de philosophie et d'histoire.* Under editors like Charles Daniel and Ambroise Matignon, this journal tried to understand with sympathy the momentous changes in the western world. Between 1864 and 1867 Matignon wrote a series of eleven articles entitled "The Teaching of the Society of Jesus on Liberty." Tracing the history of the Society's combat with Calvinism, Baius, the Jansenists, Traditionalism, and De Lamennais, he enunciated his thesis: "On the doctrinal plane, as on the practical, the Society of Jesus seems to have received a special mission, not only to maintain the divine law but also to defend and protect human liberty." [40] Because of these articles Matignon received criticism from high places. On October 9, 1866, Beckx cautioned the provincial of France, Armand de Ponlevoy, that *Études* was taking on a liberal tinge and that any future articles on liberty or other ideas reproved by the *Syllabus of Errors* should be sent to Rome for review before publication. Two years later Pope Pius IX met the members of the procura-

38 Burnichon, *La Compagnie,* I, 277; II, 19, 45.
39 Ibid., I 289; II, 76; IV, 61-62. The quote of Delvaux was provided on microfilm through the kindness of James C. Finlay, S.J. The document is in the Roman Archives of the Society of Jesus: France 6-XXII, 15.
40 J. Lecler, S.J., "Dans la crise du catholicisme liberal," *Études,* CCXCI (1956), 199-200.

tors' congregation and brought up Matignon's name. "If he were present," said the pope, "we would ask him if he means to accommodate the doctrines of the Church to those of modern society. Some people would wish to modify the *Syllabus*. This cannot be. Truth will ever be truth, and there cannot be a conciliation between truth and error." [41]

Disfavor also fell upon *Études* because of its attitude on the eve of the Vatican Council when the question of papal infallibility was under wide discussion. Since they felt a dogmatic definition would be inopportune, the editors kept a reserve and wrote little about the subject. The ultramontanists, including other Jesuits, voiced their annoyance that the magazine did not sound a clear and unequivocal call for such a definition. In 1871 superiors moved *Études* to Lyons and placed it, to the embarrassment of the recent editors, under a man of deeply traditional leanings, Henri Ramière. A period of intransigent conservatism set in as Henri, duc de Chambord, Bourbon claimant to the throne and the hope of the royalists, became one of the journal's heroes. The anti-Jesuit decree of 1880 helped to break the grip of this mentality, since it enforced a period of silence through eight years when *Études* could not be printed. In 1888 it reappeared once more, again in Paris, but now in the positive and constructive atmosphere keynoted by the pontificate of Leo XIII.

In the other burning issues of the day, of which Modernism was the most provocative, the Jesuits were also engaged. And again *Études* was a mouthpiece. Modernism, so complex, subtle, and abrasive of Christian foundations, evoked some especially fine scholarship and writing by perceptive critics, but none done with the brilliance of Léonce de Grandmaison and Jules Lebreton. With precise erudition, finely balanced prudence, sensitivity to the nuances of doctrine, avoidance of oversimplification, De Grandmaison exposed the flaws of Modernist tenets. Lebreton, with a beautiful serenity and sure grasp of dogma and its implications, rendered a superior exegesis of the decree *Lamentabili* and the encyclical *Pascendi* of Pius X.

Alongside the editor and the schoolmaster, through these hundred years, there also worked with distinction the preacher and spiritual director. Immediately after the Napoleonic era teams of Jesuit preachers moved from town to town in one of their earliest and most concentrated apostolic projects. Partic-

41 Burnichon, *La Compagnie*, IV, 153-160, 331-332.

ularly popular and effective was Nicolas MacCarthy, of an Irish family which had settled in Toulouse. From 1837 Jesuits frequently held the pulpit to which even the skeptical intelligentsia of France paid heed, that of Notre Dame of Paris. Succeeding the secular priest and future Dominican, Jean Baptiste Lacordaire, Gustave François Xavier de Ravignan, polished gentleman of keen intelligence, profound humility, and penitential spirit, gave the Lenten courses at Notre Dame from 1837 to 1847. He knew the critical and rationalistic nature of many in the throngs who listened to him. In the first two years, confining himself to the construction of a solid intellectual foundation for his profession of faith, he did not mention the name of Christ. Then, in the years that followed, he portrayed with elaborate and flowery language, undoubtedly too heavy and too ornate for critics of another age, the truth and beauty of the Christian revelation. In 1841 he essayed a bold venture. He decided to preach a mission. Throngs packed the church, and for six to seven hours a day held him in the confessional as men, away from the sacraments for years, returned.[42] De Ravignan's second successor at Notre Dame (the first was the Abbé Claude Henri Plantier), the vigorously logical and articulate Joseph Félix, preached there from 1853 to 1870. The Notre Dame conferences of both De Ravignan and Félix accurately register the philosophical structures of the nineteenth century, and in their reading, one can retrieve the philosophical preoccupations of an embroiled century. Both men showed themselves to be intellectually alert in their awareness of the current questions which clamored for an answer. They built well on the foundations laid by Lacordaire.

De Ravignan also produced one of the most telling pieces of Jesuit literature of the century. Stung to action by the weird and unreal image of a Jesuit portrayed by the assault of the 1840's, he composed a brochure entitled *The Institute of the Society of Jesus* in which he clearly and eloquently delineated the nature and spirit of St. Ignatius' organization. Respected as he was, he gained a wide and enthusiastic audience. With swelling phrases he went to the heart of the anti-Jesuit argument and insisted that a member of the Society does not by his vocation become an enemy of the fatherland. "A Jesuit I have not always been. . . . Before I became a priest and a Jesuit I was a man of my times;

42 Ibid., II, 222-229.

that I still am. A Frenchman I have not ceased to be." These words electrified Paris.[43]

In their directly spiritual ministry the French Jesuits were especially successful in their organizations, particularly the Sodalities of the Blessed Virgin and the Apostolate of Prayer. Even before the restoration of the Society, Jean Baptiste Bourdier-Delpuits organized in Paris a group of spiritual elite. In 1809 they numbered 400. Perhaps overenthusiastically Albert de Mun hailed it as "the cradle of so much of the religious life of our age." Three years after Delpuit's death in 1811, Pierre Ronsin took over its direction and guided it through a fourteen-year-period of intense Catholic apostolic life. After Ronsin's death it declined.

The Apostolate of Prayer originated in the mind of one of the preeminent Jesuits of the century, François Xavier Gautrelet, for thirty-five years spiritual director of the Jesuit scholastics at Vals. In an exhortation to the community in 1844, he outlined his plan for a pious association, a league with the object of promoting prayer for one another in union with the prayer of the Sacred Heart of Jesus. Henri Ramière, an ardent and inventive spirit, took up the idea and moved it from the drawing board to a large-scale actuality. He founded the first *Messenger of the Sacred Heart,* a magazine designed to spread devotion to the Person of Christ and his infinite love symbolized by his Sacred Heart. In 1912 separate *Messengers* in twenty-six languages were being published. In 1906 Jean Vincent Bainvel issued one of the best presentations of the place this devotion has had in the life of the Church in his *Doctrine and History of Devotion to the Sacred Heart.*

Imitating their predecessors of the seventeenth century, some Jesuits of the nineteenth had decisive parts in the foundation of new religious congregations of women. Pierre de la Clorivière, during the tumult of the French Revolution, assisted Marie Adelaide de Cicé in establishing the Daughters of the Heart of Mary. Against a background of the guillotine on the Place de la Revolution, and of Robespierre's Republic of Virtue and Reign of Terror, these nuns, dressed in lay attire, worked in hospitals, shielded priests hunted by the government, and gave solace and help to those in need. To them Clorivière, in his extensive correspondence, transmitted the Ignatian spirit. Knowing the violence of the age by the personal experience of im-

43 G. F. X. de Ravignan, S.J., *De l'existence et l'institut des Jésuites* (Paris, 1844), p. 6.

prisonment, he wrote: "Adapt yourself to circumstances which you must regard as the signs by which Divine Providence manifests to us his will." Another Jesuit director who knew the fury of mobs in revolt was Joseph Varin d'Ainville. This hopeful and joyful man helped two unusual women in the origins of their new communities, Madeleine Sophie Barat and Marie Rose Julie Billiart. He told the former, "You must learn to know the mind and heart of Jesus, and give yourself up entirely to His guidance." This Saint Madeleine did, and gave as a heritage to her companions when in 1800 she started the Religious of the Sacred Heart of Jesus. Several times, at Varin's bidding, she visited Saint Julie to encourage her in accepting the apostolic vocation the Jesuit was sure that she had. In 1805 Julie formally started the group that became known as the Sisters of Notre Dame de Namur.

Later in the century Pierre Olivaint helped Blessed Eugénie de Smet when in 1856 she founded according to the spirit and rules of St. Ignatius the Society of the Helpers of the Holy Souls in Purgatory. And still later Paul Ginhac, known for his personal austerity, encouraged Émilie d'Hoogworst in the organization of the Religious of Mary Reparatrix.

Other Jesuits picked up this difficult tradition of authentic spiritual direction. Thousands of souls in their search for the road to greater holiness felt the strong influence of the highly intelligent and spiritually sensitive Léonce de Grandmaison, the sure, original, and mystical René de Maumigny, and the expert in adaptation of principles to individual needs, Louis Poullier. Unnumbered others found spiritual guidance in the prolific writing of French Jesuits, especially in works of such high calibre as *The Graces of Interior Prayer* (1901) by Auguste Poulain.

The Society returned to Germany and the Austrian Empire in a two-pronged thrust, one from the west and south, from Switzerland into Germany, and the other, from the east and north, from Russia into Austria. Its history was one of great hardship, largely because of the internal convulsions, religious and political, within central Europe.

Germany and Central Europe

In 1810 Jesuits under the direction of Brzozowski in White Russia started a mission in Switzerland. They expanded and founded schools, at Brig in 1814, at Fribourg in 1817, at Schwyz in 1836. Then in the bitter conflict between the Catholic group, who favored a federal type of government, and the anti-clericals, who wanted a strongly centralized state, their existence in

Switzerland became one of the most controversial issues. Politics and religion became impossibly confused. The Catholics, failing to sense the strong trend toward political freedom, especially in a pluralistic state like Switzerland, insisted on officially Catholic institutions, and in 1845 the seven Catholic cantons formed "the separate alliance," the *Sonderbund.*

Against this strategy the anti-clericals reacted sharply. During the mounting tension, the Jesuits, realizing the hostility that their presence could arouse among the heirs of the Enlightenment, tried to remain unobtrusive. The Catholics of Lucerne, however, brought the Society to the forefront. Determined to show that they could not be intimidated by the anti-clericals, they importuned the Jesuits to accept the Theological Faculty at Lucerne. The Jesuits expressed reluctance. But pressed by the persistent requests, they unwisely yielded. This was one of the recent events which the anti-clericals exploited when they attained the majority in the Diet in 1847. Putting themselves forward as the champions of a menaced democracy, on July 20 they declared the *Sonderbund* dissolved. On September 3 they ordered the expulsion of the Jesuits from the country. Civil war followed. The Catholics went down in defeat. And 274 Jesuits took the road to exile.[44] But not before it had started the Province of Germany on its way, for in 1826 Fortis had carved out of the Swiss group a province for the Germans. Before mid-century, primarily because of Protestant animus in some circles and the spirit of the Enlightenment in others, the Jesuits were not able to open any colleges and confined themselves to whatever retreats and missions they could undertake from scattered residences. The National Assembly of Frankfurt (1848-1849) gave the measure of the Society's popularity in liberal circles with the resolution that it be banished forever from German soil. Catholic delegates responded strenuously in the name of liberty, and on November 30, 1848, the article of suppression was deleted from the constitution.[45]

This bold and confident stand taken by Catholics in public life manifested but one aspect of the general renaissance within the Church. As men, dried up by the naturalistic teaching of the Enlightenment, sought fresh waters for their spirits, the Jesuits, with other religious, opened up one of the golden eras of preaching in Germany by means of the immensely popular parish mission. Through Westphalia, the Rhineland, and Baden

44 Aubert, *Le pontificat,* pp. 22-24.
45 Ibid., p. 59, fn. 3.

they set up stations. Thousands assembled to hear men like Peter Roh, Peter Hasslacher, and Georg von Waldburg-Zeil. From Silesia to the Rhine scenes reminiscent of the Middle Ages took place as for a day or two villages emptied their residents who went to a neighboring parish to hear the priest. Konrad Martin, bishop of Paderborn, asserted that the revival in Catholic Germany was the glory of Roh and Hasslacher.[46] Vocations increased, and the province which numbered 324 in 1853 opened two novitiates. In the old Benedictine Abbey of Maria Laach, which a benefactor gave as a house of studies for the scholastics, these young Jesuits had a venerable reminder of the tradition of learning in the Church. To perpetuate this tradition the Society founded in 1864 the *Voces e Maria ad Lacum,* which in 1871 was renamed *Stimmen aus Maria Laach,* and in 1915 *Stimmen der Zeit.* The immediate occasion of this journal was the publication of the *Syllabus of Errors* in 1864. Not only did the German Jesuits defend the *Syllabus,* but in a series of articles, which manifested a lack of sensitivity to the various nuances of meaning inherent in a document of this nature, they drove hard for a rigid and extreme interpretation of the papal condemnations. The editors were tied to the past. In 1867, for example, Gerhard Schneemann complained that the state no longer cooperated with the Church by taking those condemned in an ecclesiastical tribunal and punishing them by the imposition of fines, scourging, and exile.[47]

The *Stimmen* also pointed the compass needle for many Catholic theologians in the direction of Rome. The strong ultramontanism he observed prompted Alexis de Tocqueville to remark that the pope was induced by the faithful to become absolute master of the Church more than they were forced by him to submit to his domination. With the *Stimmen's* editors other Jesuits were at the source of this feeling. Secular priests, trained by the Jesuits, imbibed deeply of Bellarmine. On the popular level Franz Xaver Weninger spread a sense of filial affection for the Holy Father. Strong as was this attitude, however, it met sharp challenges from several Catholic scholars, challenges which reflect another and far deeper chasm between two groups of Catholic thinkers.

46 Ibid., pp. 144-145.
47 Ibid., pp. 209, 259; J. J. Hennesey, *Catholic Historical Review,* XLVIII (1962), 178 with fn. 50; Burkhart Schneider, S.J., "Der Syllabus Pius' IX und die deutschen Jesuiten," *Archivum Historiae Pontificiae,* VI (1968), 371-392.

An insistent question was this: what should be the approach of the Catholic German renaissance toward the contemporary intellectual world?[48] Both sides wanted to win for the Church the esteem of cultivated circles and to conquer for her the mind of Germany. On the one side were those, mainly university professors, who aimed to do this by matching Protestant attainments in free scientific inquiry, especially in the use of historical methods and in adapting dogma to the modern philosophical mentality. On the other were those who, feeling that German thought since Kant had been traveling up a dead-end street, fought for a return to scholasticism and through it the elaboration of a thoroughly integrated doctrinal system. Many influential Jesuits leaned toward the second school. While Cardinal Joseph Othmar von Rauscher of Vienna encouraged them at their theological center in Innsbruck, Josef Kleutgen by his prolific writing took the lead in this movement. Pope Leo XIII called Kleutgen the Prince of Philosophers. Contemporaries believed that the Jesuit drew up the original draft of the encyclical *Aeterni Patris,* the call made by Leo for a return to the wisdom of St. Thomas Aquinas.[49]

Yet it was not completely black on one side and white on the other. In theology, for example, many Jesuits who respected this scientific movement, like Schrader and others in the Perrone-Passaglia school, integrated scholastic teaching against a background of exact understanding of the Fathers of the Church. Despite the achievements of these men, feelings became bitter between the university theologians and the Jesuits. Contributors to the *Stimmen* branded the work of the professors as not worthy of the name of theology, limited as it was to exegesis and the minutiae of patristics, and accused them of acting independently of the Holy See. The professors in turn called the Jesuits, and others too, the quartermaster sergeants of the Inquisition.[50] These conflicts added intense heat to the atmosphere which surrounded the summoning of the First Vatican Council.

By their nature removed from this kind of controversy were several scholarly enterprises undertaken by the Jesuits of the German province. Gerhard Schneemann, by a kind of research in

48 Aubert, *Le pontificat,* pp. 262-276.
49 Ibid., pp. 193-199; Augustin Kerkvoorde, O.S.B., "Kleutgen, Joseph," *Catholicisme* (Paris, 1948), VI, 1456-1457; Hocedez, *Histoire,* II, 324-328.
50 Aubert, *Le pontificat,* pp. 209-211.

which the French Jesuits of the seventeenth and eighteenth centuries, like Labbe, Cossart, and Hardouin, distinguished themselves, edited the first six volumes of the seven-volume assembly of documents of provincial church councils from 1682 to 1870. Known as *Collectio lacensis,* it was brought to completion by another German Jesuit, Theodor Granderath. Granderath included in the seventh volume nearly six hundred documents, such as diplomatic correspondence, newspaper articles, and bishops' letters which touched on the First Vatican Council. Another valuable tool for theological study, the five-volume *A Survey of Catholic Theological Literature,* was the masterpiece of the convert and Swiss, Hugo von Hurter. Among those who wrote on theology from the approach of spirituality, perhaps the best known was another Swiss, Moritz Meschler, whose works, because of their lucid expression of spiritual principles, enjoyed for a long time an honored place in the libraries of religious houses.

As so frequently happened in their history, the Jesuits in Germany saw their apostolate abruptly taken from their hands by hostile political developments. In 1872 Bismarck launched a concerted offensive against the Church. Early in this Kulturkampf he banished the Society. England, Holland, the United States, and South America received fragments of the broken province which, even in exile, continued to grow. Almost doubling the number they had in 1872, they reached 1,458 men in 1907. Although Bismarck had in the main lost the battle, anti-Jesuit legislation remained in the code of law until April, 1917. But before this, quietly and loyally Jesuits had been returning to their homeland in the grip of war, and some 535 served in one way or another with the armed forces.

The creation of the Austrian Province had deep significance for the current political attitudes in the Hapsburg regime: it signaled the turning of the tide for Josephinism. The new province had its origin in the exiles from Russia. When in March, 1820, Czar Alexander I decreed the expulsion of the Society from Russia, some of the refugees found asylum in Galicia, the Polish part of the Austrian Empire. Their official welcome by the Emperor Francis I on August 14, 1820, meant far more than the guarantee of a new home. It marked a volte-face in an important aspect of the emperor's political position. Governmental ministers in the tradition of Joseph II strongly objected to the presence of the Society in Austria but Francis, himself raised in that tradition and now appalled by the swath cut through Europe by the scythe of the French Revolution, felt that he had found in the Jesuits valuable companions-in-arms to help him bolster the authority of his throne. The excellent college, opened at Tarnopol through the skillful negotiations of Alois Landes, announced the autumn of Josephinism in the land of the Hapsburgs.[51] With the blessing of Francis' successor, Ferdinand I, the Society opened other schools at Linz and Innsbruck, and took charge of the Theresianum in Vienna. By 1846 the province numbered one hundred and fifty men. This steady progress however came to an abrupt but temporary halt during the unsettled years of revolution and reaction, 1848-1852, when the Society was forced into exile.

As among the German Jesuits, so among the Austrians ran a strong current of ultramontanism. At the University of Vienna this feeling had a celebrated defender in Klemens Schrader. Schrader, famous at the Roman College for his strong bent toward positive theology, was invited in 1857 to Vienna by Cardinal Joseph Othmar von Rauscher. There he displayed in his teaching and writing over his ten years in the Austrian capital the second prominent feature of his theological character, a strong predilection for Rome. Between 1864-1867 he presented in a series of brochures an interpretation of the *Syllabus* which was of a piece with the *Voces e Maria ad Lacum.*

Even as Bismarck uprooted the German Society, the Austrian Province continued to grow in numbers, and in 1909 Wernz created from it the new Province of Hungary with 212 men responsible for two colleges and three residences.

Poland   Poland as a nation died in 1795, not to rise again until after World War I. But it was Polish and Lithuanian Jesuits who kept the Society alive through the several years of uncertainty in White Russia. Expelled by the Czar in 1820, they continued to form a valuable unit of the Society's structure by concentrating in Galicia, the area of Poland stolen by the Austrian Empire. What was Russia's loss became Austria's gain, for they established a college which gained a high reputation at Tarnopol, followed by others at Lemberg, Neu-Sandec, and Kraków. To complement the impact of these schools in the religious and cultural life of the Hapsburg realms, they founded the distinguished review *Przeglad Powszechny.* In 1846 Roothaan created the Province of Galicia which by 1914 numbered 500 men.

51 A. Reinerman, "The Return of the Jesuits to the Austrian Empire and the Decline of Josephinism, 1820-1822," *Catholic Historical Review,* LXX (1966), 379-380, 389-390.

The history of the Belgian Jesuits in the nineteenth century had a striking resemblance to their experience in the late sixteenth century. In both periods political and religious tension marred their origins, but once stability was secured they grew into a remarkably vigorous and constructive unit of the Society. The diplomats at the Congress of Vienna placed the Belgians under the rigidly restrictive Calvinistic rule of the royal house of Holland. With the Catholic population in general the Society suffered great hardship. During the period of suppression some twenty Belgians and Dutchmen entered the novitiate in White Russia. In July 1814, Brzozowski chose Henri Fonteyne, a veteran of the old Society, to start the Belgian venture by opening a novitiate at Rumbeke-bei-Roulers. The Napoleonic Hundred Days forced them to move to Brig in Switzerland. Between 1819 and 1830 fifty young men left their native land to enter the novitiate in exile.

In 1830 the Belgians made their bid for independence. Then, as in the era of Alessandro Farnese, the highway to the Society's success was wide and open. In 1832, 105 men operated two colleges with 167 students; in 1907, 1,168 men operated fifteen colleges, each with an average of over a thousand students. Besides, 262 men were on the foreign missions. But the most audacious project of the young province was to pick up once more the work of the Bollandists. Superiors had great difficulty in recruiting talent for this exacting task, but in 1876, when the enterprise had nearly reached the point of collapse, a man of superior scholarly competence, Charles de Smedt, appeared on the scene to save it. Others who followed brought great gifts of imagination and perceptiveness, especially the brilliant Hippolyte Delehaye, who, during a half century of service and thirty years as president, brought the organization to one of the high points of its amazing history. The first great enterprise of cooperative scholarship in the modern world, the Bollandists are the sole such undertaking of the seventeenth century which in mid-twentieth century is still active and productive.[52]

Not everybody had the insight to appreciate the achievement of the Bollandists. John Adams, on June 22, 1815, while praising the industry of these Jesuits, wrote to Thomas Jefferson: "I have no doubt that the *Acta Sanctorum* is the most enormous Mass of Lies, Frauds, Hypocracy [sic] and Imposture, that ever was heaped together upon this Globe." Jefferson concurred and added: "By what chemical process M. Camus supposed that an

---

52 D. Knowles, *Great Historical Enterprises* (London, 1963), pp. 3-4.

Extract of truth could be obtained from such a farrago of false-hood, I must leave to the Chemists and Moralists of the age to divine." [53]

To the north, in Holland, a growing Catholic population and a gradual relaxation of governmental harassment of the Church eased the way for the Society's freer and wider movement. In 1849 Roothaan separated the Dutch Jesuits from the Belgians, creating a vice-province of ninety-five men in nine houses, which included the colleges at Katwijk and Kuilenburg. In 1914 the Province of Holland numbered 559 men.

If Edmund Campion and Robert Persons could have returned to their native land in 1914, they would have gasped in un-belief. Seven hundred and twenty of their religious brethren freely preached in Jesuit parishes and freely taught in Jesuit schools. One hundred years before however prospects had not been too promising.

An irksome yoke, inherited from the previous century, hung about the necks of the English Jesuits of the nineteenth century, the abrasive relations between themselves and the English bish-ops. In 1814, numbering about seventy men, they had been working in England for eleven years, ever since Pope Pius VII gave his verbal approbation to affiliate with the Society in White Russia. But until 1829, fifteen years later, most of the vicars-apostolic — John Milner was the noted exception — op-posed recognition of the Jesuits, arguing that the Society, re-membered for its militancy, would block that emancipation toward which Catholics were edging, and that the government found the Society's presence in England uncongenial. Conscious of this opposition at home, the Jesuits found little comfort in certain statements made at the Vatican. Cardinal Lorenzo Litta turned bellows on a smoldering flame when he wrote on Decem-ber 2, 1816, to William Poynter, the vicar-apostolic for the

---

53 L. Cappon, ed., *The Adams-Jefferson Letters* (Chapel Hill: University of North Carolina Press, 1959), 2 vols., II, 450-452. Quoted with permission. Erroneously Adams identified a spirit of credulity with the enterprise of the Bollandists. He failed to recognize in the Jesuit scholars that dedication to historical truth of which he was so ardent a champion. For Adams the critical spirit of the Enlightenment found its most fruit-ful form in the study of history rather than philosophy. On the philos-ophers of his time he poured his caustic contempt. He told Jefferson that the *Acta Sanctorum,* if critically examined, "would do more to open the Eyes of man kind, than all the Phylosophers of the 18th century, who were as great Hypocrites as any of the Phylosophers or theologians of Antiquity" (ibid., 450-451).

London District, that the pope intended the bull of restoration to have effect in those countries "in which the civil powers agreed to receive and recall" the Society. Yielding to an unworthy tactic to which churchmen so often succumbed and which reached back at least as far as the Arian crisis, Poynter sought the assistance of the civil government against the Society. Lord Sidmouth, the Home Secretary, obliged in 1819 and reported that the British government had "insuperable objections to the restoration of the Jesuits in England." Long and complex letters went back and forth between Rome and Great Britain. Finally in 1829 Pope Leo XII terminated the unpleasant business by writing out in his own hand that the bull *Sollicitudo Omnium* of Pius VII was in effect in England.[54]

Many of the old irritants between the hierarchy and the religious orders remained. Cardinal Henry Edward Manning, archbishop of Westminster for twenty-seven years, from 1865 to 1892, gave hostility to the Society its classic expression. In his personal notes he wrote that, to him the Jesuits represented "the continual thwarting of the English clergy," and seemed "to be a mysterious permission of God for the chastisement of England." [55] During Manning's lifetime abrasive questions about jurisdiction and discipline bedeviled the relationship between the bishops and the religious. In 1874 the tensions reached the breaking point. Peter Gallwey, the Jesuit provincial, opened a school in Manchester despite the veto of the bishop, Herbert Vaughan. Gallwey's action, canonically correct, was most inopportune, and within a year the general, Peter Beckx, closed the school. The bishops of the country then asked the decision of the Holy See on twelve specific points, all concerned in one way or another with the exemption claimed by the religious orders. In 1881 Pope Leo XIII issued the constitution *Romanos Pontifices* in which on eleven of the points he upheld the position of the hierarchy. The bishops, quite correctly and joyfully, interpreted this as a victory for their cause.

The character of the Society's ministry was in large measure determined by the condition of the Church in England. For a people, timid and hesitant after centuries of persecution and

---

54 J. H. Pollen, S.J., "The Restoration of the English Jesuits," *Month*, CXV (1910), 591-592; also his "The Recognition of the Jesuits in England," *Month*, CXVI (1910), 29-31; Basset, *English Jesuits*, pp. 376-379.

55 V. A. McClelland, *Cardinal Manning. His Public Life and Influence, 1865-1892* (New York, 1962), p. 54.

now free to worship as they would, the initial need was for the organization of parish life. To this task the Jesuits applied themselves with a wide thoroughness as they began the process of gradually withdrawing from their settlements of penal days. In the 1840's they broke out of the bounds of parish life, and in a burst of vigor and imagination under the inspiring leadership of one of their greater provincials, Randal Lythgoe, they opened colleges in Liverpool, Chichester, St. Beuno's, and Malta. Under another forward-looking provincial, the buoyant and creative Alfred Weld, they started in 1864 *The Month*, a journal for articles on various aspects of current thought and culture. Since 1901 they began to turn over their parishes to the secular clergy. As the province expanded, it grew not only in numbers but also in the rich talent and wide intellectual background which marked some of the novices, many of them converts. For fifty years after 1814 an average of a convert a year joined the Society, including the prolific writer Henry Coleridge and the admirable superior, one of the great men of the province, Edward Purbrick.

Several of these converts had exceptional literary gifts. The most accomplished was Gerard Manley Hopkins. Born in Essex in 1844, educated at Oxford where he studied under Walter Pater, baptized a Catholic by John Henry Newman in 1866, Hopkins entered the Society in 1867. A poet with a delicately tuned musical ear, he brought to his work a sensitivity to structure and a feeling for a peculiar kind of rhythm which he called "sprung rhythm." Several of his poems, especially *The Wreck of the Deutschland*, most likely have gained secure places among the masterpieces of English literature. He died in Dublin in 1889.

The Irish Jesuits had a strong cornerstone about which to build their edifice in the person of Peter Kenney. This intelligent, clear-minded organizer received a fine preparation for his responsibilities ever since 1800 when Richard O'Callaghan, then one of the three survivors of the suppressed Society, placed him and a few other boys in school at Carlow College with the hope that they would one day be members of a restored Society of Jesus. In 1803 O'Callaghan sent him to the recently opened English novitiate at Hodder. In 1805, with two other Irishmen, Kenney went to the Jesuit house in Palermo to study philosophy. When Father General Brzozowski was anxious to open a school in Ireland, he had Kenney at hand for the task. With the financial resources saved by the men of the old Society, Kenney, in 1813-14, purchased Castle Browne in Kildare, and looking back to the late fifteenth-century name of the location, *Silva de*

Clongow, called it Clongowes Wood. In 1814-1815 the school registered 110 boys.

Storm clouds, however, soon gathered. The following sentences appeared in the *Hibernian Magazine,* November 18, 1813, in reference to the passage of Castle Browne into Jesuit hands: "Ireland now stands in imminent danger. If Popery succeeds, our fairest plains will once more witness days worthy to rank with those of Bloody Mary, and the walls of Derry shall again become the lamentable bulwarks against Popish treachery and massacre." This hysteria had strong teeth. Laws of Parliament and decisions of the courts, restrictive and attenuant, almost completely thwarted through the entire century all efforts to found and endow Catholic schools and colleges.[56] Despite this discouragement the Irish Jesuits started other schools at Tullabeg and Dublin as well as an apostolic school at Mungret. In 1912 they issued the first number of their widely respected *Studies.* Fifty-eight at the time of Catholic Emancipation, in 1914 they numbered 367.

As before 1773 the foreign missions were an integral part of the restored Society's apostolate. By the end of the nineteenth century Jesuits had returned to their old overseas haunts. And they added many new names to the list. But these vast areas in the course of the century lost their old familiar markings in the rush of great climacteric changes. In North America the thirteen English colonies became a republic and extended their frontier westward across the continent; in Latin America the Spanish and Portuguese colonies broke their ties with the mother countries and formed their own governments; in the Far East China and Japan opened their doors closed for so long to foreigners; Africa became the prey in a sudden flurry of European imperial wings. In all these areas, and others like Alaska, Australia, Indonesia, the Society of the nineteenth century planted its roots, and by 1919 ten percent of its personnel were engaged in mission work. *Foreign Missions*

But political changes were not the only alterations in the mission picture. Instead of the relatively few religious communities who formerly carried the burden of the missions, an incredible number of new groups especially dedicated to this apostolate swelled the great spirit of zeal which animated the Church of the nineteenth century. Nuns joined the work in increasing numbers. And to make a difficult problem even more complex,

56 Corcoran, *Clongowes,* pp. 52-55.

Protestant missionaries, hitherto rather exiguous, increased sharply.

The Society returned to China in 1842. That year two French priests landed in Shanghai. In time the Province of France assumed responsibility for the Vicariate of Nanking, and the Province of Champagne the Vicariate of Tschi-li. True to the traditions of Ricci, Schall, and Parrenin, Jesuit scholars, in their desire to understand the Chinese people, once more studied deeply and published penetrating works on various aspects of the country's life and literature. Leo Wieger, one of the great sinologues of the time, produced a twelve-volume work entitled *Rudiments of Chinese Speech and Style* (1895-1906). At Zi-ka-wei, outside Shanghai, the Society opened in 1903 the Aurora University, which aimed at forming an elite, grounded, even though pagan, in sound philosophical thinking and freed of bias against the Catholic faith.

A major difficulty remained in the old question of the Chinese rites. Despite all the energies given to the educating of men fit to take responsible positions in public life, Catholics still ran against the stumbling block in the act of honor to Confucius exacted of those entering governmental service. This the Church had forbidden in 1704. A change came with the advent of the republic after the revolution of 1911-1912. The new government declared that the honor paid Confucius enjoyed merely a civil significance, and in view of this interpretation the Holy See in 1939 effectively abrogated the old prohibition against the Chinese rites. Under the hierarchy, the missionaries had authorization to proceed along the road of the pioneers in "adaptation." Time, social changes, and the secularization of life had absorbed the old apprehension about superstition.

If the Jesuits had not changed in their attitude of respect for the culture of China, neither had many Chinese altered their antagonistic views of Europeans. In the wake of this feeling persecution and murder of missionaries followed. European nations forced open the doors China had kept closed to outsiders, coerced her to grant special concessions in her ports, and even extorted territory from her, such as Hong Kong which Great Britain seized in 1842. Resentment against the foreigner ran high, and in these robberies many Chinese, with understandable confusion of thought, saw Christ coming not with the cross but with a sword. This anger found fierce and cruel expression in a patriotic society known as the Boxers.

In 1900 the Boxers, unleashed by governmental intrigue, descended on several Christian communities. Some 30,000 Catholics met death, and many of the individual accounts recall the dignity, nobility, and sincerity with which the Christians of the early centuries gave their lives for the faith. Many could have saved themselves by the simple statement: I renounce my religion. But this they refused to do. At Chukiaho, June 20, 1900, some 1,800 died, including two Jesuits, Léon Ignace Mangin and Paul Denn, who met the onslaught as they sat in the sanctuary of the church facing a thousand of their people. The day before, at Ou-i two other Jesuits, Remi Isoré and Modeste Andlauer, were cut down as they knelt in the little chapel of the village. The four priests and fifty-two of the faithful were beatified in 1955.[57] Turbulence and disorder were endemic to China's entry into the society of modern nations, and this created the heavy cloud of uncertainty which hung over the Church's apostolate in that vast country.

To Japan, the other favorite mission field of the Far East, the Jesuits came relatively late after Commodore Matthew Calbraith Perry had opened its doors in 1854. Over fifty years passed until, instructed by Pope Pius X to start an institution of higher education in Tokyo, the first priests arrived in 1908 and in 1913 opened Sophia University.

India, replete for the Christian with memories of St. Francis Xavier and possessing his body at Goa, had been part of the Society's history from its origin. Much of the great gains there had been lost since the suppression. Despite the efforts of the Foreign Mission Society of Paris to replace the exiled Jesuits, conditions in France, the general debilitation of religious belief, and the chaos of the revolutionary and Napoleonic years, blocked the way. Between 1777 and 1792 they sent only three priests to India; between 1792 and 1820 not one.[58]

Then, once Roothaan gave the direction, the Jesuits again entered Asia's great subcontinent. The Belgians went to Bengal and Ceylon, the French to Malabar and Madurai, the Germans to Bombay, the Italians to Mangalore. Through the century schools, seminaries, printing presses, and parishes reappeared in many areas. Several men reached heights of distinction in this reactivation of the mission, but the name which rings with the greatest clarity and has all the resonance of the zeal and drive of Francis Xavier is that of Constant Lievens. This tireless Flem-

---

57 R. Renaud, S.J., "Blessed Ignace Mangin and His Companions, Martyrs," trans. J. Cahill, S.J., *WL*, XCII (1963), 126-138.
58 M. A. Mathis, C.S.C., *Modern Missions in India* (New York, 1947), p. 10.

ing labored for thirteen years among the poor of Bengal. He gained the confidence and love of the people of Chota Nagpur through his understanding of the law of the land. Rent collectors, playing upon the ignorance of the peasants, were stealing their property. Lievens studied the intricacies of the legal structure of the province and advised the victimized people. They won case after case in court. Hundreds went to him to become Catholics. So started one of the great mass conversions in missionary history. He alone baptized 25,000. In 1891 exhaustion and the ravages of tuberculosis forced him to leave his post. He went to Belgium in the hope of regaining his health and then returning to India. But death took this extraordinary man at the age of thirty-eight at Louvain in 1893.

Lievens had labored under one of the truly great Jesuit superiors in Indian history, Silvanus Grosjean. This strong dynamic man, a born leader, was gifted with a sharp clarity of vision, the perception to discern fresh modes of development, and the initiative to seize opportunities. With striking fortitude he mastered many obstacles to his goal. During the ten years of his term as superior in Bengal the Catholic population rose from 500 to 80,000.

In Africa the Society developed its missions under the flags of nations which shared in the partition of the Dark Continent, France in Algeria and Madagascar, England in Rhodesia, Belgium in the Congo. These areas, which developed in varying degrees into strong cells within the body of the Church, had their origins in pain, tedium, and discouragement, aggravated by the political tumult of opening the continent. In the history of the faith in Madagascar, ever memorable is the name of Marc Finaz, who for two years in the guise of an engineer gradually won over a hostile court by his construction of a railroad, a telegraph system, and a gas balloon. This large and important island, agitated by native hostility to the French, suffered political tension and even revolt. Among the rebels were many who hated the missionaries because Christianity was supplanting their own divinities. For twenty-one years in this atmosphere Jacques Berthieu, a Frenchman, labored on the island of Sainte-Marie as well as Madagascar, and in his simple, direct correspondence left an inspiring memorial to the heroism of the Catholics. In March, 1896, he wrote from Alatsinary: "I have slept here under the stars with all my Christians, who are happy that I am here and determined to die with me if it is necessary, in order not to betray their conscience." Three months later he was dead, murdered for the faith. On October 17, 1965, Pope Paul VI beatified him, the latest Jesuit to be so honored by the Church.[59]

Along the Zambesi no one gave a greater example of dogged determination in the face of debilitating climate and crippling sickness than the convert, Augustus Law, who on November 25, 1880, closed his life at Umzila's Kraal, leaving in a diary the record of a mighty confidence in God. His last words were: "I do not think I could despair even if I tried." In the north of the continent Cardinal Charles Lavigerie of Algiers spearheaded a specialized mission effort by his institution in 1868 of the White Fathers, and to this project the Jesuits gave valuable assistance by providing the novice master for a considerable time. They also opened colleges at Oran and Algiers. To the East, in Egypt, the Province of Lyons set up schools in Cairo and Alexandria, and between 1879 and 1905 reconciled some 25,000 Copts to the Church. By and large the African missions of the restored Society struck deeper roots than those of the old.

When the Society was suppressed, Portugal and Spain controlled for the most part all of Central and South America. When it was restored, some twenty new nations were either actually fighting, or on the threshold of contending, for their independence in those areas. In no other part of the world had so drastic changes occurred over so vast an extent of territory. The Society's history, once nicely parcelled into neat unities within the framework of the two royal patronage systems, became fragmented into many smaller pieces. Each new country developed its own story, and in the ebb and flow of those individual national histories the Society shared.

Over the origins of South American independence hangs a provocative question: to what extent did the Jesuits stimulate revolt against the mother countries? Answers vary. Some historians return to the sixteenth century, and in Francisco Suárez they discern the creator of the intellectual temper for independence. They judge that his doctrine on civil authority, affirming as it does that government receives its authority from God indirectly and through the mediation of the people, disposed the educated classes for the break with an autocratic crown. In the late eighteenth century, Spain certainly showed its fear of this teaching and banned the offensive volumes. But the ideas it

---

59 P. Molinari, S.J., "A New Blessed of the Society of Jesus: James Berthieu, Martyr of Madagascar (1838-1896)," *Annuarium Societatis Iesu* (1965-1966), pp. 49-56.

could not put in chains, and Suárez has been given a niche in South American history as the philosopher of emancipation.

Other historians find the explosive force among the Jesuit exiles in Italy. Many were Spanish American born, and to them their own colony meant more than their mother country. Deeply attached to what they regarded as their native land and deeply resentful of the violent manner in which they were uprooted and shipped to Italy, they projected in their histories and descriptions of their countries a national awareness and consciousness which would logically evolve into secession from Spain. The two Jesuit historians, Francisco Javier Alegre and Francisco Javier Clavijero, both cultivated writers of Mexican birth, have been hailed as the intellectual leaders who prepared the way for Mexican independence.

Still other historians make a distinction between a disposing cause and an active cause. In the early period of the colonial revolt against Spain, the home government, disturbed and frustrated, saw a Jesuit rebel behind every tree. Many South American patriots clouded the atmosphere even more by linking the names of the Jesuit exiles to their cause. But, allowing for the disposing influence of the exilic writings, careful research has identified only two former Jesuits who became active plotters against Spain, the Chilean Juan José Godoy and the Peruvian Juan Pablo Viscardo.[60] The scholarly inquiries continue, but intimate knowledge of this era is still in its dawn.

The first of the infant countries to receive the Jesuits back was Mexico. Around three elderly men of the old Society a group of aspirants gathered and by 1820 thirty-two men were operating four colleges and two seminaries. The persecution of 1835 in Spain released forty-two men for Argentina. Others from Europe soon followed, to Brazil, Paraguay, Uruguay, Chile,

---

60 Mörner, *The Expulsion*, pp. 16-17; Furlong, ibid., pp. 41-46; M. Batllori, S.J., *El Abate Viscardo. Historia y Mito de la Intervención de los Jesuítas en la Independencia de Hispano-américa* (Caracas, 1953), pp. 161-171. At the International Historical Congress at Vienna in 1965, two English historians, R. A. Humphreys and J. Lynch, presented the judgment that the "popular sovereignty" doctrine of Francisco Suárez was not a living force in the Latin American break with the Spanish crown. Admitting that the possibility of the Suarezian influence had been a useful point of discussion, they claim however "that the discussion has languished from lack of evidence" ("The Emancipation of Latin America," *Comité International des Sciences Historiques. XIIe Congrès International des Sciences Historiques* [Vienna, 1965], III, 41-42).

Colombia, Ecuador. Two special marks stamped the Jesuits' Latin American experience: the endless treadmill of persecution; and the cosmopolitan nature of the missionary personnel.

Through the century the new nations were being forged in the heat of the conflict between the religion planted by the priests who landed with the conquistadores and the rationalism imparted by the books and men schooled in the ideas of Voltairian France. In 1821 the Jesuits were exiled from Mexico; back in 1834, they were again expelled five years later. Up to 1914 twice more they had to take the road to exile. Mexico's action set the tone for other nations. But persecution in one country often opened up opportunities in another. Antipathy and distrust in Argentina, for example, forced the Jesuits in 1842 to go to Paraguay and Uruguay, and in 1843 to Chile. Exiles from Colombia in 1850 started work in Ecuador. Forced two years later out of Ecuador, they started in Guatemala. This hostility to the Church carried over into the twentieth century. In Mexico especially it reached a pitiless intensity under President Álvaro Obregón (1920-1924) and President Plutarco Elías Calles (1924-1928). During the latter's rule, when public worship was halted in Mexico City, the police captured an inexhaustible worker of the hidden Church, Miguel Pro Juárez. On November 23, 1927, Pro, known for his attractive and playful manner, fell before a firing squad as he quietly said, "Viva Cristo Rey."

The second characteristic of the Latin American experience, and this was reminiscent of pre-suppression days, was the widely cosmopolitan color of the personnel. Besides the Spaniards who arrived first, the Germans went to Rio Grande do Sul in Brazil and to Chile, the Italians settled in Pernambuco, Ytu, and Nova Friburgo in Brazil, and the Portuguese started in Bahía. By their dogged refusal to surrender in the face of widespread enmity, the Jesuits gave invaluable service to the Church, horribly debilitated by their absence since the days of Pombal and Tanucci, hamstrung by an inept patronage system, and under assault by the imported Enlightenment. In 1914 there were some 1,630 Jesuits in Latin America. Impressive as this figure was, it trailed behind the pre-suppression total by 700 to 800, and showed, one hundred and fifty years after Pombal and Aranda had struck the Church, how deep that wound had been.

Across the Pacific the Society returned to the Philippine Islands on April 14, 1859, when ten Spanish priests and brothers landed at Manila. That same year the new arrivals undertook the administration of a city grammar school from which evolved the celebrated university of Ateneo de Manila. This educational enterprise they supplemented with parochial work, in the barrios, and at Culion leper colony, and with a major scientific project in the observatory, which has been a source of vast meteorological aid to the maritime peoples of the Far East. After the American conquest in 1898 Jesuits from the United States came in small numbers until 1921 when the Maryland-New York Province began a major mission effort in the Islands. In 1914 there were 172 Jesuits in the Philippines.

The United States Of all its mission areas in none did the Society grow to such impressive proportions as in the United States, which remained under Propaganda until 1908. From the five Jesuits of the infant republic in 1805, when they became affiliated with the group in White Russia, have issued the 7,442 currently in the American Assistancy. Archbishop John Carroll predicted that the Church, heartened by the religious freedom guaranteed by the American Constitution, would grow and flourish. Jean Bapst, a Swiss Jesuit who came to the United States in 1848, wrote on April 27, 1850, from Old Town, Maine, to a fellow Jesuit in Brussels, Charles Billet: "The United States is the freest country in the world. You in France and Belgium believe yourselves free. But be assured that you possess but the shadow of the liberty which we in America enjoy." Bapst was an acute observer and realized that strong strands of bigotry against the Church ran through American life. "Such is the bright side of American liberty," he told Billet. "Some other time perhaps I shall present the reverse of the medal." He himself acutely felt what "the reverse of the medal" could do when on October 14, 1854, at Ellsworth, Maine, a group of the Know-Nothing party tarred and feathered him.[61] Despite the outbursts of anti-Catholic feeling through the century, freedom generally prevailed, and on this freedom the Jesuit immigrants thrived. And Bapst went on to help in the foundation of Boston College and St. Peter's College, Jersey City.

As if gifted with foreknowledge of this expansion, John Adams wrote apprehensively to Thomas Jefferson on May 6, 1816, "I do not like the Resurrection of the Jesuits. They have a General, now in Russia, in correspondence with the Jesuits in the U.S. who are more numerous than every body knows. Shall we not have swarms of them here? In as many shapes and disguises as ever King of the Gypsies, Bamfie[l]d More Carew himself, assumed: In the shape of Printers, Editors, Writers School Masters, etc. I have lately read Pascalls Letters over again, and

61 Anonymous, "Fr. John Bapst, a Sketch," *WL,* XVII (1888), 366-367.

four volumes of the History of the Jesuits. If ever any Congregation of Men could merit, eternal Perdition on Earth and in Hell, According to these Historians though like Pascal true Catholicks, it is the company of Loiola. Our System however of Religious Liberty must afford them an Assylum. But if they do not put the Purity of our Elections to a severe Tryal, it will be a Wonder." Jefferson agreed with Adams, and on August 1, 1816, confessed that he was unhappy about the restoration of the Society "because it marks a retrograde step from light toward darkness. We shall have our follies without doubt. Some one or more of them will always be afloat. But ours will be the follies of enthusiasm, not of bigotry, not of Jesuitism." Adams returned to this theme four months later and on November 4 again confided his fears to Jefferson. "This Society has been a greater Calamity to Mankind than the French Revolution or Napoleons Despotism or Idiology. It has obstructed the Progress of Reformation and the Improvement of the human Mind in Society much longer and more fatally." [62] Adams and Jefferson, great in their contribution to the American republic but heirs to the intellectual limitations of the Enlightenment, sounded strangely like Pombal, Tanucci, and Aranda.

In 1814, at the time of the Restoration, some twenty Jesuits conducted Georgetown College and cared for small pockets of Catholics through Maryland, Pennsylvania, and New York. Fifty years later, others, from Belgium, had settled in Missouri, Ohio, Illinois, Indiana, and the Oregon Territory; still others, from France, had established themselves in Louisiana, Alabama, Kentucky, and New York; and others, from Italy, had moved into Oregon and California. And in the next decade, 1865-1875, more came from Germany to the string of cities in the North stretching from Buffalo through Cleveland, Toledo, Prairie du Chien, Green Bay, and Mankato; and others, from Italy, entered New Mexico, Colorado, Arizona, and Texas. By 1914 they numbered more than 2,000 from the Atlantic to the Pacific. Many of these pioneers were exiles, expelled from their homelands by anti-Catholic governments. Michele Accolti, who worked in Oregon and California, interpreted these sufferings in Europe as blessings for America. "And as the sea," he wrote, "in receding from the shores of one country proceeds to enrich with its waters the littoral of another, so in like manner the Society, in losing its provinces in Europe through the adversities of the

---

62 Cappon (ed.), *The Adams-Jefferson Letters,* II, 474, 484, 494; T. Hughes, *History,* II (text), 604.

times, will come to pour out its blessings on American soil." [63] Garibaldi, Bismarck, and the other Jesuit enemies were the unwitting sowers of the seed from which sprang the modern Society's most plentiful harvest.

The beginnings of this imposing growth were not assuring. In 1806 the tiny Maryland Mission opened a novitiate at Georgetown and received nine aspirants: seven scholastics, and two brothers. For several years after that, American vocations were few and superiors relied heavily on men from Europe. In 1821 Anthony Kohlmann, the Maryland superior, admitted seven Belgians into the novitiate, recently moved to White Marsh. Poverty at White Marsh was extreme and the diet was often reduced to merely potatoes and water. In 1823, when the time came to pronounce their vows, the Belgians found themselves at the distressing point of being dismissed because of lack of funds to support them. Bishop Louis Guillaume Du Bourg of St. Louis, learning of the crisis, invited them to his diocese. On rafts, Charles Van Quickenborne, the novice master, joined by another priest, three brothers, and seven novices, sailed down the Ohio River and settled at the Franco-Spanish village of St. Ferdinand de Florissant, eighteen miles outside St. Louis. From this handful grew the vice-province of Missouri with forty-five men in 1841, and the Province of Missouri with 194 men in 1863, and 487 in 1900. Back in Maryland the departure of the Belgians left an empty house at White Marsh. In 1834 the novitiate was moved to Frederick, Maryland, where vocations came in a trickle until the 1880's when sixteen to thirty entered each year. In 1833 Roothaan erected the Province of Maryland, the first province in the United States.

Maryland and Missouri became the two important watchtowers from which the Jesuits surveyed the amazing growth of the new republic and developed their strategy. By the millions immigrants poured into the Atlantic port cities. Many were Catholic. Between 1790 and 1850 some 1,071,000 Catholics entered the United States; between 1850 and 1900 five million more, increasing their proportion of the total population from one percent in 1790 to eight percent in 1850, and to almost eighteen percent in 1900.[64] Beyond the Alleghenies the Louisiana Purchase and the spoils of the Mexican War gave the United States vast areas which remained for a long time as a

63 G. J. Garraghan, S.J., *The Jesuits of the Middle United States* (New York, 1938), II, 408.

64 J. T. Ellis, *American Catholicism* (Chicago, 1956), pp. 49, 86.

challenge to the intrepidity of its citizens. Large numbers of Americans, augmented by immigrants who chose not to remain in the East, pushed back the frontier of the expanding nation. These massive shifts of population were a problem of great immediacy for the Church. With a vigor, youthfulness, and audacity that recalled the days of St. Ignatius himself, the Society, in the finest of its traditions, placed itself at the service of the Church and helped resolve this problem in the city and on the prairie, in the mountains and on the river edge, by preaching, founding parishes, writing, and by its favorite instrument, the school.

The Maryland group generally followed the pattern set by their predecessors of a thrust to the northeast, and by 1871 they had settled in the major cities between Boston and Washington. In 1808 the college at Georgetown produced its first offshoot in the New York Literary Institution. That year the discerning and knowledgeable Alsatian, Anthony Kohlmann, accompanied by Benedict Fenwick and four scholastics, opened the Institution on Mulberry Street in New York City. Soon it became a threat to Georgetown's existence. Mounting registration and its location in New York presaged that it would become the key Jesuit institution of the Maryland Mission. Twice Kohlmann moved the school, in 1809 to Broadway, and in 1810 to the present site of St. Patrick's Cathedral. But all its fair promise splintered on the rock of a manpower shortage. Unable to meet the demands of both Georgetown and New York, superiors faced a hard decision. Archbishop Carroll suggested that the New York Institution be closed. Kohlmann objected. His arguments were cogent: experts agreed that New York was the commercial center of America and would soon rival London as a port; the Catholic population of New York was larger than that of any other city; a registration of two to three hundred students was a certainty; it was Ignatian to concentrate in the large cities. He suggested that Georgetown be converted into a novitiate and that the college be transferred to New York. Brzozowski, however, supported Archbishop Carroll, and early in April, 1814, the Jesuits closed the school which of all their foundations on the eastern seaboard gave the greatest hope of wide success.[65] Thirty-three years of wasted opportunity would pass before Kohlmann's vision would be vindicated.

65 F. X. Curran, S.J., *The Return of the Jesuits* (Chicago, 1966), pp. 25-42; J. M. Daley, S.J., *Georgetown University: Origin and Early Years* (Washington, D.C., 1957), pp. 156-158, 174-180.

Georgetown, meanwhile, passed through some discouraging days, partly due to faulty administration, until it received as president, in 1812, the man known as its "Second Founder," Giovanni Grassi. This thirty-seven-year-old native of Bergamo and one of the first novices of St. Joseph Pignatelli brought a bright intelligence and zest to the task of putting order into the curriculum and organization of the college.

In Washington, Kohlmann, after his reversal in New York, opened a seminary for Jesuit scholastics in 1821. Known as the Washington Seminary, it soon received lay students who desired to pursue a classical course. The reception of these non-Jesuit students brought to a head an acute issue touching on the poverty of the Society: the need to ask for tuition in order to defray expenses. But this the *Constitutions* ([398, 478, 495]) forbade. Georgetown, as a boarding school, presented a different situation, since the request for money for the sustenance of the boarders was not a violation of the Jesuit rule. Kohlmann represented energetically to Fortis that the survival of a day-school depended on asking remuneration from the students. But this departure from the ideal of St. Ignatius the general refused to condone, and in 1827 the Seminary closed. The Seminary's vexatious quandary, experienced a little later also at St. Louis, made it clear to Roothaan that the Society faced a serious dilemma: either practically withdraw from the field of education or charge tuition. In 1833 Pope Gregory XVI gave a dispensation from this point in the Society's prescriptions on poverty.[66] In 1848, under the affectionate and engaging Belgian, Jean Blox, the seminary reopened under the new name of Gonzaga College and two years later had an enrollment of 525 students.

At Frederick, in 1829, one of the most unusual of that generation of Jesuits opened a school. John McElroy, an Irishman, who entered the Society as a brother and later studied for the priesthood, was a man of more than ordinary vision, prudence, and patience. In 1841 the Maryland Legislature incorporated his school as St. John's Literary Institute. It then had an enrollment of about one hundred and fifty boys. Whatever promise it had met disaster ten years later when, because of bad relations between the rector, Patrick Mulledy, and some students who openly rebelled, the registration suddenly dropped, and it became exclusively a day-school. But not before it had educated Enoch Louis Lowe, future governor of Maryland, the

66 Garraghan, *The Jesuits*, I, 306-308.

"Fearless Lowe" of the famous war song "Maryland, My Maryland."

One of the first American novices to join the Society after the affiliation of the Maryland group with those in White Russia was Benedict Fenwick. Appointed bishop of Boston in 1825, he invited the Jesuits to work within his jurisdiction, and then persuaded them to assume responsibility for St. James Academy, founded by a secular priest, James Fitton, in Worcester, Massachusetts. This they did in 1843, calling it the College of the Holy Cross with the West Virginian, Patrick Mulledy, as its first rector.

Philadelphia had been one of the earliest American cities associated with the Society ever since Joseph Greaton celebrated Mass there in 1732. A century later the Jesuits returned to their old St. Joseph's Church. Under the leadership of the sunny, mirthful, and expert organizer, Félix Barbelin from Lorraine, they opened St. Joseph's College in 1851 with a registration of about forty boys. Of all St. Joseph's rectors none made a more lasting impression than the Swiss, Burchard Villiger, who through forty years, by his large-mindedness and audacity, built up the faith in Philadelphia. He erected the impressive Church of the Gesù, which was dedicated in 1888, and then moved the college into a spacious building at Stiles Street and Seventeenth Street.

Colleges in other cities were opened during this same period. One year after Barbelin opened St. Joseph's, the tactful and paternal Irishman, John Early, started Loyola College in Baltimore. In 1847 John McElroy, experienced builder from Frederick, Maryland, arrived in Boston, where there was a mounting Irish population, to be pastor of St. Mary's Church. One objective he had was to find land for a college. On Harrison Avenue, a house for Jesuit scholastics was opened in 1860 under the guidance of the cultivated Swiss, Jean Bapst. Three years later superiors converted this scholasticate into a school for externs, and Boston College soon entered into the Catholic and public life of the city.

Meanwhile, in the Midwest, the small group of Belgians who had left Maryland in 1823 faced problems of a vastly different nature. On the frontier they had immediate experience of the unrest, crudeness, and violence which marked that area of the country, and in their correspondence with the general and in their records they penned vivid pictures of those hard and rude days when drunkenness, gambling, fighting, and passion degraded the civic community. Peter Verhaegen, witness of the

483

general inconstancy of the population, wrote to Roothaan in 1831: "We live in the youngest of the United States. Year by year there is a great outpouring of settlers from all sides. All things in the State seem to take on the character of infancy and change and instability." [67] On Charles Van Quickenborne fell the responsibility of guiding the Mission during its uncertain beginnings. Formidable in zeal and fortitude, he nevertheless hampered his work by personal qualities of gloominess, secretiveness, and at times an incapacity to invite confidence. "Hard on himself and hard on others" was the description of a fellow Jesuit.[68] Yet this resolute pioneer carried the mission through some of its darkest hours. In the new cities which were rapidly expanding these Jesuits brought the civilizing force of education, and within twenty-five years after Van Quickenborne's arrival they were conducting colleges in St. Louis, Cincinnati, Grand Coteau, and Bardstown. And within the half-century after that, they were operating others at Milwaukee, Chicago, Mankato, Detroit, Omaha, and St. Marys, Kansas.

In 1818 diocesan priests founded St. Louis Academy. In 1820, three years before the arrival at Florissant of Van Quickenborne and his community, they began to take steps for the transfer of the Academy to the Jesuits. In 1828 Van Quickenborne, who had been receiving boys into the seminary classes at Florissant since 1825, took over the administration of the diocesan college and housed it on a new campus at Washington Avenue and Ninth Street. There classes opened in November, 1829. Peter Verhaegen was the rector. He brought to his assignment a genial spirit and a practical sense of affairs which carried the institution through many arduous days.[69] In 1840, in Cincinnati, the Missouri Jesuits accepted from Bishop John Purcell a school which he had started earlier and named it St. Xavier College. In 1848, two years after the departure of their French brethren, they undertook two schools in Kentucky, St. Joseph's in Bardstown and St. Aloysius in Louisville. Despite the courage and energy of Johann Emig, a direct man from Hesse-Darmstadt, who left a deep impression at Louisville, Roothaan felt that the Missouri Vice-province was over-expanding. To Bishop Martin J. Spalding of Louisville the general wrote with candor. "I say, Bishop, that the College was started in too great a hurry. And,

---

67 Ibid., 300.
68 Ibid., 384-385.
69 Ibid., 282-294; G. E. Ganss, S.J., *The Jesuit Educational Tradition and Saint Louis University* (St. Louis, 1969), pp. 1, 34-36.

in truth, the great plague of the Society in your part of the world is this, that we undertake too many things and do not leave time for the training of subjects, as it is necessary to do. As a result, the latter cannot go through their studies properly and as a matter of fact many find themselves ruined in this regard. . . . I understand quite well how urgent are the needs; but if things go on there at this pace, I cannot help entertaining very great fears for the future of that portion of the Society where the harvest is gathered before it is ripe and where one must look for grass instead of grain. This is my chief solicitude and I do not fail to preach on this subject continually in my letters." [70] Roothaan's concern was well-grounded, and the Missouri Jesuits, by a maneuver of shortening their educational lines, withdrew from Louisville in 1858 and from Bardstown ten years later.

Not long after these reverses, however, the Society of the Midwest moved in other directions and opened some of its more enduring schools: St. Ignatius, now Loyola University, in Chicago in 1870; Detroit in 1877; Creighton, Omaha, in 1878; Marquette, Milwaukee, in 1881. These colleges became colonies of order, culture, and religion amid the restive and unsettled conditions of a people engaged in the mammoth task of creating new American cities.

In three other ways these European Jesuits played an important role on the frontier: in the erection of parishes among the settlers; in conducting parish missions for the immigrants; in bringing the faith to the Indians.

Van Quickenborne started the parochial work by taking charge, in 1823, of St. Ferdinand's parish in Florissant. That same year the Jesuits moved into four other parishes. Through their correspondence run the names of the freshly hewn towns in Missouri, Iowa, Illinois, and Wisconsin, where they labored: Council Bluffs, Sugar Creek, Washington, Jefferson City, Dubuque, Quincy, Mill Seat, Palmyra. Of all the parochial organizers the greatest was the Dutchman Arnold Damen, powerful in body and large in vision, who in 1857 went to Chicago and with the thousands of immigrants built up the vibrant and humming parish of the Holy Family.[71]

Damen's name became a household word not only in Chicago but also through the rest of the Midwest because of his forceful and effective manner of conducting parish missions.

70 Garraghan, *The Jesuits*, III, 273-274.
71 Ibid., 396-416.

Joined by a fellow Dutchman, the striking teacher of rhetoric, Cornelius Smarius, he kept the faith alive in the hearts of thousands who had left their familiar and ancient religious environment in Europe. The two preachers moved even to the eastern seaboard where in 1863 they gave a most fruitful mission at the church of St. Francis Xavier in New York, during which twenty-two priests heard confessions and seventy persons became converts.[72] As notable as the pair from Holland was the Austrian, Franz Xaver Weninger, who came to the United States in 1848 and preached for nearly forty years to the German-speaking people, from Buffalo westward and into the Mississippi valley.

Presence on the frontier inevitably meant awareness of the Indians. Van Quickenborne, even while in Maryland, felt a deep desire to work among the natives, and from Florissant he began to minister to the Osage tribe. In 1835 he contacted the Kickapoo at the confluence of the Missouri River and Salt Creek; in 1838 Verhaegen arrived among the Potawatomi at Council Bluffs. So began the apostolate among the redmen of the West in which the Society is still engaged.

For his charity and understanding of these peoples, dismayed over the conquest of their lands by the advancing white man, no one gained the respect of the Indians as did Peter De Smet, one of the Belgian novices who had traveled from Maryland to Missouri in 1823. His is one of the most honorable names in the story of America's tortured dealings with the red man. On March 27, 1840, the diarist of St. Louis University wrote: "The day eagerly desired of the Indians that dwell beyond the Rocky Mountain has dawned at last! For today Rev. Father De Smet departed to carry to them the light of faith and announce to them the way of salvation. . . ." The Flatheads, settled between the Rocky Mountains and the Pacific, had incorporated into their tribe two Iroquois who had been instructed by priests of the suppressed Society. These Iroquois spoke affectionately of their old teachers and inspired a desire for the Blackrobes among the Flatheads, who then sent to St. Louis for a priest. De Smet's journey was the answer. For many years this practical, energetic, enterprising man led the way in starting mission stations deep in the Oregon Territory. His letters, vivid in detail, bring to life once more the exciting years of the Wild West. From his pen came sharply accurate pictures of the Missouri River with its twists and turns and turbulent waters, the buffalo, antelope, polecat, snakes of the prairie, the rugged splendor of

72 Ibid., II, 89.

the Rockies. No more graphic memory of the relationship between the red men and the United States government remains than that of the redoubtable Belgian, in 1868, riding alone, save for a small escort of friendly Sioux and his interpreter, along the Yellowstone River into the camp of 5,000 Sioux intent on war against the white man, and by the power of his persuasion and the integrity of his character inducing Sitting Bull to order his braves to bury their hatchets. One of De Smet's Jesuit companions, Nicolas Point, a close and precise observer, recorded what he saw in his diary and in his paintings, in which he showed with vivid color and rich detail various phases of Indian life, on the hunt, at home, at play, at prayer.[73] Other Jesuits followed De Smet and Point, and soon the fortunes of tribes like the Flatheads, the Blackfeet, the Coeur d'Alènes, the Winnebagos, the Yakimas, the Nez Percés entered into the narrative of the Society's annals.

These records are an important part of the larger history of the United States and the development of the Old Oregon country. They register the penetration of civilization, peace, and religion, with the Jesuits as spearheads, into a vast area furrowed by barbarism, war, and superstition. The Blackrobes, in the tradition of the pre-suppression Society, envisaged a series of stable Indian communities. Learning from the experience of the Hudson's Bay Company, they planned, for purposes of mutual support and the warding off of a sense of isolation, various ways to keep open the avenues of communication through the vast plains and in the rugged mountains. They met many obstacles, and the Indians themselves were among the more serious. Nation differed from nation, but a widespread ignorance, volatility, and stubborn resistance to the exacting moral teaching of Christianity frustrated the missionaries.

The Jesuits, however, did not capitulate. Blackrobe surveyors and farmers measured tracts of land, cultivated and fenced them in; Blackrobe architects and artisans raised barns, mills, shops, and chapels; Blackrobe craftsmen produced bricks, chisels, soap, and grindstones; Blackrobe husbandmen raised cattle, pigs, and poultry; Blackrobe doctors vaccinated against smallpox and cholera; Blackrobe musicians taught the clarinet, flute,

---

73 Ibid., 252; III, 78-79. Joseph P. Donnelly, S.J., has published an English translation of Point's diary and an attractive set of reproductions, in color, of his paintings in *Wilderness Kingdom. Indian Life in the Rocky Mountains: 1840-1847. The Journals and Paintings of Nicolas Point, S.J.* (New York, 1967).

piccolo and accordion, and changed Indian songs into sacred chant.[74]

The effort was gallant but the Jesuits never realized their dream of an Oregon Paraguay, for between 1840 and 1880 most tribes continued to roam. Nevertheless, the fixed and stable community did attain a certain status as the center to which the Indian could go and from which the priest went out on his wide-ranging expeditions. Discouraged as the Jesuits confessed themselves to be, they and their achievements received warm tribute from explorers, traders, and soldiers as a beautiful and inspiring page in an otherwise grim story.

De Smet entered the Oregon Territory not only from the East but also from the Pacific side. As great a beggar for men and money in Europe as he was a frontiersman in America, — he crossed the Atlantic at least sixteen times — he returned from Europe in 1844 with five Jesuits, including the three Italians, Michele Accolti, Giovanni Nobili, and Antonio Ravalli, and six Sisters of Notre Dame de Namur. They made the long ocean journey across the Atlantic, around Cape Horn, and northward on the Pacific. In early August they dropped anchor in the mouth of the Columbia River. The new arrivals were in Oregon only four years when their attention was drawn southward toward California. There, in 1848, gold had been discovered. Settlers in Oregon picked up stakes and joined the rush. Accolti and Nobili followed and on December 8, 1849, put into San Francisco Bay. Accolti, an exuberant, vivacious, friendly man, construed the situation well: "Gold, gold, gold, it's the watchword of the day . . . Old and young, women and children, layfolk and ecclesiastics, all have on their lips only the word *gold.*" And about San Francisco, "whether it ought to be called Madhouse or Babylon I am at a loss to determine . . ."[75] To this agitated town the two priests tried to bring the Gospel by their preaching. In 1851, at the urgent invitation of the Dominican Bishop, José Allemany, Nobili with amazing courage and a minimum of resources took over the Santa Clara Mission, originally one of the Franciscan chain, in order to start a school there.

Other Italians followed, and in 1854 Beckx placed both Oregon, known as the Rocky Mountain Mission, and California under the Province of Turin. Some of these men lived in the

74 R. I. Burns, S.J., *The Jesuits and the Indian Wars of the Northwest* (New Haven, 1966), pp. 48-60.
75 Garraghan, *The Jesuits*, II, 392-393.

saddle, roving among the settlers and the Indians. Giuseppe Giorda and Luigi Folchi became familiar figures far and wide through the Northwest because of their missionary excursions. A man of vision, who saw in the construction of the Northern Pacific Railroad the future importance of Spokane, Giuseppe Cataldo, obtained property near the Spokane River for a school. In 1887 Gonzaga College opened. Four years later, in 1891, in Seattle, Victor Garrand, a Frenchman, started the school of the Immaculate Conception which, in 1898, changed its name to Seattle College. In San Francisco, in 1858, Antonio Mareschi opened St. Ignatius College, now the University of San Francisco. In 1911 the Society accepted St. Vincent's College in Los Angeles from the Vincentians and called it Loyola College. American youths joined these Italian pioneers in increasing numbers, and in 1909 Wernz as general formed from Oregon and California the Province of California with 378 men.

Another immense front in the country's expansion was in the Southwest, in a territory where the Church had been present since the era of the Spanish conquistadores. Other Italian Jesuits, Neapolitans, moved into New Mexico, Arizona, Colorado, and Texas. In 1866 Bishop Jean Lamy, the hero of Willa Cather's *Death Comes for the Archbishop*, spoke to Beckx in Rome and asked for help. The general assigned this project to the Naples Province. Donato Gasparri, Rafaello Bianchi, and two brothers, who were joined in the United States by Livio Vigilante, recently at Holy Cross College, made up the first expedition. They traveled with the bishop, and both Vigilante and Gasparri recorded their recollections of the dangers, excitement, and wonder of travel along the Santa Fe trail, replete with details about fording rivers, finding corpses and burned ruins left by Indians, and crossing the sandy mesas of the Southwest. On August 15, 1867, they arrived at Santa Fe.[76] Lamy assigned them to parish work in Bernalillo. A year later they transferred to Albuquerque. Gasparri was the soul of the mission and the inspirer of its wide development. Faced by the increasing Protestant population brought in by the new railroad, he founded in 1873 a press, *Revista Católica*, which provided valuable books of instruction and devotion for the faithful. Twice these Italians founded a college, in 1878 at Las Vegas, New Mexico, and in 1884 at Morrison, Colorado, but in each instance they were forced to close it. In 1887 they made another attempt, this

76 Sister Lilliana Owens, *Jesuit Beginnings in New Mexico* (El Paso, 1950), pp. 85-95, 96, 108.

time at Denver, where they opened Sacred Heart College. This venture endured, and in 1921 assumed the name of Regis College. In 1914 the New Mexico-Colorado Mission numbered ninety-three men. In 1919 Ledochowski as general divided the Mission between the Missouri and New Orleans Provinces.

New Orleans had its memories of the French Jesuits of the pre-suppression Society. In that earlier period the missionaries had penetrated the interior of the continent through the mouth of the Mississippi in the south and by the thread of the St. Lawrence in the north. This pattern they repeated in the nineteenth century. On February 7, 1831, one of the most enterprising pioneers, Pierre Chazelle, arrived at New Orleans. For fourteen years Chazelle was to labor in Louisiana, Kentucky, Montreal, Toronto, and Wisconsin, and help lay the foundations of four future Jesuit provinces.[77] With him on his arrival at New Orleans were two priests and a brother. Their destination was Kentucky to which they were invited by Benedict Joseph Flaget, Bishop of Bardstown. Léon de Neckère, the bishop of New Orleans, naturally tried to keep the Jesuits in his own understaffed diocese. Chazelle compromised, and when he started for Kentucky in April, 1831, he left two of his companions in Louisiana. Six years later, in 1837, with Bishop Antoine Blanc, De Neckère's successor, eight more Jesuits arrived from France. The following year they opened St. Charles College at Grand Coteau, Louisiana, under the supervision of Nicolas Point. In 1847, led by François de Sales Gautrelet, brother of François Xavier Gautrelet, the founder of the Apostolate of Prayer in France, they assumed control of Spring Hill College at Mobile, Alabama, an institution previously in the care of the Eudist Fathers.

It was in the Northeast however that the French Jesuits found their most promising opportunity. Kentucky became the stepping-stone to New York City. In 1832 Chazelle accepted from William Byrne, a secular priest, St. Mary's Seminary, twenty miles from remote and sleepy Bardstown, and converted it into a Jesuit school. Other Jesuits from France followed and in 1842 opened St. Ignatius Literary Institution in Louisville. Soon after this, Bishop John Hughes of New York sent them an invitation which opened before them a completely new and enticing horizon. He asked them to take charge of St. John's College, which he had founded in the Fordham area above New York City. They accepted. In 1846 they closed their two schools in Ken-

---

77 Curran, *The Return,* pp. 81-84, 96-97.

tucky and went to Fordham where Auguste Thébaud became the first Jesuit president.[78]

The move to New York, thirty-three years after Anthony Kohlmann closed his New York Literary Institution, gave the Society its most important center on the Atlantic seaboard from which to expand. And expansion started almost immediately. In 1847, the year after the arrival at Fordham, John Larkin, an Englishman and member of this French mission, and, in the judgment of a contemporary, an exquisitely urbane gentleman whose "refined taste, self-possession, composure" were excelled only by those of James Russell Lowell, started another school in downtown New York near Elizabeth and Walker Streets.[79] By 1850 the site of the school was shifted to West 16th Street where, under the patronage of St. Francis Xavier, it quickly became the largest Jesuit institution on the Atlantic Coast. From the Frenchmen in New York and those in Canada Beckx formed, in 1869, the New York-Canada Mission. One of the last achievements of this Mission while Jean Bapst was superior was the establishment of St. Peter's College in Jersey City, chartered in 1872 with Victor Beaudevin as rector and opened in 1878. The following year the general divided the Mission, attaching New York to the Maryland Province and Canada to the English Province. The Maryland-New York Province broadened the scope of its educational apostolate by inaugurating in quick succession three new schools, Loyola in New York City, in 1900; Brooklyn Preparatory in 1908; and Regis, New York City, in 1914, the last being the only American Jesuit high school which is endowed and fulfills the Ignatian ideal of offering a free education.

Germans constituted a large part of the immigrants who settled in a large belt that stretched from Buffalo westward under the Great Lakes and into the Mississippi valley. To care for their former countrymen the German Province created the Buffalo Mission in 1869. From that time until the Mission was divided thirty-eight years later, in 1907, between the Maryland-New York and Missouri Provinces, the German Jesuits, many exiles because of Bismarck's Kulturkampf, built a strong and durable unit of the American Church. In less than thirty years they started five colleges, Canisius in Buffalo in 1870, St. Ignatius in Mankato, Minnesota, in 1876; Sacred Heart (now

78 Ibid., 98-102; R. I. Gannon, S.J., *Up to the Present. The Story of Fordham* (New York, 1967), pp. 33-38.

79 Gannon, *Up to the Present*, pp. 46-47.

Campion) at Prairie du Chien, Wisconsin, in 1880; St. Ignatius (now John Carroll University) in Cleveland in 1886; and St. John Berchmans in Toledo in 1898.

The Society's organization in America during the second decade of the twentieth century had moved far from the five men of the Maryland Mission of 1805. Four Provinces and the New Mexico-Colorado Mission, with over 2,000 members, reached from the Atlantic to the Pacific. In tribute to the maturity of the American Society, the general assigned them foreign missions in Alaska, British Honduras, and Jamaica, and in 1909 approved the bold venture of launching the weekly *America,* which under a series of talented editors has become one of the most alert, perceptive, and intelligent organs of the Catholic press in the English-speaking world.

The most evident symbol of the Jesuits' service to the Church in the United States has been the school. This service demanded self-sacrifice and intrepidity of heroic proportions, because it was with the utmost scarcity of money and physical resources that the presidents and their staffs started and kept these institutions running. The wealthy American Catholic was rare. Nicolas Point was able to build St. Charles College, Grand Coteau, largely because of a gift of 2,000 bricks by the Religious of the Sacred Heart. Burchard Villiger, rector of St. Joseph's College, Philadelphia, recalled in his diary "all these subscriptions, concerts, lectures, fairs, and excursions" in order to erect a building.[80] Victor Garrand told how the Irish and Germans of Seattle constructed, under his supervision, a combination church and school, each nationality trying to outdo the other. "The Irish want to convince me," he noted, "that their devotion is superior to that of the Germans, and these latter pretend to be better than the Irish." [81] The account books of the treasurers tell, in their own impersonal way, an inspiring story of the courage and dedication of the Jesuit educators of the nineteenth century.

If poverty evoked a magnificent resiliency in these men, the evolving structure of American education brought out a great capacity for adaptation to the conditions peculiar to the rapidly expanding republic. Guided by the American developments, they took the European Jesuit college which they knew, and from it they made the American Jesuit high school and the

---

80 F. X. Talbot, S.J., *Jesuit Education in Philadelphia, Saint Joseph's College, 1851-1926* (Philadelphia, 1927), p. 79.

81 W. N. Bischoff, S.J., *The Jesuits in Old Oregon, 1840-1940* (Caldwell, Idaho, 1945), p. 195.

American Jesuit college. The European organism with which they started, designed for boys about nine to seventeen years of age, embraced the "lower studies" of the *Ratio studiorum,* which were basically the three years of Latin grammar, the year of "humanities," and the year of "rhetoric." A lineal descendent of the original Jesuit *collège* (France), *colegio* (Spain), *Kolleg* (Germany), and *collegio* (Italy), it shared its ancestry with the non-Jesuit secondary schools, such as the *lycée* and the *gymnasium,* which too evolved from the pre-1773 Jesuit system. In the American colonies schools like Harvard, William and Mary, and Yale had a strikingly similar design in their origins.

This fundamentally simple structure, however, could not survive within the educational pattern that developed in the United States during the nineteenth century. The span of elementary school lengthened to eight years; educators designed a unit called the high school, usually for students from fourteen to eighteen years of age, and then the college of four years of literary, scientific, and philosophical studies that led to the Bachelor of Arts degree. This organization the Jesuits adopted. They took the initial step when they added philosophy to "rhetoric," or the final year of the "lower studies." Eventually they united "grammar" into a high school of four years. "Humanities" and "rhetoric" and scholastic philosophy they organized into the four-year college which matched that of their American associates. By 1910 they had generally established this division. By the creation of the American Jesuit high school and the American Jesuit college, they brought a fresh contribution to the Society's educational tradition.

During this period of adaptation certain differences of judgment arose between the Jesuits of the East and those of the Midwest, and a little later those of the West. These differences focused mainly on the position of the Latin and Greek languages in the curriculum. New York and St. Louis, 1,000 miles apart— the same as between Vilna and Paris — differed socially, economically, and culturally. Along the Atlantic seaboard, where society with its relatively long established cities was more stable, and where an intellectual tradition symbolized by Harvard, William and Mary, Yale, and King's College (Columbia) had taken root, and where the ties to Europe were more immediate, the Jesuit high schools and colleges preserved with ease and naturalness the classical curriculum. In the Midwest the Jesuit pioneers labored in a strikingly dissimilar milieu. During the era of the great western frontier, in the Society's tradition of adaptability, they endeavored to meet the educational need of

493

that vast area. What Latin meant at Messina, or Paris, or Vienna in the sixteenth century could never have the same urgency in the American Midwest of the nineteenth century. Consequently, at an early date, the school at St. Louis offered, besides the classical subjects, courses in "mercantile education" with a distinct emphasis on mathematics. Peter Kenney, the Irish visitor of the Missouri Mission during 1831-1832, noted his unfavorable impressions of the lack of enthusiasm for the classical languages. Another Jesuit, speaking of the *Ratio studiorum*, made the observation, "It is a document rarely met with in our houses." The faculty at St. Louis could not overcome the general apathy for the Latin and Greek languages. Roothaan took a dismal view of the school's direction, but did not seem to realize that St. Louis was not another Rouen, or Augsburg, or Naples. Peter Verhaegen tried to explain that, with the constant shifting of families the town could enjoy no stability, and that, things in general "are all new and must be molded into shape. The study of languages, if you except English and French, has no great attraction for the young." [82] Toward the close of the century, in cogently argued articles, members of the Maryland-New York and Missouri Provinces engaged each other on the question of keeping Greek as a requisite for the academic diploma. Strong as these disagreements were, they nevertheless were rooted in an identical aspiration, that of achieving Ignatian flexibility and alertness to local needs, in the one instance along the northeastern Atlantic seaboard, in the other west of the Appalachian Mountains.

Nothing sharpened Jesuit awareness of American procedures and attitudes in education more than certain new institutions which gradually achieved a pervasive influence over the colleges and high schools, the standardizing or accrediting agencies. These forced the Jesuits to realize that they must cooperate with the other educators of the nation if they would not be left isolated outside the mainstream of American life, and that there was much which they could learn from others. In 1896 J. Havens Richards, president of Georgetown, wrote that, "we must be on the alert to adjust our colleges to the altered circumstances of the times. We must be prepared to modify our schedules." The general, Wernz, authorized this flexible approach when he admitted that the pre-suppression program in Jesuit schools was a thing of the past. The great variety of subject-matter, he re-

82 Garraghan, *The Jesuits,* I, 324-325; III, 116-117; Ganss, *The Jesuit Educational Tradition,* pp. 20, 25-29, 31-38.

alized, had broken the old uniformity, but he called on the modern Jesuits to imitate the first members of the Society in adopting the best methods of the age. Before 1917 few Jesuit high schools had requested recognition by the standardizing agencies. But that year all those of the Missouri Province were directed by superiors to make application.[83]

In many ways, therefore, as they moved into the early decades of the twentieth century, the Jesuit high schools and colleges reflected both their Renaissance origins and the spirit of American life. The men who built the bridge between sixteenth century Europe and nineteenth century America were in the main Europeans. With but three exceptions, Holy Cross' Patrick Mulledy, Marquette's Joseph Rigge, and Rockhurst's Michael Dowling, the first rector of every Jesuit college started before 1900 was a foreigner. Even at John Carroll's Georgetown the first to hold the office of president was an Englishman, Robert Plunkett. The American Jesuit of today is reaping the harvest of those dogged men who for several decades crossed the Atlantic in the perennial missionary tradition of the Church. Up to 1870 all the superiors of the Missouri Mission and Vice-province, save for the Irishman, William Stack Murphy, were Belgians. Like the nation itself, the Society's organizational units in the States became melting pots for various nationalities. In 1846 the Missouri Vice-province had forty-five Irishmen (all but five were brothers), forty-two Belgians, sixteen Dutchmen, sixteen Americans, thirteen Germans, eleven Italians, nine Frenchmen, and two Spaniards.[84]

The individual history of each of the Jesuit institutions was shaped by no common form. Some few, like St. Marys, Kansas, and St. Charles, Grand Coteau, Louisiana, converted into houses of study for Jesuit scholastics; others, like Xavier in New York, Gonzaga in Washington, D.C., and Campion at Prairie du Chien, closed their collegiate department and continued as high schools; others, like St. John's, Toledo, and St. Joseph's, Bardstown, were transferred to the diocesan clergy; and a few, like St. Ignatius', Mankato, and Guadalupe in Seguin, Texas, failed to develop as Jesuit schools. In Kentucky, despite three ventures, the Society never struck permanent roots. All these schools, their individual fortunes notwithstanding, had a common trait. They bore witness to the fact that the Society, in the cities, on the frontier, among the immigrants, had entered, with

---

83 McGucken, *The Jesuits,* pp. 140-145.
84 Garraghan, *The Jesuits,* I, 506.

others, into the mighty task of keeping the Church abreast of the advancing young nation.

To the north of the United States, Jean de Brébeuf, Isaac Jogues, Noël Chabanel, and the other heroes of the seventeenth and eighteenth centuries had returned in 1842 to the land of the St. Lawrence in the persons of the French Jesuits. The leader of the party of six priests and three brothers was Pierre Chazelle. Three years earlier Chazelle had traveled from Kentucky to Montreal to conduct a retreat for eighty-three priests. On all sides he received requests for the return of the Blackrobes. Bishop Ignace Bourget, coadjutor of Montreal, played on the inspiring memories of the past in his *Appeal to the Jesuits* (1841) which he sent to Roothaan. The general could not refuse. And Chazelle's group of 1842 was the answer. For three years Chazelle created new mission posts in areas familiar to the authors of the old *Jesuit Relations*. On his way to Sault Sainte Marie he took sick, and on September 4, 1848, died at Green Bay in Wisconsin. He had lived as a true follower of Brébeuf, Ménard, Le Jeune, and Allouez in his desire to extend the Church's presence in the wilds of Canada. More and more Jesuits took up the work Chazelle had started, and in 1907 Wernz set up the Canadian province, which by 1914 numbered almost 400 men.[85]

In other areas too throughout the world the Society became established. In 1914 there were 217 Jesuits in Armenia and Syria, 102 in Australia, 78 in Indonesia, 22 in Egypt, 16 in the Greek islands. Officially listed as missionaries were the 42 in Albania and the 81 in Denmark and Sweden.

Conclusion   Between the suppression and the restoration of the Society two mighty revolutions had occurred, the American and the French. These upheavals gave new direction to the world. The Society's experience, as it moved out of the twilight of an age with which it was familiar and into the dawn of the modern day, eludes any single and simple formula. In some nations, especially in Europe and Latin America, it suffered terribly at the hands of secularist doctrinaires who, in the name of a kind of totalitarian democracy, aimed to get control of religion and chain it to their own purposes. In other nations, notably the United States where, in a pluralistic society, there developed a strong consensus for the separation of church and state, it prospered in the fresh air of religious freedom.

85 Curran, *The Return*, pp. 89-97.

In the former class the Society encountered nations traditionally one in their Catholicity, now divided in two, one part loyal to the ancient faith, the other committed to the laical proposition. There were two Frances, two Italies, two Spains.[86] Catholics, generally, in preserving their ties with the faith of their fathers, also looked back with nostalgia to the old regime, and so lost the feel for the pulse of the times and the sense of change in history. Many Jesuits identified themselves with this mentality. There is a touch of irony in the wistful looking back of these men toward a royal kind of government, which only shortly before had done them to death. But other Jesuits thought differently. Having found the American democratic tradition, they entered vigorously into the enormous constructive enterprise of building a free Church within the expanding American Republic.

Education and the missions regained their previous positions as major facets of the apostolate, but the changed structure of the world forced the Society to adopt altered modes of action. No longer could the schools give a free education; no longer could they exert the wide range of cultural and religious influence of earlier centuries. Unlike the pre-1773 school, founded by an individual or a civic community, the post-1814 Jesuit school, most frequently without a financial sponsor because of the impoverished state of the aristocracy, or the neutral or even hostile policy of a government, established its fiscal bases in the tuition exacted of the students. No longer part of a social fabric which guaranteed its permanence, it was forced to receive from the Holy See a dispensation from the *Constitutions* and require compensation of its pupils. And, again unlike the pre-1773 school, that of the restored Society never regained its former paramount position in the cultural life of a number of nations when the Society had been among the main depositories of learning in Europe. Schools under state auspices increased in unprecedented numbers. And within the Church other religious communities, as well as the diocesan clergy, took up the task of education.

On the foreign missions, Christian charity and zeal, comparable to the high levels attained by earlier men, were poured out and lavished on lands far distant from Europe. The men of the new Society proved to be true sons of St. Francis Xavier. But the old frameworks were altered, and even dismantled. The

86 J. C. Murray, "Leo XIII on Church and State," *Theological Studies*, XIV (1953), 9-10.

last page in the history of the two Royal Patronages had been turned. In Latin America older skirmishes with avaricious royal governors or slave traders gave way to philosophical encounters, often within a political context, with the imported ideas of the French Enlightenment. In the United States a religiously neutral government provided a freedom to the Church never experienced under the great Catholic monarchies. In the Far East two great empires, China and Japan, once more opened their long-closed gates to the Gospel. In many areas the Catholic missionary found a competitor in a Protestant apostle. No earlier century ever demanded such drastic adjustment.

To complicate this adjustment an old hazard reappeared. Under a new but equally invidious form arose the familiar danger of Christianity being identified with Europe and European political power or culture. The Society's expansion into mission lands coincided with the vast colonial splurge which the European nations made in Asia and Africa. Soldiers, traders, administrators left home in droves in the Europeanization of the rest of the world. Priests and religious went too, and from this common movement resulted the sorry entanglement of interests and objectives. Western rule and the Church were two birds in parallel flight. Under these circumstances some mission areas, especially where Catholic powers were the colonizers — under British Protestant rule the Church could more readily disassociate herself from white rule — became seed beds of future trouble, because, when nationally conscious eyes began to look with aversion on the European presence, the Church too fell within that field of vision.

Chapter 8

THE TWENTIETH CENTURY

A FEW LINES OF HORACE INTIMATE the character and shape which this chapter must take. Asinius Pollio had started to write an account of the then quite recent turbulent events in the Roman Republic. Horace warned Pollio: "You are treating a subject full of perilous risk; you are walking into fires that lie beneath deceptive ashes." [1] Some of the more important issues which engaged the Society through the first six decades of the twentieth century remain burning coals. As live questions they are still before the forum and elude a clearly defined and balanced historical perspective. Only time will disclose the soundness or unwisdom of policies, the impact of international and national events, the success or failure of enterprises and experiments. This chapter can therefore be only brief and schematic.

During the fifty years, 1914-1964, two generals governed the *The Generals* Society. Wlodimir Ledochowski, forty-nine-year-old Pole, born in Loosdorf under Austrian rule, was elected on February 11, 1915, by the Twenty-sixth General Congregation and held office for twenty-seven years until his death on December 14, 1942. His rule began during World War I and terminated during World War II. During this period he convened two general congregations, the Twenty-seventh in 1923 to adapt the Society's *Constitutions* to the new Code of Canon Law, and the Twenty-eighth in 1938 to obtain a vicar to assist him in governing the order. Since his death occurred during war, a general congregation could not assemble until 1946 when, on September 15, John Baptist Janssens, a fifty-seven-year-old Belgian, was elected. In 1957 Janssens, whose health gradually worsened in

---

1 Periculosae plenum opus aleae
  Tractas et incedis per ignes
  Suppositos cineri doloso (*Odes*, Book II, Ode 1).

his closing years, convened a general congregation which provided him with the help of a vicar, John L. Swain, a Canadian. After eighteen years in office Janssens died on October 5, 1964.

Through these fifty years the Society's growth was steady. The 16,894 men of 1914 became 35,788 in 1964. But this growth was not universal throughout the order. In France and Italy numbers steadily declined while in the United States they mounted sharply. In 1964 there were more American Jesuits, over 8,000, than Germans, French, Italians, Austrians, Belgians, and Dutch combined. But then a reverse trend, which was experienced also by most other religious groups, set in. In 1965 the American Jesuits numbered 8,469; in 1966, 8,393, a drop of seventy-six. In the same two years the experience of the Society as a whole mirrored that of the Americans. In 1965 the Society throughout the world numbered 36,038; the next year, 35,929, a loss of one hundred and nine.

Both generals witnessed historical events of awesome proportions, which convulsed the world and shook the structure of the Society. With the rest of the continent the European provinces suffered deep wounds during the two World Wars and the decades after each. In 1932 the Republic of Spain abruptly cut the thread of the Society's apostolate there and sent 2,640 men into exile. During and after World War II the Russian conquest of the Baltic states and domination of Central Europe practically crippled — and in some instances erased — ten of the Society's provinces, vice-provinces, and missions. Outside Europe the Communist sweep in China pulled down the structure erected by a century of toil. In Africa and Asia new nations, taking control of education, created delicate problems for the missionaries, who had relied so considerably on the school as a key instrument in their apostolate. In some of these newly created countries, a full-blown nationalism created an atmosphere of hostility to the foreigners.

Both generals, perceptive and realistic men, squarely faced the alterations brought into human society by the rapid advances of science, industry, and technology. In their directives they insisted that the Society come to grips with these mundane problems so pregnant with spiritual and moral implications. Janssens expressed himself with particular clarity about the Society's objectives in the modern world in June, 1947, when he addressed a letter to his fellow religious. In his forthright and pointed style, which placed some of his letters among the best issued by the generals since St. Ignatius, he expounded the rules which should guide the Society's choice of ministries in the present day. Overwhelmed by requests for help since the close of World War II, the general pointed out that all could not be accepted and that a choice had to be made. Echoing St. Ignatius, he recalled that the supreme norm must ever be "catholic and universal" and where the greater service can be given the Church.

Ledochowski and Janssens did not only summon the members of the Society to laborious work and energetic activity. In a strong tradition, rooted in the convictions of St. Ignatius and preserved through the centuries in the letters of the generals and the writings of the Society's spiritual masters, they kept before the modern Jesuit his fundamental obligation to be a man of deep prayer and intimate union with God.

The response of the Jesuits to the desires of their superiors that they confront the modern challenges was generous and intelligent, and long before Pope John XXIII "opened the windows," they had built up an immense deposit of research and reflection which expressed the spirit of *aggiornamento* and helped to create the theological and spiritual climate which enabled Vatican Council II to carry out its exacting responsibilities. With dedication they joined others in the arduous task of vitalizing the sacred sciences and enabling the Church to speak with freshness and in an idiom comprehensible to modern man. For example, Émile Mersch, Sebastian Tromp, and Henri de Lubac explored deeply the inner life of the Church, the meaning of the mystical body of Christ, the balance between the visible and invisible aspects of the Church's nature. These Jesuits were among the large number of theologians, from the religious orders and secular clergy, whose ideas were mirrored in some of the more significant ecclesial documents of modern times such as the encyclical *Mystici corporis* of Pope Pius XII and the Dogmatic Constitution on the Church, *Lumen gentium,* of Vatican Council II.

A fresh school of philosophy, known as Transcendental Thomism, with a sensitivity for the modern emphasis on evolution and personalism, began to rethink the heritage of the Angelic Doctor. The Belgian, Joseph Maréchal, who drew much inspiration from two other Jesuit thinkers, Pierre Rousselot and Pierre Scheuer, founded this movement about forty years ago. Two of the more influential of the Society's scholars of the present day, Bernard Lonergan and Karl Rahner, whose profundity as theologians flows in large measure from their power as philosophers, have shaped much of their thought within the school of Transcendental Thomism. Rahner, also a profound student of existentialism, has incorporated some of its principles within the structure of his theological reflection. And of Lonergan's *Insight* the learned Benedictine bishop, B. Christopher Butler, observed that it could possibly form a bridge between Christian and non-Christian thinkers.[2]

Patristic, liturgical, hagiographic, and scriptural studies received further depth and amplitude from the contributions of Jesuit scholars. Jean Daniélou and Claude Mondésert continued the familiar Jesuit penchant for the Fathers of the Church. Joseph Jungmann with his sure mastery of the sources placed the liturgical movement, so much a Benedictine creation, in clear historical perspective and carefully noted its changes and modulations through the centuries. No one more than Hugo Rahner, honored in 1961 on his sixtieth birthday with a *Festschrift* which listed 720 titles of his published books, articles, and reviews, grasped the significance of mysticism in St. Ignatius' life and thus gave a new and profound dimension to modern Ignatian studies. Of Georg Schurhammer, octogenarian expert on St. Francis Xavier and author through sixty years of 343 books, articles, monographs, and reviews, Charles R. Boxer, distinguished historian at King's College, London, wrote: "Few living scholars can look back on so productive a life, and one, moreover, in which quality has never been sacrificed to quantity. His name is revered by students of mission history and Orientalists from the Black Forest to Japan. . . ."[3] The Magna Carta of the new scriptural age, the encyclical *Divino afflante Spiritu,* issued by Pope Pius XII in 1943, both reflected Jesuit thought and opened the way for an impressive body of Jesuit scholars in the sacred writings.

The explosive influence of scientific studies, the development of nuclear energy, and the exploration of outer space have created an intellectual anxiety and disquiet which the French Jesuit, Pierre Teilhard de Chardin, analyzed as a fear that man has lost all significance and is trapped in a corner from which there is no escape. To find the key to Teilhard's optimism, men, in the most diverse intellectual climates, assiduously study his many works. A geologist and paleontologist absorbed in the process of evolution, Teilhard, also the theologian, believed that, as it is in man that the evolutionary process finds its consumma-

2 B. Christopher Butler, O.S.B., "The Role of Philosophy," *The Tablet* (London), CCXXII, No. 6686 (July 13, 1968), 692.
3 C. R. Boxer in *AHSJ,* XXXV (1966), 262, reviewing G. Schurhammer's *Gesammelte Studien,* 4 vols. (Rome, 1963-1965).

tion, so man reaches his own climax in Christ, God and Man. The Teilhardian vision of Christ as center of the world has assisted many to unify their thought and close the chasm which has been widening between science and theology.

Pope Paul VI described the Declaration on Religious Freedom as "one of the major texts" of the Second Vatican Council. The Declaration, in its manifestation of a sense of history and its awareness that twentieth-century man has arrived at a twofold consciousness, personal and political, in the realization of his dignity as a person and in his aspiration to live in freedom under a limited government, echoes the writings of John Courtney Murray. Murray, an American, hailed as one of the architects of this Declaration, clarified through several years of study the links between religious freedom and limited constitutional government as well as between freedom of the Church and freedom of the people. With a sensitivity to developments in history, he demonstrated the inadequacy of certain nineteenth-century concepts to answer the questions about religious freedom in the current age, and with a feel for the peculiar history of the United States he enunciated the truth of American democracy's compatibility with Catholicism. His reflections were a milestone in the development of Catholic thought.

Closely tied to the Church's attitude on religious freedom is her encouragement of the ecumenical spirit. In their ability to comprehend the theological positions of non-Catholics, two Jesuits, Augustine Cardinal Bea and, in the United States, Gustave Weigel, won great respect for the Church. And for years before the Council's stress on the dignity of man, in the United States John La Farge pioneered for interracial justice.

Since the pontificate of Leo XIII the popes in a series of penetrating documents have been developing the Church's teaching on the social and economic order. Among these documents certain encyclicals, such as *Rerum novarum, Quadragesimo anno,* and *Mater et Magistra,* have distinguished places. Papal social teaching evolved in large measure from the storehouse richly stocked with the thought and study of Catholic scholars. Several Jesuits, especially Germans, made unique contributions to this repository of ideas. Regarded by many as the father of modern Catholic social thought was Heinrich Pesch of Cologne. This prodigious scholar and author, who died in 1926, opponent of economic liberalism and advocate of what has been called Christian solidarism, built an integrated economic theory based on Aristotelian-Thomistic philosophy. Several distinguished Catholics preceded Pesch in their social activity, but he, with the tool of the modern science of economics, erected on his social philosophy an economic system which he elaborated in his monumental work of five volumes, *Manual on the National Economy* (1905-1923). Pesch was the link between *Rerum novarum* of 1891 and *Quadragesimo anno* of 1931, discerning commentator of the former and sourcebook for the latter. Two other German Jesuits, Gustav Gundlach and Oswald von Nell-Breuning, carried on Pesch's school of thought with profundity of learning, and this they saw spread from Rome to penetrate other parts of the world.

All these men served the Church with distinction, meeting the highest demands of the Ignatian tradition as it was carried onward and enriched by the intelligence of Canisius, Bellarmine, Laynez, Salmerón, Maldonado, Lessius, Van Papenbroeck, Ripalda, Suárez, Petau, Sirmond, Gretser, Ricci, De Nobili, Vieira, Stattler, Passaglia. Others less known but expertly trained in the natural sciences, sociology, economics, literature, history, staffed schools throughout the world. In 1969 11,594 Jesuits, or approximately a third of the Society, were engaged as teachers or administrators in 4,672 schools with 50,000 non-Jesuit teachers and administrators and more than a million and a quarter students.[4] Historians of the future, in their review of the first six decades of the twentieth century, quite conceivably will judge them to have been among the more impressive and brilliant periods in the Society's history.

On the missions the number of Jesuits steadily increased: 11.7% of the Society's personnel in 1929, 12.7% in 1934; 14.8% in 1940, 19.4% in 1964. Janssens was not satisfied with this. In one of his last letters to the Society, dated July 31, 1964, he wrote: "It would not be too much if, as happens in some otherwise flourishing provinces, 30 to 35% were sent to the foreign missions."[5] In contrast to the situation before the suppression, vocations from the peoples of the old mission lands mounted strikingly. In 1966, of the 484 men in the Philippine Province, 242 or exactly 50% were Filipinos. In 1948, of the 888 Jesuits in China, 269, or a little more than a third, were Chinese. In 1962 the Province of Indonesia numbered 237, almost half of whom were natives. The winds of change were blowing over the mission apostolate.

4 W. J. Mehok, S.J., "Jesuits: International Educators," *Jesuit Educational Quarterly*, XXXII (1969-1970), 277. About half of these schools are small parochial schools with a Jesuit administrator but no other Jesuits.
5 *ActRSJ*, XIV (1964), 460.

What these statistics revealed was that the missionaries had arrived at a welcome clarification, in theological terms, of the precise objective of their enterprise. In earlier centuries a few scholars did concentrated studies on the question of missionary work. Ramón Lull in the thirteenth century, the Jesuit José de Acosta in the sixteenth century, and several popes since Gregory XV established the Sacred Congregation of Propaganda in 1622 contributed to the reflective literature on the missions, but only gradually, from the obscure perceptions of the nineteenth century and through the patient work of Catholic and Protestant scholars, did a theology of the missions, modern and cognizant of the changing social, cultural, and political order in the world, emerge. Especially influential in the creation of the movement toward a scientifically theological understanding of the missions was the German, Robert Streit, O.M.I., who died in 1930. Two who built on Streit's work were the Alsatian secular priest and professor of Church History at Münster, Josef Schmidlin, who died in 1943, and the Belgian Jesuit, Pierre Charles, who died in 1954.

Charles with his trenchant and energetic style advanced and refined the meaning of missiology. Positing, after careful analysis, the objective to be the establishment of a visible and stable Church, wide in its extension, universal in its function, one in its discipline, part of the national life, maintained by its own people, Charles and his disciples did much to endow missionary activity with an intelligible theological basis.[6] In 1923 at Louvain, Charles initiated the collection *Xaveriana,* a series of monographs on the theology, history, and methodology of the missions. At the Gregorian University in Rome the faculty of Missiology was created in 1932, and in 1943 the annual collection *Studia Missionalia* was inaugurated. As a practical implementation of the scholar's thought, the Society encouraged, as the statistics quoted above indicate, an indigenous clergy. Had this theology matured during earlier centuries, a different and happier story of the missions could very probably be told.

The Society in the United States, no longer dependent on help from Europe, sent many of its own men abroad. In 1968 American Jesuits were in Japan, Taiwan, Korea, India, Ceylon,

---

6 The drastic changes in the modern world have prompted new directions in thought about the nature of the missions. Vatican Council II in the Decree on the Church's Missionary Activity, *Ad gentes,* takes account of several of these advances in the science of missiology within the past thirty years.

Iraq, the Philippines, the Caroline and Marshall Islands, Jamaica, British Honduras, Nigeria, Zambia, and several countries of South America. In 1966 they were expelled from Burma; in 1969 from Iraq.

This capacity of the American Society to help in other countries reflected its own increased domestic resources. As in the previous century, it was the school which was the most visible sign of the Jesuit presence in the life of the Church. In 1968, within the United States, including Puerto Rico, the Society conducted fifty-two high schools, ten colleges, and eighteen universities. So wide was the labyrinth of modern educational changes and experiments into which these Jesuit institutions entered, that had Ledesma, Des Freux, Pontanus, or De Jouvancy been suddenly dropped into the classrooms of Boston College High School or Seattle Preparatory School, or on the campus of Fordham University or St. Louis University, they would have been completely bewildered. Educational development, especially since the second World War, erased forever the simple lines inherited from Collège Louis-le-Grand, Colegio Imperial de Madrid, and the English College of St. Omers of the eighteenth century.

The presence of the Jesuit colleges and universities on the American educational scene testified to one of the more striking instances of adaptation in the history of the Society, comparable to the initial election to embrace the humanism of the sixteenth century and place it at the service of the Church. Confronted with the novel opportunity offered by the American educational system, the Society, without dropping secondary schools, adopted the American college and university and their wider intellectual responsibilities. This was the uniquely American contribution to the history of Jesuit education.

Schools stimulate scholarship, and scholarship generates writing, and writing begets journalism. The number of learned periodicals, edited or sponsored by Jesuits, and all of relatively recent inception, gave a measure of the intellectual maturing of the Society in the United States. *Theological Studies, Traditio, International Philosophical Quarterly, Review for Religious, Theology Digest, Thought, New Testament Abstracts* became vehicles for the presentation of worthy scholarship and fresh thinking.

The schools by their size and number cast a shadow over other Jesuit activities which were important parts of the Society's corporative enterprise in the United States. These latter included retreat houses for men and boys, mission bands dedicated to preaching, the more popular magazines like *America* and *Jesuit Missions*. And there were others. In 1942, for example, there were in the United States one hundred and two Jesuit parishes, fifteen mission centers and ninety-nine mission stations for the Indians, forty-eight chaplaincies in hospitals and sanatoria, four chaplaincies in mental hospitals, and twelve in prisons and penitentiaries. During World War I thirty-nine American Jesuits received commissions in the armed forces. At the end of World War II two hundred and forty-three were in uniform. One of them, Joseph T. O'Callahan, received the nation's highest award for heroism in combat, the Congressional Medal of Honor, for his gallantry during the fiery ordeal of the U.S.S. *Franklin* on January 19, 1945.[7]

A number of the non-scholastic ministries felt, as did the schools, the impact of the changes on the American scene. In December, 1967, the Society closed the *Sacred Heart Messenger,* one of its older apostolic tools. Started just a little over a century earlier, in 1866, the *Messenger* served the growing American Church well as it fed an audience starved for Catholic literature. A perennial pioneer in printing innovation, such as the use of color, the *Messenger* also opened the way for several other Jesuit journals. For fifty years Brother Claude Ramaz with keen technical skill preserved the magazine's widely known trim and fine appearance. To its last editor, Daniel F. X. Meenan, studies revealed that to continue in the field, then filled with more than five hundred Catholic journals, quality would have to be sacrificed. Rather than do this, he and his advisors reached the painful decision to terminate operations. The *Messenger's* passing marked the close of an era in the American Church. A companion in its demise was *Jesuit Missions,* the pacesetter among Catholic mission magazines in the United States. Both were in a way casualties in the reevaluation by Jesuits of their apostolic tools called for by the general congregation of 1965-1966.

On May 7, 1965, the Thirty-first General Congregation convened to elect a successor to Janssens. The delegates, numbering a little over two hundred, had a further responsibility because, coming together between the third and fourth sessions of the

The Thirty-First General Congregation, 1965–1966

7 E. J. Reiser, S.J., "Parochial and Allied Ministries in the American Assistancy," *WL,* LXXII (1943), 306-317; G. F. Giblin, S.J., *Jesuits as Chaplains in the Armed Forces 1917-1960* (Woodstock, 1961), pp. 2, 10, 84-85.

Second Vatican Council when the spiritual climate was one of renewal and adaptation to the needs of the modern world, they had to direct the Society's vision toward the horizons opened by the Council. Because of the unusually heavy load of business the Congregation, in an unprecedented step, met in two sessions, the first from May 7, 1965, to July 15, 1965, and the second from September 8, 1966, to November 17, 1966.

Before the election of the general, Maurice Giuliani of France gave the customary exhortation to the delegates. "We need a general," Giuliani said, "who will ever keep the Society united with the world to which the word of salvation is to be carried effectively. It will not be enough for our general to be taken up with continuing and enlarging particular works which arise out of local needs, but if his vision is fixed on the universal good, he will assist us, as companions of Jesus, to embrace the entire world in all its fullness and to cooperate in the redemption of our age."

The man chosen by the congregation on May 22, 1965, matches Giuliani's ideal of openness to the universal needs of the Church, for in the entire history of the Society there has been no general who brought to the office the breadth of experience and knowledge of the world as does Pedro Arrupe. Fifty-eight years old when elected, this native of Bilbao, the fifth Spaniard and the first Basque to be general after St. Ignatius, knows from first-hand experience Europe, North and South America, and Asia. A medical student before he entered the Society at Loyola in 1927, he had a minimal part of his Jesuit training in Spain, because in 1932 the republican government sent the Jesuits into exile. He pursued the Society's program of studies in Belgium, Germany, Holland, and the United States. In 1939 he went to Japan. On August 6, 1945, when the atom bomb struck Hiroshima, he was instructor of novices at the novitiate in the outskirts of the city. Because of his skill and devotion in aiding those injured by the explosion, he excited widespread admiration. In 1954 Janssens appointed him head of the Vice-province of Japan, and in 1958, when Japan was made a full province, the provincial. For eleven years, therefore, Father Arrupe had guided the expanding Jesuit apostolate in Japan when he became general.

After Arrupe's election the delegates began their work on a massive volume of business. Two dominant influences gave direction to the congregation: Vatican Council II and Pope Paul VI. The Council, penetrated with the spirit of renewal, revealed to the delegates the mind and mood of the Church in the mid-twentieth century. In its decree on the adaptation and renewal of the religious life, *Perfectae caritatis,* it focused on two basic ways for the renewal of religious communities: first, an ever constant return to the sources of Christian life and the original inspiration of the founder; and second, adjustment to modern times.

Pope Paul received the delegates at the inception of their meetings and expressed a wish which gave a clear orientation to the Society in its approach to the modern apostolate and shaped several of the major decrees. Reminding the delegates that Jesuit strength lay in its spiritual resources, he called on the Society to employ its energies against one of the most serious maladies of the modern world, the widespread denial, in one form or another, of Almighty God. Then before the congregation's second session, on August 6, 1966, he issued his forward-looking motu proprio *Ecclesiae sanctae,* which gave valuable guidelines for the practical implementation of *Perfectae caritatis.*

The Congregation responded to the call of the Council in an open, positive, and constructive way. Its documents, save the few essentially juridical in nature, adopted the scriptural and pastoral language of the conciliar decrees, expressed a fresh appreciation of the legacy of St. Ignatius and at the same time manifested a mature awareness of the intellectual, social, and spiritual problems of the present age. Through the legislation ran a strong thread of unity in the constantly recurring idea: the character of the Society is essentially apostolic; the Society of Jesus is a group of men called to union with Christ in his redeeming mission. The influence of this insight, realized by St. Ignatius and his companions in the experience of the Spiritual Exercises, was strongly pervasive. The decrees, solidly based on documents of the Society's beginning, evoked a heightened awareness of the roots of Jesuit life. They were, in a sense, a rediscovery of the Ignatian thrust.

At the conclusion of the congregation Pope Paul received the delegates. He recalled the special character of Jesuit history, stamped as the Society was "for the service of the Catholic Church and the Apostolic See." This mission he renewed. "Yes, it is time, most beloved sons," he said. "Go forth in faith and ardor; Christ chooses you, the Church sends you, the pope blesses you." [8]

Jesuits throughout the world began the task of integrating the

8 *AAS,* LVIII (1966), 1178.

decisions of the congregation with their personal endeavors for renewal. As general, Father Arrupe indicated that he expected action. He said, "I do not want to defend any mistakes Jesuits might have made, but the greatest mistake would be to stand in such fear of making error that we would simply stop acting." [9]

Epilogue   Dom David Knowles, former Regius professor of Modern History at Cambridge University, once wrote that, when we think of the Jesuits, "we feel the impression of that mighty impulse, perhaps the greatest single religious impulse since the preaching of the apostles, which spread over Europe from Manresa." [10] This is one attempt to formulate a general judgment about the history of the Society of Jesus. To be more precise and to indite a more sharply defined formula is immensely difficult. The problem is to embrace within a single proposition the interior spirit and the external activity of thousands of men through more than four centuries of history who taught Latin and Greek at Collège Louis-le-Grand; composed astronomical tables at the Imperial Court of Peking; paddled down the St. Lawrence River in New France; built St. Michael's baroque church in Munich; lectured on philosophy and theology at the Gregorian University in Rome; died on the gallows at Tyburn in England; adopted the role of the sanyassi in India; developed communities of Amerindians in Paraguay; gave their lives in the service of the plague-stricken in Andalusia; taught in large universities from Boston to San Francisco. Three marks may help to elucidate the Society's identity more precisely.

The first mark: apostolic action. One of the more dominant features of Catholic Reform spirituality was its intense activity.[11] Men and women of the sixteenth century, motivated by the desire to labor for the salvation of souls, gave themselves to works of charity and mercy. From this spiritual milieu emerged the Theatines, the Barnabites, the Capuchins, and the Ursulines. The Jesuits had their origins at the same time. St. Ignatius, from his personal mystical insights about the character of the Society of Jesus and from his experience of the needs of the Church, insisted on apostolic activity as a hallmark of the Jesuit vocation. His enterprise merged gracefully and perfectly with the mood of the Church. This apostolic character the Society preserved through the years. And this the Thirty-first

---

9 *New York Times*, Nov. 25, 1966, p. 10.
10 D. Knowles, O.S.B., *The Benedictines* (New York, 1930), p. 2.
11 Evennett, *The Spirit of the Counter-Reformation*, pp. 31-32.

General Congregation reaffirmed in 1965-1966. It was apostolic action of a distinctive quality, shaped and determined as it was by the principle that God's greater glory was ever the objective— *ad maiorem Dei gloriam.*

The second mark: a penchant for Christian humanism. Early in its history the Society forged a harmonious accommodation of Christian revelation and human worth. The Jesuits made their own what Henri Bremond called that "cast of mind," which, while it reveres every teaching of Christianity, nevertheless prefers to stress those truths which are most consoling to man as manifestations of the Infinite Goodness.[12] They affirmed positively the dignity, beauty, and worth of human nature created anew by the Redemption. In 1951 Pope Pius XII said that "the profession of Christian truth and fidelity to the fundamental tenets of the Catholic faith are indissolubly bound up with the sincere and constant assertion of human nature's most authentic and exalted values. . . . True religion and profound humaneness are not rivals. They are sisters." [13] Two years later John Courtney Murray, in another context, synthesized this principle as follows: "The *res sacra* which grace would achieve is likewise *res humana* in the full sense. In the stage of growth proper to its earthly pilgrimage the Body of Christ finds organic place for developed human values." [14] These statements underline an essential quality of the Jesuit style. And this style characterized areas other than that of thought and learning. Jesuits also labored as masons, metallurgists, architects, and farmers with the purpose of making life more human for others. Through more than four centuries the Society anticipated the pastoral constitution on *The Church in the Modern World,* which enunciated this principle: "Christians, on pilgrimage toward the heavenly city, should seek and savor the things which are above. This duty in no way decreases, but rather increases, the weight of their obligation to work with all men in constructing a more human world. In fact, the mystery of the Christian faith furnishes them with excellent motives and helps toward discharging this duty more energetically and especially toward uncovering the full meaning of this activity, a meaning which gives human culture its eminent place in the integral

12 Bremond, *Histoire littéraire,* I, 11-13.
13 *AAS,* XLIII (1951), 169.
14 J. C. Murray, S.J., "Christian Humanism in America," *Social Order,* III (1953), 240.

vocation of man." [15] This "cast of mind" helped to shape other characteristically Jesuit attitudes: an openness to diverse cultures of the world and a readiness to accommodate to constantly shifting situations.

The third mark: a common spiritual ideal. All Jesuits received their spiritual formation according to the basic intuitions and experiences of St. Ignatius as he transmitted them in the *Spiritual Exercises* and the *Constitutions* of the Society. The month engaged in making these Exercises was a cardinal experience. From this major event in the life of each emerged a group of men who, in greater or lesser degree, grasped the rich import of this ideal: to be with Jesus — in order to serve.[16] This service was not of an ordinary kind. Of its nature it demanded excellence and high competence. This ideal was the profound internal force that bound Jesuits through the centuries and over continents into one clearly identifiable fellowship. José de Anchieta of the sixteenth century, Henry Garnet of the seventeenth, Pedro de Calatayud of the eighteenth, Constant Lievens of the nineteenth, Ruppert Mayer of the twentieth could meet and instinctively appreciate the basic spiritual point of departure of one another.

Despite their unity the Jesuits were strikingly diverse. Differences of nationalities often led to friction. On the missions Italians and Portuguese clashed. So did Germans and Portuguese. Pierre Coton the Frenchman, Robert Persons the Englishman, Stanislaw Naruszewicz the Pole, Francisco Javier Alegre the Mexican, Daniel Lord the American, Hippolyte Delehaye the Belgian, Jakob Balde the German, all differed one from the other in temperament, talent, and background. On important intellectual issues Jesuits sometimes split. Some adopted the philosophy of Descartes. Others attacked it. Some championed the indirect power of the pope in temporal affairs. Others opposed it. Yet a basic, deep, and pervasive spiritual unity transcended the disagreements of the moment and the sharp contrast of personalities.

These three marks, apostolic action, Christian humanism, and the interior ideal of being with Jesus — in order to serve — may help to explicate the singular identity that the Society of Jesus has preserved through over four centuries of history.

---

15 Section 57. Translation from *The Documents of Vatican II,* ed. W. M.
  Abbott, S.J., (New York: America Press, copyrighted 1966), p. 262.
16 *DeGuiJes,* p. 594.

REFERENCE MATTER

Appendix

Abbreviations

Bibliography

Index

APPENDIX

List of the Generals and General Congregations

1. Ignatius of Loyola, Apr 19, 1541 – July 31, 1556
2. Diego Laynez, July 2, 1558 – Jan 19, 1565
3. Saint Francis Borgia, July 2, 1565 – Oct 1, 1572
4. Everard Mercurian, Apr 23, 1573 – Aug 1, 1580
5. Claudio Aquaviva, Feb 19, 1581 – Jan 31, 1615

6. Muzio Vitelleschi, Nov 15, 1615 – Feb 9, 1645
7. Vincenzo Carafa, Jan 7, 1646 – June 8, 1649
8. Francesco Piccolomini, Dec 21, 1649 – June 17, 1651
9. Luigi Gottifredi, Jan 21, 1652 – March 12, 1652
10. Goswin Nickel, Mar 17, 1652 – July 31, 1664
11. Giovanni Paolo Oliva, Vicar June 7, 1661
    General, July 31, 1664 – Nov 26, 1681
12. Charles de Noyelle, July 5, 1682 – Dec 12, 1686
13. Tirso González, July 6, 1687 – Oct 27, 1705

14. Michelangelo Tamburini, Jan 31, 1706 – Feb 28, 1730
15. Frantisek Retz, Nov 30, 1730 – Nov 19, 1750
16. Ignazio Visconti, July 4, 1751 – May 4, 1755
17. Luigi Centurione, Nov 30, 1755 – Oct 2, 1757
18. Lorenzo Ricci, May 21, 1758 – Aug 16, 1773
19. Tadeusz Brzozowski, Aug 7, 1814 – Feb 5, 1820
20. Luigi Fortis, Oct 18, 1820 – Jan 27, 1829
21. Jan Roothaan, July 9, 1829 – May 8, 1853
22. Pieter Beckx, July 2, 1853 – Mar 4, 1887
23. Anton Anderledy, Vicar Sept 24, 1883
    General Mar 4, 1887 – Jan 18, 1892
24. Luis Martín, Oct 2, 1892 – Apr 18, 1906
25. Franz Wernz, Sept 8, 1906 – Aug 19, 1914
26. Wlodmir Ledochowski, Feb 11, 1915 – Dec 13, 1942

27. John Baptist Janssens, Sept 15, 1946 – Oct 5, 1964

28. Pedro Arrupe, May 22, 1965

---

1. June 19 – Sept 10, 1558
2. June 21 – Sept 3, 1565
3. Apr 12 – June 16, 1573
4. Feb 7 – Apr 22, 1581
5. Nov 3, 1593 – Jan 18, 1594
6. Feb 21 – Mar 29, 1608
7. Nov 5, 1615 – Jan 26, 1616
8. Nov 21, 1645 – Apr 14, 1646
9. Dec 13, 1649 – Feb 23, 1650
10. Jan 7 – Mar 20, 1652

11. May 9 – July 27, 1661

12. June 22 – Sept 6, 1682
13. June 22 – Sept 7, 1687
14. Nov 19, 1696 – Jan 16, 1697
15. Jan 20 – Apr 3, 1706
16. Nov 19, 1730 – Feb 13, 1731
17. June 22 – Sept 5, 1751
18. Nov 18, 1755 – Jan 28, 1756
19. May 9 – June 18, 1758

20. Oct 9 – Dec 10, 1820
21. June 30 – Aug 17, 1829
22. June 22 – Aug 31, 1853
23. Sept 16 – Oct 23, 1883

24. Sept 24 – Dec 5, 1892
25. Sept 1 – Oct 18, 1906
26. Feb 2 – Mar 18, 1915
27. Sept 8 – Dec 21, 1923
28. Mar 12 – May 9, 1938
29. Sept 6 – Oct 23, 1946
30. Sept 6 – Nov 11, 1957
31. May 7 – July 15, 1965
    Sept 8 – Nov 17, 1966

ABBREVIATIONS

used in the footnotes[1]

AAS—*Acta Apostolicae Sedis*
ActRSJ—*Acta Romana Societatis Iesu*
AHSJ—*Archivum Historicum Societatis Iesu*
Cons—*The Constitutions of the Society of Jesus*
ConsSJComm—*The Constitutions of the Society of Jesus*. Translated,
      with an Introduction and a Commentary, by G. E. Ganss, S.J.
DeGuiJes—De Guibert, *The Jesuits: Their Spiritual Doctrine and
      Practice*
DocInd—*Documenta Indica*
DTC—*Dictionnaire de théologie catholique*
EppMixt—*Epistolae Mixtae ex variis Europae locis, 1537–1556.*
EppXav—*Epistolae S. Francisci Xaverii*
FN—*Fontes narrativi de Sancto Ignatio*
IdeaJesUn—Ganss, *St. Ignatius' Idea of a Jesuit University*
MonBras—*Monumenta Brasiliae*
MonBroet—*Epistolae PP. Paschasii Broëti, Claudii Jaji, Joannis Codurii
      et Simonis Rodericii S.J.*
MonFabri—*Fabri Monumenta*
MonNad—*Epistolae P. Hieronymi Nadal*
MonPaed (1965)—*Monumenta paedagogica S.J., I (1540–1556)*
MonSalm—*Epistolae P. Alphonsi Salmeronis*
SdeSI—*Scripta de Sancto Ignatio*
RAM—*Revue d'ascétique et de mystique*
SMV—*Sommervogel, Bibliothèque de la Compagnie de Jésus*
WL—*Woodstock Letters*

---

[1] For more complete descriptions of the above books, particularly those
   of the 100 volume series Monumenta Historica Societatis Iesu, see
   ConsSJComm, pages 358-362.

This bibliography lists only those books and periodicals to which actual reference is made in the footnotes. The authors' names can also be found in the Index.

Abbott, Walter M., S.J., editor. *The Documents of Vatican II*. New York, 1966.

Alegre, Francisco Javier, S.J. *Historia de la Provincia de la Compañía de Jesús de Nueva España*. Edited by Ernest Burrus, S.J., and Félix Zubillaga, S.J., 4 vols. Rome, 1956-1960.

Amann, Émile. "Malabares (Rites)," *Dictionnaire de Théologie Catholique*, IX, ii, 1704-1745.

————"Pazmany, Pierre," *Dictionnaire de Théologie Catholique*, XII, i, 97-100.

Annales de la Propagation de la Foi, X (1837), 101-103.

Anonymous. "Fr. John Bapst. A Sketch." *Woodstock Letters*, XVII (1888), 361-372.

Astráin, Antonio, S.J. *Historia de la Compañía de Jesús en la Asistencia de España*. 7 vols. Madrid, 1902-1925.

Aubert, Roger. *Le pontificat de Pie IX (1846-1878)*. Paris, 1952.

Bangert, William V., S.J. *To the Other Towns. A Life of Blessed Peter Favre, First Companion of St. Ignatius*. Westminster, Md., 1959.

Basset, Bernard, S.J. *The English Jesuits. From Campion to Martindale*. New York, 1968.

Batllori, Miguel, S.J. *El Abate Viscardo. Historia y Mito de la Intervención de los Jesuitas en la Independencia de Hispanoamérica*. Caracas, 1953.

————"La irrupción de Jesuitas españoles en la Italia dieciochesca." *Razon y Fe*, CXXVI (1942), 108-130.

Beales, A.C. F. *Education under Penalty*. London, 1963.

Beccari, Camillo, S.J., editor. *Rerum Aethiopicarum Scriptores Occidentales Inediti*. 15 vols. Rome, 1907-1917.

Bednarski, Stanislaus, S.J. "Déclin et renaissance de l'enseignement des Jésuites en Pologne." *Archivum Historicum Societatis Jesu*, II (1933), 199-223.

Bischoff, William N., S.J. *The Jesuits in Old Oregon*. Caldwell, Idaho, 1945.

Blet, Pierre, S.J. "Jésuites et libertés gallicanes en 1611." *Archivum Historicum Societatis Jesu,* XXIV (1955), 165-188.

————Jésuites Gallicans au XVIIᵉ siècle?" *Archivum Historicum Societatis Jesu,* XXIX (1960), 55-84.

Bober, Andreas, S.J., and Bednarz, Miecislaus, S.J. "Relatio de caedibus Patrum ac Fratrum, S.J. in Provincia Poloniae a P. Joanne Zuchowics, S.J., collecta A.D. 1665 (1648-1665)."*Archivum Historicum Societatis Jesu,* XXIX (1960), 329-380.

Bolton, Herbert E. "The Jesuits in New Spain." *The Catholic Historical Review,* XXI (1935), 257-282.

Borowy, W. "Polish Literature in the Eighteenth Century." *The Cambridge History of Poland from Augustus II to Pilsudski (1697-1935),* 177-194. Cambridge (England), 1941.

Bouyer, Louis. *Liturgical Piety.* Notre Dame, Indiana, 1954.

Boxer, Charles R. *The Christian Century in Japan.* Berkeley, 1951.

————*The Golden Age of Brazil 1695-1750.* Berkeley, 1962.

————*A Great Luso-Brazilian Figure. Padre António Vieira, S.J., 1608-1697.* London, 1957.

————A book review of the *Gesammelte Studien* of Georg Schurhammer, S.J. *Archivum Historicum Societatis Jesu,* XXXV (1966), 259-262.

Bremond, Henri. *Histoire littéraire du sentiment religieux en France depuis la fin des guerres de religion jusqu' à nos jours.* 12 vols. Paris, 1924-1936.

————*The Thundering Abbot. Armand de Rancé Reformer of La Trappe.* Translated by F.J. Sheed. London, 1930.

Brodrick, James S.J. *The Progress of the Jesuits.* London and New York, 1947.

————*Robert Bellarmine. Saint and Scholar.* Westminster, Md., 1961.

Brou, Alexandre, S.J. A book review of *Histoire Politique et Religieuse d'Abyssinie* by J.B. Coulbeaux. *Archivum Historicum Societatis Jesu,* I (1932), 376.

————"Le point final à la question des rites chinois." *Études* CCXLII (1940), 275-288.

Brucker, Joseph, S.J. *La Compagnie de Jésus. Esquisse de son Institut et de son Histoire.* Paris, 1919.

————"Dechamps ou Agard de Champs, Étienne." *Dictionnaire de Théologie Catholique,* IV, i, 175-176.

Burnichon, Joseph, S.J. *La Compagnie de Jésus en France: 1814-1914.* 4 vols. Paris, 1914-1922.

Burns, Robert I., S.J. *The Jesuits and the Indian Wars of the Northwest.* New Haven, 1966.

Burrus, Ernest, S.J. "Pedro de Mercado and Mexican Jesuit Recruits." *Mid-America,* XXXVII (1955), 140-152.

Butler, B. Christopher, O.S.B. "The Role of Philosophy." *The Tablet* (London), CCXXII, No. 6686 (July 13, 1968), 692.

Canisius, Peter St. *Beati Petri Canisii Societatis Jesu epistulae et acta.* Collegit et adnotationibus illustravit O. Braunsberger, S.J. 8 vols. Freiburg-im-Breisgau, 1896-1923.

Cappon, Lester, editor. *The Adams-Jefferson Letters.* 2 vols. Chapel Hill, 1959.

Carr, Raymond. *Spain 1808-1939.* Oxford, 1966.

Caussade, Jean-Pierre, S.J. *Self-abandonment to Divine Providence.* Translated by Algar Thorold. Introduction by David Knowles. London, 1959.

Cerri, Urbano. *An Account of the State of the Roman-Catholick Religion Throughout the World.* Translated by Sir Richard Steele. London, 1716.

Certeau, Michel de, S.J. "Crise social et réformisme spirituel au début du XVIIᵉ siècle: 'Une nouvelle spiritualité chez les Jésuites français.'" *Revue d'ascétique et de mystique,* XLI (1965), 339-386.

Chatellain, J.C. Vital. *Le Père Denis Petau d'Orléans. Sa Vie et ses Oeuvres.* Paris, 1884.

Cheke, Sir Marcus. *The Cardinal de Bernis.* London, 1958.

————*Dictator of Portugal.* London, 1938.

Cognet, Louis. *De la Dévotion Moderne à la Spiritualité Française.* Paris, 1958.

————*Le Jansénisme.* Paris, 1964.

Corcoran, Timothy, S.J. *Clongowes Record.* Dublin, 1932.

————"Early Irish Jesuit Educators." *Studies,* XXIX (1940), 545-560; XXX (1941), 59-74.

Cordara, Giulio, S.J. "Julii Cordarae de Suppressione Societatis Jesu Commentarii." *Atti e Memorie della R. Academia di Scienze Lettere ed Arti in Padova* XL (1923-1924), 35-79; XLI (1924-1925), 41-173. Edited by G. Albertotti.

Costa, Horacio de la, S.J. *The Jesuits in the Philippines, 1581-1768.* Cambridge (Mass.), 1961.

————"The Development of the Native Clergy in the Philippines." *Theological Studies,* VIII (1947), 219-250.

Costa, Manuel da, S.J. "The Last Years of a Confessor of the Faith, Father David Wolf." *Archivum Historicum Societatis Jesu,* XV (1946), 127-143.

Coulbeaux, Jean B. *Histoire Politique et Religieuse d'Abyssinie.* 3 vols. Paris, 1929.

————"Éthiope (Église d')." *Dictionnaire de Théologie Catholique* V, i, 922-969.

Crétineau-Joly, Jacques. *Histoire religieuse, politique et littéraire de la Compagnie de Jésus.* 6 vols. Paris, 1844-1846.

Curran, Francis X., S.J. *The Return of the Jesuits.* Chicago, 1966.

Cushner, Nicholas, S.J. *Philippine Jesuits in Exile. The Journals of Francisco Puig, S.J., 1768-1770.* Rome, 1964.

Dainville, François de, S.J. *La Naissance de l'Humanisme Moderne.* Paris, 1940.

————"Effectifs des collèges et scolarité aux XVIIᵉ et XVIIIᵉ siècles dans le nord-est de la France." *Population,* X (1955), 455-488.

————"Collèges et fréquentation scolaire au XVIIᵉ siècle." XII (1957), 467-494.

————"S. Ignace et l'Humanisme." *Cahiers Universitaires Catholiques* (1956), 458-479.

Daley, John M., S.J. *Georgetown University: Origin and Early Years.* Washington, 1957.

Daniel-Rops, Henri. *The Church in the Eighteenth Century.* Translated by John Warrington. London and New York, 1964.

Dansette, Adrien. *Religious History of Modern France.* Translated by John Dingle. 2 vols. New York, 1961.

Delanglez, Jean, S.J. *The French Jesuits in Lower Louisiana, 1700-1763.* Washington, D.C., 1935.

Delattre, Pierre, S.J. and Lamalle, Edmond, S.J. "Jésuites wallons, flamands, français, missionaires au Paraguay (1608-1767)." *Archivum Historicum Societatis Jesu,* XVI (1947), 98-176.

D'Elia, Pasquale M., S.J. *Galileo in China.* Translated by Rufus Suter and Matthew Sciascia. Cambridge, Mass., 1960.

————"Cina." *Enciclopedia Cattolica,* III, 1646-1667.

Desautels, Alfred, S.J. *Les Mémoires de Trévoux et le mouvement des idées au XVIIIᵉ siècle.* Rome, 1956.

Devitt, Edward I., S.J. "The Suppression and Restoration of the Society of Jesus in Maryland." *Woodstock Letters* XXXIII (1904), 371-381; XXXIV (1905), 113-130; 203-235.

Dickens, Arthur G. *The Counter Reformation.* London and New York, 1969.

Dominion, Helen. *Apostle of Brazil.* New York, 1958.

Donnelly, Joseph, S.J. *Jacques Marquette, S.J. 1637-1675.* Chicago, 1968.

————*Wilderness Kingdom. Indian Life in the Rocky Mountains: 1840-1847. The Journals and Paintings of Nicolas Point, S.J.* Translated and Introduced by Joseph Donnelly, S.J. New York, 1967.

Donohue, John W., S.J. *Jesuit Education: An Essay on the Foundations of its Idea.* New York, 1963.

Dudon, Paul, S.J. *St. Ignatius of Loyola.* Translated by William J. Young, S.J. Milwaukee, 1949.

————"The Resurrection of the Society of Jesus." Translated by Gerald McCool, S.J. *Woodstock Letters,* LXXXI (1952), 311-360.

Dugout, Ignace Henri, S.J. *Nos Martyrs. Catalogue des Pères et Frères de la Compagnie de Jésus qui, dans les Fers ou dans les Tourments, ont sacrifié leur Vie pour leur Foi ou leur Vocation.* Paris, 1905.

————*Victimes de la charité Catalogue des PP. et FF. de la*

Comp. morts de maladies contagieuses contractées au service des malades. Paris, 1907.

Duhr, Bernhard, S.J. *Geschichte der Jesuiten in den Ländern Deutscher Zunge.* 4 vols. in 6 parts. Munich-Regensburg, 1907-1928.

Dumas, Gustave, S.J. *Histoire du Journal de Trévoux.* Paris, 1936.

————"Voltaire's Jesuit Chaplain." *Thought,* XV (1940), 17-25.

Dunne, George H., S.J. "What Happened to the Chinese Liturgy?" *The Catholic Historical Review,* XLVII (1961), 1-14.

Dunne, Peter M., S.J. and Burrus, Ernest, S.J. "Four Unpublished Letters of Anton Maria Benz, Eighteenth Century Missionary to Mexico." *Archivum Historicum Societatis Jesu,* XXIV (1955), 336-378.

Égret, Jean. "Le procès des Jésuites devant les parlements de France (1761-1770)." *Revue Historique,* CCIV (July, 1950), 1-27.

Ellis, John Tracy. *American Catholicism.* Chicago, 1956.

Evennett, H. Outram. *The Spirit of the Counter-Reformation.* Edited by John Bossy. Cambridge (England), 1968.

Fauchier-Magnan, Adrien. *The Small German Courts in the Eighteenth Century.* London, 1958.

Favre, Blessed Pierre, S.J. *Bienheurex Pierre Favre: Mémorial.* Traduit et commenté par Michel de Certeau, S.J. "Collection Christus," No. 4. Paris, 1959.

Ferroli, Domenico, S.J. *The Jesuits in Malabar.* 2 vols. Bangalore, 1939, 1951.

————*The Jesuits in Mysore.* Kozhikode, 1955.

Fiorito, M. A., S.J. "Ignatius' Own Legislation on Prayer." *Woodstock Letters,* XCVII (1968), 149-224.

Foley, Henry, S.J. *Records of the English Province of the Society of Jesus.* 8 vols. London, 1877-1882.

Forbes-Leith, William, S.J. *Memoirs of Scottish Catholics during the XVII and XVIII Centuries.* 2 vols. London and New York, 1909.

Fouqueray, Henri, S.J. *Histoire de la Compagnie de Jésus en France des origines à la suppression (1528-1762).* 5 vols. Paris, 1910-1925.

Frias, Lesmes, S.J. *La Provincia de España de la Compañía de Jesús. 1815-1863.* Madrid, 1914.

————*La Provincia de Castilla de la Compañía de Jesús desde 1863 hasta 1914.* Bilbao, 1915.

————"La Compañía de Jesús Suprimida en España hace un Siglo." *Archivum Historicum Societatis Jesu,* V (1936), 203-230.

Furlong, Guillermo, S.J. "The Jesuit Heralds of Democracy and the New Despotism." *The Expulsion of the Jesuits from Latin America,* 41-46. Edited by Magnus Mörner, New York, 1965.

Gannon, Robert I., S.J. *Up to the Present. The Story of Fordham.* New York, 1967.

Ganss, George E., S.J. *The Jesuit Educational Tradition and St. Louis University: Some Bearings for the University's Sesquicentennial.* St. Louis, 1969.

————*Saint Ignatius' Idea of a Jesuit University: A Study in the History of Catholic Education.* 2d ed. rev. Milwaukee, 1956.

García-Villoslada, Ricardo, S.J. *Manual de Historia de la Compañía de Jesús.* 2d ed. Madrid, 1954.

Garraghan, Gilbert J., S.J. *The Jesuits of the Middle United States.* 3 vols. New York, 1938.

Garstein, Oskar. *Rome and the Counter-Reformation in Scandanavia, 1539-1583.* Oslo, 1964.

Gay, Peter. *The Enlightenment: An Interpretation.* Vol. I, *The Rise of Modern Paganism.* Vol. II, *The Science of Freedom.* New York. 1967, 1969.

Giblin, Gerard F., S.J. *Jesuits as Chaplains in the Armed Forces 1917-1960.* Woodstock (Maryland), 1961.

Godfrey, John J., S.J. "Sir William Jones and Père Coeurdoux: a Philological Footnote." *Journal of the American Oriental Society,* LXXXVII (1967), 57-59.

Gomes, Joaquim Ferreira. "Pedro da Fonseca: Sixteenth Century Portuguese Philosopher." *International Philosophical Quarterly,* VI (1966), 632-644.

Grausem, J. P. "Ruiz de Montoya, Diego." *Dictionnaire de Théologie Catholique,* XVI. i, 163-167.

Groh, John E. "Antonio Ruíz de Montoya and the Early Reductions in the Jesuit Province of Paraguay." *The Catholic Historical Review,* LVI (1970), 501-533.

Guibert, Joseph de, S.J. *The Jesuits: Their Spiritual Doctrine and Practice.* Translated by William J. Young, S.J., Chicago, 1964.

Guillermou, Alain. *Les Jésuites.* Paris, 1963.

Guitton, Georges, S.J. *Le Père de la Chaize.* 2 vols. Paris, 1959.

Gurr, John E., S.J. *The Principle of Sufficient Reason in Some Scholastic Systems.* Milwaukee, 1959.

Halecki, Oscar. *From Florence to Brest (1439-1596).* Rome, 1958.

Hales, Edward E. Y. *Mazzini and the Secret Societies.* New York, 1956.

————*Pio Nono.* London, 1954.

————*Revolution and Papacy 1769-1846.* London, 1960.

Hamm, Victor M. "*Father Dominic Bouhours and Neo-Classical Criticism.*" *Jesuit Thinkers of the Renaissance.* Edited by Gerard Smith, S.J. Milwaukee, 1939.

Hans, N. "The Dissolution of the Society of Jesus in the Eighteenth Century and its Financial Consequences." *Education and Economics: The Year Book of Education,* (1956), 137-146.

Harney, Martin P., S.J. *The Jesuits in History.* New York, 1941.

————"Cardinal Peter Pázmány." *Thought*. XI (1936), 225-237.

Haskell, Francis. *Patrons and Painters. A Study in the Relations between Italian Art and Society in the Age of the Baroque.* New York, 1963.

Hastings, Adrian. *The World Mission of the Church.* London, 1964.

Hay, Malcolm. *Failure in the Far East.* Philadelphia, 1957.

Hazard, Paul. *European Thought in the Eighteenth Century.* Translated by J. Lewis May. New Haven, 1954.

Hemphill, Basil, O.S.B. *The Early Vicars Apostolic of England 1685-1750.* London, 1954.

Hennesey, James J., S.J. "James A. Corcoran's Mission to Rome: 1868-1869." *The Catholic Historical Review,* XLVIII (1962), 157-181.

————"National Traditions and the First Vatican Council." *Archivum Historiae Pontificiae,* VII (1969), 491-512.

————"A Prelude to Vatican I: American Bishops and the Definition of the Immaculate Conception." *Theological Studies,* XXV (1964), 409-419.

Hering, Hollis W. "A Study of Roman Catholic Missions in China—1692-1744." *New China Review,* III (1921), 106-126; 198-212.

Hicks, Leo, S.J. "Father Persons and the Seminaries in Spain." *The Month,* CLVII (1931), 193-204; 410-417; 497-506; CLVIII (1931), 26-35; 143-152; 234-244.

Hill, Elizabeth. "Biographical Essay." *Roger Joseph Boscovich. Studies of His Life and Work on the 250th Anniversary of His Birth.* Edited by Lancelot Law Whyte. London, 1961.

Hocedez, Edgar, S.J. *Histoire de la théologie au XIXᵉ siècle.* 3 vols. Paris, 1947-1952.

Hoffmann, Hermann. *Friedrich II von Preussen und die Aufhebung der Gesellschaft Jesu.* Rome, 1969.

Hughes, Philip. *Rome and the Counter-Reformation in England.* London, 1944.

————*The Reformation in England.* Vol. III, *True Religion Now Established.* London, 1954.

Hughes, Thomas, S.J. *History of the Society of Jesus in North America, Colonial and Federal.* 4 vols. London and New York, 1907-1917.

Humphreys, R. A. and Lynch, John. "The Emancipation of South America." *Comité International des Sciences Historiques. XIIᵉ Congrès International des Sciences Historiques.* 5 vols. Vienna, 1965, III, 39-56.

Huonder, Anton von, S.J. "German Jesuit Missionaries in the Seventeenth and Eighteenth Centuries." *Woodstock Letters,* XXIX (1900). This is an article signed B and based on Huonder's *Deutsche Jesuitenmissionäere des 17 und 18 Jahrhunderts.* Freiburg-im-Breisgau, 1899.

Ignatius of Loyola, St. *The Constitutions of the Society of Jesus.* Translated, with an Introduction and a Commentary, by George E. Ganss, S.J. St. Louis, 1970.

Irsay, Stephen d'. *Histoire des universités Françaises et étrangères des origines à nos jours.* 2 vols. Paris, 1933.

Janssen, Johannes. *History of the German People at the Close of the Middle Ages.* Translated by M. A. Mitchell and A. M. Christie. 16 vols. St. Louis, 1905-1910.

Jemolo, A.C. *Church and State in Italy 1850-1950.* Translated by David Moore, Oxford, 1960.

Jungmann, Josef, S.J. *The Mass of the Roman Rite: Its Origins and Development.* Translated by Francis A. Brunner, C. SS. R. 2 vols. New York, 1951, 1955.

Karrer, Otto, S.J. "Borgia's Influence on the Development of Prayer-Life in the Society of Jesus." Translated by Walter J. Babo, S.J. *Woodstock Letters,* XCVI (1967), 340-364.

Kenyon, J. P. *Robert Spencer, Earl of Sunderland, 1641-1702.* London, 1958.

Kerkvoorde, Augustin, O.S.B. "Kleutgen, Joseph." *Catholicisme,* VI, 1456-1457.

Knowles, Dom David, O.S.B. *The Benedictines.* New York, 1930.

————*From Pachomius to Ignatius. A Study in the Constitutional History of the Religious Orders.* Oxford, 1966.

————*Great Historical Enterprises.* London, 1963.

Krahl, Joseph, S.J. *China Missions in Crisis. Bishop Laimbeckhoven and His Times 1738-1787.* Rome, 1964.

Kratz, Wilhelm, S.J. *El tratado hispano-portugués de límites de 1750 y sus consecuencias. Estudio sobre la abolición de la Compañía de Jesús.* Translated from German by Diego Bermúdez Camacho. Rome, 1954.

————"Exjesuiten als Bischöfe, (1773-1822)." *Archivum Historicum Societatis Jesu,* VI (1937), 185-215.

Lallemant, Louis, S.J. *La vie et la doctrine spirituelle du Père Louis Lallemant, S.J. Introduction et notes par François Courel, S.J.* Paris, 1959.

Lamalle, Edmond, S.J. "La Propagande du P. Nicolas Trigault en Faveur des Missions de Chine." *Archivum Historicum Societatis Jesu,* IX (1940), 49-120.

Lancashire, Douglas. "Anti-Christian Polemics in Seventeenth Century China." *Church History,* XXXVIII (1969), 218-241.

Larère, Charles, S.J. "La suppression de la mission de la Guyane Française (1763-1766)." *Archivum Historicum Societatis Jesu,* IX (1940), 208-226.

Latourette, Kenneth S. *A History of Christian Missions in China.* London, 1929.

————*A History of the Expansion of Christianity.* Vol. III, *Three Centuries of Advance, A.D. 1500-1800.* New York and London, 1951.

Launay, Adrien. *Mémorial de la Société des Missions-Étrangères*. 2 vols. Paris, 1912.

Laures, Johannes, S.J. *The Catholic Church in Japan*. Tokyo and Rutland (Vermont), 1954.

Le Bachelet, Xavier, S.J. "Jésuites. La Théologie dogmatique dans la Compagnie de Jésus." *Dictionnaire de Théologie Catholique*, XIII, 1043-1069.

Lecler, Joseph, S.J. *Histoire de la tolérance au siècle de la Réforme*. 2 vols., Paris, 1955.

————"Dans la crise du catholicisme libéral." *Études*, CCXCI (1956), 196-211.

Leite, Serafim, S.J. *Páginas de História do Brasil*. Rio de Janeiro, 1937.

Leturia, Pedro de, S.J. "Conspectus Chronologicus Vitae Sancti Ignatii." *Estudios Ignacianos. Revisados por el P. Ignacio Iparraguirre, S.J.* 2 vols. Rome, 1957.

————*Iñigo de Loyola*. Translated by Aloysius Owen, S.J. Syracuse, 1949.

Lewey, Guenter. "The Struggle for Constitutional Government in the Early Years of the Society of Jesus." *Church History*, XXIX (1960), 141-160.

Lewis, Clifford M., S.J. and Loomie, Albert J., S.J. *The Spanish Jesuit Mission in Virginia, 1570-1572*. Chapel Hill, 1953.

Loomie, Albert J., S.J., *The Spanish Elizabethans*. New York, 1963.

Lopetegui, León, S.J. *El Padre José de Acosta, S.J., y las misiones*. Madrid, 1942.

Lubac, Henri de, S.J. *The Splendour of the Church*. Translated by Michael Mason. New York, 1956.

Lynch, John. *Spain under the Habsburgs*. Vol II, *Spain and America 1598-1700*. New York, 1969.

McClelland, Vincent A. *Cardinal Manning. His Public Life and Influence, 1865-1892*. New York and Toronto, 1962.

————"Scots Jesuits and Episcopal Authority 1603-1773." *Dublin Review*, No. 507 (1966), 111-132.

McGucken, William, S.J. *The Jesuits and Education*. Milwaukee, 1932.

McMahon, Thomas J. "Joseph Anthony Masdeu, S.J. A Distant Herald of Aeterni Patris?" *Theological Studies*, III (1942), 163-188.

McNally, Robert E., S.J. "St. Ignatius, Prayer, and the Early Society." *Woodstock Letters*, XCIV (1965), 109-134.

Mâle, Émile. *L' art religieux de la fin XVIᵉ siècle, du XVIIᵉ et du XVIIIᵉ siècle*. Paris, 1951.

Martín, Luis. *The Intellectual Conquest of Peru. The Jesuit College of San Pablo, 1568-1767*. New York, 1968.

Massachusetts Peace Society. *Correspondence of the Massachusetts Peace Society with the Emperor of Russia and Prince Alexander Gallitzin*. London, 1817.

Mathis, Michael A., C.S.C. *Modern Missions in India*. New York, 1947. This is Volume 4, No. 8 of *A Mission Academia Study*.

Matignon, Ambroise, S.J. "Les Doctrines de la Compagnie de Jésus sur la Liberté. La Lutte contre Jansénisme." *Études,* VIII (1866), 1-26.

Maynard, Michel Ulysse. *The Studies and Teaching of the Society of Jesus at the Time of Its Suppression, 1750-1773.* Translator not given. Baltimore and London, 1855.

Mehok, William J., S.J. "Jesuits: International Educators." *Jesuit Educational Quarterly,* XXXII (1969-1970), 275-281.

Messineo, S., S.J. "Il P. Luigi Taparelli d'Azeglio et il Risorgimento Italiano." *Civiltà Cattolica,* XCIX (1948), 492-502.

Molinari, Paul, S.J. "A New Blessed of the Society of Jesus: James Berthieu, Martyr of Madagascar (1838-1896)." *Annuarium Societatis Jesu,* (1965-1966), 49-56.

Moody, Joseph N. Book review of *The Development of Technical Education in France, 1500-1850* by Frederick B. Artz. *The Catholic Historical Review,* LV (1969), 476-477.

Mörner, Magnus, editor. *The Expulsion of the Jesuits from Latin America.* New York, 1965.

Mulcrone, Thomas F., S.J., "Boscovichian Opportunities in the History of Science and Mathematics." *Bulletin of the American Association of Jesuit Scientists,* XLIII (Dec. 1966), 1-4.

Munby, A.N.L. *Portrait of an Obsession. The Life of Sir Thomas Phillipps, the World's Greatest Book Collector.* London, 1967.

Murray, John Courtney, S.J. "Christian Humanism in America." *Social Order,* III (1953), 233-244.

————"The Church and Totalitarian Democracy." *Theological Studies,* XIII (1952), 525-563.

————"St. Robert Bellarmine on the Indirect Power." *Theological Studies,* IX (1948), 491-535.

————"Leo XIII on Church and State: The General Structure of the Controversy." *Theological Studies,* XIV (1953), 1-30.

Navarrete, Domingo, O.P. *The Travels and Controversies of Friar Domingo Navarrete.* Edited by James B. Cummins. 2 vols. Cambridge (England), 1962.

Needham, Joseph. *Chinese Astronomy and the Jesuit Mission: An Encounter of Cultures.* London, 1958.

O'Brien, Charles H. "Idea of Religious Toleration at the Time of Joseph II. A Study of the Enlightenment among Catholics in Austria." *Transactions of the American Philosophical Society Held at Philadelphia for Promoting Useful Knowledge,* new series, LIX Part 7. (1969), 5-80.

O'Neill, George, S.J. *Golden Years on the Paraguay.* London, 1934.

Orcibal, Jean. *Louis XIV et les Protestants.* Paris, 1951.

Owens, Sister Lilliana. *Jesuit Beginnings in New Mexico.* El Paso, 1950.

Oxford Companion to Art, 11th edition. Harold Osborne, editor. Oxford, 1970.

Oxford Companion to the Theatre, 3rd edition. Phyllis Hartnoll, editor. London, 1967.

Padberg, John W., S.J. *Colleges in Controversy. The Jesuit Schools in France from Revival to Suppression, 1815-1880.* Cambridge (Mass.), 1969.

Palmer, Robert R. *Catholics and Unbelievers in Eighteenth Century France.* Princeton, 1939.

——————"The French Jesuits in the Age of the Enlightenment." *American Historical Review,* XLV (1939), 44-58.

Pappas, John N. *Studies on Voltaire and the Eighteenth Century.* Vol. III, *Berthier's Journal de Trévoux and the Philosophers.* Edited by Theodore Besterman. Geneva, 1957.

Pascal, Blaise. *Les provinciales ou les lettres écrites par Louis de Montalte à un provincial de ses amis et aux RR.PP. Jésuites.* Edited by Louis Cognet. Paris, 1965.

Pastor, Ludwig von. *The History of the Popes from the Close of the Middle Ages.* Translated by Ralph E. Kerr and E. F. Peeler. 40 vols. St. Louis, 1891-1953.

Paul VI, Pope. "An Appeal to the Laity, given at Frascati, Sept. 1, 1963." *The Pope Speaks,* IX (1963), 176-177.

Peers, E. Allison. *Spain, the Church and the Orders.* London, 1939.

Persons, Robert, S.J. *Letters and Memorials of Father Robert Persons, S.J.* Edited by Leo Hicks, S.J., London, 1942.

Petau, Denis, S.J. *Dogmata Theologica Dionysii Petavii e Societate Jesu.* Editio Nova, J. B. Fournials. 5 vols. Paris, 1845.

Petrucelli della Gattina, Ferdinando. *Histoire Diplomatique des Conclaves.* 4 vols. Paris and Brussels, 1864-1866.

Pinkerton, Robert. *Extracts of Letters from the Rev. Robert Pinkerton on his Late Tour in Russia, Poland, and Germany; to promote the Object of the British and Foreign Bible Society. Together with a Letter from Prince Alexander Galitzin, to the Right Honourable Lord Teignmouth.* London, 1817.

Pirri, Pietro, S.J. "Civiltà Cattolica, La." *Enciclopedia Cattolica,* III (1949), 1759-1762.

Plattner, Felix A., S.J. *Jesuits Go East.* Translated by Lord Sudley and Oscar Blobel. Westminster (Maryland), 1952.

Pollen, John H., S.J. "English Colleges in Eighteenth Century Spain." *The Month,* CXIX (1912), 190-193.

——————"A Jesuit 'Free School' in London 1688." *The Month,* CXXVIII (1916), 264-267.

——————"The Recognition of the Jesuits in England." *The Month,* CXVI (1910), 23-36.

——————"The Restoration of the English Jesuits." *The Month,* CXV (1910), 585-597.

——————"An Unobserved Centenary." *The Month,* CXV (1910), 449-461.

Poncelet, Alfred, S.J. *Histoire de la Compagnie de Jésus dans les anciens Pays-Bas.* 2 vols., Bruxelles, 1927.

Ponlevoy, Armand de, S.J. *Vie du R.P. Xavier de Ravignan de la Compagnie de Jésus.* 2 vols. Paris, 1862.

Pouliot, Léon, S.J. *Étude sur les Relations des Jésuites de la Nouvelle-France (1632-1672)*. Montreal, 1940.

Pourrat, Pierre. *Christian Spirituality*. Translated by S. P. Jacques, W. H. Mitchell, and D. Attwater. 4 vols. Westminster (Maryland), 1922-1955.

Prat, Jean Marie, S.J. *Maldonat et L'Université de Paris*. Paris, 1856.

Purdie, Edna. "Jesuit Drama." *The Oxford Companion to the Theatre*, 3rd edition, Edited by Phyllis Hartnoll, 505-515. London, 1967.

Rahner, Hugo, S.J. *The Spirituality of St. Ignatius Loyola. An Account of Its Historical Development*. Translated by F. J. Smith, S.J. Westminster (Maryland), 1953.

Ranke, Leopold von. *The History of the Popes, their Church and State, and especially of their Conflicts with Protestantism in the Sixteenth and Seventeenth Centuries*. Translated by E. Foster. 3 vols. London, 1847-1851.

Ravignan, Gustave François Xavier de, S.J. *Clément XIII et Clément XIV*. Paris, 1854.

————*Clément XIII et Clément XIV. Volume Supplémentaire. Documents historiques et critiques*. Paris, 1854.

————*De l'existence et l'institut des Jésuites*. Paris, 1844.

Reilly Connor, S.J. "A Catalog of Jesuitica in the 'Philosophical Transactions of the Royal Society of London' (1665-1715)." *Archivum Historicum Societatis Jesu*, XXVII (1958), 339-360.

Reinerman, Alan. "The Return of the Jesuits to the Austrian Empire and the Decline of Josephinism, 1820-1822." *The Catholic Historical Review*, LXX (1966), 372-390.

Reiser, Edward J., S.J. "Parochial and Allied Ministries in the American Assistancy." *Woodstock Letters*, LXXII (1943), 306-317.

Renaud, Rosario, S.J. "Blessed Ignace Mangin and his Companions, Martyrs." Translated by Joseph Cahill, S.J. *Woodstock Letters*, XCII (1963), 115-138.

Rickaby, Joseph, S.J. "Clement the Eleventh and the Chinese Rites." *The Month*, LXXIII (1891), 70-79.

Riedl, Clare C. "Suarez and the Organization of Learning." *Jesuit Thinkers of the Renaissance*. Edited by Gerard Smith, S.J. Milwaukee, 1939.

Riga, Peter. "The Ecclesiology of Johann Adam Möhler." *Theological Studies*, XXII (1961), 563-587.

Rochemonteix, Camille de, S.J. *Les Jésuites de la Nouvelle-France au XVIIᵉ siècle*. 3 vols. Paris, 1895.

Rodrigues, Francisco, S.J. *A Formação intellectual do Jesuita*. Porto, 1917.

————*História da Companhia de Jesus na Assistência de Portugal*. 4 vols. Porto, 1931-1950.

————"A Companhia de Jesus em Portugal e nas Missões. Esbôço

Histórico." *Revista de História*, X (1921), 161-201.

————"Nas missões do extremo-oriente. Quatro missionarios do padroado português." *Brotéria*, XX (1935), 301-315.

————"O. P. António Vieira. Contradicçoes e Applausos. (Á Luz de Documentação Inedita.)" *Revista de História*, XI (1922), 81-115.

Roman Archives of the Society of Jesus: France 6-XXIII, 15.

Rouleau, Francis, S.J. Book Review of *Science and Civilization in China*. Vol. III. *Mathematics and the Sciences of the Heavens and the Earth* by Joseph Needham. *Archivum Historicum Societatis Jesu*, XXX (1961), 299-303.

————"Maillard de Tournon, Papal Legate at the Court of Peking. The First Imperial Audience (31 December 1705)." *Archivum Historicum Societatis Jesu*, XXXI (1962), 264-323.

Roustang, François, S.J., editor. *An Autobiography of Martyrdom. Spiritual Writings of the Jesuits in New France*. Translated by Sister M. Rennelle, S.S.N.D. St. Louis, 1964.

Ruhan, Anthony, S.J. "The Origins of the Jesuit Tertianship." *Woodstock Letters*, XCIV (1965), 407-426.

Scaduto, Mario, S.J. *Storia della Compagnia di Gesù in Italia*. Vol. III, *L'epoca di Giacomo Lainez. Il Governo 1556-1565.* 1964.

Schneider, Burkhart, S.J. "Der Syllabus Pius' IX und die deutschen Jesuiten." *Archivum Historiae Pontificiae*, VI (1968), 371-392.

Schurhammer, Georg, S.J. "Thomas Stephens (1549-1619)." *Gesammelte Studien*, II, *Orientalia*. 367-376. Edited by László Szilas, S.J. 4 vols. Lisbon and Rome, 1963.

Scorraille, Raoul, S.J. *François Suarez de la Compagnie de Jésus*. 2 vols. Paris, 1911.

Sebes, Joseph, S.J. *The Jesuits and the Sino-Russian Treaty of Nerchinsk*. Rome, 1961.

Servière, J. de la, S.J. *Les anciennes missions de la Compagnie de Jésus en Chine*. Shanghai, 1924.

Simon-Diaz, José. *Historia del Colegio Imperial de Madrid*. 2 vols. Madrid, 1952.

Smith, Sydney, S.J. "The Suppression of the Society of Jesus." A series of nineteen articles in *The Month*, XCIX-CII (Feb., 1902-Aug. 1903).

Sorel, Albert. *Europe Under the Old Regime*. Translated by Francis H. Herrick. New York, 1964.

Steinman, Jean. *Pascal*. London, 1965.

Stierli, Josef, S.J. "Devotion to Mary in the Sodality." Translated by Joseph Vetz, S.J. and Gustave Weigel, S.J. *Woodstock Letters*, LXXXII (1953), 16-45.

Symlie, James H. "American Protestants Interpret Vatican Council I." *Church History*, XXXVIII (1969), 459-474.

Talbot, Francis X., S.J. *Jesuit Education in Philadelphia, Saint Joseph's College, 1851-1926.* Philadelphia, 1927.

Thayer, William R. *The Life and Times of Cavour.* 2 vols. Boston and New York, 1911.

Tisserant, Eugène. *Eastern Christianity in India: a History of the Syro-Malabar Church from the Earliest Time to the Present Day.* Translated by E. R. Hambye, S.J. Westminter, Md. 1957.

Trappes-Lomax, Michael. *Bishop Challoner.* London and New York, 1936.

Turner, F. C. *James II.* London, 1948.

Villaret, Émile, S.J. "Les premières origines des Congrégations mariales dans la Compagnie de Jésus." *Archivum Historicum Societatis Jesu,* VI (1937), 25-57.

Watkin, Edward I. "The Splendour of Baroque." *The Tablet* (London), CCXXII (1968), 386-388.

Wedgwood, Cicely V. *The Thirty Years War.* New Haven, 1939.

Wilckens, Ricardo Krebs. *El pensamiento histórico, político y económico del Conde de Campomanes.* Santiago de Chile, 1960.

————"The Victims of a Conflict of Ideas." *The Expulsion of the Jesuits from Latin America,* 47-52. Edited by M. Mörner. New York, 1965.

Wilkins, Kathleen Sonia. *Studies on Voltaire and the Eighteenth Century.* Vol. LXVI, *A Study of the Works of Claude Buffier.* Edited by Theodore Besterman. Geneva, 1969.

Wittkower, Rudolf and Jaffe, Irma B., editors. *Baroque Art: The Jesuit Contribution.* New York, 1972.

Zalenski, Stanislaus, S.J. *Les Jésuites de la Russie-Blanche.* 2 vols. Translated from Polish by Alexandre Vivier, S.J. Paris, 1886.

Zubillaga, Félix, S.J. *La Florida. La Misión Jesuítica (1566-1572) y la Colonización Española.* Rome, 1941.

————"La Provincia Jesuítica de Nueva España. Su fundamento económico: siglo XVI." *Archivum Historicum Societatis Jesu,* XXXVIII (1969), 3-169.

INDEX

The numbers refer to pages

531

in Portugal, 366-372
in Portuguese colonies, 371
in Spain, 383-390
in Spanish colonies, 390-392
throughout the world, 393-410
See also Exile, Jesuits in
Surin, Jean Joseph, S.J., 309
Sutcliffe, Matthew, 55
Swain, John L., S.J., 500
Sweden, 79-82, 137
Sweiten, Gerhard van, 310
Swift, Dean Jonathan, 324
Sylva, Melchior de, S.J., 161
Symlie, James H., 448
Szilas, László, 150
Syro-Chaldean Christians in India, 151, 240

T

Tacchi Venturi, Pietro, S.J., 440
Talbot, Francis X., S.J., 492
Talon, Jean, 264
Tamaral, Nicolás, S.J., 349
Tamburini, Michelangelo, S.J., 279, 282-284, 295, 339, 346, 361
Tanner, Adam, S.J., 133
Taño, Francisco Díaz, S.J., 259
Tanucci, Bernardo, 383-387, 392, 401, 405
Taparelli d'Azeglio, Luigi, S.J., 442
Tapia, Gonzalo, S.J., 165
Tarin, Jean, 200
Tekakwitha, Kateri, 267
Teles, Baltasar, S.J., 198
Thayer, William R., 441
Thébaud, Auguste, S.J., 490
Theological Doctrines by Denis Petau, S.J., 213
Theology, Jesuits and, 56, 58, 68, 70, 75, 78, 114-116, 129-133, 140, 192, 194, 212, 223, 288, 292, 305, 312, 444, 446, 456, 458, 464, 501

Thérèse Couderc, St. Marie Victoire, R.C., 211
Thirty Years War, 217-221
Thwaites, Reuben, 265
Tillot, Guillaume du, 393
Tilly, Johann Tzerclaes, graf von, 218, 220
Tisserant, Cardinal Eugène, 151, 240
Tocqueville, Alexis de, 431, 463
Tokugawa Iemitsu, 241
Tokugawa Ieyasu, 156
Toledo, Francisco de, S.J., 55, 100-102, 114, 122
Tongiorgi, Salvatore, S.J., 449
Torites, Melchior, S.J., 133
Torre, Giuseppe della, S.J., 421
Torres, Cosme de, S.J., 33-37
Torres Rubio, Diego de, S.J., 96
Torrigiani, Cardinal Luigi, 368, 385, 394
Tour, Charles de la, S.J., 125
Tournély, François Eléonor de, 420
Tournemine, René-Joseph, S.J., 298
Tournon, Carlo Tomasso Maillard de, 280, 329-332, 336-340
Tournon, François Cardinal de, 65
Toyotomi Hideyoshi, 154-156
Trappes-Lomax, Michael, 322
Treatise on the Power of the Supreme Pontiff by Robert Bellarmine, S.J., 126
Trent, Council of, 23, 48, 58
Trigault, Michel, S.J., 245
Trigault, Nicolas, S.J., 186, 243
Tromp, Sebastian, S.J., 501
Truchses, Eusebio, S.J., 277
Truchsess von Waldburg, Cardinal Otto, 24
Tupi Indians, 38
Turner, F. C., 234
Tyrannicide, Jesuits and, 117, 126, 375